Configuring
Windows® 2000 Server

ISBN 0-13-085858-7

PRENTICE HALL PTR MICROSOFT® TECHNOLOGIES SERIES

NETWORKING

- Microsoft Technology: Networking, Concepts, Tools
  Woodard, Gattuccio, Brain

- NT Network Programming Toolkit
  Murphy

- Building COM Applications with Internet Explorer
  Loveman

- Understanding DCOM
  Rubin, Brain

- Web Database Development for Windows Platforms
  Gutierrez

PROGRAMMING

- Introduction to Windows 98 Programming
  Murray, Pappas

- Developing Professional Applications for Windows 98 and NT Using MFC, Third Edition
  Brain, Lovette

- Win 32 System Services: The Heart of Windows 98 and Windows NT, Third Edition
  Brain

- Multithreaded Programming with Win32
  Pham, Garg

- Visual Basic 6: Design, Specification, and Objects
  Hollis

- ADO Programming in Visual Basic 6
  Holzner

- Visual Basic 6: Error Coding and Layering
  Gill

- Visual C++ Templates
  Murray, Pappas

- Introduction to MFC Programming with Visual C++
  Jones

- MFC Programming in C++ with the Standard Template Libraries
  Murray, Pappas

- COM-CORBA Interoperability
  Geraghty, Joyce, Moriarty, Noone

- Distributed COM Application Development Using Visual Basic 6.0
  Maloney

- Distributed COM Application Development Using Visual C++ 6.0
  Maloney

- Understanding and Programming COM+: A Practical Guide to Windows 2000 DNA
  Oberg

- ASP/MTS/ADSI Web Security
  Harrison

- Microsoft Site Server 3.0 Commerce Edition
  Libertone, Scoppa

- Building Microsoft SQL Server 7 Web Sites
  Byrne

ADMINISTRATION

- Windows 2000 Registry
  Sanna

- Configuring Windows 2000 Server
  Simmons

- Tuning and Sizing NT Server
  Aubley

- Windows NT Cluster Server Guidebook
  Libertone

- Windows NT 4.0 Server Security Guide
  Goncalves

- Windows NT Security
  McInerney

- Supporting Windows NT and 2000 Workstation and Server
  Mohr

- Zero Administration Kit for Windows
  McInerney

- Designing Enterprise Solutions with Microsoft Technologies
  Kemp, Kemp, Goncalves

MICROSOFT® TECHNOLOGY SERIES

SIMMONS

Configuring Windows 2000 Server

PH PTR Prentice Hall PTR, Upper Saddle River, NJ 07458
www.phptr.com

Library of Congress Cataloging-in-Publication Data

Simmons, Curt, 1968–
    Configuring Windows 2000 Server / Simmons [sic].
        p. cm. — (Microsoft technology series)
    ISBN 0-13-085858-7
    1. Microsoft Windows 2000 server. 2. Operating systems (Computers) I. Title.
    II. Series.

    QA76.76.063 S55855   1999
    005.7'13769—dc21   99-054466

Editorial/Production Supervision: MetroVoice Publishing Services
Acquisitions Editor: Jill Pisoni
Editorial Assistant: Linda Ramagnano
Development Editor: Ralph Moore
Cover Design Director: Jerry Votta
Cover Designer: Anthony Gemmellaro
Buyer: Maura Goldstaub
Series Design: Maureen Eide
Marketing Manager: Lisa Konzelmann
Art Director: Gail Cocker-Bogusz
Project Coordinator: Anne Trowbridge

PH PTR

© 2000 by PrenticeHall PTR
Prentice-Hall, Inc.
Upper Saddle River, New Jersey 07458

Prentice Hall books are widely used by corporations and government agencies for training, marketing, and resale. The publisher offers discounts on this book when ordered in bulk quantities. For more information, contact:

   Corporate Sales Department,
   Prentice Hall PTR
   One Lake Street
   Upper Saddle River, NJ 07458
   Phone: 800-382-3419; FAX: 201-236-7141
   E-mail (Internet): corpsales@prenhall.com

Reprinted with corrections March, 2000.

All rights reserved. No part of this book may be reproduced, in any form or by any means, without permission in writing from the publisher.

Printed in the United States of America

10 9 8 7 6 5 4 3 2

ISBN 0-13-085858-7

Prentice-Hall International (UK) Limited, *London*
Prentice-Hall of Australia Pty. Limited, *Sydney*
Prentice-Hall Canada Inc., *Toronto*
Prentice-Hall Hispanoamericana, S.A., *Mexico*
Prentice-Hall of India Private Limited, *New Delhi*
Prentice-Hall of Japan, Inc., *Tokyo*
Pearson Education Asia Pte. Ltd., *Singapore*
Editora Prentice-Hall do Brasil, Ltda., *Rio de Janeiro*

DEDICATION

This book is dedicated to my grandmother, the late Lucille Crain, who always encouraged me to chase dreams.

CONTENTS

PREFACE   xxi

ACKNOWLEDGMENTS   xxv

PART ONE   Introducing Windows 2000 Server

ONE   Overview of New Features in Windows 2000 Server   3

Management   4
- Microsoft Management Console   4
- The Active Directory   5
- Application Installation Service   7
- Group Policy Editor   7
- Intellimirror   7
- Web Based Enterprise Management   7
- Windows Scripting Host   8

Application and Publishing Services   8
- Web Application Services   8
- Message Queuing Services   8
- Transaction Services   9
- Web Publishing Services   9
- Indexing   9
- Streaming Media   9

Networking   10
- Dynamic Domain Name System   10
- Network Address Translator   10

       Asynchronous Transfer Mode and Fibre Channel   *10*
       Windows Quality of Service   *11*
       IP Telephony   *11*
       Services for Macintosh   *11*
File System   *11*
       NTFS Enhancements   *11*
       Remote Storage Services and Removable Storage Manager   *12*
       Enhanced Backup Utility   *12*
Print Services   *12*
Improved Scalability   *12*
       Enterprise Memory Architecture   *13*
       SMP Scalability and I2O Support   *13*
       Job Object and Clustering   *13*
Security   *13*
       Kerberos Authentication   *13*
       Public Key Certificate Server   *14*
       Smart Card   *14*
       Security Configuration Editor   *14*
       IP Security Protocol   *14*
Setup Tools   *14*
Summary   *15*

TWO   Installing Windows 2000 Server   *17*

Hardware Requirements for Windows 2000 Server   *17*
Getting Windows NT Server 4.0 Ready to Upgrade   *18*
       Install Service Pack 4 or 5   *19*
       Convert FAT Disks to NTFS   *20*
       Install TCP/IP and Remove Unnecessary Protocols   *20*
       Install and Implement DHCP   *20*
       Install DNS   *23*
       Review Hardware   *23*
       Review Users and Groups   *23*
Installing Windows 2000 Server   *23*
       About Domain Controllers   *24*

Contents **ix**

      Performing the Windows 2000 Upgrade 24
      Installing a Clean Copy of Windows 2000 Server 26
Summary *30*

PART TWO Hardware and Disk Management

THREE A Tour Around the Interface 33

Desktop *34*
    Start Menu 34
    My Briefcase 36
    Internet Explorer 36
    Recycle Bin 36
    My Network Places 36
    My Documents 37
    My Computer 37

Control Panel *37*

Accessories *40*
    Accessibility 41
    Communications 41
    System Tools 41
    Other Features 43

Administrative Tools *43*
    Component Services 43
    Computer Management 43
    Configure Your Server 45
    Data Sources 46
    DHCP Manager 46
    Distributed File System 48
    DNS Management 48
    Event Viewer 48
    File Manager 48
    Internet Services Manager 49
    Licensing 49
    Performance 49
    Routing and Remote Access 49

Contents

    Terminal Services Licensing 51
    WINS 51
  Active Directory Administrative Tools *51*
  Summary *53*

FOUR Configuring and Managing Hardware 55

Understanding Plug and Play 55
Add/Remove Hardware Wizard 57
Device Manager 60
  General Tab 61
  Advanced Tab 62
  Driver Property Sheet 63
  Resources Property Sheet 64
  Other Tabs 66
Using Control Panel 66
  Fax 66
  Game Controllers 68
  Keyboard and Mouse 68
  Phone and Modem Option 68
  Printers 70
  Scanners and Camera Properties 71
Hardware Profiles *71*
Using System Information 72
Summary *74*

FIVE Disk Management 75

File Systems 75
Dynamic and Basic Disks 76
  Upgrading a Basic Disk to a Dynamic Disk 78
Managing Dynamic Volumes 80
  Volume Properties 81
  Configuring Simple Volumes 83

Contents **xi**

  Configuring Spanned Volumes 88
  Configuring and Managing Striped Volumes 89
Fault Tolerance Solutions *90*
  Creating Mirrored Volumes 90
  Deleting a Mirrored Volume 90
  Removing a Mirrored Volume 90
  Breaking a Mirrored Volume 91
  Repairing a Mirrored Volume 91
  Creating RAID-5 Volumes 91
  Deleting RAID-5 Volumes 91
  Reactivating RAID-5 Volumes 92
  Repairing RAID-5 Volumes 92
Disk Tools *92*
  Disk Cleanup 92
  Disk Defragmenter 93
  Error Checking 93
  Maintenance Wizard 94
Summary *95*

SIX Interface and System Settings 97

Start Menu and TaskBar *97*
Configuring Settings Using Control Panel *99*
  Accessibility Options 99
  Display 101
  Folder Options 102
  Internet Options 104
  Regional Options 107
  Sounds and Multimedia 108
  System 109
Summary *112*

SEVEN The Registry and Backup Operations 113

The Structure of the Registry *114*

    HKEY_LOCAL_MACHINE 115
    HKEY_USERS 115
    HKEY_CURRENT_USER 115
    HKEY_CLASSES_ROOT 116
    HKEY_CURRENT_CONFIG 116
  Using the Registry Editors 116
    Using Regedt32 116
    Using Regedit 118
  Backup Options in Windows 2000 Server 119
    Backup Types 119
    Using Windows Backup 121
  Summary 132

EIGHT Remote and Removable Storage 133

Storage Concepts 133
  Understanding Libraries 134
  Understanding Media Pools 134
  Understanding Media States 135
Setting Up and Using Remote Storage 135
  Volume Management 136
  Managing Media 139
Using Removable Storage 140
  Configuring and Managing Libraries 140
  Configuring Media Pools 142
  Configuring and Managing Physical Media 143
  Configuring Queued Work and Operator Requests 144
  Configuring Removable Storage Security 148
  Using Removable Storage Command Line 149
Summary 151

PART THREE Networking

NINE Configuring the Active Directory 155

Features of the Active Directory 155

  Scalability 156
  DNS Integration and Standard Naming 156
  Extensibility 156
  Security 156
Active Directory Organization 156
  Domain 157
  Organizational Units 157
  Objects 157
  Tree 157
  Forest 157
  Sites 158
Active Directory Design 159
  Global Catalog 159
  Schema 159
  Namespace 160
  Naming Conventions 160
Installing the Active Directory 161
Using the Active Directory Administrative Tools 164
  Active Directory Users and Computers 164
  Active Directory Domains and Trusts 168
  Active Directory Sites and Services 172
Active Directory Schema 178
Summary 179

TEN Configuring Network Communication *181*

Installing Protocols in Windows 2000 Server 181
TCP/IP 182
  TCP/IP Review 183
  Configuring TCP/IP 184
  Installing and Configuring TCP/IP Simple Services 186
NWLink 187
Using Other Protocols 188
  NetBEUI 189
  AppleTalk 189
  DLC 189

Network Monitor Driver   190
Streams Environment   190
Adjusting Protocol Bindings   *190*
Quality of Service (QoS) Admission Control   *191*
Installing QoS   192
Installing the Packet Scheduler   192
Configuring QoS Policies   192
Summary   *198*

ELEVEN   Installing and Configuring DHCP   *199*

How DHCP Works   *199*
Reviewing DHCP Terminology   *200*
Installing DHCP   *201*
Configuring the DHCP Server   *201*
    DHCP Server Properties   *201*
    Authorizing a DHCP Server   *202*
    Creating Scopes and Superscopes   *203*
    Configuring DHCP Options   *209*
The DHCP Database   *210*
Summary   *211*

TWELVE   Configuring DNS   *213*

Understanding DNS   *213*
    DNS Zones   214
    DNS in Windows 2000 Server   216
Installing DNS   *216*
Configuring DNS   *219*
    Connecting to Another Computer   219
    Removing a DNS Server   219
    Creating a New Zone   219
    Manually Updating a Server   219
    Clearing the Cache   220
    Configuring the DNS Server Properties   220

Contents **XV**

        Configuring Zone Properties   *225*
        Configuring Resource Records   *227*
Summary   *229*

THIRTEEN   Configuring WINS   *231*

How WINS Works   *231*
Using WINS in Windows 2000   *232*
Installing WINS   *233*
Configuring the WINS Server   *233*
        Adding a WINS Server to the Console   *233*
        WINS Properties   *233*
        Server Status   *234*
        Examining Server Statistics   *235*
        WINS Server Properties   *235*
        Using Server All Tasks Functions   *238*
        Managing WINS Registrations   *240*
        Managing Replication   *244*
Summary   *246*

FOURTEEN   Configuring Routing and Remote Access   *247*

Overview of Remote Access   *247*
        Dial-up Connectivity   *248*
        Virtual Private Networks   *248*
        New Features of Remote Access   *251*
Overview of Routing   *251*
Installing Routing and Remote Access   *252*
Configuring Routing and Remote Access   *255*
        Adding a Server   *255*
        Server Properties   *255*
        Routing Interfaces   *258*
        Dial-in Clients   *258*
        Ports   *258*
        IP Routing   *258*

Contents

       Remote Access Policies   261
       Creating a New Remote Access Policy   267
Summary   268

FIFTEEN   Connecting with Apple and Novell Systems   269

Apple Macintosh Interoperability   269
       Installing the Services for Macintosh   270
       Macintosh User Accounts   270
       Configuring AppleTalk   271
       Creating and Managing Macintosh Accessible Volumes   273
Interoperability with Novell NetWare   277
       Installing NWLink   277
       Configuring NWLink   277
       Installing GSNW   278
       Configuring GSNW   278
       Directory Service Migration Tool   280
Summary   281

SIXTEEN   Overview of Windows 2000 Security Features   283

New Security Features in Windows 2000   283
Authentication   284
     Kerberos V5   284
     Secure Socket Layer/Transport Layer Security (SSL/TLS)   285
     NT LAN Manager (NTLM)   285
Active Directory Object-based Access Control   285
Encrypting File System   285
     Encrypting or Decrypting a File or Folder   286
     Configuring Recovery Agents   287
Security Policies   288
     The Security Template Snap-in   288
     Configuring the Policies   289

The Security Configuration and Analysis Snap-in   *290*
Certificates   *292*
   Installing the Certificate Authority   *292*
   Managing Certificates   *294*
Summary   *298*

SEVENTEEN   IP Security   *299*

IP Security Features   *299*
   IPSec Policy Agent   *300*
   Tunneling with IPSec   *301*
Configuring IPSec   *301*
   Creating an IP Security Policy   *303*
   Creating New IPSec Policy Rules   *306*
   Managing Filter Lists   *310*
   Checking Policy Integrity   *312*
   Restoring Default Policies   *312*
   Importing or Exporting Policies   *312*
Summary   *313*

PART FOUR   Managing Clients and Performance

EIGHTEEN   Configuring User, Computer, and Group Accounts   *317*

Understanding User and Computer Accounts in Windows 2000   *317*
User Accounts   *318*
   Creating Domain User Accounts   *318*
   Configuring Account Properties   *320*
   Managing User Accounts   *326*
Configuring and Managing Computer Accounts   *328*
   Configuring Computer Account Properties   *328*
   Managing Computer Accounts   *330*
Understanding Groups   *331*
   Types of Groups   *331*
   Group Scopes   *331*

Understanding Builtin Groups 332
Configuring Groups 333
    Creating a New Group 333
    Configuring Group Properties 333
Summary 338

NINETEEN   Configuring Profiles and Policies   339

Understanding User Profiles 339
Managing User Profiles 340
    Setting Up a Roaming User Profile 340
    Configuring a Custom Roaming User Profile 341
    Making a Profile Mandatory 342
Understanding Group Policies 343
Understanding Group Policy Components 344
    Group Policy Objects 344
Group Policy Structure 345
Configuring Group Policies 346
    Working with Administrative Templates 347
    Setting Policies Using Administrative Templates 349
Configuring Software Settings 351
Configuring Windows Settings 353
Configuring GPO General Properties 355
Summary 358

TWENTY   Managing Shared Resources   359

NTFS Permissions 359
    Assigning NTFS Permissions 362
    Advanced Access Permissions 364
Managing Shared Folders 368
Distributed File System 370
    Configuring Dfs 371
Summary 376

TWENTY-ONE Additional Client Technologies 377

Intellimirror 377
Remote Installation Services 379
    Setting Up Remote Installation Services 379
    Configuring General Remote Install Properties 382
    Creating a Remote Client Boot Disk 387
    Invoking a Network Service Boot 387
    Creating a Remote Installation Preparation Image 388
Synchronization Manager 389
    Setting Up Client Computers to use Offline Files 390
    Making a File or Folder Available Offline 390
    Setting Up Synchronization Manager 391
Indexing Service 394
    Installing the Indexing Service 395
    Configuring the Indexing Service 395
    Creating a New Catalog 397
    Performing Manual Catalog Scans 397
    Checking Indexing Service Performance 398
    Retrieving a List of Unindexed Documents 399
    Preventing an NTFS Directory or Document from Being Indexed 399
Summary 400

TWENTY-TWO Printing 401

Printing Overview 401
    New Windows 2000 Print Features 402
Setting Up Printers 403
    Printer Properties 404
Setting Up Client Computers 411
Printing to Macintosh and UNIX Servers 412
Summary 412

TWENTY-THREE Auditing   *413*

Auditing in Windows 2000   *413*
   Configuring Auditing   414
   Auditing File and Folder Access   417
   Auditing Access to Active Directory Objects   418
   Auditing Printer Access   419
Configuring Logs   *420*
Summary   *423*

TWENTY-FOUR Performance Monitor and Network Monitor   *425*

Performance Monitor   *425*
   Using Counters   426
   Performance Monitor Properties   428
   Performance Logs and Alerts   431
Network Monitor   *435*
   Installing Network Monitor   435
   Using Network Monitor   436
Summary   *437*

INDEX   439

PREFACE

Unless you have been completely removed from the computing world during the past two years, you have no doubt heard a lot about Windows 2000 Server. Windows 2000 Server, previously named Windows NT 5.0, is Microsoft's next generation of server software. Some of the things you have heard during Microsoft's development of this new operating system are true—some are not—and the rumors that have followed its development have been many.

This book is designed to be your companion. You may have installed Windows 2000 Server and decided you need a little extra help in getting it to play the way you want it to, or perhaps you are still staring at that installation CD, afraid of what the new operating system may do to your server.

As the title suggests, this book helps you configure the various services and functions of Windows 2000 Server, as well as find your way around the new interface. I address every major configuration topic in this book. Some of them are easy and some are not, but this book is designed to help you get your system up and running as quickly as possible. Although you can upgrade Windows NT to Windows 2000 Server, the new operating system is much more than an upgrade, and Windows 2000 Server functions very differently than Windows NT does. In other words, you have a learning curve to go through, but hopefully this book will make that learning curve much easier.

What You Should Know First

This book is not a beginner's book, but you don't have to have five degrees in computer science either. In this book, I assume that you are familiar with Windows NT Server 4.0 and have worked with its various services and functions. I also assume you have a fundamental command of networking technologies and protocols.

However, if you are somewhat new to server software and Microsoft networking, you can still use this book and you will learn a lot as you do. I have tried to discuss and explain everything simply so you can get the information you need to make your server behave in the way you want.

What's in the Book

This book includes major topics and issues concerning the configuration of Windows 2000 Server. Some of the chapters may appear to be basic, but this operating system is significantly different from Windows NT 4.0, and you will find that most components of the system work somewhat differently.

This book focuses on the local operating system, but it also explains the configuration options for the local machine's place in a complex network. Microsoft's domain structure and networking approach is different with the release of Windows 2000 Server, so you may also benefit from reading a book about Windows 2000 networking as well.

The following bulleted list tells you what you can expect to see in each chapter:

- Chapter 1, Overview of Windows 2000 Server, points out the new features and enhancements you can expect to see in Windows 2000 Server.
- Chapter 2, Installing Windows 2000 Server, walks you through the software installation and points out some important pre-installation actions.
- Chapter 3, A Tour Around the Interface, gives you a chance to explore the new interface in Windows 2000 Server.
- Chapter 4, Configuring and Managing Hardware, shows you how to setup hardware devices on your system.
- Chapter 5, Disk Management, explores the new disk management features and configuration options in Windows 2000 Server.
- Chapter 6, Interface and Systems Settings, explores the configuration of the interface and system settings, such as memory and Control Panel.
- Chapter 7, The Registry and Backup Operations, shows you how to use registry tools and the new Windows 2000 Backup utility.
- Chapter 8, Remote and Removable Storage, examines the new remote and removable storage features available in Windows 2000 Server.
- Chapter 9, Configuring the Active Directory, explores the configuration of the Active Directory, the new, powerful directory service in Windows 2000.
- Chapter 10, Configuring Network Protocols, shows you how to install and configure standard network protocols, such as TCP/IP, NWLink, and others.
- Chapter 11, Installing and Configuring DHCP, examines the use and configuration of DHCP for Windows 2000 networks.
- Chapter 12, Configuring DNS, explores the functionality of Dynamic DNS in relation to the Active Directory.
- Chapter 13, Configuring WINS, discusses the purpose of WINS in Windows 2000 networks and shows you how to implement WINS in Windows 2000 Server.

- Chapter 14, Configuring Routing and Remote Access, explores the configuration and functionality of RAS and RRAS in Windows 2000 Server.
- Chapter 15, Connecting with Apple and Novell Systems, shows you how to connect with Macintosh and Netware clients and servers.
- Chapter 16, Windows 2000 Security, introduces the new security features in Windows 2000 Server, such as Kerberos, EFS, and Certificate Services.
- Chapter 17, IP Security, examines the functionality of IP Security, how it works, and how to use it in your network.
- Chapter 18, Configuring User, Computer, and Group Accounts, shows you how to use the Active Directory and configure and manage network accounts.
- Chapter 19, Configure Profiles and Policies, discusses the use and configuration of profiles and policies in Windows 2000.
- Chapter 20, Managing Shared Resources, shows you how to manage and secure shared resources, including the configuration of Distributed File System.
- Chapter 21, Additional Client Technologies, shows you how to use new client management technologies, such as Intellimirror, on your network.
- Chapter 22, Printing, explores the configuration of print devices and the new print features in Windows 2000.
- Chapter 23, Auditing, shows you how auditing can be a powerful tool for system administrators.
- Chapter 24, Performance Monitor and Network Monitor, shows you how to use the new interface for Performance Monitor and Network Monitor.

ACKNOWLEDGMENTS

I would like to thank everyone at Prentice Hall, especially Jill Pisoni, for the opportunity to write this book. As always, I owe a huge debt of gratitude to my agent, Margot Maley, who keeps book opportunities coming my way. Thanks to Ariel Silverstone for the eagle eye. Finally, thanks to my wife Dawn, who takes care of life's little details on a daily basis so I can keep focused on my work.

PART ONE

Introducing Windows 2000 Server

In This Part

▶ **CHAPTER 1**
Overview of New Features in Windows 2000 Server

▶ **CHAPTER 2**
Installing Windows 2000 Server

Welcome to *Configuring Windows 2000 Server.* This part introduces you to the major components and new features you will find in Windows 2000 Server and the major topics you can expect to learn about in this book. Also in this part, we will explore the installation requirements and steps for installing Windows 2000 server either as a clean installation or as an upgrade to another Windows operating system.

ONE

Overview of New Features in Windows 2000 Server

What new features are available in Windows 2000 Server? A lot! If you are upgrading from Windows NT 4.0 to Windows 2000 Server, you will find that Windows 2000 Server functions differently and looks significantly different from the Windows NT generation. Windows 2000 Server is Microsoft's answer to the next generation of high-end server operating systems and networking solutions. Windows 2000 Server is designed to move networking environments into the twenty-first century, making use of new technologies, protocols, and the explosive use of the Internet. Before we get into the nuts and bolts of configuring the various components and services in Windows 2000 Server, this chapter gives you an overview of the changes that have been made from Windows NT 4.0 and the new services and components that have been added. A firm understanding of Microsoft's approach with this operating system and what you can expect in terms of operation will greatly help your efforts in configuring Windows 2000 Server for your network environment.

Microsoft's major goals with Windows 2000 Server are to deliver a scalable server system that provides fast and reliable service for standard file and print services, Web support, security, system tools, and automated administrative tasks. In short, Windows 2000 Server is designed to be more manageable, comprehensive, and the best choice for long-term investment. Windows 2000 Server provides centralized management and allows organizations to slowly deploy its various features if they so choose. As with previous versions of Windows NT, Windows 2000 Server maintains compatibility with other operating systems and client-side software.

The following sections, give a brief overview of the major changes and new features Windows 2000 Server offers to organizations that require complex, yet manageable, networking solutions. In later chapters, we consider the configuration for these various components and new features.

Management

Server management is a major concern and time-consuming task for system administrators. Microsoft addresses this issue in Windows 2000 Server by including a number of tools to help system administrators quickly and easily manage the tasks and services in Windows 2000 Server. The following sections take a look at the major new management features.

Microsoft Management Console

If you have used some of Microsoft's BackOffice products, such as Internet Information Server, Proxy Server, or Systems Management Server, you are familiar with the Microsoft Management Console (MMC). The MMC is a stripped-down GUI interface in which multiple products can function through the use of snap-ins. A snap-in is a management tool that connects with the MMC. On its own, the MMC does not have any management functionality, but with the snap-ins, various server components can be grouped and managed in one location.

Windows 2000 Server is fully integrated with the MMC, and all server components and services function as snap-ins to the MMC. By using this design, all services and server applications have the same look and feel. For example, in Windows NT 4.0, the DHCP Manager and the DNS Manager each have a different GUI interface with differing menus. To use each service, you have to learn what the menus offer and how to configure the service. By integrating the server software and all of its services into the MMC, all services have the same appearance and configuration standards. This conformity greatly reduces administrative time since all of the Windows 2000 Server functions are located in one place and it simplifies the Windows 2000 Server interface. As you can see in the figure, the MMC looks similar to the standard Explorer interface. In Figure 1.1, you see a basic MMC interface without any snap-ins.

So, because Windows 2000 Server functions as an MMC snap-in, the initial look and feel of the server is significantly different from Windows NT Server 4.0, but over the long term, the MMC is much easier to use and initially learn. In turn, this feature reduces management time and simplifies server management.

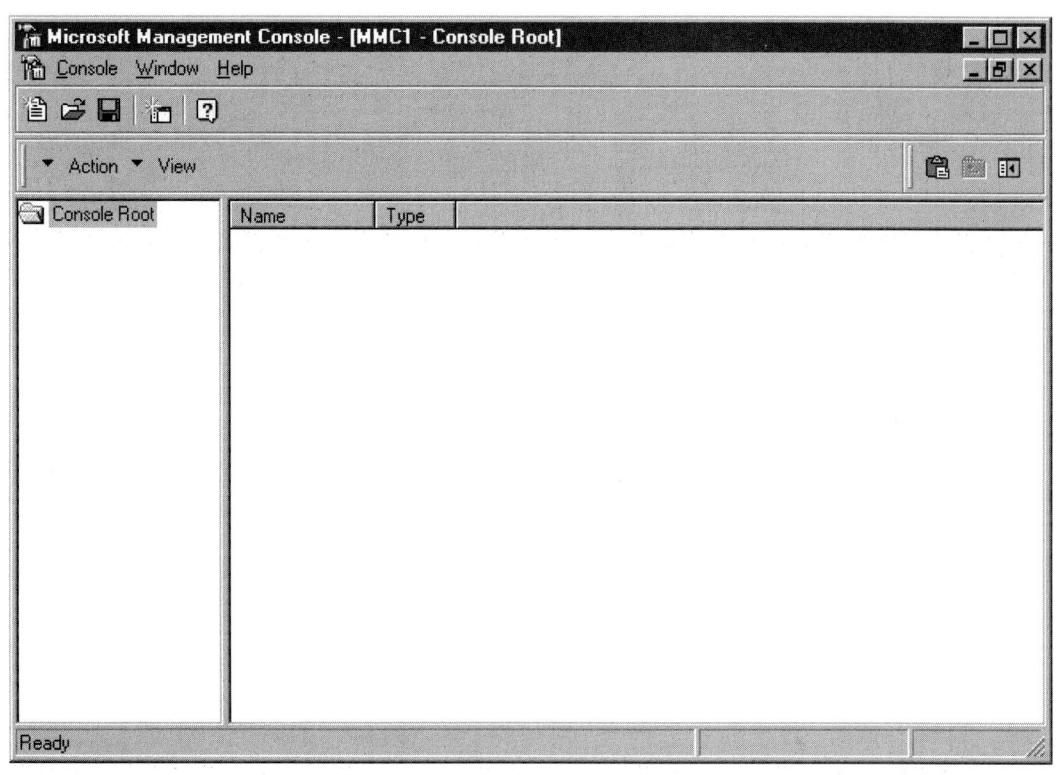

FIGURE 1.1 Microsoft Management Console standard interface

The Active Directory

One of the greatest new features of Windows 2000 Server is the Active Directory, which is the directory service. A "directory" in and of itself is simply a listing of information about particular objects. In terms of a file system, the directory stores information about each of the files so users can find the particular files they want. You can think of the directory service as an index or even a table of contents. The directory service stores multiple directories and makes the information found in the directories available to users.

The Active Directory takes the concept of a directory service a step further in that it provides security, distribution, and replication features. The Active Directory is organized in a hierarchy structure beginning with "objects." Active Directory objects can be any number of network resources, such as users, groups, computers, or files. The objects are stored in the Active Directory Database and are organized by "organization units" (OU). An OU is a logical grouping of objects that can be accessed by network users. In order to find what OU is needed and what OU contains what

FIGURE 1.2 Active Directory hierarchy structure

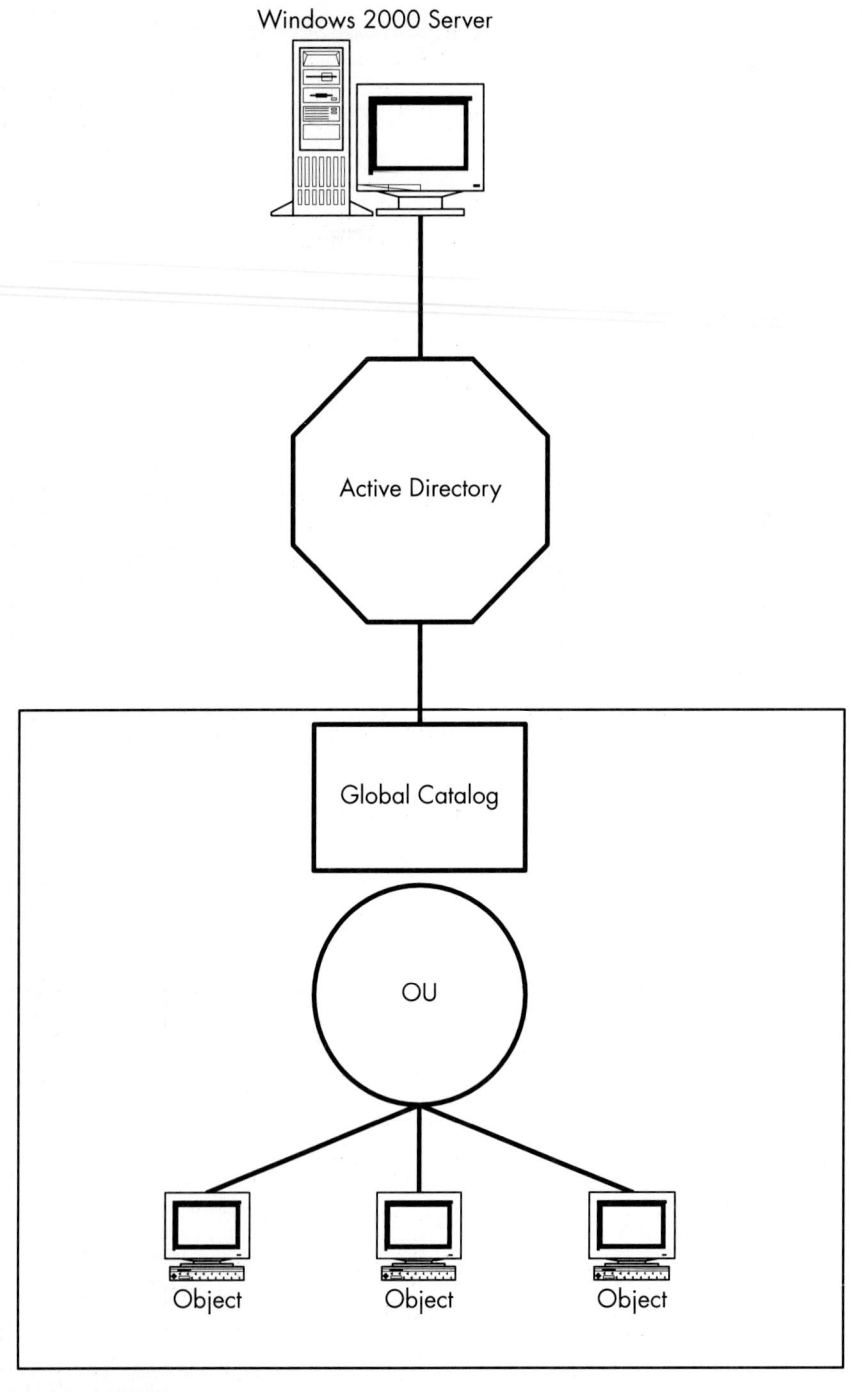

objects, the Active Directory contains a "global catalog" that is searchable. This way, users can easily find whatever objects they may need. Figure 1.2 shows the hierarchy structure of the Active Directory.

The Active Directory is designed to logically and easily manage large amounts of information so the information can be easily located and accessed. Chapter 9 is devoted to explaining the functionality and configuration of the Active Directory.

Application Installation Service

In large networking environments, the management of shared applications can be a harrowing experience. Windows 2000 Server helps reduce the management burden as well as common DLL conflicts between applications with the Application Installation Service. With the Application Installation Service, you can specify a set of applications to be available to a user or a group of users. This feature makes remote deployment and management of applications much easier and reduces the number of potential problems.

Group Policy Editor

Another great administrative burden is the management of individual and group policies. Depending on the policy requirements of your network, configuring and managing policies can be a time-consuming task. Windows 2000 Server eases this burden by introducing the Group Policy Editor. The Group Policy Editor allows administrators to set policies for individual users and groups to a site, domain, or even an OU in the Active Directory. This approach allows you to streamline user profiles, operating system updates, and even application installation, which are then enforceable through the Active Directory. The Group Policy Editor is an MMC snap-in.

Intellimirror

Intellimirror is a group of management tools that allows individual user data, system settings, and operating system settings to move with the user from desktop to desktop or site to site. This feature is accomplished through intelligent local caching and the maintenance of the data and settings on the server. This way, a user is assured that his or her data and settings remain intact and available, regardless of the desktop used. Through the use of intelligent caching available in Windows 2000 Professional, the user has access to his or her settings and data, regardless of whether the user is connected to the network or not.

Web Based Enterprise Management

The Desktop Management Task Force developed the Web Based Enterprise Management (WBEM) standard. The standard seeks to simplify the development and use of drivers and applications and to provide more administrative control. Windows 2000 Server fully supports the WBEM standard.

Windows Scripting Host

The Windows Scripting Host (WSH) is another management tool that allows system administrators or even users to automate a number of user tasks, such as connecting or disconnecting to or from a network server, creating shortcuts for standard applications and files, as well as other typical tasks. The WSH provides a way to automate these tasks.

Application and Publishing Services

Windows 2000 Server offers several new application and publishing services that provide additional functionality. Specifically, one of Microsoft's goals with Windows 2000 Server is to provide seamless integration with the Internet and web components. A number of the new features focus on this goal. The following sections give you a brief overview of the new application and publishing services.

Web Application Services

The Web Application Services use Active Server Pages (ASP) to allow an organization to develop a web-based front end to their server-based applications. ASP combines ActiveX scripts and components to create dynamic web-based applications. ASP allows component-based web application development in any language, such as VBScript or JAVA. ASP in Windows 2000 Server includes several new features, such as enhanced flow control, which allows developers to tightly control program flow; error handling functions that allow developers to trap errors in a custom error message file; and server scriptlets, which allow developers to turn script procedures into reusable COM components that can be used with other web applications. Also, ASP in Windows 2000 Server includes performance-enhanced objects of ASP's typical components. With Web Applications Services, organizations can create a web-based approach to server applications.

Message Queuing Services

Windows 2000 Server Message Queuing Services help developers create and deploy applications that run more smoothly over unreliable networks. Additionally, the Message Queuing Services helps applications running on different platforms to interoperate with the Windows network more easily. The Message Queuing Services function with the Active Directory to store information about message queues in order to increase communication reliability.

Transaction Services

The new Transaction Services in Windows 2000 Server enable developers to create distributed transaction applications. The Transaction Services provide the foundation for developers so that complex transactions can be completed across distributed networks. This foundation makes certain that updates to different data sources, such as SQL, are correct. The Transaction Services reduce development time and expense by allowing developers to focus their attention on the business problems.

Web Publishing Services

Windows 2000 Server Web Publishing Services integrate the server with the Internet or Intranet. Internet Information Server 5.0 installs with Windows 2000 Server as a networking service and allows organizations to take advantage of the latest Internet technologies, such as Dynamic HTML, XML, HTTP 1.1 and others so that Windows 2000 Server provides the built-in capabilities to create and publish complex web sites and information on the Internet or Intranet. The new group of Web Publishing Services includes other features such as a Certificate Wizard to manage SSL security and a Permission Wizard to help administrators establish permissions on restricted web sites.

Indexing

The new indexing services in Windows 2000 Server allow users to find the information they need quickly and easily. The new indexing services function in a cross-platform manner; users can perform full text searches and find the information they need whether that information is stored in a typical file, a web, or even another format or language. As with other new components, indexing helps bring full integration to complex networks offering a variety of information in a variety of formats or languages.

Streaming Media

A final new application and publishing feature of Windows 2000 Server is support for streaming media. As this technology has become more popular on the Internet, Windows 2000 Server provides delivery of streaming media for web users or Intranet sites. Streaming media includes audio and video as well as other multimedia types that can be delivered over the network. With support for Streaming Media, the network can take advantage of other Microsoft components, such as NetShow.

Networking

Of course, the networking services provided by any server define the functionality of network components and user access. Windows 2000 Server offers a number of new networking components that significantly changes portions of the networking environment from Windows NT 4.0. This section gives you an overview of the major new networking components offered in Windows 2000 Server.

Dynamic Domain Name System

Domain Name System (DNS) is a set of protocols and services that allows the use of "friendly" names instead of having to remember a host or computer's Internet Protocol (IP) address. DNS is used to resolve Internet names, such as www.xyzcompany.com to an IP address, such as 131.107.2.200. The friendly name makes communication much easier since users can remember a language-based name instead of a numerical representation. So, the function of the DNS server is to resolve the friendly name to its corresponding IP address.

An additional feature of DNS in Windows 2000 server is Dynamic DNS. Dynamic DNS can automatically edit and replicate the DNS database when a change occurs in the DNS configuration. Windows 2000 Server uses Dynamic DNS as its domain naming service so that you can use the same naming convention seen on the Internet for your domain. In this design, you can connect to computers on the local network using the same naming convention as you would connect to computers on the Internet. DNS is integrated with the Active Directory so that the Active Directory fits with the Internet or Intranet for quick local or remote name resolution.

Network Address Translator

With the integration of Dynamic DNS into the Active Directory, the network must protect its internal IP addresses against external users. The Network Address Translator (NAT) is a new service that hides IP addresses that are internal from external networks by translating the internal IP address to a public external address. This action hides the internal IP structure and also allows a local network to use unregistered IP addresses for internal communication.

Asynchronous Transfer Mode and Fibre Channel

Asynchronous Transfer Mode (ATM) is an advanced WAN transmission technology that provides packet switching of high-speed data transmissions of fixed cell sizes. ATM can transfer voice, data, video, imaging, and other multimedia products at about 155 Mbps with a theoretical limit of 1.2 Gbps.

Fibre Channel provides 1 Gbps data transfer that combines typical transport protocols, such as IP, and high-speed I/O into one connectivity solution. Both of these emerging technologies are supported in Windows 2000 Server.

Windows Quality of Service

Windows Quality of Service (QoS) is a set of services designed to provide a guaranteed delivery system for IP traffic. QoS provides a set of service requirements the network must meet while transferring data.

IP Telephony

Windows 2000 Server provides TAPI 3.0, which further integrates IP and telephony. This approach allows developers to create new telephony applications that work the same over the Internet as they do traditional phone lines.

Services for Macintosh

Windows NT provided file and print services for Macintosh clients. Windows 2000 Server further extends this relationship by allowing Macintosh clients to use TCP/IP to access shares on a server that is running File Services for Macintosh. This approach more fully integrates the Macintosh client into the Windows network.

File System

Windows 2000 Server provides a number of new services and functions to manage files and protect files from hard disk failures. The following sections give you an overview of the major new improvements.

NTFS Enhancements

NTFS is Windows NT's file system that has gained popularity over the past few years because of its extensive file security. Windows 2000 Server provides an enhanced version of NTFS that supports file encryption as well as the ability to add disk space to a volume without rebooting the server. Other enhancements apply to user management and are discussed in the next three sections.

DISTRIBUTED FILE SYSTEM SUPPORT

Microsoft Distributed File System (DFS) is a new server component that makes finding information and data easier for users. With DFS, users can view a single directory tree that includes several file servers or groups of files.

DISTRIBUTED LINK TRACKING

Distributed Link Tracking solves problems with files that have received a name or path change. Distributed Link Tracking resolves the shortcut files and OLE links for the name or path changes.

DISK QUOTAS

You can manage the amount of space in NTFS volumes with disk quotas. By using disk quotas, you can limit the amount of space that is used or monitor the amount of space used on disk partitions.

Remote Storage Services and Removable Storage Manager

Windows 2000 Server provides Remote Storage Services (RSS), which automatically checks the amount of storage space available on the server's local hard disk. When the storage availability on that disk moves below the necessary level, RSS can automatically remove local data that has been copied to a remote disk to make room. Windows 2000 Server also provides a Removable Storage Manager (RSM), which allows multiple applications to share tape or disk drives.

Enhanced Backup Utility

The new Backup Utility in Windows 2000 Server allows files to be backed up to a wide range of media, such as Zip disks, CD-ROMs, tape drives, and external hard disks.

Print Services

Windows 2000 Server provides better print services through the Active Directory. Printers can be organized in the Active Directory as objects so they are easy to locate and use. Additionally, Windows 2000 Server supports over 2,500 different printers, which makes configuration and printer selection much easier. Finally, Windows 2000 Server makes use of the Internet Printing Protocol (IPP), which allows users to print to a URL over the Internet or Intranet while providing printer information in an HTML format.

Improved Scalability

Scalability is a term that has become popular in ever expanding computer networks during the past several years. Hardware and software that is "scalable" can grow with the network and meet the rising needs of the network. There are several new enhancements to Windows 2000 Server to make it even more scalable than Windows NT 4.0. The following sections give you a short overview of some of the major improvements.

Enterprise Memory Architecture

Windows 2000 Server now supports accessing up to 32 Gb of memory on 64-bit processors, such as those offered on Alpha and Intel platforms. The memory architecture allows applications to keep more data in memory, which provides greater performance.

SMP Scalability and I20 Support

Windows 2000 Server offers improved SMP scalability so that it functions more quickly on RISC and Intel processors. Also, Windows 2000 Server offers support for the I20 architecture, which uses a dedicated processor with its own memory so that it can take processing tasks off the main CPU. This architecture greatly improves I/O performance, especially when used with CPU intensive tasks such as client/server processing.

Job Object and Clustering

Windows 2000 Server includes a new extension to the process model known as a "job." The Job objects are named, securable, and sharable objects that control the attributes of the processes associated with those job objects. Job objects allow several processes to be managed as one unit. Windows 2000 Server also supports new clustering services. Available in the Enterprise edition, clustering allows two or more servers to be connected to form one server. This action creates higher availability and computing power.

Security

Windows 2000 Server provides several new tools and enhancements for the ever increasing security needs of today's advanced networks. The following sections give you an overview of the new security enhancements and tools.

Kerberos Authentication

Kerberos Version 5 authentication protocol provides a single log-in model to Windows 2000 Server. Kerberos is an Internet standard and it replaces NTLM as the primary security protocol for access to resources within a domain or across domains. Kerberos provides a number of security benefits, including both client and server authentication, reduction of server load, and the allowance of proxy software to help manage authentication.

Public Key Certificate Server

Windows 2000 Server provides a Public Key Certificate Server built in to Windows 2000 Server. This technology allows organizations to use a public key to encrypt data. The Public Key Certificate Server solution provides organizations that use Public Key Certificates with a certificate server for their own site instead of relying on other companies that provide key certificates.

Smart Card

Microsoft has implemented smart cards, a component of the public-key infrastructure. Smart cards enhance the security of single log-on, storage, and other software solutions. Smart cards allow you to protect private keys, passwords, personal data, and other private information. The smart cards included in Windows 2000 Server conform to the ISO standard and will help reduce incompatibility problems that have been common in the past.

Security Configuration Editor

The Security Configuration Editor included in Windows 2000 Server allows administrators to create a security template that can be applied to many computers. This template feature saves administrators time and provides a more uniform approach to security configurations within a network.

IP Security Protocol

Windows 2000 Server supports the IP Security protocol for encrypting TCP/IP traffic. IP Security Protocol can be used for encrypted transmissions within the Intranet and can also be used with Point to Point Tunneling Protocol (PPTP) when creating Virtual Private Networks over the Internet.

Setup Tools

Windows 2000 Server includes a few new tools to help with setup problems. First, Windows 2000 Server includes Advanced System Recovery (ASR). ASR allows an administrator to save a complete copy of their system settings so those settings can be recovered in the event of a disk crash or some other disaster. Another tool now included with Windows 2000 Server is the Driver Incompatibility Wizard. The Driver Incompatibility Wizard identifies incompatible hardware drivers and points the user to a web site that may update the driver. Finally, Windows 2000 Server is Plug and Play compliant, which makes the addition of new devices much easier.

Summary

This chapter gave you a brief look at the major changes and new features in Windows 2000 Server. Windows 2000 Server offers improvements and new services in virtually every category, from management to networking, and is designed to be the next generation of powerful server software to meet the needs of complex networks in the twenty first century.

The following chapters address the configuration of Windows 2000 Server so that it can provide the functionality, security, and service needs of your growing network.

TWO

Installing Windows 2000 Server

It's no secret that operating system installations can be terrifying events. If you are still holding that Windows 2000 Server installation CD-ROM and feel some trepidation about installing it onto your Windows NT 4.0 Server that works just as you want it to, you are certainly not alone. From experience, you know that an installation can be a bumpy ride, and it may take days of work to fix issues or problems that occur. This chapter can help you get the server software installed with minimal problems and make your work easier.

The key to avoiding problems when installing Windows 2000 Server is planning. Before the installation, you must make certain that your system is ready for the installation. This action alone will prevent a number of potential problems and issues. Keep in mind that Windows 2000 Server is more than a version upgrade. The operating system is different from Windows NT, and it functions significantly different. With that said, the first two sections of this chapter help you make certain you are ready to install the server software.

Hardware Requirements for Windows 2000 Server

Regardless of whether you will be upgrading to Windows 2000 Server from Windows NT Server or performing a clean installation, you need to make certain your computer meets the hardware requirements. As you are probably aware, Microsoft's hardware recommendations are bare-bones minimum, so I have also included my own experience in recommending minimum hardware. Check your system against Table 2.1 to make certain your hardware can support Windows 2000 Server.

TABLE 2.1 Windows 2000 Server Minimum Hardware Requirements

Hardware Component	Requirement
Processor	166-MHz Pentium or higher. In reality, the faster the processor, the better
RAM	64 MB minimum, at least 128 MB (or more) recommended (4 Gb maximum)
Hard Disk	2-GB (or larger) hard disk with a minimum of 500 MB of free space
Monitor	VGA or higher resolution
CD-ROM	12x or higher

For additional hardware, you should make certain that your devices are compatible with Windows 2000 Server. Setup automatically checks your system and reports any potential conflicts, but to avoid this problem, you should check your system in advance. Windows 2000 Server is Plug and Play compliant, but any non-Plug and Play devices should be checked against the hardware compatibility list at http://www.microsoft.com/hwtest/hcl or on your Windows 2000 Server CD-ROM.

Getting Windows NT Server 4.0 Ready to Upgrade

If you are installing Windows 2000 Server on a machine with no operating system, you can skip over this section until you need it and move to the "Performing a Clean Installation" section. If you are upgrading your system from Windows NT 4.0, then you should read and follow the instructions in this section carefully. You can also upgrade Windows NT 3.51 and Windows NT 4.0 Terminal Server to Windows 2000 Server. You cannot upgrade to Windows 2000 Server from earlier versions of NT without first upgrading that version to at least 3.51.

For the most part, installing Windows 2000 Server on a Windows NT 4.0 Server computer is not a difficult process. Windows 2000 Server automatically keeps your users and groups, system settings, and existing application if they are compatible with Windows 2000 Server. However, there are a few issues and changes you should make to the system to help ensure a painless installation. The following sections give you specific actions and instructions to get your Windows NT 4.0 Server computer ready for a Windows 2000 Server installation.

Install the Latest Service Pack

In the fall of 1998, Microsoft released Windows NT 4.0 Service Pack 4. Service Pack 4 (SP4) contains a number of additions and fixes as well as tools that are implemented in Windows 2000 Server. In the summer of 1999, Service Pack 5 was released, then Service Pack 6. Service Pack 5 and 6 contain additional Y2K fixes and make some enhancements of updates included in Service Pack 4. If you are going to upgrade to Windows 2000 Server, you should at least have Service Pack 4 installed.

Service packs are available on CD-ROM from Microsoft, or you can download them from their web site. However, some components are only available on the CD-ROM. The following list gives you an overview of the major changes and additions that are made by installing SP4, 5 or 6.

- Support for Windows 2000 Server NTFS. As mentioned in Chapter 1, Windows 2000 Server contains an enhanced version of NTFS that supports encryption technology.
- Year 2000 updates. SP4 contains updates for known issues with Y2K compatibility in Windows NT 4.0.
- User Profile Quotas. SP4 allows you to limit the size of your users' profiles.
- Protocol Enhancements. SP4 contains a number of enhancements for widely used networking protocols in Windows NT 4.0 such as DHCP, WINS, RRAS, and PPTP.
- Windows NT 4.0 Option Pack Updates. If you are using the Windows NT 4.0 Option Pack, SP4 contains fixes for minor issues with Option Pack components.
- Security Configuration Manager. SP4 includes the Security Configuration Manager (SCM) that allows you to streamline security setting and user rights. The SCM is an MMC snap-in and is available on the CD-ROM version of SP4. You can also download the SCM from microsoft.com as a separate component.
- Euro Key Patch. SP4 provides the new euro currency symbol and updates core fonts.
- Microsoft Data Access Components. SP4 provides Y2K updates to Data Access components. This update is available on the CD-ROM or through a full SP4 download.
- Microsoft Web Based Enterprise Management (WBEM). WBEM is an industry initiative to develop standardized technology for accessing management information in enterprise environments. SP4 installs Windows Management Instrumentation (WMI) that conforms to the WBEM standard. This option is available only on the SP4 CD-ROM.

Since you are moving to Windows 2000 Server, it's a good idea to install SP4 or 5 before beginning the Windows 2000 Server installation and install the WBEM and SCM components if possible. As with all service packs, you should check microsoft.com for updates or hot fixes that may need to be applied to SP4 or 5.

Convert FAT Disks to NTFS

Windows 2000 Server supports FAT (File Allocation Table) disks and FAT32, but it is optimized for the new version of NTFS. NTFS provides a high level of security options that are not supported in FAT. Before installing Windows 2000 Server, you should seriously consider converting any FAT disks to NTFS, so you can make use of the new security enhancements as well as support any BackOffice products that require an NTFS partition.

To convert a FAT drive to NTFS, use the convert.exe utility provided in Windows NT. The conversion will preserve any data stored on the FAT volume, but the process is one-way; you cannot return to FAT without reformatting the disk. To use the convert utility, simply use the following syntax at the command line:

```
CONVERT driveletter: /FS:NTFS
```

Install TCP/IP and Remove Unnecessary Protocols

TCP/IP is the primary protocol used by Windows 2000 Server. Due to the server's design and its Active Directory features, TCP/IP is required for many major functions such as directory replication. Windows 2000 Server continues to support other protocols, such as NetBEUI and NWLink, but you should remove any protocols that are not required by applications or particular network clients. If TCP/IP is not currently installed on your server, you should install the protocol using the Protocols tab on the Network Properties page and reapply the current service pack.

Install and Implement DHCP

Dynamic Host Configuration Protocol (DHCP) is used to dynamically assign IP addresses to network clients. DHCP makes the implementation of TCP/IP much easier because the server can lease an IP address to a client and ensure that no IP addresses are duplicated on the network. Since this process is done automatically and dynamically as needed, administrators do not have to worry about manually assigning IP addresses or the possibility of duplicate IP addresses within the network. In Windows 2000 Server, DHCP is also used to automatically register server and client computers with DNS so that they can be easily found on the network using host naming conventions.

To install DHCP on your NT server, complete the following steps:

1. Access the Services tab on the Network Properties sheet.
2. Click the Add button. Windows NT generates a list of network services that can be added. Select DHCP Server and click OK.
3. Setup prompts you for the location of the installation files. Normally,

you will need to access your CD-ROM drive or a network share point. Type the appropriate location and click OK.

4. Setup copies the necessary files and prompts you to reboot your computer.
5. Reapply the current service pack.

Once you have DHCP installed, you need to establish a DHCP scope and configure your client computers to contact the DHCP server for an IP address. To configure a DHCP scope, complete the following steps:

1. Click Start → Programs → Administrative Tools (Common) → DHCP Manager. The DHCP Manager opens.
2. Click the Server menu, then click Add.
3. Type the IP address of your server in Add DHCP Server to Server List dialog box. Click OK.
4. Expand the DHCP Servers list and highlight your server, as shown in Figure 2.1.

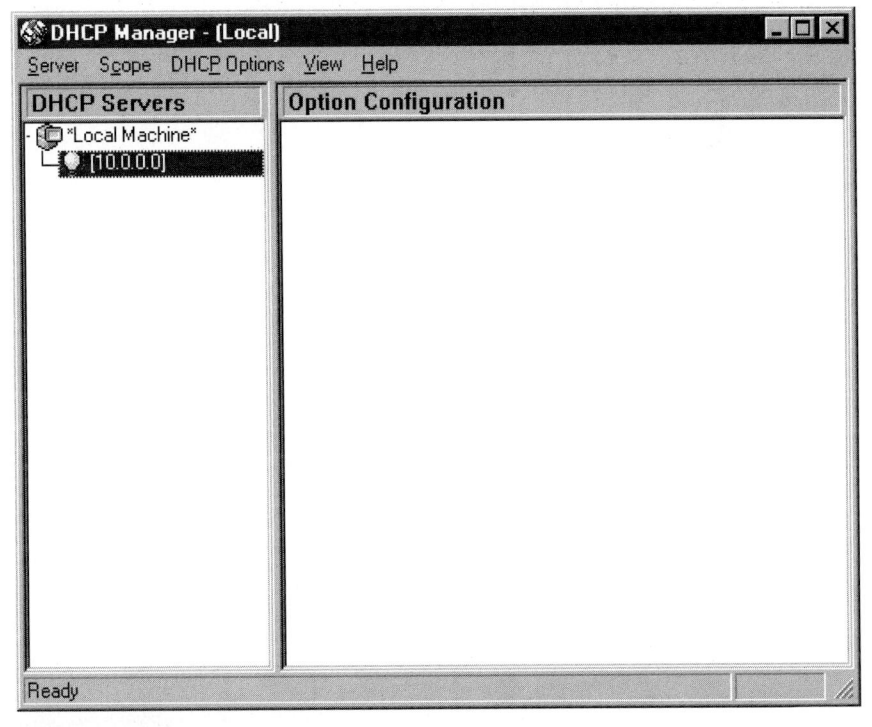

FIGURE 2.1 DHCP Server Manager servers list

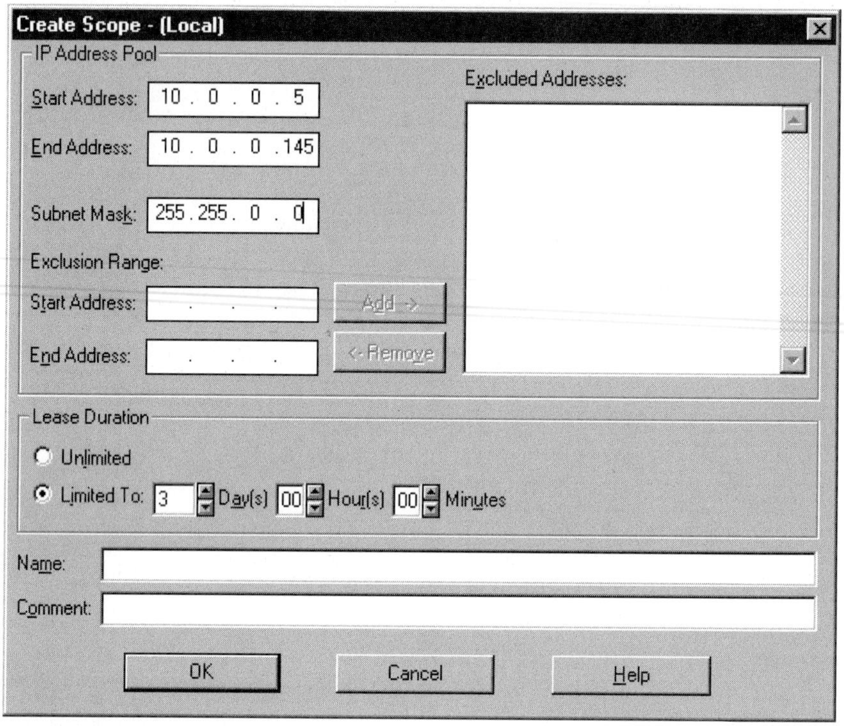

FIGURE 2.2 DHCP Scope

5. Click on the Scope Menu and select Create. The Create Scope dialog box appears. Enter the IP addresses you want assigned to network clients in the Start and End Address boxes. The range you enter must have the same network ID. You should also enter an appropriate subnet mask for the scope. Figure 2.2 shows you an example. You can also specify an exclusion range if necessary, and you can configure the lease duration as desired for your network. Click OK.

6. A dialog box appears telling you that the scope has been created but has not yet been activated. Click the Yes button to activate.

You can configure several other components of DHCP, such as the router and default gateway you want to use. To learn more about the additional configuration options, consult the Windows NT 4.0 help files.

Once you have a DHCP scope configured, you need to configure the client computers to contact the DHCP Server for an IP address. In Windows NT 4.0 Workstation, right click Network Neighborhood and choose properties. Click the Protocols tab, highlight TCP/IP protocol, then click the properties button. On the properties sheet, select the Obtain an IP address from a DHCP Server radio button. Windows 95 and 98 computers are configured in a similar fashion.

Once client computers begin contacting the DHCP Server for an IP address, you can use the IPCONFIG command line utility (or WINIPCFG for Windows 95 or 98) to view the DHCP assignment for each client. On the client computer, type IPCONFIG/ALL at the command line to get this information.

Install DNS

As mentioned in Chapter 1, DNS is integrated with the Active Directory and replaces WINS for primary name resolution. Before installing Windows 2000 Server, you should install the DNS service. You do not have to worry about configuring DNS at this time, but you should at least install the service on your Windows NT 4.0 Server. To install DNS, follow the same steps as you did to install DHCP, but select DNS from the network services list.

Review Hardware

Before installing Windows 2000 Server, you should review the hardware in your system and make certain you have the most updated drivers. Windows 2000 Server is Plug and Play compliant and also supports the Universal Serial Bus (USB), but in order to avoid potential hardware problems, make sure you have current drivers. Refer to the first section in this chapter to see the minimum hardware requirements for Windows 2000 Server.

Review Users and Groups

Finally, before you install Windows 2000 Server, carefully examine your users and groups. You should gather current records and attempt to streamline groups so you do not have repetitive groups or permissions. This action will make your work with the Active Directory much easier to implement.

Installing Windows 2000 Server

You can install Windows 2000 Server as a clean installation or as an upgrade over Windows NT 4.0, NT 3.51, or Terminal Server 4.0. For the most part, the two installation options work similarly. If you are installing Windows 2000 Server as a clean installation, you will be asked to provide more information about your network and the role of the server. If you are installing Windows 2000 Server as an upgrade to Windows NT 4.0, make sure you read and follow the instructions in the first section of this chapter, "Getting Windows NT 4.0 Ready for Installation," so that your system is ready for the installation.

You won't see too many surprises when you begin the installation—most of the screens you will see are somewhat familiar to previous installations, and the setup program does most of the work for you. This section assumes you are installing Windows 2000 Server as an upgrade to Windows NT 4.0, and the following steps follow the upgrade installation. If you are performing a clean installation, refer to the next section.

About Domain Controllers

Once you upgrade to Windows 2000 Server, you can easily change the role of your server as you please. Windows 2000 allows you to use the Active Directory to dynamically change the role your server plays in the network—from a domain controller, a member server, or a standalone server—as many times and as often as you need. This is a big change from previous versions of NT, which required you to reinstall the operating system to change a server's role.

Windows 2000 Server offers three server roles: domain controller, member server, or a standalone server. There are no longer Primary Domain Controllers (PDC) and Backup Domain Controllers (BDC). When you upgrade Windows NT PDCs and BDCs, they simply become "domain controllers," or the BDC can become a member server based on your choice. An NT standalone server can become a member server or a standalone server in the Windows 2000 network.

If you currently have more than one server, with one being a PDC and the other(s) being BDCs, you must upgrade the PDC first so that it becomes an Active Directory domain controller. The good news is that you can mix Windows 2000 and Windows NT environments. The upgraded server will appear as an Active Directory domain controller to other Windows 2000 servers but still appears as a PDC to Windows NT servers and clients. This feature allows you to slowly implement Windows 2000 into your network, test each server thoroughly, and "learn as you go" while maintaining a fully functional network.

Performing the Windows 2000 Upgrade

Before upgrading to Windows 2000 Server, you should perform a complete backup of all of your files, and you need to uncompress any DriveSpace or DoubleSpace volumes before running setup. If disk mirroring is configured, you need to disable it before running the set up program. Also, if you are using an uninterruptible power device, disconnect it from your computer before running setup. To install Windows 2000 Server as an upgrade over Windows NT or Terminal Server, follow these steps:

1. Insert the Windows 2000 Server CD-ROM into your CD-ROM drive. Autorun will launch a GUI installation window and a dialog box appears telling you an older version of Windows is running on your machine. Click the Yes button to upgrade. If autorun does not automatically launch, double-click the Setup icon on the CD-ROM.

2. Windows 2000 Server launches the setup wizard and begins with a window asking if you would like to upgrade to Windows 2000 Server or perform a clean installation. Select the Upgrade to Windows 2000 radio button and click the Next button.
3. The next screen presents you with the Microsoft licensing agreement for Windows 2000. Read the agreement, click the "I accept the agreement" radio button, then click the Next button. Setup will not continue unless you accept the agreement.
4. Setup examines your system to determine which files to copy; then it begins the file copy process. Once the file copy process has completed, setup reboots your computer.
5. After your computer reboots, the MS-DOS portion of setup begins. The MS-DOS portion begins by loading necessary installation files and then performs a search for previous versions of Windows.
6. Next, setup examines your hard disks, then reboots the computer.
7. Setup continues in MS-DOS mode by loading additional files and drivers. Then, setup checks your hard disk(s) again and deletes unneeded files.
8. Setup now creates a list of files that it needs to copy and begins the file copy process. The file copy process is rather lengthy and will take several minutes.
9. After the files are copied, setup initializes the Windows 2000 configuration and saves the default configuration; then the computer is rebooted.
10. Next, Windows 2000 begins for the first time and launches a hardware detection and driver installation for your system. This process takes several minutes and the screen may flicker a few seconds during the process.
11. Next, setup installs Windows 2000 components and upgrades existing services. This takes several minutes.
12. Setup continues by installing start menu items, registering the components, and saving the settings. Temporary setup files are deleted and the computer reboots.
13. Windows 2000 Server begins for the first time by preparing the network connections. If WINS and DHCP were installed on your Windows NT 4.0 Server, you will receive a message telling you that these services cannot start because they have to be converted to a Windows 2000 format. Click OK for the conversions to take place.
14. Next, the Active Directory installation wizard appears. Click the Next button to begin the installation of the Active Directory.
15. Setup gives you a window asking you if you want to create a new domain tree or create a new child domain in an existing Windows

2000 Server domain tree. If you do not want to join an existing Windows 2000 domain tree, click to create a new domain tree and click the Next button.

16. The next windows asks you if want to create a new forest of domain trees or place this new domain tree in an existing forest. If you do not want to join an existing forest, click to create a new forest of domain trees and click the Next button. Also, you can refer to Chapter 9 to learn more about tree and forests in the Active Directory.

17. Next, the Active Directory installation Wizard asks you to provide a full DNS name for the new domain. If you have a DNS name registered with an Internet naming authority, you can use that name. If not, you need to decide what name you will use. You may choose to use the name of your domain with a .com extension, such as corp.com. If you are unsure about the naming convention you should use, refer to Chapter 9.

18. The next window gives you a recommended location for the Active Directory databases. You can accept the recommendation or change it by using the browse buttons.

19. The next window gives you a recommendation for the location for the Shared System Volume which stores the server's copy of the domain's public files. These files are replicated to all domain controllers. Accept the suggested location or click the browse button to enter a new location.

20. The system configures the Active Directory.

21. The Active Directory wizard completes its tasks. Click the Finish button. The system is rebooted for the final time and the upgrade is complete.

Installing a Clean Copy of Windows 2000 Server

You can install Windows 2000 Server on a computer that does not have an operating system. Before doing so, you should make certain that your system meets at least the minimum hardware requirements listed in Table 2.1 at the beginning of this chapter. You can also install a copy of Windows 2000 Server in a separate partition on an existing system so that you have a dual-boot configuration, such as Windows NT 4.0 or Windows 2000 Professional. The major issue with dual-boot configurations is file system choice. For example, if you dual-boot Windows 98 and Windows 2000, Windows 98 will not be able to see the Windows 2000 partition if it is formated with NTFS. Additionally, because NTFS is enhanced in Windows 2000, even Windows NT will not be able to read some of its encryption features. The advantage of dual-boot configurations is you can use software that is written for a particular system. For example, you can dual-boot Windows 2000 Server and

Windows 98 to use applications specifically written for Windows 98. In this case, Windows 98 will not be able to see the NTFS partition. If you are considering dual-booting, see the Windows 2000 Server setup notes on your CD-ROM for more information about known issues and problems.

CREATING BOOT DISKS

Before beginning the installation, you will need to create a set of boot disks so you can launch the installation program on the blank machine. You can create setup disks using the Windows 2000 Server CD-ROM on any computer running any version of Windows or MS-DOS. You will need four blank, formatted 3.5-inch 1.44-MB floppy disks, and you should label the disks. To create the setup disks, follow these steps:

1. Insert a blank disk into the floppy disk drive.
2. Insert the Windows 2000 CD-ROM into the CD-ROM drive.
3. Click Start ➤ Run and type

   ```
   d:\bootdisk\makeboot.exe
   ```

   Where "D" is the drive letter of your CD-ROM drive.
4. The system will begin creating the boot disks and prompt you to remove and replace floppy disks as needed. The system will also tell you which disk each floppy disk becomes, such as 1, 2, 3, and 4. Make sure you label the disks appropriately.

INSTALLING FROM A NETWORK SHARE

If you are installing Windows 2000 Server from a network share, you will need to access the network share, locate the 1386 (or Alpha) folder, then run WINNT.EXE. The installation process will then occur from the network shared folder.

SETUP OPTIONS

As with Windows NT, you have a number of setup options with Windows 2000 Server. This section explains the major setup options you may want to consider before actually installing Windows 2000 Server. As with Windows NT, you can modify how winnt.exe or winnt32.exe runs by using a number of setup switches. As with Windows NT, running Winnt from the command prompt installs Windows 2000. Tables 2.2 and 2.3 give you the setup switches you can use for both winnt.exe and winnt32.exe respectively.

TABLE 2.2   WINNT.EXE Setup Switches

Switch	Explanation
/a	Enables Accessibility Options
/I	Specifies the .inf file of the Setup information file
/1	Creates the $Winnt.log file containing a list of file copy errors
/r	Specifies an optional folder to be installed
/rx	Specifies an optional folder to be copied
/s	Specifies the location of the Windows 2000 files
/t	Specifies a drive that will hold the temporary installation files
/udf	The Uniqueness Database file that modifies the answer file for unattended setup

TABLE 2.3   WINNT32.EXE Setup Switches

Switch	Explanation
/s	Specifies the location of the Windows 2000 files
/syspart: drive_letter	Allows you to copy setup startup files to a hard drive, mark the drive as active, then install the drive in another computer (You must use the /tempdrive switch with /syspart.)
/tempdrive: drive_letter	Tells setup to place temporary files on a specified drive and to install Windows 2000 on that drive
/copydir: folder_name	Creates additional folders in the folder that contains the Windows 2000 files
/copysource: folder_name	Creates a temporary folder in the folder that contains the Windows 2000 files
/cmd	Tells setup to carry about a specific command before setup is complete
/debug	Creates a debug log at the level specified
/I	Specifies the .inf setup information file
/x	Stops setup from creating setup boot floppies
/unattended	Upgrades the previous version of Windows in unattended mode. All user settings are imported from the previous installation.
/r	Installs an additional directory within the tree where Windows 2000 files are installed
/e	Tells setup to execute a specific command after setup is complete
/udf:id	Specifies the Uniqueness Database File for use during an unattended installation

If you choose to use any of the setup switches or run an unattended installation, you should review additional documentation on the Windows 2000 Server CD-ROM or from your Windows NT Server CD-ROM.

INSTALLATION

Now you are ready to run the installation program to install a clean copy of Windows 2000 Server. To install Windows 2000 Server, follow these steps:

1. Insert the Setup Disk 1 into the disk drive and turn on the computer. You will be prompted for the remaining three disks until the setup program is loaded. If your CD-ROM drive supports it, you may be able to boot off of the CD-ROM.
2. Setup restarts the computer and begins a text-based portion of setup. Setup prompts you to select a partition in which to install Windows 2000 Server. Select an existing partition or create a new one using any unpartitioned space.
3. Next, setup prompts you to select a file system for the new partition. Then setup formats the partition with the file system you selected.
4. After the disk is formatted, setup begins copying files to the hard disk then restarts the computer.
5. Setup detects and installs the hardware on your system.
6. The setup wizard appears and asks you for the following information:
   - Computer name: Enter a computer name of up to 63 characters. Windows operating systems earlier than Windows 2000 will only see the first 15 characters.
   - Licensing: Select either Per Server or Per Seat licensing.
   - Your name and organization.
   - Regional Settings: Enter your regional settings so that Windows can configure your language and keyboard settings.
   - Administrator account and password. The password can be up to 256 characters long and should be at least 7 for optimal security. Use a mixture of letters and numbers.
   - Optional Component Selection: You have several optional components you can select to install with Windows 2000 Server. Table 2.4 gives you an overview of these components.
   - Display Settings: Allows you to configure the desktop.
   - Time and Date.
7. Once this information is collected, Setup installs the networking components, which includes detection of your network adapter card.
8. Setup prompts you to choose typical or custom network settings. A typical selection includes Client for Microsoft Networks, File and

TABLE 2.4 Windows 2000 Server Optional Components

Component	Description
Certificate Services	Allows you to create X.509 digital certificates
IIS	Selected by default. IIS allows you to host Internet or Intranet webs and ftp sites.
Message Queuing Services	Provides developers with a simplified programming model and built-in transactional support
Indexing Service	Enables dynamic full-text searches of data stored on your computer on other network computers
Networking Options	Includes standard networking options including DHCP, DNS, TCP/IP, and additional file and print services
Remote Installation Service	Allows you to remotely install Windows 2000 Professional on a remote client computer
Terminal Services	Provides components and tools to host Windows-based terminals
Transaction Server	Selected by default, the transaction server installs the DCOM-based MTS Transaction Manager.

Printer Sharing for Microsoft Networks, and TCP/IP. If you select custom, you can select additional components, or you can always install them later as needed.

9. Next, Setup will prompt you to join a domain or workgroup. Make your selection and click Next.
10. Setup continues the installation and reboots Windows 2000 Server.
11. After rebooting, you are prompted to press CTRL + ALT + DEL and enter your password to logon to Windows.

Summary

Installing Windows 2000 Server does not have to be a painful experience. The foremost key is to make certain that your computer hardware can support Windows 2000 Server and will perform in a satisfactory manner. If your computer components are up-to-date, the Setup program can do most of the work for you and provide an easy installation. As with most installations, planning is the key.

PART TWO

Hardware and Disk Management

In This Part

▶ **CHAPTER 3**
A Tour Around the Interface

▶ **CHAPTER 4**
Configuring and Managing Hardware

▶ **CHAPTER 5**
Disk Management

▶ **CHAPTER 6**
Interface and System Settings

▶ **CHAPTER 7**
The Registry and Backup Operations

▶ **CHAPTER 8**
Remote and Removable Storage

Windows 2000 Server includes several new hardware and disk management features, from Plug and Play support to remote file storage. In this section, you will learn about configuring hardware devices, disk management and fault tolerance, interface and system settings, backup operations, and remote and removable storage solutions.

THREE

A Tour Around the Interface

At first glance after installing Windows 2000 Server, you may think it is a hybrid of Windows 98. In fact, Windows 2000 Server combines the best features of Windows NT, Windows 98, MMC integration, and several new surprises as well. This chapter gives you a first look at the interface and helps you discover the new design and location of familiar tools and services.

After installing Windows 2000 Server, one of the first questions (or series of questions) is usually "Where is User Manager? Where do you add or remove protocols? How do you add network services?" These questions are normal because most of Windows 2000 Server's interface locations and designs are different from those of Windows NT. However, after you pass the learning curve, you will probably agree that the new design is much easier and streamlined.

Although the desktop area, as shown in Figure 3.1, looks very familiar, the system is significantly different.

The following sections give you a quick tour around the Windows 2000 Server interface. We will explore the various configuration options for each of these in later chapters, but for now, it's a good idea to be able to find your way around the system.

34 Chapter three • A Tour Around the Interface

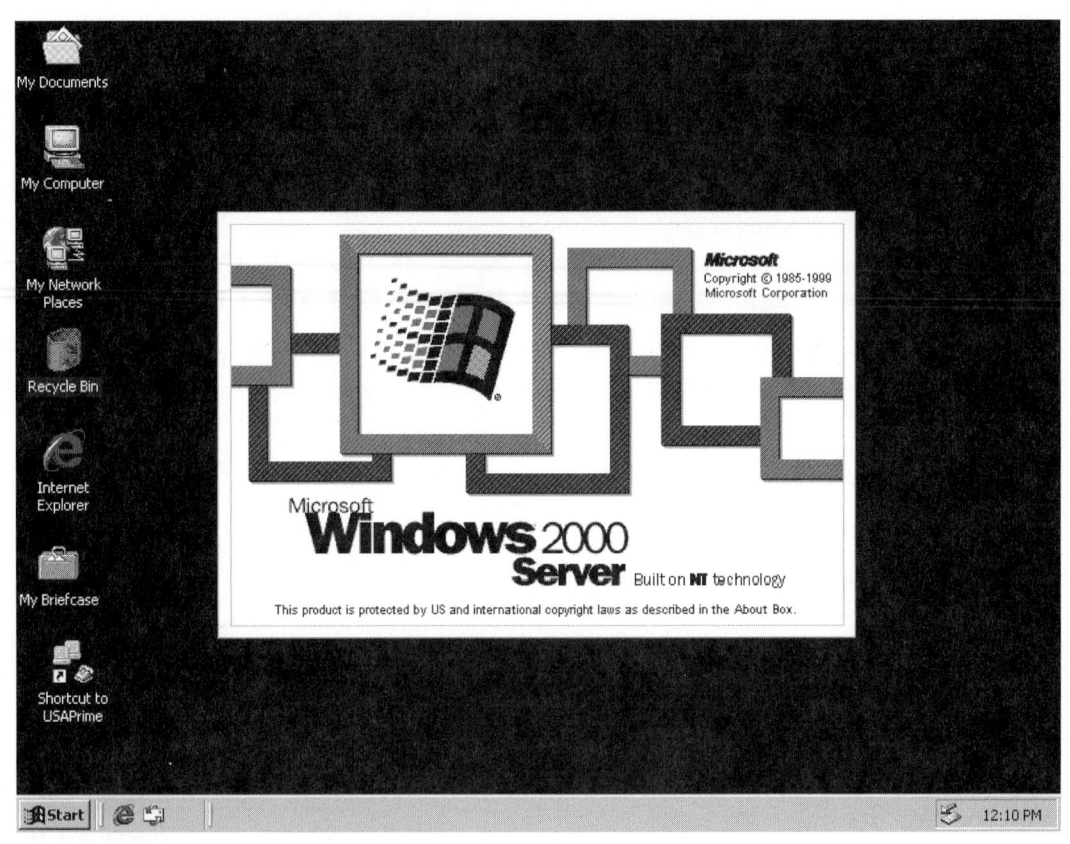

FIGURE 3.1 Windows 2000 Desktop

Desktop

The first section we will explore concerns the desktop icons. These are the most familiar to you if you have used any Windows operating system. However, there are some differences from Windows NT.

Start Menu

The Start Menu in Windows 2000 Server looks very similar to that of Windows 98 and contains the following options:

- Shut Down: The Shut Down option presents you with a drop-down menu with the options of Shutting down the computer, restarting the computer, or logging off the current account.
- Run: The run command allows you to access local or network drives, folders, or shares.

- Help: The help option opens Windows 2000 Server help files. The help files in Windows 2000 Server contain a number of useful features, such as checklists, hyperlinks that automatically help you configure system components, hyperlinks to other portions of the help files, and hyperlinks that take you to information on Microsoft's web site. The new help interface is shown in Figure 3.2.
- Search: The Search Menu is expanded in Windows 2000 Server to allow you to search for files and folders, the Internet, printers, how to use Microsoft Outlook, or people.
- Settings: The Settings Menu allows you to access quickly the Control Panel, Network and Dial-up Connections folder, Printers, or the Taskbar and Start Menu.
- Documents: The Documents Menu contains a list of recently used or modified documents.
- Programs: The Programs Menu is your starting point to all program files within Windows 2000 Server.

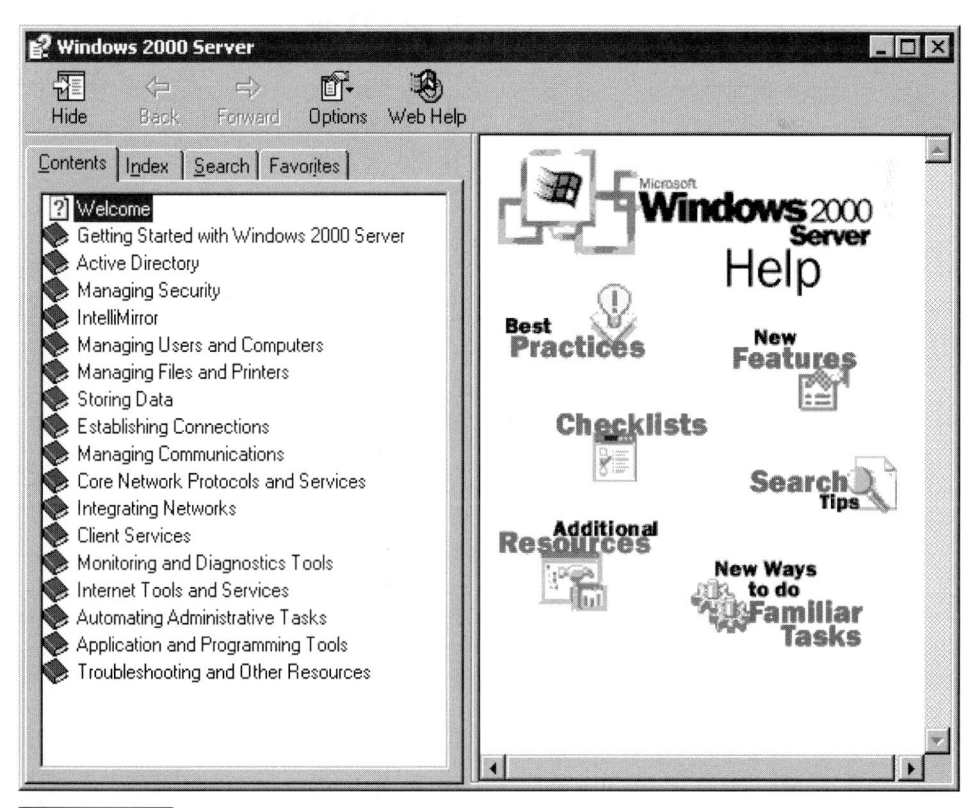

FIGURE 3.2 Windows 2000 Help

- Windows Update: The Windows Update, introduced in Windows 98, launches Internet Explorer and a connection to Microsoft's update site. The site contains documentation, fixes, patches, critical updates, and add-on components for Windows 2000 Server.
- Additional Options: Depending on the software you have installed, additional options may appear, such as a New Office Document icon to immediately launch Microsoft Word.

My Briefcase

My Briefcase appears in Windows 2000 Server. My Briefcase allows you to work on files on multiple computers and synchronize those files so that you have the most current version of the file available.

Internet Explorer

The Internet Explorer browser appears as a desktop icon and is also available on the taskbar.

Recycle Bin

The Recycle Bin appears on the desktop and contains additional information about files that are placed in the Recycle Bin, such as the file's original location, the date it was deleted, and the type of file.

My Network Places

My Network Places replaces Network Neighborhood. In My Network Places, as shown in Figure 3.3, you can browse computers near you, browse the entire network, or use the Add Network Place wizard, which helps you connect to a network share or an FTP site. The Entire Network option also contains a handy search utility so you can easily find a desired computer, printer, person or shared file or folder, or you can view the entire contents that leads you into the Active Directory. Notice in Figure 3.3 that the folder contains hyperlinks to additional places where you can configure related components.

If you right click the My Network Places icon and select Properties, the window in Figure 3.3 opens again. Instead of a properties sheet with Services, Protocols, Bindings, etc. where you spent a lot of time in Windows NT. What you have to do now is right click Local Area Connection from within the My Network Places window and select Properties. Then, you get a general connection properties sheet where you can configure as well as install and uninstall additional services. If you have used Windows 95 or 98, this window will look very familiar.

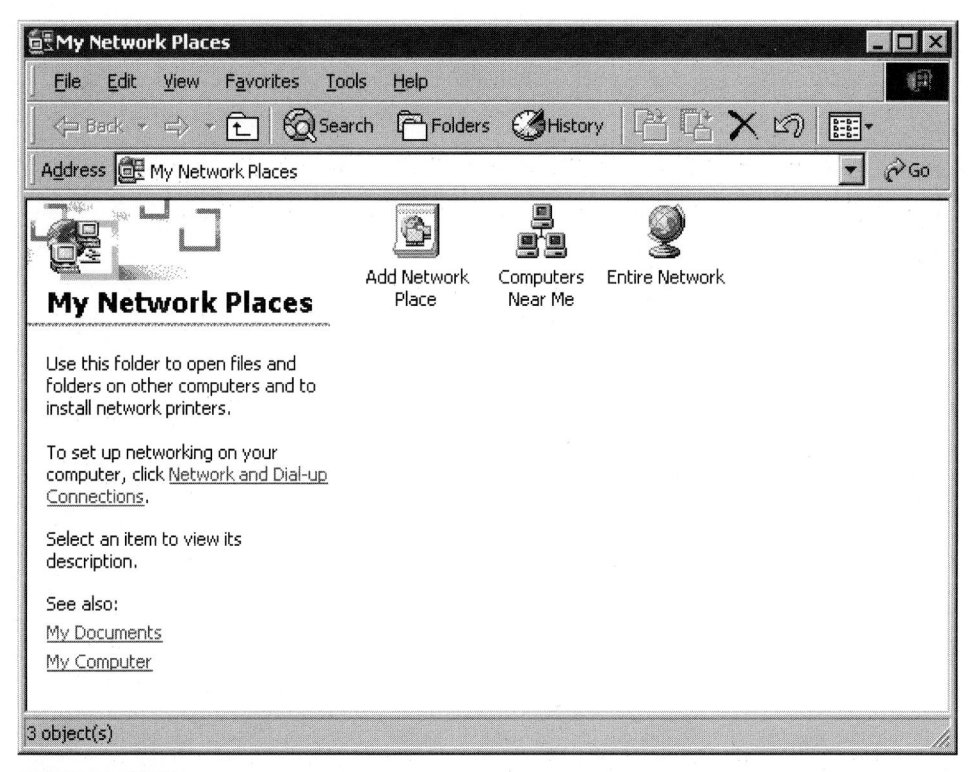

FIGURE 3.3 My Network Places

My Documents

My Documents allows you to store current files, including pictures, in an easily accessible location.

My Computer

My Computer allows you to access your hard drives, floppy disk drive, and compact disk drives. My Computer also allows you to access the Control Panel.

Control Panel

Now let's take a look at what is available in the Control Panel. Some of the icons you see in the Control Panel are familiar, some of them are new, and some that you might expect are no longer available, as you can see in

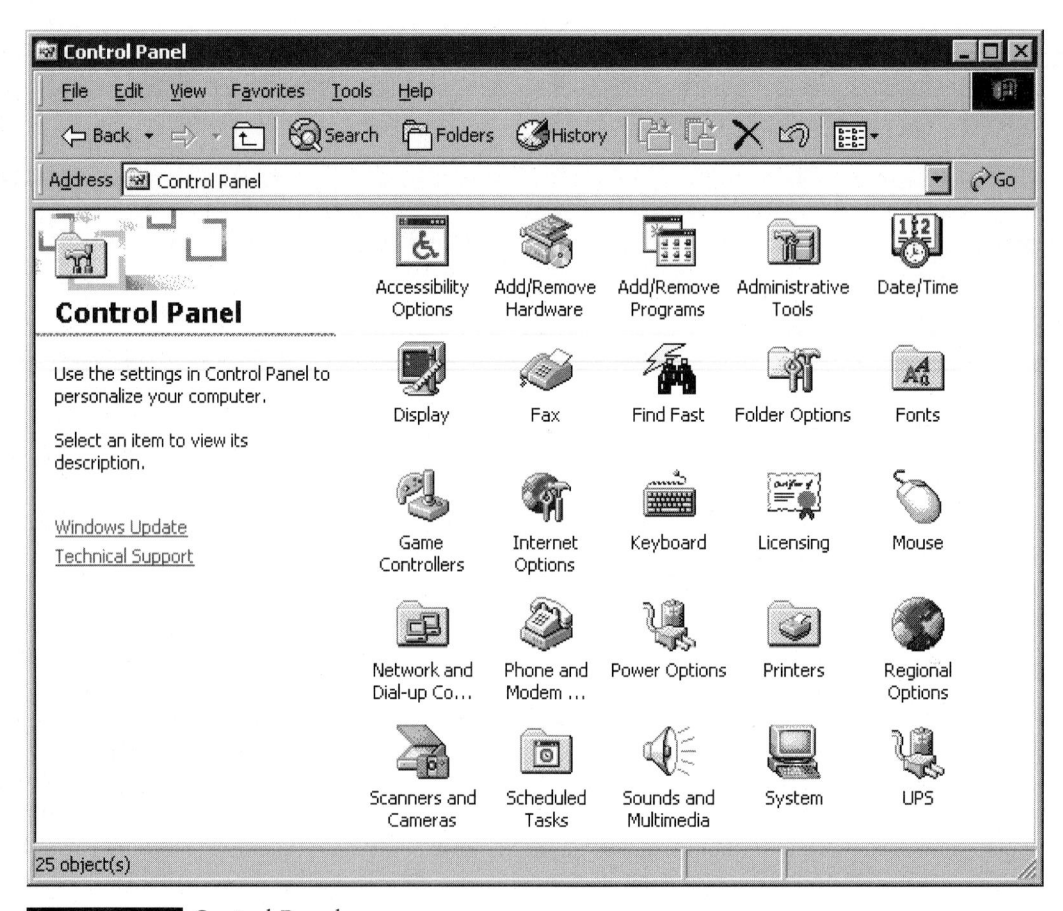

FIGURE 3.4 Control Panels

Figure 3.4. The following bulleted list gives you a brief overview of the Control Panel icons and what you can do with each:

- Accessibility Options: This option allows you to customize your computer with features that make the computer more accessible to those with disabilities.
- Add/Remove Hardware: This option, first introduced in Windows 98, provides you with a wizard so that you can easily install or remove hardware devices.
- Add/Remove Programs: This options allows you to easily see what programs are currently installed on your system, so you can add or remove them as necessary. As you can see in Figure 3.5, the interface is somewhat different, but it does provide you with additional information, such as usage frequency, when you highlight a particular component.

two • Hardware and Disk Management **39**

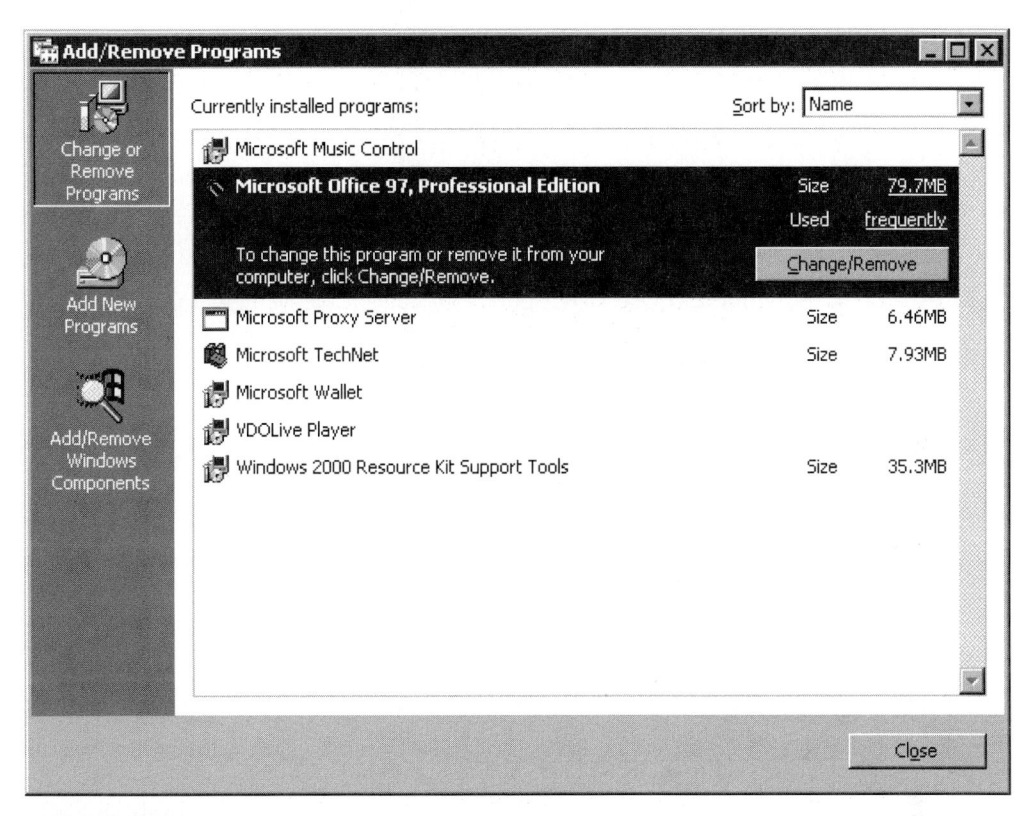

FIGURE 3.5 Add/Remove Programs Interface

- Administrative Tools: This option is new and contains shortcuts to a number of tools such as Component Services, Computer Management, DHCP Manager, and many others. We will explore these in more detail later in this chapter and in subsequent chapters.
- Date/Time: Allows you to adjust the date and time of your server.
- Display: The Display option allows you to make changes to the appearance of your server, such as the background, screen saver, appearance of icons, and the settings. You can also add and remove various web components and effects as well.
- Fax: Allows you to configure information about the fax user and additional fax properties.
- Fast Find: Fast Find provides a content indexer that tracks file changes to your system.
- Folder Options: Folder options allow you to choose how Windows should display your folders and files. For example, you can use web content and web views or select classic desktop appearance.

- Fonts: This folder contains the current fonts in use on your system.
- Game Controllers: Allow you to add, remove, and configure game controller hardware.
- Internet Options: This icon provides you with Internet Explorer's Properties sheet so you can figure a variety of Internet access options.
- Keyboard: Allows you to configure your keyboard.
- Licensing: Allows you to review and change your licensing options.
- Mouse: Allows you to configure your mouse.
- Network and Dial-Up Connections: This folder is new and contains your current dial-up connections, local area connections, and a Make New Connection wizard.
- Phone and Modem: Allows you to configure telephone dialing rules and modem properties.
- Power Options: Allow you to configure energy saving settings for your server.
- Printers: This folder provides you with information about printers that are currently installed and it also contains the Add Printer wizard.
- Regional Options: Allow you to configure your display for languages, numbers, currency, and other regional options.
- Scanners and Cameras: Allow you to configure and troubleshoot installed scanners and cameras.
- Scheduled Tasks: This folder allows you to configure certain tasks, such as cleaning up your hard disk, to run automatically at certain times.
- Sounds and Multimedia: Allow you to choose various sounds and multimedia options.
- System: This icon opens the system properties sheet that contains information about your system, network identification, hardware, user profiles, and advanced system options.
- UPS: Allows you to configure Uninterruptible Power Supplies that may be attached to your computer.

Accessories

Now let's move to the program files, beginning with Accessories. When you click Start ➤ Programs, you will notice right away that there is no longer a Windows Explorer in this locaton. However, the other listings in Programs are similar to what you have seen in Windows NT 4.0. The Accessories option provides the typical items you are used to seeing, such as the Calculator, Paint, Notepad, and Imaging, but there are some new features as well.

Accessibility

Windows 2000 Server includes some new accessibility features that make using the computer easier for users with certain disabilities. These are outlined in the following list:

- Accessibility Wizard: The Accessibility Wizard provides a simple way for users to setup accessibility options.
- Magnifier: Enlarges selected text by following your mouse movements.
- Narrator: The Narrator reads on-screen dialog boxes, text, menus, and buttons aloud if the computer has a sound card and speaker installed.
- On-Screen Keyboard: Accessibility options now include an on-screen keyboard that can be used by your mouse, as shown in Figure 3.6.
- Utility Manager: The Utility Manager allows you to control other Accessibility Options, such as the Magnifier and Narrator. You can use the Utility Manager to start the tools when Windows starts or start non-running utilities.

Communications

The Communications Menu that appears under Accessories provides you with an easy way to access Hyper Terminal, the Internet Connection Wizard, NetMeeting, Network and Dial-up Connections, and the Phone Dialer.

System Tools

The System Tools you see here were first used as menu items in Windows 98 and they continue in Windows 2000 Server. You will no doubt find these items helpful:

- Backup: Windows 2000 Server contains an enhanced backup tool that is available in the System Tools menu. We will address this utility in detail in a later chapter.

FIGURE 3.6 On-Screen Keyboard

- **Character Map:** This tool is used to view characters that are available in a selected font. This tool allows you to manage the character sets.
- **Disk Cleanup:** This tool searches your hard drive and removes temporary or unnecessary files. You can specify what kind of files you would like removed.
- **Disk Defragmenter:** A Disk Defragmenter is now included in Windows 2000 Server as an MMC snap-in. The Defragmenter, as shown in Figure 3.7, gives you information about your drives and allows you to defragment as needed. As you can see in the figure, the snap-in gives you display information about the amount of fragmentation on the selected disk.
- **Scheduled Tasks:** A Scheduled Tasks wizard is also included that allows you to schedule the tools, such as Disk Defragmenter, to automatically run at certain times and intervals.

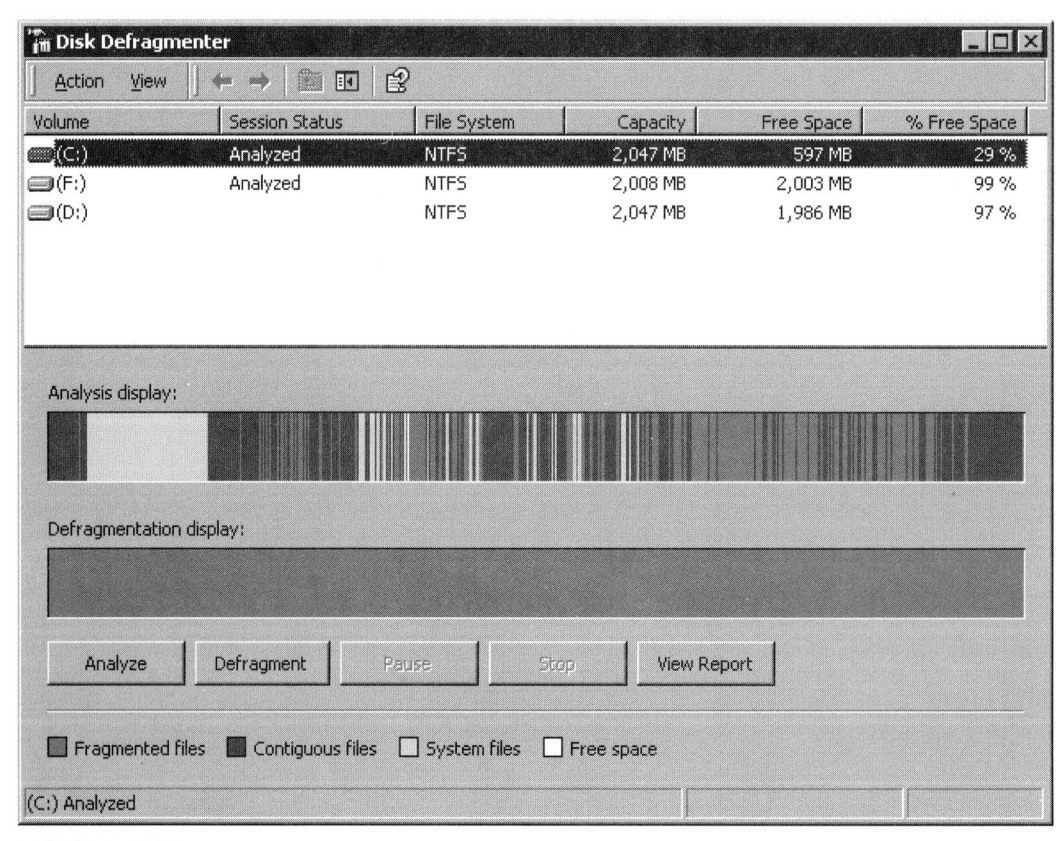

FIGURE 3.7 Disk Defragmenter

Other Features

The Accessories menu also includes some other tools and options that were not previously available in this menu:

- Address Book: You now have a system address book where you can store the names of people, email addresses, business and home phone numbers. This feature is similar to the address book you see in Microsoft Outlook.
- Synchronize: This feature allows you to update the network copy of materials that were edited offline, including documents, email messages, and even calendars.
- Windows Explorer: Wondering where the lost Windows Explorer is located? It's now available in the Accessories menu and is maintained for backwards compatibility.

Administrative Tools

Here's what you have been waiting for—administrative tools. We will work with and configure these throughout the book, but this section will give you an introduction to what is now available and where some of the former tools have moved. This section covers the general administrative tools. For an overview of the Active Directory administrative tools, see the following section. To access the Administrative Tools, click Start ➤ Programs ➤ Administrative Tools. The following sections give you an overview of each.

Component Services

Component Services is an MMC snap-in that allows you to access the Event Viewer log files and the Services on the local machine, as shown in Figure 3.8.

As you can see in the right pane, the services basically function the same as they did under the control panel in Windows NT 4.0. If you select a service, right click it, and choose Properties, you can make modifications to the way the service runs as needed. The Properties sheet contains several tabs to configure the service and how it starts-up, but it also includes a Dependencies tab, as shown in Figure 3.9.

Since some services may be dependant on other services, this tab lets you know what other services will be affected if you stop a particular service and what system components need the service.

Computer Management

Computer Management allows you to stop services, manage local disks, manage local users, and provides additional tools to manage local and

44 Chapter three • A Tour Around the Interface

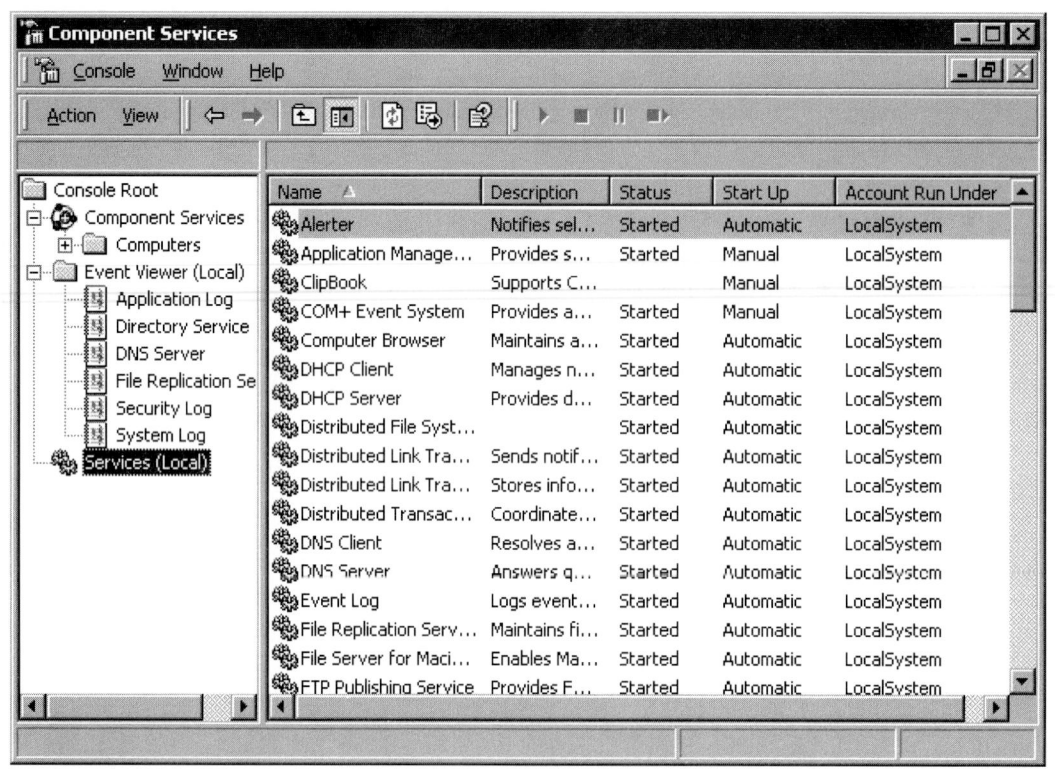

FIGURE 3.8 Component Services

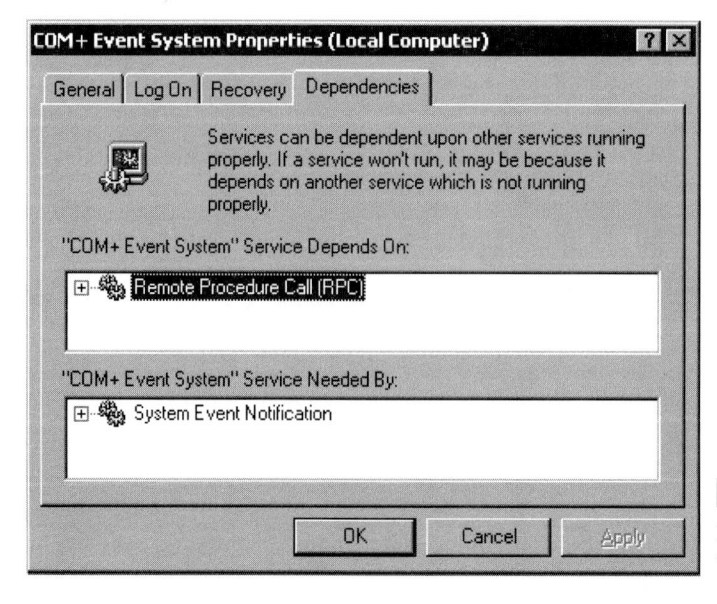

FIGURE 3.9 Dependencies Tab

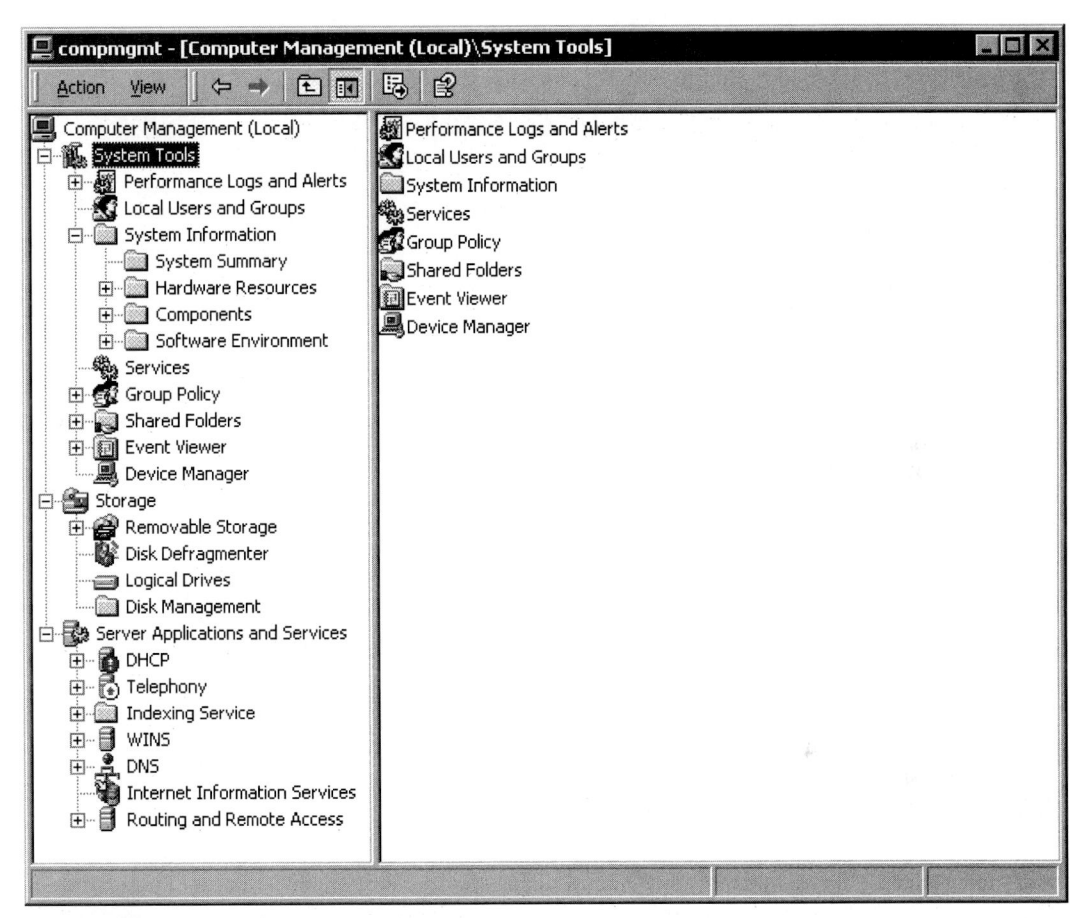

FIGURE 3.10 Computer Management

remote computers. The Computer Management feature is an MMC snap-in, as shown in Figure 3.10.

As you can see in Figure 3.10, you have the option of configuring a number of system tools and components such as Performance logs and alerts, local users and groups (for non-domain controllers), System Information, services, and hardware devices. You can also access local drives and various server applications and services from this snap-in.

Configure Your Server

The Configure Your Server option provides you with a variety of wizards and help files so you can initially learn how to configure the most common components of the Windows 2000 Server. You can use the wizard to install services as needed, and if the service is already installed, the wizard will

46 Chapter three • A Tour Around the Interface

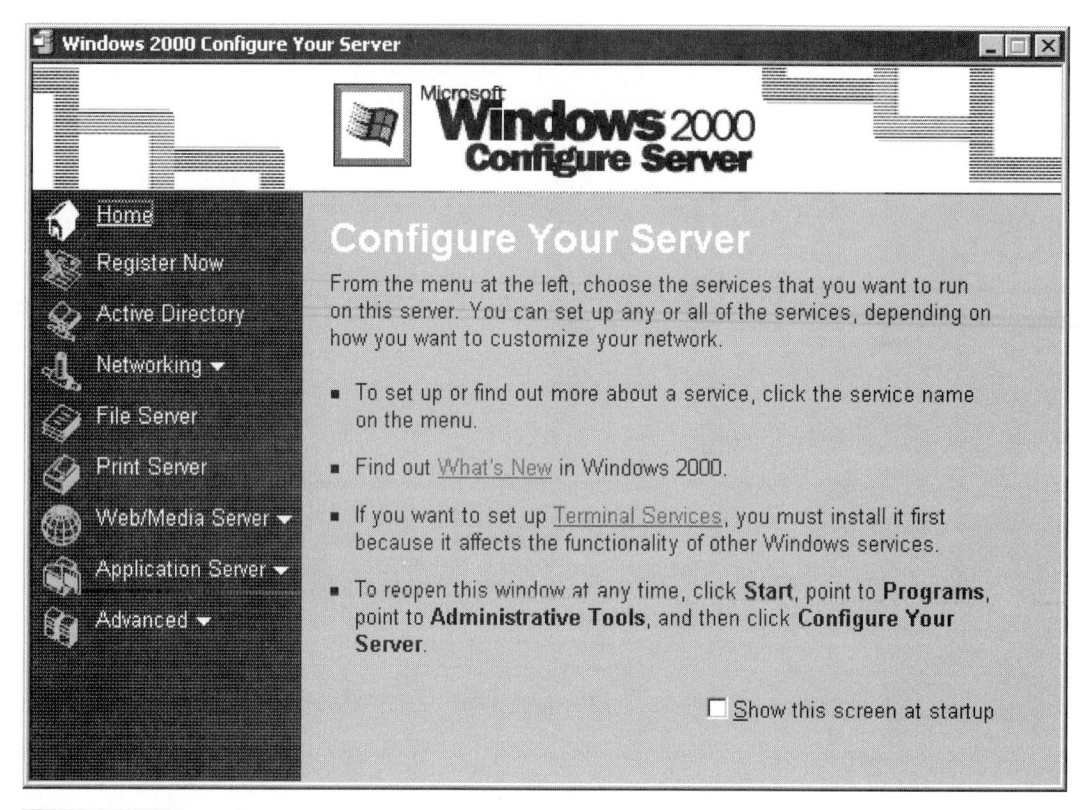

FIGURE 3.11 Configure Your Server

help you manage the service or learn more about it. Figure 3.11 shows you Home screen.

Data Sources

The utility Data Sources allows you to add, remove, and configure Open Database Connectivity (ODBC) data and drivers. ODBC is a programming interface that enables applications to access data in systems that use Structured Query Language (SQL) as the standard for data access. The Data Sources window allows you to configure data access depending on the needs of your organization. The Data Sources window is shown in Figure 3.12.

DHCP Manager

DHCP is an integrated part of the Active Directory Services, and you can manage your DHCP scopes, leases, address pool, and reservations from the DHCP Manager. As with other components, the DHCP Manager is now an MMC snap-in, as shown in Figure 3.13.

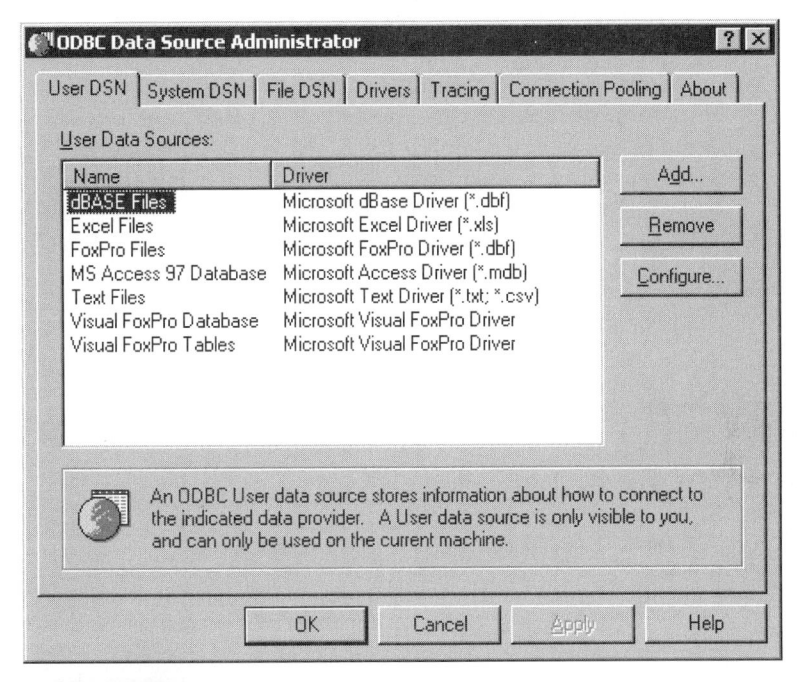

FIGURE 3.12 Data Source Administrator

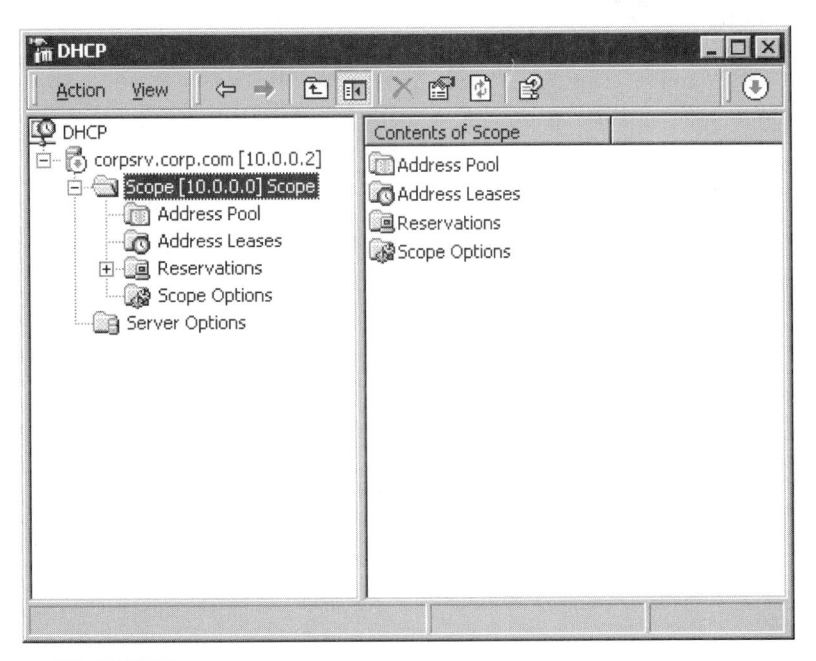

FIGURE 3.13 DHCP Manager

Distributed File System

Distributed File System is an MMC snap-in that allows you to create and manage distributed file systems that connect shared folders and files on different computers. The Distributed file system (Dfs) is a single hierarchical file system that distributes its contents across an enterprise network. This design provides a tree structure so that resources can be easily found, regardless of their location on the network. Figure 3.14 shows you the interface for managing the Dfs.

DNS Management

DNS Management is a major component of Windows 2000 Server with Dynamic DNS being an integrated part of the Active Directory. The DNS Management snap-in allows you to manage your DNS service on your server. The interface is shown in Figure 3.15.

Event Viewer

As in Windows NT, you can use Event Viewer to examine system events. The Event Viewer provides information, warnings, and stop errors with an explanation of the event. The Event Viewer continues to be an excellent troubleshooting tool, and it is even easier to use in Windows 2000 Server.

File Manager

File Manager continues to be a part of Windows 2000 Server as it is easy to manage your files and shared folders.

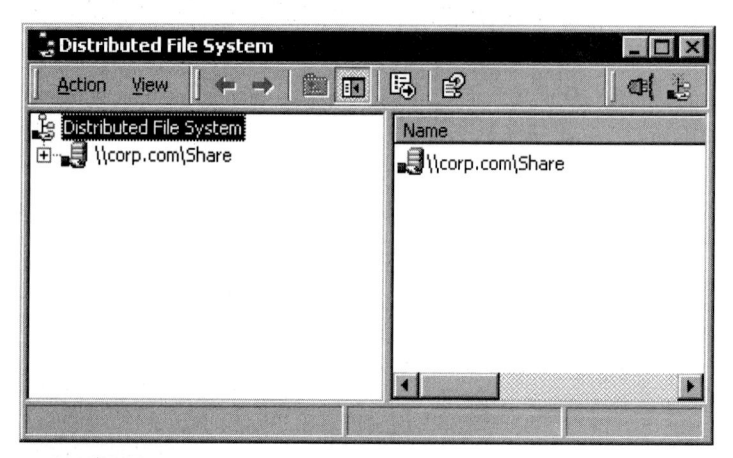

FIGURE 3.14 Distributed File System

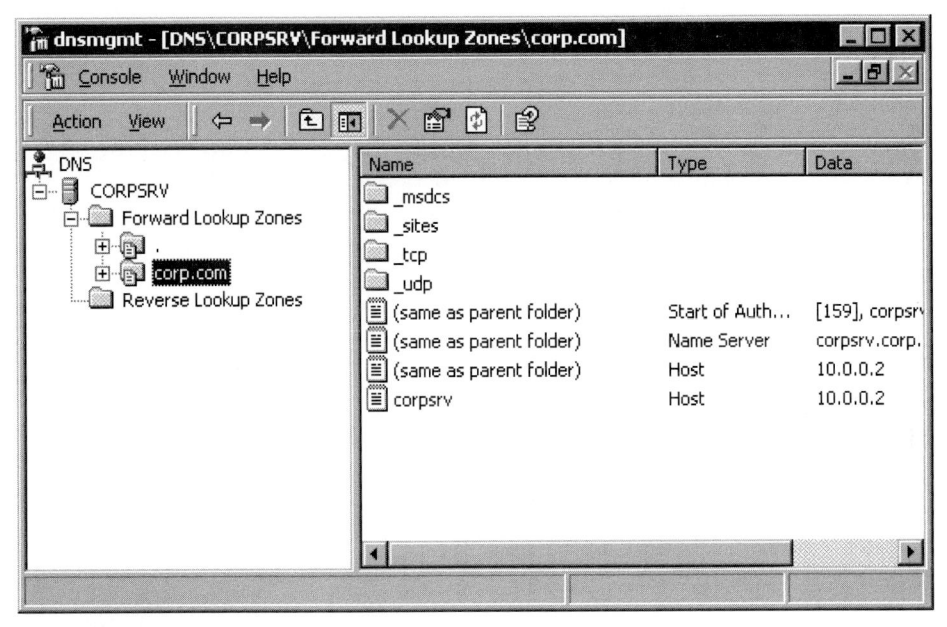

FIGURE 3.15 DNS Management

Internet Services Manager

Internet Services Manager is an MMC snap-in that is now built into Windows 2000 Server so you can manage Internet Information Server. This feature allows you to easily maintain web sites both on the Internet and the Intranet.

Licensing

You can continue to manage your server license through the licensing window as you did in Windows NT.

Performance

Performance Monitor now appears as an MMC snap-in. You can add counters to be charted as you did in Windows NT and log the results as necessary. The new interface is shown in Figure 3.16.

Routing and Remote Access

You can manage RAS and RRAS through the Routing and Remote Access snap-in. This interface allows you to configure these services as well as ports and RAS policies. The interface is shown in Figure 3.17.

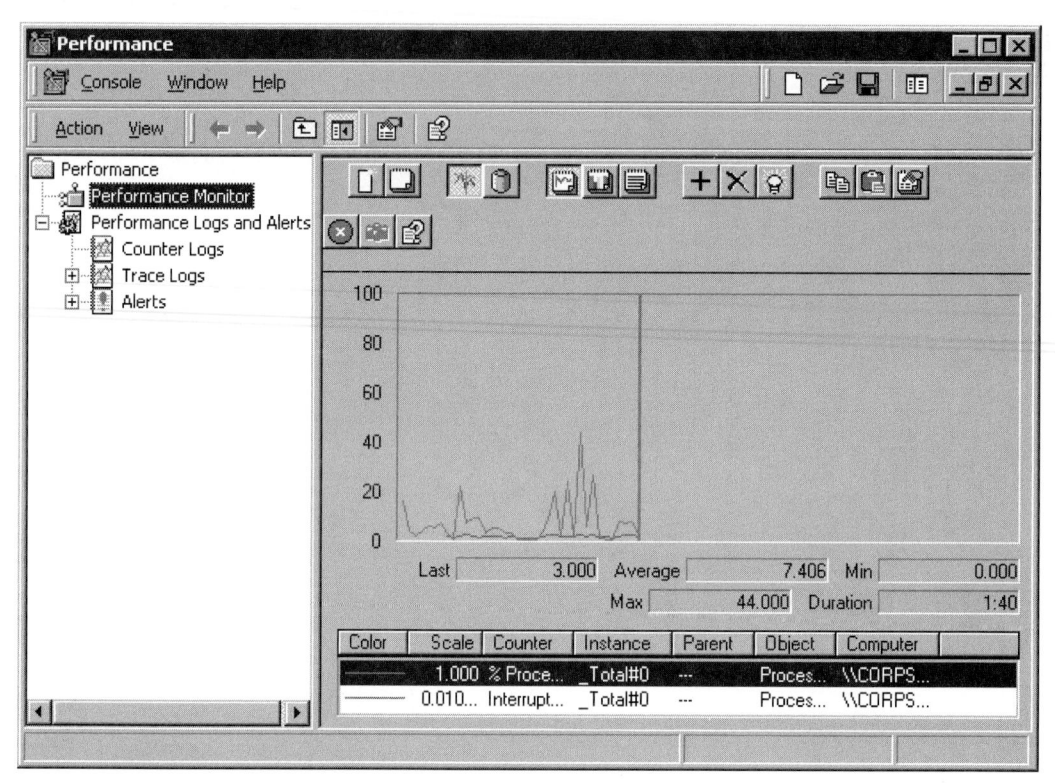

FIGURE 3.16 Performance

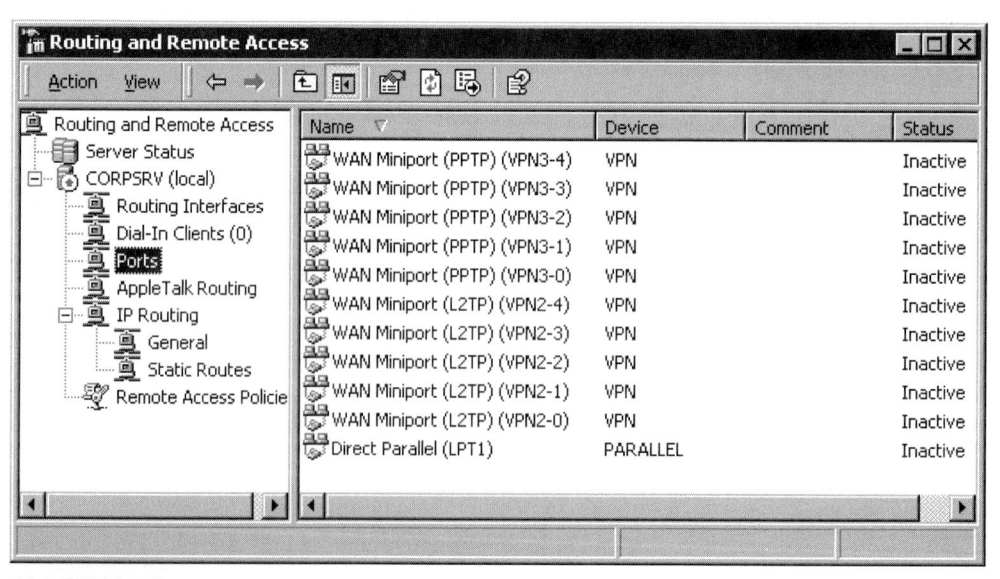

FIGURE 3.17 Routing and Remote Access

Terminal Services Licensing

If you have terminal services on your network, you can use this tool to manage client access licensing.

WINS

Finally, you can manage WINS through the WINS MMC snap-in. As in Windows NT, WINS resolves NetBIOS names to IP addresses automatically on your network. The snap-in allows you to view and manage active registration and also replication partners.

Active Directory Administrative Tools

You will learn all about the Active Directory in Chapter 9, but for now, I would like to introduce the four Active Directory administrative interfaces. As with most other tools, the Active Directory uses the MMC and functions

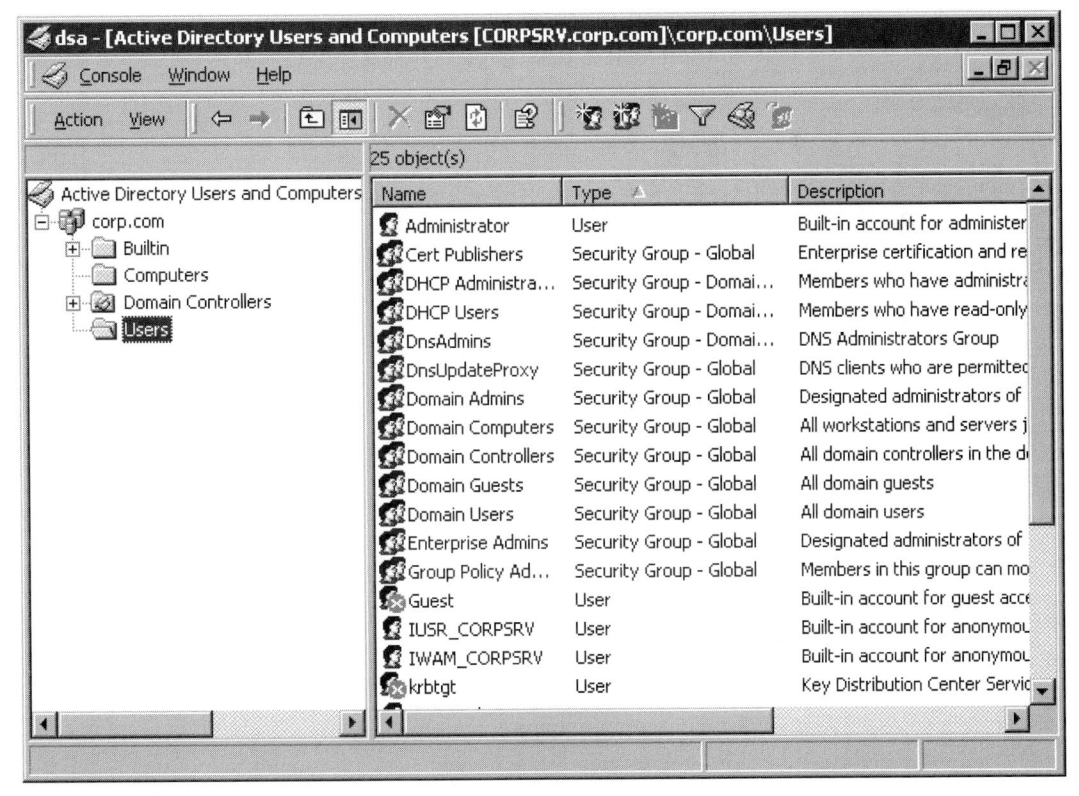

FIGURE 3.18 Active Directory Users and Computers

as snap-ins. You can access the Active Directory administrative tools by clicking Start ➤ Programs ➤ Administrative Tools. The four snap-ins are described in the following bulleted list:

- Active Directory Users and Computers: This snap-in allows you to manage accounts, organizational units, group policies, and other directory objects, as shown in Figure 3.18. Through this interface, you can manage individual accounts by right clicking on the account and choosing properties, or you can add or remove accounts as necessary. All of these configuration options are discussed in later chapters.
- Active Directory Domains and Trusts: This snap-in allows you to add, modify, or remove domains and domain trust relationships in the directory. Domains and trust relationships in Windows 2000 are fully explained in Chapter 9.
- Active Directory Sites and Services: This snap-in allows you to create site definitions and manage directory replication and publishing among domain controllers, as shown in Figure 3.19.
- Active Directory Schema: The final Active Directory snap-in allows senior administrators and developers to view, create, or modify object classes and attributes in the schema. This interface allows you to manage the attributes that are indexed in the global catalog. This snap-in is available via the resource kit.

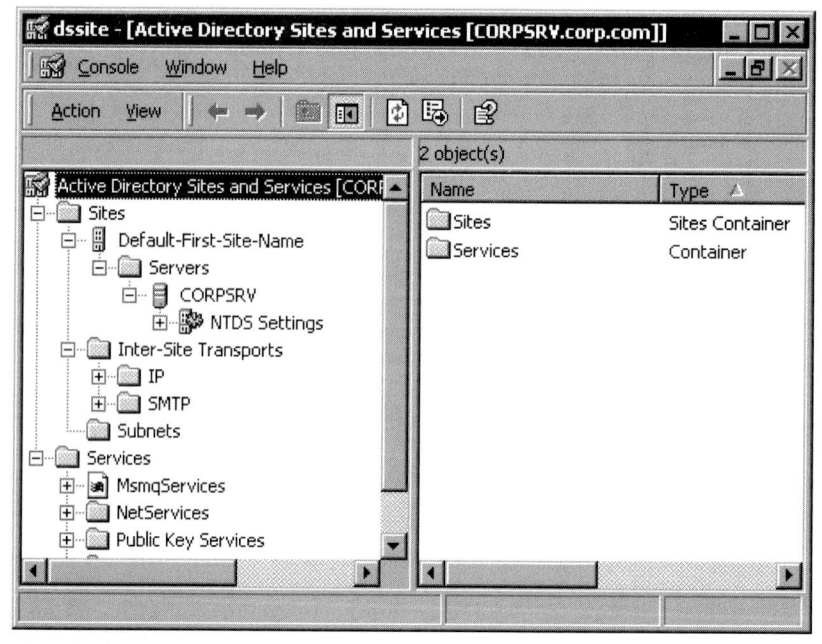

FIGURE 3.19 Active Directory Sites and Services

Summary

Windows 2000 provides an integrated interface that retains some features of Windows NT, but it is significantly different. However, most of the new interfaces make an administrator's work easier once the initial learning curve is mastered. Overall, the new interface allows you to easily configure and manage the many services and functions of Windows 2000 Server.

FOUR

Configuring and Managing Hardware

One of the major difficulties with Windows NT was getting various hardware devices to work. Windows NT was not Plug and Play compliant, and when you wanted to add a new piece of hardware, you had to carefully check the Hardware Compatibility List (HCL) or carefully read the manufacturers' packaging to see if you could get the hardware to work on your system.

Windows 2000 Server leaves that legacy behind and provides a Plug and Play compliant system that supports a wide range of devices. In fact, you can install new hardware just as easily in Windows 2000 Server as in Windows 98.

In this chapter, we explore how to add, remove, configure, and manage hardware devices in Windows 2000 Server.

Understanding Plug and Play

Plug and Play first came onto the scene with Windows 95. The goal behind Plug and Play (PnP) technology was to allow users to add and remove hardware easily without having to know a lot about hardware configuration or troubleshooting. A PnP system is designed to take care of the hardware needs with very little intervention from the user. A PnP system automatically detects new hardware and attempts to install it.

PnP has changed a lot since Windows 95. Windows 95 achieved PnP operation through the use of Advanced Power Management (APM) BIOS (Basic Input Output System) or a Plug and Play BIOS. Both of these were designed for Windows 95 PnP, and we know that the design was less than perfect. PnP is much more stable now due to an OnNow design initiative called Advanced Configuration and Power Interface (ACPI), which defines the system board and BIOS interface and allows not only PnP, but also power management and other configuration capabilities. In Windows 2000, you can expect to see the following PnP features:

- Automatic adaptation to hardware changes. Windows 2000 Server automatically detects hardware changes in your system and seeks to install or remove those devices as the changes occur.
- Automatic hardware resource allocation. In times past, installing a new piece of hardware required you to have a good handle on the resources the hardware might need, such as DMA channels, IRQs, I/O ports, and so forth. PnP handles all of these issues for you and assigns the new hardware resources it needs while preserving the resource allocation of other devices.
- Automatic driver loading. PnP systems automatically load appropriate drivers for PnP devices.
- Hardware Wizard. Windows 2000 Server provides a Hardware Wizard so that adding and removing hardware is an easy task.

When new hardware is added to the system, Windows 2000 Server gives you a dialog box stating that Windows has found new hardware and is attempting to install it. In Figure 4.1, a new modem has been added, and Windows has detected it. If Windows can install the appropriate driver for the device, it will do so automatically. If not, the system will prompt you for help to provide a driver for the device.

Generally, installing new hardware requires three basic steps:

1. Attach the device to your computer, either internally or externally. You should follow the manufacture's guidelines so that you attach the device to the correct port or slot.

FIGURE 4.1 Found New Hardware

2. Install device drivers and software. If the device is Plug and Play, Windows will be able to automatically take care of this task. In the case of older legacy hardware that is not Plug and Play aware, you can use the new Add/Remove Hardware Wizard described in the next section to install the hardware.

3. Configure the device and settings. This action involves accessing the properties sheet for the device and configuring it as needed. Later sections in the chapter examine how to configure various hardware devices.

Add/Remove Hardware Wizard

If you have used Windows 98, you are familiar with the Add/Remove Hardware Wizard. Windows 2000 Server's version of the wizard is basically the same, and it makes your management of hardware devices much easier. You can launch the wizard by accessing the Add/Remove Hardware icon in the control panel. The wizard begins, as shown in Figure 4.2.

When you click the Next button, you are presented with two radio buttons that allow you to either add or troubleshoot a device or uninstall or

FIGURE 4.2 Add/Remove Hardware Wizard Opening Screen

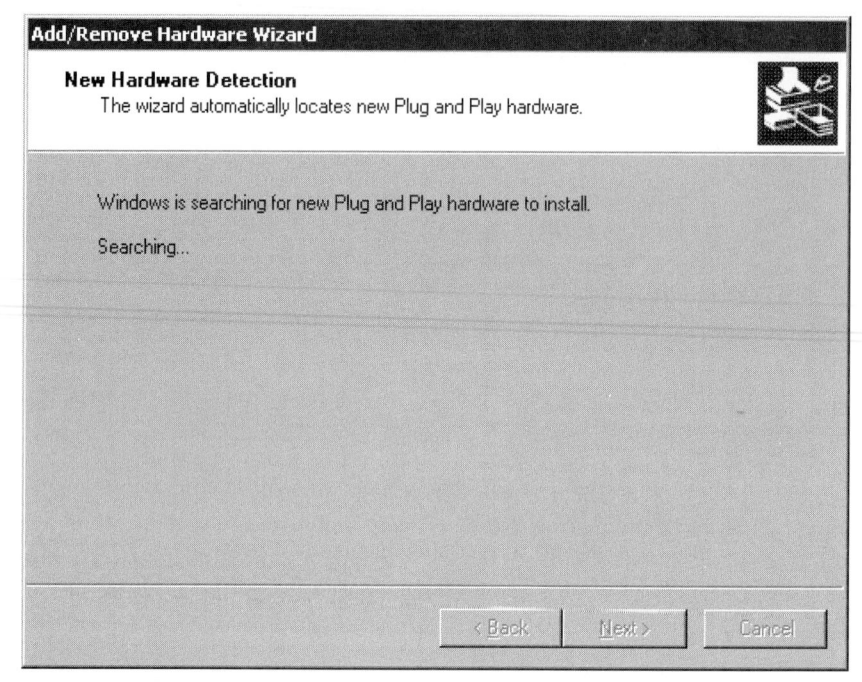

FIGURE 4.3 Add/Remove Hardware searches for new devices.

unplug a device. If you choose to uninstall a device, you will be able to select the device from a list and simply click to uninstall it from the system. If you choose to install a device, Windows attempts to find the device, as shown in Figure 4.3. If it can find it, the wizard will complete the installation for you.

If Windows cannot find any new Plug and Play devices on your system, the wizard continues by allowing you to select the device that you want to add, as shown in Figure 4.4.

If you select the device you want to add, for example, "Imaging Device," Windows will once again search for the device on your system. If Windows finds the device, it will install it for you. If it does not, the wizard presents you with a window listing choices of manufacturers and models, as shown in Figure 4.5. You can then select your device from the list so Windows can install it, or you can click the Have Disk button to install the software from either a CD-ROM or floppy disk.

two • Hardware and Disk Management

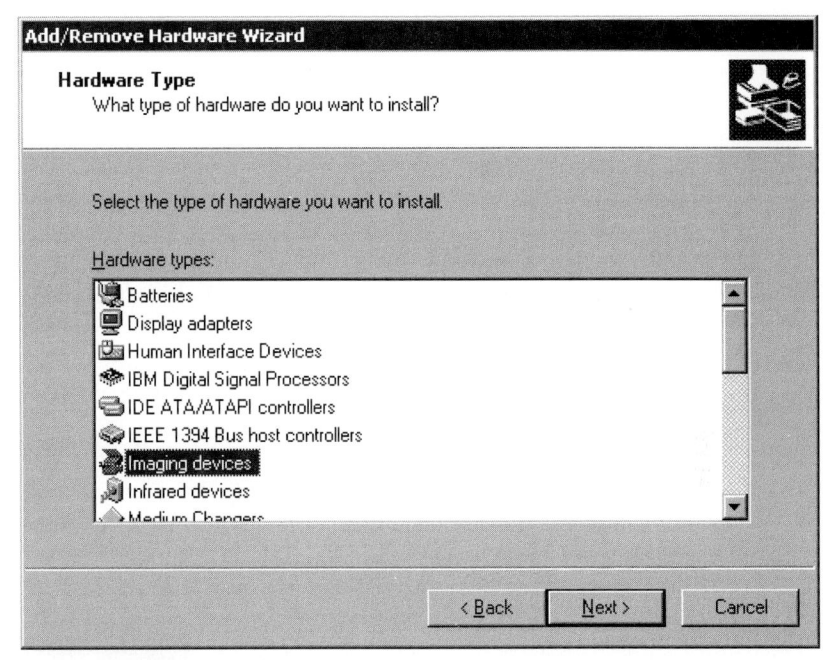

FIGURE 4.4 Hardware types

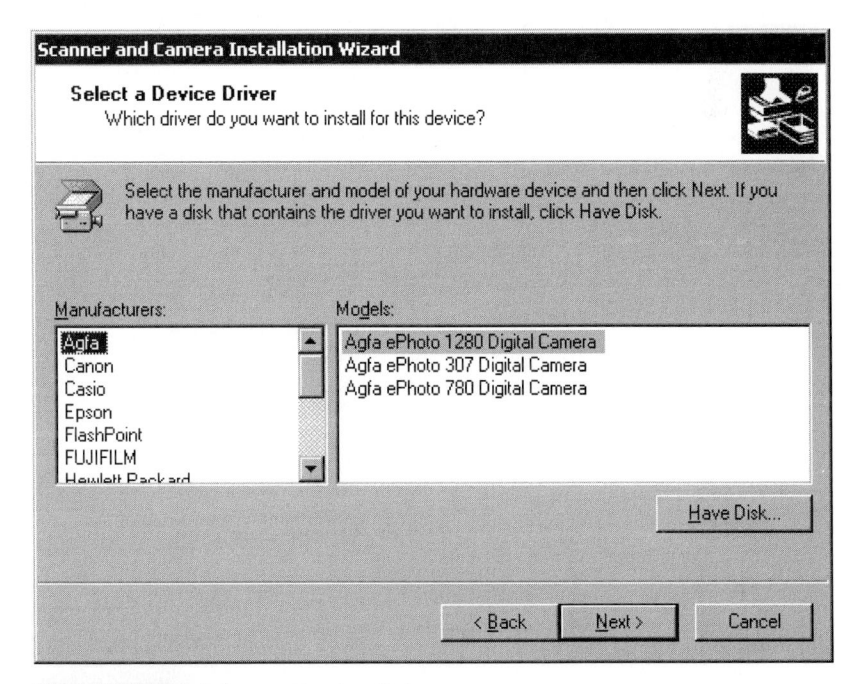

FIGURE 4.5 Select a Device Driver

Device Manager

Device Manager in Windows 2000 Server is similar to the device manager provided in Windows 98. With Device Manager, you can manage or reconfigure devices that are already installed on your system. Device Manager also gives you information about devices that are not working properly. The Device Manager is located in the Computer Management console. Click Start → Programs → Administrative Tools → Computer Management. When the console opens, expand System Tools and select Device Manager, as shown in Figure 4.6.

As you can see, the Device Manager view gives you categories of hardware. You can expand the categories by clicking the category to see the devices that are actually installed on your computer, as shown in Figure 4.7.

If you select a device and right-click it, or select a device and click the Action menu, you have the options of disabling the device, uninstalling the device, scanning for hardware changes, or viewing the properties sheet.

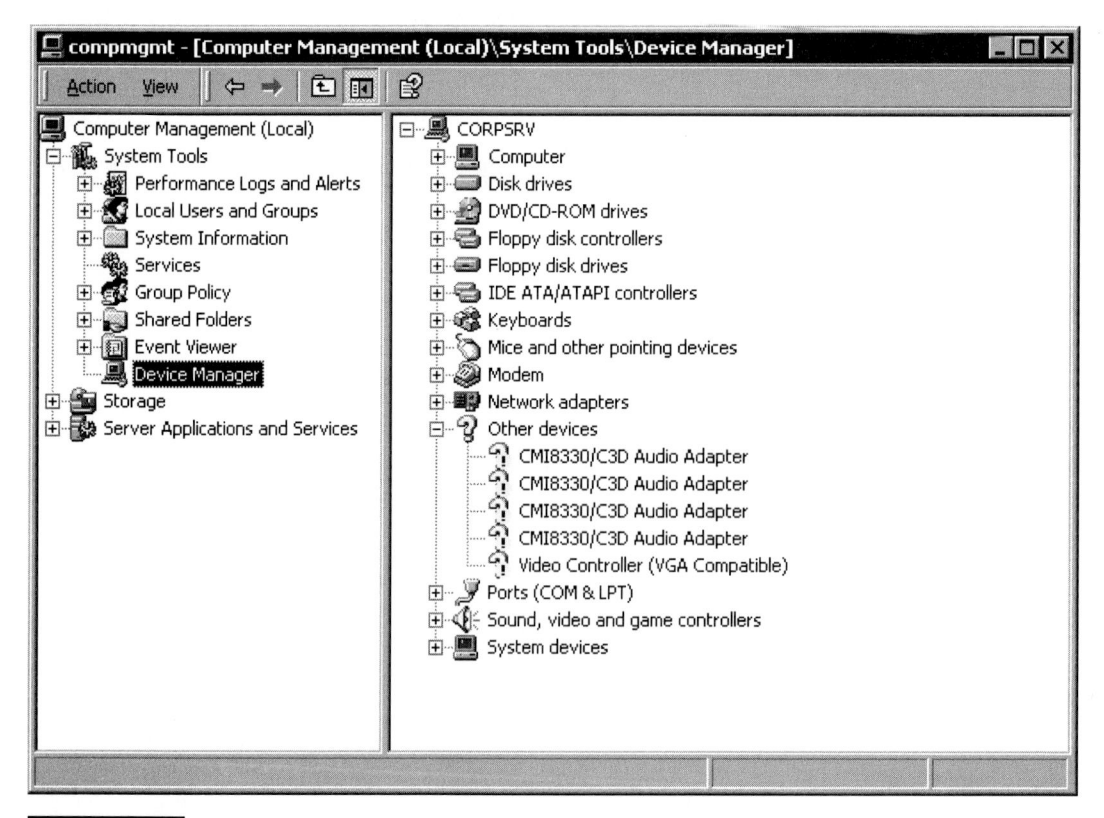

FIGURE 4.6 Device Manager

two • Hardware and Disk Management   61

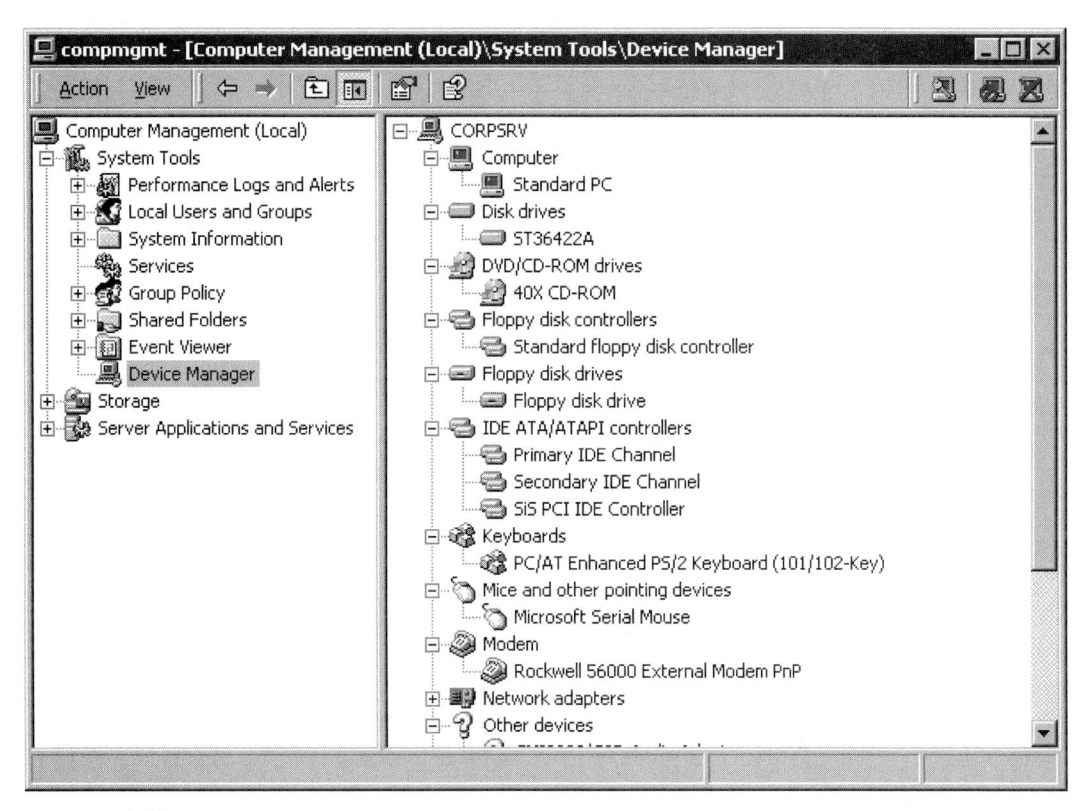

FIGURE 4.7   Expanded tree

You can also double-click the icon to get the properties sheet for each device you have installed on your computer. The Properties sheet for each device allows you to check the status of devices, troubleshoot the device, or make driver update changes. The following sections give you an overview of what you can do on each tab of the device properties sheets.

General Tab

A typical General tab for a network adapter is shown in Figure 4.8.

The General Property sheet gives you information about the device, its status, troubleshooter, and a device usage drop-down menu. If you launch the troubleshooter, you are taken to the Windows 2000 help files, which guide you through a series of questions to attempt to help you resolve the problem you are having with the device. The device usage drop-down menu allows you to tell Windows whether or not to use the device—in other words, you can use this menu to temporarily disable a device if necessary.

FIGURE 4.8
Device Properties

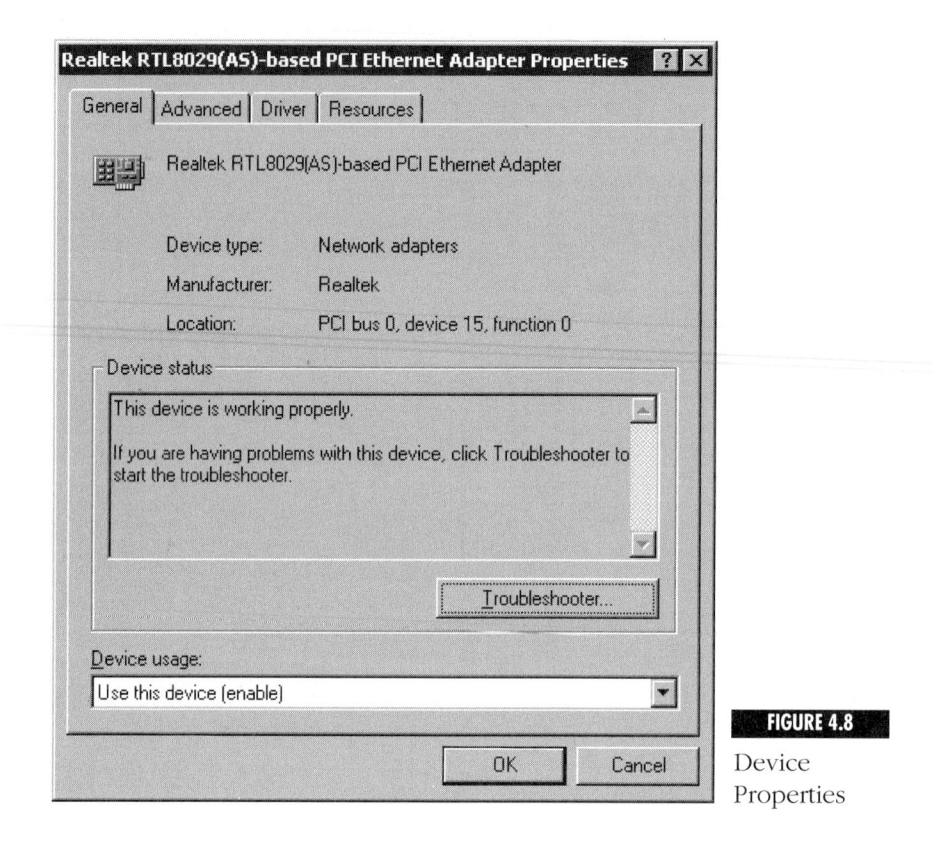

If the device is not working properly, Windows will display the icon in yellow with a question or exclamation point. If you access the properties of the device, the General tab will give you information that may help you resolve the problem. For example, in Figure 4.9, the drivers for the video controller are not installed. You can use the General Property sheet for a problematic device to attempt to reinstall the driver by clicking the Reinstall Driver button.

If you choose to reinstall the driver, the Upgrade Device Driver Wizard launches and searches for a suitable driver that you specify from a floppy disk or CD-ROM.

Advanced Tab

Some device properties sheets contain an Advanced Property sheet with specific information about that particular device. For example, the network adapter properties Advanced Property sheet, allows you to reconfigure certain properties. The properties are available in the left pane and the changes you can make are available in drop-down menu, as shown in Figure 4.10.

two • Hardware and Disk Management

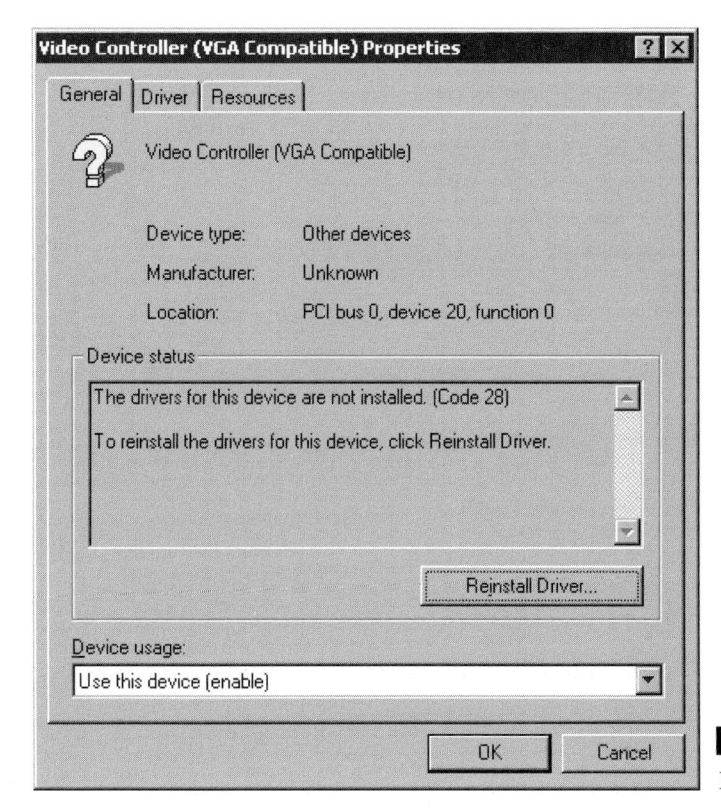

FIGURE 4.9
Problem device

Other devices contain differing settings. For example, the modem properties Advanced Property sheet allows you to add extra initialization commands and some of the devices do not contain an Advanced Property sheet at all.

Driver Property Sheet

The Driver Property sheet gives you information about the current driver that is installed for the device. On this property sheet, you have the option of uninstalling, updating, or reading more information about the details of the driver. As on the General Property sheet, if you click the Update Driver button, the wizard begins to help you update the current driver. This is the easiest way to reconfigure a device to use a new or updated driver, as they are published by the manufacturer.

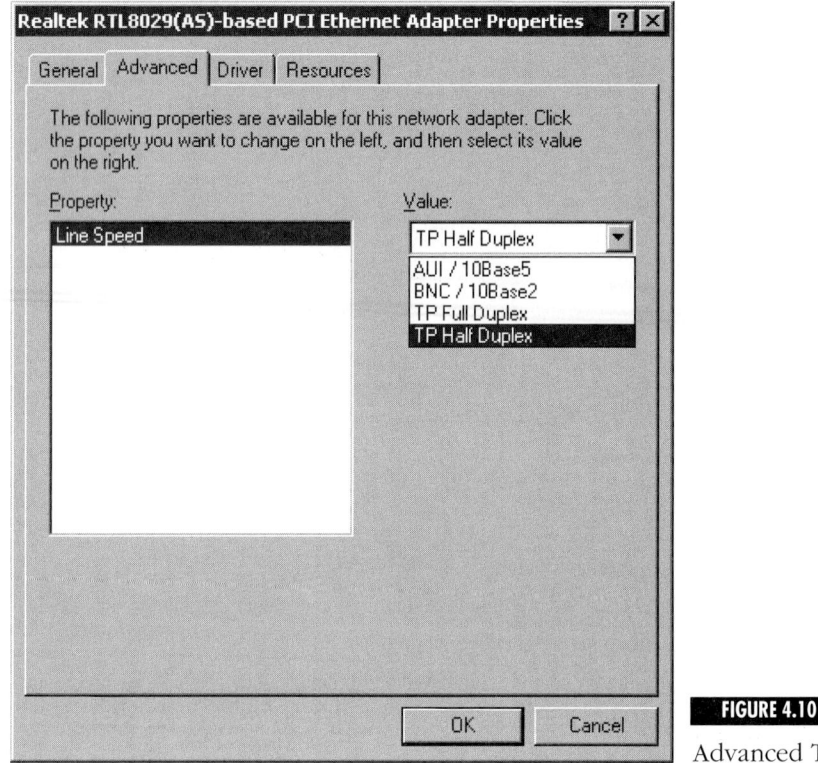

FIGURE 4.10
Advanced Tab

Resources Property Sheet

The Resources Property sheet gives you information about the system resources the device uses, as shown in Figure 4.11. For example, the network adapter card in Figure 4.11 uses IRQ 11 and the I/O Range settings are displayed.

As you can see, there are no conflicts with the service. If there were one, it would appear in the conflicting device list. Manually changing the settings with the Change Settings button may resolve the resource conflict. Under normal circumstances, Windows 2000 does a good job of managing device resources, but when a combination of legacy and PnP hardware is used, there can be resource conflicts that have to be manually resolved. In these cases, an IRQ conflict is most common, where two devices attempt to use the same IRQ. When there are system resource problems, use the console view menu to change the way Device Manager displays the information. For example, in Figure 4.12, I selected View ➤ Resources by type, which gives me a list of resources. If I expand the tree, I see which device is using which resource. This feature makes troubleshooting resources, such as IRQ conflicts, much easier.

two • Hardware and Disk Management 65

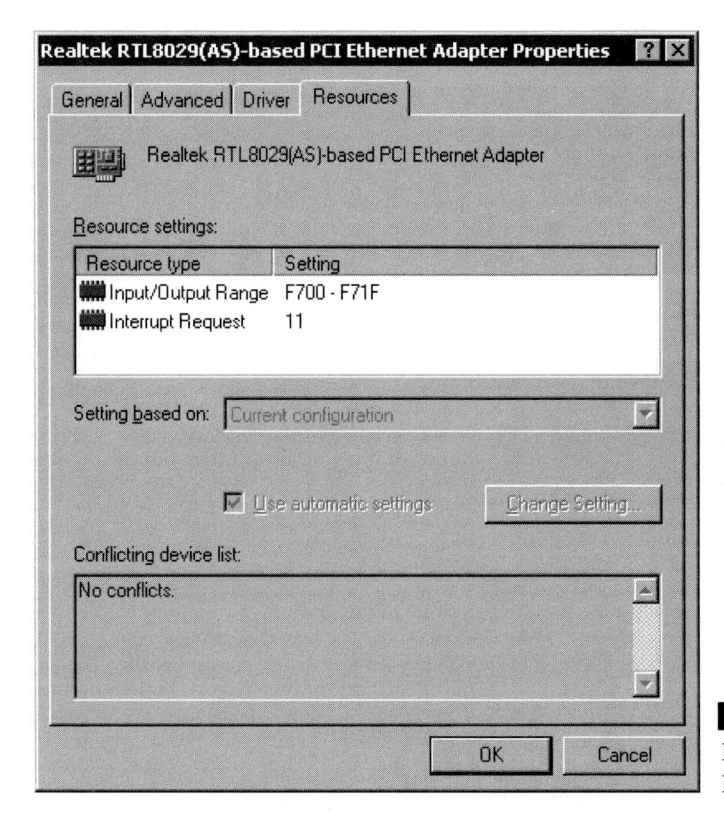

FIGURE 4.11 Resources Properties

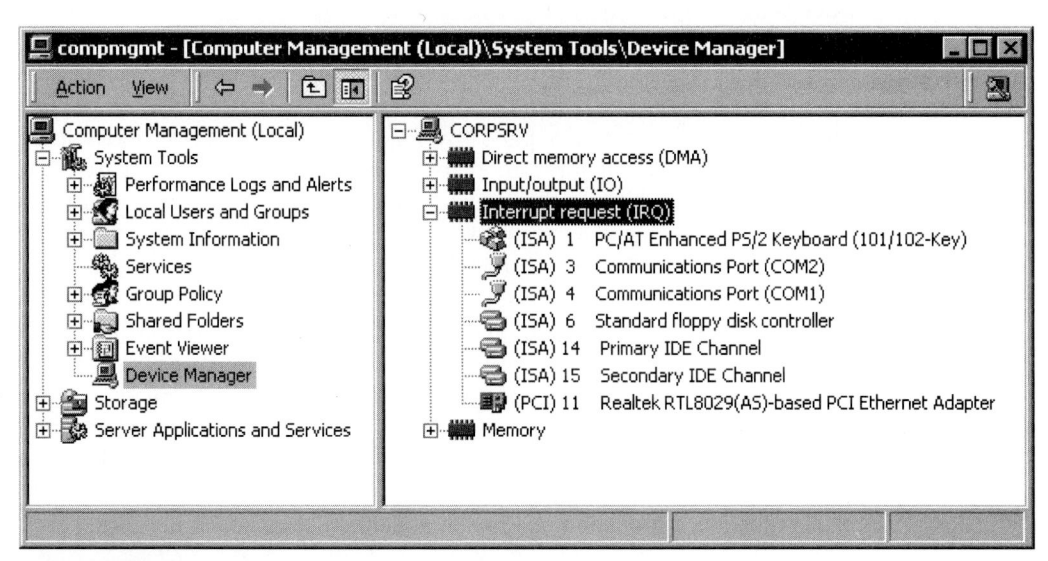

FIGURE 4.12 Resources by type

Other Tabs

Depending on the hardware device you select, other tabs may be available as well. For example, the modem properties sheet contains a Modem sheet that allows you to control the modem volume, maximum port speed, and the dial. It also contains a diagnostics sheet that allows you to query the modem to check for communication problems. See the next section for more information about configuring modems.

Using Control Panel

Aside from the Add/Remove Hardware Wizard and Device Manager, a number of hardware devices can be added, removed, or configured directly from icons in Control Panel. These devices are usually ones that contain the most configuration options or requirements. This section takes a look at those hardware devices that are accessible from Control Panel.

Fax

Fax properties device in Control Panel allows you to configure fax services for devices—such as a modem—that can send and receive fax data. The Fax Properties sheet contains a User Information sheet, where you can type information about yourself to be included on your fax cover pages, a Cover Pages tab that allows you to add and delete various cover pages as needed, a Monitor tab where you can configure Windows to give you a notification when a fax is sent or received, and an Advanced Options tab. The Advanced tab contains a Launch Fax Service Management button. This button takes you to the Fax Service Management console snap-in, as shown in Figure 4.13.

If you double-click the Devices icon, any fax devices installed on your system will appear in the right pane. By right-clicking the device and selecting Properties, you can configure various properties concerning faxing. First, on the General Properties sheet, you can enable or disable both the sending and receiving of faxes. You may want your computer only to send faxes or receive faxes, or you can select both check boxes for both options. If you choose to receive faxes, you can also set the number of times the line rings before answering. The Received Faxes Properties sheet gives you the options of automatically printing the fax when it is received, saving it to a folder, which by default is located in the My Documents folder, or sending the fax to a local e-mail inbox.

In addition to devices, you can also configure fax logging options in the Fax Service Management console. The logging options include inbound, initialization/termination, outbound, and unknown log files. If you select a category in the right pane, as shown in Figure 4.14, and right-click it, you can choose the level of logging for that particular category.

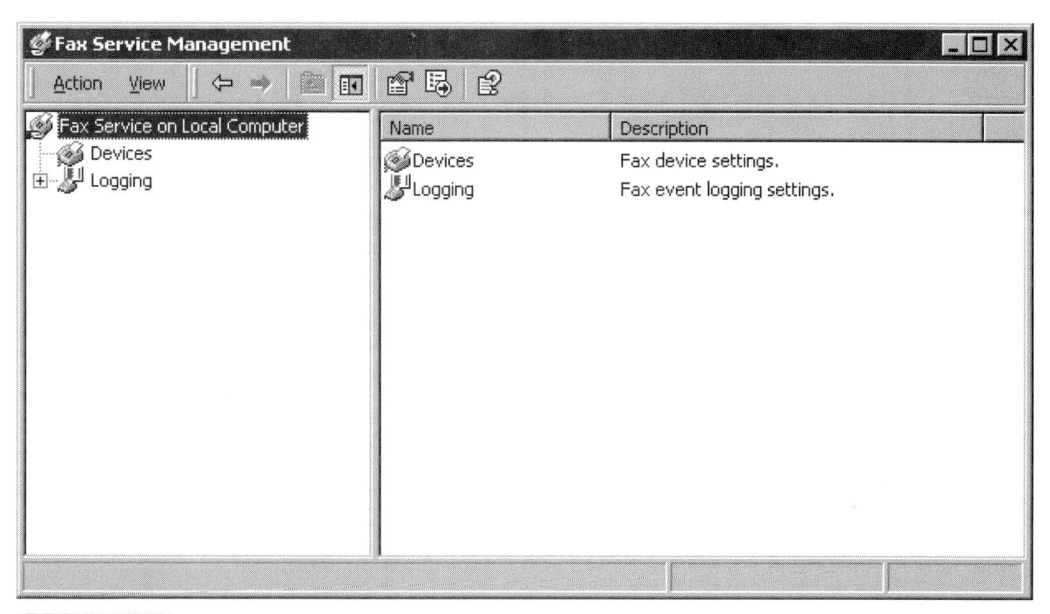

FIGURE 4.13 Fax Service Management

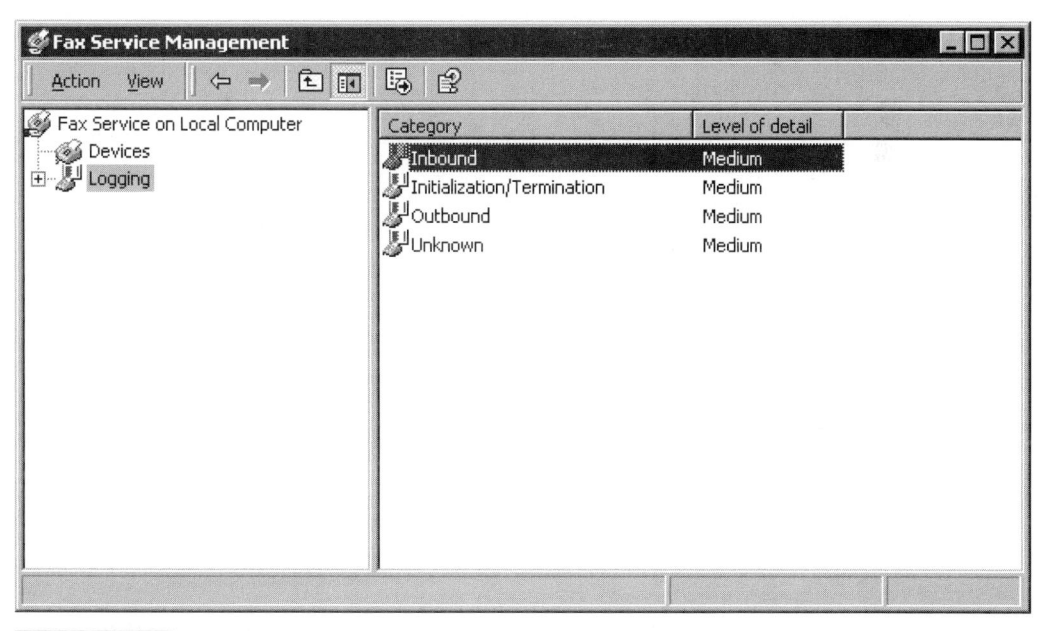

FIGURE 4.14 Fax Logging

Game Controllers

Windows 2000 Server supports various game controllers for which an icon is included in Control Panel. The Game Controllers properties page contains two properties sheets: General and Advanced. The General sheet provides list of installed game controllers and buttons to add, remove, troubleshoot, refresh, or view properties for a particular controller. The Advanced sheet allows you to modify the Controller ID assignment and port if necessary. The Troubleshooting button opens the Help files, which can help you resolve conflict issues if you have multiple game controllers on your system.

Keyboard and Mouse

As with Windows NT, the keyboard and mouse icons remain in Control Panel, so you can configure them as desired. The Keyboard Properties sheet allows you to configure the speed at which the keyboard responds to keystrokes and the speed of the blinking cursor. The Input Locales tab allows you to configure language options and Hot Keys as desired, and you can further troubleshoot keyboard problems using the Hardware tab.

The Mouse Properties sheet contains a number of tabs that allow you to select right- or left-handed control, the mouse response speed, pointers, and the mouse motion. As with the Keyboard Properties sheet, these settings are self-explanatory.

Phone and Modem Option

As you are probably aware, modems can be one of the more tricky hardware devices to configure, but modem installation and configuration is significantly easier in Windows 2000. The phone and modem options in Control Panel gives you three tabs: Dialing Rules, Modems, and Advanced.

DIALING RULES

The Dialing Rules property sheet, as shown in Figure 4.15, gives you a list of dialing locations you have specified.

This feature is especially useful if you have several locations from which you are dialing. For each location, you can specify a number of dialing rules. You can use the Add button or Edit button to add a new rule or edit an existing one. Both take you to a New or Edit Location properties page, as shown in Figure 4.16.

The three Property sheets available are: General, Area Code Rules, and Calling Card, and they allow you to configure the location as needed. On the General Property sheet, you can specify a location name, country/region, and how to access an outside line. The Area Code Rules tab allows you to set how a number is to be dialed. This feature is useful for areas that have multiple area codes that are all local calls. This way, you

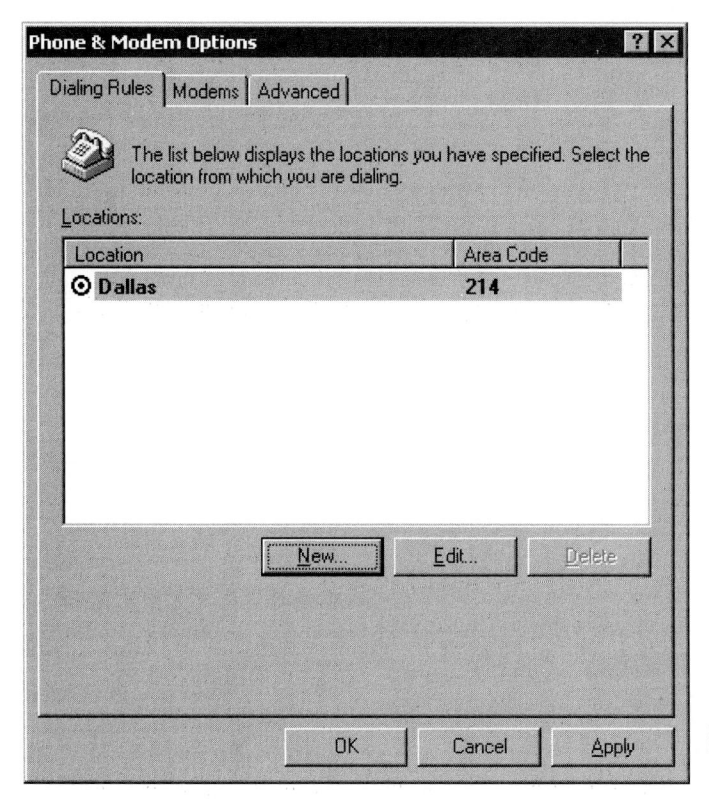

FIGURE 4.15
Dialing Rules

can specify which area codes should be dialed without a "1" in front of the area code. The Calling Card tab allows you to configure your computer to use a calling card for the location if necessary so that your computer can negotiate the long distance call.

MODEMS

The Modems Property Sheets of the phone and modem options presents you with a list of the modems that are installed on your computer. From this window, you add a new modem, remove an existing modem, or view the properties sheet for an existing modem. If you click the Add button, the Install New Modem Wizard launches and you can allow Windows to try to detect your new modem or you can manually install it from a list. If you click the Properties button, you are given General, Diagnostics, and Advanced Property Sheets—all of which are available in Device Manager as well.

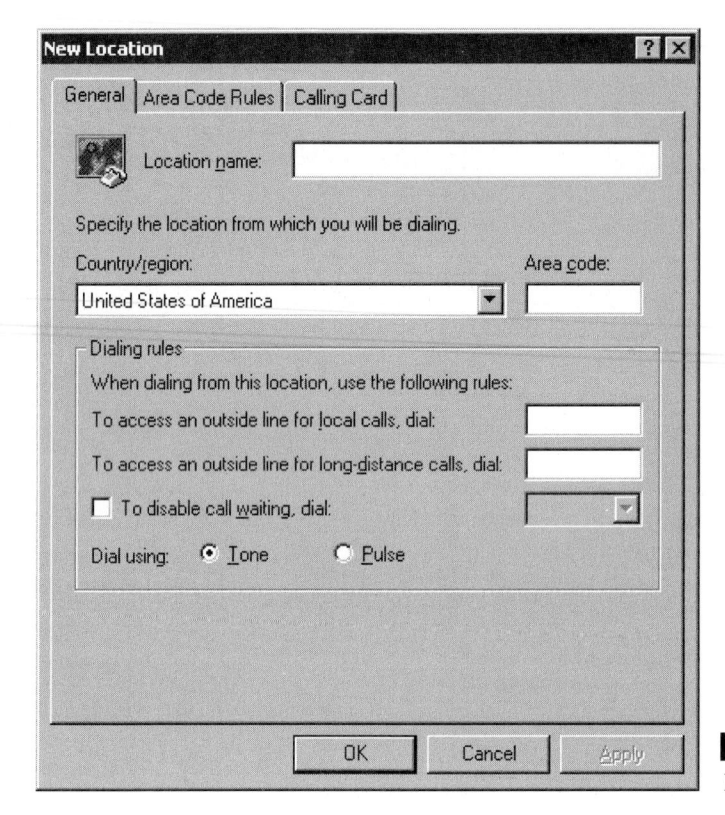

FIGURE 4.16
New Location

ADVANCED

The Advanced Property Sheet allows you to add, remove, or configure telephony drivers that are installed on your server. If you select a driver and click the Configure button, you can select gateway or proxy services if applicable.

Printers

The printers folder, located in Control Panel, allows you to configure local or network printers for your computer. As in Windows NT 4.0, the Add Printer wizard returns, which allows you to set up a printer on your computer or connect to a shared network printer. The wizard is self-explanatory, so we will not discuss it here.

Once a printer is setup, you can right-click the printer icon to access the properties page. On the properties sheet, you can configure general settings, share the printer, assign ports, and configure color management, security, and other general printer settings. Some of the sheets are self-explanatory, but I have pointed out the important configuration options available on some of the tabs in the following list:

- Security: The Security sheet allows you to configure printing rights for network users. For example, you can assign print rights to "everyone," but you can also assign the roles of manage printers and manage documents to specific users. To make these changes, simply select the user(s) from the list and check the appropriate permissions boxes as desired.
- Advanced: The Advanced sheet has several options. First, you can use the radio buttons to allow the printer to be available at all times, or you can set the time of day the printer is available to users. You can also use a series of radio buttons displayed to spool the documents so the program finishes printing faster. You have the option to start the printing immediately or wait until the last page is spooled. Also, you can print directly to the printer. There are also check boxes that allow you to control what the printer does with the documents and to allow spooled documents to print first. At the bottom of the tab, you can click the Printing Defaults button to choose portrait or landscape printing, Print processor, where you can change which processor is used, or you can click the Separator Page to generate a separator page between print jobs.

Scanners and Camera Properties

Windows 2000 Server provides a Scanners and Camera Properties interface in response to the wide use of scanners and digital cameras. The Properties sheet provides you with one tab that lists the devices currently installed, with buttons to add, remove, troubleshoot, or view the device specific properties.

Hardware Profiles

A hardware profile is a set of instructions Windows 2000 uses to determine which hardware devices and which settings should start when you start your computer. The first hardware profile, called Profile 1, is created when you install Windows 2000 Server, and it contains every device that is installed on your computer at the time of setup. With a server, you normally would not have multiple hardware profile settings since the server typically remains in one location. However, for mobile computing, hardware profiles are very beneficial to users who move from location to location.

You can manage hardware profiles in Windows 2000 by double-clicking System in Control Panel, then accessing the Hardware tab, as shown in Figure 4.17.

The Hardware tab provides quick access to the Hardware Wizard, Device Manager, and Hardware Profiles by clicking on the Hardware Profiles button. On the Hardware tab that appears, you can configure new hardware

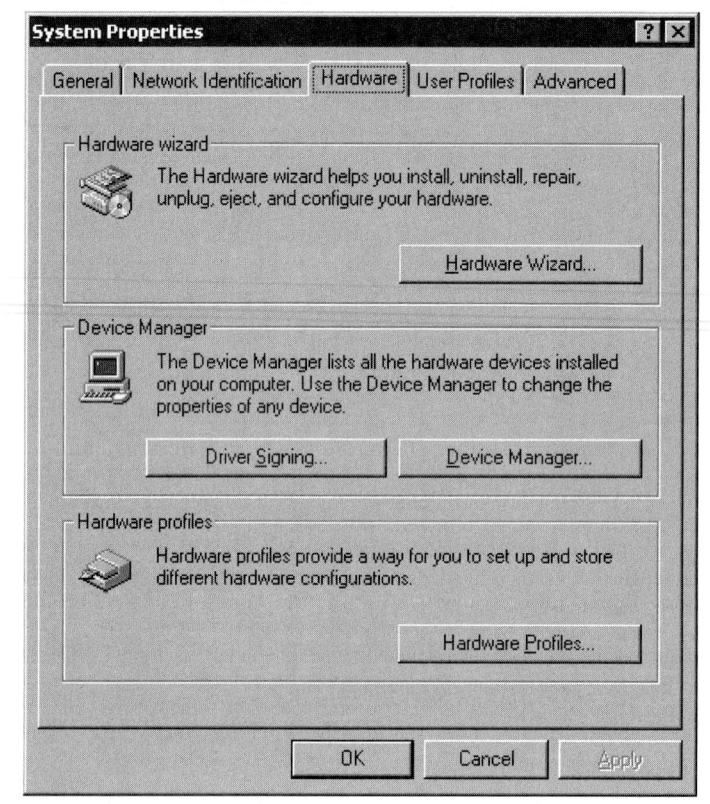

FIGURE 4.17
Hardware tab

profiles, copy or rename a profile, decide how to select a profile at start-up if there are multiple profiles, and view the properties of a selected hardware profile. As previously mentioned, hardware profiles primarily affect mobile users, and a number of settings available are designed specifically for this task.

Using System Information

If you have used Windows 98, you may be familiar with System Information, a tool that was introduced with the operating system. The purpose of System Information is to give you one interface that reports a variety of information about the system, problems it may be experiencing, and information about the hardware. A MMC console version of System Information is included in Windows 2000 Server, and you can use System Information to find various information about your system and troubleshoot problems.

two • Hardware and Disk Management **73**

System Information is accessible in the Computer Management Console. Click Start ➤ Programs ➤ Administrative Tools ➤ Computer Management to open the console. If you expand the System Tools tree and then expand System Information, you will see information for Hardware Resources, Components, and the Software Environment. You can use the Hardware Resources and Components sections to gain additional information about the hardware or hardware-related problems on your system.

The Hardware Resources folder contains the following subfolders:

- Conflicts/Sharing—contains information about hardware conflicts in your system, such as conflicting IRQ settings
- DMA—information about DMA channel assignment
- Forced Hardware—a list of forced hardware
- I/O—a list of address ranges, device using the address range, and the status of each
- IRQs—a list of what device is using what IRQ, as shown in Figure 4.18
- Memory—a list of the memory ranges, devices, and status

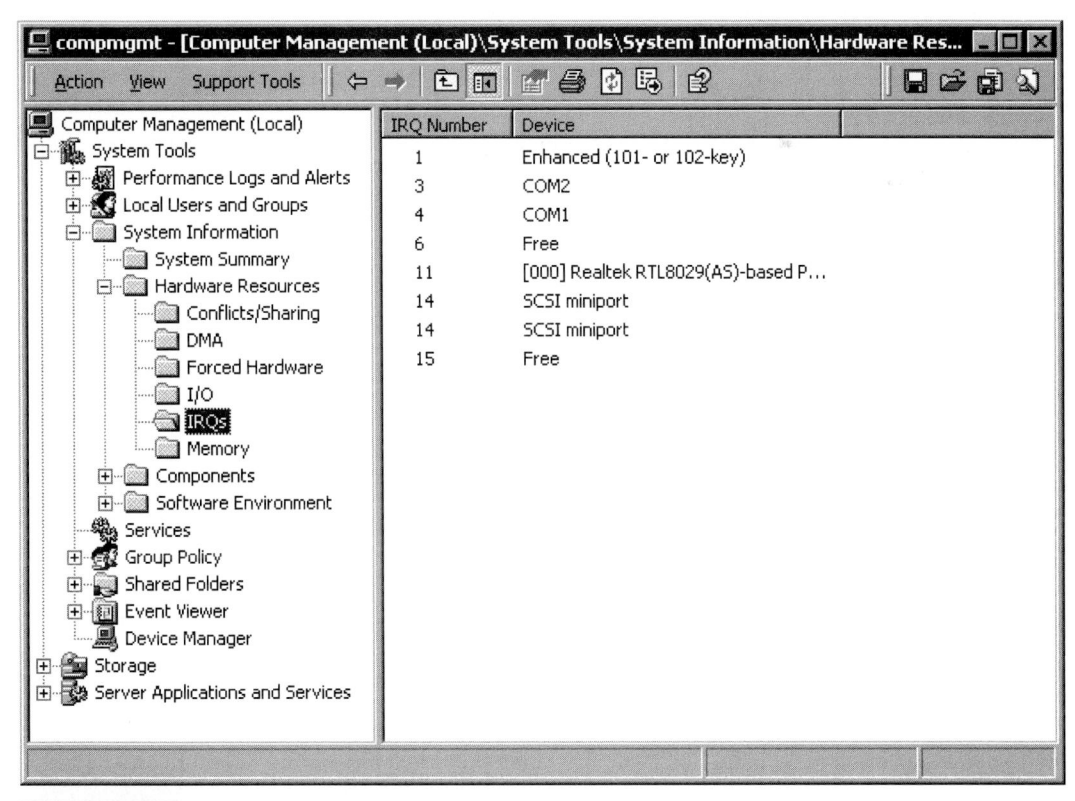

FIGURE 4.18 System Information

You can also use the Components folder to gain additional information about devices that are connected to your server. This folder gives detailed information about modems, infrared devices, USB devices, and a number of other system devices. It also contains a section that reports any problem devices.

Although System Information does not help you configure any devices, it does provide a fast way to gain an overall look at the hardware devices on your system and find any problems that may exist.

Summary

Windows 2000 Server makes installing, configuring, and troubleshooting hardware easy. Because Windows 2000 Server provides a Plug and Play compliant system, your hardware choices are greatly expanded. The major tools provided in Windows 2000 Server to configure hardware are the Add/Remove Hardware Wizard, Device Manager, Control Panel icons, and System Information. With the use of these tools and Windows 2000's ability to self-configure Plug and Play hardware, major hardware conflicts and difficulties are becoming a thing of the past.

FIVE

Disk Management

Disk Management in Windows 2000 Server is significantly different from Windows NT Server 4.0. You will see some familiar features and functions concerning fault tolerance and general disk management, but there are several new technologies and features you will have to get a handle on to properly manage your system hard disk(s). This chapter tells you about these new technologies and features and shows you how to configure your hard disks in Windows 2000 Server for optimal performance.

File Systems

Windows 2000 Server supports FAT, FAT32, and NTFS. The NTFS file system provided in Windows 2000 Server is an enhanced version that supports the additional security features of Kerberos. When you installed Windows 2000 Server setup retained your file system from Windows NT (if the installation was an upgrade). Unless you have specific reasons for using FAT or FAT32, you should implement NTFS on all of your disk drives. NTFS allows you to use a variety of security and file storage features in Windows 2000 Server and is your best performance choice.

You can format any partitions (with the exception of the boot or system partition) using the Disk Management tool in Windows 2000 Server. To format or reformat any drives, follow these steps:

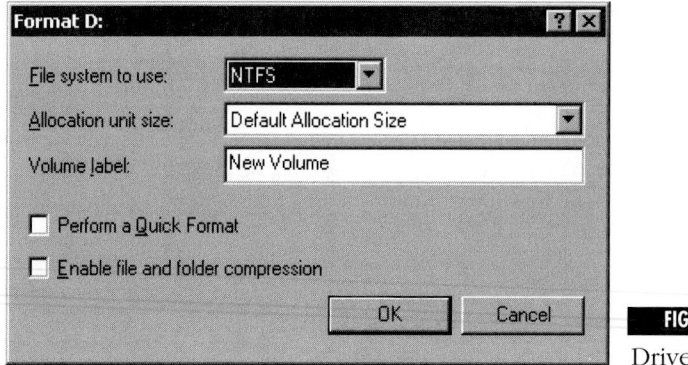

FIGURE 5.1
Drive Format

1. Click Start → Programs → Administrative Tools → Computer Management. The console window opens.
2. Expand the Storage tree and double-click Disk Management. The Disk Management utility appears in the right pane.
3. Right click the partition you want to format or reformat and choose Format.
4. A window appears, as shown in Figure 5.1 asking you to choose the file system, allocation unit size, and a volume label. For the file system, you can choose FAT, FAT32, or NTFS. Make your selections and click OK.
5. A dialog box appears telling you that formatting will erase all data on the partition. Click OK to continue or Cancel to quit.

Dynamic and Basic Disks

Windows 2000 Server now provides support for "dynamic" disks as well as basic disks. A dynamic disk is not restricted to four primary partitions per disk, and several disk management tasks discussed later in the chapter can only be performed on dynamic disks. A basic disk is simply partitions and logical drives (and volumes) that were created with Windows NT 4.0 or earlier, such as volume sets, stripe sets, mirror sets, and stripe sets with parity. In Windows 2000, these volumes are now called spanned volumes, striped volumes, mirrored volumes, and RAID-5 volumes.

> **for review**
>
> **Windows NT Disk Solutions**
>
> A quick review of the storage and fault tolerant solutions provided in Windows NT will help you with the content later in this chapter.
>
> Volume Set. A volume set is a collection of partitions that are treated as one partition. This storage solution allows you to combine 2 to 32 areas of unformatted free disk space to create one logical drive.
>
> Stripe Set. A stripe set is like a volume set, but a stripe set combines unformatted free space on 2 to 32 physical drives to create one logical drive. Data is written across the disks in 64K blocks. This evenly distributes data on the disks and speeds performance. Stripe Sets, however, do not provide any inherent fault tolerance.
>
> Mirror Set. A mirror set duplicates a partition and moves the duplicate copy onto another physical disk. In other words, a mirror set maintains two complete copies of the partition at all times. In this case, if one physical disk fails, the data remains on the other physical disk.
>
> Stripe Set with Parity. A stripe set with parity (RAID 5) requires 3 to 32 physical drives. The data is written in rows across the disk with a parity bit. In the event of a single disk failure, the data can be regenerated using the parity bit.

Dynamic disks in Windows 2000 Server offer you more management flexibility without the partition limitation of basic disks. Dynamic disks can contain an unlimited number of volumes, but they cannot contain partitions or logical drives.

Also, once you upgrade to Windows 2000 Server from Windows NT Server, Windows 2000 Server further limits what you can do with a basic disk. The following list tells you what you can and cannot do with basic disks in Windows 2000 Server:

You can:

- check disk properties and run most administrative tools
- view volume and partition properties
- change drive-letters for disk volumes or partitions
- share information and establish security restrictions
- create new primary partitions or extended partitions
- create and delete logical disks within an extended partition
- format a partition and mark it as active
- delete volume sets, stripe sets, and stripe sets with parity
- break a mirror set
- repair a mirror set or stripe set with parity

You cannot:

- create new volume, stripe, mirror sets, or stripe sets with parity
- extend existing volumes and volume sets

Basically, Windows 2000 Server allows you to keep your disk configuration when you upgrade from Windows NT 4.0. You can manage your basic disks and repair fault-tolerant solutions; however, you are limited to the current configuration. You really cannot make any significant changes to the disk or establish new volume or stripe sets, and you cannot implement new fault-tolerant solutions.

I should also mention here that Windows 2000 has introduced two other terms concerning disk management: online and offline. A disk that is up and running is referred to as online, while a disk that has errors that are preventing it from running is considered offline. Windows 2000 allows you to make configuration changes to online disks without rebooting the server—in most instances anyway.

Upgrading a Basic Disk to a Dynamic Disk

Windows 2000 Server keeps your disk configuration if you upgrade from Windows NT 4.0, so your disk will be a basic disk. You can choose to upgrade the basic disk to a dynamic disk so that you have full access to the disk management tools available in Windows 2000 Server. The next question is naturally, "Should I upgrade?" There is one basic rule to determine whether or not you should upgrade your basic disk to a dynamic disk. If your computer also runs MS-DOS, Windows 98 or earlier, or Windows NT 4.0 or earlier, you should not upgrade your disk because these operating systems cannot access dynamic volumes. If your system only runs Windows 2000, then you should upgrade the basic disk to a dynamic disk. This action will allow you to more effectively manage your disk in Windows 2000 Server.

Any disk that you upgrade to dynamic must have at least 1 MB of unformatted free space at the end of the disk otherwise, the upgrade will fail. Disk Management uses this free space when creating partitions or volumes on a disk, but partitions or volumes created with Windows NT may not have this free space readily available. Once you perform the upgrade, your Windows NT partitions become dynamic volumes, which you cannot change back to partitions. If you have Windows NT volume sets, mirror sets, striped sets, or striped sets with parity on your disk, the upgrade will change those to Windows 2000's spanned volumes, striped volumes, mirrored volumes, or RAID-5 volumes. Remember that once the upgrade is complete, the disk cannot be accessed by operating systems that exist on the computer other than Windows 2000. Also, before performing the upgrade, the following issues should be taken into consideration:

- Boot Partition: You can upgrade a basic disk containing the boot partition to a dynamic disk. The boot partition becomes a simple boot volume after the upgrade is complete.
- System Partition: You can upgrade a basic disk containing the system partition to a dynamic disk. The system partition becomes a simple system partition when the upgrade is complete.
- Removable Media: You cannot upgrade removable media to dynamic volumes.
- Volumes on multiple disks: If a basic disk contains any volumes that span multiple disks, as in a stripe set with parity, you must also upgrade the other disks that contain parts of the volume.
- Disks with sector sizes larger than 512 bytes: You cannot upgrade a basic disk to a dynamic disk if the sector size of the disk is greater than 512 bytes.
- You cannot change a dynamic disk back to a basic disk without deleting all of the volumes first. This action deletes all of the data on the disk. Once the volumes have been deleted, you can right-click on the disk and choose Revert to Basic Disk.

To upgrade a basic disk to a dynamic disk, follow these steps:

1. To make sure your data is protected from any failure, perform a backup before upgrading the disk.
2. Click Start ➤ Programs ➤ Administrative Tools ➤ Computer Management. The Console Window opens.
3. Expand the Storage tree and double-click Disk Management. The Disk Management interface appears in the right pane with a display of your disk(s).
4. Right-click the disk you want to upgrade. Make sure you are right-clicking the disk and not a partition of the disk. Click Upgrade to dynamic disk.
5. The upgrade takes place, and you are prompted to reboot your computer. You must reboot for the upgrade to complete the boot and system partition upgrades.
6. Once the upgrade is complete, Disk Management will display the disk as dynamic, as shown in Figure 5.2.

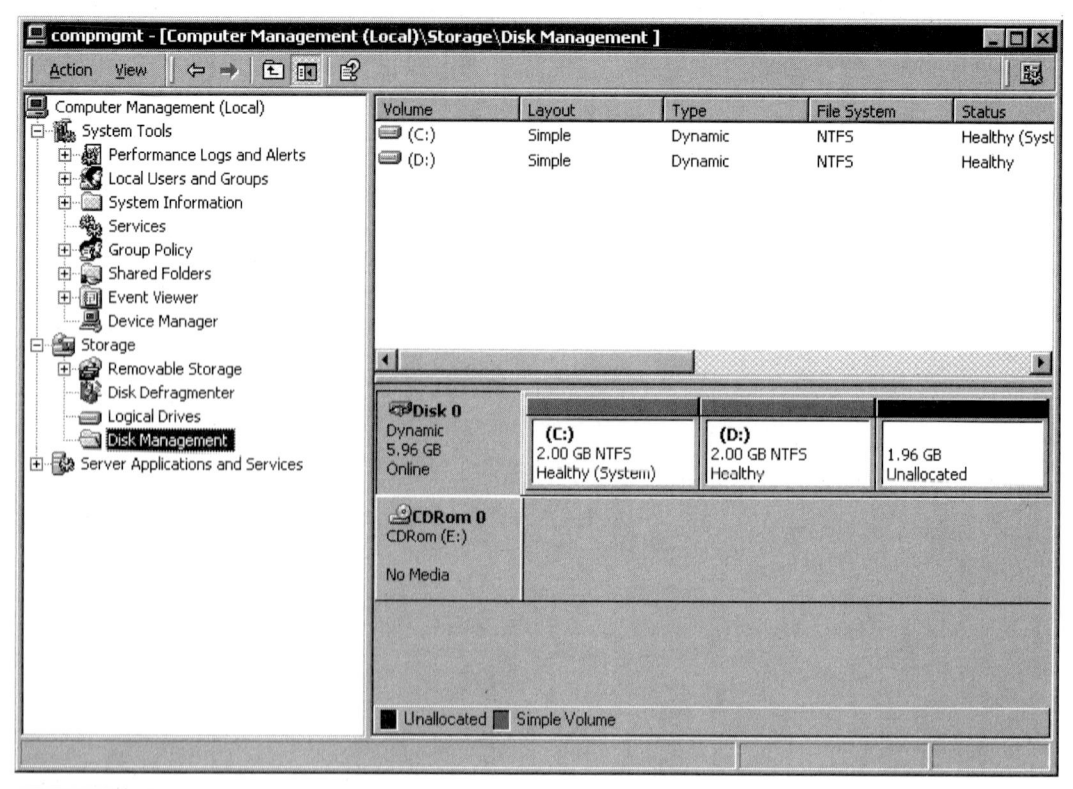

FIGURE 5.2 Dynamic Disk Upgrade

Managing Dynamic Volumes

Dynamic disk volumes are managed through the Disk Management interface as shown in Figure 5.2. In the top part of the right pane, the volume label is displayed with additional information about the disk: Layout, Type, File System, Status, Capacity, and Free Space. The status label gives you information about the disk and may display as follows, depending on the condition of the disk:

- Healthy: The volume is accessible and has no known problems.
- Healthy (At Risk): The volume is accessible, but I/O errors have been detected on the disk. In this case, all volumes on the disk are displayed as Healthy (At Risk). The underlying disk is displayed as Online (Errors). Normally, you can return the disk to Online status by reactivating the disk. This can be done by right-clicking on the disk and choosing Reactivate Disk.

- Initializing: The volume is being initialized and will be displayed as Healthy once the initialization is complete. This status does not require any action.
- Re-synching: The status indicator occurs on mirror volumes when re-synchronization between the two disks is occurring. When the resynchronization is complete, the status returns to Healthy, and no action is required.
- Regenerating: In the case of RAID-5 volumes, this status indicator occurs when data is being regenerated from the parity bit. This status does not require any action.
- Failed Redundancy: This status indicator appears when the underlying disk is no longer online. In this case, the data is no longer fault tolerant in either the mirror volume or RAID-5 volume. In order to avoid potential data loss, the volume should be repaired (see the Fault Tolerance section later in this chapter).
- Failed Redundancy (At Risk): This status is the same as Failed Redundancy, but the underlying disk status is usually Online (Errors). To correct the At Risk problem, Reactivate the disk so that its status returns to Online.
- Failed: The volume cannot be automatically started, and the volume needs to be repaired.

Volume Properties

You can access a volume's properties sheet by right clicking the volume in Disk Management and selecting Properties. The Properties Sheet, as shown in Figure 5.3, gives you a variety of information about the volume and configuration options, which are described in the following list:

- General: The General Property sheet contains information about the disk, such as the file system, used space, free space, and a pie chart showing you how much free space is available. You have the option of launching Disk Cleanup (described in the Disk Tools section later in this chapter) and also the options of compressing the drive or indexing the drive.
- Tools: The Tools Property sheet allows you to run Error-Checking, Backup, and De-fragmentation. Error-Checking and De-fragmentation are described in the Disk Tools section later in this chapter and Backup is discussed in Chapter 7.
- Hardware: The Hardware tab contains standard information about the disk hardware, its status, and buttons to troubleshoot the hardware or view its properties.
- Sharing: The Sharing tab allows you to configure standard sharing options for the volume. You can share the volume, limit the number

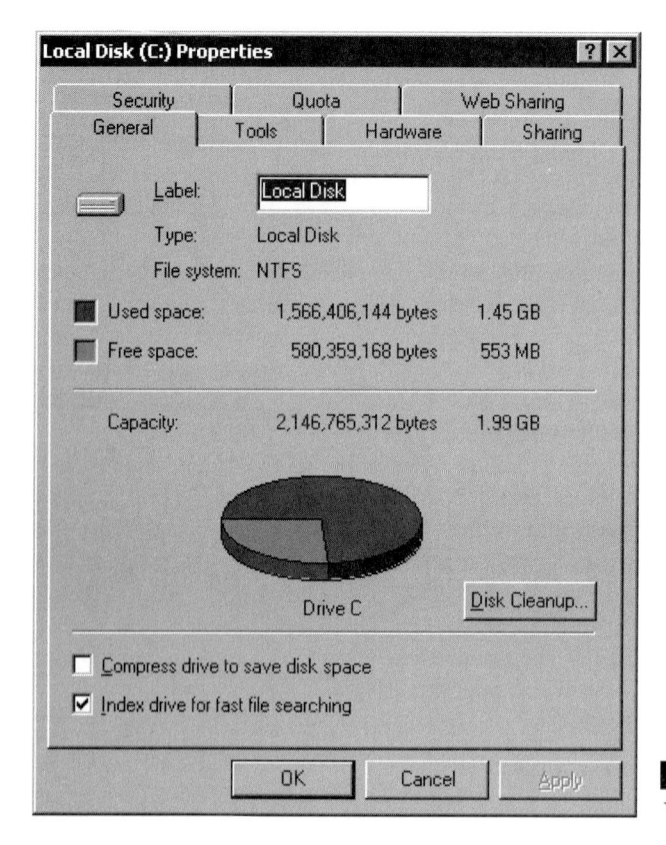

FIGURE 5.3
Volume Properties

of users, set the permissions, and configure caching so that the volume can be accessed offline. The caching option is normally used for documents and folders that users need to access. The caching option allows these documents to remain available even if the disk goes offline.

- Security: The Security tab allows you to configure security options for users who access the volume or deny permissions to groups or particular users. The Security tab is shown in Figure 5.4.
- Quota: Disk Quota which is new in Windows 2000 Server, provides a way to manage how much disk space each user is allowed. This feature forces users to be more conservative with storage and delete unnecessary files and folders. The Quota Property sheet appears in Figure 5.5. Once you enable quota management in the check-box provided, you can deny disk space to users who exceed the quota limit. The Limit disk space boxes allow you to set the quota as well as to set a warning level so users will receive notification when they are close to their limits. Logging options are available at the bottom of the win-

two • Hardware and Disk Management

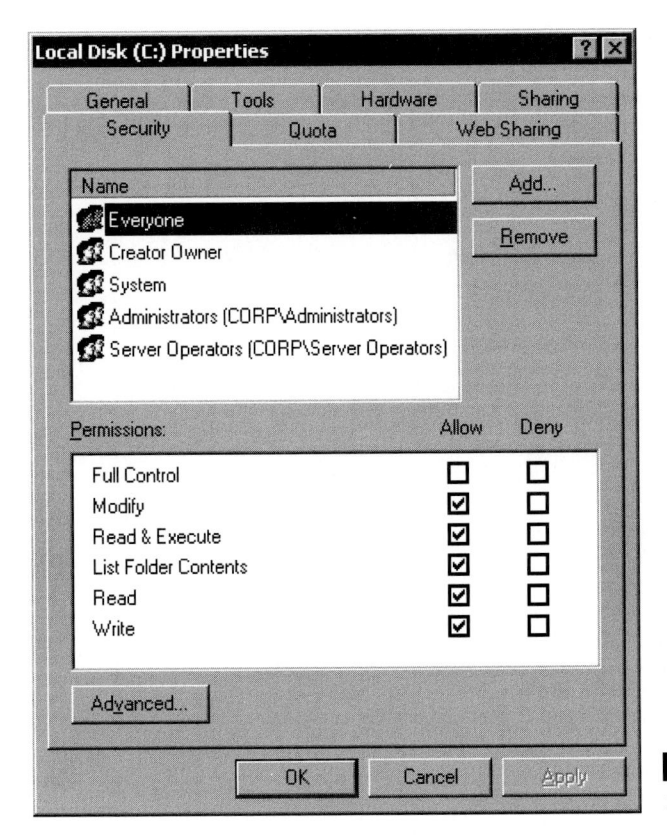

FIGURE 5.4
Security Tab

dow, and a Quota Entries button enables you to view quota events and usage. Although quota restrictions are a good way to manage disk space, you should make certain that quota restrictions are large enough for the needs of your users.
- Web Sharing: The Web Sharing tab allows you to share the volume on a web site. You can use the Aliases box to create aliases for the volume. This feature could be used to share the volume on an Intranet so that users can access the volume by clicking on the alias.

Configuring Simple Volumes

Managing simple volumes is relatively easy, and Windows 2000 Server provides several wizards to help you configure your simple disk volumes as desired. The following sections show you how to accomplish several tasks concerning simple volumes.

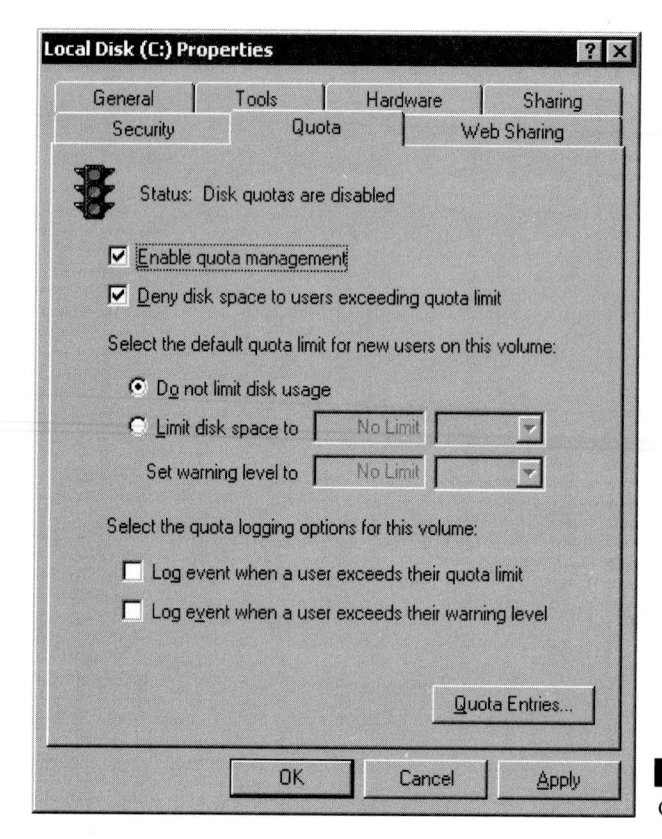

FIGURE 5.5
Quota Tab

CREATING A NEW SIMPLE VOLUME

To create a new volume, follow these steps:

1. Click Start → Programs → Administrative Tools → Computer Management. The Console opens.
2. Expand the Storage tree, and double-click Disk Management.
3. On the disk where you want to create a new volume, right click the disk (not one of the volumes) and choose New Volume. This action launches the Create New Volume Wizard.
4. The Wizard's opening screen gives you a brief introduction. Click Next.
5. The Select Volume Type screen appears. Click the Simple Volume radio button and click Next.
6. The Select Disks screen appears. In this window, select the dynamic disk on which you want to create volumes and the size of the volume, as shown in Figure 5.6. Make your selections and click Next.

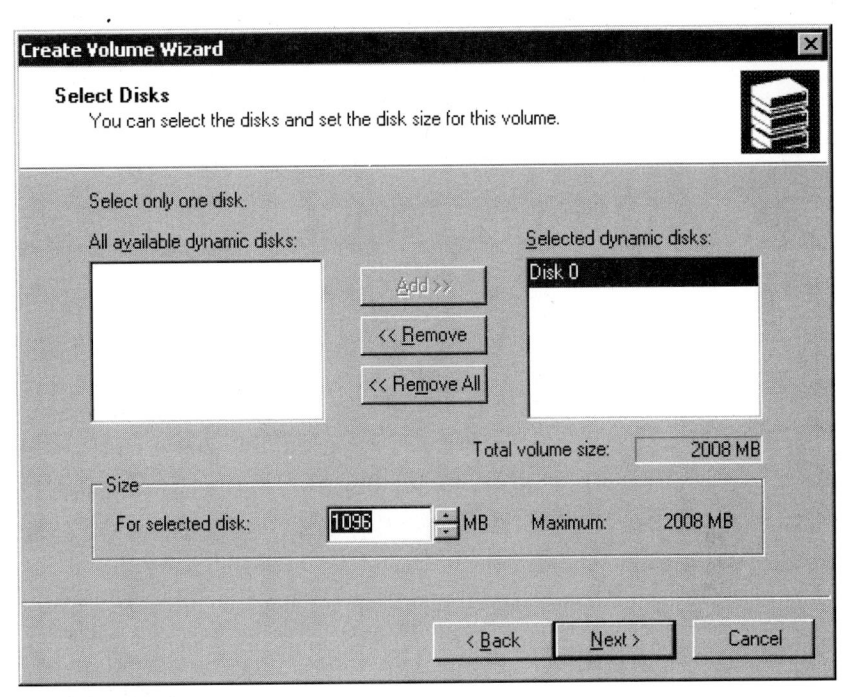

FIGURE 5.6 Select Disks

7. The Assign Drive Letter or Path window appears. In this window, you can assign a drive letter or drive path if desired. Make your selection and click Next.

8. The Format Volume window appears. In this window, you can choose to either format the volume or not. If you decide to format the volume, you can choose the file system, allocation unit size, and the volume label. After making your choices, click Next.

9. The wizard ends with a summary of the choices you make. Click the Finish button to create the volume. The new volume appears in the Disk Management window.

DELETING A SIMPLE VOLUME

To delete a simple volume, follow these steps:

1. Click Start ➤ Programs ➤ Administrative Tools ➤ Computer Management. The Console opens.
2. Expand the Storage tree, and double-click Disk Management.

3. Right-click the volume you want to delete and click Delete Volume.
4. A dialog box appears asking if you are sure you want to delete the volume. Click Yes. The volume is deleted.

EXTENDING A SIMPLE VOLUME

You can easily extend a simple volume, but it has to be either formatted with NTFS or contain no file system; you cannot extend volumes formatted with FAT or FAT32. To extend an existing simple volume, follow these steps:

1. Click Start ➤ Programs ➤ Administrative Tools ➤ Computer Management. The Console opens.
2. Expand the Storage tree, and double-click Disk Management.
3. Right-click the volume you want to extend and choose Extend Volume.
4. The Extend Volume Wizard begins. Click Next.
5. The Select Disks window appears. In the Size box, choose the size of the extended volume as desired.
6. The wizard displays the changes you have made. Click Finish to extend the volume.

CHANGE DRIVE LETTER AND PATH

You can change the drive letter for a simple volume by following these steps:

1. Click Start ➤ Programs ➤ Administrative Tools ➤ Computer Management. The Console opens.
2. Expand the Storage tree, and double-click Disk Management.
3. Right-click the volume on which you want to change the drive letter, and select Change Drive Letter and Path.
4. The current drive letter and any paths are listed in the dialog box, as shown in Figure 5.7. Click the Modify button.
5. In the Assign Drive letter drop down menu, select the new drive letter and click OK.

You can also use the same process to assign a mounted path or change an existing mounted path; and it allows you to mount a local drive at an empty folder on a local NTFS volume. This action causes Windows 2000 to assign a drive path to the drive rather than to the drive letter. You are not limited to the 24-drive letter limit (C through Z). Using a mounted path, you work around such a restriction and ensure that no failures occur due to changes made to the drive path. This action allows a number of pos-

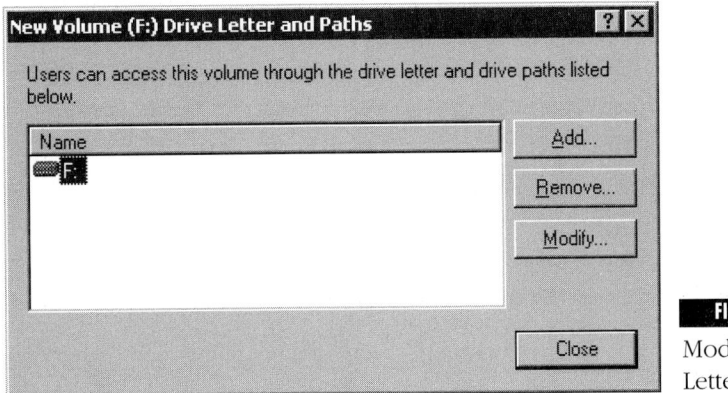

two • Hardware and Disk Management

FIGURE 5.7
Modify Drive Letter or Path

sibilities, including mounting your CD-ROM drive so it is accessible from C:\CD-ROM, or even moving the Program Files folder to another volume that has more space while retaining the path of C:\Program Files.

To configure a mounted path, follow these steps:

1. Click Start → Programs → Administrative Tools → Computer Management. The Console opens.
2. Expand the Storage tree and double-click Disk Management.
3. Right-click the volume on which you want to change the drive letter and select Change Drive Letter and Path.
4. The current drive letter and any paths are listed in the dialog box. Click the Add button.
5. In the Mount this volume at an empty folder which supports drive paths dialog box, enter the path or browse to it, as shown in Figure 5.8. Then, click OK. The mounted path now appears as a drive instead of as a folder where you had configured it to reside, as shown in Figure 5.9.

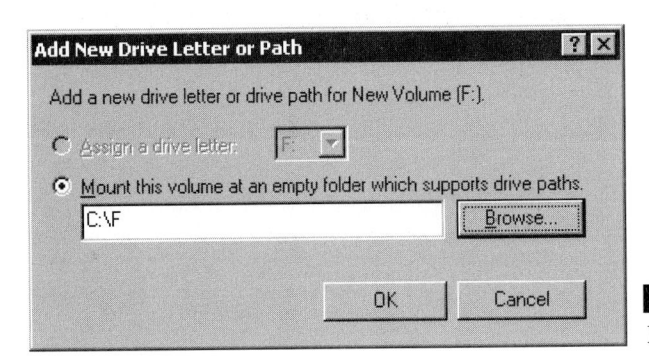

FIGURE 5.8
New Mounted Path

Chapter five • Disk Management

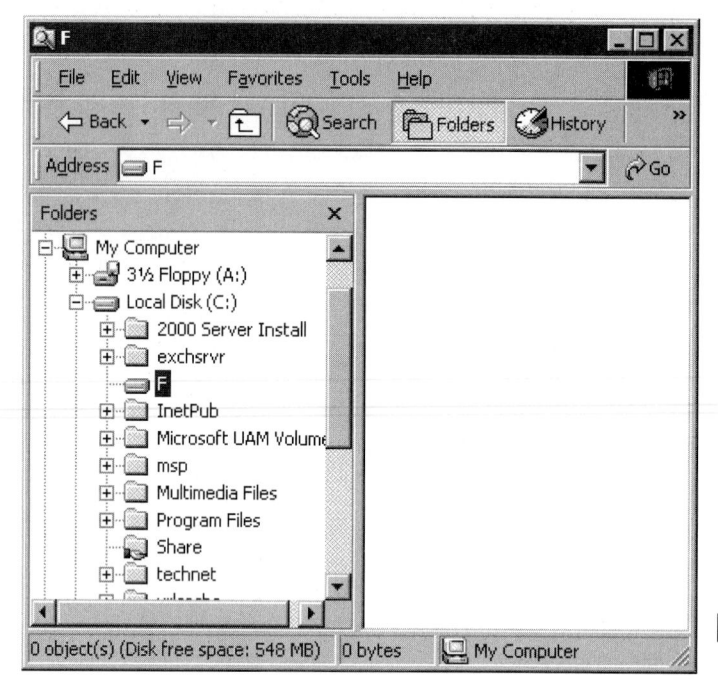

FIGURE 5.9
Mounted Path

Configuring Spanned Volumes

Spanned volumes, formerly called volume sets, allow you to combine disk space from more than one physical disk to create one logical volume. A spanned volume is a storage solution that helps you make the most of small pieces of disk spaces but does not have any inherent fault tolerance—if one disk fails, the entire volume is lost. In a spanned volume data is written to the first disk until the disk is full, then data is written to the second disk, and so forth. The following sections explain how to configure and manage spanned volumes.

CREATING A SPANNED VOLUME

To create a spanned volume you need at least two dynamic disks with a maximum of 32 dynamic disks. Spanned volumes cannot be mirrored or striped.

To create a spanned volume, follow these steps:

1. Right-click an area of unformatted free space on the first disk that will be included in the spanned volume. Choose Create Volume.
2. The Wizard appears. Select the Spanned Volume radio button and click Next.
3. The Wizard will ask you to select additional areas on other hard disks to create the volume; then it will present you with a summary at the end. Click Finish.

DELETING A SPANNED VOLUME

You can easily delete a spanned volume, but do remember that deleting the volume deletes all data stored in the spanned volume. In other words, you cannot delete a portion of a spanned volume. To delete a spanned volume, follow these steps:

1. Click Start ➤ Programs ➤ Administrative Tools ➤ Computer Management. The Console opens.
2. Expand the Storage tree, and double-click Disk Management.
3. Right-click the spanned volume you want to delete and click Delete Volume.
4. Windows will ask you to confirm the delete order before deleting the spanned volume.

EXTENDING A SPANNED VOLUME

You can extend a spanned volume in the same way you extend a simple volume. The spanned volume has to be formatted with NTFS or not contain a file system; you cannot extend a spanned volume formatted with FAT or FAT32. To extend a spanned volume, follow the instructions in the Extending a Simple Volume Section.

Configuring and Managing Striped Volumes

Striped volumes, formerly called stripe sets, store data on two or more physical disks. Data is written across the disks in 64 K blocks in a stripe fashion. Striped volumes are storage solutions that do not provide any fault tolerance, but they do improve hard disk access speed.

CREATING A STRIPED VOLUME

You can create a striped volume the same way you create a spanned volume. You need a minimum of two dynamic disks with a maximum of 32. Striped volumes do not provide fault tolerance, and they cannot be mirrored or extended. To create a striped volume, follow the steps in the Extending a Spanned Volume Section with the exception that you should choose to create a striped volume rather than a spanned volume.

DELETING A STRIPED VOLUME

You can delete a striped volume in the same way you delete a spanned volume. Remember that deleting a striped volume deletes all of the data in the volume; you cannot delete only a portion of a striped volume. For specific steps to delete a striped volume, follow the instructions in the Deleting a Spanned Volume.

Fault Tolerance Solutions

Windows 2000 Server supports mirrored volumes and RAID-5 volumes on dynamic disks. These solutions allow you to recover data in the event of a hard disk failure. The following sections show you how to configure both mirrored volumes and RAID-5 volumes.

Creating Mirrored Volumes

A mirrored volume, formally called a mirror set, requires two identically sized physical disks and creates a complete copy of one disk onto the other disk by using the Windows 2000 fault tolerance driver, FTDISK.SYS. Each time changes take place on the disk, the mirror is updated so there is always exact data redundancy. A mirror set is an effective solution, but it reduces disk space by fifty percent (called "overhead") since you have to have a separate disk reserved for the mirror. If the primary disk fails, the system switches to the mirror disk so that operations can continue. To create a mirrored volume, follow these steps:

1. In Disk Management, right click an area of unformatted free space and click Create Volume.
2. The Create Volume Wizard appears. Click Next.
3. The Volume Types window appears. Click Mirrored volume.
4. The wizard will ask you to select another volume of equal size on another physical disk. You will also be asked to format the volume and assign a drive letter.
5. Once the wizard finishes, you are presented with a summary. Click Finish to create the mirrored volume.

Deleting a Mirrored Volume

You can delete a mirrored volume in the same way you delete other volumes in dynamic disks. Remember that deleting a mirrored volume deletes all of the data both on the primary disk and on the mirror.

Removing a Mirrored Volume

You can remove a mirrored volume so that the mirrored disk can be used for other purposes. Once you remove the mirror, the mirror becomes unallocated space. This action, of course, removes the fault tolerance of the mirror. To remove a mirror, right-click on the mirror and click Remove.

Breaking a Mirrored Volume

You can also break a mirror relationship. When you do this, both the primary disk and the mirrored disk become two simple volumes with the same data. The mirror is no longer fault tolerant at this point. To break a mirrored volume, follow these steps:

1. Click Start ➤ Programs ➤ Administrative Tools ➤ Computer Management. The Console opens.
2. Expand the Storage tree, and double-click Disk Management.
3. Right-click the mirrored volume, then click Break Mirror.

Repairing a Mirrored Volume

When a mirrored volume's status in Disk Management is Failed Redundancy, the volume is no longer fault tolerant and needs to be repaired. There are two ways to attempt to repair a mirrored volume, depending on the problem:

1. If one of the underlying disks' status is Offline, then you need to reconnect the disk and repair the mirrored volume. In Disk Management, right-click the offline disk and click Reactivate disk. If this does not solve the problem, then you can break the mirrored volume and create a new mirror on another physical disk.
2. If the underlying disks' status is Online (Errors) and the volume's status is Failed Redundancy, then you need to reactivate the disk. Right-click the disk with errors and click Reactivate disk. The mirrored volume's status should first change to Regenerating and then to Healthy.

Creating RAID-5 Volumes

RAID-5 volumes, formerly called stripe sets with parity, are fault-tolerant solutions that write data in a stripe across three or more physical disks. As the data is written, a parity bit is included that can be used to regenerate the data should one of the physical disks fail. A RAID-5 volume is a good fault tolerant solution that has less cost per megabyte than a mirrored volume. RAID-5 volumes cannot be extended or mirrored. To create a RAID-5 volume, follow the steps in the "Creating Mirrored Volumes" section. You need at least three dynamic disks that have free unformatted areas the same size.

Deleting RAID-5 Volumes

You can delete a RAID-5 volume just as you would any other dynamic volume. Deleting a RAID-5 volume deletes all of the information in the volume.

Reactivating RAID-5 Volumes

If there are problems with one of the physical disks, such as Offline or Online (Errors) status, you can right click the disk and choose Reactivate Disk to attempt to resolve the problem. Once this is done, the RAID-5 volume's status should change to Regenerating and then to Healthy.

If the disk containing the RAID-5 volume cannot be reactivated this way, then you can replace a disk region by right-clicking the failed portion of the RAID-5 volume and clicking Repair Volume. This action will allow you to move the failed portion to another physical disk that has enough unallocated space to repair the volume. The regeneration process will take place and be displayed as Healthy once it is complete.

If there is a catastrophic failure of one of the RAID-5 disks, then that disk becomes an orphan. At this point, you can regenerate the data from the orphan by using the other RAID-5 disks. To perform this action, you should select an area of free space on another disk that is at least the same size as the orphan so that the data can be regenerated to the new disk.

Repairing RAID-5 Volumes

If one of the physical disks has an Offline or Online (Errors) status, you can attempt to repair the RAID-5 volume be reactivating the offending disk. This is done in the same manner as the mirrored volume.

Disk Tools

Windows 2000 Server includes several new tools to help you manage and resolve problems with your hard disks. Some of these tools first came on the scene in Windows 98, and you will find them very beneficial. You can run the disk tools by accessing the properties sheets for each disk with the Computer Management Console, My Computer; or you can access them by clicking Start ➤ Programs ➤ Accessories ➤ System Tools. The following sections show how to access the tools from the disk's properties sheet, and give you an overview of each tool, and show you how to use them.

Disk Cleanup

Over time, your hard disk collects a lot of files and fragments that are not needed. These files take up disk space that can be used for other purposes,

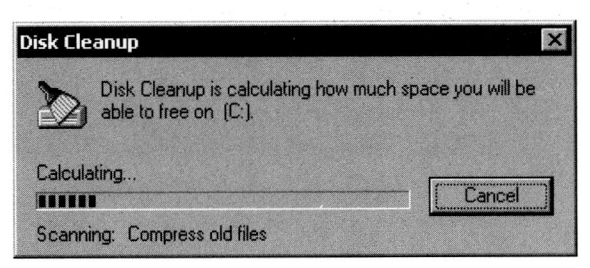

FIGURE 5.10
Disk Cleanup inspection

so Windows 2000 includes a Disk Cleanup tool. It allows you to specify cleanup options on the drive you select and even allows you to uninstall no longer needed programs.

The Disk Cleanup is accessed from the General tab of the disk's properties sheet by using the Disk Cleanup button. If you click the button, Disk Cleanup examines the disk and determines how much space can be freed, as shown in Figure 5.10.

Once the examination is complete, Disk Cleanup gives you a list of files that can be deleted. Typically, the utility will give you a list of downloaded program files, temporary Internet files, Recycle bin items, and an option to compress old files on your drive. After making the selections you want, the utility will delete or compress the items, as chosen by you. You can also click the More Options tab to clean up Windows components that you do not use or programs that are no longer used or needed. These options launch the Add/Remove Programs interface and the Windows Components Wizard where you can select components to remove from your system.

Disk Defragmenter

Windows 2000 Server includes a disk de-fragmentation utility. Fragmentation occurs over time as files are changed, added, and deleted in your system. Instead of the files being stored in a contiguous format, they are separated and stored in pieces wherever there is available space. This causes your system to work harder and often slower as it retrieves data from the hard disk.

You can access the Disk Defragmenter on the Tools menu of the disk's properties sheet. The Disk Defragmenter allows you to analyze a drive by selecting the drive and clicking the Analyze button. System files are displayed in green, contiguous files are displayed in blue, and fragmented files are displayed in red. As you can see in Figure 5.11, this drive needs to be de-fragmented.

To defragment a drive, simply click the Defragment button.

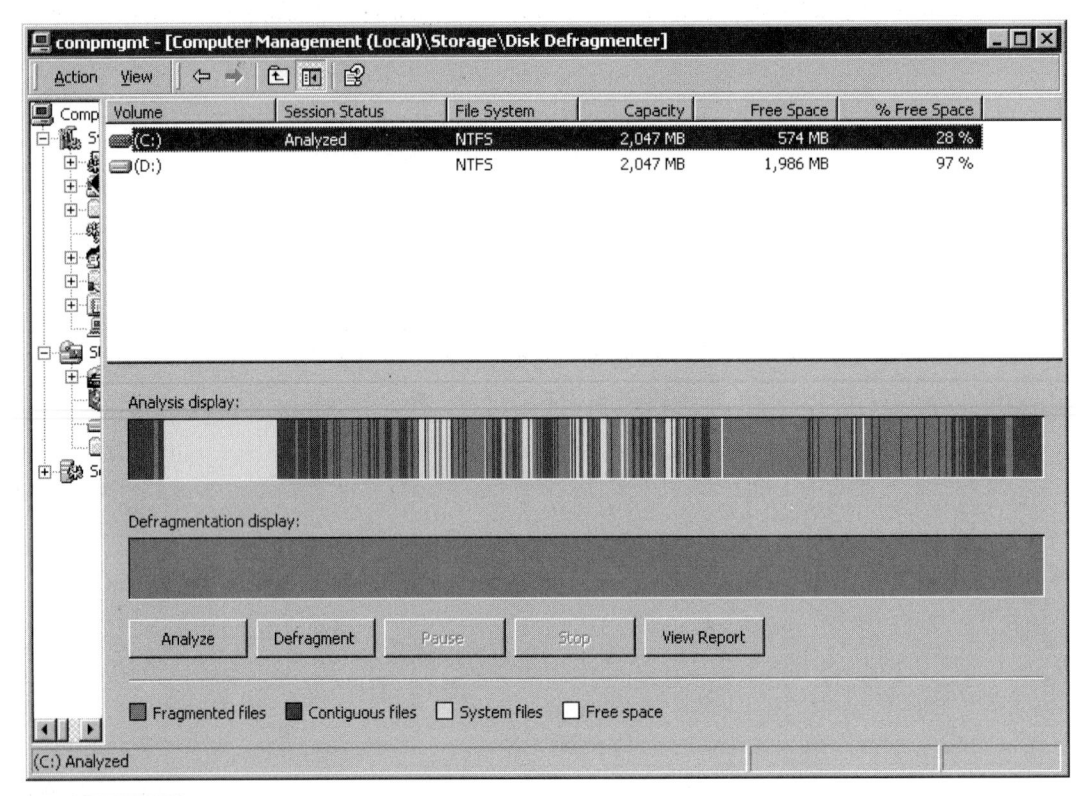

FIGURE 5.11 Disk Defragmenter

Error Checking

The Error Checking tool checks your disk for file system errors and bad sectors. The Error Checking tool scans for these problems and automatically attempts to repair them. You can access the Error Checking tool from the Tools menu of the disk's properties sheet.

Summary

Windows 2000 Server provides a number of enhancements to managing hard disks. Windows 2000 supports both basic disks and the new dynamic disks which does not limit the number of volumes you can create. Windows 2000 supports FAT, FAT32, and the new NTFS. Through the use of storage solutions such as spanned volumes and striped volumes, you can more easily manage disk space usage, and Windows 2000 supports mirrored volumes and RAID-5 volumes for fault tolerance. Additionally, Windows 2000 Server provides a number of disk tools, such as Error Checking, Cleanup, and Disk Defragmenter to keep your hard drives working correctly and efficiently.

SIX

Interface and System Settings

As you can imagine, configuring your interface and system settings is one of the easiest tasks you can perform with your server. Interface and system settings refer to a diverse collection of settings that affect how your desktop, icons, and folders appear, how the system handles applications and memory, and how your server accesses and uses the Internet. Although configuring your interface and system settings is much easier than the complex server services and networking options we explore in the following chapters, your system settings do affect how your system operates and how the interface appears. In this chapter, you learn how to configure your interface and system settings so that they meet your needs.

Start Menu and TaskBar

You can easily customize what items appear in the Start Menu and what items appear on the Taskbar. To configure these options, click Start ➤ Settings ➤ Taskbar and Start Menu. A window appears that has two tabs; General and Advanced.

On the General tab, as shown in Figure 6.1, you can use the check boxes to select what taskbar options you would like to use.

The check-box options are:

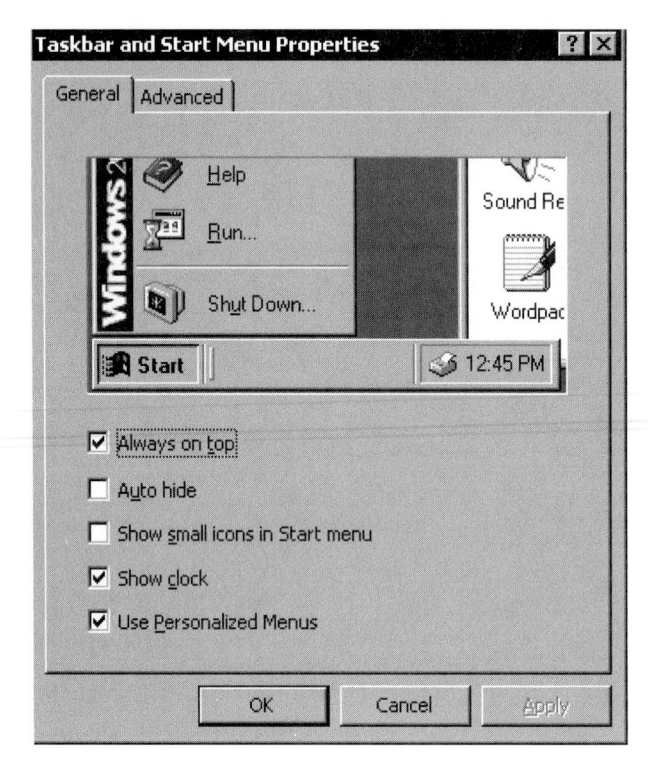

FIGURE 6.1
Taskbar Options

- Always on top: This option does not allow other windows to cover the taskbar.
- Auto hide: This option hides the taskbar when it is not in use.
- Show small icons in Start Menu.
- Show clock.
- Use personalized menus.

If you click on the Advanced tab, you can customize what items appear in the Start Menu. The Advanced tab is displayed in Figure 6.2.

If you click the Add button, the Create Shortcut Wizard appears so that you can add shortcut items to your Start Menu. Once you select an item to include, the wizard prompts for the location it should be placed in the Start Menu folders. After you make your selection, the wizard asks you to name the new addition, then the wizard adds the item to the Start Menu. In a likewise manner, you can remove items from the Start Menu by using the Remove button.

The Advanced button opens all items in the Start Menu and displays them in an Explorer window if you desire to make significant changes to the contents. The Re-sort button allows you to change the order in which the various Start Menu items appear, and the Clear button allows you to remove all records of recently accessed documents, programs, and web sites. In the Start Menu settings scroll box, you can select the major settings

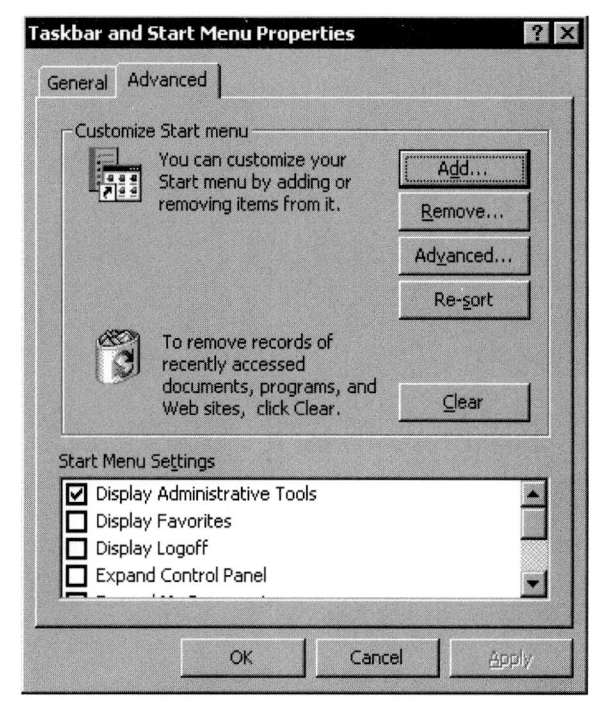

FIGURE 6.2 Start Menu Options

for the Start Menu, such as whether or not to display Administrative Tools, expand the Control Panel, and so forth.

Configuring Settings Using Control Panel

The bulk of your system settings can be configured from icons in the Control Panel. Most of these settings are simple, and the following sections show you what is available and how to configure the settings.

Accessibility Options

The Accessibility Options in Windows 2000 are designed to make your system, keyboard, and mouse easier to use, especially for people who have certain disabilities. The Accessibility Options Properties sheet has five tabs with various configuration options:

- Keyboard: The Keyboard tab allows you to configure three major keyboard helps. First, you can use StickyKeys. StickyKeys allow you to configure your keyboard so that you can use Shift, Ctrl, or Alt keys by pressing one key at a time. In other words, the keys "stick" so you do not have to press a series of keys at the same time for various commands. You can also use FilterKeys. FilterKeys filter, or ignore, brief or repeated keystrokes and also slow the repeat rate. Finally, you can use ToggleKeys that allow you to hear tones when you press Caps Lock, Num Lock, or Scroll Lock. In addition, the Keyboard tab has a checkbox that allows you to show extra keyboard help in programs.

- Sound: On the Sounds tab, you can configure windows to use the SoundSentry and ShowSounds. The SoundSentry tells Windows to generate a visual warning when the system makes a sound, and the ShowSounds tells your programs to display captions for any sounds or speech they make.
- Display: You can configure your display to use high contrast and adjust the settings so that colors and fonts are easy to read. Select the High Contrast check box and click the Settings button to adjust the display settings.
- Mouse: You can configure your system to use MouseKeys so that you can control the mouse movement with keys on your keyboard. Select the checkbox and click the Settings button to adjust the response speed.
- General: The General tab, as shown in Figure 6.3, allows you to configure several global options.

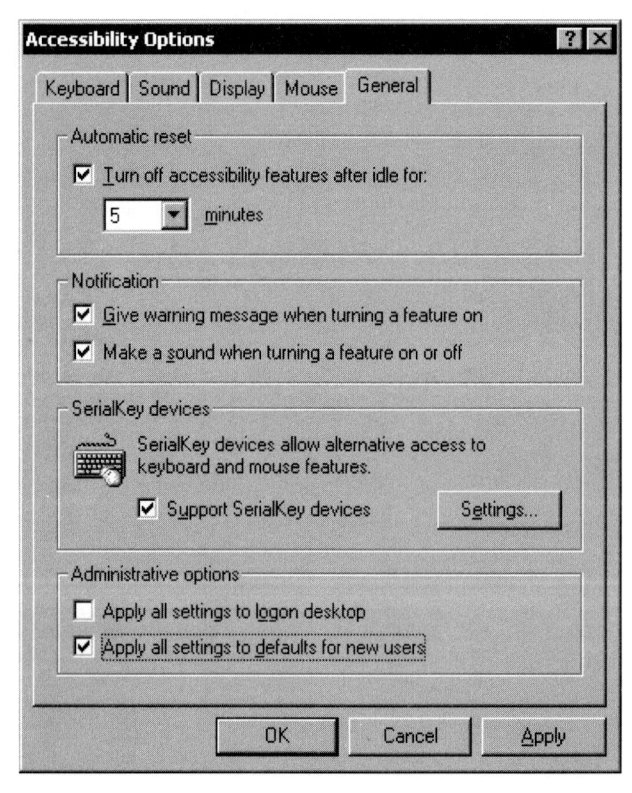

FIGURE 6.3
Accessibility Options General Tab

First, you can use the Automatic reset check-box to turn off the Accessibility features if they are idle for a specific time you specify. The Notification area allows you to tell Windows to play a sound or give a message when features are turned on or off. The SerialKey devices allow you to access the keyboard and mouse through an alternate device, such as special input devices designed for handicapped persons, attached to your machine, and the Administrative options enable you to apply the Accessibility settings when you logon to the desktop and even set the settings as defaults for new users.

Display

The Display Properties icon in the Control Panel allows you to configure a number of display options in Windows 2000 Server. You have several built-in options that were first available with the Internet Explorer 4.0 Active Desktop. The following sections tell you about each of these.

BACKGROUND

The Background Property sheet is the same as in Windows NT, but Windows 2000 provides a number of new wallpaper selections, or you can use your own graphics files or HTML files for backgrounds. If you have any pictures or graphics files in the My Pictures folder in the My Documents folder, those are automatically displayed in the selection list. You can also browse for additional pictures or HTML files to be displayed.

SCREEN SAVER

The Screen Saver Property sheet allows you to select a screen saver of your choice. If you click the Settings button, you specify certain colors and shapes depending on the screen saver you select. If you click the Power button, you can specify power settings that turn off your monitor and hard disks after a specified period of time, if your hardware supports power management. Also, when using screen savers, keep in mind that many of them available (especially those that use OpenGL) use a lot of system memory and resources.

APPEARANCE

The Appearance Property sheet is the same as in Windows NT 4.0. You can use this tab to specify the colors for your desktop, windows, scrollbars, menus, and so forth.

WEB

First introduced in Internet Explorer 4.0, you can now use the Active Desktop to view web content on your desktop. This feature allows you to view HMTL files that you have created, or you can view Internet content directly on your desktop. To configure this option, select the Show Web content on my Active Desktop check-box, then click the New button. A simple wizard appears asking you to type the location of the local web page or the Internet web page you want to view.

EFFECTS

The Effects Property sheet allows you to choose the appearance of your desktop icons and other visual effects. If you click the Change Icon button, you are shown the current icons in use, and you have an option to Browse to select alternate icons. The Visual Effects section presents you with a number of check boxes that allow you to enhance the windows and icons that appear on your system.

SETTINGS

The Settings Property sheet is the same as in previous versions of NT, with the exception of the "Test" button. Since Windows 2000 is Plug and Play, you don't need to manually test your settings any longer. On this tab you can select the number of colors and screen area size. If you click the Advanced tab, you can specify additional settings for your monitor or troubleshoot performance.

Folder Options

Windows 2000 Server gives you flexible options of how you choose to view your folders and the files in them. You can access the Folder Options icon in the Control Panel to view the folder options that are available, as shown in Figure 6.4.

The following Property Sheets and configuration options are available:

- General: The General Property sheet allow you to choose whether or not to display web content on the desktop or enable web content in folders. If you do not want this feature, you can choose the Use Windows classic desktop radio button. You can also choose to browse folders so that each folder opens in the same window or multiple windows open. You can choose to single click items to open them in the same way you click on a hyperlink on a web page.
- View: The View Property sheet presents you with a number of check boxes and radio buttons so that you can specify what information is presented in files and folders. This feature allows you to view system files, full file paths, and a number of additional features.
- File Types: This Property sheet shows you all of the file types registered in the system. You can add or delete the file types as needed, but the default settings are usually best. The Advanced button allows you to specify certain icons for file types and always shows the file extension, if desired.

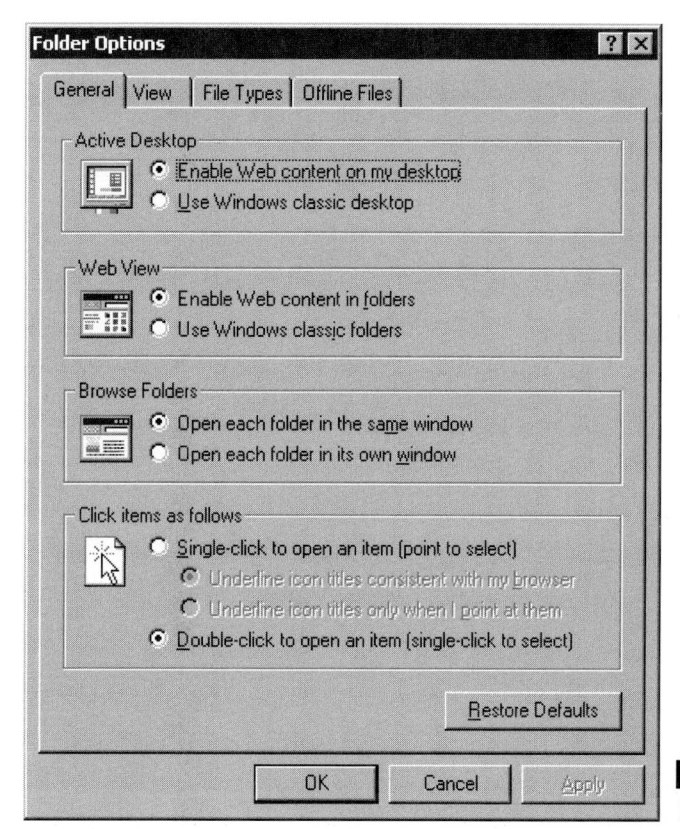

FIGURE 6.4
Folder Options

- Offline Files: In Windows 2000, you can view files that are stored on a network computer even when your computer is offline. This property sheet, shown in Figure 6.5, is a new feature in Windows 2000 server, and it functions by caching files on your local machine in much the same way that Internet files are temporarily stored on your hard drive.

As you can see in Figure 6.5, you can use the check boxes to enable offline files, synchronize the files before logging off, enable reminders, and even place a shortcut to offline files on the desktop. You can also specify the amount of local disk space to be used for temporary offline viewing. The default is ten percent. The Advanced button allows you to configure Windows to notify you when a network connection is lost and to create an exception list. The Advanced options allow you to specify how your computer should behave when a particular computer goes offline. The View Files button allows you to see what offline files are currently stored, and the Delete button allows you to delete offline files when they are no longer needed.

Chapter six • Interface and System Settings

FIGURE 6.5
Offline Files

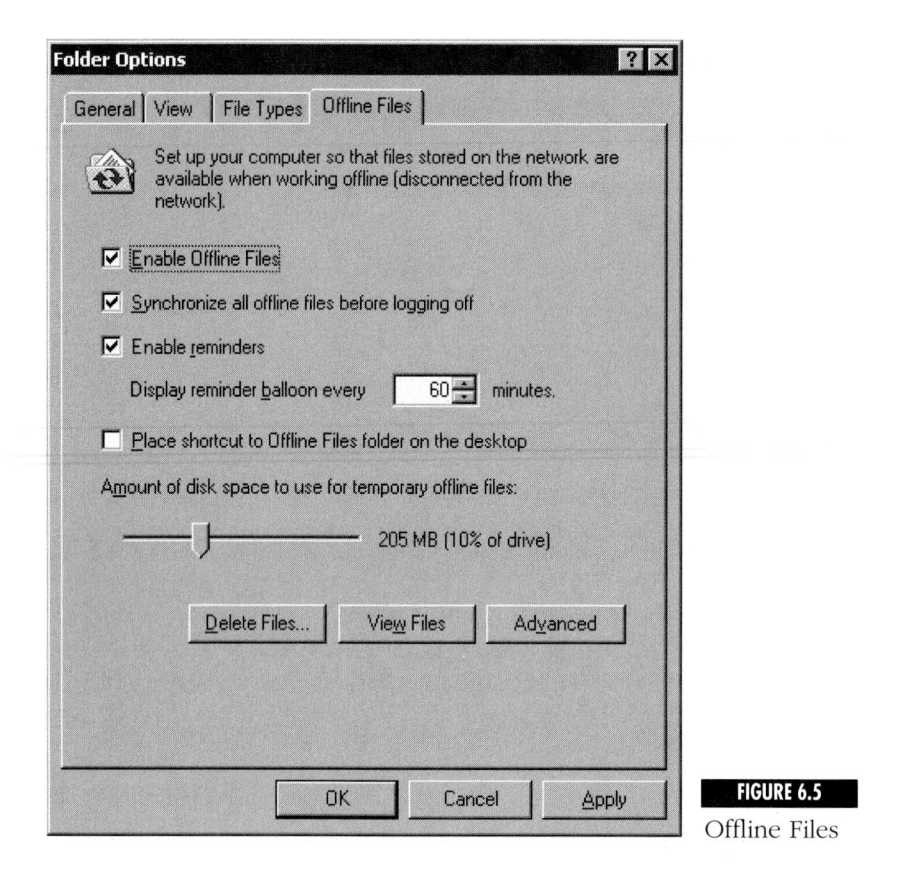

Internet Options

You manage Internet Explorer's settings from within Internet Explorer or through the Internet Options icon in the Control Panel. The properties sheet is the same in either location, as shown in Figure 6.6.

There are a lot of configuration options with Internet Explorer, and most of them are self-explanatory. The following bullet points give you an overview of each tab and what you can configure on each of them:

- General: The General Property sheet has three sections; Home page, Temporary Internet files, and History. In the Home page section, you can specify a URL to which IE automatically connects upon launching the browser. The Temporary Internet files allows you to delete the current files by clicking on the Delete Files button. If you click on the Settings button, you can configure how long temporary Internet files remain on the disk and how much disk space can be used by Temporary Internet files.

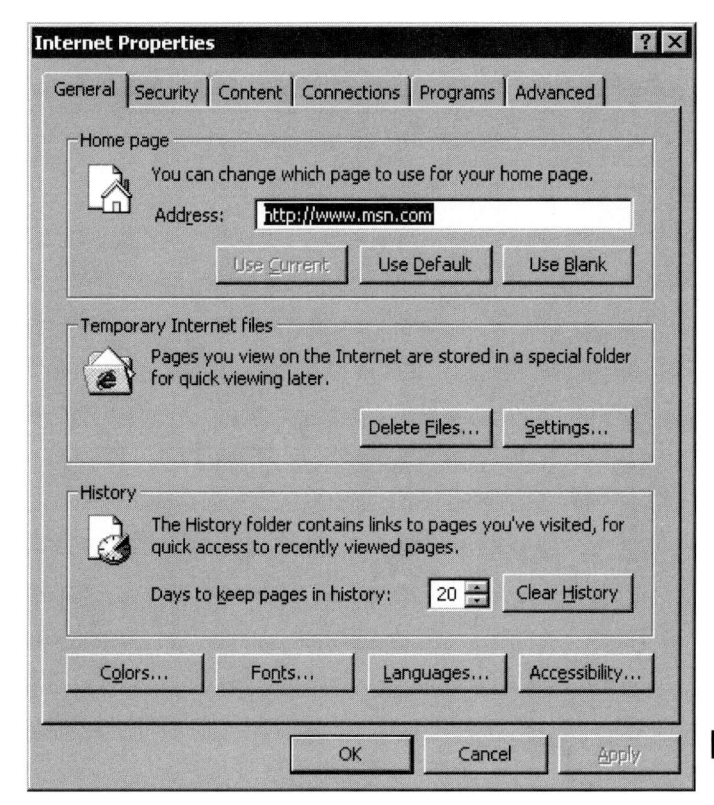

FIGURE 6.6
Internet Options

- Security: The Security Property sheets allows you to configure zone security (low, medium-low, medium, high) for the four zones; Internet, Local Intranet, Trusted sites, and Restricted sites. A default zone security is included for each zone, but you can change it by using the sliding bar, as shown in Figure 6.7. A description is also included for each security level.
- Content: This property sheet contains three sections; Content Advisor, Certificates, and Personal Information. If you click the Enable button in the Content Advisor section, you are given a Content Advisor Properties sheet with four tabs, as shown in Figure 6.8.

On the Ratings tab, you select a category and adjust the slider bar to control what kind of information can be viewed. The other properties sheets on the Content Advisor allow you to enable or block certain sites and configure general information.

On the Content Properties sheet, the Certificates section allows you to use digital certificates that are generated by certificate publishers. A digital certificate is a security measure that allows visitors to your web site to

Chapter six • Interface and System Settings

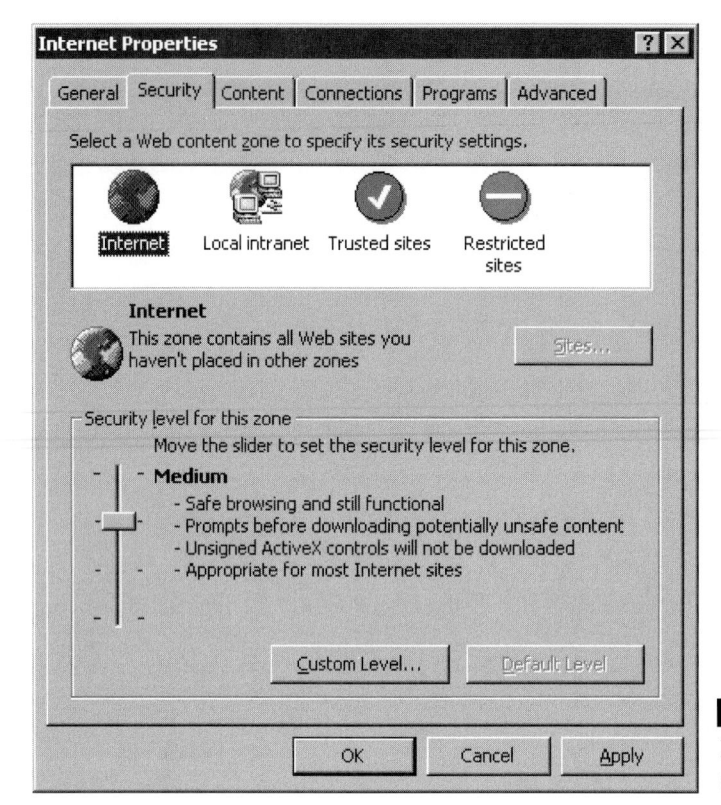

FIGURE 6.7
Internet Zone Security

download information that is authentic. The Personal Information section stores information about Microsoft Wallet and a personal profile.

- Connections: The Connections tab allows you to configure how Internet Explorer reaches the Internet. If you are using a modem, you can use the Dial-Up settings section to add or remove phone book entries so that IE knows which connection to use. You can also use the Setup button to launch a wizard to help you establish an initial connection. The Local Area Network (LAN) settings section can be used by clicking its button to configure a connection to a proxy server that provides Internet access to your organization.
- Programs: The Programs tab allows you to specify which program should be used automatically for the HTML editor, E-mail, newsgroups, Internet call, calendar, and the contact list. Simply use the drop-down menu for each program to select what you would like to use.
- Advanced: The Advanced tab gives you a series of check-boxes to further configure the performance of IE. For example, you can enable page hit counting and page transitions, always underline hyperlinks, and so forth. Simply check the boxes you want to enable.

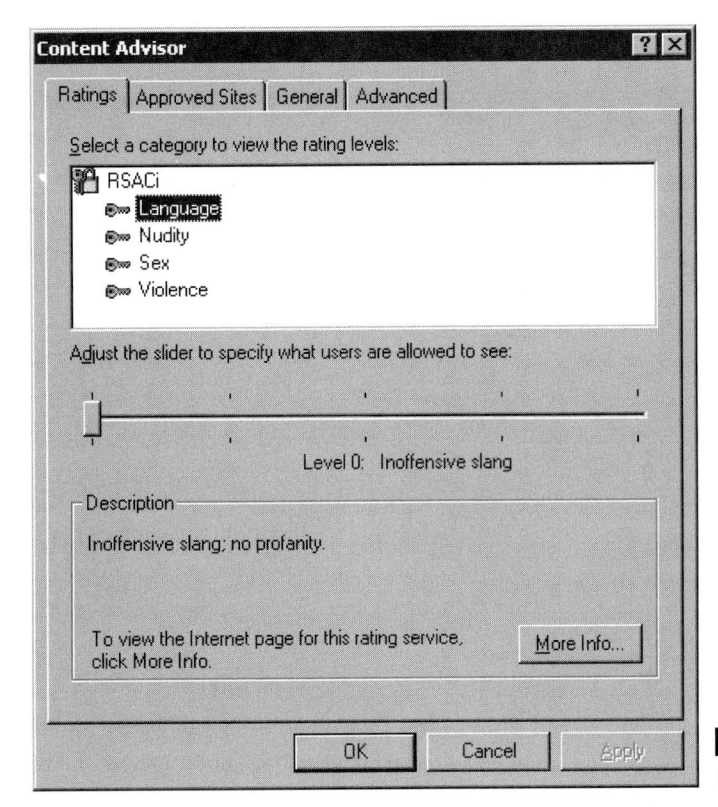

FIGURE 6.8
Content Advisor

Regional Options

The Regional Options, as shown in Figure 6.9, allows you to configure various regional options that affects a number of components in your system.

The following list gives you an overview of what configuration options are available on each property sheet:

- General: On the General Property sheet, you can select from the drop-down menu your country location, and the Language settings section allows you to select what language should be used on your computer.
- Numbers: The Numbers Property sheet allows you to configure, through the use of drop-down menus, the manner in which numbers and symbols are displayed on your system.
- Currency: As with the Numbers Property sheet, the drop-down menus allow you to manage the way currency is displayed on your system.
- Time: The Time Property sheet also contains drop-down menus so that you can configure how your system displays the time.
- Date: The Date Property sheet allows you to configure the way your system displays the current date, such as in a short or long format.

FIGURE 6.9 Regional Options

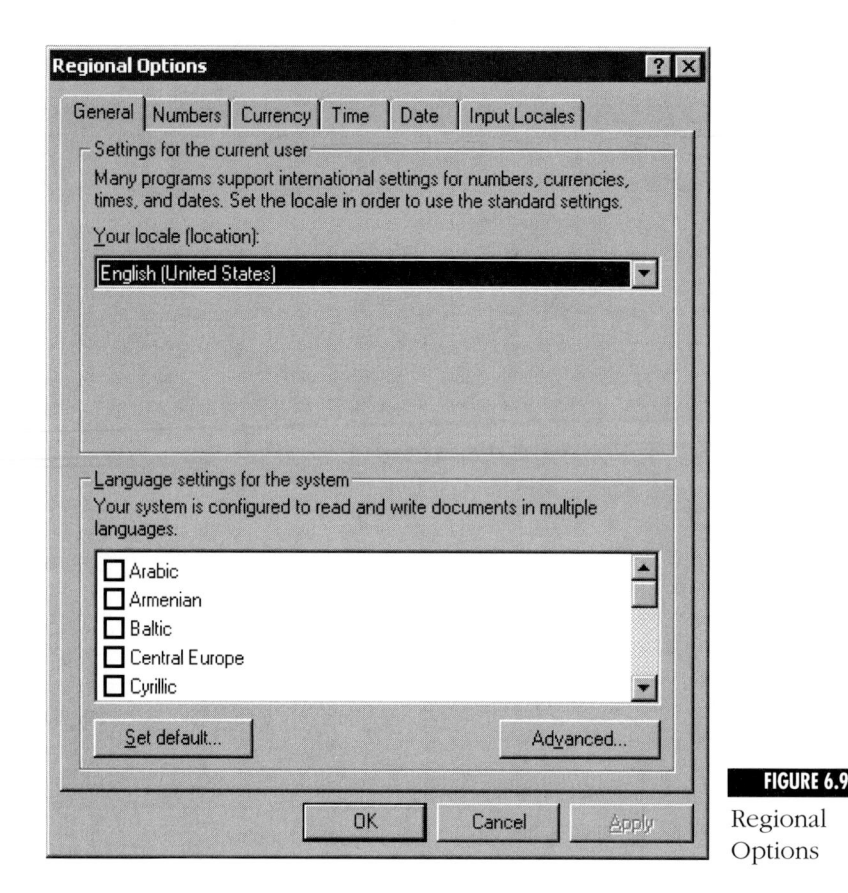

- Input Locales: The Input Locales tab allows you to configure additional locale settings. Depending on the language selection on the General tab, a number of settings are built-in, but you can click the Add button to further refine keyboard settings. You can also use the Hot Key section to use Hot Keys that contain locale input information.

Sounds and Multimedia

You can control the way your system uses sounds and multimedia components. Depending on the hardware you have installed, you have several options in the Sounds and Multimedia properties, as explained in the following bullet list:

- Sounds: The Sounds Property sheet allows you to choose what sounds Windows uses for a program close, a critical stop, E-mail notification and so forth. If you select the sound event from the list, you can use the drop-down menu to select the sound you would like played for

that particular event. You can also use the Browse button to use a custom sound.
- Audio: The Audio Property sheet has three areas; sound playback, sound recording, and MIDI music playback. Each of these sections gives you a simple drop-down menu so you can choose the system device you want to use for each of these.
- Speech: This property sheet allows you to configure speech input and output engines that may be installed on your system. If you have these devices installed, you can control the pronunciation and configure general property settings for the devices.
- Hardware: The Hardware Property sheet gives you a list of hardware devices installed on your system that are used for sound and multimedia. If you select a device from the list, you can view its properties sheet or click the Troubleshoot button to attempt to resolve problems with the device.

System

The System Properties sheets, now available in the Control Panel, is virtually the same as in Windows NT 4.0. You can also access System Properties by right-clicking My Computer and selecting properties. The following list tells you what you can do with each Properties sheet:

- General: The General Properties sheet gives you the operating system version, the name of the person or company the OS is registered to, and basic hardware information about the computer. You cannot configure anything on this tab.
- Network Identification: This properties sheet tells you the role of your computer on the network. You can change the name and role of the computer from this tab, if the computer is not a domain controller. If the computer is a domain controller, you can use the Active Directory to change the role and name of the computer.
- Hardware: The Hardware Property sheet presents you with buttons to launch the hardware wizard, device manager, or hardware profiles. Refer to Chapter 4 for more information about each of these tools.
- User Profiles: This property sheet lists the current profiles in use and allows you to delete any profiles you choose. It also allows you to change the profile type to either a local profile or a roaming profile by using the Change Type button; or you can use the Copy to button to copy the profile to a different location.
- Advanced: On the Advanced Property sheet, you have the option of configuring the system performance, environment variables, and startup and recovery by clicking the appropriate button, as shown in Figure 6.10. The following list shows you how to configure each of these:

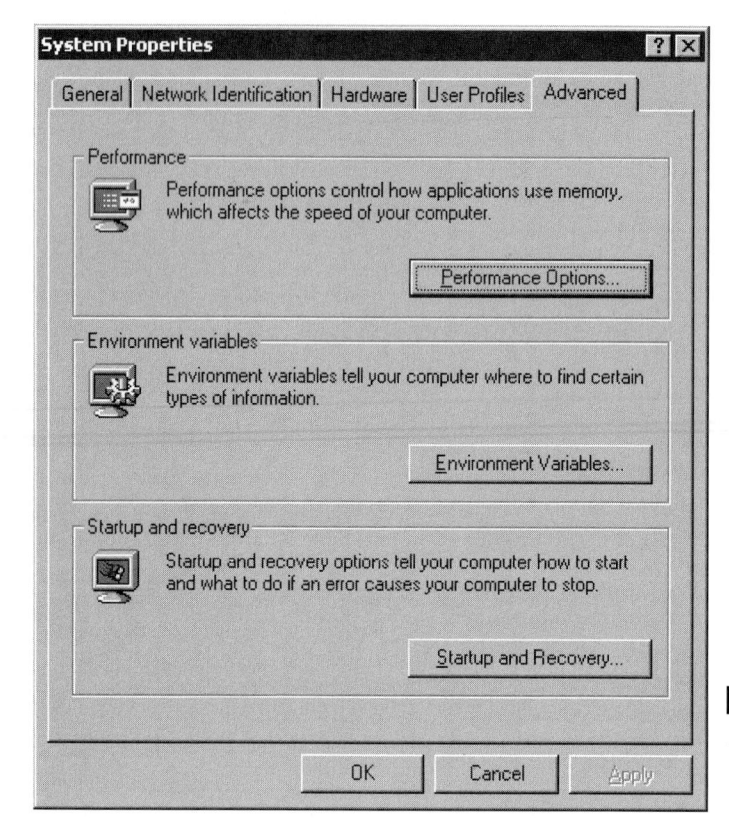

FIGURE 6.10
Advanced System Properties

- Performance: If you click the Performance Options button, you can choose to optimize either the performance for applications or background services by clicking the appropriate radio button. By default, the background services button is selected. You should carefully consider using the default setting unless you have a specific reason to optimize performance for applications. Doing so may affect system performance negatively. You also have the option of changing your virtual memory settings. Remember that virtual memory allows your system to use a portion of your hard disk for memory storage in the event the physical RAM becomes low. If you click the Change button, you are taken to the Virtual Memory sheet as shown in Figure 6.11.

On this sheet, you are given information about your current virtual memory settings with the option to change them by using the Set button. Under normal circumstances, you should leave

two • Hardware and Disk Management

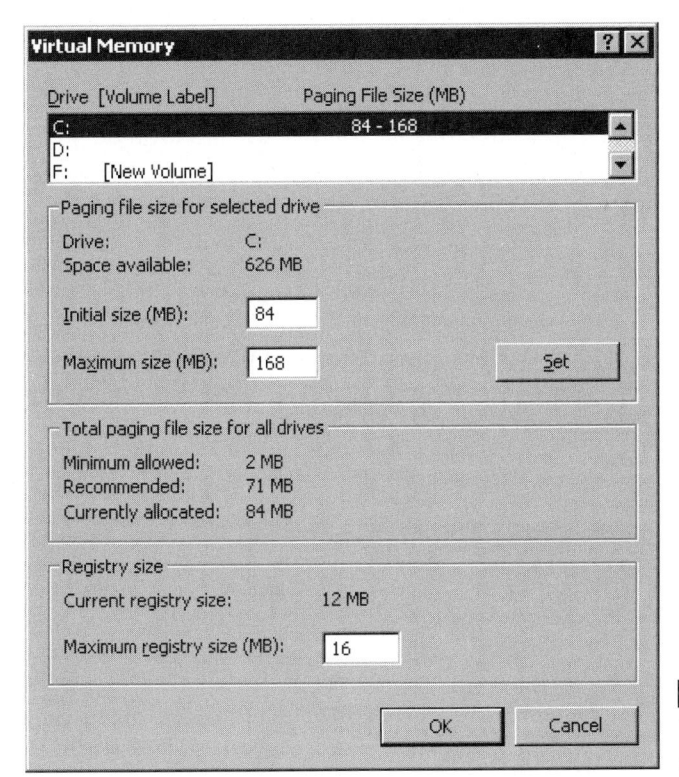

FIGURE 6.11
Virtual Memory Sheet

the virtual memory settings at the default level: making the level too low or too high will usually have a negative impact on system performance. Remember, if memory is becoming a problem on your system, the best solution is always to add more RAM rather than to alter the virtual memory settings.

- Environment Variables: If you click the Environment Variables button, you are presented with both the user and system variables. Environment variables are displayed as strings that contain information such as the drive or path name. The variables listed control how programs behave and where they store information. You can add, delete, or edit the variables as desired by clicking the appropriate buttons, but you can only change system variables if you have administrative privileges. The user variables are different for each user and are defined by the system settings and additional settings that are configured by the user. Windows does a good job of managing its own system variables, so this is not normally something you would want to change.

- Startup and recovery: By clicking the Startup and Recovery button, you can make a few changes to system startup and recovery. First, if you dual-boot Windows 2000 Server with another operating system, you can use the drop-down menu to select the default operating system that should be loaded. The rest of the tab gives you check boxes to alter the actions Windows performs should there be a system stop. Your options include writing an event to the system log, sending an administrative alert, writing debugging information (the default location is C:\WINNT\MEMORY.DMP), overwriting the existing .DMP file, or writing kernel information only, and also automatically rebooting your system. These options can be selected by clicking the appropriate check-box.

Summary

In this chapter, we examined the configuration of your system and interface settings. In Windows 2000 Server, most major settings for your system and interface can be set through icons in the Control Panel, and most are very easy to configure. Windows 2000 Server makes it easy for you to configure your interface and system settings, allowing you to spend more time on networking and server service configuration and issues.

SEVEN

The Registry and Backup Operations

This chapter explores two related topics—the Windows 2000 registry and the backup operations available in Windows 2000 Server. Concerning the registry, one of your major skills as an administrator is the backup of the system registry and critical files for your organization. The first three sections of this chapter explore the Registry and the editing of it; and the rest of the chapter explores the various backup options, including backing up the registry.

As you have seen so far, there are many differences and changes in Windows 2000 Server from Windows NT. The registry, however, is one area of Windows 2000 Server that is not different from Windows NT. The registry both looks and functions just the same way in Windows 2000 Server as it does in Windows NT. Microsoft's recommendations for using and editing the registry also remain the same in Windows 2000 Server—stay out if at all possible! Any changes you make to the registry go into effect immediately; and an incorrect registry edit can cause system-wide problems and even failure to boot. Windows 2000 Server does a much better job than Windows NT of helping you configure the various components of your system, so your need to use the registry to make configuration changes should be almost non-existent.

Occasionally, however, you may find the need to wade into the registry. In this chapter, I give you an overview of the structure of the registry and show you how to use the Windows 2000 Server registry editors.

The Structure of the Registry

The registry is essentially a system-wide database. The registry contains all of the hardware information and software settings for your server and provides the operating system with appropriate initialization information for the various hardware and software components. The registry stores information about drivers and protocols; and every time a change is made to the system, it is stored in the registry. Every time information about that change is needed by the system, it is read from the registry.

The registry is organized in a hierarchical tree structure, similar to what you have seen with MMC snap-ins. An example of one of the registry subtrees is shown in Figure 7.1, and you should familiarize yourself with the following registry components:

- Subtree: A subtree is a major storage category in the registry. You can think of the subtree as the same as the root folder of a hard disk. There are two primary subtrees in Windows 2000: HKEY_LOCAL_MACHINE and HKEY_USERS; but to make system information easier to find, there are three others as well: HKEY_CURRENT_USER, HEKY_CLASSES_ROOT, and HKEY_CURRENT_CONFIG.
- Keys: Keys are similar to folders. A key contains particular information about hardware or software settings.
- Subkeys: A subkey is like a subfolder. This subkey resides within a key and may further define information about the key.
- Entry: Every key or subkey contains at least one entry. Any entry contains information about the subject of the key or subkey and is made up of a name, data type, and a value.
- Hive: A hive is a collection of entries, keys, and even subtrees.

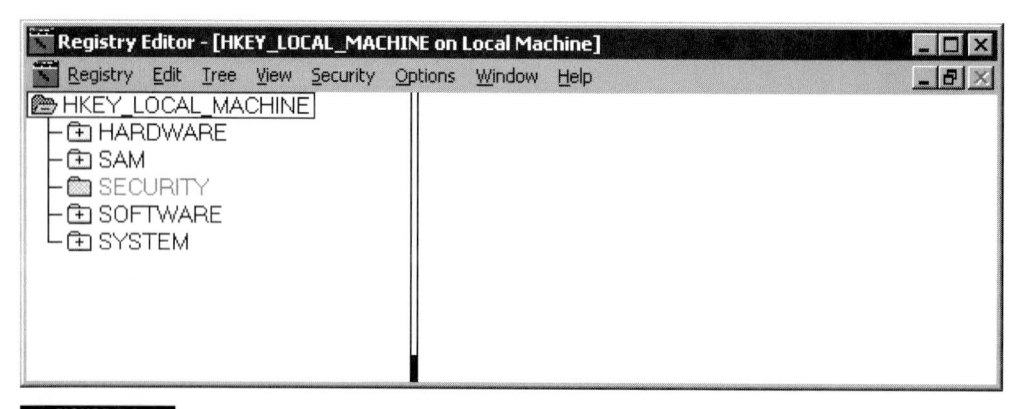

FIGURE 7.1 HKEY_LOCAL_MACHINE Subtree

- Data Types: An entry's value is defined by a data type. The following list gives you the data types that may appear in an entry:
  - REG_DWORD: A single value that is represented by a string of one to eight hexadecimal digits.
  - REG_SZ: A single value that is interpreted as a string that should be stored.
  - REG_EXPAND_SZ: This data type is like REG_SZ, except that Windows can replace or update a variable.
  - REG_BINARY: One value that is exhibited as a string of hexadecimal digits.
  - REG_MULTI_SZ: A string that allows for multiple values.
  - REG_FULL_RESOURCE_DESCRIPTOR: This data value stores information about the hardware components and their drivers.

The key to finding the information in the registry is to have a firm grasp of the kind of information that is stored in each subtree. The following sections give you an overview of each subtree and the kind of information contained in each.

HKEY_LOCAL_MACHINE

HKEY_LOCAL_MACHINE is a primary key that holds information about the local machine. This subtree holds all data about system configuration, operating system data, hardware devices and drivers, startup data, and applications. HKEY_LOCAL_MACHINE contains five major keys, with each key containing a number of subkeys. The major keys are Hardware, SAM, Security, Software, and System.

HKEY_USERS

HKEY_USERS contains information about user settings and default user settings. HKEY_CURRENT_USER is a child of HKEY_USERS, and all data that affects users is stored in this subtree. The subtree contains a default key and keys about the users. With each key, you will find information about the Control Panel, environment, Remote Access and a number of other keys that affect user settings.

HKEY_CURRENT_USER

As mentioned previously, HKEY_CURRENT_USER is a child of HKEY_USERS. This subtree contains setting information about the current user. When a user logs on, the account information for the user is retrieved from Ntuser.dat to invoke settings and hardware profiles. It supercedes any settings in HEKY_LOCAL_MACHINE so that users can keep their individual system settings.

HKEY_CLASSES_ROOT

HKEY_CLASSES_ROOT points to the Classes subkey under the Software key in HKEY_LOCAL_MACHINE. It contains information about system software settings, such as Object Linking and Embedding (OLE) data.

HKEY_CURRENT_CONFIG

This subtree contains information about the active hardware on the system. HKEY_CURRENT_CONFIG uses the Software and System hives to load information about hardware settings so that proper device drivers and hardware settings are loaded and implemented at startup.

Using the Registry Editors

As in Windows NT, you have access to two registry editors in Windows 2000—Regedt32 and Regedit. Regedt32 allows you to search and manually edit the registry as needed while also providing a read-only mode so that you do not accidentally make changes you did not intend to make. Regedit does not contain the read-only mode, and it does not support REG_EXPAND_SZ or REG_MULTI_SZ, but it does provide an Explorer-oriented interface that is easier to use. The next two sections give you an overview of what you can do with these tools.

Using Regedt32

As I mentioned previously, the registry is designed for troubleshooting but not configuration. You should make all configuration changes to your system using the Control Panel, Active Directory Tools, and other tools and properties sheets. Improper editing of the registry can cause a system failure which will require reinstallation of Windows 2000. Any changes you make to the registry are saved automatically and take effect immediately.

You can access either Regedt32 or Regedit by typing either one at the run dialog box. Regedt32 is the recommended registry editor for Windows 2000. Once you open Regedt32, you can expand the subtree you desire to view.

Regedt32 provides a number of menu options to help you use the registry editor and find the information you require. The following list explores the major options on each menu:

- Registry: the Registry menu contains several useful features. You can use Select Computer to open the registry on a remote computer. Windows 2000 Server allows this remote access to the Administrators' group. You can select the Save Key options which saves the part of the registry that you select so that you can test changes. The Save

Subtree As allows you to save the subtree in a text-file for searching. You cannot save this text-file back to registry data, however.
- Edit: The Edit menu allows you to add a registry key, add a value, or delete a selected object. As you can imagine, you should exercise great care when using the Edit menu.
- Tree: The Tree menu allows you to expand the tree as needed. You also expand the tree by double-clicking on the key or subkey you want to expand.
- View: The View menu allows you to change how you view the data in each subtree. By default, you can see both the tree and the data for the keys in the left and right panes. However, you can use the View menu to view the tree only or the data only or split the two. Also, you can use the Find Key option to perform a key search within the Subtree.
- Security: The Security menu, which is not available in Regedit allows you to configure permissions, auditing, and ownership of the registry. If you click the Permissions button, you can alter the permissions of what groups or users can do with the Registry Editor. As you can see in Figure 7.2, only the Administrators, Creator Owner, or System users have full control of the Registry by default.
- Options: The Options menu allows you to select the font used in the registry editor. Also, you have the options of auto refresh, read-only mode, and save settings on exit from Registry Editor. The read-only mode is an important feature of this menu.

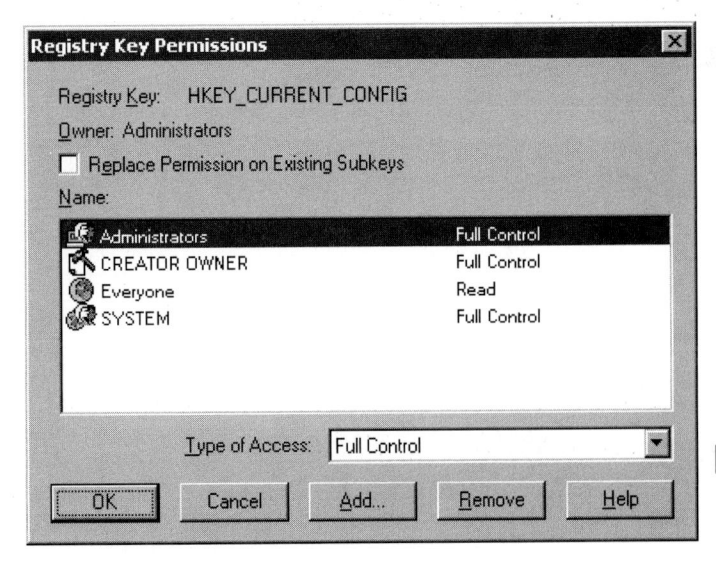

FIGURE 7.2

Registry Key Permissions

Using Regedit

Regedit does not contain all of the tools of Regedt32, and it does not have a read only mode. However, for browsing purposes, Regedit is easier to use because it mimics an Explorer window, as shown in Figure 7.3.

The major advantage of using Regedit in Windows 2000 is the expandable interface and the fact that all subtrees appear in the left pane instead of individual windows. Beyond that, you simply do not have as many options in Regedit as in Regedt32. The following list tells you what is available in each menu:

- Registry: The Registry menu allows you to import or export a registry file, or you can connect or disconnect to a network registry.
- Edit: On the Edit menu, you can point to New and add a new key, string value, binary value, or DWORD value. The rest of the Edit menu allows you to delete or rename a selected item, and you can copy a key name. The Edit menu also contains a Find function to help you locate a desired key or subkey.
- View: On the View menu, you can choose to view the status bar, choose the Split view, or choose to Refresh the registry.
- Favorites: The Favorites menu allows you to select a subtree or key and add it to, or remove it from the favorites list.

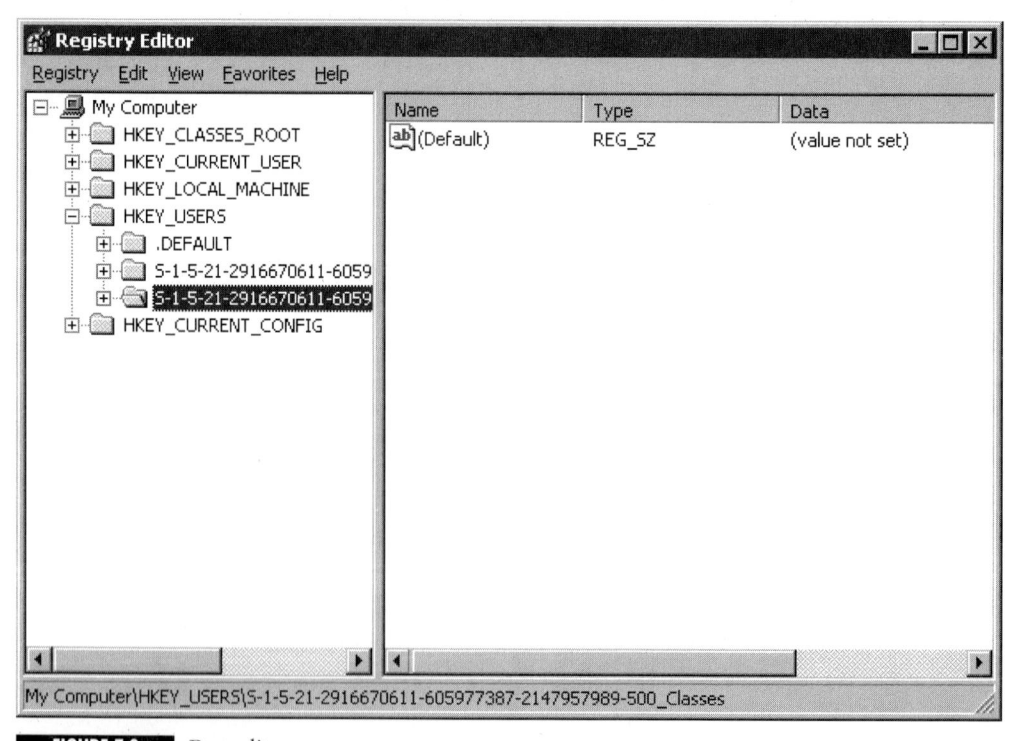

FIGURE 7.3 Regedit

Backup Options in Windows 2000 Server

The purpose of backing up data and system information, such as the registry, is to restore that data should a system failure or data loss of some kind occur. If data is properly backed up on a regular basis, that data can be restored in its entirety regardless if the data is a single file or an entire disk. To make backup operations easy, Windows 2000 Server includes a backup tool called Windows Backup that is accessible from Start ➤ Programs ➤ Accessories ➤ System Tools ➤ Backup.

There is no one correct way to backup data. The goal is to be able to restore critical data at any given moment, so the type of backup you choose to use and the frequency of backup depends on the needs of your company. You don't need to backup files that rarely change on a regular basis, but daily backups of constantly changing data is of utmost importance in order to restore the most current version of that data.

Windows 2000 Server allows you to choose your backup media such as tape backup and removable media such as Zip drives, CD-ROMS, or hard drives on remote computers. Windows 2000 includes Remote Storage Services (RSS) and a Remote Storage Manager (RSM), which you will learn about in the next chapter.

Backup Types

Windows Backup provides five types of backup that enable you to manage and plan your backup sessions. If you have used backup in Windows NT, you will recognize them. The following bullet list tells you about the five backup types:

- Normal: In a normal backup, all files and folders that you select are backed up. A normal backup does not use markers to determine which files have been backed up, any existing markers are removed, and the file is marked as having been backed up. This type of backup is the fastest to restore, but backup time can be slow depending on the amount of data involved.
- Copy: A copy backup is similar to a normal backup in that all files and folders selected are backed up. A copy backup does not look at markers, and it does not clear existing markers. You can use the copy backup if you do not want the markers cleared, as they may affect other backup types.
- Differential: In a differential backup, only selected files and folders that contain a marker are backed up since the last full backup. A differential backup does not clear the existing markers.
- Incremental: An incremental backup is like a differential backup in that it backs up selected files and folders with a marker since the last full backup, but an incremental backup clears the existing markers.

- Daily: In a daily backup, all selected files and folders that have changed during the day are backed up. A daily backup does not look at or clear markers, but this is an effective way to backup files and folders that have changed during the day.

Determining how to backup your files is an important planning step. The most effective solutions normally use a combination of backup types, and each design has its advantages and disadvantages. For example, you can use normal and differential backups together. A normal backup can be performed on Monday and a differential backup performed on the following week days. If there is a failure on Saturday, only Monday's backup and Friday's backup have to be used to reconstruct the data. This combination takes more time to backup but less time to restore. Or, you could use normal and incremental backup in the same manner. In the case of a failure, each incremental backup would have to be restored since it clears the markers. This solution takes less time to backup, but more time to restore the data. The key question is to determine the speed of restoration you need should a failure occur. Typically, faster restoration solutions take more backup time on a daily basis.

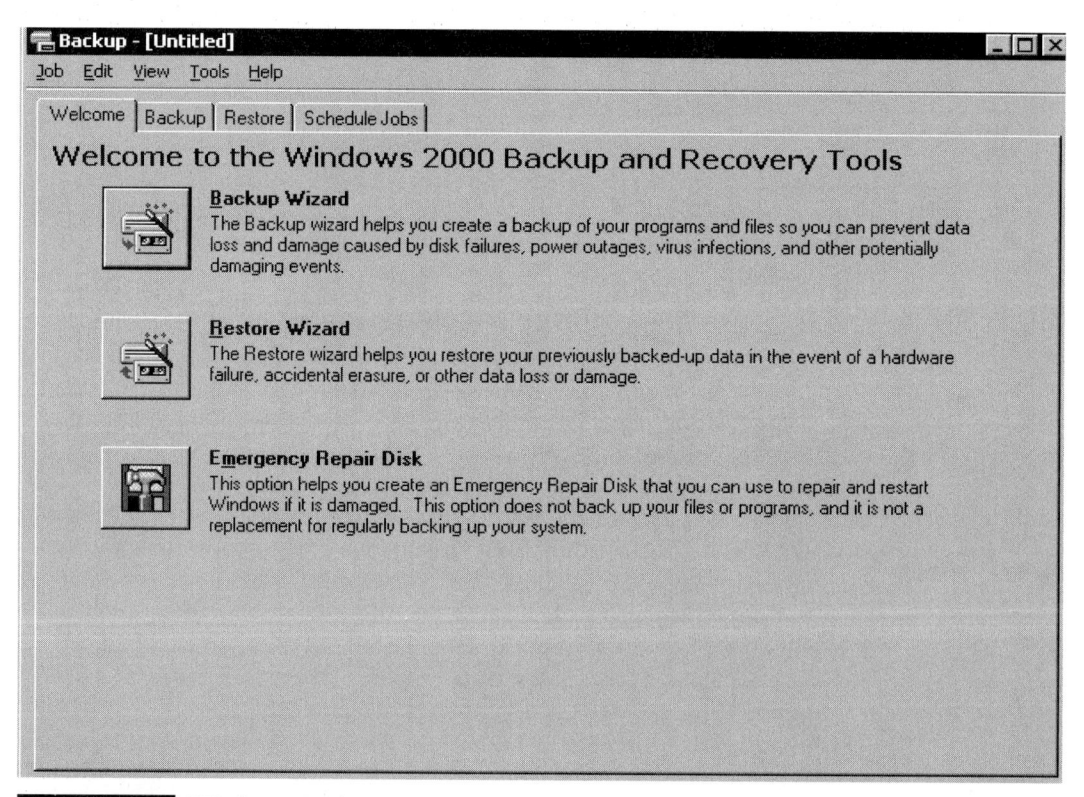

FIGURE 7.4 Windows Backup

Using Windows Backup

You can access Windows Backup by clicking Start ➤ Programs ➤ Accessories ➤ System Tools ➤ Backup. Windows Backup appears, as shown in Figure 7.4. As you may imagine, backup operations are dependent on user rights. If you are an administrator or a backup operator in a local group, you can back up any file or folder on the local server to which the group applies. If you are an administrator or backup operator on a domain controller, you can back up any file or folder in the domain if there is a two-way trust relationship, with the exception of System State data which can only be backed up on the local machine.

The Welcome tab, shown in Figure 7.4, gives you four button options: Backup Wizard, Restore Wizard, ASR Preparation Wizard, and Emergency Repair Disk. The following sections examine each of these options.

BACKUP WIZARD

You can use the Backup Wizard to create a backup plan for your files and programs to protect against a catastrophic failure. To use the Backup Wizard, click the Backup Wizard button to begin the process and follow these steps:

1. After clicking the Backup Wizard button, the wizard begins. Click Next.
2. The second screen asks you what you want to backup. You have the following options, as shown in Figure 7.5.

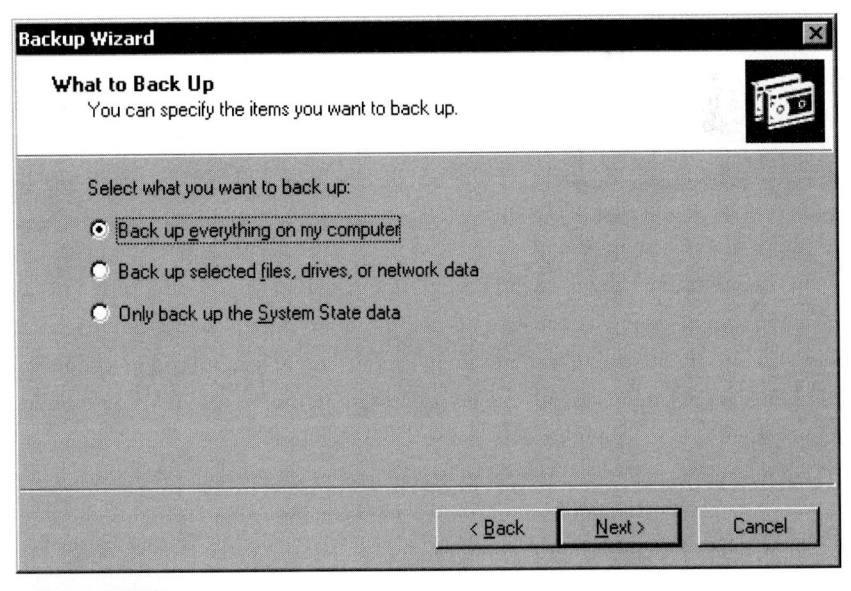

FIGURE 7.5 What to Back Up Window

a. Back up everything on my computer: This option backs up all files on the local machine except certain power-management files that are not backed up by default.

b. Back up selected files, drives, or network data: This option backs up the files and programs you select. You can use this option to back up any network shares or disks also.

c. Only back up the System State data: This option backs up the registry, COM + class registration components, the SAM database, system boot files, and Certificate Server on the local computer. If the server is a domain controller, the Active Directory and the SYSVOL directory are also backed up. If you choose the System State data option, all of the data relevant is backed up—in other words, you cannot choose which components to backup. If using Certificate Server, note that certificate server cannot be running or the backup operation will fail. Using the System State data option also backs up the registry.

3. If you choose back up selected files, drives, and network data, you are taken to the Items to Back Up window, as shown in Figure 7.6. This Explorer-based window allows you to backup selected files or

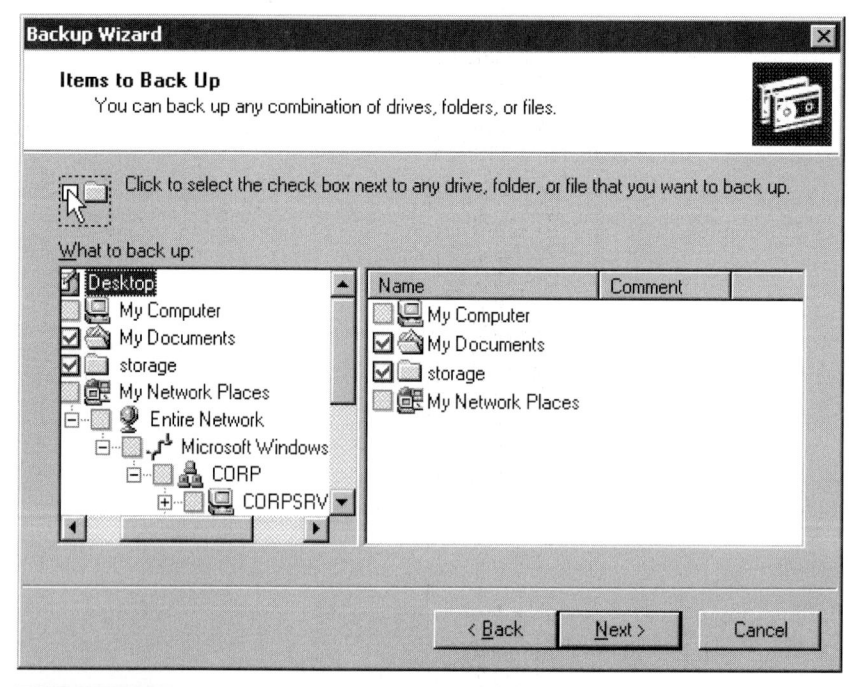

FIGURE 7.6 Items to Back Up

two • Hardware and Disk Management

disks or even network data by using the checkboxes provided. By expanding My Network Places, you can choose any network drive or individual files as desired. Make your selections and click Next.

4. If you choose to back up everything on your computer or Only back up System State data on your domain controller, you are taken to the Where to Store the Backup window shown in Figure 7.7. In the Where to Store the Backup, shown in Figure 7.7, use the Browse button to select your backup media, then click Next.

5. The next window gives you a summary of the selections you made. If you click the Advanced button before clicking finish, you can specify additional backup options. This feature allows you to specify the type of backup, as shown in Figure 7.8. This window allows you to select the type of backup you would like to perform. If you use the drop down menu, you can select normal, copy, incremental, differential, or daily backup. Make your selection and click Next.

6. The next window presents you with two check boxes, one to verify data after backup and one to use hardware compression, if available. Make your selection and click Next.

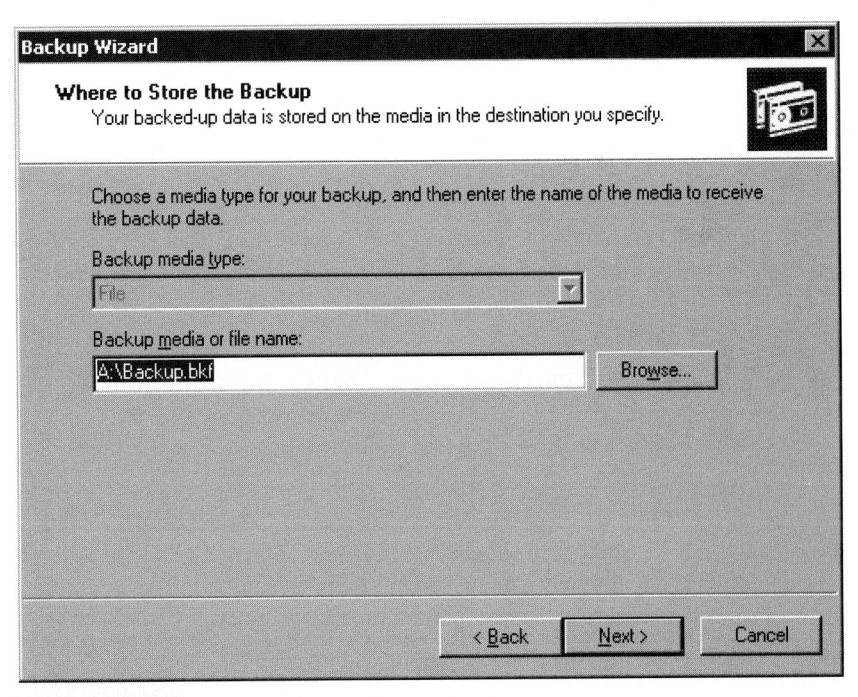

FIGURE 7.7 Where to Store the Backup

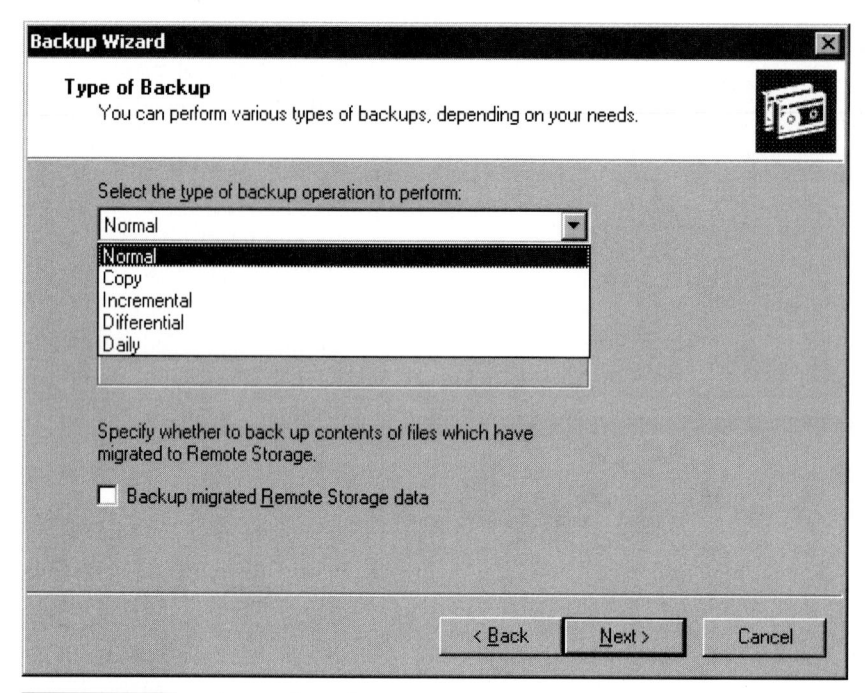

FIGURE 7.8 Advanced Back up Options

7. The next window, Media Options, allows you to select radio buttons that tell Windows to append the backup to existing backup on the media, or overwrite the old backup file with a new one. Make your selection and click Next.
8. The Backup Label window appears. On this page, you can accept the default labels or create your own. The default media name is **media created on** *date* **at** *time*. Click Next.
9. The When to Backup window asks you when you want to run the backup. You can select the Now radio button or the Later button and specify a start date for the job. Click Next.
10. You return to the final summary page of the wizard. Review your selections and click Finish.
11. The Backup Wizard estimates the size of the backup job and begins the job to the selected media. When the backup is complete, Windows Backup creates a summary file and directory information in a backup set catalog, which is stored on the backup media.

In addition to using the Backup Wizard, you can also click the Backup tab in Windows Backup. It presents you with a screen where you can select

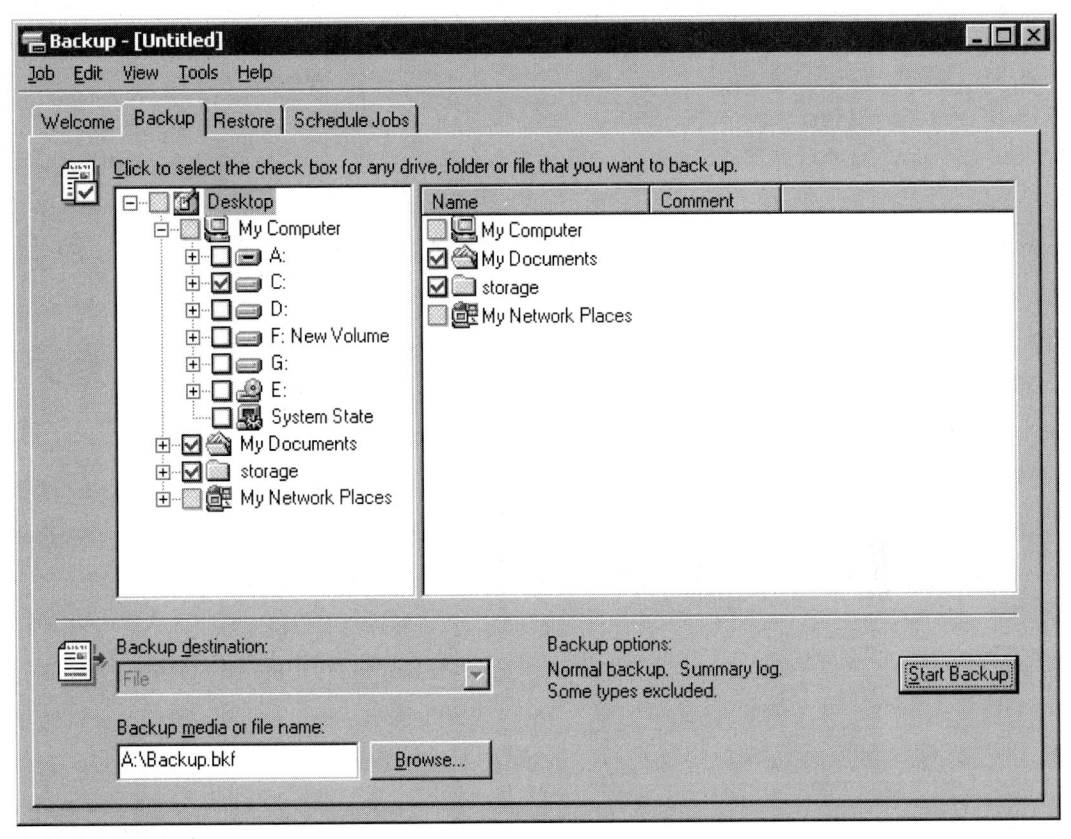

FIGURE 7.9 Backup Tab

drives, files, folders, and network drives or files and start the backup process immediately without the wizard, as shown in Figure 7.9.

From this view, when you click the Start Backup button, you are given a condensed window of several options available in the wizard, shown in Figure 7.10.

On the Backup Job Information window, you can specify the label and append or replace the previous backup jobs. You can also click the Advanced button to select the type of backup you want to perform. If you click the Schedule button, you will be asked to first save the backup job and provide your administrator password to complete the action. Once you do this, you are taken to the Schedule Job window shown in Figure 7.11 where you can select the time and date you wish to perform the backup.

RESTORE WIZARD

Once you have completed a backup job, you can restore the backup by using the Restore Wizard. You can restore data on either FAT or NTFS vol-

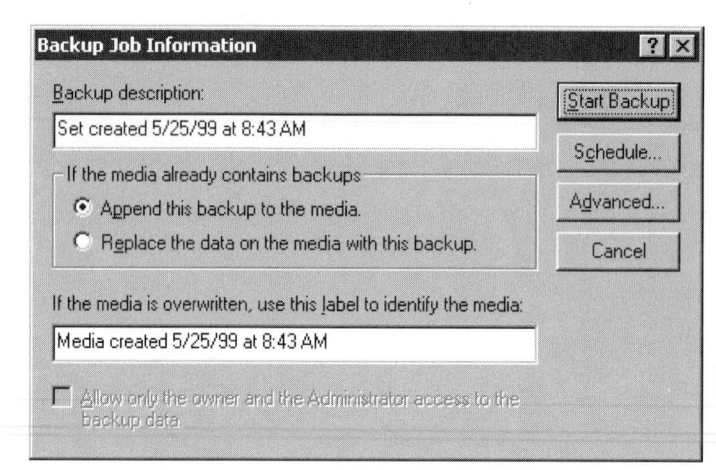

FIGURE 7.10
Backup Job Information

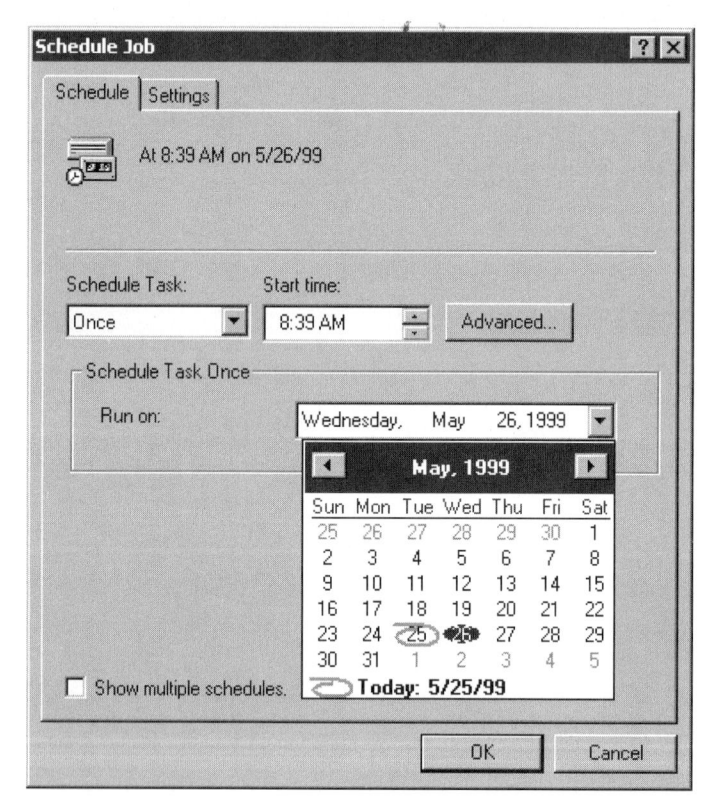

FIGURE 7.11
Schedule Window

umes, but if you have data backed up on an NTFS volume, you should restore it to an NTFS volume. If you restore it to a FAT volume, you could lose some data, and you will lose certain features, such as access permis-

two • Hardware and Disk Management   **127**

sions, encryption file system settings, disk quota information, mounted drive information, and possibly other information that is specific to NTFS.

Begin the Restore Wizard by clicking on the Restore Wizard button on the Welcome tab, then follow these steps:

1. After clicking the Restore Wizard button, the wizard begins. Click Next.
2. The What to Restore window appears, as shown in Figure 7.12. In the What to Restore pane, select the items you want to restore, and click Next.
3. The summary window appears. If you click the Advanced button, you can specify additional actions for your restore operation. The first window asks you where you want to restore the files. By default, the original location is selected, but you can use the drop-down menu to select an alternate location or a single folder. Click Next.
4. The How to Restore window asks you if you would like to restore files that already exist. The default and recommended selection is to not replace the file from backup since the file still exists in the original location. This action prevents backup from replacing newer files with older files from the backup job. Click Next.
5. The Advanced Restore Options window appears. Here, you can choose to restore security, restore Removable Storage Management

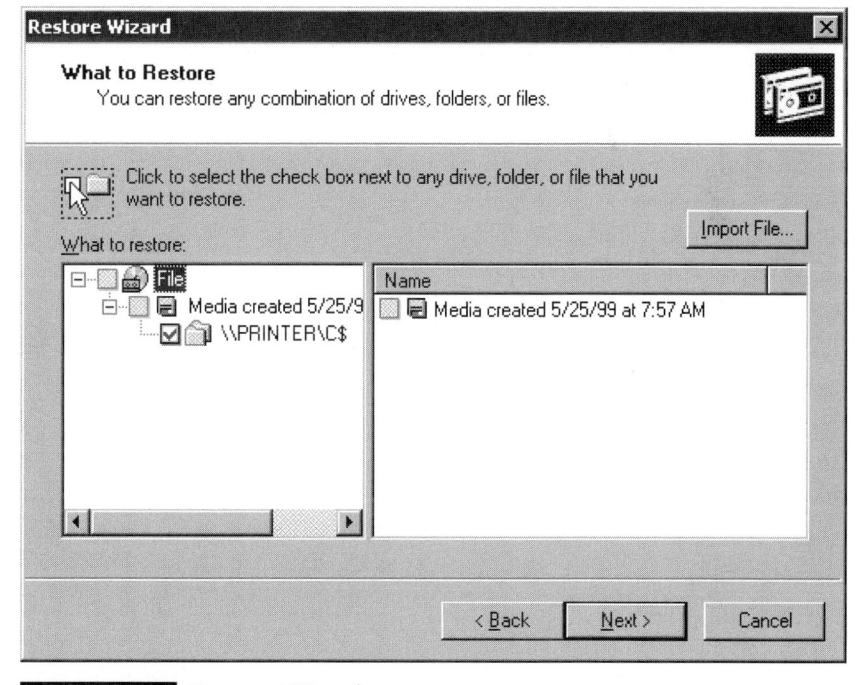

FIGURE 7.12   Restore Wizard

database, or restore junction points instead of the folders and file data they represent. Make your selections and click Next.

6. You now return to the summary page. Review your selections and click Finish.
7. You are asked to confirm the media path where the backup job resides, then click OK.
8. The restoration process begins.

As with the backup process, you can also access the Restore tab of Windows Backup. It is the same window as seen in the wizard so you can quickly select what job to restore. If you click the Start Restore button, you can access the Advanced options in the wizard, or you simply start the Restore process. Once you are comfortable with the restore process, you can use this tab instead of the wizard.

If you are restoring System State data, you should be aware of a process called "authoritative restore." If you have more than one domain controller in your organization where your Active Directory is replicated to the other domain controllers, an authoritative restore ensures that your restored data is replicated to those other domain controllers. The authoritative restore updates the Active Directory sequence number so that the restored data does not appear as "old" to the other domain controllers. If this is the case, the data will not be replicated, and the restored data will actually be updated with replicated data from other servers. The authoritative restore corrects such an issue by updating the sequence number so that the data is current. To use authoritative restore, you restore your System State data in a usual restore operation, but you then need to run Ntdsutil available on the Windows 2000 Server CD-ROM so that the sequence numbers will be updated. You need to run this utility before you reboot your server.

EMERGENCY REPAIR DISK

You can also use the Windows Backup to create an Emergency Repair Disk (ERD). The ERD saves settings and files that can help you start Windows in the event of a failure. The ERD is not a replacement for a backup plan, and it does not protect your data in the event of a failure. You should keep a current ERD at all times—any time you make a system change, such as a new service pack, you should recreate the ERD so that it is current. In order to create an ERD, you will need at least one 1.44 MB floppy disk. To create the ERD, click the Emergency Repair Disk button on the Welcome tab. You are prompted to insert the blank floppy disk into your drive. After doing this, click OK. The ERD is created.

CHANGING DEFAULT BACKUP OPTIONS

Windows provides a number of default backup settings, which you can alter as needed using Windows Backup. If you access the Tools menu and select Options, you are given a window with several tabs, as shown in Figure 7.13. The following list tells you what options are available on each tab.

- General: on the General Property sheet, you have several checkboxes which affect how Windows handles backup jobs and storage media:
  - Compute selection information before backup and restore operations—allows backup to determine the size of the backup operation.
  - Use the catalogs on the media to speed up building restore catalogs on disk.
  - Verify data after the backup completes.
  - Show alert message when I start Backup and Removable Storage Management is not running.
  - Show alert message when I start Backup and there is compatible Import media available.
  - Show alert message when new media is inserted into Removable Storage Management.
  - Always move new import media to Backup pools. This feature automatically moves new media detected by Removable Storage to Backup media pools. You can learn more about Removable Storage in Chapter 8.
- Restore: the Restore Property sheet allows you to choose whether restoration should not replace a file that already exists on the computer, replace the file only if the file is older, or always replace the file.
- Backup Type: the Backup Type Property sheet again allows you to choose either normal, copy, differential, incremental, or daily backup.
- Backup Log: the Backup Log Property sheet allows you to select the type of backup log that is generated. By default, a Summary log is selected, but you can select a detailed log or no log at all.
- Exclude Files: the Exclude Files Property sheet allows you to select files that are excluded from the backup process.

FIGURE 7.13
Backup Options

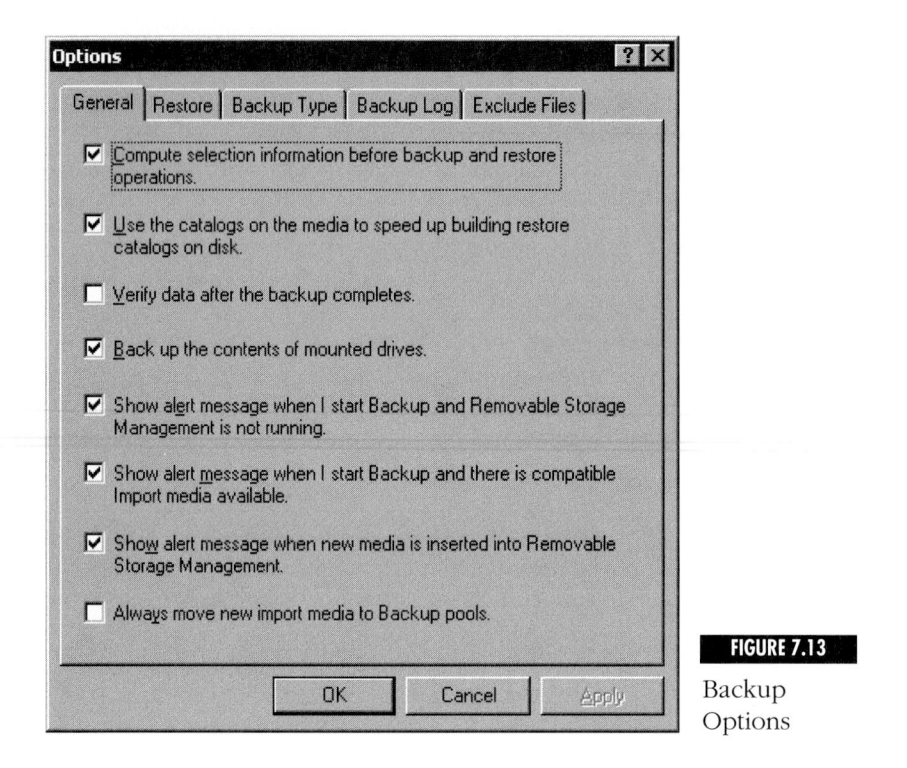

USING THE COMMAND LINE

You can use the command prompt to perform backup operations, or you can use a batch file. This is accomplished using the ntbackup command.

two • Hardware and Disk Management

The ntbackup command syntax is listed below and an explanation of the parameters are listed in Table 7.1 for easy reference.

```
Ntbackup backup [systemstate} "bks file name" /J {job name}
/P {pool name} /G {guid name} /T {tape name} /N {media
name} /F {file name} /D {set description} /DS {server name}
/IS {server name} /A /V {Yes or No} /R {yes or no}
/L:f|s|n /M {backup type} /RS {yes or no} /HC {on or off}
```

TABLE 7.1 NTBACKUP Command Line Parameters

Parameter	Explanation
systemstate	Specifies that you want to backup System State data.
Bks file name	Specifies the name of the selection information file to be used.
/J	Job name. Specifies the name of the job to be used in the log file.
/P	Pool name. Specifies the media pool. You can learn more about media pools in Chapter 8.
/G	Guide name. Overwrites or appends to this tape. Do not use with the /P parameter.
/T	Tape name. Overwrites or appends to this tape. Do not use with the /P parameter.
/N	Media name. Specifies the new tape name. Do not use with the /A parameter.
/F	File name. The logical disk path and file name. Do not use with the /P, /G or /T parameters.
/D	Set Description. Specifies a label for each backup set.
/DS	Server name. Backs up the Directory Service file for a specified Exchange Server.
/IS	Server Name. Backs up the Information Store file for a specified Exchange Server.
/A	Specifies an append operation which is used with either the /G or /T parameter. Do not use /A with /P.
/V	Yes or No. Verifies the data after the backup is complete.
/R	Yes or No. Restricts access to the tape to the owner or Administrators.
/L	f, s, or n. Specifies f–full, s–summary or n–no log for the log file created.
/M	Backup Type. Specifies the backup type (normal, copy, incremental, differential, or daily).
/RS	Yes or No. Backs up the Removable storage database. You can learn more about removable storage in Chapter 8.
/HC	On or Off. Specifies whether or not to use hardware compression, if it is available.

Summary

This chapter gave you an overview of the structure of the registry and explored using the Regedt32 and Regedit. It then explored Windows Backup and the functions of the backup utility. Windows 2000 Server's enhanced backup utility makes backing up data much easier. ASR gives you additional protection against a system failure, and an ERD can be used to restore system settings. With these tools, you can manage Windows 2000 Server more easily and protect your local machine and network against data loss.

EIGHT

Remote and Removable Storage

Disk storage space is an ongoing issue in networking environments. Even with the large hard drives available today, file storage continues to pose a problem in many environments. Microsoft addresses this issue by providing remote storage on tape drives and removable media drives in Windows 2000. This technology makes it easy for you to gain additional storage space without having to purchase more hard disks.

Remote storage is not the same as backup. Remote storage is designed to be a storage solution to extend a hard drive, but a regular backup plan should still be in place and followed. In the following sections, you first learn how remote and removable storage work and the benefits that can be gained, then you learn how to configure and manage Remote and Removable Storage in Windows 2000.

Storage Concepts

Remote storage works by moving eligible files from your local hard disk volumes to a remote storage location. When the space on your local, or managed, volume falls under the level you specify, remote storage automatically removes the content from the original file and moves it to the remote storage location. The file still appears on your local drive, but the file size is zero since the file actually resides in a remote location. When the file is needed, remote storage recalls the file and caches it locally so the file can be accessed. Since response time is slower than if the file were actually stored on your local volume, you specify the files or the parameters for the files that should be stored remotely so that your most commonly used files remain on the local volume.

Removable storage allows you to extend your local volumes by using removable storage media to store information. Removable Storage Manager handles this process and keeps track of the location of data stored on removable media, such as CD-ROMs, digital audio tape (DAT), Zip disks, and DVD.

Understanding Libraries

Removable storage organizes data in libraries so that it can track the storage location of individual files. There are two major types of libraries. The first are the Robotic libraries, often called changers or jukeboxes, that hold multiple tapes or disks and can automatically switch between tapes and disks as needed. For example, a ten-CD stereo player can automatically mount the various CDs loaded to the CD drive. The second type are Stand-alone libraries, which are single drives that hold one tape or disk at a time and must be manually changed by the administrator. Remote storage can also manage and track offline media not currently contained in a library. For example, you could store some of the disks or tapes in a file folder until they are needed. Even though the disks or tapes are not currently available, remote storage is aware of them and still considers them a part of the storage library.

Understanding Media Pools

A media pool is a collection of media, such as tapes or disks, that contain the same properties. Media can be organized into pools that have the same management policies. Each media pool can hold either media or other media pools. This design allows you to configure properties that apply to a group of media. A media pool can span a number of libraries, and you can even create media pools that are designed to hold other media pools. This structure allows you to design your media pools as best fits your organization.

There are two major classes of media pools: system and application. System media pools include unrecognized media pools, or blank media, import media pools, which remote storage recognizes, but which have not been used in the system, and Free Media pools, which contain media that is not currently used by applications. Application media pools contain media created by applications and are controlled by those applications (or an administrator). A typical example is Backup. Windows Backup may use one media pool for full backup storage and another for differential backup storage. Unrecognizable media must be moved into Free Media pools before it can be used, and Import media pools can be used once they are catalogued.

Removable storage classifies media in one of two ways. Media can either be classified physically (such as a tape or a disk) or logically. Logical media refers to media that has more than one side, such as double-sided CD-ROM. Removable storage sees each side as a separate medium, and each side can belong to different media pools if needed.

Understanding Media States

Media states define the status of each tape or disk within the removable storage system as to whether the media is working or not. Media states are broken into two categories: physical states and side states. The physical states show the operational condition of the media, such as idle, in use, loaded, mounted, and unloaded. The side states show the usage of the tape or disk instead of its current physical state. For example, a side state can be listed as allocated, available, completed, imported, reserved, etc.

Setting up and Using Remote Storage

Remote storage is not installed on your Windows 2000 Server by default, but you can specify for it to be set up during installation. If this has not been done, you can install remote storage by completing the following steps. Before you perform the steps, you must be logged on as an administrator, and there must be a remote storage media available in a free media pool (see the "Using Removable Storage" section for more information), and you must format volumes managed by remote storage with the Windows 2000 version of NTFS.

1. Click Start ➤ Settings ➤ Control Panel. Double-click Add/Remove Programs.
2. In Add/Remove programs, click Add/Remove Windows Components. The Windows Components Wizard begins. Click Next.
3. Select the Remote Storage check box and click Next. Windows copies the files and installs Remote Storage. Click Finish and reboot your computer.
4. When your computer reboots, log on with an account that has administrative privileges, then click Start ➤ Programs ➤ Administrative Tools ➤ Remote Storage.
5. Right-click Remote Storage in the left pane and click Set-up.
6. The Remote Storage Setup Wizard begins. Click Next.
7. Set-up checks for logon security privileges and a supported media device.
8. Select the device or devices you want to use for remote storage, and then complete the steps in the wizard.

Once you have set-up remote storage, you can manage it within the remote storage snap-in, which includes both remote and removable storage. As explained in the wizard, you cannot manage the System volume, but you did specify which volumes remote storage manages during set-up. At this point, remote storage can manage these volumes by copying selected files to remote storage that you specify while leaving the original files cached on your local volumes. You can automatically copy files with the schedule you provide, or you can do this manually as needed. The following sections, show the tasks you can perform with remote storage and how to perform those tasks on your server.

Volume Management

In order to use remote storage effectively, you will have to make some decisions about how you want remote storage to function. The first thing you need to decide is the parameters you want remote storage to use when determining which files to move to remote storage and which to leave on the local volume. You can specify the following criteria so that remote storage can determine which files to store:

- Minimum file size
- Elapsed time since the file was last accessed
- Exclude or include files based on a specified folder and subfolders, file type, file name, or wildcard characters

Remote storage gives you a set list of file inclusion and exclusion rules that cannot be changed, but you can create, remove, or edit your own rules. The following sections show how to configure various file selection parameters.

BASIC FILE SELECTION

To change the file size and file time parameters, follow these steps:

1. Right-click on the volume you want to manage and click Settings.
2. On the Settings tab, under File Criteria in Larger Than, click the Up or Down arrow to adjust the file size value.
3. Under File Criteria in Not Accessed In, click the Up or Down arrow to change the time value.

ADDING A FILE RULE

You can add your own file rules by following these steps:

1. Right-click the appropriate volume and click Include/Exclude Rules.
2. On the Include/Exclude tab, click Add.

3. In Path box, type the full path to the file.
4. In File Type, type the file name extension.
5. To exclude files when the rule is applied, click Exclude matching files, or to include files when the rule is applied, click Include matching files.
6. You can also apply the rule to any files stored in subfolders by clicking the Apply rule to subfolders check box.

CHANGING OR DELETING A FILE RULE

You can easily change or delete a file rule by following these steps:

1. Right-click the appropriate volume and click Include/Exclude Rules.
2. To edit a rule, click the rule you want to edit and click Edit, then change the settings and click OK.
3. You can delete a rule, select the rule and click Remove, then click OK.

CHANGING THE PRIORITY OF FILE RULES

To change the priority of file rules, follow these steps:

1. Right-click the applicable volume, then click Include/Exclude Rules.
2. On the Include/Exclude tab, select the applicable rule.
3. Click the Up or Down arrow to adjust the rule priority.

ADDING OR REMOVING VOLUMES FOR MANAGEMENT

Aside from creating and editing rules and rule management, you may also need to add new volumes that you would like remote storage to manage from time to time. This is an easy task and one that you can perform at any time after you run the remote storage setup wizard. Remember that you may need to adjust the file criteria and rules for that volume. To add the new volume, double-click remote storage in the console tree and right-click Managed Volumes. Point to New, then click Managed Volumes. Follow the instructions that appear in the Add Volume Wizard.

You can also remove volumes from remote storage management as needed. In this case, you either keep the remote files in storage and allow remote storage to recall them as necessary. Remote storage simply does not continue to manage the volume and remove files to remote storage any longer. Or you can have all the volume's data in remote storage moved back to the volume. To perform this action, right-click the appropriate volume and click Remove. Follow the wizard's instructions to determine what Remote Storage should do with the stored volume files.

SETTING FREE SPACE

You determine how you want remote storage to respond to storage conditions of the volume. Once the volume drops below an amount of free space that you specify, remote storage automatically begins deleting cached data from files that have already been copied to remote storage. This way, remote storage can manage the volume by keeping the amount of free space desired available. You can adjust the free space setting on a volume by right-clicking the applicable volume and clicking Settings. Then, on the Settings tab in Desired Free Space, click the Up or Down arrow to increase or decrease the free space value. You can also create free space immediately if it is needed. This action tells remote storage to remove all cached data from the volume, which creates immediate free space. To perform this, right-click the applicable volume, click Tasks, then click Create Free Space.

SETTING THE RUNAWAY RECALL LIMIT

The Runaway recall limit is the maximum number of successive file recalls a user can make on a file during the same session. Once a user makes a file recall, if the user requests another recall within 10 seconds, the count is increased. This causes the file to be copied back to the managed volume and moved out of remote storage. The runaway recall limit stops this from occurring by limiting the number of successive recalls a user can make with less than 10 seconds between each recall. Therefore, the file remains in remote storage but is still accessible. To set the runaway recall limit, follow these steps:

1. Right-click Remote Storage in the console tree and click Properties.
2. On the Recall Limit tab, change the value in Maximum number of successive recalls by clicking the Up or Down arrows.
3. To exclude users with administrative permissions from the limit, click the Exempt administrators from this limit check box.

SETTING VALIDATION

Validation in remote storage means that the data stored in the remote storage media correctly points to the correct file on the managed volume. Validation is automatically performed two hours after a backup program is used to restore a file, and validation can also detect whether a file has moved from one volume to another. Validation should be performed on a regular basis, and one of the easiest ways to do this is to use validation with Windows 2000 Scheduled Tasks. To manually validate a volume, right-click the appropriate volume, point to All Tasks, and then click Validate Files.

CHANGING THE FILE COPY SCHEDULE

You can change remote storage's default schedule used to copy files, which was initially created during set-up. To change the schedule, follow these steps:

1. In the console tree, right click Remote Storage and click Change Schedule.
2. In the Remote Storage File Copy Schedule dialog box, click the arrow in Schedule Task, and click an interval.
3. In Start time, set the start time using the Up or Down arrows.
4. In Schedule Tasks Daily change the value in Every by clicking the Up or Down arrow.

In a case where you need to copy files without waiting for the scheduled time, right-click the appropriate volume and click Copy Files to Remote Storage.

Managing Media

In addition to setting up and managing Remote Storage so that it functions in an appropriate manner to meet your needs, there are a few actions concerning the management of the remote storage media you may need to perform. Remote storage supports all SCSI class 4mm, 8mm, and DLT tape libraries. All libraries used by remote storage exist in a single media application pool which is created during remote storage set-up. This media is used for all storage procedures.

For fault tolerance, you should consider creating copies of the media so that your stored files can be recalled should there be a problem with the media master set. Remote storage can automatically create copies of the media master set, called media copy sets, so you have redundant copies at all times. This process can occur only if there are two or more drives in the tape library—one functions as the media master while the other functions as the media copy. You can also use additional drives to create additional copies if desired. To adjust the number of media copies you would like to create, right-click Remote Storage and click Properties. On the Media Copies tab, adjust the Number of media copy sets value by using the Up or Down arrow. In the case of a failure or corruption with the media master, the data can be recreated using a media copy. To recreate the media master, right-click on Remote Storage and click Media. In the details pane, right-click one of the media shown and click Properties. Click the Recovery tab and click Re-create Master. Follow the wizard that appears.

Finally, if you are using a media master and media copy sets, synchronization of the two should be performed regularly so that the copy always accurately reflects the master. To synchronize the media copies, right-click Media in the console tree and click Synchronize Copies Now. Follow the wizard that appears.

Using Removable Storage

As mentioned earlier in the chapter, removable storage allows you to store data on removable disks such as Zip disks and CD-ROMs. Removable storage can use jukeboxes or individual media drives, which can be grouped together in media pools. Removable storage functions by configuring libraries to keep track of the location data stored. Even if, for example, a Zip disk is removed and put in another physical location, the library is still aware of that disk and data on it.

Configuring and Managing Libraries

Removable storage automatically configures all libraries whenever you add or remove a library, but Removable Storage allows you complete control over library management. The following sections show you how to manage and configure these options.

ENABLING OR DISABLING A LIBRARY OR DRIVE

You can easily enable or disable a library by following these steps:

1. Expand Removable Storage in the Remote Storage Management Console.
2. In the Console Tree, double-click Physical Locations.
3. Right-click the library you want to enable or disable and click Properties.
4. On the General tab of the Properties sheet, click the Enable library check box to enable it, or clear the box to disable it.

To enable or disable a drive, follow these steps:

1. Expand Removable Storage, expand Physical Locations, expand the library you want to enable or disable, and select Drives.
2. In the details pane, right-click the drive and click Properties, shown in Figure 8.1.
3. On the General Property sheet, click the Enable Drive check box to enable the drive, or clear it to disable the drive.

CHANGING MEDIA TYPES

To change a media type, follow these steps:

1. Double-click Physical Locations.
2. Right-click the library you want to change and click Properties.

two • Hardware and Disk Management   **141**

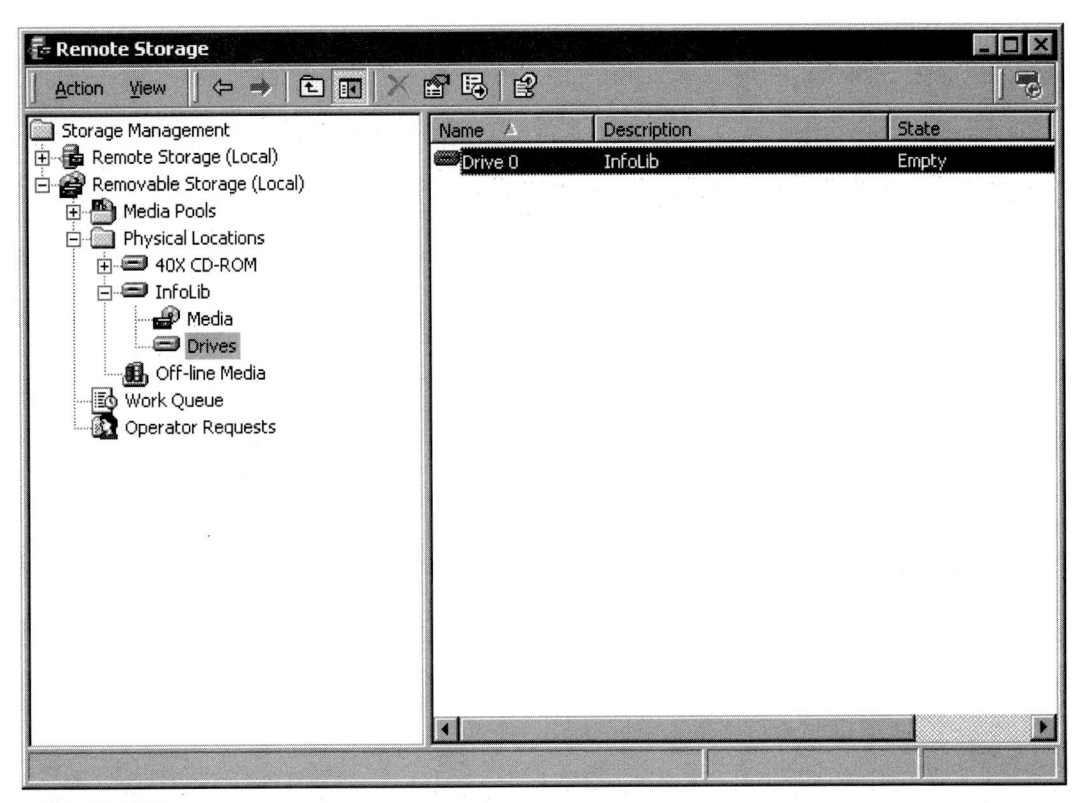

FIGURE 8.1   Drive Properties

3. Click the Media Property sheet and click Change.
4. In the Change Media Types dialog box, you can add a new media type by selecting the entry in Available types and clicking Add, or you can remove an existing media by clicking Remove in Selected Types, shown in Figure 8.2.

CREATING A LIBRARY INVENTORY

Removable storage allows you to create either a Fast Inventory or a Full Inventory of all media in a library. A Fast Inventory is created by reading bar codes if a bar-code reader is present, or by checking slots that have changed status from either occupied or unoccupied. A Full Inventory is performed when removable storage mounts each media in the library and reads the identifier. To create a library inventory, simply double-click Physical Locations and right-click the library you want to inventory, then click Inventory.

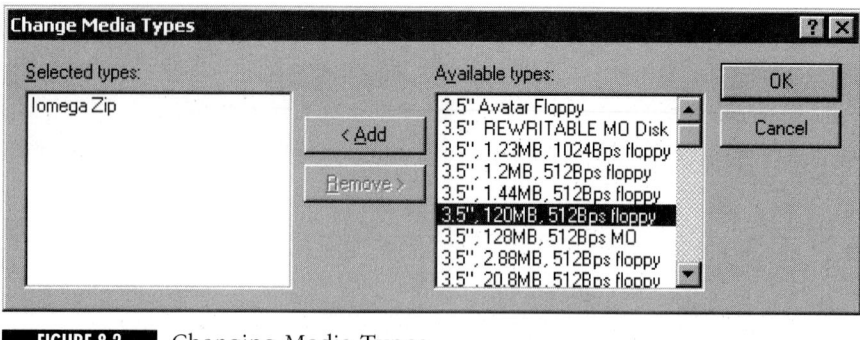

FIGURE 8.2 Changing Media Types

If you want to change the inventory method from Fast to Full or vice versa, right-click the library and click Properties. On the General Property sheet, select None, Fast, or Full.

CLEANING LIBRARIES

Removable storage can manage the cleaning of both standalone drives and robotic libraries. In this design, the robotic library can contain one cleaner cartridge, which removable storage can use to periodically clean the drive. If this is done, removable storage keeps a count of the number of times the cleaner cartridge is used and will generate an operator request when the cartridge needs to be replaced. For a standalone drive, you must manually insert a cleaner cartridge, then click Drives and in results pane, right-click the drive and click Mark as Clean. This action tells removable storage that the drive has been cleaned, so it can keep a record of the cleaning. To clean a robotic library, right-click on the library you want to clean and click Cleaner Management, then follow the instructions in the Cleaner Management Wizard. The wizard will prompt you to insert a cleaner cartridge, and you should always use the wizard to insert a cleaner cartridge.

Configuring Media Pools

Once you have configured your libraries, you need to configure your media pools so they function in an organized manner and are appropriate for the needs of your environment. The following sections show you how to perform various tasks in order to configure your media pools.

CREATING OR DELETING A NEW MEDIA POOL

To create a new media pool, follow these steps:

1. In the console tree, right-click Media Pools and click Create Media Pool. If you want to create another media pool within a media pool, right-click the media pool and click Create Media Pool.

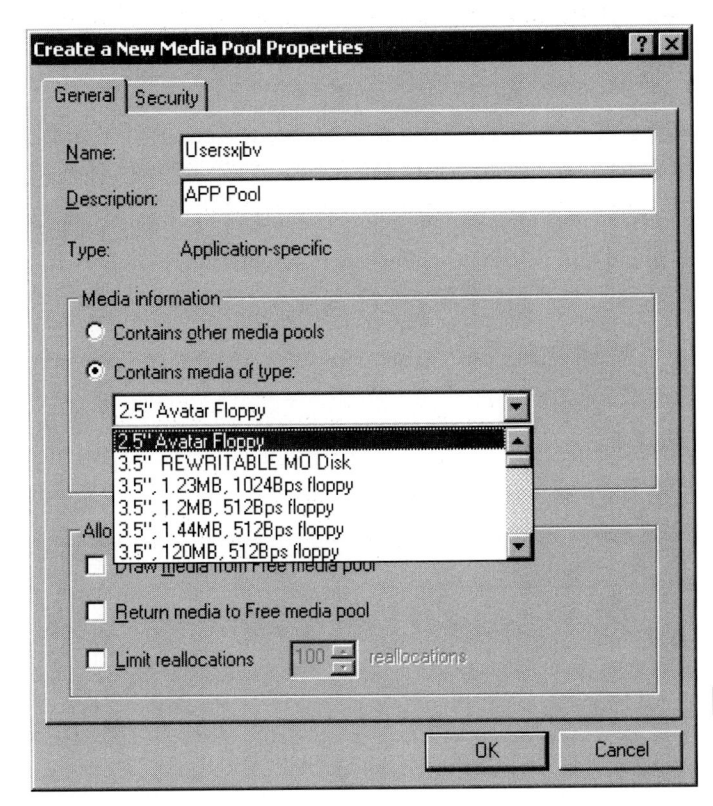

FIGURE 8.3
Media Pool Properties

2. Type a name and description on the General page.
3. Click the Contains Media of Type radio button, then select the media from the drop-down menu as shown in Figure 8.3.
4. In the Allocation/Deallocation policy, choose the Draw media from free media pool check box if desired, or choose automatically return media to free media pool when no longer needed by clicking the Return media to free media pool check box, or choose both if desired.
5. To set an allocation limit for the media in the media pool, click the Limit reallocations check box and adjust the value as desired.

If you want to delete an application media pool, simply right-click it and choose delete. You cannot delete the free, import, or unrecognized media pools.

Configuring and Managing Physical Media

Removable storage allows you to completely manage and control tapes and disks in your libraries. Once you create and configure various media pools as needed, you move media into a specific media pool, but you do need to leave enough media in the free media pool so that it can be used by applications as needed.

A tape or a disk can be inserted or ejected from a robotic library using either a library door or an insert/eject port. A library door gives you unrestricted access to the media in the library while an insert/eject port allows you controlled access by inserting or ejecting the media through a port. The library then uses a transport to move the media to a storage slot. Additionally, you have full control in terms of disk mounting and dismounting, and the same media can be mounted or dismounted many times before it is deallocated.

The following sections will show the control options to manage your media.

INSERTING, EJECTING, OR MOUNTING A TAPE OR DISK

To insert a tape or disk into a robotic library, double-click on Physical Locations, then right-click the appropriate library, then click Inject. Follow the Media Inject Wizard to insert the new tape or disk. To insert a tape into a standalone drive, manually insert the tape.

To eject a tape or disk from standalone drive, right-click the appropriate library in Physical locations and click Eject. To eject a tape or disk from a robotic library, in the console tree, expand Physical Locations, expand the appropriate library, then select Media. In the right pane, right-click the tape or disk you want to eject and click Eject.

To mount a tape or disk, navigate once again to media, then in the right pane, right-click the tape or disk you want to mount and click Mount. To dismount from a standalone drive, perform the same steps but click Dismount. To dismount a tape or disk in a robotic library, navigate to Physical Storage, Physical Locations, the appropriate library, Drives. In the right pane, right-click the drive you want to dismount the tape or disk and click Dismount.

Configuring Queued Work and Operator Requests

In remote storage, the work queue provides a list of all requests made to the library from an application or remote storage. If you expand removable storage in the console tree and click on Work Queue in the list, you will see a list of operations that have been performed at the state of that operation, as shown in Figure 8.4.

The work queue can display five different states for the operation:

- Completed: the operation has been completed successfully.
- Failed: the operation request has failed.
- In Process: the operation is currently being completed.

two • Hardware and Disk Management   145

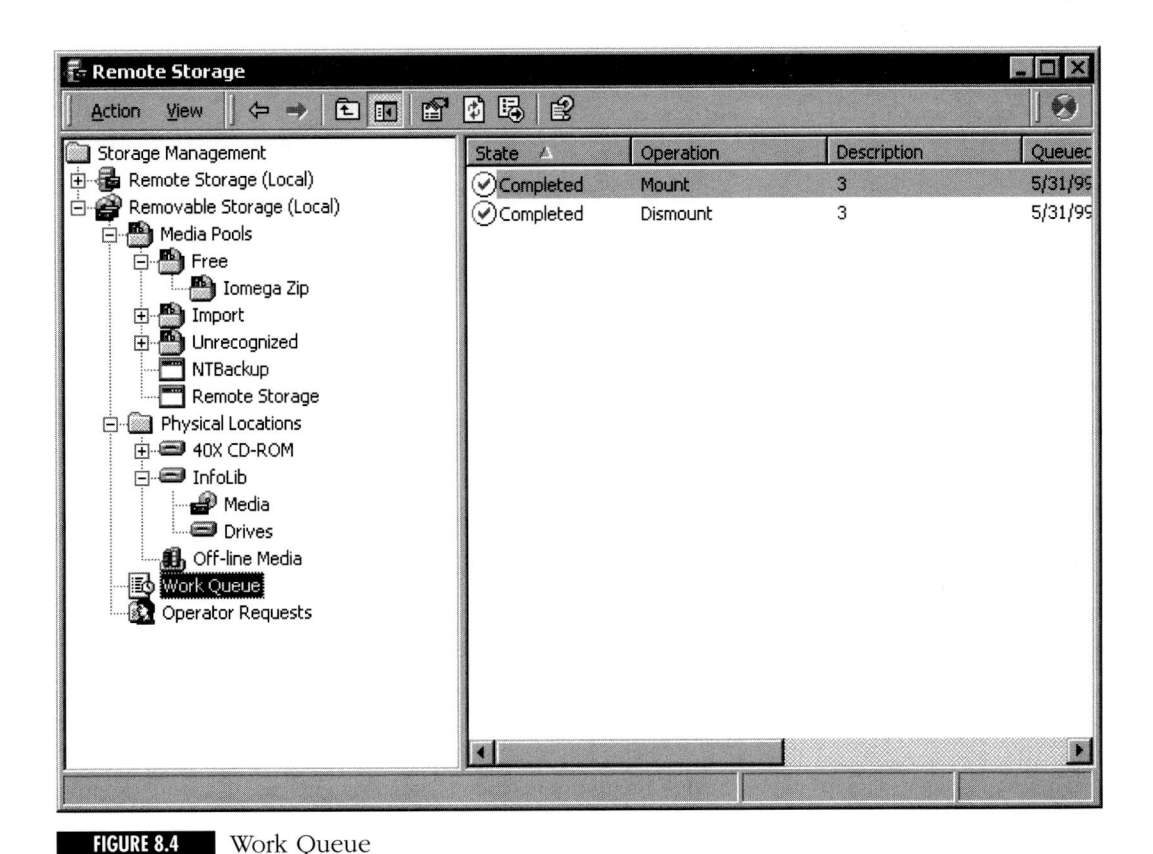

FIGURE 8.4   Work Queue

- Queued: the operation has been requested and is waiting for Remote Storage to examine the request.
- Waiting: the operation is waiting for service by Remote Storage.

The Queued Work Properties sheet, which can be accessed by right-clicking Queued Work and selecting Properties, simply allows you to automatically delete completed requests and specify whether or not you want to keep or delete failed requests. By default, the requests are deleted after one hour, but you can change that by selecting the amount of time you want in the dialog box, shown in Figure 8.5.

You can also right-click any operation in the list and click Properties to find out more information about the operation, when it was completed, or who initiated the request. Also, you can re-order the work queue item by right-clicking it and choosing Re-order Mounts. This allows you to move the item to the front or end of the work queue. You can also cancel an operation request by right-clicking the request and clicking Cancel Request.

A related topic to the work queue is Operator Requests. An operator request is a message that requests that some task or action can be complet-

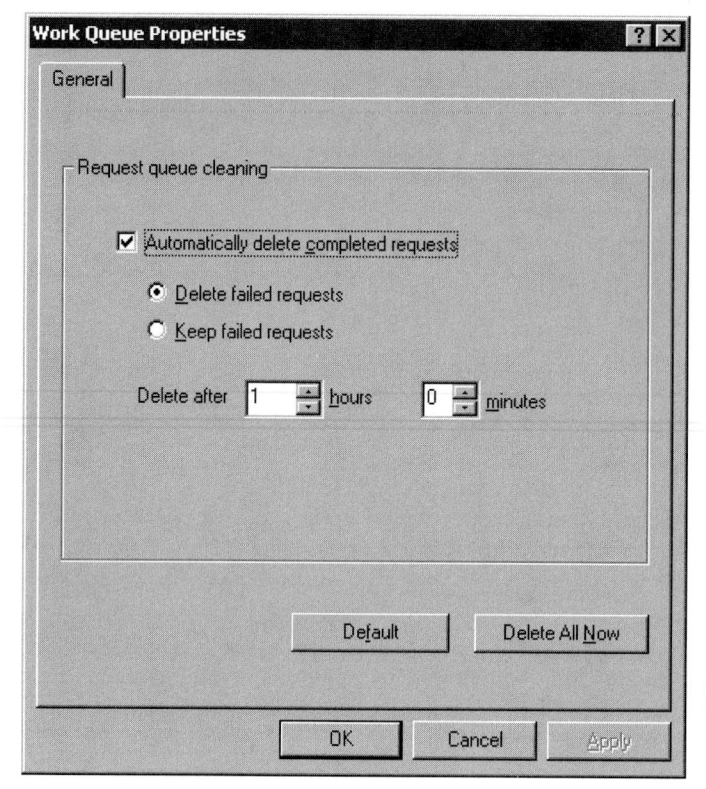

FIGURE 8.5
Work Queue Properties

ed. Remote storage or remote storage aware programs can generate operator requests when an application begins a mount request for a medium that is offline, a library fails, there are no available media online, or a drive needs cleaning but usable cleaner cartridges are not available.

You can complete or refuse an operator request as desired, and if you refuse a request that was generated by a remote storage aware application, remote storage will notify the application that the request has been refused. The Operator Requests icon appears in the Removable Storage console tree, and the following sections show you to manage operator requests.

RESPONDING TO AN OPERATOR REQUEST

To respond to an operator request, follow these steps:

1. In the console tree, double-click Operator Requests.
2. In the right pane, double-click the request you want to answer.
3. In the Operator Request dialog box, click Complete to complete the request, then perform the requested action, or to refuse, click Refuse. This cancels the request.

two • Hardware and Disk Management   **147**

DELETING OPERATOR REQUESTS

You can delete an operator request by right-clicking on Operator Requests and clicking Properties. This gives you the same kind of properties sheet as the Queued Work. To adjust how the operator requests are deleted, adjust what is deleted and how long it should be kept by clicking the appropriate radio buttons.

CHANGING OPERATOR REQUESTS DISPLAY

You can change how operator requests are displayed by following these steps:

1. Right-click Removable Storage in the console and click Properties.
2. On the General Property sheet, you have two check boxes, as shown in Figure 8.6. You can choose to send the operator requests to the Messenger service so that they are displayed in a pop-up window, and you can choose to tray icon for pending operator requests, which displays an icon on the taskbar for requests that are waiting to be serviced. Click the selections you want to use.

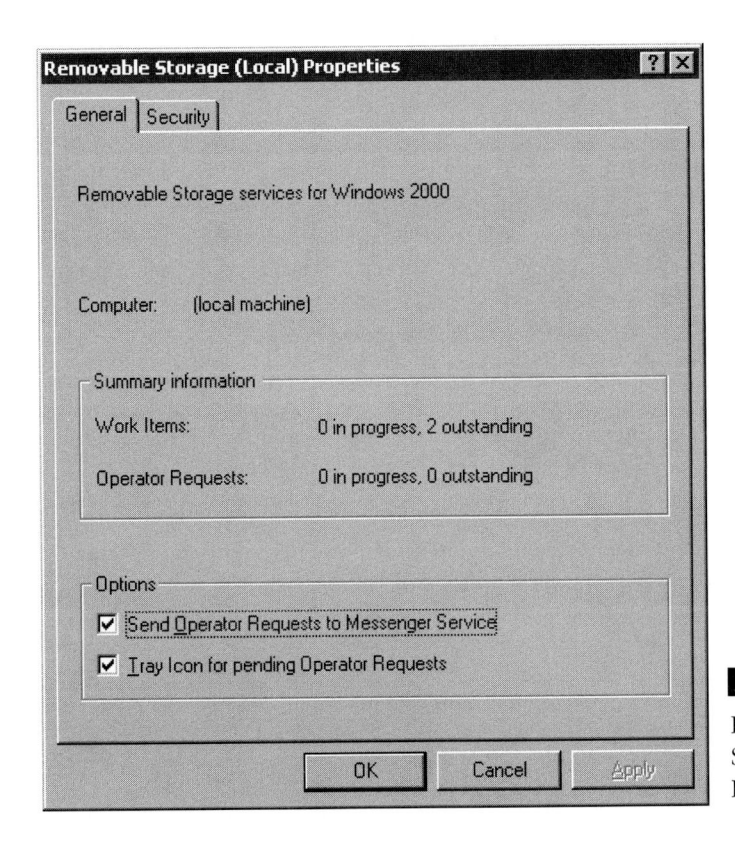

FIGURE 8.6

Removable Storage Properties

Configuring Removable Storage Security

You can easily configure Removable Storage security by right-clicking Removable Storage in the console tree, clicking Properties, then clicking the Security tab, shown in Figure 8.7.

You can further refine security by configuring this same interface for each library. Simply right-click on the library and choose Properties, then choose the Security Property sheet. In this way, you can allow one user certain rights to one library and restrict rights to others.

By default, members of the System and Administrators Group have Use, Modify, and Control permissions, Backup Operators have Use and Modify permissions, and Users have Use permission. You can change these default settings as needed, and you can click the Add button to specify individual user settings or add new groups. As with any user access permissions and security, careful consideration should be made before implementing a security plan for remote storage.

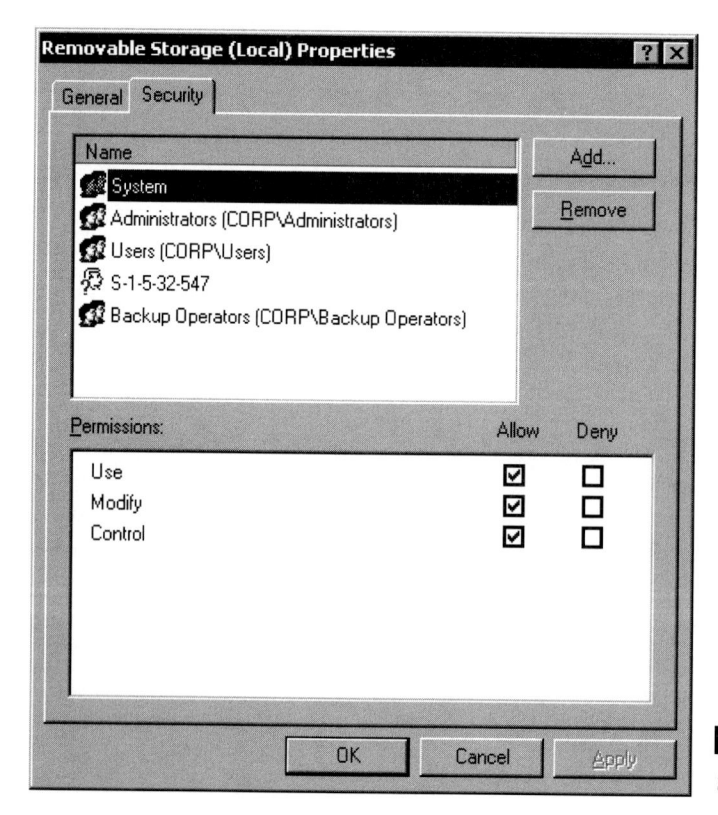

FIGURE 8.7

Security Tab

Using Removable Storage Command Line

As with many other Windows 2000 components, you have the option of administering removable storage at the command line. This feature allows you to write batch scripts for applications that do not support the removable storage API. The command line syntax is

```
rsm {allocate|deallocate|deletemedia|dismount|help|mount|view}
```

Each command has its own argument switches that can be used in conjunction with the command. You should keep in mind that no spaces are allowed after an argument switch or in the names or information following a switch. Also, all commands are case sensitive and you can use only one command at a time. The following sections explain the argument switches that can be used with each command.

ALLOCATE

The Allocate command allows you to allocate media to a particular media pool. The argument switches for the allocate command are as follows:

- /m: media pool name
- /n: logical media name (optional)
- /p: media side to allocate (optional)
- /t: time-out value (optional)

The syntax for the allocate command is:

```
rsm allocate /mmediapoolname [/ppartid /nlogicalname /ttimeout]
```

DEALLOCATE

You can use the deallocate command to deallocate media from a media pool. The deallocate command has the following argument switches:

- /l: Logical media ID (if the /n switch was used when the media was allocated, it can be reused here in place of the logical media ID)
- /n: Logical media name

The syntax for the deallocate command is:

```
rsm deallocate /llogicalmediaid /nlogicalmedianame
```

DELETEMEDIA

The deletemedia command allows you to delete data on the tape or disk from the removable storage database. The deletemedia command has the following argument switches:

- /p: The physical media ID
- /n: The physical media name

The syntax for the deletemedia command is:

`rsm delemedia /pphysicalnameid /nphysicalmedianame`

DISMOUNT

The dismount command is used to dismount the medium from a drive. The logical media name can be used to specify the logical medium if it was assigned during the allocate command using the /n switch. If not, then the logical media ID must be used. The /l and /n argument switches are used with the dismount command, and the syntax is as follows:

`rsm dismount /llogicalmediaid /nphysicalmedianame`

MOUNT

The mount command allows you to mount a medium on a drive and is specified by the /l or /n switch. The mount command also contains the following optional switches:

- /d: Drive ID (if you do not assign this, Removable Storage assigns a drive)
- /p: Priority from 1 to 100, which specifies the drive-mount priority
- /t: Time-out value

The syntax for the mount command is:

`rsm mount /llogicalmediaid /nlogicalmedianame [/ddriveid /ppriority /ttimeout]`

HELP

The help command allows you to get argument switch and syntax information for each command. The syntax for the help command is:

`Rsm help {allocate | deallocate | dismount | mount | view |rsm}`

VIEW

The view command displays a list of media pools or a list of logical media. The view command contains the following argument switches:

- /c: Object type, such as media pool
- /I: Object ID

The syntax for the view command is:

`rsm view /cobjecttype /iobjectid`

Summary

Remote and removable storage in Windows 2000 Server provides you with advanced storage solutions that allow you to conserve local disk space. Through remote storage's caching features, you can remotely store information as though it were located on your local volumes, and removable storage allows you to utilize removable tape and disk solutions through the use of libraries. Both of these solutions help you manage storage and access to stored information.

PART THREE

Networking

In This Part

▶ **CHAPTER 9**
Configuring the Active Directory

▶ **CHAPTER 10**
Configuring Network Communication

▶ **CHAPTER 11**
Installing and Configuring DHCP

▶ **CHAPTER 12**
Configuring DNS

▶ **CHAPTER 13**
Configuring WINS

▶ **CHAPTER 14**
Configuring Routing and Remote Access

▶ **CHAPTER 15**
Connecting with Apple and Novell Systems

▶ **CHAPTER 16**
Overview of Windows 2000 Security Features

▶ **CHAPTER 17**
IP Security

Networking technologies are perhaps the most important component of Windows 2000 Server. In this section, you learn how to configure the Active Directory, basic network protocols, DHCP, DNS, WINS, RAS, as well as connectivity with NetWare and Apple operating systems. You also learn about the new security features in Windows 2000 Server.

NINE

Configuring the Active Directory

One of the major problems with networks today is finding and managing resources. As networks have grown both in size and complexity, users are faced with trying to find the right server that has the right resource, and administrators are faced with the daunting task of ensuring that all of the servers and resources are available to the network users. When networks were smaller, this wasn't as big of a problem, but in today's large, distributed networking environments, directory services have become just as complex.

Windows 2000 Server answers this problem through its new directory service, the Active Directory. The Active Directory stores all network resources, such as users, files, printers, and databases, in one structured location so they are easy to locate and use. Since Windows 2000 networks contain only Domain Controllers and not PDCs and BDCs, all servers maintain an exact copy of the database at all times through replication. So, the Active Directory is Microsoft's answer to directory services in today's complex computing environments.

Features of the Active Directory

The Active Directory contains several important features that make it easier to administer and use. The following sections give you a brief overview of these features.

Scalability

The Active Directory is highly scalable. It's directory services function just as well in a small environment as in a large distributed network. Because the Active Directory is scalable, it can grow with your organization, and it is capable of supporting basically an unlimited number of objects.

DNS Integration and Standard Naming

Windows 2000 domain names are DNS names because the Active Directory uses DNS as its naming and location service. Windows 2000 Server supports Dynamic DNS, which means that clients running dynamically assigned IP addresses can register with the DNS service so that the DNS table is updated dynamically. The Active Directory also directly supports HTTP and LDAP. LDAP enables you to easily find objects within the Active Directory by searching, and HTTP enables you to view objects in the Active Directory as web pages. The Active Directory also supports e-mail names (RFC 822) such as *myname@mycompany.com* and the UNC naming convention. Due to these open standards, the Active Directory is easy to use and can function with foreign directory services.

Extensibility

The Active Directory is "extensible," which means that administrators can customize the classes and objects that appear in the Active Directory to meet the needs of the organization. This action is performed using the Active Directory Schema snap-in, discussed later in this chapter, or through the Active Directory Services Interface (ADSI).

Security

The Active Directory is fully integrated with the security features of Windows 2000 Server. With this new design, access control can be enabled on each object and even on each property of that object. This design allows you to completely control what users can access within the Active Directory.

Active Directory Organization

The Active Directory allows you to design a directory structure that meets the needs of your organization, and care should be taken before implementing a structure so that it does provide an organized and logical approach. The key to remember is that the Active Directory allows you to organize your directory on a searchable basis so that users can find the resources they need without being aware of the network's physical design and location of various servers. In order to accomplish this, the Active Directory is organized in a tree-like structure that logically holds the resources. This organization is explained in the following sections and illustrations.

Domain

The organizational structure of the Active Directory is based on the domain. This structure follows the network's domain structure, and each domain stores only the information about its objects. For practical purposes, each domain is essentially unlimited in the number of resources it can contain, with a theoretical limit of about 10 million. The domain also acts as a security boundary so that rights to the resources within that domain can be controlled. This is accomplished through an Access Control List (ACL). The ACL for the domain contains all of the permissions for resources within the domain.

Organizational Units

The resources for the domain are organized into Organizational Units (OU). You can think of an OU as a file folder that holds appropriate files. OUs contain logical groupings of resources, such as files, printers, databases, applications, and other domain resources.

Objects

Organization Units contain objects, or resources. An object can be any domain resource such as files, applications, or even users. Objects can be even further organized into classes that group certain kinds of objects together. As you can see in Figure 9.1, objects fit into OUs, and OUs fit into a domain.

Tree

A tree is a grouping of one or more Windows 2000 domains. A tree, though usually made up of several domains, is still one unit in that it shares a contiguous namespace. This means that the domain name of a child domain falls within the DNS naming scheme. For example, the parent domain may be named xyzcompany.com while the child domain is named acct.xyzcompany.com. All domains within the tree also share the same global catalog—a listing of objects within that domain.

Forest

A forest is a logical grouping of trees. Since a tree is still one unit, a forest is several units that do not share a contiguous namespace. A noncontiguous name space does not follow the naming scheme of other trees. For example, sales.corp.com and sales.corpau.com do not share a contiguous name space. Trees within the forest may use differing naming structures and they operate independently of each other, but the forest still shares one global catalog so users can find resources in different trees.

FIGURE 9.1
Domain organization

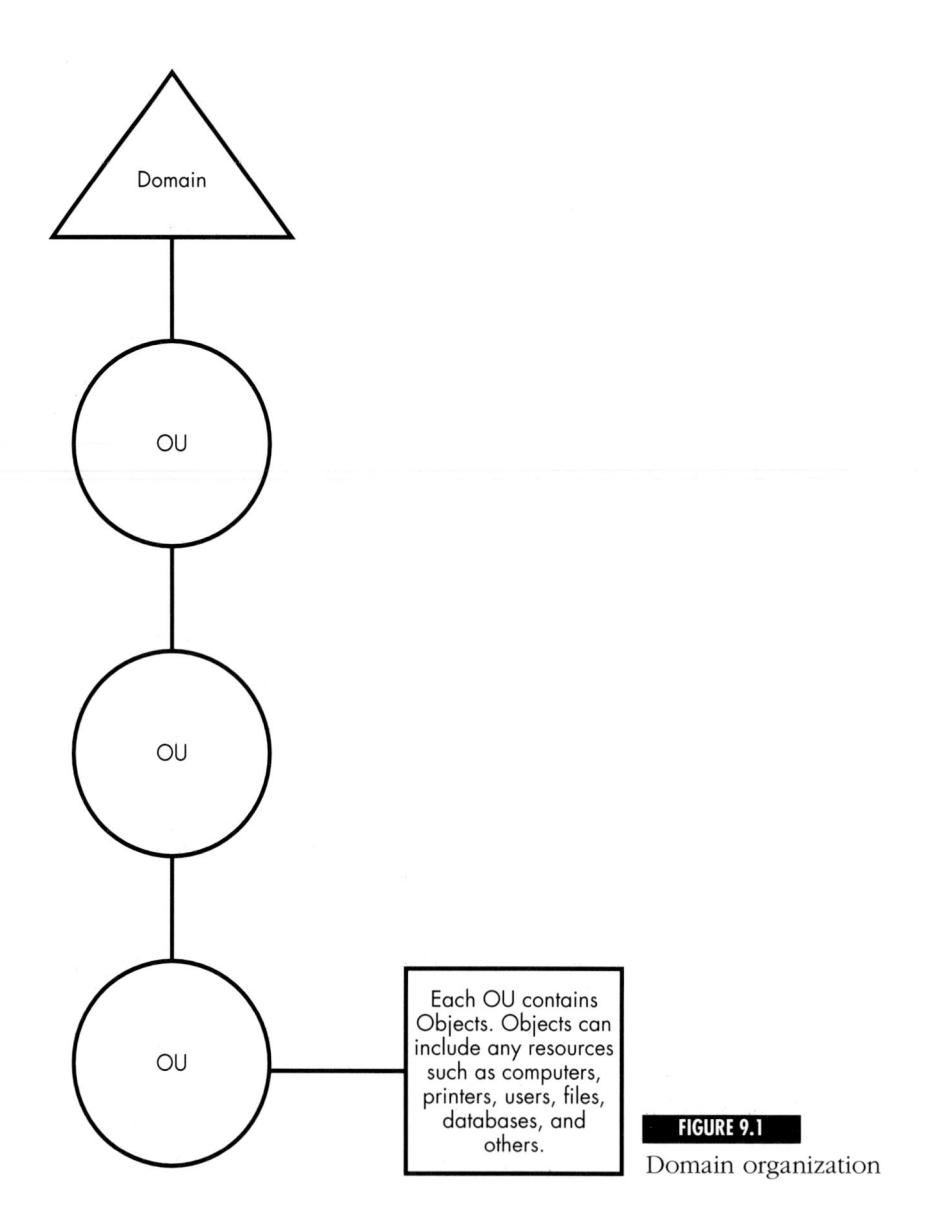

Sites

A site houses the physical structure of the Active Directory. The Active Directory users see objects not in terms of a site, but in trees and domains. The site, however, is maintained for administrative purposes, primarily for replication. Sites are connected to each other through high-speed links so that directory replication can occur between sites. The Active Directory uses multimaster replication, which means there is not a domain controller that is the master replicator, but all domain controllers work in a peer fashion to replicate changes in their domain resources to the other domain.

Active Directory Design

Now that you have an understanding of the Active Directory's organization, let's take a look at some design features that further refine how the Active Directory functions.

Global Catalog

As mentioned previously, the Active Directory uses a global catalog that enables users to find information in any domain, tree, or forest. The global catalog is automatically generated for each domain through the replication process. The global catalog is a service as well as a storage location that contains replicas of objects as well as their attributes. By definition, the attributes of each object enable a user to perform a search to find the object without knowing the exact name of the object. For example, in the global catalog, a user can search for "printer" without having to know the name of the particular printer he or she would like to use.

When the Active Directory is installed on the first domain controller in a new forest, the domain controller by default is the global catalog server. The global catalog server stores a copy of the global catalog. Additional servers can be specified as global catalog servers; however, it should be noted that the more global catalog servers, the more replication and query traffic you will have on your network. Yet, additional global catalog servers do help speed response time in busy networks.

Schema

The Active Directory Schema is a list of definitions that determine what objects and what information about those objects can be stored in the Active Directory. The schema defines these objects through classes, class properties, and attributes. For each class of objects, the schema defines what attributes those objects must have to be listed in a particular class. For example, a computer class will hold certain attributes that objects must meet in order to be an instance of that class. These attributes are provided by default but can be manipulated and changed as needed. For each object in each class, certain attributes for that object are defined. For instance, a user in the user class will contain attributes such as first name, last name, logon name, e-mail address, and so forth. Due to the attributes, users can access the global catalog to search for a particular resource only by providing attributes.

The schema is considered extensible, in that you can define new objects and new attributes as needed, and you can define new attributes for existing objects. This can be accomplished through the Schema Manager snap-in or through programming via the Active Directory Services Interface (ADSI).

Namespace

Since Active Directory names are DNS names, They allow you to use a standard naming format, such as *mycompany.com*. By definition, a namespace is an area by which names can be resolved. All objects belonging to the namespace carry the same naming scheme and can be resolved to the object the name represents. This is how the Active Directory knows that server1.mycompany.com actually refers to a particular server in a particular location. A contiguous namespace exists if all child objects inherit the namespace of the parent. A disjointed namespace does not follow this inherited format. Figure 9.2 gives you an example of a contiguous namespace.

Naming Conventions

Every object in the Active Directory contains a "name." The Active Directory uses four major naming conventions to identify objects in it.

First, the Active Directory gives every object a Distinguished Name (DN). The DN is unique from all other objects and contains enough infor-

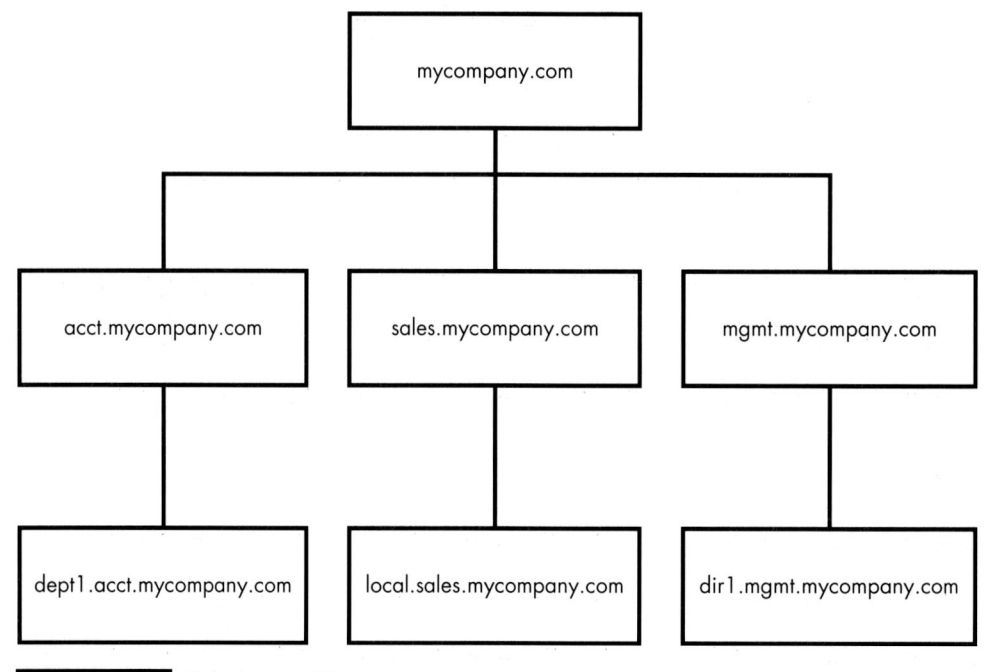

FIGURE 9.2 Contiguous Namespace

mation for a user to retrieve the object from the directory. The DN contains the name of both the domain and the path to that particular object. The DN is made up of several attributes, such as a DomainComponentName (DC), OrganizationalUnitName (OU), and a CommonName (CN). Because the DN contains these attributes, the Active Directory can locate a particular object beginning from the domain name and working its way down. For example, let's say you want to access the shared folder "Sales Presentations." The DN in the Active Directory would read:

```
/DC=COM/DC=mycompany/OU=Sales/CN=Shares/CN=Sales Presentations
```

Next, the Active Directory uses Relative Distinguished Names (RDN). The RDN is the part of the DN that is an attribute of the actual object. In the above example, Sales Presentations is an attribute (Common Name) of the shared folder. You can have the same RDN for two objects, but they cannot belong to the same OU. For example, you can have a folder RDN called "Presentations" in the Sales OU and in the Marketing OU, but you cannot have two of the same RDNs in the Sales OU.

Then, the Active Directory uses a Globally Unique Identifier (GUID), which is a 128-bit number that is unique from all others. A GUID is assigned to an object upon creation, and it never changes regardless of how often an object is moved or renamed.

Finally, the Active Directory uses User Principal Names (UPN), which are short, friendly names of the object. A UPN looks like a typical e-mail address. The Common Name of an object is combined with the domain for a short UPN, such as *KarenSmith@mycompany.com*.

Installing the Active Directory

Now that we have taken a brief conceptual overview of the Active Directory structure and organization, let's move to the installation and configuration of the Active Directory. This section shows you how to install the Active Directory on your server.

You can easily install the Active Directory by accessing Configure Your Server in Administrative Tools, or by running dcpromo.exe at the command line. Either selection launches the Active Directory Installation Wizard that guides you through the process of installing the Active Directory. If the Active Directory is already installed on your server, running the Installation Wizard removes the Active Directory and demotes your server from a domain controller to a member server.

When you run the installation, you have the option of joining an existing domain and an existing domain tree, or you can create a new domain and create a new domain tree and forest, depending on the needs and design of your organization. To install the Active Directory, follow these steps:

1. Click Start ➤ Programs ➤ Administrative Tools ➤ Configure Your Server. The Window opens. Click Active Directory. Or click Start ➤ Run and type cmd in the dialog box to open the command prompt, then type dcpromo.exe. This begins the Active Directory Installation Wizard. Click Next.
2. The Domain Controller Type window appears, as shown in Figure 9.3. Select the radio button for your server either to be a domain controller in a new domain or to become an additional domain controller in an existing domain. Select the appropriate radio button and click Next.
3. If you selected the option to join an existing domain, you are prompted for the appropriate name and password. Set-up will then locate the domain you are joining and proceed with the installation. If you are creating a new domain, you are presented with a Create or Join Forest domain. If you would like to create a new forest of domain trees, click the appropriate radio button, or if you would like to place the new domain tree in an existing forest, click the appropriate radio button and click Next.

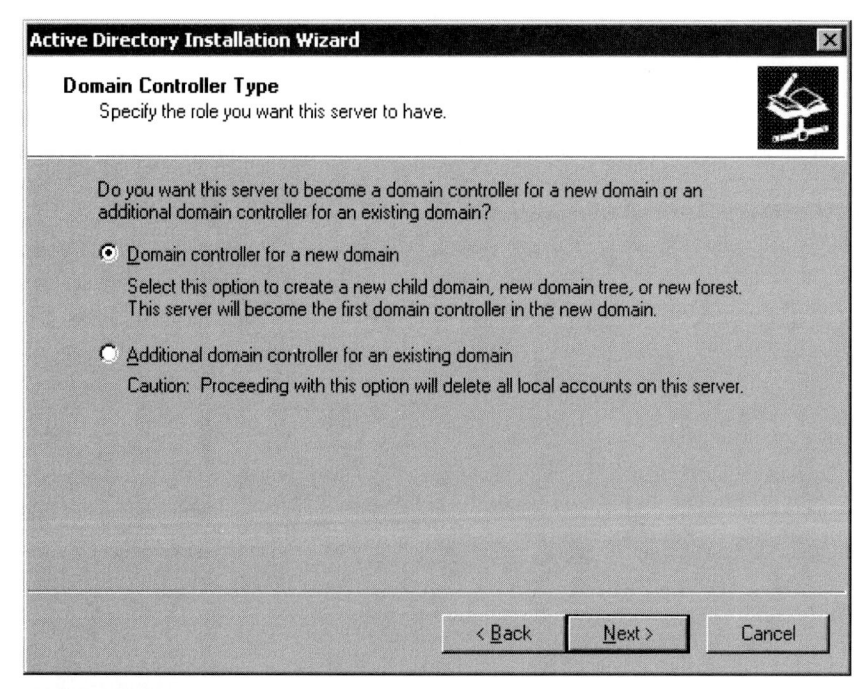

FIGURE 9.3 Domain Controller Type

4. If you chose to join an existing forest, you are prompted for a user name and password. If you chose to create a new forest of domain trees, you are given the New Domain Name dialog box. In this box, you need to type the full DNS name for the new domain, as shown in Figure 9.4. You have the option of creating a new DNS name or using one that is already assigned to your company by an Internet naming authority, such as the InterNIC. Type the name you wish to use for the new domain and click the Next button.

5. The NetBIOS Domain Name dialog box appears. Windows 2000 maintains compatibility with NetBIOS naming for previous versions of Windows operating systems. You are presented with the Domain NetBIOS name as it will appear to these systems. Click Next.

6. The Database and Log Locations window appears. The default location, C:\WINNT\NTDS, is presented for both the Active Directory database and the Active Directory log. You can change this location to another disk for better performance. Change the locations as desired and click Next.

7. The Shared System Volume window appears. Sysvol stores the server's copy of the domain's public folders, and you are given the default location of C:\WINNT\SYSVOL. You can change the default location if desired. Click Next.

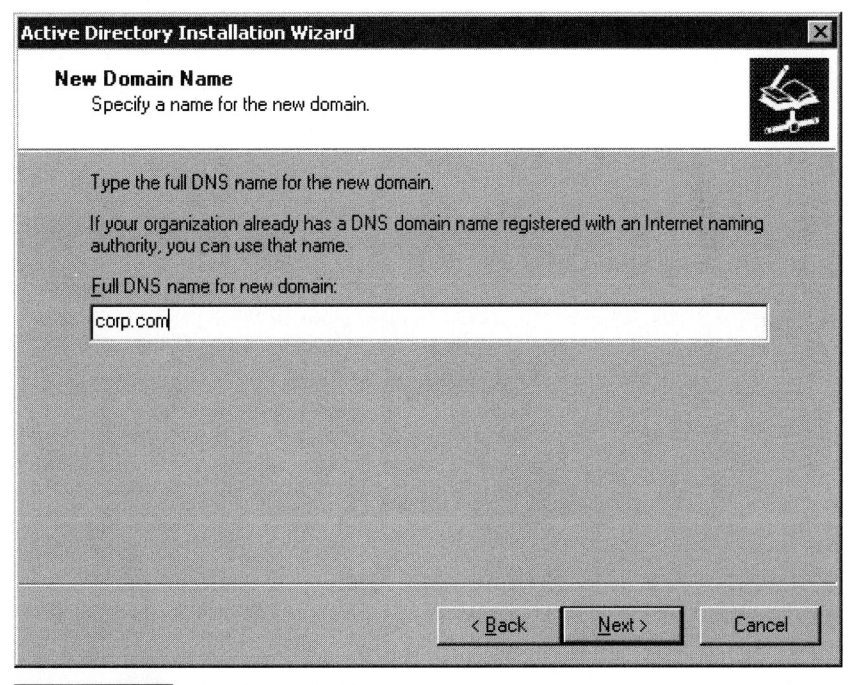

FIGURE 9.4   New Domain Name

8. The Windows NT 4.0 RAS Servers window appears. Windows 2000 recommends that you slightly weaken RAS permissions if those users will access the new domain through Windows NT 4.0 RAS. You can choose to weaken the permissions or not, but it is recommended that you weaken them. Make your selection and click Next.
9. A summary page appears. Review the configuration selections you made and click Next.
10. Set-up configures and starts the Active Directory. This process takes several minutes.
11. When set-up is finished, you are presented with a final wizard page. Click Finish and restart your computer.

Using the Active Directory Administrative Tools

The Active Directory contains four MMC snap-ins that enable you to administer and configure the Active Directory. Each of the snap-ins focuses on a particular aspect of Active Directory configuration and management. The following sections introduce you to each of these and show you the configuration options of each.

Active Directory Users and Computers

The Active Directory Users and Computers snap-in is used to manage and configure user accounts, computers, OUs, and related directory objects. The snap-in is available by clicking Start → Programs → Administrative Tools → Active Directory Users and Computers, as shown in Figure 9.5. From this interface, you can perform a number of tasks.

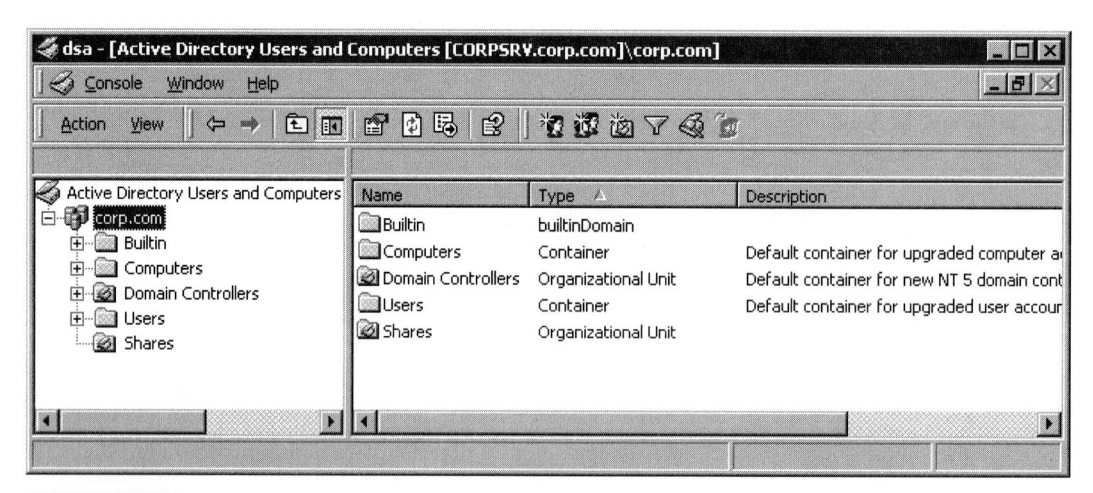

FIGURE 9.5 Active Directory Users and Computers

The following sections focus on various configuration and management options you have in the Active Directory Users and Computers.

ADDING AN ORGANIZATIONAL UNIT

You can easily add an organizational unit to your domain tree by following these steps:

1. In the console tree, expand the domain node.
2. Right-click either the domain node or a folder within the domain node where you want to add an OU.
3. Point to New and click Organizational Unit.
4. Type the name of the OU in the window that appears and click OK.

DELEGATING CONTROL OF AN ORGANIZATIONAL UNIT

One of the benefits of Windows 2000 Server is that it allows you to delegate control of a number of administrative tasks. You can delegate control of an OU to a user or group you select by following these steps:

1. In the console tree, expand the domain node.
2. Right-click the organizational unit and click Delegate Control. The Delegation of Control Wizard begins. Click Next.
3. The next window tells you that you can delegate control of any folder, although it is recommended that you delegate control at the level of the domain or organizational unit. This approach simplifies administration and avoids the problem of having too many people who have control over sub-organizational units. The name of the OU you want to delegate appears in the dialog box. Click Next.
4. The Group or User Selection window appears. You can delegate control of the OU to any user or group you choose. Click the Add button.
5. The User accounts in the domain appear, as shown in Figure 9.6. Select the user or group desired, click the Add button, then click OK.
6. The user or group you selected appears in the Group or User Selection window. Click Next.
7. The Predefined delegations window appears. In this window, as shown in Figure 9.7, you can select what predefined tasks you would like to delegate. Make the selections as desired and click Next.
8. A summary of the selections you have made in the wizard appears. Review your selections and click Finish.

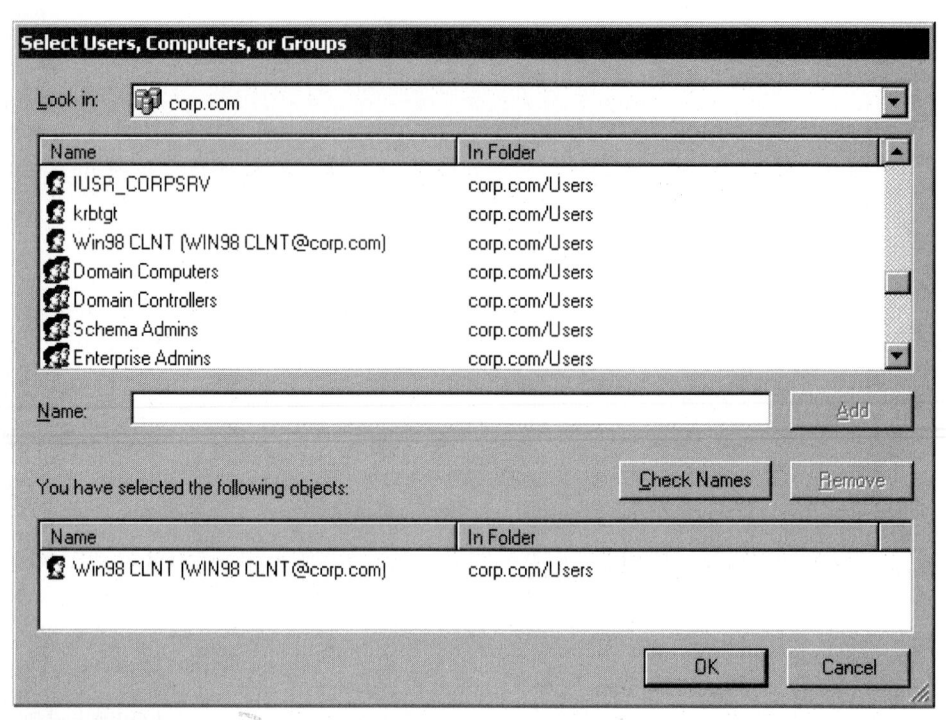

Chapter nine • Configuring the Active Directory

FIGURE 9.6 Group or User Selection

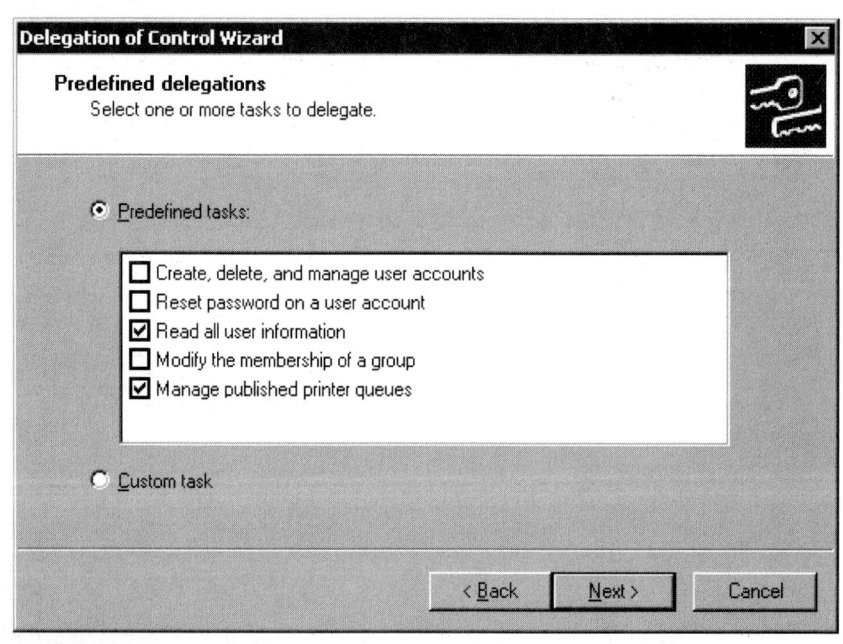

FIGURE 9.7 Predefined Delegations

three • Networking

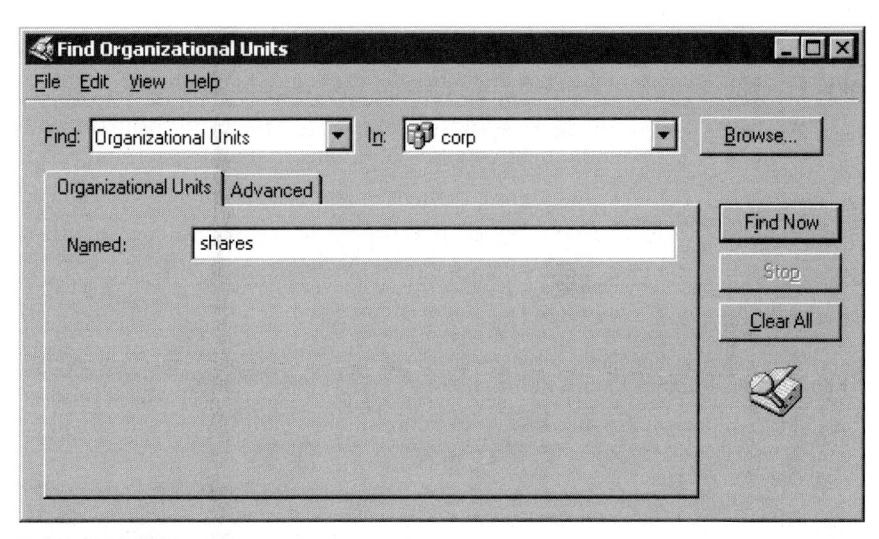

FIGURE 9.8 Find Organizational Units

DELETING AN ORGANIZATIONAL UNIT

You can easily delete an organizational unit as needed by right-clicking on the OU and selecting Delete. You will be asked to confirm the delete order by clicking either Yes or No.

FINDING AN ORGANIZATIONAL UNIT

In large organizations, finding the organizational unit you need could be a time-consuming task. The Active Directory contains a simple find window to help you find the OU desired. To find an OU, follow these steps:

1. In the console tree, right-click the domain node and click Find.
2. The Find Users, Contacts, and Groups window appears. In the Find drop-down menu, select Organizational Units. In the In drop-down menu, select the appropriate domain, or you can search the entire directory if necessary. Type the name of the OU in Named dialog box, as shown in Figure 9.8.
3. Click the Find Now button.

MOVING AN ORGANIZATIONAL UNIT

You can move an organizational unit into another organizational unit or into a different container in the domain tree. To move an OU, follow these steps:

1. In the console tree, expand the domain node.
2. Right-click the OU and click Move.
3. The Move window appears. Expand the domain and select the folder where you want to move the organizational unit. Click OK.

RENAMING AN ORGANIZATIONAL UNIT

You can easily rename an organizational unit by right-clicking it and choosing Rename. Then, type the new name.

CHANGING DOMAIN CONTROLLERS

If you have multiple domain controllers, you can easily change to another domain controller in the Active Directory. To do this, click on the Action menu and click Change Domain Controller, then select the domain controller from the list.

ADDING CONTACTS

You can publish contacts in the Active Directory. This functions a lot like an e-mail address book. If you right-click on the OU where you want to add the contact, point to New, and click Contact, you are given the Create New Object (Contact) window where you can enter the person's name. Once you do this, you can access the contact in the Active Directory. If you right-click on the contact and click Properties, you can input additional information such as the telephone number, e-mail address, organization, home page, and other properties. Once you configure the additional entries, you can access the contact with the Active Directory and by right-clicking on the contact, you can directly send mail or access his or her home page.

ADDING USERS, GROUPS, AND SHARES

You use the Active Directory Users and Computers snap-in to add, remove, and manage users, groups, and shares as well. These topics are covered in detail in Chapter 18.

Active Directory Domains and Trusts

The second administrative tool for managing and configuring the Active Directory is the Active Directory Domains and Trusts snap-in. You can access this snap-in by clicking Start ➤ Programs ➤ Administrative Tools ➤ Active Directory Domains and Trusts. Use this tool to manage domain trust relationships, user principal name suffixes, and to manage domain modes. In addition to these primary tasks, you can also configure support for mixed mode domains (Windows 2000 and Windows NT) and alter the domain controller that performs the single operations master role.

As mentioned previously, a network that has one domain is easier to manage, but this is often impractical in today's complex computing environments. In multiple domain environments, different administrators can administer their own domains which may have different requirements and needs from those of another domain. Also, multiple domains in different geographical locations are often easier to manage. However, the multiple domain model does have more overhead, so your organization should carefully weigh the options before implementing more than one domain. Because of the Active Directory's scalability, multiple domains are often just an organizational issue as opposed to issues with directory services.

If your organization has more than one domain, you can establish a trust relationship between domains that are not a part of your domain's Active Directory. This trust relationship enables user authentication and resource access to the other domain. As with Windows NT, you can establish an external one-way trust relationship, where there is a trusting and a trusted domain. This design access is one way users in the trusted domain can access resources in the trusting domain, but users in the trusting domain cannot access resources in the trusted domain. This relationship between a Windows 2000 Server and a Windows NT Server, is called an external nontransitive trust. A one-way trust is established only between two domains; additional one-way trust must be established if there are other domains as well. This model is used for domains that are not a part of the same tree. You can also create external transitive trusts. In this model, the trust relationship works both ways. The transitive trust is a feature of the Kerberos authentication protocol, and simply means that if Domain 1 trusts Domain 2 and Domain 2 trusts Domain 3, then Domain 1 automatically trusts Domain 3. Domains that reside in the same tree automatically participate in a transitive trust relationship with one another.

The following sections show you how to use and configure various aspects of the Active Directory Domains and Trusts snap-in.

CHANGING THE DOMAIN MODE

Windows 2000 has two domain modes: mixed and native. Mixed mode allows you to use Windows NT domain controllers in a mixed Windows 2000 and Windows NT environment. Once all domain controllers are Windows 2000, the network becomes a pure Windows 2000 network, and you can change the mode to native mode. Mixed mode is enabled by default for backwards compatibility. Once you change your domain mode to native, you can no longer perform down-level replication to NT Servers, you can no longer add new down-level domain controllers to the domain, and all domain controllers begin acting as peers. Once you make the change to native mode, you cannot return to mixed mode. To change your server from mixed mode to native mode, follow these steps:

1. Click Start ➤ Programs ➤ Administrative Tools ➤ Active Directory Domains and Trusts. The snap-in opens.
2. Click the domain you want to administer and click the Action menu, then select Properties. The Domain Properties sheet opens, as shown in Figure 9.9.
3. The Domain Operation tells you that the domain is running in mixed mode. To change the mode, click the Change Mode button.
4. A warning message appears telling you that you cannot change the domain back to mixed mode once the operation is complete. Click Yes to complete the operation or No to cancel.

UPN SUFFIXES

You can use the Active Directory Domains and Trusts snap-in to add user principal name (UPN) suffixes. A UPN suffix is the part of the user principal name that identifies a domain containing the user account. The UPN suffix must be the DNS name of the domain. To add a new UPN suffix, click the

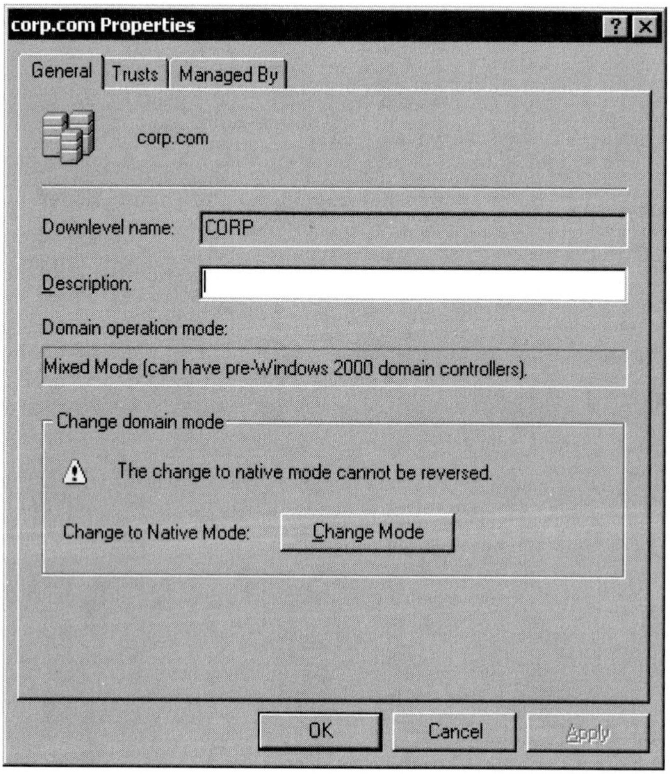

FIGURE 9.9
Domain Properties

Action menu and select Properties. On the UPN Suffixes tab, type an alternative UPN suffix for the domain and click the Add button.

CREATING DOMAIN TRUSTS

To create domain trusts, complete the following steps. These steps must also be completed on the domain that forms the other half of the trust relationship.

1. Click on the domain in which you want to create a trust, click the Action menu, and select Properties.
2. Click on the Trusts tab.
3. To configure the domain as a trusting domain, click Domains trusted by this domain and click the Add button. Supply the DNS name of the domain and the administrator password in the appropriate dialog boxes. To configure the domain as a trusted domain, click Domains that trust this domain and click Add. Supply the DNS name of the domain and the administrator password in the appropriate dialog boxes.

CONNECTING TO ANOTHER DOMAIN CONTROLLER

To connect to another domain controller from within the Active Directory Domains and Trusts snap-in, follow these steps:

1. In the left pane, click the Active Directory Domains and Trusts, then click the Action menu and click Connect to Domain Controller.
2. The Change Domain Controller dialog box appears, as shown in Figure 9.10.
3. You select either the Any DC radio button or the Specify Name button and enter the name of the server. Click OK to connect.

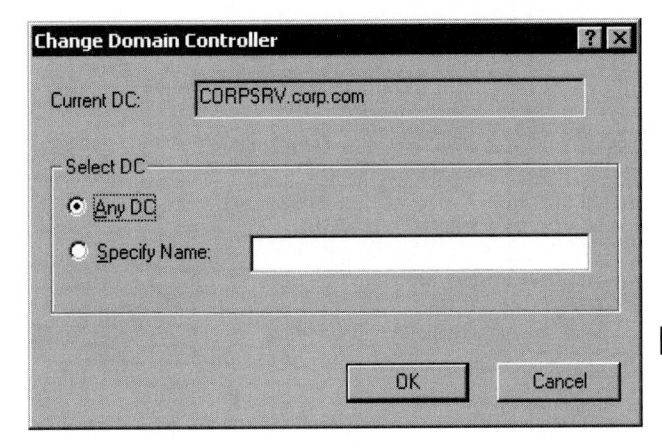

FIGURE 9.10 Change Domain Controller

CHANGING THE OPERATIONS MASTER

The operations master makes certain that all domain names are unique. One server in the enterprise performs this action, and you can use the Active Directory Domains and Trusts snap-in to change the operations master as needed. To change the operations master, follow these steps:

1. In the left pane, select Active Directory Domains and Trusts. Click the Action menu and click Change Operations Master.
2. The Change Operations Master window appears, as shown in Figure 9.11. This window tells you the current operations master and whether or not the master is online. To change the master, click the Change button and make your selection.

Active Directory Sites and Services

A site is physical grouping of computers on a particular subnet. WAN networks use sites to better manage their network structure and directory replication among domain controllers. Typically, different sites reside in different locations, such as a New York site or a Boston site. The Active Directory Sites and Services tool is used to manage physical sites and Active Directory replication between them. It is important not to confuse domains and sites. A domain is a logical grouping of users and computers while a site is a physical grouping of users and computers. A site can contain multiple

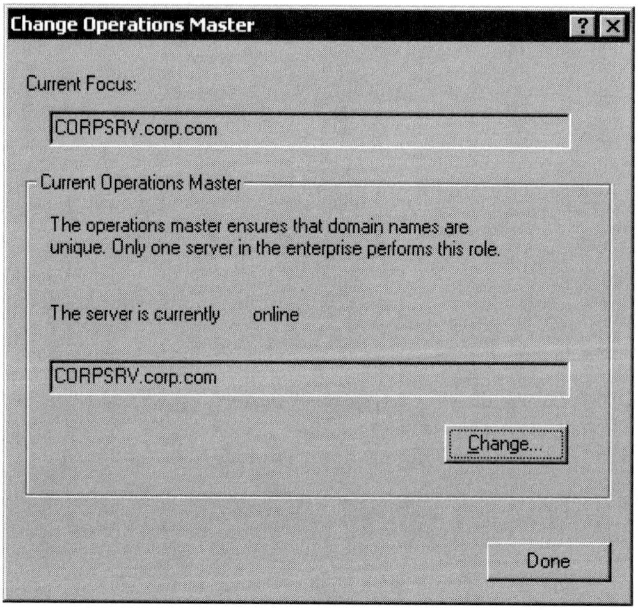

FIGURE 9.11 Change Operations Master

domains if desired. In terms of the Active Directory, users do not browse the network's site structure. Sites are maintained within the Active Directory for administrative purposes, namely directory replication. You can access the sites and services snap-in by clicking Start ➤ Programs ➤ Administrative Tools ➤ Active Directory Sites and Services. The following sections show you the configuration options available.

CREATING A NEW DOMAIN CONTROLLER

To create a new domain controller in a site, follow these steps:

1. In the left pane, expand the Sites folder and expand the site where you want to add the new domain controller.
2. Right-click Servers, point to New, then click Server.
3. You are presented with a dialog box. Enter the new server in the name box and click OK.

SELECTING A QUERY POLICY

To select a query policy, follow these steps:

1. In the left pane, expand the Sites folder, then expand the site folder that contains the domain controller of the policy you want to change.
2. Expand the Server folder and expand the domain controller of the policy you want to change.
3. Right-click NTDS Settings and click Properties, as shown in Figure 9.12. From the drop-down menu, select the query policy you want to use and click OK.

ENABLING OR DISABLING A GLOBAL CATALOG SERVER

You can enable or disable a global catalog server from the Sites and Services snap-in. Follow these steps:

1. In the left pane, expand the Sites folder and expand the site folder that contains the domain controller that you want to make a Global catalog.
2. Expand the server folder and expand the domain controller you want to enable or disable as a global catalog.
3. Right-click NTDS Settings and click Properties. Select the Global Catalog Server check box to enable the global catalog server or deselect it to disable the global catalog server. Click OK.

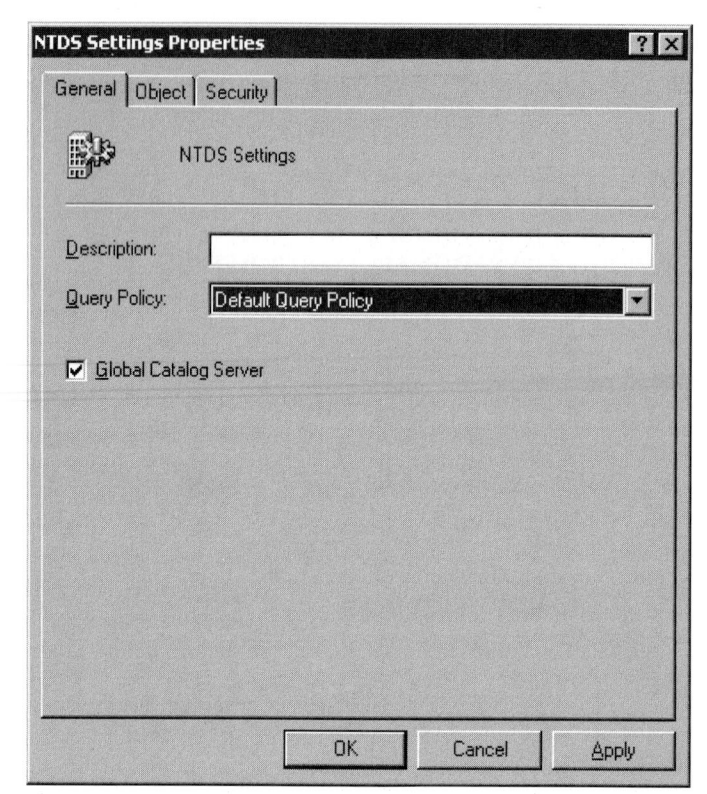

FIGURE 9.12
Query Policy

MOVING A DOMAIN CONTROLLER BETWEEN SITES

You can easily move a domain controller between sites as needed. Simply right-click the domain controller you want to move to a different site and click Move. From the provided list, click the site where you want to move the domain controller and click OK. Each site must contain at least one domain controller, and the move should reflect the site on which the domain controller physically resides.

DESIGNATING A PREFERRED BRIDGEHEAD SERVER

A preferred bridgehead server handles the replication data transfer to and from a site. The bridgehead server then sends this data to the other domain controllers in the site. To designate a server as a preferred bridgehead server, follow these steps:

1. Expand the Sites folder and expand the site that contains the domain controller that you want to make a preferred bridgehead server.
2. Expand the Servers folder and right-click the domain controller you want to make a preferred bridgehead server and click Properties.

3. Click the transport(s) you want the server to use for the preferred bridgehead, and click the Add button to move them to the preferred bridgehead window, as shown in Figure 9.13. Click OK when you are done.

REPAIRING A DOMAIN CONTROLLER

You can use the Sites and Services snap-in to attempt to repair a domain controller by following these steps:

1. Expand the Sites folder and expand the site that contains the domain controller you want to repair.
2. Expand the Servers folder and expand the domain controller you want to repair.
3. Right-click NTDS Settings, point to All Tasks and click Repair Domain Controller. Click the components of the domain controller that need to be repaired and click OK.

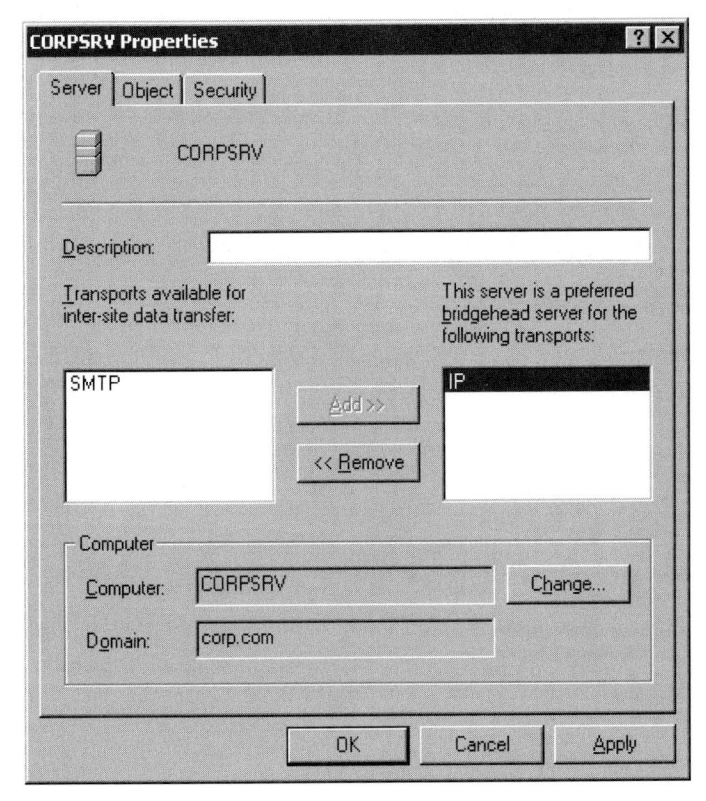

FIGURE 9.13 Server Properties

REMOVE A NONOPERATIONAL SERVER

You can easily remove a nonoperational server from a site by expanding the site, selecting the domain controller, and using the Action Menu, click Delete.

CHANGING FORESTS

You can change to a different forest in the Sites and Services snap-in by right-clicking Active Directory Sites and Services and pointing to Change Forest. In the root domain, enter the new forest.

CHECKING REPLICATION TOPOLOGY

You can check the replication topology by following these steps:

1. Expand the Sites folder and expand the site that contains the domain controller you want to check.
2. Expand Servers and expand the server you want to check.
3. Right-click NTDS Settings and click Check Replication Topology from All Tasks. The replication is checked and reported to you.

CREATING AND RENAMING A SITE

You can create a new site by right-clicking the Sites folder and clicking New Site. You will need to name the new site and assign a site link object as prompted. Next, associate a subnet for the new site and move a domain controller to this new site. Once the site is created, you can right-click the site to perform various actions, such as delegate control, rename, or delete a site.

CREATING A SUBNET

You can create a new subnet by expanding the Sites folder and right-clicking the Subnets folder. Click New Subnet. In the name box, type the network/bits-masked name and select a site object for the subnet, as shown in Figure 9.14. Of course, subnets created must reflect actual subnets that exist in your network. Once the subnet is created, you can right-click it to get the properties sheet where you can further refine the configuration.

CONFIGURING INTER-SITE TRANSPORTS

An inter-site transports is a link you configure that connects two or more sites. If you expand the Inter-Site Transports container, you will see containers for IP or SMTP. If you expand the IP container, you will see the Default IP Site Link, which contains all of your configured sites. You can also create new site links by right-clicking the IP container and clicking New Site link.

FIGURE 9.14 Create New (Subnet)

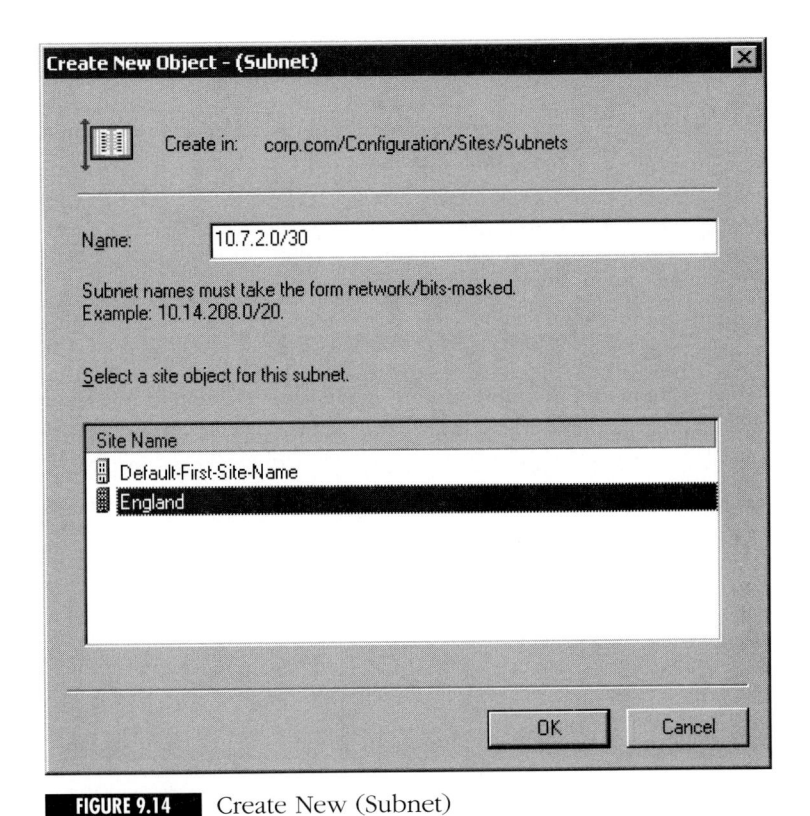

In the window provided, select the sites you want to include in the new site link and use the Add button to move them to the Sites in the Site Link window. There must be at least two sites to configure a site link.

Site links link two or more sites, and site link bridges link two or more site links. You can create site link bridges by right-clicking on the IP container and clicking New Site Link Bridge. In the same manner as sites, move the Site links you want to bridge into the Site Links in this Site Link Bridge window using the Add button. As with all components of this tool, you should carefully plan how you will link your sites together and how you will connect your site links using bridges. The goal is to make certain that all sites are connected for replication.

SELECTING A DIFFERENT LICENSING COMPUTER

The Active Directory automatically configures a licensing computer for the site, and the computer does not have to be a domain controller. For performance sake, it's best if the licensing computer resides in the same site. To change the licensing computer, follow these steps:

1. Expand the Sites folder and click the site whose licensing information you want to configure.
2. Right-click Licensing Site Settings. This action displays the Properties dialog box. Click Change to select an alternate computer.

Active Directory Schema

The Active Directory schema is a list of definitions, called metadata, that determines what objects and what attributes for those objects are stored in the Active Directory. You can alter and change the Active Directory schema using the Active Directory Schema Manager MMC snap-in, which is available in the Windows 2000 Resource Kit on your Windows 2000 CD-ROM. This section will give you a brief overview of the Schema Manager and how it functions, but it should be noted here that modifying the Active Directory schema requires careful planning and can cause extensive problems if the schema is modified incorrectly. Therefore, schema modification should be left to highly skilled administrators and programmers.

The Active Directory Schema manager is available on the Windows 2000 Resource Kit on your CD-ROM. To use the Schema manager, you must install the resource kit. Access your CD-ROM, open the Support folder, then open the Reskit folder. Double-click Setup to install the resource kit. Once the resource kit is installed, you can access it by clicking Start ➔ Programs ➔ Resource Kit. You have online books or tools management console to choose from. Select the Tools Management console.

Expand the Microsoft Resource Kits container in the left pane, expand Windows 2000 Resource Kit, then expand Tools A to Z. Double click Active Directory Schema. The Schema Manager opens.

The console contains the Schema manager root, and containers for classes and attributes. From this management tool, you can define new classes and associate those classes with attributes, or you can alter attributes. As mentioned earlier, schema modification is a complex and serious action, and it is beyond the scope of this book to explain development of the Active Directory. Microsoft recommends that modification of the schema be performed only when absolutely necessary due to the serious implications throughout the directory. By default, write access to the schema is limited to members of the Schema Administrators Group that exist in the forest root domain. Schema modification should be left to those individuals with proper training and expertise in directory development.

Summary

This chapter gave you an overview of the Active Directory and explored the configuration of the Active Directory using the four Active Directory administrative tools. Remember that most major Windows 2000 Server components are integrated with the Active Directory. Later chapters discuss the configuration of those functions and services individually.

TEN

Configuring Network Communication

A protocol is a set of rules that define how computers communicate with each other on a network. Without these rules of communication behavior, network communication would be hopeless and computers would not be able to communicate with each other. You will not see a lot of differences in the way you configure and manage protocols in Windows 2000 Server from Windows NT, but you will see some new network communication features. This chapter explains these features and shows you how to configure network communication.

Installing Protocols in Windows 2000 Server

You install protocols in Windows 2000 Server in much the same way as you did in Windows NT. You can do this by opening My Network Places, then right-clicking Local Area Connection and clicking Properties. The Properties interface gives you a General Property Sheet, which is different from Windows NT, but will look very familiar if you have used Windows 98. The General Property Sheet is shown in Figure 10.1.

The selected components show you which protocols and servers are currently in use by the local area connection. You can select any component and click Uninstall to remove it, and you can select any component and click Properties to view the Properties sheet for that particular component. If you click the Install button, Windows presents you with a Select Network

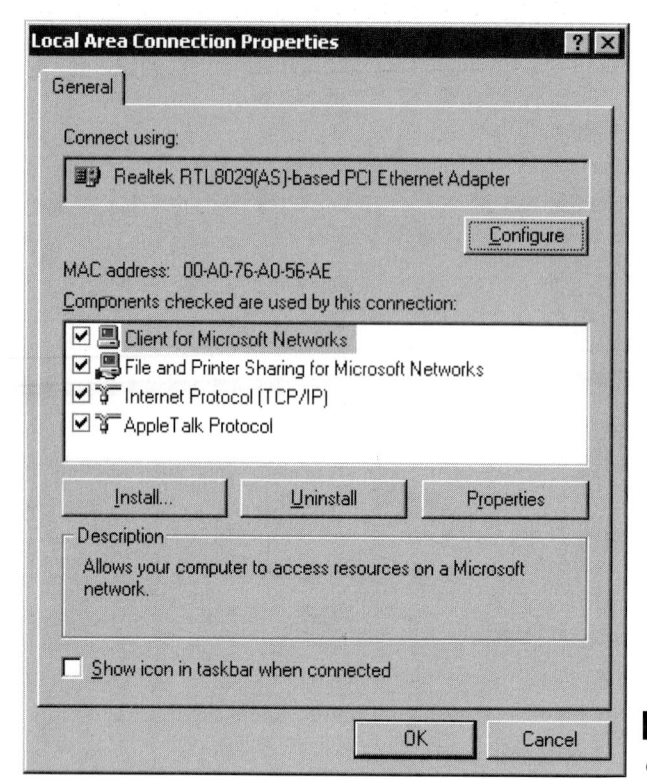

FIGURE 10.1
General Properties tab

Component Type dialog box so that you can select the type of component you want to install. Click Protocol and click the Add button. Windows generates a list of protocols that can be added to the system. From the provided list, simply select the protocol you want to install and click OK. Windows will install the protocol and may prompt you for the location of the set-up files if necessary. You may have to reboot your system. Since all protocols are installed in this same way, the rest of the chapter focuses on configuring various protocols that you may choose to install.

TCP/IP

TCP/IP (Transmission Control Protocol/Internet Protocol) is the de facto standard for Internet communication, and over the past several years, TCP/IP has become the network protocol of choice for local area networks. This is due in part to LAN integration with the Internet and TCP/IP's scalability. TCP/IP is rather complex and it is beyond the scope of this book to explain the structure and features of TCP/IP. The next section does, however, give you a general review of TCP/IP, its components, and new features supported in Windows 2000.

TCP/IP Review

TCP/IP is a protocol suite, which means it is made up of many individual protocols that all function together. These individual protocols provide you with vast functionality for many services and features. There are over 100 protocols in the TCP/IP protocol suite, and Table 10.1 reviews some of the major ones.

TABLE 10.1 Common TCP/IP Protocols

Protocol	Explanation
TCP	Transmission Control Protocol. TCP is responsible for connection-oriented transmissions.
IP	Internet Protocol. IP provides connectionless packet delivery.
UDP	User Datagram Protocol. UDP provides connectionless communication and does not guarantee that packets will be delivered.
SMTP	Simple Mail Transfer Protocol. SMTP provides e-mail delivery services.
NNTP	Network News Transfer Protocol. NNTP provides news services.
FTP	File Transfer Protocol. Provides file transfer and directory management.
HTTP	Hypertext Transfer Protocol. HTTP is responsible for delivery of HTML documents.
ICMP	Internet Control Message Protocol. ICMP is used by TCP/IP utilities to request certain responses from network components.
Telnet	Telnet provides terminal emulation services.

TCP/IP functions by using three major components that must be configured for each TCP/IP client on the network:

- IP Address: An IP address is a 32-bit address that identifies the host. The computer's IP address is different from all other computer IP addresses on the network and is represented as an octet, such as 10.0.0.2. The IP is made up of the host ID and the network ID.
- Subnet Mask: A subnet mask hides the network portion of the IP address from the host portion of the IP address. In networks that use multiple subnets, the subnet mask determines to which subnet a particular host belongs.
- Default Gateway: The default gateway is the IP address of the computer or router that can send packets to another subnet or network.

When configuring any computer on a TCP/IP network, at least the IP address and a default subnet mask must be supplied. Windows 2000 Server provides you with three ways to accomplish this task:

- **Manual:** you can manually assign an IP address, subnet mask, and default gateway for each computer. This method is impractical in large networks for the general client population, but you should consider assigning a static IP address to your servers so that their IP addresses will not change.
- **Dynamic:** You can use Dynamic Host Configuration Protocol (DHCP) to dynamically assign an IP address to network client computers. To learn more about DHCP and DHCP configuration, see Chapter 11.
- **Automatic Private IP Addressing:** Windows 2000 Server includes a new feature that allows you to implement an automatic private IP address to network clients. This method is effective in small environments so that manual configuration or use of DHCP is not needed. The automatic private IP feature automatically assigns network clients an IP address in the range of 169.254.0.0 to 169.254.255.255, which is a reserved IP address range established by the Internet Corporate for Assigned Names and Numbers (ICANN). This way, clients can use an IP address that will not conflict with other routable addresses.

As in Windows NT, you still have access to the wide assortment of TCP/IP utilities that help you manage and troubleshoot TCP/IP, such as PING, IPCONFIG, NETSTAT, and ARP.

Configuring TCP/IP

You configure TCP/IP on Windows 2000 Server in the same way you did in Windows NT. In My Network Places, right-click the connection you want to configure and click Properties. Select Internet Protocol in the list and click Properties. The Internet Protocol Properties sheet appears as shown in Figure 10.2.

By default, the Obtain an IP address automatically radio button is selected. When this radio button is selected, the computer attempts to locate a DHCP server for an IP address. If the computer cannot locate a DHCP server, then the computer uses AutoNet to assign itself an automatic private IP address in the 169.254.0.0 to 169.254.255.255 address range so that it can have connectivity on the network. The automatic private IP addressing feature is enabled by default in Windows 2000, but you can disable it using the registry if you prefer to do so. To disable the automatic private IP addressing feature, open regedt32 and navigate to HKEY_LOCAL_MACHINE\SYSTEM\CurrentControlSet\Services\Tcpip\Parameters\Interfaces\adapter_name, then create an entry called IPAutoconfigurationEnabled: Reg_DWORD and assign a value of 0 to the selected network adapter.

If you need to manually configure the TCP/IP settings for the computer, which is often necessary for servers, then you should enter a unique IP address and an appropriate subnet mask as well as default gateway if needed. Additionally, the server can obtain the DNS server address automatically

FIGURE 10.2 Internet Protocol Properties

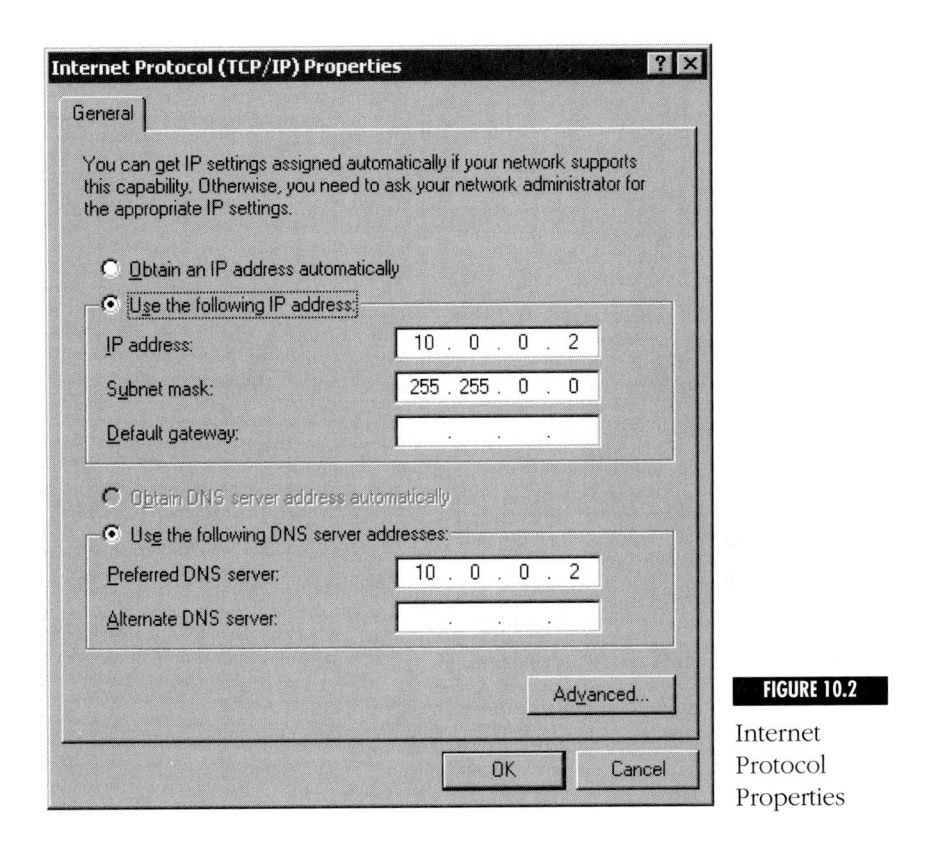

or you can manually enter the IP address of the DNS server and an alternate server if one exists.

If you click the Advanced button, you have some additional configuration options. First, you have an IP Settings tab. On this tab, you can add or change the IP address(es) or default gateway(s) for your server. By using the Add, Edit, or Remove buttons, you can configure these values as needed. The DNS tab allows you to specify the DNS server use order so that you can configure a certain DNS server to appear at the top of the list. You also have some additional DNS settings you can configure which will be discussed in Chapter 12. The WINS tab enables you to perform the same kind of configuration, and you can learn more about WINS in Windows 2000 in Chapter 13. Finally, the Options tab enables you to further configure optional settings such as IP security and TCP/IP filtering, as shown in Figure 10.3.

If you select an item in the list and click the Properties button, you can further configure the component. For example, with IP security, you can choose not to use IP security, or you can select a security policy to use by clicking the appropriate radio button. TCP/IP filtering allows you to restrict TCP, UDP, and IP ports if you desire to do so. You can learn more about TCP/IP security features in Windows 2000 Server in Chapter 17.

FIGURE 10.3
TCP/IP Advanced Options

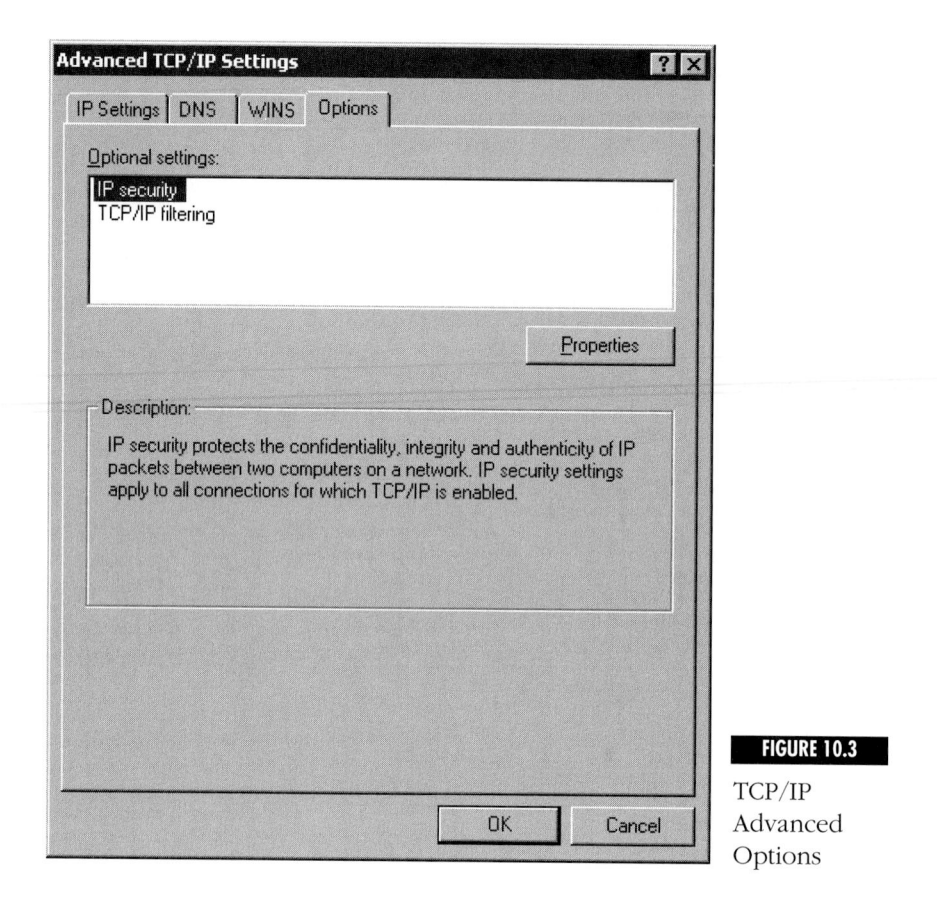

Installing and Configuring TCP/IP Simple Services

TCP/IP simple services provide you with Windows 2000 utilities software to support optional TCP/IP services that are known as "elective" Internet standards. Typically, you do not need TCP/IP simple services unless you need your server to support communication with other systems that use the services offered in Simple TCP/IP. The optional services provided with TCP/IP Simple Services are Character Generator (CHARGEN), which sends data in ASCII printable characters; and Daytime, which returns messages containing the day of the week, month, year, and current time. Next, simple TCP/IP services include Discard, which discards all messages received on a particular port without a response; Echo, which echoes back data from any messages it receives on a particular server port; and Quote of the Day, which returns a quotation as one or more lines in a text message.

To install TCP/IP simple services, follow these steps:

1. Right-click My Network Places and click Properties.
2. In the Network and Dial-up Connections window, click the Advanced tab and click Optional Networking Components.
3. In the Scroll box, double-click Network Services.
4. Click the Simple TCP/IP Services check box and click OK.
5. Click Next.
6. Setup configures the component and prompts you for the location of the setup files.
7. Click Finish.

NWLink

NWLink is Microsoft's answer to communication in mixed Microsoft and Novell networks. The NWLink protocol is Microsoft's implementation of Novell's Internetwork Packet Exchange/Sequenced Packet Exchange (IPX/SPX) protocol and is used in NetWare environments. With NWLink, you can allow your Windows clients to access NetWare servers and you can allow NetWare clients to access Windows 2000.

As in Windows NT, you will need to install File and Print Services for NetWare (FPNW) on the Windows 2000 Server to allow NetWare clients access to file and print resources (see Chapter 15), and you configure the NWLink protocol the same way in Windows 2000 as you did in Windows NT.

Once the NWLink protocol is installed, you can configure it by selecting it from the Local Area Connection Properties list, then clicking the Properties button. This takes you to a General Property sheet, as shown in Figure 10.4.

There are three components involved in configuring NWLink: frame type, network number, and internal network number. The network number and frame type are automatically selected by Windows 2000 when you install NWLink, and a generic internal network number is also supplied by default, as you can see in Figure 10.4. If you run FPNW, IPX routing, or any other NetWare service that uses the Service Advertising Protocol (SAP) agent, you will need to change this default internal number to a correct internal number for your network.

The Frame Type tells the computer how the network adapter card should format the data. This frame type must match the frame type of the NetWare server for communication to take place, and this is a common communication error in mixed Microsoft and Novell environments. Windows will attempt an auto detection for the network frame type, but

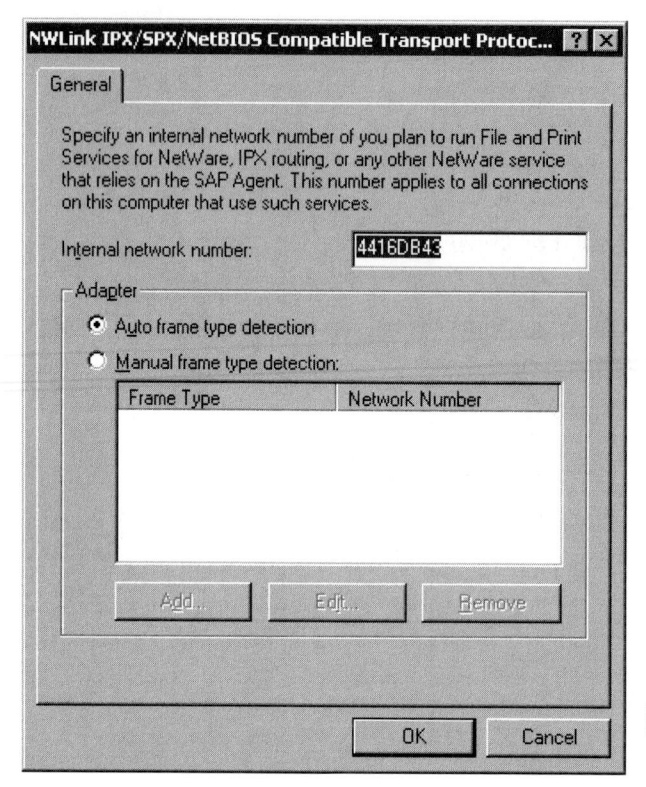

FIGURE 10.4

NWLink Properties

you can also click the manual frame type detection and enter the appropriate frame type by using the Add button. For example, the typical frame type for an Ethernet network is either 802.3 or 802.2, depending on the version of NetWare that is running. Consult the NetWare documentation for more information about frame types.

The Network Number is required for each frame type and must be unique for each segment in the network. All computers on the same segment must use the same network number for communication to take place. Windows 2000 automatically detects a network number during NWLink installation, and you use the *ipxroute config* command at the command prompt to gain this information, as shown in Figure 10.5.

Using Other Protocols

Windows 2000 supports a number of additional protocols that provide you with connectivity to other systems and services. The following sections gives you an overview of these.

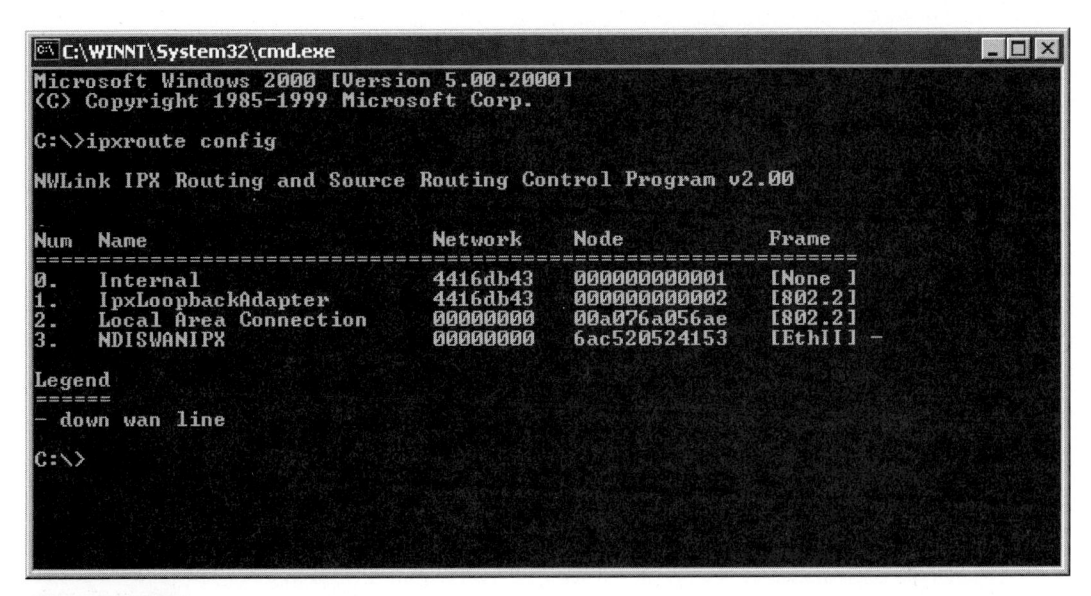

```
C:\WINNT\System32\cmd.exe

Microsoft Windows 2000 [Version 5.00.2000]
(C) Copyright 1985-1999 Microsoft Corp.

C:\>ipxroute config

NWLink IPX Routing and Source Routing Control Program v2.00

Num  Name                     Network    Node           Frame
===============================================================
0.   Internal                 4416db43   000000000001   [None ]
1.   IpxLoopbackAdapter       4416db43   000000000002   [802.2]
2.   Local Area Connection    00000000   00a076a056ae   [802.2]
3.   NDISWANIPX               00000000   6ac520524153   [EthII] -

Legend
======
- down wan line

C:\>
```

FIGURE 10.5 Ipxroute config

NetBEUI

NetBIOS Extended User Interface (NetBEUI) is a small, fast protocol that was developed by IBM for workgroups and small LANs. NetBEUI is not routable, so it has widely been replaced by TCP/IP implementations. Windows 2000 still supports NetBEUI for backwards compatibility and it can be installed in the same way as other protocols. There are no configuration options for the protocol.

AppleTalk

The AppleTalk protocol allows clients running Macintosh systems to connect to a Windows 2000 Server if Services for Macintosh are also installed. Windows 2000 now supports connectivity with Macintosh clients running TCP/IP. For more information about connectivity with Macintosh, see Chapter 15.

DLC

Data Link Control (DLC) allows communication with IBM mainframes and some print devices such as some Hewlett-Packard printers that can connect directly to the network. DLC is still supported in Windows 2000, and there are no configuration options once installation is complete.

Network Monitor Driver

The Network Monitor Driver allows operability of the Network Monitor Agent that can be used to collect and display network statistics for your server.

Streams Environment

The Streams Environment protocol allows transport drivers in Streams environments, such as UNIX, to port to Windows.

Adjusting Protocol Bindings

"Bindings" allow protocols and services to function with particular network adapter card(s) in your server. If a protocol or service is bound to the network adapter card, the network adapter card can use that protocol or service for communication and functionality. The same protocol or service can be bound to several network adapter cards if necessary.

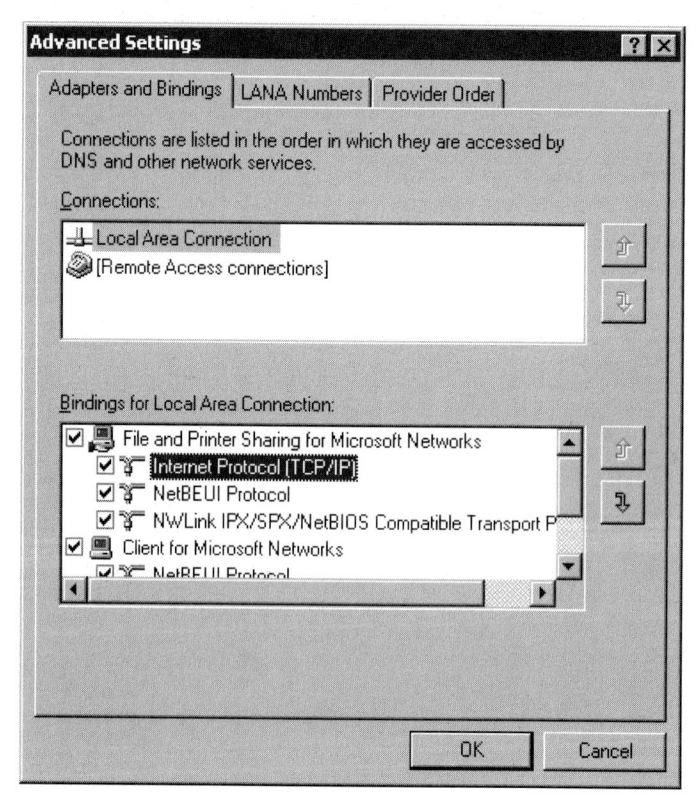

FIGURE 10.6
Advanced Settings

You can make adjustments to the bindings of your network adapter cards as needed, and you can also adjust the binding order of a particular card. This action is useful for performance purposes since you should have the protocols and services you most commonly use bound at the top of the list. Because the computer will attempt connectivity with the protocol bound first, then the protocol bound second, and so forth, the most commonly used protocol should appear first in the list.

You can easily make these adjustments by right-clicking My Network Places and clicking Properties. In the Network and Dial-up Connections window, click on the Advanced menu and select Advanced Settings. The Advanced Settings window appears, as shown in Figure 10.6.

To adjust the binding order, simply select the appropriate connection in the Connections window, then click on the protocol you want to adjust and use the arrow buttons to move it up or down in the list. You can also unbind a protocol from an adapter by clearing the check box next to the protocol. Once you do this, the adapter will not be able to use the protocol.

Quality of Service (QoS) Admission Control

Although protocols enable network communication, complex networks today are often in need of communication control. With the amount of network traffic and the types of advanced traffic, conserving bandwidth is often an issue. Quality of Service (QoS) Admission Control gives you the ability to decide how subnet resources are used, when they are used, and who can use them. In other words, QoS allows you to manage network bandwidth at the subnet level. This is accomplished through policy-based administration so that you can determine how network bandwidth is used and who can reserve it. This service is particularly useful to control applications, such as real-time multimedia, that may consume more bandwidth than the subnet can handle. QoS is based on the Subnet Bandwidth Management (SBM) standard, and all clients that are SBM enabled can use the QoS to request priority bandwidth. SBM enabled clients are Windows 2000, Windows 98 and any client running the SMB client software.

However, QoS poses some deployment problems in that every piece of hardware on the network must support QoS. This includes switches, routers, and client computers. When all equipment supports the service, it provides better network quality by giving more bandwidth to applications that need it while reducing bandwidth for background processes that are not time critical.

Installing QoS

You can install QoS by following these steps:

1. Access Add/Remove Programs in Control Panel.
2. Click Add/Remove Windows Components.
3. On the Windows Components page, double-click Networking Services, then select QoS Admission Control Service from the list.
4. Click OK, then click Next.
5. The service is installed.
6. Click Finish.

Installing the Packet Scheduler

You will need to install the QoS packet scheduler on all end-systems that make reservations on the QoS subnet. To install the packet scheduler, follow these steps:

1. Right-click My Network Places and click Properties.
2. Right-click the local area connection you want to use and click Properties.
3. Click the Install button.
4. Select Service, then click the Add button.
5. Select the QoS Packet Scheduler from the list and click OK.
6. The Service is installed. Click the Close button.

Configuring QoS Policies

To start the QoS Admission Control snap-in, click Start → Programs → Administrative Tools → QoS Admission Control. The snap-in opens, which contains a container for Enterprise settings and one for Subnetwork Settings, as shown in Figure 10.7.

The first action you will need to take is to create QoS subnets. Your local subnet may already appear, or you may need to add subnets on your network that will be QoS subnets. If you expand the Subnetwork Settings container, you can see any subnets that currently exist. To add a new subnet, right-click on the Subnetwork Settings Container and click Add Subnetwork. A dialog box appears asking for the IP address of the subnet you want to create. Enter the IP address and click OK.

Once you have subnets added, you need to access the properties pages for the subnet and configure QoS properties. Right-click on the subnet you want to configure and click Properties. The properties sheets appear with five tabs.

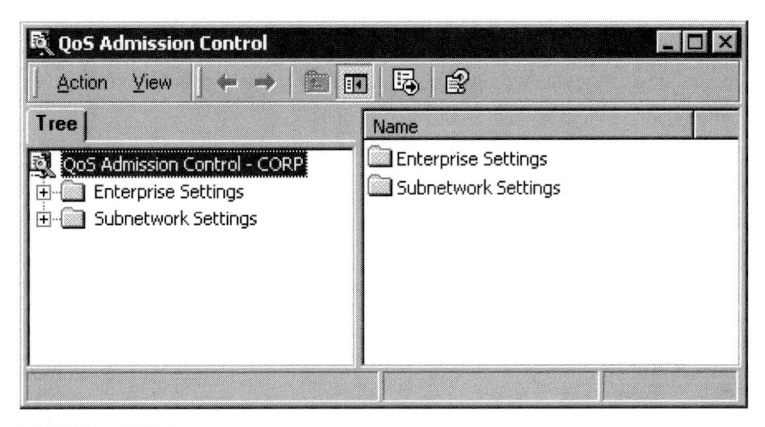

FIGURE 10.7   QoS Admission Control

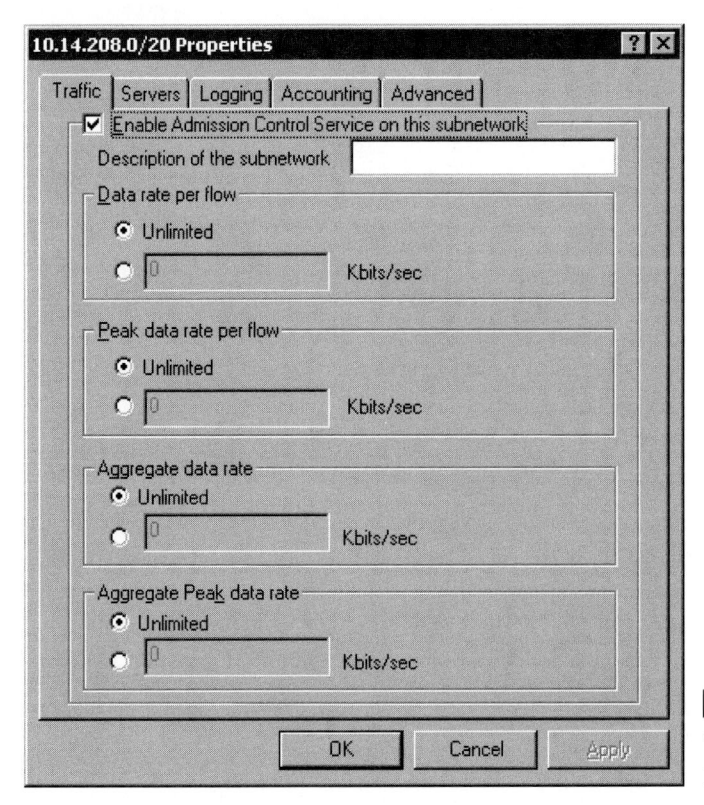

FIGURE 10.8 Traffic Properties

On the Traffic Property sheet, as shown in Figure 10.8, you can check the Enable Admission Control Service on this subnetwork check box to enable QoS. You can enter a description of the network if desired. In the next several sections, you can use the radio buttons to specify traffic

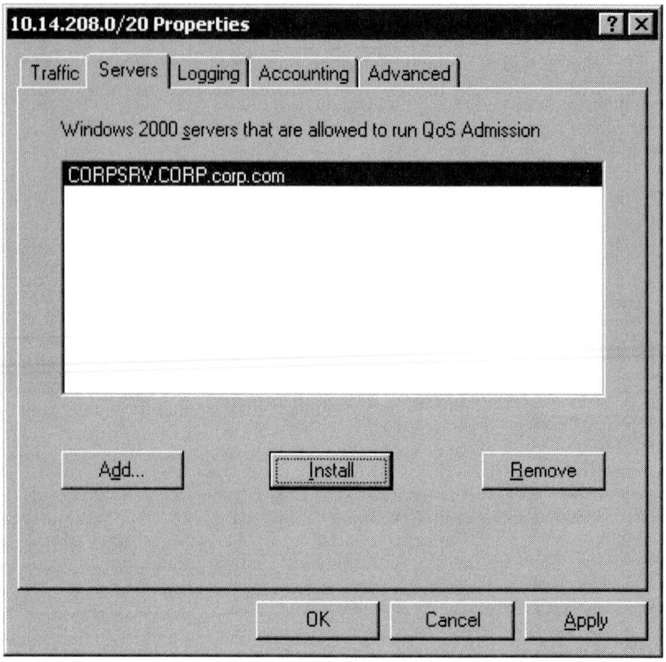

FIGURE 10.9
Server Properties

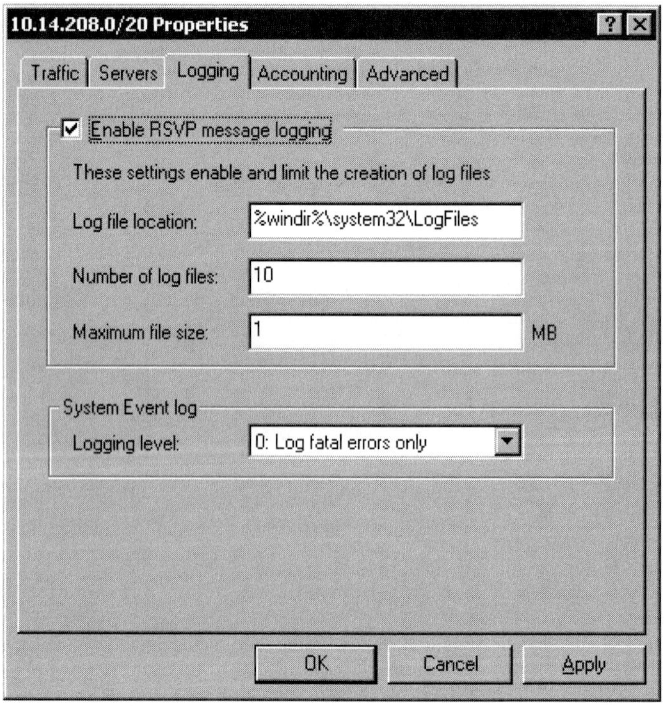

FIGURE 10.10
Logging Properties

amounts. The defaults for all settings is "unlimited," but you can specify a maximum amount in kilobytes.

On the Servers Properties sheet, you can add which servers are allowed to run the QoS Admission control service, as shown in Figure 10.9. Use the Add, Remove, and Install buttons to make your changes.

On the Logging Properties sheet, you can choose to enable RSVP message logging and specify log file locations. RSVP logging records all QoS bandwidth reservations made by QoS clients. The Logging Property sheet is shown in Figure 10.10.

Next, the Accounting Properties sheet allows you to log accounting activities for QoS. This feature gives you the opportunity to see who is using network resources and information about those sessions, such as duration and addressing information. Click the Enable Accounting checkbox, as shown in Figure 10.11, to use this option.

The Advanced Properties sheet allows you to configure the designated subnet bandwidth manager (DSBM) properties. These properties include election priority, keep alive intervals, dead interval, and so forth. The DSBM also checks for new policy information in the Active Directory. The default is every 30 minutes. The Advanced Properties sheet is shown in Figure 10.12.

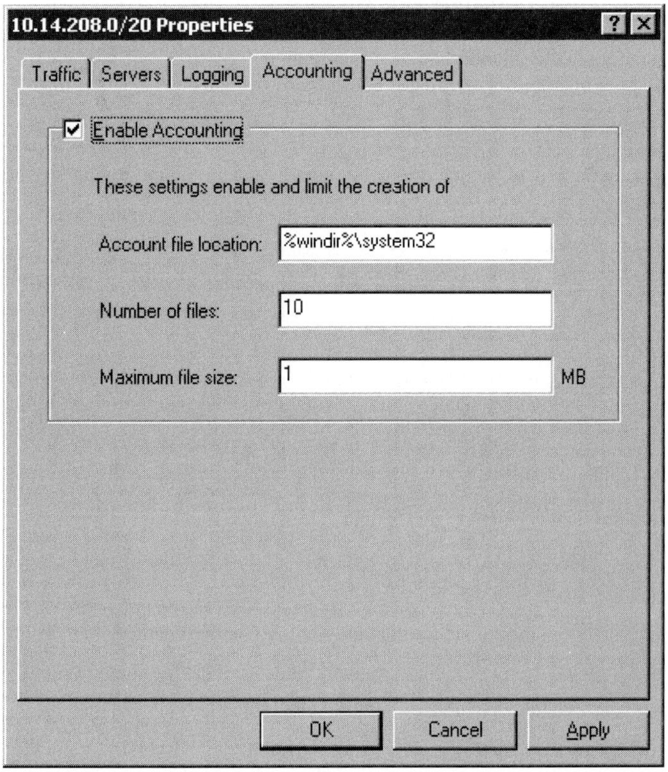

FIGURE 10.11 Accounting Properties

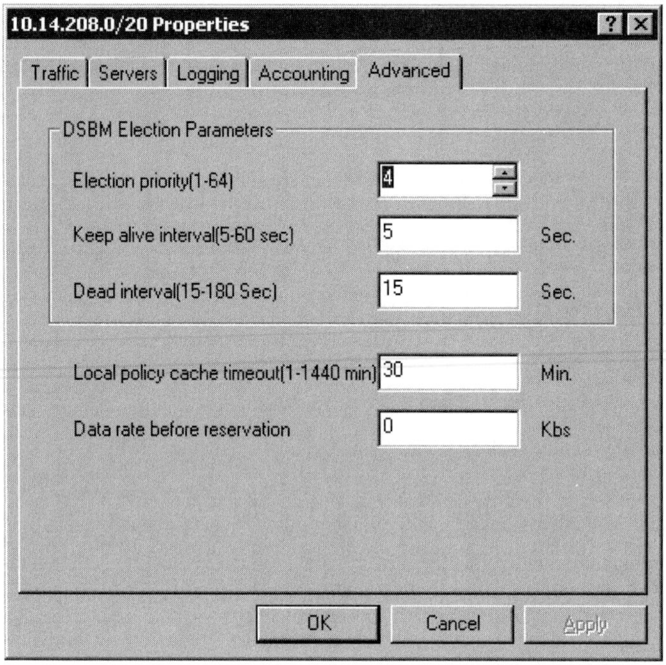

Chapter ten • Configuring Network Communication

FIGURE 10.12
Advanced Properties

Once you have the subnets configured, the next step is to configure the QoS policies for the subnets. The policies determine what QoS actions users can perform. You can configure the policies at the enterprise level or on a per subnet basis. To configure policies at the enterprise level, use the Enterprise settings container, and to configure polices at the subnet level, use the Subnetwork container. The default polices for the enterprise or for each subnet contain an un-authenticated user policy and an Any authenticated user policy. All properties sheets for the polices are the same.

If you double-click one of the policies in the details pane, you see General, Flow limits, and Aggregate limits tabs. On the General Properties page, you can control the flow direction by using the drop-down menu. You can select either send, receive, or send and receive. The send and receive option enforces QoS settings whether the user is sending or receiving data. Next, you can adjust the service level. You can select Best Effort, which gives no guarantee of adequate network resources, Controlled Load, which helps control network congestion, or Guaranteed Service, which guarantees network resources, or you can select All to use all of the Service options.

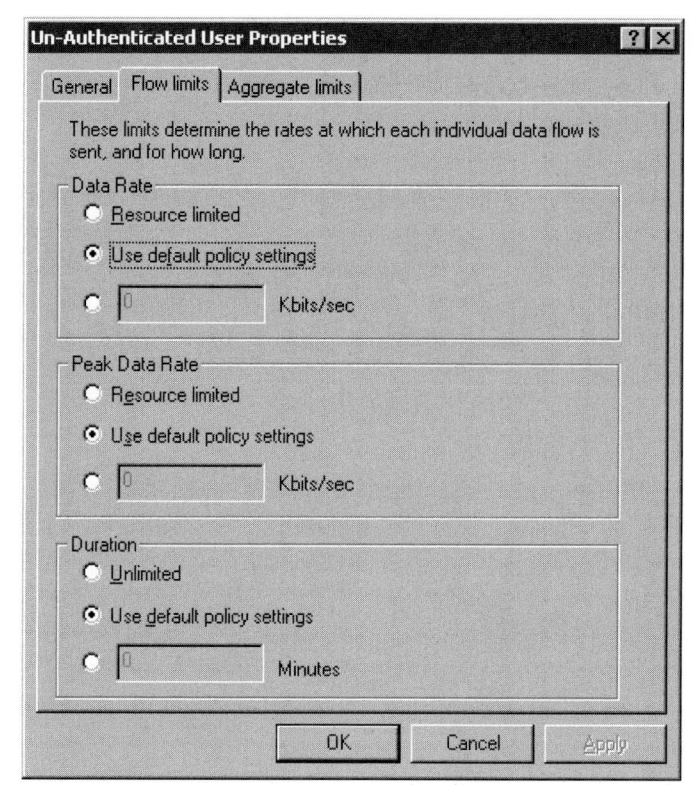

FIGURE 10.13
Flow Limits Properties

On the Flow Limits Properties sheet, you can adjust the flow limits for each data flow, or you can use the default policy settings. If you adjust these settings, you can alter the data rate, peak data rate, and the duration of the data flow by using the appropriate radio buttons. Figure 10.13 shows the Flow Limits Properties sheet.

The final sheet, Aggregate Limits, as shown in Figure 10.14, allows you to adjust settings for the number of flows that are allowed as well as the total data flow rates.

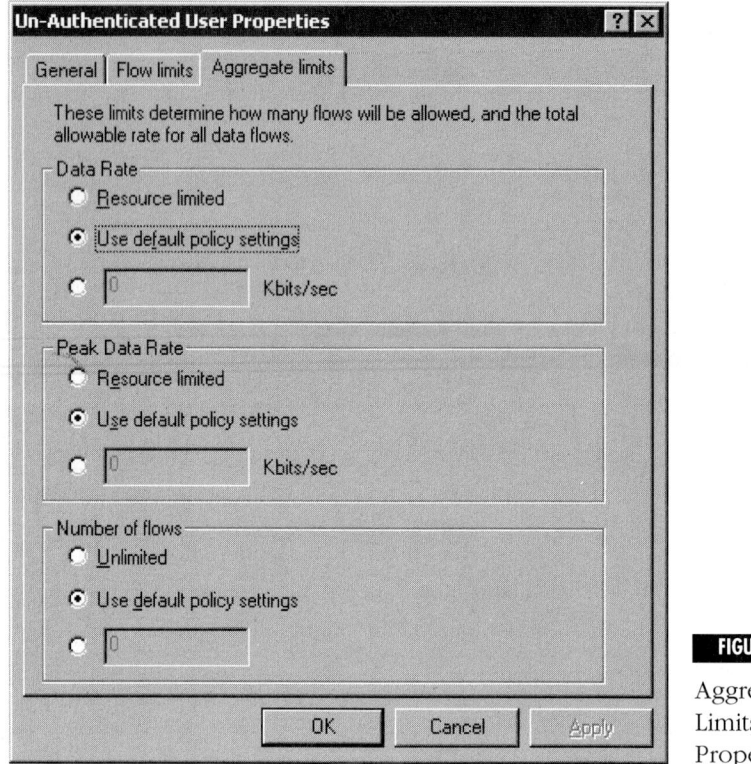

FIGURE 10.14
Aggregate Limits Properties

Summary

Configuring network protocols in Windows 2000 is easy. If you are using TCP/IP, proper planning will reduce potential problems with implementation, and other protocols should not be installed or bound if they are not needed in your network. Fortunately, you can easily add, remove, or adjust the bindings for network protocols and services as needed in Windows 2000. Windows 2000 also provides additional network communication support with QoS.

E L E V E N

Installing and Configuring DHCP

Dynamic Host Configuration Protocol (DHCP) is a TCP/IP standard designed to dynamically assign IP addresses and IP information to network clients. DHCP eliminates the need for manual TCP/IP client configuration, which greatly reduces administrative overhead by reducing the possibility of IP address errors or duplicate IP addresses. DCHP is an extension of the BOOTP protocol that enables diskless clients to automatically configure TCP/IP. Each time a network client starts, the DHCP Server is contacted so that it can provide an IP address, subnet mask, and other optional components such as a default gateway and DNS server address. This chapter shows you how to install and configure DHCP on your Windows 2000 Server.

How DHCP Works

Each network client must have a unique IP address and correct subnet mask information. The DHCP server can dynamically assign this information to network clients by leasing an IP address for a specified period of time. The leased IP address is taken from a pool of IP addresses that you configure. The DHCP server keeps track of the leased IP addresses as well as the IP addresses available for lease to network clients. This way, no duplicate IP addresses are provided to clients. There is a four-step process involved in leasing an IP address to a network client:

1. **DHCPDISCOVER:** The process begins when the client issues a broadcast message that looks for a DHCP Server. The discover message contains the computer's name and MAC address so that the DHCP Server can respond to the client.
2. **DHCPOFFER:** The DHCP Server(s) responds to the discover request by making an IP address offer. The DHCP Server reserves an IP address for the client so that it can be issued if the client accepts the offer. The client receives the offer(s) and accepts the first offer it receives.
3. **DHCPREQUEST:** After the client accepts an offer, the request message is sent (broadcast) accepting the offer from a particular DHCP server. All DHCP servers whose offer was not accepted retract the offer so that the reserved IP addresses are now available to other clients.
4. **DHCPACK:** The DHCP server whose offer was accepted sends an acknowledgement message with a valid IP address and lease time information. The client can now fully implement TCP/IP, participate on the network and is considered a DHCP client.

Reviewing DHCP Terminology

You are probably familiar with most of the terms in Table 11.1, but you should review them before moving any further in the chapter. We will use these terms in our discussion of the installation and configuration of DHCP.

TABLE 11.1 DHCP Terminology

Term	Definition
Scope	A DHCP scope is the full range of IP addresses that are available for leasing. The scope is normally used in reference to a particular DHCP Server residing on a particular subnet and not to the entire network environment.
Superscope	A Superscope is a grouping of scopes used to support logical IP subnets residing on one physical subnet. The Superscope contains child scopes, which must be configured individually.
Address Pool	The IP address that is available for lease within a scope is called an Address Pool.
Exclusion Range	An Exclusion Range is a range of addresses within the scope that are not available for lease. This range is normally reserved for static server IP addresses.
Reservation	A reservation is used to permanently assign a particular IP address to a particular client. This option is normally used for hardware devices that need to keep the same IP address.
Lease	A lease is a period of time a client may use an IP address. Before the IP address expires, the client attempts to renew the lease with the DHCP Server.

Installing DHCP

To install DHCP Server on your Windows 2000 Server, follow these steps:

1. Click Start ➤ Programs ➤ Administrative Tools ➤ Configure Your Server.
2. Expand Networking in the left pane and click DHCP. In the right pane, click Start.
3. The Windows Component Wizard begins. Click Next.
4. Click Networking Services in the scroll box and click the Details button.
5. Select Dynamic Host Configuration Protocol by clicking the check box, then click OK.
6. Click Next. Windows begins the installation process.
7. Click Finish.

Configuring the DHCP Server

The DHCP Manager functions as a MMC snap-in in Windows 2000 Server. You can access the DHCP console by clicking Start ➤ Programs ➤ Administrative Tools ➤ DHCP Manager. The following sections show you how to configure the DHCP Server.

DHCP Server Properties

You can access the properties sheet for the DHCP Server by selecting the server in the console tree, clicking the Action menu, then clicking Properties. The Properties sheet, as shown in Figure 11.1, gives you General Property sheets, Dynamic DNS Property sheets, and Advanced Property sheets.

The General Property sheet allows you to enable auto refresh of DHCP statistics. This feature allows you to automatically see current lease or scope information. To enable auto refresh, click the check box and adjust the refresh interval, which is every 10 seconds by default. Next, DHCP logging creates a daily log file that can be used for troubleshooting purposes. By default, the log file is created, but you can choose not to generate a log by clicking the check box to clear it. Also, the General tab allows you the options of showing the BOOTP folder and showing authorization warning messages.

The DNS Property sheet allows you to automatically update DNS so that client names and IP addresses match. This option is enabled by default. See the "Creating Scopes and Superscopes" section later in the chapter for more information about DNS.

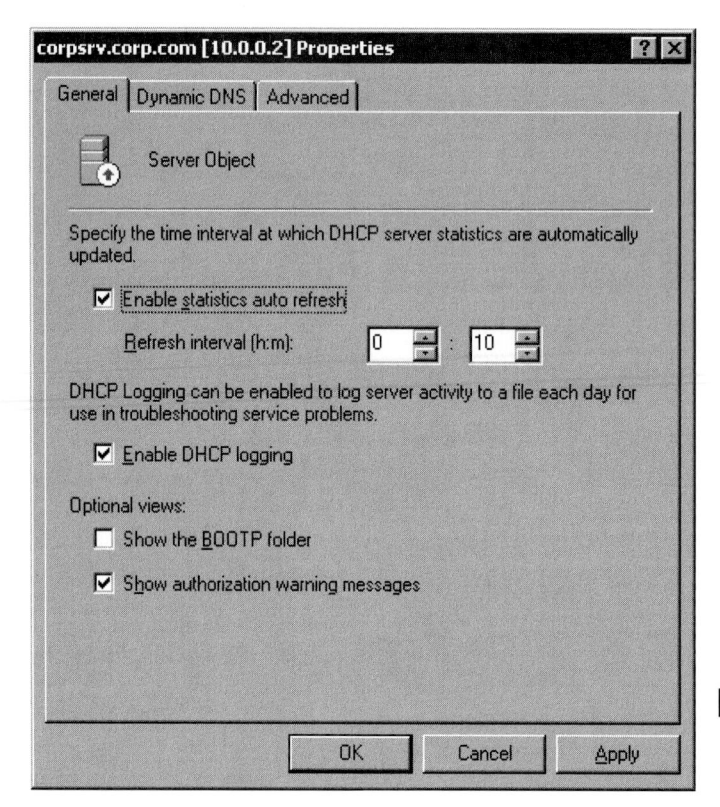

FIGURE 11.1
DHCP Server Properties

The Advanced Property sheet, as shown in Figure 11.2, allows you to configure conflict detection.

Conflict detection is used by the DHCP server to determine whether there is an IP address conflict before leasing the IP address to the client. For example, if a static client uses a TCP/IP address that is available for lease, DHCP can detect this IP conflict. The selection box allows you to set how many times conflict detection should run before the lease is provided. The default is 0. Also, you can accept the default locations of the audit file path and the database path or use the Browse buttons to change the location. Finally, the Advanced tab allows you to change the server connections binding by clicking on the bindings button. Typically, the server will be bound to the local area connection, but this can be changed to an alternate connection if necessary.

Authorizing a DHCP Server

Your first step to setting up the DHCP Server is to authorize the DHCP server to participate in the Active Directory. This enhancement allows DHCP to integrate with the Active Directory security features. The authorization

FIGURE 11.2 Advanced Tab

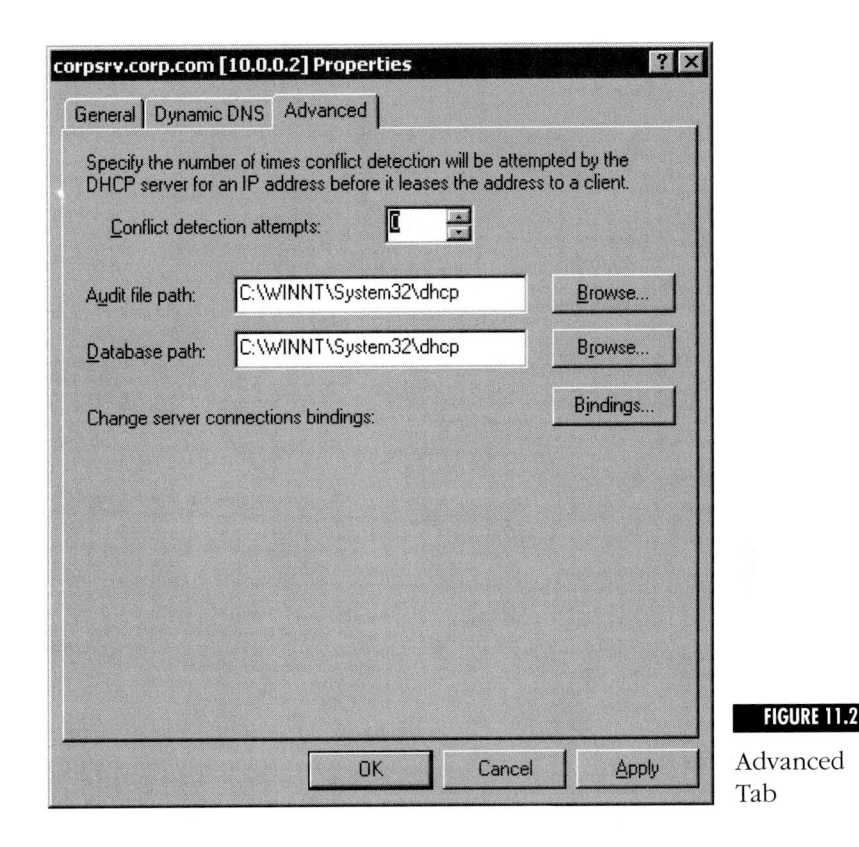

process prevents unauthorized, or "rogue," DHCP servers from leasing IP addresses to clients. The Active Directory can determine whether the DHCP server can be authorized to participate on the network and lease IP addresses to clients. To authorize a DHCP server to participate on the network, right-click on the server in DHCP Manager, point to All Tasks, and click Authorize. Likewise, you can de-authorize a server in the same manner.

Creating Scopes and Superscopes

A scope determines the IP address range and additional IP configuration information that can be provided to clients. To create a new scope in DHCP Manager, right-click on the DHCP Server, point to New, then click Scope. The Create Scope Wizard begins. To complete the wizard, follow these steps:

1. Click Next on the opening wizard screen.
2. Enter a scope name and a comment if desired and click Next.
3. On the Address Range window, enter a valid IP address range and

subnet mask that you want to use for the scope, as shown in Figure 11.3. Click Next.

4. In the Add Exclusions window, enter a start address and end address for an exclusion range if one is desired. Click Next.

5. In the Lease Duration window, enter a lease time. The default time is 8 days. If you would like to make changes to the default lease time, adjust the boxes using the arrow buttons. Click Next.

6. The DHCP Options window appears. If you would like the DHCP Server to provide optional information such as the IP address of the DNS and WINS server and a default gateway, click the Yes button. Click Next.

7. The Gateways window appears. Enter the IP address(es) of the gateways available if desired and click Next.

8. The DNS window appears. If you want DHCP to supply the domain name and DNS Server's IP address, enter this information, click Add, then click Next.

9. The WINS window appears. If you want DHCP to supply the IP address of the WINS server to clients, then enter the IP address and click Add, then click Next.

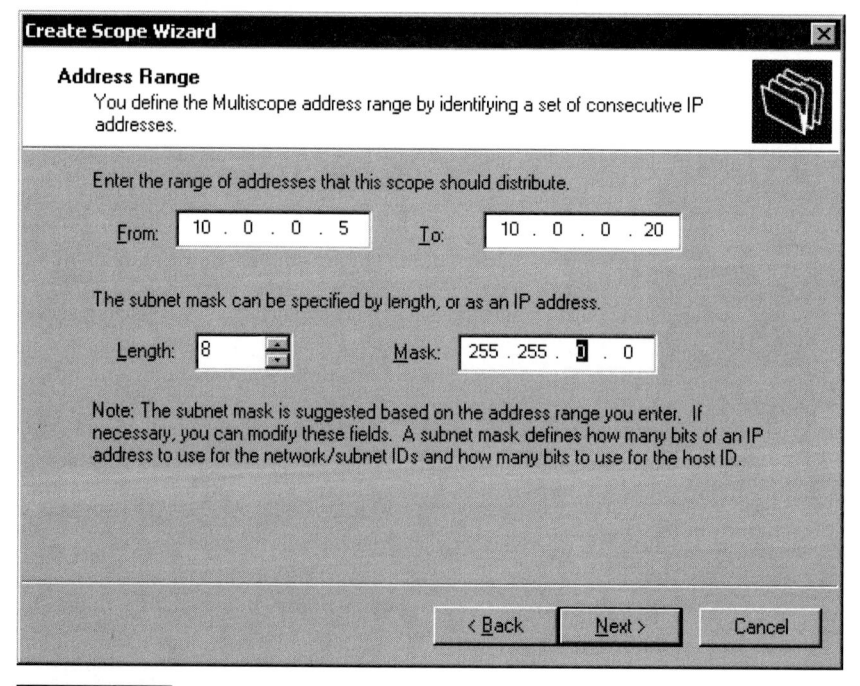

FIGURE 11.3 Address Range

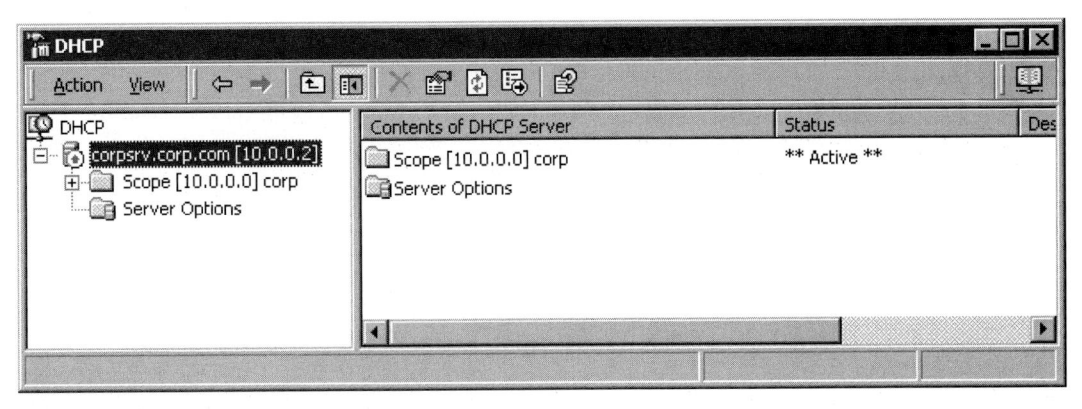

FIGURE 11.4 Active DHCP Scope

10. The Activate Scope window appears. If you want to activate the scope now, click Yes, then click Next, then click Finish. The scope now appears as "active" in the DHCP Manager, as shown in Figure 11.4.

Once the scope is configured, you can expand Scope in the left console pane to see the Address Pool, Address Leases, Reservations, and Scope Options. If you right-click on the Scope and click Properties, you are provided with that scope's particular properties sheet. The General tab gives you the same information you selected when creating the scope, but you can easily change the address range or lease information if desired. If you click the DNS tab, as shown in Figure 11.5, you have the option to enable dynamic update of DNS client information in the Active Directory. This option is selected by default, and should be used to fully integrate DNS client information so that the Active Directory is always current.

Enabling dynamic update of DNS client information maintains the client DNS information according to IP address lease, such as Name to IP address or IP address to Name. Because the IP address lease for clients may change once the lease expires, the dynamic update ensures that a particular IP address can be resolved to the correct client, or vice versa.

The Advanced Property sheet allows you to dynamically assign IP addresses to DHCP clients, DHCP or BOOTP clients, or to BOOTP clients only. This is a new feature in Windows 2000 Server to provide for dynamic support of BOOTP clients. Once a selection is made, adjust the lease time as desired.

RECONCILING THE SCOPE

If you suspect there are missing IP addresses within the scope, DHCP Manager can check the scope for inconsistencies. If you right-click the

FIGURE 11.5

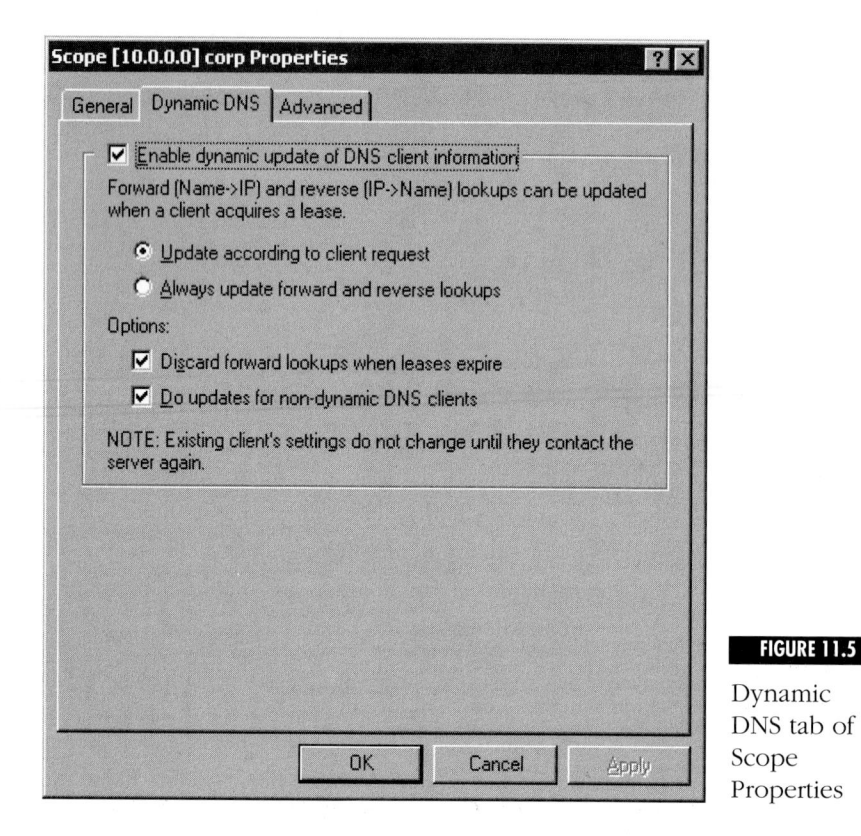

Dynamic DNS tab of Scope Properties

scope, point to All Tasks, then click Reconcile, a dialog box appears telling you to click the Check button. If there are inconsistencies, they will be listed in the dialog box, and if not, a message appears telling you the database is consistent.

ADDING A RESERVATION

Once the scope has been created, you can still add a reservation if desired. Expand Scope in the console tree and right-click Reservations. Point to New and click Reservation. A dialog box appears asking you to enter the client's IP address, MAC address, and name. Once you enter this information and click Add, the reservation is made so that the client can always use a particular IP address. This feature is particularly useful for hardware devices in which you want the IP address reserved, such as routers or gateways.

ADDING A NEW EXCLUSION RANGE

After the scope has been created, you can still create a new exclusion range if necessary. To create a new exclusion range, right-click on Address Pool in the console tree, point to New, and click Exclusion Range. A dialog box appears where you can enter the IP address range.

CREATING A SUPERSCOPE

A Superscope allows you to extend the number of IP addresses you can use in a network or subnet by grouping distinct scopes under a single name. A superscope allows you to support DHCP clients on a single physical network segment where multinets exist. A multinet is a single physical network segment where multiple logical IP networks are used. A superscope also allows you to support DHCP clients on the far side of a DHCP or BOOTP relay agent. Essentially, this configuration allows your DHCP server to provide leases from more than one scope to clients on a single network segment.

Superscopes are easy to create and manage and require very little configuration. To create a superscope, follow these steps:

1. In the console tree, right-click the DHCP server, point to New, then click Superscope.
2. The Superscope wizard begins. Click Next.
3. Enter a name for the Superscope and click Next.
4. Select one or more scopes in the window to add to the superscope. Click Next.
5. Click Finish. The Superscope appears in the console tree.

Once you have created the superscope, you can always add more scopes to the superscope by right-clicking the superscope in the console tree, pointing to New, and clicking Scope. Remember that the superscope is an administrative tool to help you logically group and organize several scopes. You should plan carefully before implementing superscopes to make certain they benefit the structure of your organization.

CREATING A MULTICAST SCOPE

Multicasting is the process of sending a message to multiple clients. A multicast scope is a group of IP multicast network addresses that are distributed to multiple computers in a network. Multicast DHCP (MDHCP) is an extension of the typical DHCP lease assignment that allows you to use Class D multicasting IP addresses (range of 224.0.0.0 to 239.255.255.255). Multicast addresses are considered a "group" address in that they are shared by many computers. In this manner, communication can be sent to all computers with a multicast address as a group in much the same way you would group network users together or an e-mail distribution list. The Class D IP addresses are reserved for multicasting. MDHCP and DHCP function together, although the two services are not interconnected. In other words, clients configured to receive a DHCP lease can also participate in the multicast to receive a multicast IP address. However, each client must have a DHCP Class A, B, or C address before participating in a multicast group.

To create a multicast scope, follow these steps:

1. Right-click the DHCP Server, point to New, and click Multicast Scope.
2. The Multicast Scope Wizard begins. Click Next.
3. Give the scope a name and a descriptive comment if desired and click Next.
4. Input the address range of the multicast scope. The default TTL is 32, but you can adjust this as needed. Enter a scope ID number that clients can use to access the scope, as shown in Figure 11.6. Click Next.
5. You can specify an exclusion range if desired. Enter the range and click Next.
6. Next, you select the Lease duration. The default is 8 days, but you can adjust this value or use the Unlimited button. Click Next.
7. On the final window, click the check box to activate the multicast scope now, then click Finish.

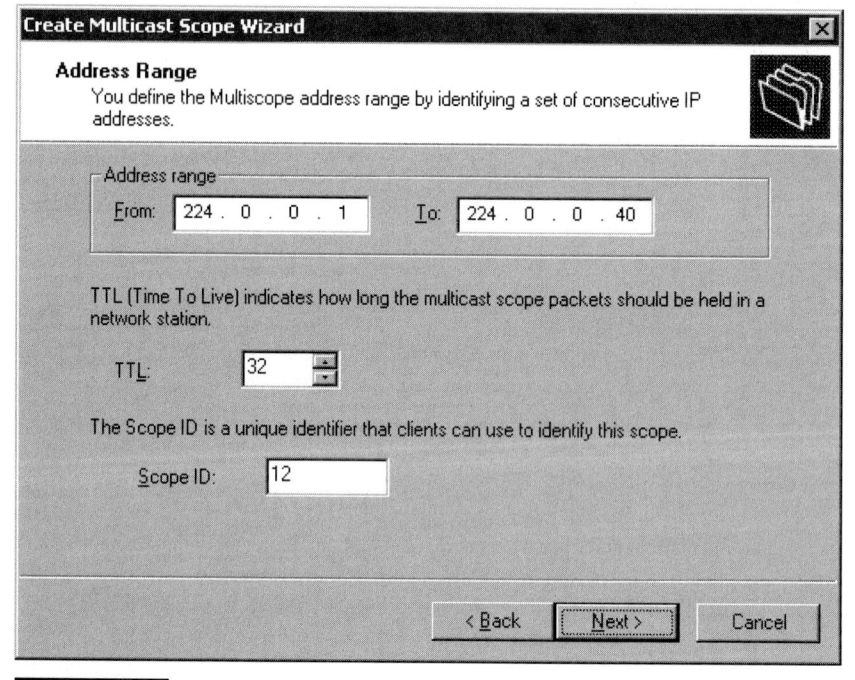

FIGURE 11.6 Address Range window

Configuring DHCP Options

As in Windows NT, DHCP still offers you a number of options that enable you to refine the leasing process and the type of data that is returned to the clients. You can assign options at four levels within DHCP: server options, scope options, class options, and reserved client options. DHCP configures its default options, but you manipulate the default options at each of these levels. By default, the options needed for Microsoft DHCP clients are automatically configured, such as:

- 003 Router: The IP address of the router or default gateway.
- 006 DNS Servers: The IP address of the DNS servers.
- 015 Domain Name: The DNS domain name.
- 044 WINS/NBNS Servers: The IP address of the WINS server.
- 046 WINS/NBT Node Type: The TCP/IP over NetBIOS name resolution strategy to be used. The options are B-node (broadcast), P-node (peer), M-node (mixed), H-node (hybrid).
- 047 NetBIOS Scope ID: The local NetBIOS scope ID.

In normal circumstances, the default options will be all you need for your network; however, if you have DHCP clients who need additional information configured with their lease, you can specify the additional class options as needed. You can define additional classes that are specific to your network by right-clicking on the DHCP Server, and clicking Define User Class or Define Vendor Class for vendor specific DHCP settings. You can also click Set Pre-defined Options to adjust standardized options that affect every client. The options classes include DHCP Standard Options (default), Microsoft Windows 2000 Options, Microsoft Windows 98 Options, or Microsoft Options. You can use the option name to set additional information options such as Cookie Server, Log Server, IRC Servers, and so forth. The Pre-defined DHCP Options and Values window is shown in Figure 11.7.

In addition to defining class and option values, you can adjust the default scope options as well. This feature is useful if you want additional information sent to DHCP clients within a particular scope. If you expand the Scope in the console tree, click on Scope Options, then right-click Scope Options and click Configure Options, you see a basic and advanced tab. Both of these tabs look similar to those in Figure 11.7, and you can select on an additional option, then enter the values as needed. For example, if you select 008 Cookie Servers, you are prompted to enter the IP addresses and name of the Cookie Server. Once this is configured, DHCP clients will be provided with this information when they lease an IP address from the DHCP Server.

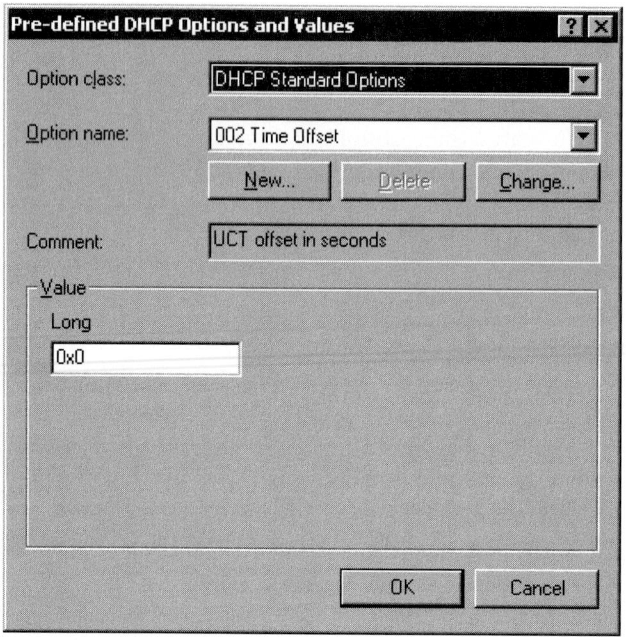

FIGURE 11.7 Predefined DHCP Options and Values

The DHCP Database

The DHCP database in Windows 2000 is enhanced for greater performance and ease of administration. The database files are automatically created when the DHCP Server is installed and the following files are automatically created in the Winnt\System32\Dhcp directory:

- Dhcp.mdb: The DHCP Server database file.
- Dhcp.tmp: A temp files used as a swap file during database index maintenance.
- J50.log and J50*.log: Log files used by DHCP to recover database information.
- J50.chk: A checkpoint file.

The DHCP database is dynamic and is updated when there is a change in a client's lease or renewal, and the database is backed up by default every 15 minutes. If you want to change the default backup time, change the BackupInterval value in the registry by navigating to HKEY_LOCAL_MACHINE\SYSTEM\CurrentControlSet\Services\DHCPServer\Parameters.

If there is a problem or failure of the DHCP database, DHCP automatically restores the database when the DHCP Server service is restarted. You can manually restore the database by setting the RestoreFlag value to 1 in the registry, then restarting the DHCP Service. To do this, navigate to HKEY_LOCAL_MACHINE\SYSTEM\CurrentControlSet\Services\DHCPServer\Parameters.

Summary

DHCP is a powerful tool that enables you to dynamically assign unique IP addresses and related IP information to network clients. DHCP functions by leasing an IP address from a pool of IP addresses within a scope to network clients as needed. By this design, network clients using the DHCP service are assured of a valid IP address and participation on the TCP/IP network.

TWELVE

Configuring DNS

Domain Name System (DNS) is a name resolution strategy designed to resolve domain names and host names to IP addresses. As we have discussed earlier in the book, each computer on a network or on the Internet must have a unique IP address. Because humans are language-based creatures, we would have a difficult time remembering the IP address of every computer we might want to communicate with. To solve this problem, DNS provides a way to use friendly names to communicate with computers while DNS handles the name-to-IP address resolution.

You are most familiar with DNS from the Internet. All Internet names, such as microsoft.com, abcnews.com, and the multitude of others use the domain name system. However, DNS is no longer restricted to the Internet—it has been adopted by private networks as well. Windows 2000 will only further the use of DNS since it is integrated with the Active Directory and now has dynamic functionality. This chapter gives you an overview of DNS, and then shows you how to install and configure DNS on your server.

Understanding DNS

DNS functions by using a naming scheme called the "domain name space." A "name space" means that the naming convention used shares common traits and attributes. For example, everyone in the "Smith" family would have a common name space because they all have the last name of Smith. The DNS domain name space uses a hierarchical structure to define DNS names and host names and organize the DNS database. Each node in the name space, called a domain, represents a section of the database.

The DNS domain name space is organized by the root domain, top-level domain, second-level domain, and host name. Each of these domains creates the hierarchy of the DNS database. The following bulleted list gives you an overview of the domains:

- Root Domain: The Root domain is represented by a period (.) and is the foundational unit of organization in the domain name space.
- Top-Level Domain: Top level domains represent the type of organization or may provide a country code. Common examples of top-level domains are com, edu, org, net, gov, mil, au, and jp.
- Second-Level Domain: Second-Level domains are names that normally represent the business or organization. Second-Level domains must be unique. Some examples are yahoo.com, aol.com, and ucla.edu.
- Host Names: Second-Level domains can be further subdivided by host names. A host name points to a particular computer within the Second-Level domain. For example, corp.com may have hosts such as server1, server2, and server3. In order to specify server2, the name space would read server2.corp.com.

Domains can be subdivided, so there are child domains and parent domains. For example, corp.com can be subdivided as acct.corp.com or sales.corp.com. The acct and sales subdomains are divisions of the corp.com parent domain.

The names in the database are resolved by beginning at the top of the hierarchy and working through the name space until the final domain is reached. At this point, an IP address can be returned. On the Internet, this process usually requires several different servers to resolve the name to an IP address. Figure 12.1 gives you a look at the hierarchical resolution process for server1.acct.corp.com.

DNS Zones

As you can imagine, the size of the DNS database can quickly get out of hand. In order to organize and manage the database, it can be divided into zones, although not required. A zone allows you to section the domain name space into smaller pieces that can be more easily managed. Typically, a zone represents a division within an organization. For example, at corp.com, the sales division and accounting division could be divided into DNS zones so that one administrative group can handle sales.corp.com while another can handle acct.corp.com. Each zone contains its own database file that functions independently of the other zones. A zone, however,

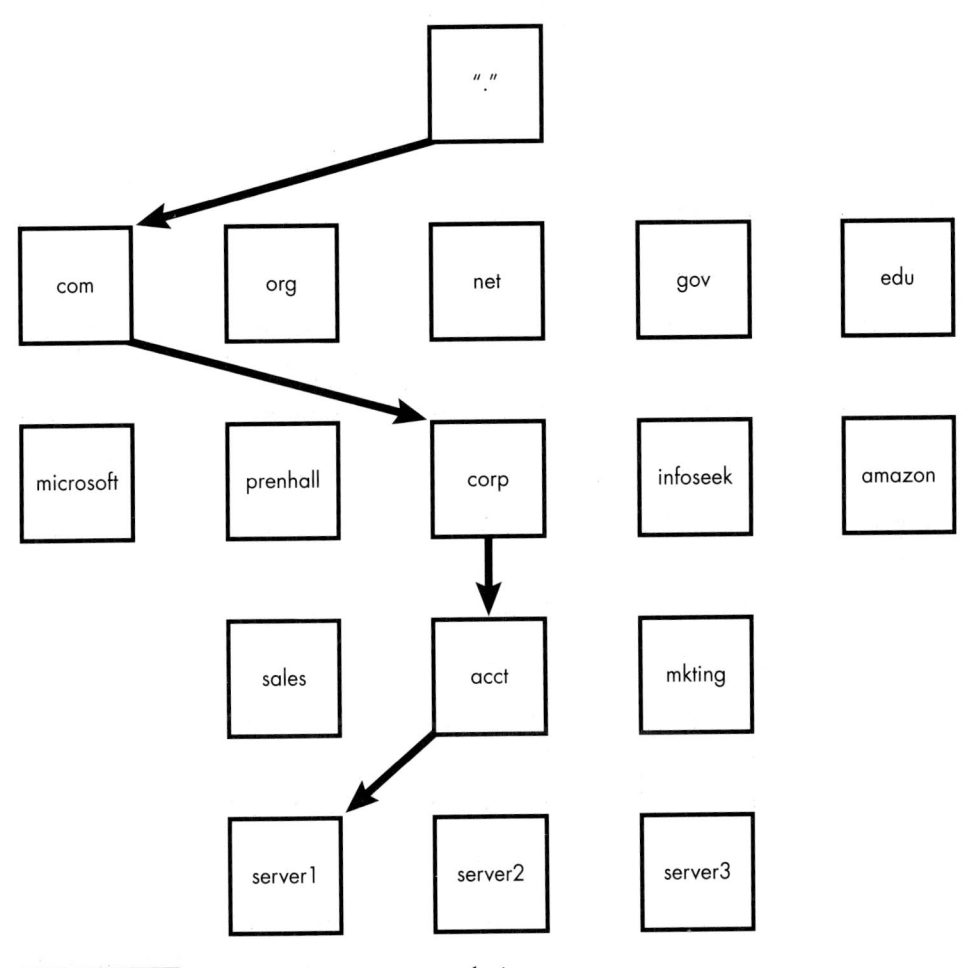

FIGURE 12.1 Domain name space resolution

does have to exist in a contiguous name space. For example, you can create zones from sales.corp.com and acct.corp.com, because sales and acct belong to the contiguous name space of corp.com, but you cannot create zones from sales.corpusa.com.jp and acct.corp.com, because the name space is not contiguous.

Resolution for zones is handled by a name server(s) that contains the zone database file. There may be multiple name servers within a zone, and the name servers can also store information for one zone or multiple zones. One of the servers, however, has the primary zone database file for the zone; the other servers can perform zone transfers, provide fault tolerance, and reduce the load on the primary name server. The name server for the zone is called an authoritative name server because it has authority over the domain name space that the zone covers. You can think of authoritative servers as company managers. There could be three divisions of a company that work together, but each division has its own manager—or authority.

DNS in Windows 2000 Server

Windows 2000 Server provides several enhancements to DNS that make it function more effectively and efficiently. You will see the following features when working with DNS in Windows 2000.

- The most important feature is dynamic ability. In the past, DNS was a static database that had to be manually altered for changes to take place. Dynamic DNS (DDNS) in Windows 2000 can make changes to the database file as they occur without manual manipulation from an administrator.
- Active Directory Integration: The Active Directory uses DNS to resolve names and locate Windows 2000 domain controllers. The Active Directory can be used to manage and integrate zone database files from one central location. Any time you install the Active Directory on a domain controller, DNS is automatically installed and configured for integration with the Active Directory.
- Unicode Character Support: Original DNS names had to be represented using ASCII-based characters. This design has a number of limitations, especially in international naming. To solve this problem, Windows 2000 expands the character support to include UTF-8, a Unicode naming format. The UTF-8 protocol extends ASCII and incorporates most of the world's languages and writing systems.
- WINS Integration: In a Windows 2000 environment, you no longer need WINS since Windows 2000 computers use DNS instead of NetBIOS for name resolution. However, in mixed environments where WINS is required, DNS can now use a WINS lookup to resolve names that cannot be resolved by the DNS name space. This feature is highly useful in mixed environments where Windows 2000, earlier versions of Windows, and UNIX operating systems are present. In order to accomplish this, you add two resource records, a WINS and WINS-R record, to the zone where you want WINS lookup to occur.

Installing DNS

You can install DNS either by accessing Start ➤ Programs ➤ Administrative Tools ➤ Configure Your Server, or through Add/Remove Programs in Control Panel. To install DNS, select it from the components list under Networking Components, then click OK to begin the installation. Once you begin the installation, Windows configures your system for DNS and installs the component. Once the installation is complete, click Finish.

Once the installation is complete, you will need to set-up DNS and configure server zones. This is done through a wizard. Click Start → Programs → Administrative Tools → DNS Management. The Configure DNS Server Wizard appears. Follow these steps:

1. Click Next on the Welcome screen.
2. The Root Servers window appears. If the server cannot find other DNS root servers on the network, a window appears asking to select a radio button. You have the option of selecting "This is the first DNS server on this network," which makes the server a root server, or you have the option of supplying the IP address of the root server. Make your selection and click Next.
3. The Add Forward Lookup Zone window appears. The Forward Lookup Zone is a database that helps resolve names to IP address and locate network services. You should choose to create the Forward Lookup Zone by selecting the appropriate radio button and clicking Next.
4. The Select a Zone Type Window appears, as shown in Figure 12.2. You have the option of integrating the zone into the Active Directory, storing it in a standard text file, or creating a replica of the existing zone. You may choose to integrate the zone into the Active Directory

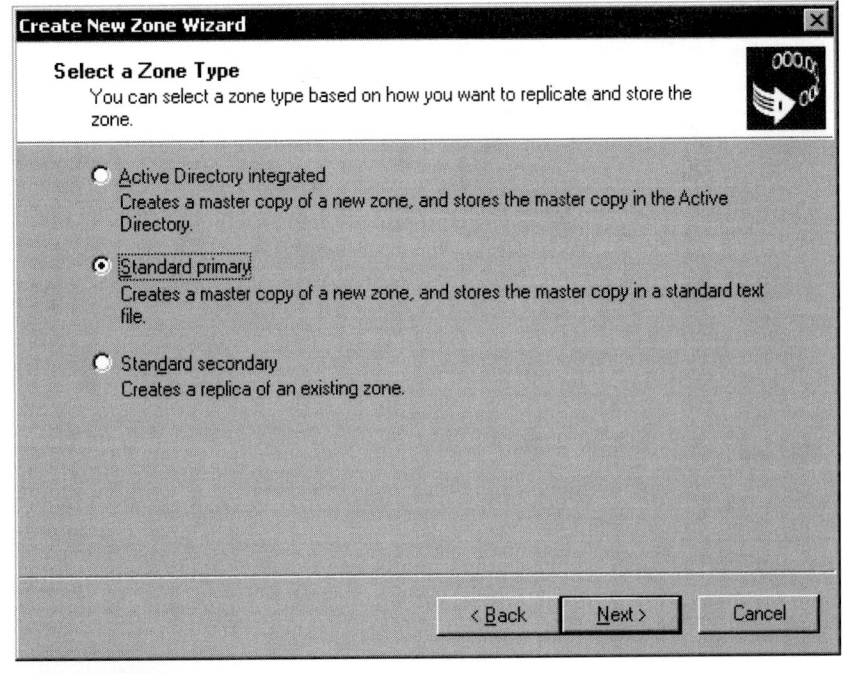

FIGURE 12.2 Select a Zone Type Window

Chapter twelve • Configuring DNS

if you have fully integrated the Active Directory into your environment. By default, the Standard primary selection is chosen. Make your selection based on your network's needs and click Next.

5. The Zone Name window appears. Type the name of the zone and click Next.

6. The Add Reverse Lookup Zone window appears. The Reverse Lookup Zone helps resolve IP addresses into names. This action allows for "reverse lookup" in that IP addresses are resolved to names instead of names to IP addresses. If you want to add a reverse lookup zone, click Yes, then click Next.

7. If you selected Yes, you are again presented with the Select a Zone Type window. Make your selection and click Next.

8. The next window asks you to enter the network ID of the reverse lookup zone. Enter the class network and subnet mask used in your network in the appropriate boxes and click Next.

9. The final window appears. Click Finish.

Once the nine steps above are complete, the DNS Management console appears, as shown in Figure 12.3.

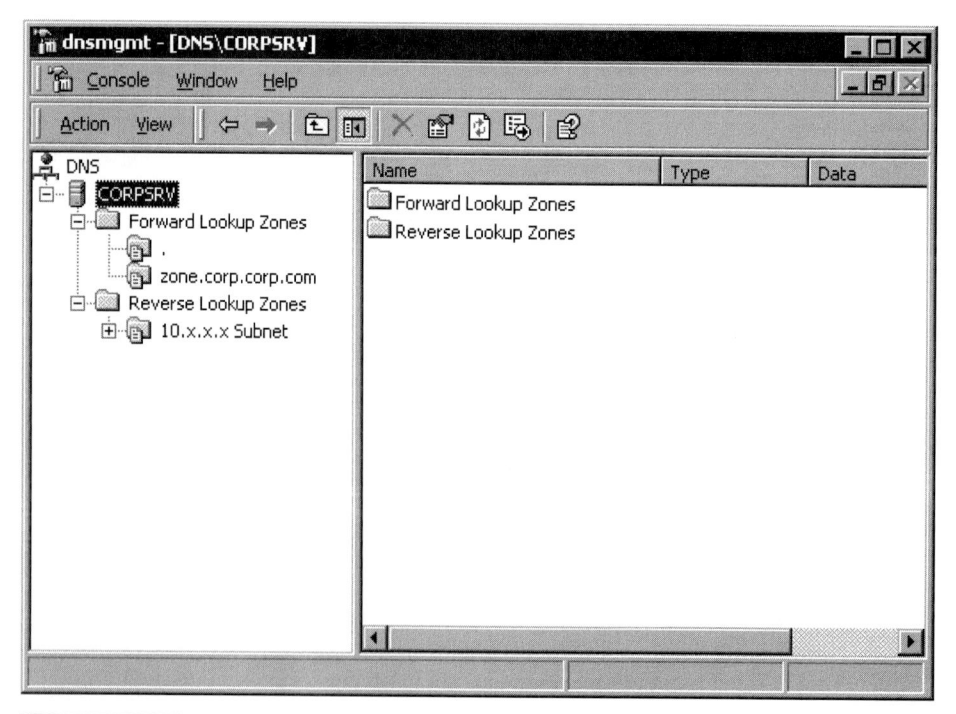

FIGURE 12.3 DNS Management Console

Configuring DNS

Since the Initial Installation and Configuration Wizard helps you establish your DNS server, general configuration of DNS is not difficult. The following sections show how to adjust or change your DNS configuration in the DNS Management Console.

Connecting to Another Computer

If you want to connect to another computer from within the DNS Management console, right-click on DNS at the top of the console tree and click Connect to another Computer. The Choose Target Machine window appears. Select either the This Computer radio button or click the Another Computer button and specify the target computer name, then click OK.

Removing a DNS Server

You can remove a DNS Server from the DNS Management Console by clicking the server you want to remove, then clicking the Action menu and clicking Delete. You will be asked to confirm the delete order. Click OK.

Creating a New Zone

You can create a new DNS zone by right-clicking on the appropriate DNS server in the console tree and clicking Create a new Zone. The Create New Zone Wizard appears. Follow these steps to create the new zone:

1. Click Next on the Welcome screen.
2. In the Select a Zone Type window, select whether to integrate the zone with the master copy in the Active Directory, use a Standard primary zone, or create a Standard secondary zone, then click Next.
3. Select the Zone lookup type as either forward lookup or reverse lookup. Click Next.
4. Type the name of the zone and click Next.
5. Choose a File name for the DNS server zone. You can accept the new file name that entered in step 4 or click the existing file radio button to load an existing file copied from another computer. Click Next, then click Finish.

Manually Updating a Server

You can manually update a server's data files. The data files are normally written at update intervals and when the DNS Server is shut down, but you can choose to immediately update all of the DNS changes to the data files within the zone. To perform this action, right-click the DNS Server you want to manually update and click Manually Update Server Data Files.

Clearing the Cache

You can easily clear the DNS Server's cached files by right-clicking on the Server and clicking Clear Cache. Once the cache is cleared, the server will refer to the DNS database files for update information.

Configuring the DNS Server Properties

The DNS Server Properties sheet presents you with a number of configuration options for the DNS Server. You can access the properties sheet by right-clicking on the DNS Server and clicking Properties. The following sections look at the configuration options available on each tab.

INTERFACES

The Interfaces Property sheet, as shown in Figure 12.4, allows you to restrict the DNS Server to listen only to selected IP addresses. By default,

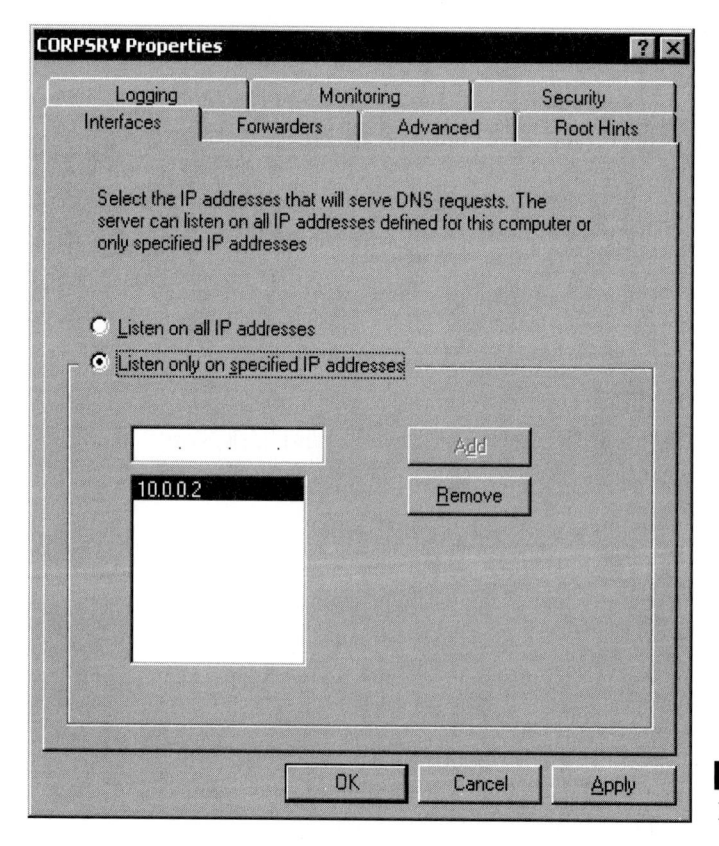

FIGURE 12.4

Interfaces tab

the DNS Service listens for all DNS messages on all configured IP addresses for the server. If your server has multiple IP addresses, you can restrict which IP address the server listens to. If your server has multiple IP addresses and you want to create this restriction, click on the Listen only on specified IP addresses radio button and add the IP address(es) you want the server to listen to.

FORWARDERS

A DNS Server that is configured to provide recursive service for other DNS Servers is called a "forwarder." A forwarder helps resolve DNS names that cannot be resolved by the server. The Forwarders Property sheet, shown in Figure 12.5, allows you to configure the server to pass any resolution query it cannot resolve to another server(s). To designate forwarders, click the Enable forwarders check box. If you want the DNS Server to only use forwarders, click the Operate as slave server check box as well. Next, type the IP address(es) of the DNS Servers you want to forward resolution queries to and click the Add button.

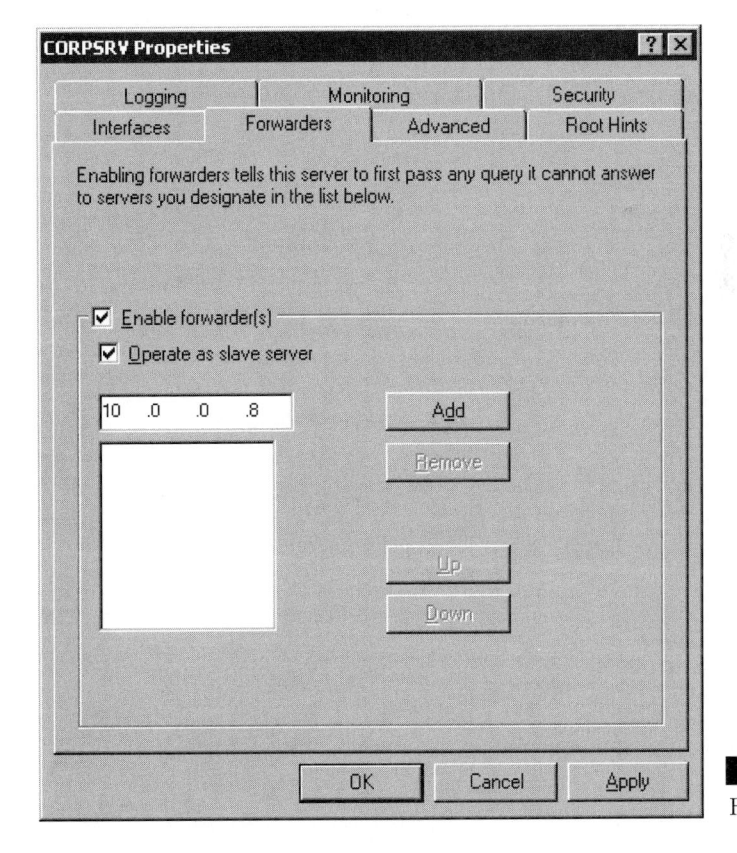

FIGURE 12.5 Forwarders

ADVANCED

The Advanced Property sheet allows you to configure several DNS Server advanced options, shown in Figure 12.6. First, you have a list of check boxes that you can select or deselect. By default, the Bind Secondaries (which binds secondary DNS servers), Enable Round Robin, and Enable Netmask Ordering are selected. You can also choose to use Disable Recursion, Fail On Load If Bad Zone Data, and Secure Cache Against Pollution. You can also use the drop-down menu to change the name-checking method. DNS supports three methods for checking DNS names:

- Strict RFC: This method strictly enforces the use of the RFC compliant rules for all DNS names. Any names that are not RFC compliant are treated as errors.
- Non RFC: This method allows names that are not RFC compliant to be used with the DNS Server.
- Multibyte: This method uses the Unicode 8 bit translation encoding scheme.

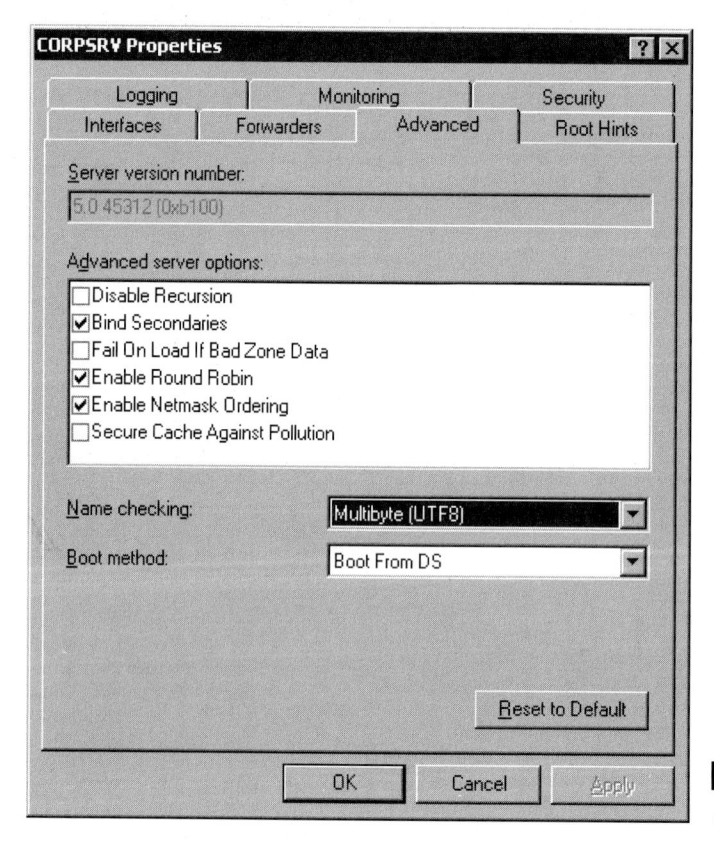

FIGURE 12.6

Advanced tab

By default, the server will use the non-RFC type, which is the most lenient. The non RFC-type provides the greatest amount of interoperability with other DNS Servers.

You can also use the Advanced Property sheet to change the loading method used by the DNS Server. If you click the drop-down menu, you can select From Registry, From File, or From DS. By default, the registry option is used. However, you can also specify to load from a file. If you use this option, the file must be a text file named Boot.dns and located in the DNS folder in %system%\WINNT\System32. You can also choose to load the DNS Service from the Active Directory if the database is integrated with the Active Directory.

ROOT HINTS

Root hints are used to help the DNS Server discover and use other servers that manage other subtrees or domains located at a higher level in the domain namespace. The root hints are necessary for the authoritative server to find servers at levels above them or servers that are authoritative for remote domain name trees. By default, the Root Hints tab contains a list of hints generated from the cache.dns file. The default list helps the DNS server locate other upper level servers on the Internet. If you are using DNS in a private network, you can use this property sheet to edit the entries so that they point to appropriate DNS servers on your network. If you are using root servers, they do not need root hints and you can delete the cache.dns file on the root server. For other servers, you can select the hint and click the Edit button to make changes as necessary for your environment.

LOGGING

You can use the Logging Property sheet to select debug options. These options help you gain a detailed analysis of issues or problems that can occur with DNS operation. By default, none of the options are selected, and you should not use any of the debug options unless needed. They tend to use a lot of disk space and may affect your server's performance. To use an option, simply select it in the check box. The log is located in the Dns.log file located in the Dns folder. The following list explains the debug logging options available:

- Query: logs all queries received by the DNS service from clients.
- Notify: logs all notification messages received by the DNS service from other servers.
- Update: logs all dynamic updates received by the DNS service.
- Questions: logs the contents of the question part of each DNS query message.
- Answers: logs the contents of the answer part of each DNS query message.
- Send: logs the number of DNS query messages sent by the DNS service.

- Receive: logs the number of DNS query messages received by the DNS service.
- UDP: logs the number of DNS requests received by the DNS service on a UDP port.
- TCP: logs the number of DNS requests received by the DNS service over a TCP port.
- Full packets: logs the number of full packets written and sent by the DNS service.
- Write through: logs the number of packets written through by the DNS service and back to the zone.

MONITORING

The Monitoring Property sheet, as shown in Figure 12.7, allows you to test simple and recursive queries as well as establish automatic testing. If you click either the Simple query or Recursive query check box and click the Test Now button, a message is generated in the bottom window telling you whether or not the test was successful. You can also click the Automatic testing check box and assign the amount of time between tests.

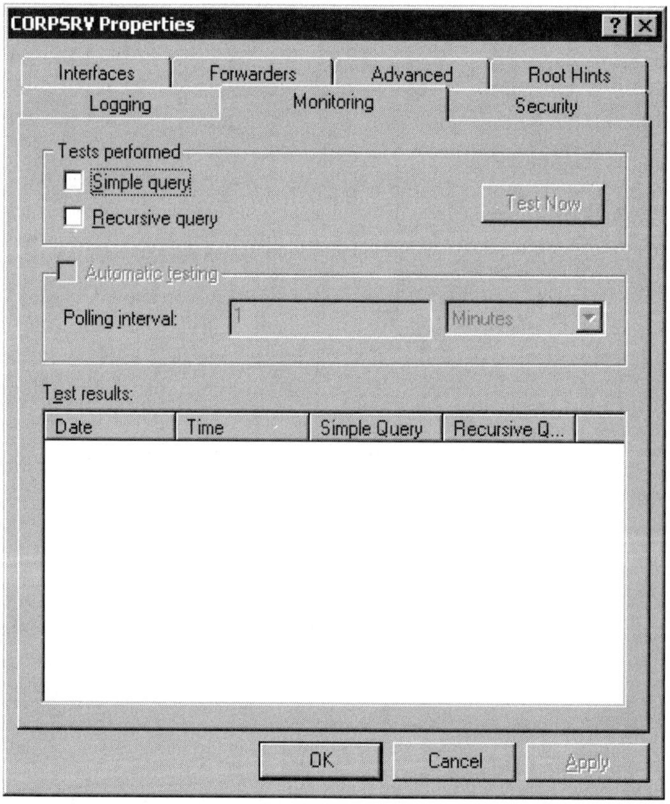

FIGURE 12.7 Monitoring Property Sheet

SECURITY

The Security Property sheet gives you the typical security window you have seen in other areas of configuration. You can use this tab to assign different levels of permission and control to groups of individuals for the DNS Service.

Configuring Zone Properties

For each zone you create, you can access the properties sheet for the zone to further configure options. If you right-click on the zone you want to configure and select Properties, you are provided with a properties sheet with six tabs. The following sections show you what configuration options are available on each.

GENERAL

The General Property sheet, shown in Figure 12.8, allows you to manage the zone and configure dynamic updates for the zone.

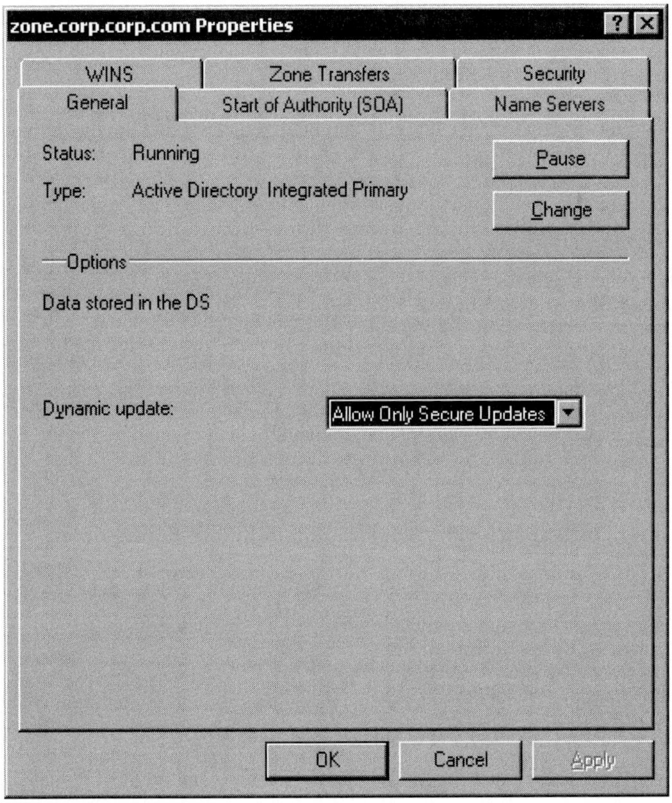

FIGURE 12.8
General Property Sheet

The status information tells you whether the zone is running or not, and you can use the Pause button to pause the zone on the DNS server. The Type field tells you the type of zone that is currently configured. As you can see in Figure 12.8, this zone is an Active Directory Integrated Primary zone. You can click the Change button to change the zone type to Standard Primary, Standard Secondary, or Active Directory integrated.

In the second half of the sheet, you can select the type of dynamic updates you want to use. Through the use of Dynamic DNS (DDNS), DNS database updates occur automatically as changes are made by name servers or clients. You can configure authorized servers to dynamically update the database as needed. This feature allows DHCP IP to name mappings to be dynamically updated in the database, along with other changes that may occur. On the General tab, you have the option of selecting either None, Allow updates, or Allow only secure updates (this option appears only if the zone is Active Directory integrated).

START OF AUTHORITY (SOA)

The Start of Authority (SOA) Property sheets allows you to configure the SOA resource record, should changes need to be made. The SOA is a default resource record that is created with any zone, and it defines which name server is the authoritative name server within the domain. The Start of Authority (SOA) Property sheet, shown in Figure 12.9, allows you to make adjustments to the properties of the SOA record.

As you can see in Figure 12.9, you can adjust the primary server, responsible person, and refresh, retry, and expire intervals as necessary.

NAME SERVERS

The Name Servers Property sheet allows you to add authoritative name servers to a zone. The name servers (NS) record is automatically created when a new primary zone is created. You can add other authoritative servers for the zone by typing the server(s) IP address and clicking Add.

WINS

You can also specify DNS to use WINS resolution for names not found in DNS by clicking the check box on the WINS Property sheet and entering the IP address of the WINS server. The Advanced button allows you to alter the cache timeout and lookup timeout values if necessary. You learn more about the role of WINS in Windows 2000 in Chapter 13.

ZONE TRANSFERS

The Zone Transfers Property sheet allows you to configure zone transfers from this particular zone. DNS allows a namespace to be divided into

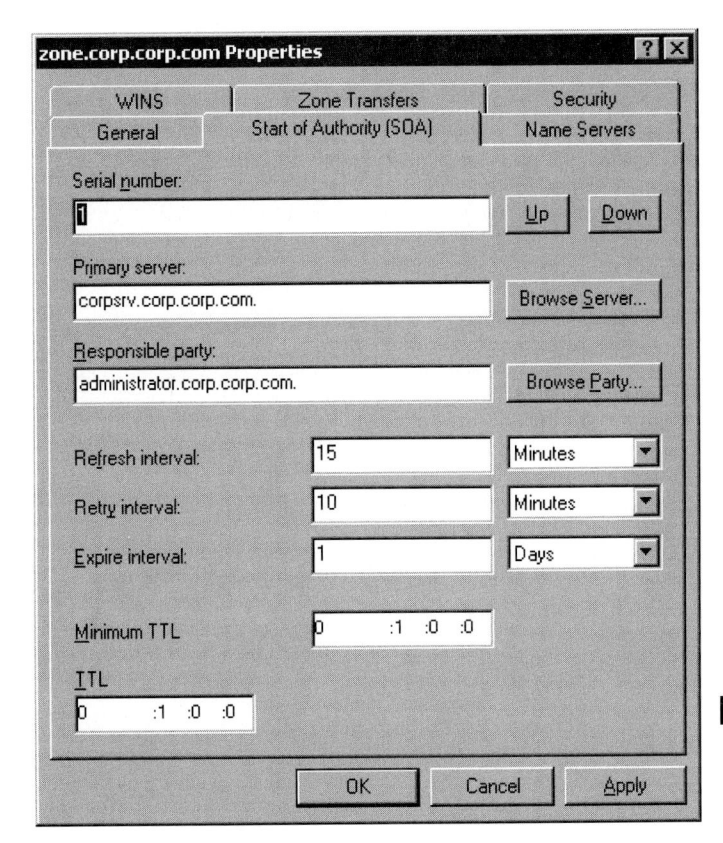

FIGURE 12.9
Start of Authority (SOA)

zones. Zone transfers are required to replicate and synchronize all copies of the zone used at each server configured to host the zone. If this does not happen, name resolution errors or failure for a particular zone can occur should a single zone server fail. In the Zone Transfers Property sheet, as shown in Figure 12.10, you can configure the zone to perform zone transfers to any server, only to servers in the NS record, from a specified list, or not at all.

SECURITY

The Security Property sheet is the same as other security property sheets in most other system properties. You can use the Security Property sheet to manage control and access of the zone by groups and users.

Configuring Resource Records

Each Zone database file contains resource records, which are entries in the database that affect the zone's operation and performance. When a Zone is

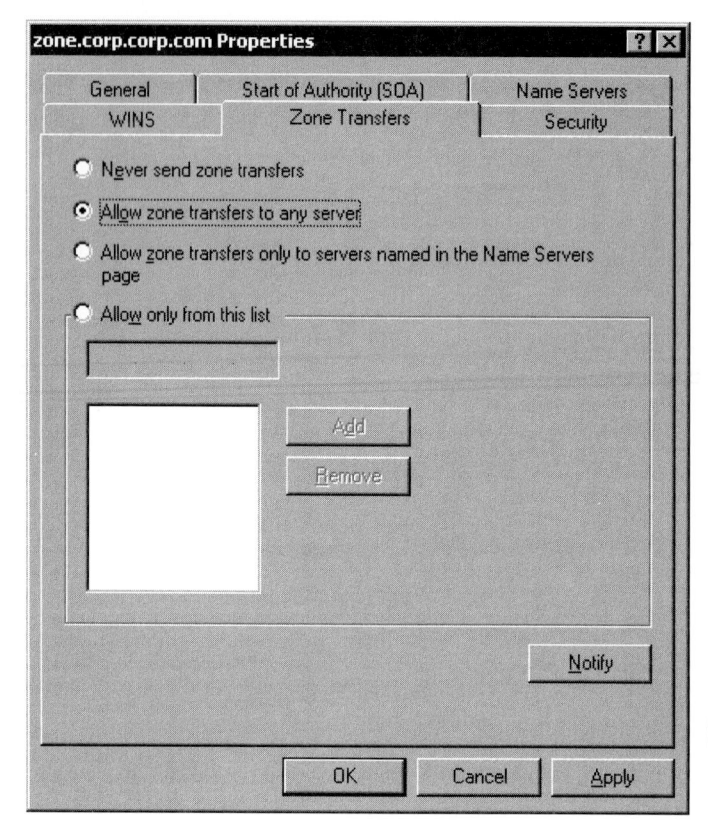

FIGURE 12.10
Zone Transfers Tab

created, DNS creates two resource records, the Start of Authority (SOA) and the Name Server (NS) records. The SOA record defines which name server is the authoritative source for data within the domain. The NS record lists the name servers that are assigned to a domain. You can add and configure additional resource records as needed, depending on the needs of your organization. The following list gives you an overview of the major resource records you can use:

- Host (A): Lists the host name to IP address mappings for a forward lookup zone.
- Pointer (PTR): Points to another part of the namespace, such as an IP address to name mapping.
- Service (SRV): Lists which servers are hosting a certain service.
- Alias (CNAME): Provides a canonical, or an alternate name, for a host.
- Mail Exchanger (MX): Specifies mail hosts for a domain and the order in which the mail hosts should be used.
- Host Information (HINFO): Identifies the CPU and operating system in use by the host.

You can add resource records by right-clicking on the appropriate zone, pointing to New, and selecting the type of record from the list you want to create. You can also select Other Record to select an alternate record from a list. Select the record you want to create and click the Create Record button. Each record will ask you to enter information appropriate for that record.

Summary

Windows 2000 Server uses DNS is an integrated part of the Windows 2000 environment and heavily used in the Active Directory. DNS functions as the primary name to IP address resolution strategy in Windows 2000 Server and allows you to fully implement domain naming schemes into your LAN. Windows 2000 also offers dynamic functionality in that DNS can update the DNS database as changes occur. These features make DNS name resolution a power tool in Windows 2000.

THIRTEEN

Configuring WINS

Windows Internet Naming Service (WINS) provides computer names to IP address resolution in networks using NetBIOS to communicate. A WINS Server allows a client computer to register its name and IP address so that the server can resolve the name to the IP address for other clients. As with DNS, WINS allows you to use "friendly" computer names on your network without having to know the IP address of each client you might want to communicate with.

In Windows 2000, name resolution occurs through DNS, so WINS is provided for backwards compatibility with earlier versions of Windows, such as Windows NT and Windows 9x. In a network where there are servers running Windows 2000 and all clients are running Windows 2000 Professional, WINS is unnecessary, but most environments contain a mix of operating systems, and in this case, WINS will need to be implemented.

This chapter provides an overview of WINS, then shows you how to implement and configure WINS on your Windows 2000 Server.

How WINS Works

WINS clients register their computer names and IP addresses with a WINS Server. This information is then stored in the WINS database so that the server can provide computer name to IP address resolution for clients attempting to communicate with each other. When a WINS client starts, it registers its NetBIOS name and IP address with the WINS server specified. When this information changes, such as in the case of a new DHCP lease, the client updates its NetBIOS to IP information with the WINS Server. When a WINS client needs to contact another client or resource, the resolution request is sent to the WINS server instead of to a broadcast message. The WINS Server resolves the request and returns the NetBIOS to IP address mapping to the client. The client then uses the IP address to contact the client or resource.

All WINS database records are temporary so that another client can use the same name as it becomes available. Because the record is temporary, the WINS client has to renew its lease before it expires. If the client does not renew the lease, the WINS server makes the lease available to another client. The WINS client attempts to renew its lease after one-eighth of the lease time (TTL) has expired. If the client is not successful, the client continues trying to renew its lease at two-minute intervals. If the client is still not successful when half of the lease time has expired, the client attempts to contact a secondary WINS server to renew its lease if a secondary server is configured for use. The WINS client repeats the two-minute process with the secondary WINS Server until successful, or it then reverts again to the primary WINS Server.

When a WINS client is shut down properly, it sends a name release request to the WINS server so that the name and IP address are free on the network.

Using WINS in Windows 2000

To implement WINS on a Windows 2000 Server, you need to have a static IP address, subnet mask, and default gateway. You may also need to configure static mappings for non-WINS clients on remote networks and enable WINS support on the DHCP Server.

The following operating systems can be WINS clients:

- Windows 2000.
- Windows 9.x.
- Windows NT 3.5 or later.
- Windows for Workgroups 3.11 running TCP/IP-32.
- Microsoft Network Client version 3.0 for MS-DOS with the real-mode TCP/IP driver.
- LAN Manager 2.2c for MS-DOS.

Installing WINS

As with other Windows 2000 components, you can install WINS by accessing Control Panel ➤ Add/Remove Programs, and then by clicking Add/Remove Windows Components. Click Next when the wizard begins, then select Networking Components and click the Details button. Click the Windows Internet Naming Server and click Next. WINS is installed on your system. Click Finish. Once WINS is installed, you can manage it by accessing the WINS snap-in by clicking Start ➤ Programs ➤ Administrative Tools ➤ WINS, shown in Figure 13.1.

Configuring the WINS Server

For the most part, WINS takes care of itself and will not require a lot of configuration. It is designed to reduce overhead and function without a lot of attention. The following sections, show what configuration options are available in the WINS console and point out some configuration options you may want to consider.

Adding a WINS Server to the Console

You can add WINS servers to the console by right-clicking WINS at the top of the console tree and clicking Add Server. In the dialog box that appears, enter the NetBIOS name or IP address of the server and click OK.

WINS Properties

You can access the overall WINS Properties sheet by right-clicking WINS at the top of the console tree and clicking Properties. A General Properties sheet appears, as shown in Figure 13.2, where you can specify that the server be

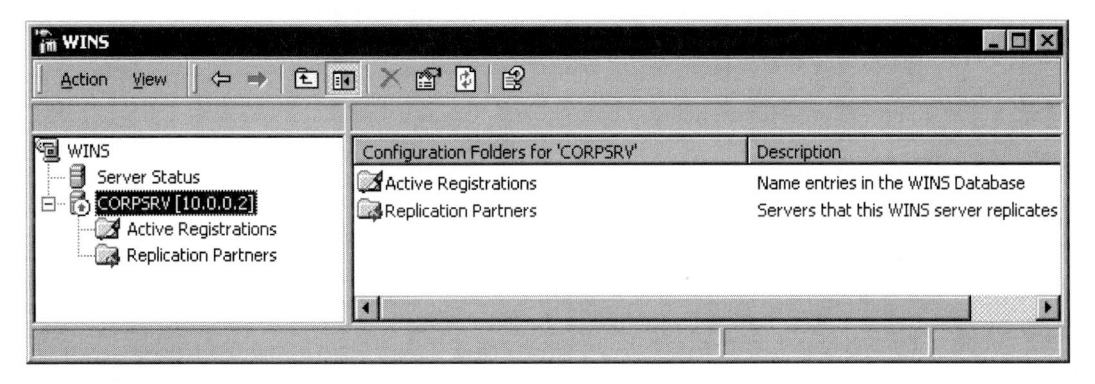

FIGURE 13.1 The WINS Console

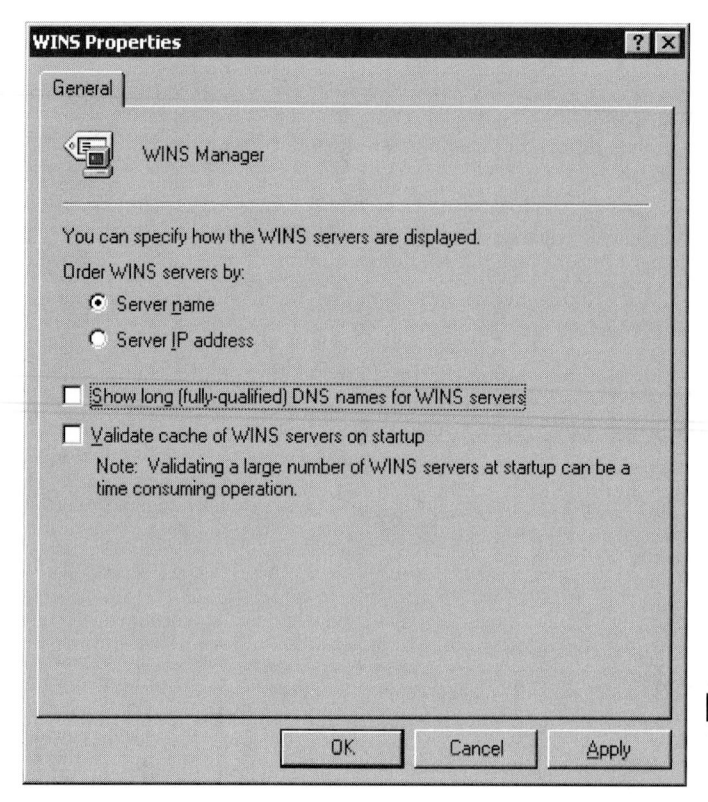

FIGURE 13.2
WINS General Properties

displayed by name or IP address. You can also choose to show fully qualified domain names (DNS FQDN) for WINS Servers. For example, if you choose this option, the NetBIOS name of Corpsrv would be displayed as corpsrv.corp.com. You can also choose to validate the cache of the WINS Servers on startup. Neither of these options is selected by default, and cache validation may take up a lot of server processing time.

Server Status

If you double-click on Server Status in the console tree, you are given the results in the right pane. The results give you the name(s) of the WINS server(s), the status (up or down), and the date and time of the last update. If you right-click on Server Status in the console tree and select Properties, you are presented a General page, shown in Figure 13.3. By default, status checks each server in the WINS server list every five minutes. You can change this number if desired.

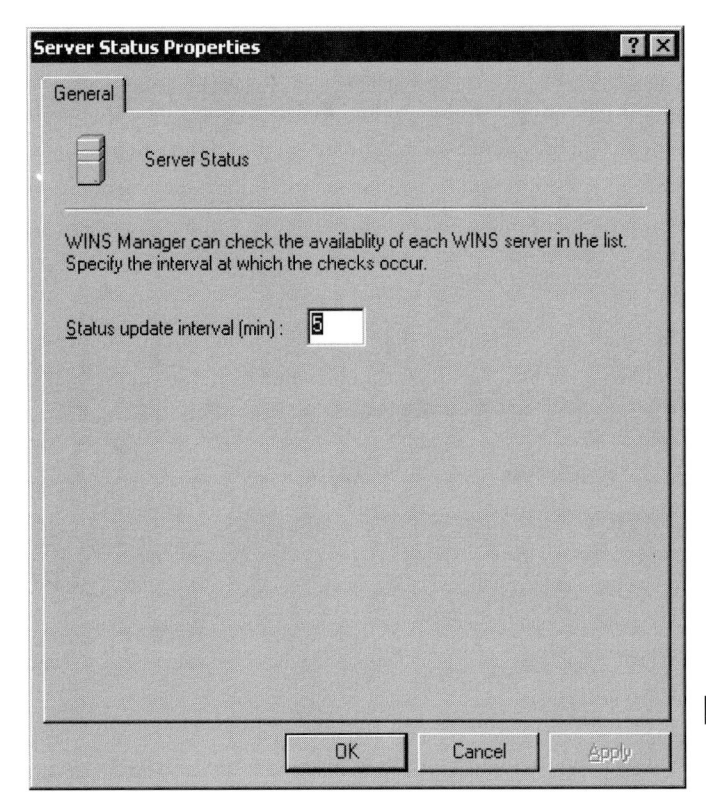

FIGURE 13.3 Server Status Properties

Examining Server Statistics

If you select a WINS Server in the list and right-click the server name, then click Show Server Statistics, a window appears that presents you with the description of various events and the details. This feature can be useful for troubleshooting, and an example is presented in Figure 13.4.

WINS Server Properties

You can access the properties sheet for each WINS Server by right-clicking on the Server and clicking Properties. The properties sheet has four tabs, which are examined in the following sections.

GENERAL

On the General Property sheet, shown in Figure 13.5, you can control the server statistics auto-refresh by adjusting the time that server statistics are automatically updated. You can also choose to back up the WINS database by browsing to a back-up path.

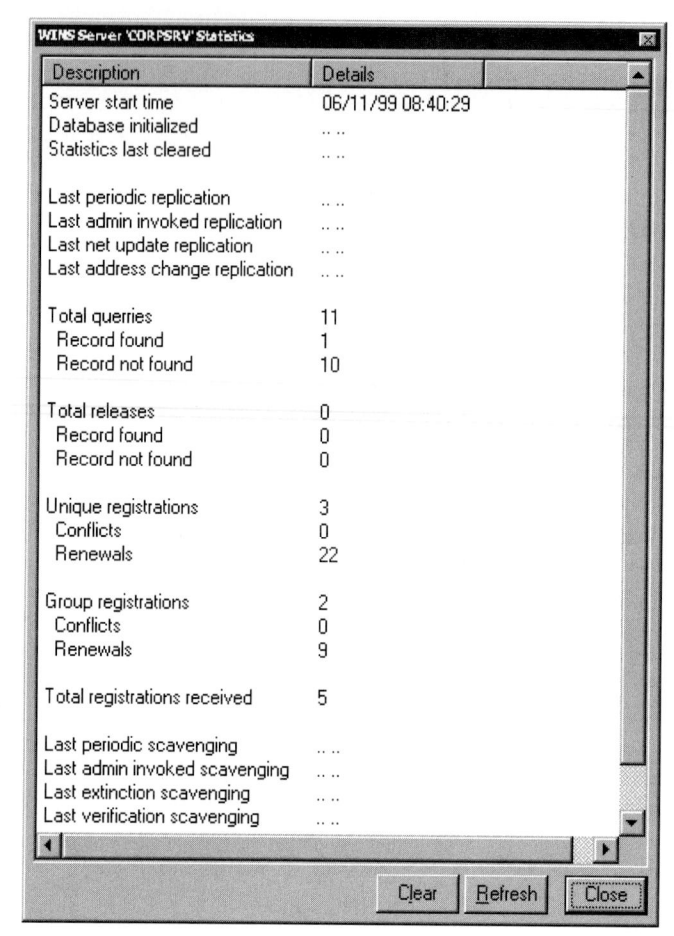

FIGURE 13.4
Server Statistics

INTERVALS

The Intervals Property sheet, shown in Figure 13.6, allows you to adjust the name record settings, such as the renew, extinction, and verification intervals as well as the extinction timeout.

DATABASE VERIFICATION

You can also check the Enable Periodic Database Consistency Checking to allow the Server to check the WINS database for consistency. You can adjust the check intervals as desired on this page.

ADVANCED PROPERTIES

In the Advanced Property sheet, shown in Figure 13.7, you can adjust logging options as needed. WINS stores changes to the database in a tempo-

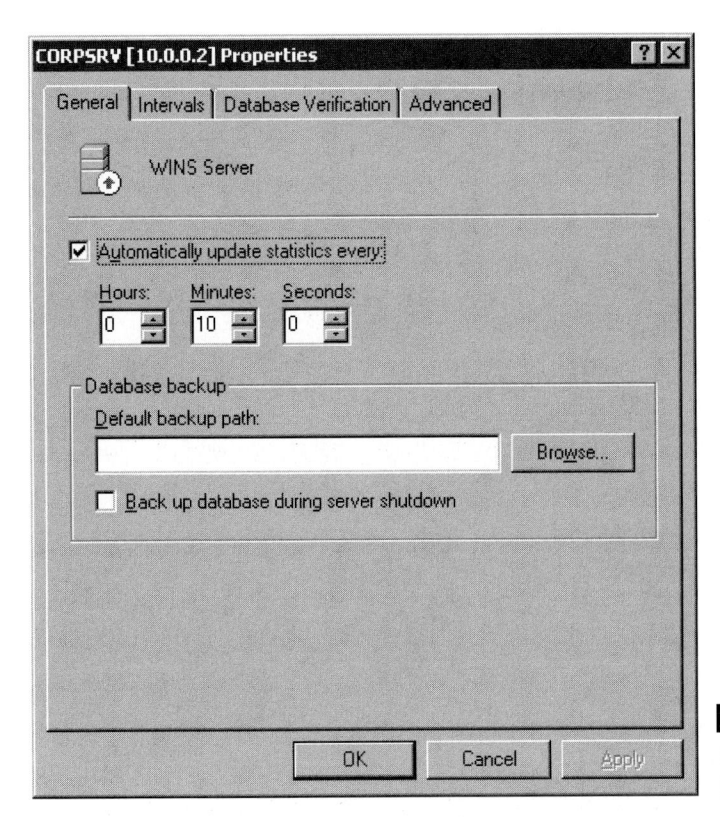

FIGURE 13.5 General Properties

rary file called jet.log in order to improve performance when handling a large "burst" of database changes. If you do not want to use the jet.log temporary file, you can disable it by deselecting the check box, but in most cases, you should allow WINS to use jet.log. In the middle of the page, you can enable burst handling and set a level, which is medium by default. Burst handling occurs when a certain number of client name registrations and refresh requests occur. This action helps improve performance so the server can handle the communication load. The following list tells you how many registrations and requests can occur before burst handling takes effect for the setting you choose:

- Low: 00 registration and name refresh requests in the burst queue before burst-handling mode begins.
- Medium: 500 registration and name refresh requests in the burst queue before burst-handling mode begins.
- High: 1000 registration and name refresh requests in the burst queue before burst-handling mode begins.
- Custom: allows you to enter the desired number of registration and name refresh requests in the burst queue before burst-handling mode begins.

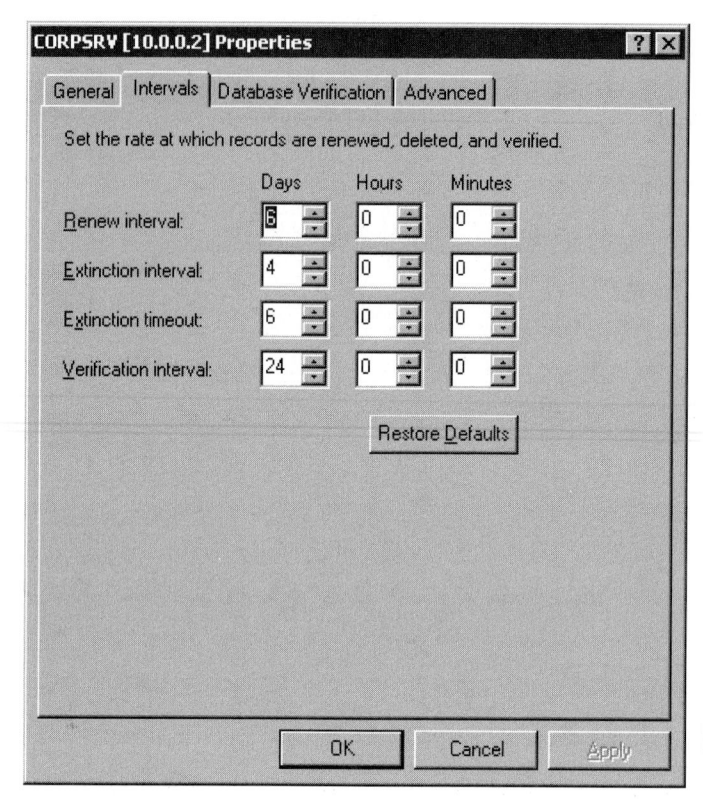

FIGURE 13.6
Intervals Tab

Additionally, the Advanced Property sheet allows you to disable LAN Manager compatibility by deselecting the check box at the bottom of the properties page.

Using Server All Tasks Functions

If you right-click on a WINS Server and point to All Tasks, you have several options you can perform. These actions can be performed by simply clicking on the selection. The following list tells you what each action does:

- Scavenge WINS Database: The WINS database periodically needs to remove outdated information. This action, known as "scavenging," cleans out old records. WINS automatically scavenges the database by the properties defined in the Name Record tab in the Server's Properties sheets, but you can force the scavenge manually by using All Tasks.
- Check WINS Database Consistency: A consistency check helps maintain database integrity among several WINS servers. This process is scheduled by default, but you can manually check the consistency

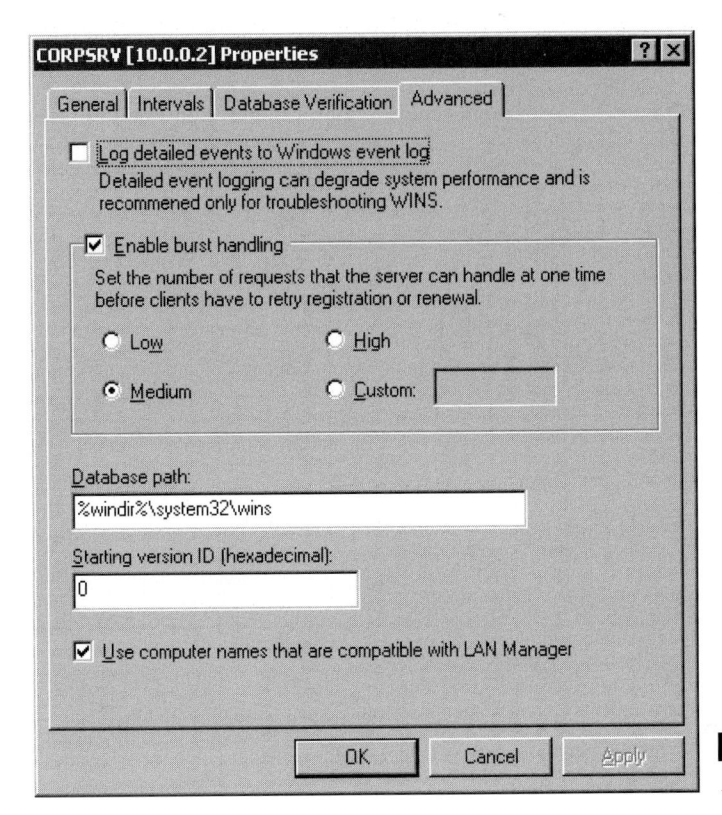

FIGURE 13.7
Advanced Tab

using All Tasks. The process, however, can be intensive and should be performed during off-peak hours.
- Check Version Number Consistency: This operation makes certain each server has the correct version number consistency to ensure that all servers have been tested for consistency.
- Send Push Replication Trigger: The push replication trigger allows you to immediately start a push replication to other WINS Servers. Click Send Push Replication Trigger in All Tasks, then enter the NetBIOS name or IP address in the dialog box provided, then click OK.
- Send Pull Replication Trigger: The pull replication trigger allows you to immediately start a pull replication from another WINS Server. Click Send Pull Replication Trigger in All Tasks, then enter the NetBIOS name or IP address in the dialog box provided, then click OK.
- Backup WINS Database: You can manually back-up the WINS database using this option. By default, the back-up path is the root folder on your volume, such as C:\. The WINS back-up file is called Wins.mdb.
- Restore WINS Database: This action allows you to restore a previously backed up WINS database.

Chapter thirteen • Configuring WINS

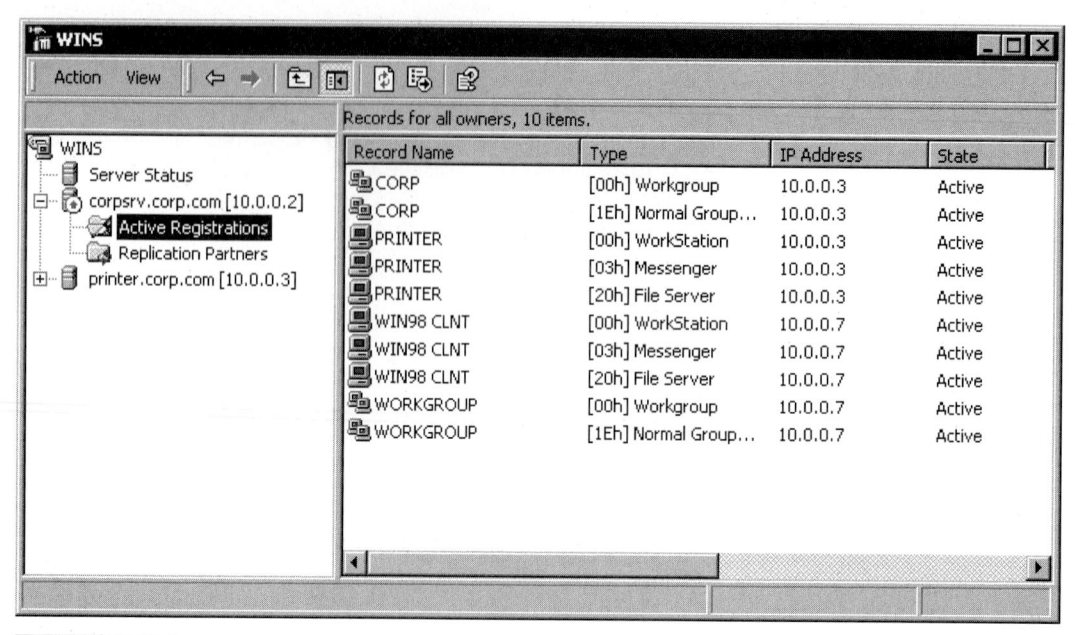

Record Name	Type	IP Address	State
CORP	[00h] Workgroup	10.0.0.3	Active
CORP	[1Eh] Normal Group...	10.0.0.3	Active
PRINTER	[00h] WorkStation	10.0.0.3	Active
PRINTER	[03h] Messenger	10.0.0.3	Active
PRINTER	[20h] File Server	10.0.0.3	Active
WIN98 CLNT	[00h] WorkStation	10.0.0.7	Active
WIN98 CLNT	[03h] Messenger	10.0.0.7	Active
WIN98 CLNT	[20h] File Server	10.0.0.7	Active
WORKGROUP	[00h] Workgroup	10.0.0.7	Active
WORKGROUP	[1Eh] Normal Group...	10.0.0.7	Active

FIGURE 13.8 Active Registrations

Managing WINS Registrations

If you expand the WINS Server, you will see a folder called Active Registrations, and by double-clicking on the object, the details pane will show you the WINS registrations for that server that are active, as shown in Figure 13.8.

For each record in the details pane, you can right-click on the record and click Properties to see the record state, expiration, IP address, and server owner of the record, as shown in Figure 13.9.

If you right-click on Active Registrations, you have a number of management options to help you manage the WINS registrations. The following sections explore these options.

QUICK FIND RECORDS

The quick find option presents you with a dialog box to search for WINS records. The dialog box asks you to "enter names beginning with" to search for name matches. You can also click the Mixed Case Search check box to perform mixed searches.

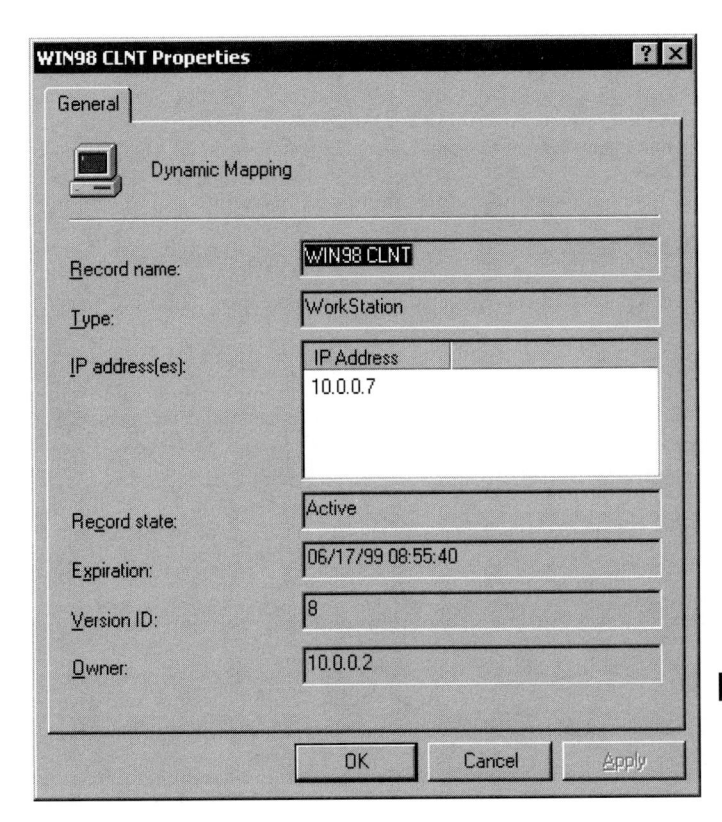

FIGURE 13.9
Dynamic Mapping Properties

VIEW RECORDS

The View records option allows you to see all records that exist or all records for a selected owner, as shown in Figure 13.10. Once you make your selection, press OK and the records will appear in the console's details pane.

The Record Types Property sheet, shown in Figure 13.11, allows you to view records based on type. By default, all record types are selected for display, but you can deselect records that you choose to help you refine the view.

STATIC MAPPINGS

You can create static mappings in the WINS database by pointing to New, then clicking Static Mapping. This option presents you with a Static Mapping sheet, shown in Figure 13.12, which allows you to enter the computer name, scope, type (either unique, group, domain name, Internet Group, or Multihomed), and the IP address. This action gives you permanent computer name to IP mapping for a particular computer.

Chapter thirteen • Configuring WINS

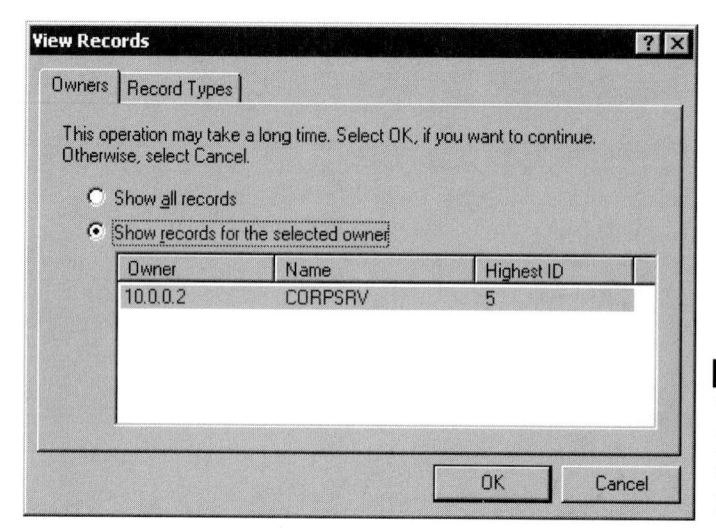

FIGURE 13.10
View Records Owners Properties

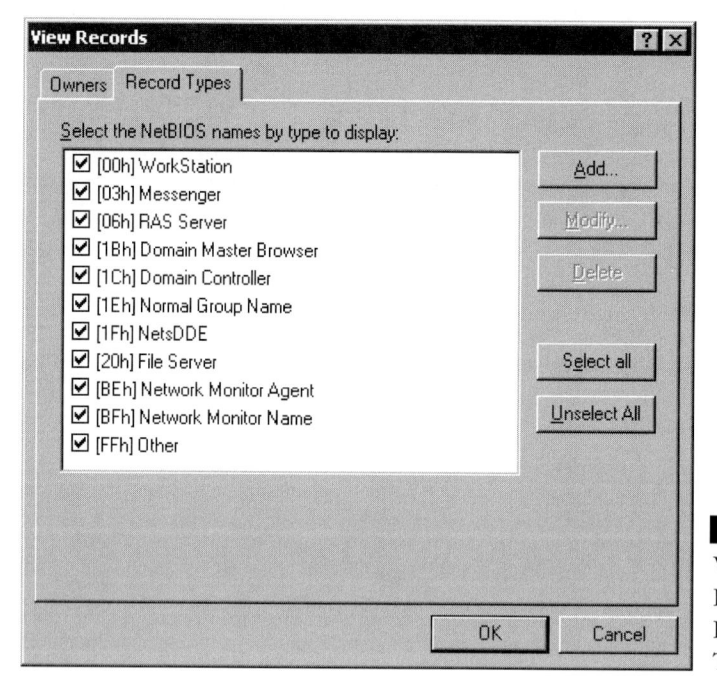

FIGURE 13.11
View Records Record Types Tab

ALL TASKS

The All Tasks option allows you to perform three actions. First, you can import an LMHOSTS file. If you click this option, you are prompted to browse for the location of the LMHOSTS file to import. Next, you can check

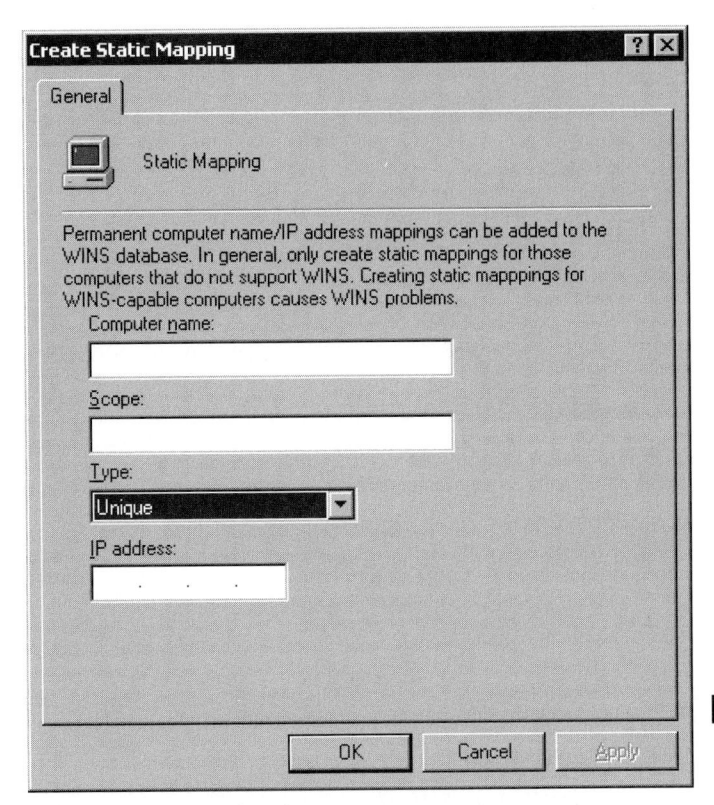

FIGURE 13.12
Create Static Mapping

FIGURE 13.13
Delete Owner

Registered Names, which queries a list of name records on a set of WINS Servers. This allows you to check for inconsistencies between records. Finally, you can delete an owner of a group of active registrations if desired. This option, shown in Figure 13.13, lets you delete the selected owner and all of its records, or you can select the option to tombstone all records for the selected owner. Tombstoning marks a record as inactive for a period of time before the record is deleted. This allows the tombstone to be replicated to other servers so the record that can be deleted from all WINS Servers.

Managing Replication

One of the most important WINS management tasks is ensuring that replication among WINS Server's is configured and performing in an acceptable manner. The following sections show you how to perform replication tasks.

ADD A REPLICATION PARTNER

To add a replication partner, expand the WINS Server where you want to add the partner, then right-click on Replication Partners, point to New, then select Replication Partner. Enter the name or IP address of the WINS server you want to add as a replication partner and click OK.

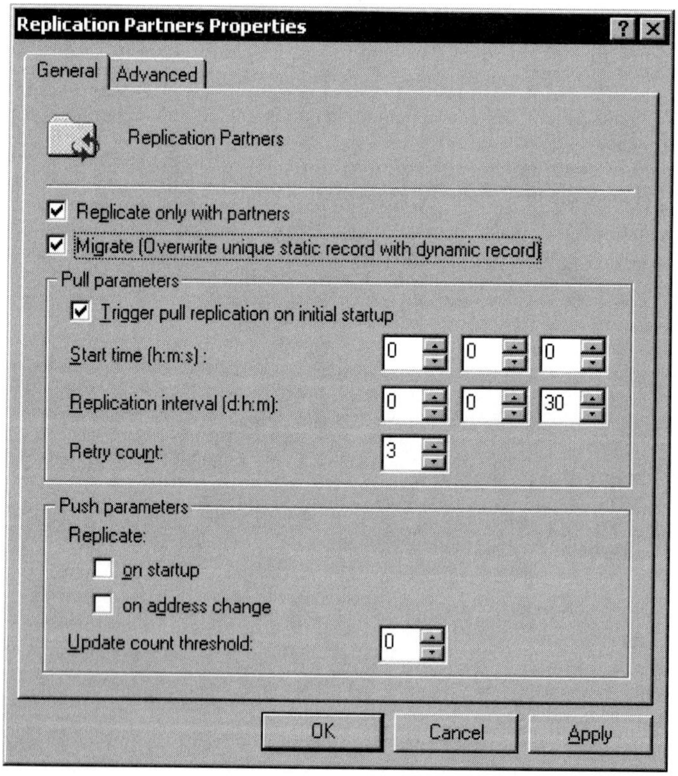

FIGURE 13.14

Replication Partners General

FORCING REPLICATION

To force replication between partners, expand the Server on which you want to force replication, right-click Replication Partners, point to All Tasks, and click Replicate Now. A message appears asking if you are sure you want to start replication. Click Yes.

REPLICATION PARTNER PROPERTIES

You can further configure replication by accessing the properties sheet. Expand the Server you want to administer and right-click on Replication Partners, then click Properties. The Properties sheet appears and contains two tabs, General and Advanced.

On the General Property sheet, shown in Figure 13.14, you can replicate only with partners and migrate, which overwrites unique static records with dynamic records. Next, you can configure pull and push parameters. By default, a pull replication is triggered on initial startup, and you can configure the amount of time that passes between pull triggers. The default replication interval is 30 minutes. For push triggers, you can replicate on startup and on address change if desired. Neither of these options is selected by default.

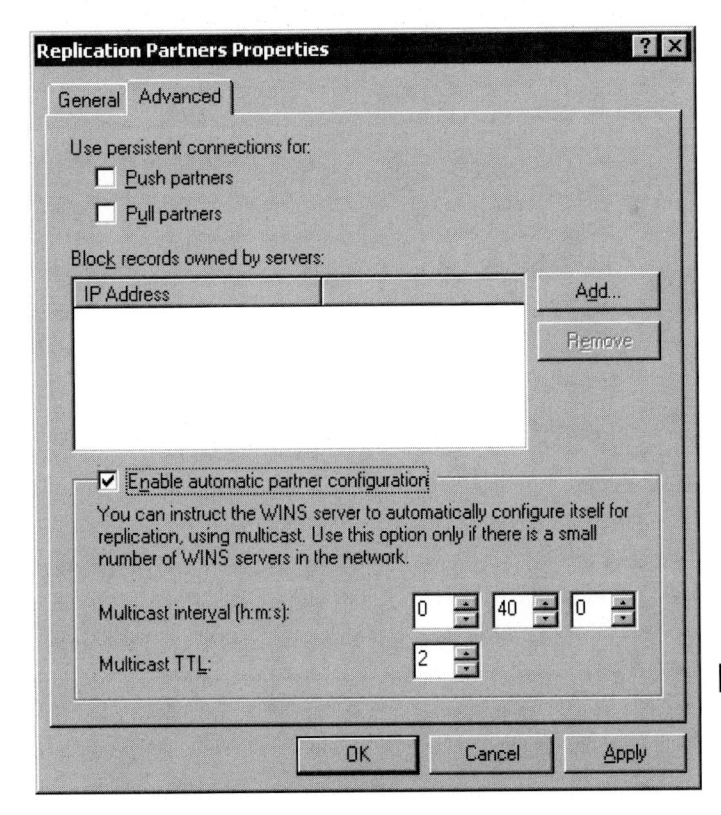

FIGURE 13.15 Replication Partners Advanced

On the Advanced Property sheet, shown in Figure 13.15, you can configure persistent connections for push or pull partners, or both if desired. You can also use the dialog box to block replication records from certain servers. Click the Add button and enter the server IP address to block records owned by certain servers. The bottom section of the screen allows you to enable automatic partner configuration. This configuration allows a WINS server to automatically configure itself as a push/pull partner with other WINS Servers found on the network. This feature uses multicasting, and in order for this feature to work, your routers must support multicasting for servers on different subnets to be discovered. The default multicast interval is every 40 minutes, and the default multicast TTL is 2.

Summary

WINS in Windows 2000 Server provides down-level functionality for systems other than Windows 2000. WINS provides computer name to IP address mappings so that computer names can be resolved to IP addresses. The WINS Manager functions as an MMC snap-in and can be configured for a variety of needs and environmental variables.

FOURTEEN

Configuring Routing and Remote Access

Remote Access Service (RAS) and Routing and Remote Access Service (RRAS) in Windows 2000 allow remote clients to gain access to the network through either dial-up connections or virtual private connections. These remote clients, once authenticated, then gain access to network resources as though they are physically connected to the LAN. Remote access has become more and more important in today's complex networks where many people travel with laptop computers or work from a home office. Routing and Remote Access is much more than simple dial-up connectivity; depending on the configuration of the service, the remote clients can have just as much access to the network as the clients who are physically located and connected to the network.

Typically, routing and remote access has not been an easy component to configure in Windows NT. In Windows 2000, the services are more complex, but are somewhat more manageable through the MMC snap-in provided. This chapter explores the functions and configuration of Routing and Remote Access Service in Windows 2000 Server.

Overview of Remote Access

As mentioned in the introduction to this chapter, Remote Access allows clients to connect to a Remote Access Server in order to gain network resources as though connected directly to the network. A client can access the Remote Access server in two different ways: dial-up and virtual private networking.

Dial-up Connectivity

Windows 2000 Server can be configured as an RAS dial-up server that provides access to the LAN or WAN. You can configure the dial-up server to permit clients to access the entire network once they are authenticated, or you can restrict the clients to shares and information available on the dial-up server only. Obviously, the latter option provides greater security, but it is also the most restrictive to dial-up clients.

With dial-up networking, clients access the server using a modem, a modem pool, ISDN connection, or even an X.25 connection. During configuration of the server, you determine what protocols the dial-up clients can use. Available protocols include TCP/IP, IPX, AppleTalk, and NetBEUI. The following client operating systems can access a Windows 2000 dial-up server:

- Windows 2000
- Windows NT
- Windows 9.x
- Windows For Workgroups
- MS-DOS
- LAN Manager
- Macintosh

Dial-up clients must have dial-up hardware configured as well as the RAS software.

Virtual Private Networks

A Virtual Private Network (VPN) allows you to create a virtual communication session with a remote network as though you are directly connected to the network. A VPN allows you to send secure data across a shared or public network, such as the Internet. VPNs are cost effective solutions to communicate with remote networks when a dedicated WAN link is not needed or is too expensive. A VPN is also a solution for individual users who travel and need to connect the LAN from various locations through the Internet. VPNs are configured through the Routing and Remote Access Service console by allowing TCP traffic for VPNs and by configuring desired security features.

HOW VPNs WORK

VPNs function by using either the Point to Point Tunneling Protocol (PPTP) or the Layer Two Tunneling Protocol (L2TP) with IP Security (IPSec). The PPTP or L2TP allows a LAN protocol, such as IPX or NetBEUI, to travel over an IP network by encapsulating the LAN protocol with a Point to Point

| IP Header | PPP Header | Encrypted PPP data such as IP datagram, IPX datagram, NetBEUI frame |

FIGURE 14.1 PPTP Frame

Protocol (PPP) header. The header information provides generic routing, such as a source and destination IP address, so the LAN data can travel over the public network. The data contained in the data frame is encrypted for transit so that no one on the public network is able to read the packet data. The encryption is accomplished through the use of encryption keys, which are contained on each side of the VPN (such as the client and server.) Figure 14.1 gives you a graphical representation of a PPTP frame.

By sending the PPTP frame over the Internet, companies can use the Internet as an inexpensive resource to send secure data.

A VPN can be created by either using remote access so that a user makes a remote access VPN connection or by using a router-to-router connection. The server authenticates the remote access client and authenticates itself to the client so the VPN connection can occur. At this point, the remote access server and the remote client initiate a VPN session, and the client can access network resources (depending on permissions) as though the client were directly connected. Client computers running Windows 2000, Windows NT 4.0, or Windows 9.x can be used to create VPNs with a server running Windows 2000. A router-to-router connection can also be established so that two routers initiate a VPN. This action allows you to connect two LAN segments without a WAN link. Clients on both networks can use the connection as though directly connected to the remote network (depending on permissions). Windows 2000 Server and Windows NT 4.0 Servers with routing and remote access installed can be configured to function as VPN routers to connect to other Windows 2000 Servers functioning as routers. In either case, a connection can be made using dial-up WAN or dedicated WAN links so the Internet can be used to transfer the data, as shown in Figure 14.2.

VPNs can also be configured for use over an intranet. In this situation, if a certain LAN department is not directly connected to the LAN for security purposes, a VPN can be established over the intranet for secure communication. This configuration allows you to allow either client VPN establishment or router VPN establishment.

VPNs are configured as other components in the routing and remote access console. You can learn more about using L2TP over IPSec in Chapter 17.

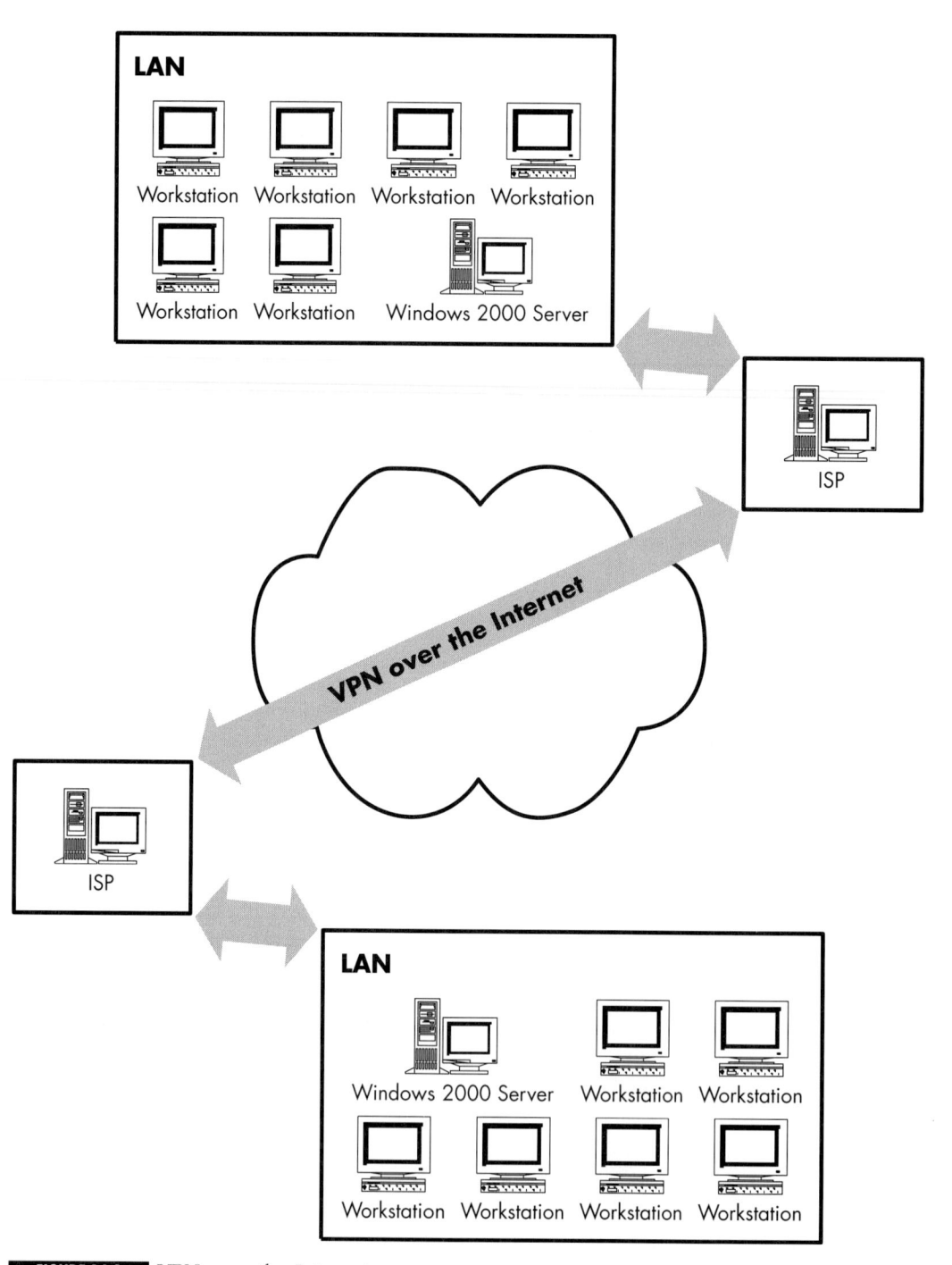

FIGURE 14.2 VPN over the Internet

New Features of Remote Access

Remote Access in Windows 2000 Server provides several new features that enable tighter security and management. The following list gives you an overview of the new features in Windows 2000:

- MS-CHAP Version 2: RAS in Windows 2000 supports Microsoft Challenge Handshake Authentication Protocol version 2, which provides greater security for logon and authentication information. MS-CHAP version 2 generates encryption keys during the RAS connection negotiation.
- EAP: Extensible Authentication Protocol (EAP) is now supported in Windows 2000 RAS. EAP allows the use of third-party authentication software and is an important part of smart card deployment.
- L2TP: Layer 2 Tunneling Protocol (L2TP) is an additional standard to PPTP and is used in conjunction with IP Security. To learn more about L2TP and IP Security, see Chapter 17.
- Macintosh support: Windows 2000 supports dial-up connections for Apple Macintosh computers that use either PPP or AppleTalk Remote Access Protocol (ARAP).
- IP Multicast: RAS now supports IP multicast to allow a RAS server to forward IP multicast traffic between connected RAS clients, the Internet, or the LAN.
- BAP and BACP: Bandwidth Allocation Protocol (BAP) and Bandwidth Allocation Control Protocol (BACP) allow you to dynamically drop or add PPP links depending on traffic flow. These protocols help you control and reduce the amount of bandwidth that is being used by RAS clients.
- Active Directory integration: As with most Windows 2000 components, remote access is integrated with the Active Directory for easier management and control.
- Policies: Remote Access in Windows 2000 allows you to set policies that control RAS connections. For example, you can specify the time of day remote access connections are allowed, limit the session time, the type of authentication required, and so forth.
- Account Lockout: RAS now supports account lockout. As with standard accounts, you can configure RAS to lock an account after a certain number of failed logon attempts.

Overview of Routing

The Routing and Remote Access Service (RRAS) was first introduced by Microsoft in 1996 as a free add-on component. In Windows 2000, Routing and the Remote Access Service are fully integrated and not considered two separate components. The routing feature allows you to route information within the local network or even over the Internet. Routing is fully integrated with Windows 2000 and functions on a wide variety of hardware platforms and with a wide variety of network adapters. Routing in Windows 2000 supports numerous protocols and provides an open platform for internetworking. The following list gives you an overview of the Routing features supported in Windows 2000:

- Multiple protocol unicast routing for IP, IPX, and AppleTalk.
- Standard IP routing protocols and services, such as RIP, RIP for IPX, and SAP for IPX.
- Internet Group Management Protocol router and proxy services for IP multicast traffic.
- IP network address translation (NAT) services.
- IP and IPX packet filtering.
- Demand dial routing over dial-up WAN links.
- VPN support for PPTP and L2TP.
- DHCP Relay Agent for IP support.
- IP-in-IP tunnel support.
- SNMP management capabilities.
- Extensive network support from analog modems to 100 Mbps Ethernet.

Installing Routing and Remote Access

Routing and Remote access is integrated with the Windows 2000 Server system and is present after an initial Windows 2000 Server installation. At this point, you need to install routing and remote access for the server itself, and you can also install and manage routing and remote access for other servers within the same interface with appropriate permissions.

To install RAS, click Start ➤ Programs ➤ Administrative Tools ➤ Routing and Remote Access. Double-click Routing and Remote Access in the Console tree, then right-click the server name for which you want to install remote access. Click Install Routing and Remote Access. Complete these steps:

1. When the wizard begins, click Next.
2. On the Routing and Remote Access screen, select the Enable this server as a router and select the Enable Remote Access check boxes if you want to install both Routing and Remote Access service on the server, as shown in Figure 14.3.
3. On the next screen, you can select whether to enable all devices present on your computer for remote access, enable all devices for rout-

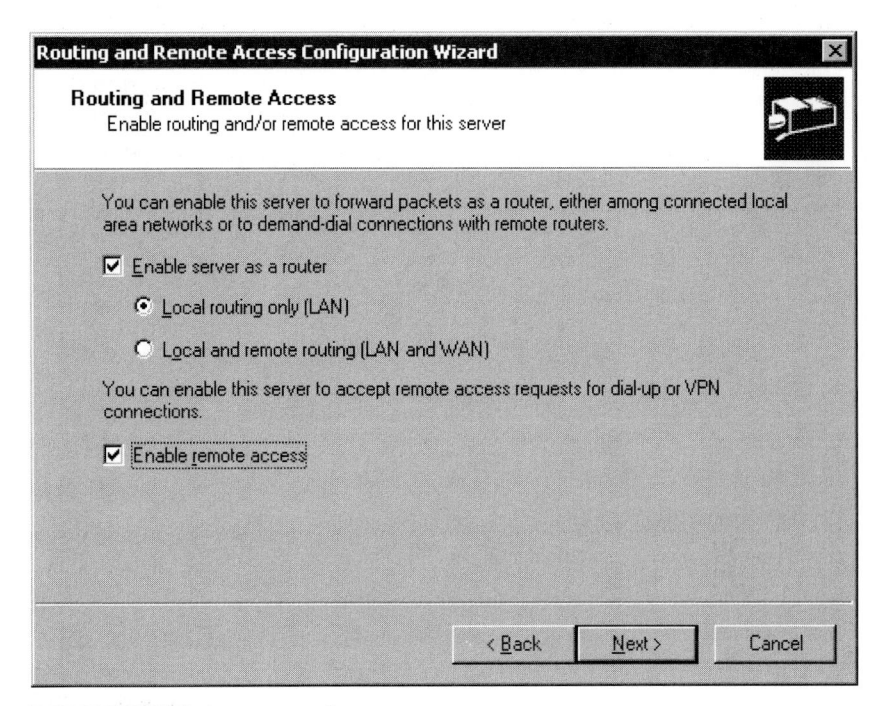

FIGURE 14.3 Routing and Remote Access

ing, enable all devices for both routing and remote access, or you can choose to configure each device individually. Click the radio button of your selection and click Next.

4. The Authentication and encryption window appears, shown in Figure 14.4. Make your selection to either allow all authentication methods or only allow methods that secure the user's password.

5. The Remote Access window appears, shown in Figure 14.5. The list box shows you which protocols that have been loaded on your server. Select each protocol and click either Access this server only or Access entire network, depending on what rights you want to grant to dial-up clients.

6. The TCP/IP Server Settings for Remote Access window appears. In this window, you can select the Use DHCP radio button so that remote clients gain their IP configuration information from DHCP, or you can enter a static pool of IP addresses so that remote clients do not become DHCP clients. Make your selection and click Next.

7. Click the Finish button.

8. A dialog box appears telling you that Routing and Remote Access service has been installed. Click Yes to start the service.

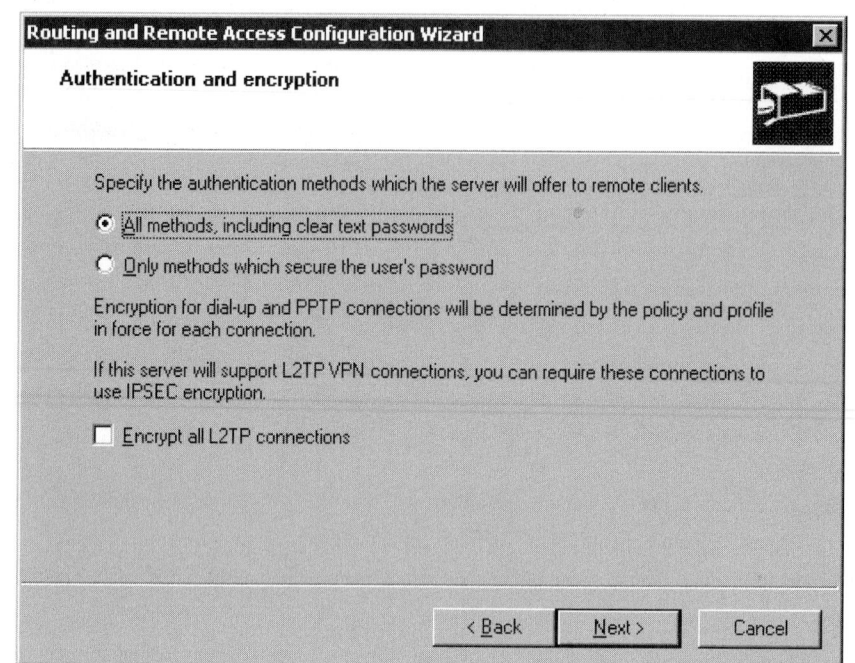

FIGURE 14.4
Authentication and Encryption

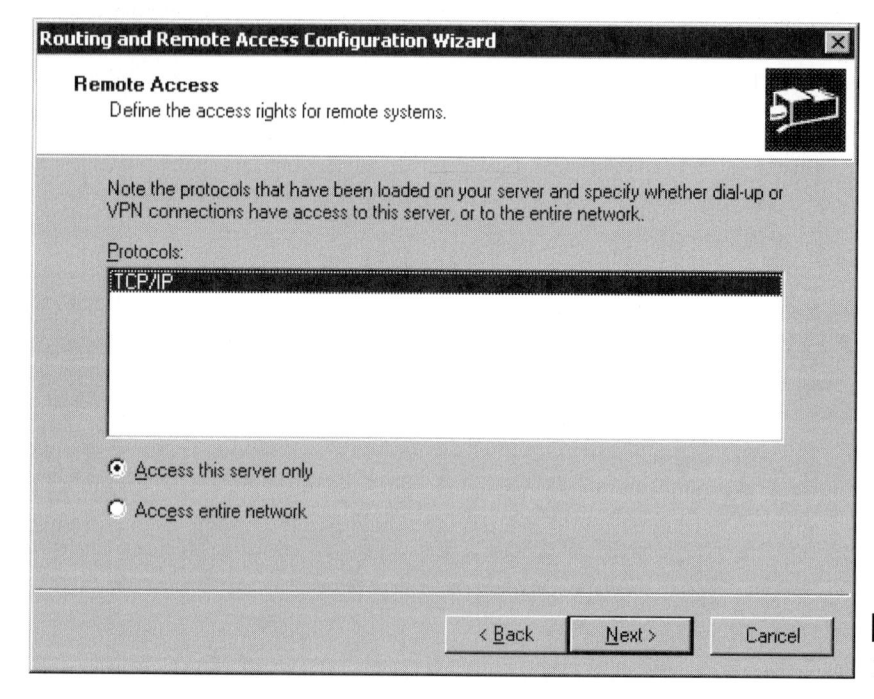

FIGURE 14.5
Remote Access

Configuring Routing and Remote Access

You configure all routing and remote access options in the Routing and Remote Access MMC console, which is accessible from Administrative Tools. The following sections show you how to configure a number of routing and remote access options.

Adding a Server

If you right-click on Routing and Remote Access at the top of the console tree, and click Add Server, you can add another routing and remote access server to the server list. This feature allows you to manage several routing and remote access servers from one location. When you click Add Server, a dialog box appears, shown in Figure 14.6.

The window allows you to add a server to this computer, or another machine on the network (by entering the server name or IP address), or you can search the directory and add all routing and remote access servers in the domain.

Server Properties

You can access the routing and remote access server's properties by right-clicking on the server name in the console tree and selecting Properties. The properties sheet presents you with five tabs, which are explained in the following sections.

GENERAL

The General Properties gives you the same information you entered during installation. You can change this information by clearing or checking either

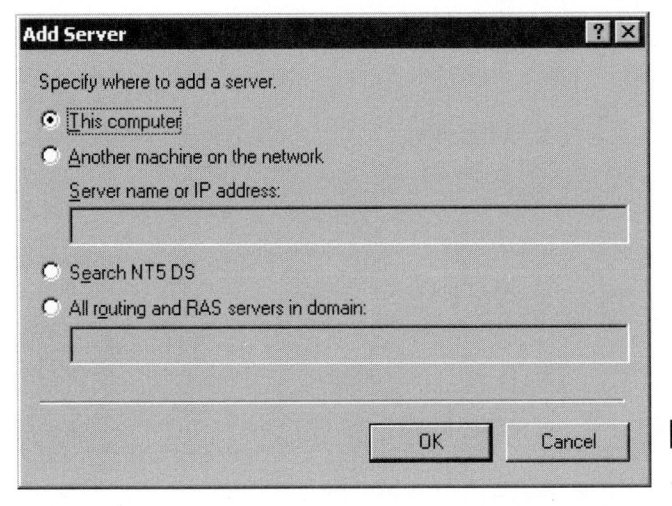

FIGURE 14.6
Add Server

the Enable this server as a router or Enable remote access server check boxes. For both routing and remote access to be available, both check boxes need to remain selected.

SECURITY

The Security Properties, shown in Figure 14.7, allows you to select what authentication protocols and security you want to use.

By selecting the appropriate check boxes, you can enable EAP, MS-CHAP v2, MS-CHAP, CHAP, SPAP, PAP, or you can even allow unauthenticated access. If you want to use EAP, you can click the Details button to view a list of currently installed EAP methods. You can also click the check box to allow the use of IP security for L2TP connections. In the authentication provider drop-down menu, you can select the available authentication provider, such as Windows authentication or RADIUS (Remote Authentication Dial-In User Service) if a RADIUS server is in use. The Accounting Provider determines how you want to log authentication information. By default, "none" is selected, but you can choose to log the information through Windows accounting or RADIUS if a RADIUS server is in use.

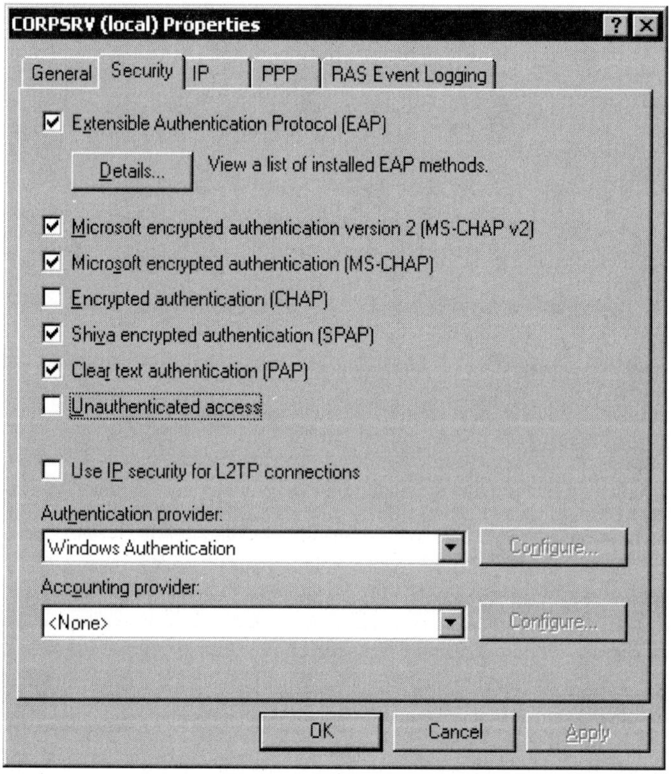

FIGURE 14.7

Security Tab

IP AND IPX

The IP Properties presents you with the same information you entered during routing and remote access installation. In the IP section, you can allow remote computers running IP to access the routing and remote access server only, or you can allow the computer to access the entire network, depending on which radio button you select.

You can also use this property page to define the IP addressing for remote access clients. You can allow the remote access clients to receive an IP address and IP configuration information from the DHCP server, or you can enter a static pool of addresses that can be used. If NwLink is used on your network, you will see a similar IPX tab.

PPP

The PPP Properties allows you to configure which PPP negotiation options should be used during a connection, as shown in Figure 14.8. Policies, however, will override the selection depending on the specifications for those policies.

The options are available to enable multilink control with dynamic BAP/BACP, LCP (Link Control Protocol), which enables callback, and software compression. By default, all options are selected.

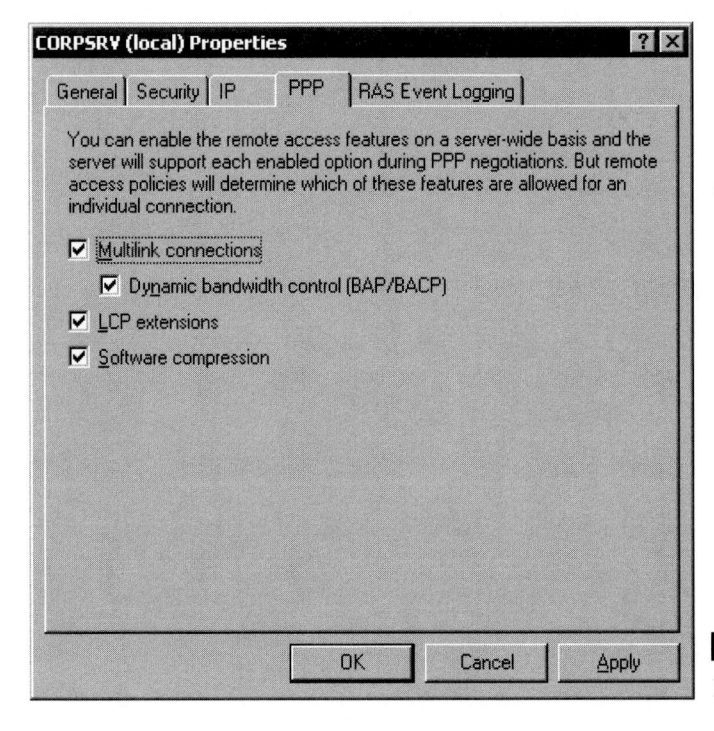

FIGURE 14.8
PPP Tab

RAS EVENT LOGGING

The RAS Event Logging Properties provides you with four radio buttons so that you can configure logging as needed; the four radio buttons are disable event logging, log errors only, log errors and warnings, and log maximum amount of information.

Routing Interfaces

If you expand the server name in the console tree, you will see a Routing Interfaces object if Routing is installed. If you double-click on the Routing Interfaces icon, you will see the routing interfaces currently configured for your server. You can right-click on any of the interfaces to set the credentials, connect or disconnect, enable or disable, or access refresh or help. If you right-click on the Routing Interfaces icon in the left pane, then point to New, you can configure a new demand dial interface or tunnel (IP only). Either of these options will ask you for the interface name, and I should note that WAN routing is required to add a demand-dial interface.

Dial-in Clients

The dial-in clients icon that appears under the server name in the console tree allows you to view the clients that are currently connected to the remote access server. In the right pane of the console tree, the user name, duration of the connection, and the number of ports in use by the user are listed.

Ports

If you right-click on the Ports icon that appears under the server name in the console tree and click Properties, as shown in Figure 14.9, you can view the ports that are currently used by the remote access service.

You can select each port and click the Configure button to specify information about the port, as shown in Figure 14.10. You can see that PPTP is installed by default, but you will need to configure the ports to allow VPN connections. For each port, you can allow the device to accept inbound remote access calls, or use demand dialing for both inbound and outbound access. You can also adjust the port limit if dynamic ports are supported.

IP Routing

The IP Routing icon under the remote access server contains two divisions: general and static routes. If you right-click the General icon, point to New, then select Interface, you can install a new routing interface if new routing hardware is available for use. You can also point to New and click Routing Protocol to install a new routing protocol. When you choose to install a new routing protocol, a window appears, shown in Figure 14.11, which

three • Networking **259**

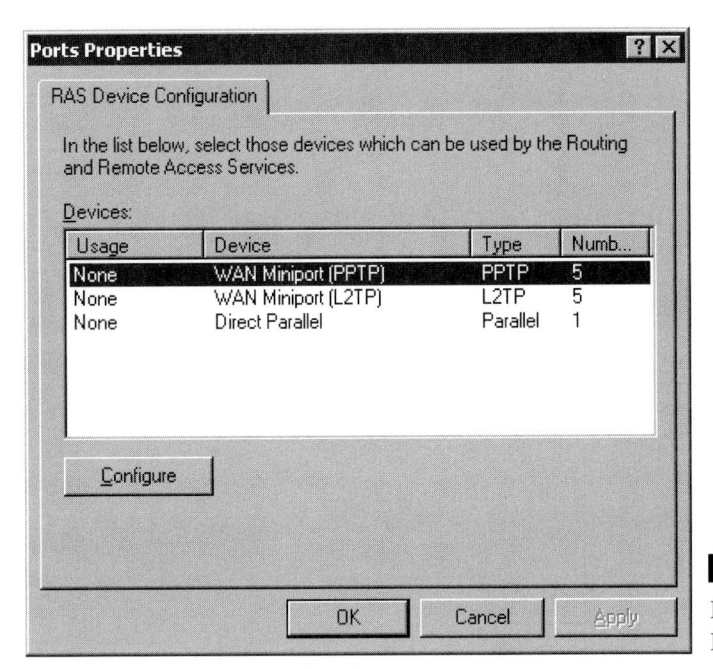

FIGURE 14.9
Ports Properties

FIGURE 14.10
Configure Ports

allows you to select the new protocol from a list for installation. Once you select the protocol, you can further define properties for the protocol by accessing its properties sheet. Most of the property sheets are very similar and are self-explanatory.

FIGURE 14.11
New Routing Protocol

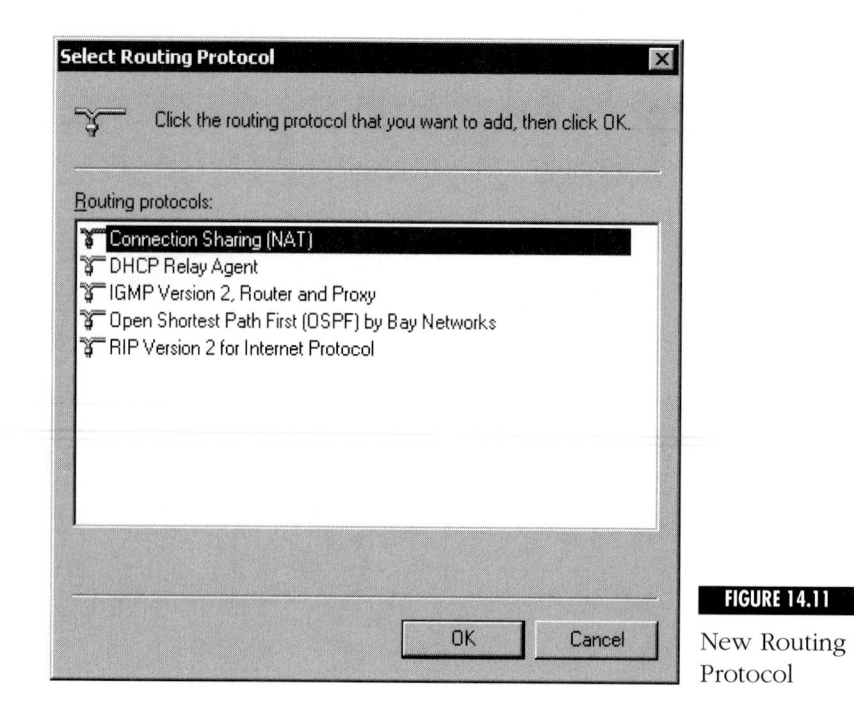

The General IP Routing component also allows you to view TCP/IP information, show the multicast forwarding table, and show the multicast statistics. To view any of these, right-click on General and select the desired information from All Tasks.

The General IP routing component also contains a properties sheet with General, Preference Levels, and Multicast Scopes tabs. The General Properties sheet allows you to select a logging option for General IP routing. From the radio button available, you can select disable event logging, log errors only, log errors and warnings, or log the maximum amount of information. The Preference Levels tab, shown in Figure 14.12, allows you to adjust the level of the routing protocols in use. By using the raise and lower level buttons, you can move a protocol up or down in the list. Protocols with lower levels are preferred over ones in higher levels.

The final property sheet, Multicast Scopes, allows you to configure multicast scopes for multicast functions within routing. To add a scope, click the Add button, then enter the scope name, IP address, and subnet mask.

The second IP routing component is Static Routes. If you right-click Static Routes under IP Routing in the console tree, then point to New, you can add a new static route. In the window that appears, you can select the interface where you want to add a new static route, then enter the destination IP address, network mask, gateway, and metric number. You can

FIGURE 14.12 Preference Levels

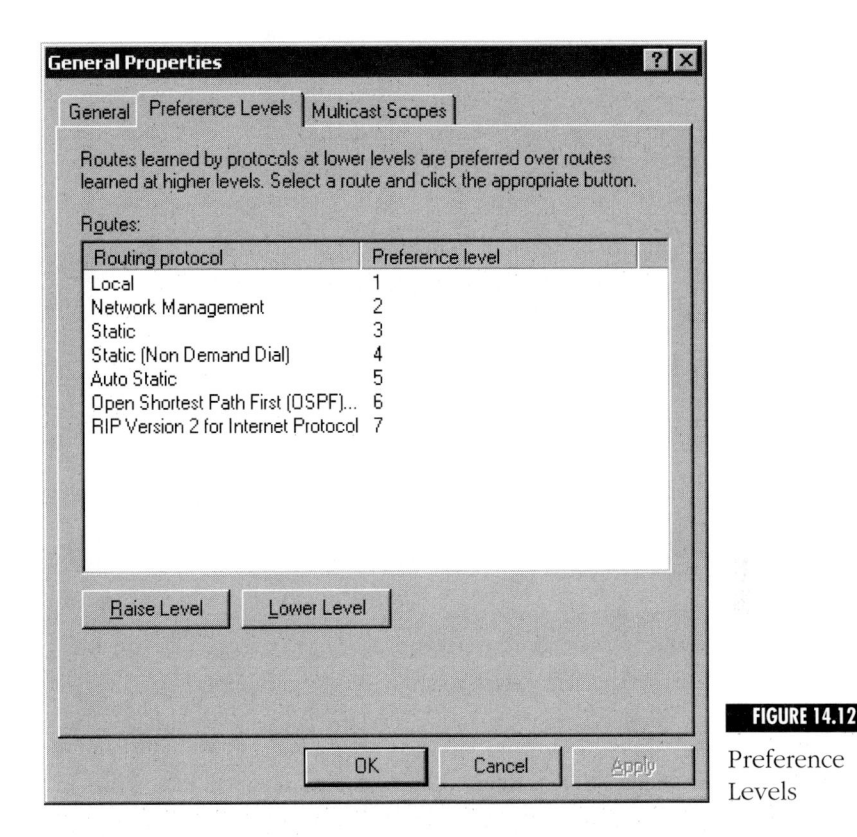

click the Use this route to initiate demand dial connections check box if you want to enable this feature.

Remote Access Policies

Remote access policies determine how the remote users can dial-in and how they can access the network. When you install routing and remote access, you have a default policy titled "Allow access if dial-in permission is enabled." If you click Remote Access Policies, then double-click this policy in the details pane, you can see the settings for the policy, shown in Figure 14.13.

You can make changes to this policy, remove it, or you can click the Edit Profile button to make additional changes to the profile. If you click the Edit Profile button, you are presented with an Edit Dial-in Profile Properties sheet that has six tabs. The following sections show you what you can configure on each property sheet.

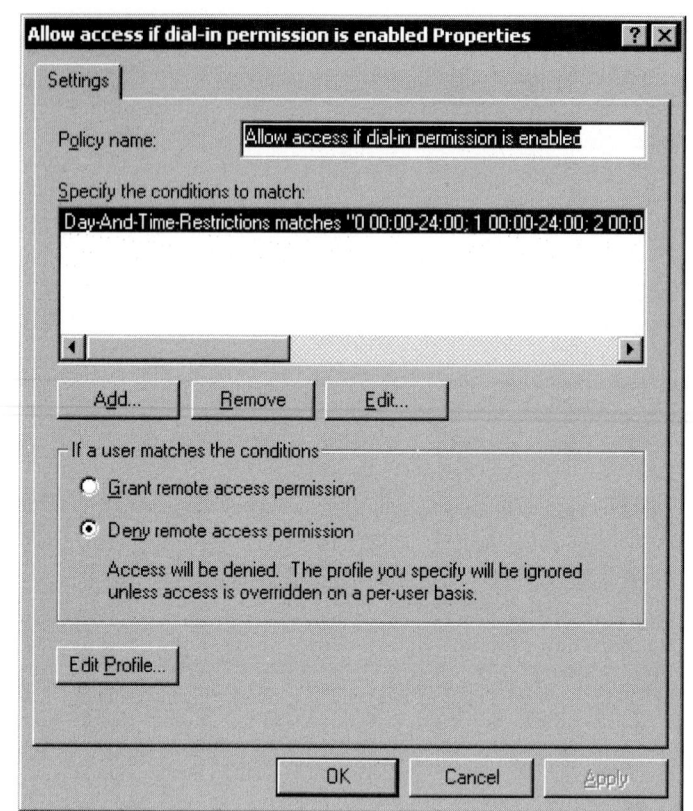

FIGURE 14.13
Policy Settings

DIAL-IN CONSTRAINTS

The Dial-in Constraints sheet, shown in Figure 14.14, allows you to restrict various components of dial-up connectivity. First, you can use the checkboxes to disconnect the call if it is idle for a certain period of time (which you enter), and you can restrict the amount of access time as well. In the center of the properties sheet, you can restrict the days and times the users can access the dial-up server. To make changes, click the check box, then click the Edit button. You can clear the grids that appear on the days and hours you wish to restrict dial-in availability. Next, you can restrict dial-in to a certain number by clicking the check box and entering the number, and you restrict the dial-in media to a certain type if desired.

IP

The IP Property sheet allows you to further configure IP addresses and policies for the dial-up server. This property sheet, shown in Figure 14.15, allows you to specify that the server must supply the IP address, the client

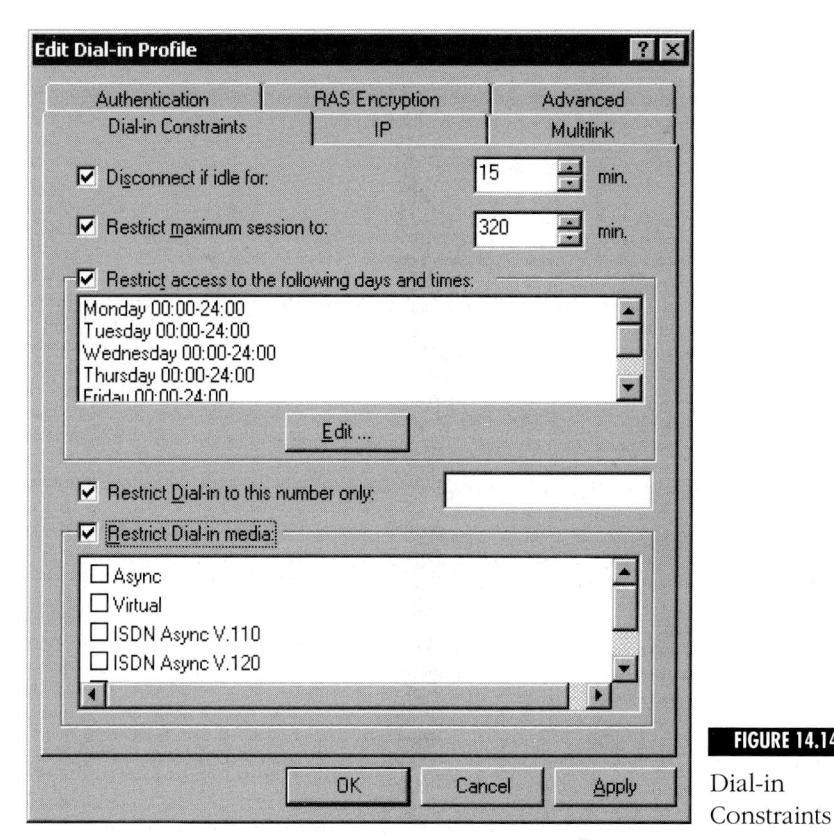

FIGURE 14.14
Dial-in Constraints

may request an IP address, or you can allow the server's settings to define the policy.

Also, you can define IP packet filters. Packet filters restrict certain kinds of IP traffic that you do not want used over the connection. If you click the From Client button, you are taken to an IP Packet Filters Configuration sheet, shown in Figure 14.16, that allows you to filter protocols.

If you click the Add button, you can enter the destination network or source network IP address and subnet mask, then select a protocol from the drop-down list, then click OK. Once you make your selection, you can select either the Permit all traffic except those listed below or the Deny all traffic except those listed below radio buttons. In Figure 14.13, all traffic is permitted except ICMP. However, I could turn this around, set-up a TCP filter and allow only TCP traffic by using the second radio button. In the same manner, you can click the To client button on the IP Properties sheet and configure filters for traffic passed to the client. As with all filtering, you should carefully examine your need to use packet filters before implementing them, as this action may halt certain TCP traffic that needs to pass.

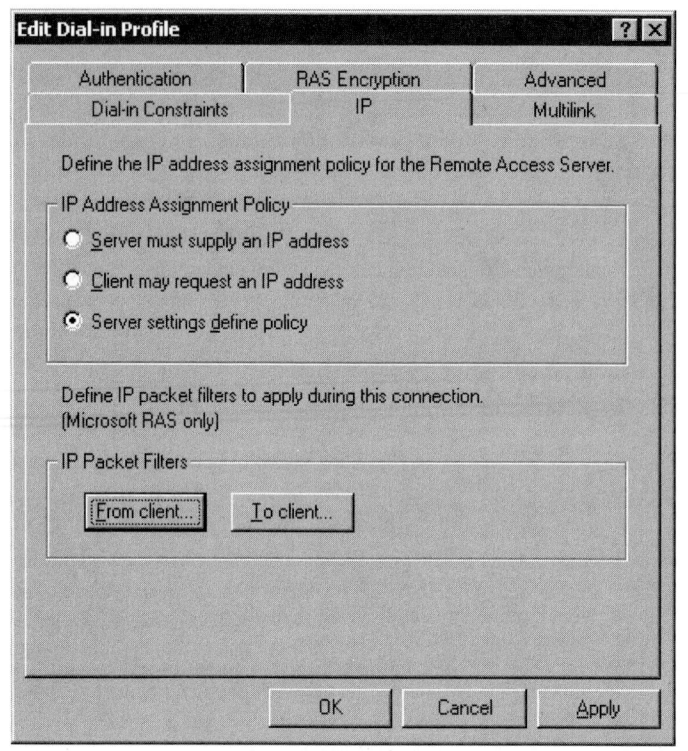

FIGURE 14.15

IP Properties

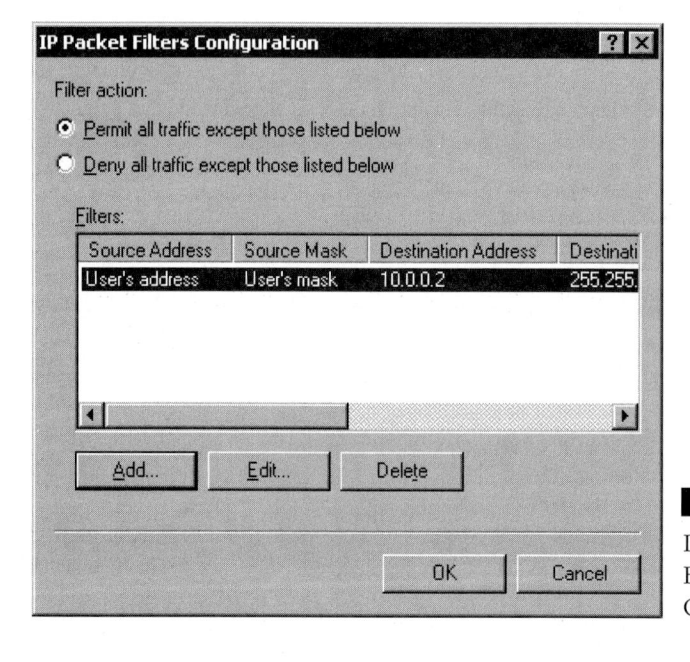

FIGURE 14.16

IP Packet Filters Configuration

MULTILINK

Multilink allows you to configure several devices, such as modems, to work as one device. This approach increases bandwidth for the connection. You can use the Multilink Property sheet to configure multilink settings for the routing and remote access server. The Multilink Property sheet, shown in Figure 14.17, allows you to use either default server settings, disable multilink, or allow multilink. You can limit the maximum number of ports that can be used for a multilink connection by adjusting the dialog box. Also, you can specify whether or not to require Bandwidth Allocation Protocol (BAP) usage for multilink connections. BAP allows your server to reduce the multilink connection by one line if the traffic falls under a certain percentage of the bandwidth for a certain period of time. You can use the dialog boxes to configure this option, such as 50 percent capacity for 2 minutes. When the capacity is 50 percent or under for two minutes, BAP will reduce one of the multilink lines.

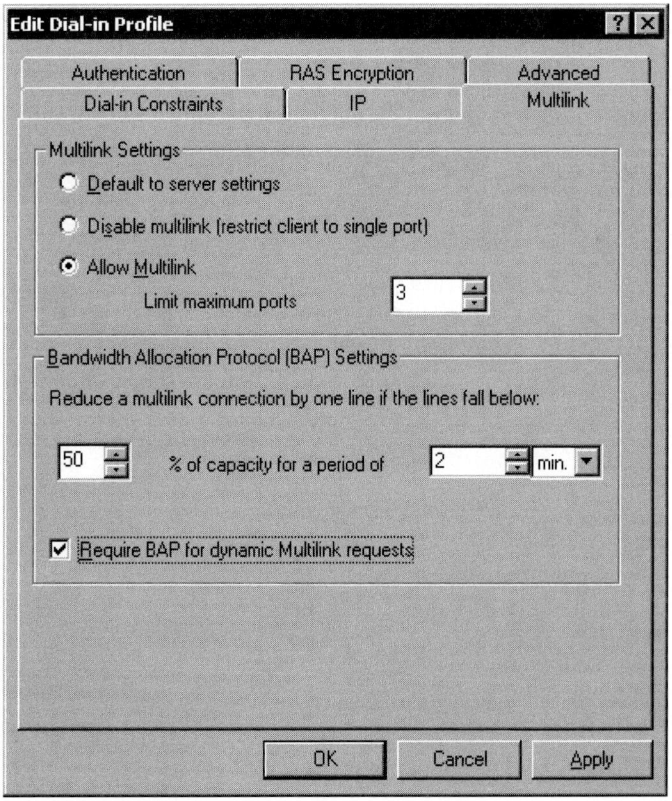

FIGURE 14.17
Multilink

AUTHENTICATION

The Authentication Property sheet offers the same information you have seen under the server properties sheet. You can use this tab to enable EAP, MS-CHAP v2, MS-CHAP, PAP, SPAP, ARAP, and you can allow unauthenticated access if desired.

RAS ENCRYPTION

The RAS Encryption Property sheet allows you to further define the type of RAS encryption to be used. You have three choices: prohibit encryption, allow IP Security (IPSec) or Microsoft Point-to-Point Encryption (MPPE), or require encryption, in which case you can choose between IPSec or MPPE. You can learn more about IPSec and MPPE in Chapter 17.

ADVANCED

The Advanced Property sheet allows you to add other connection attributes that further define your remote access policy. To add an attribute, simply

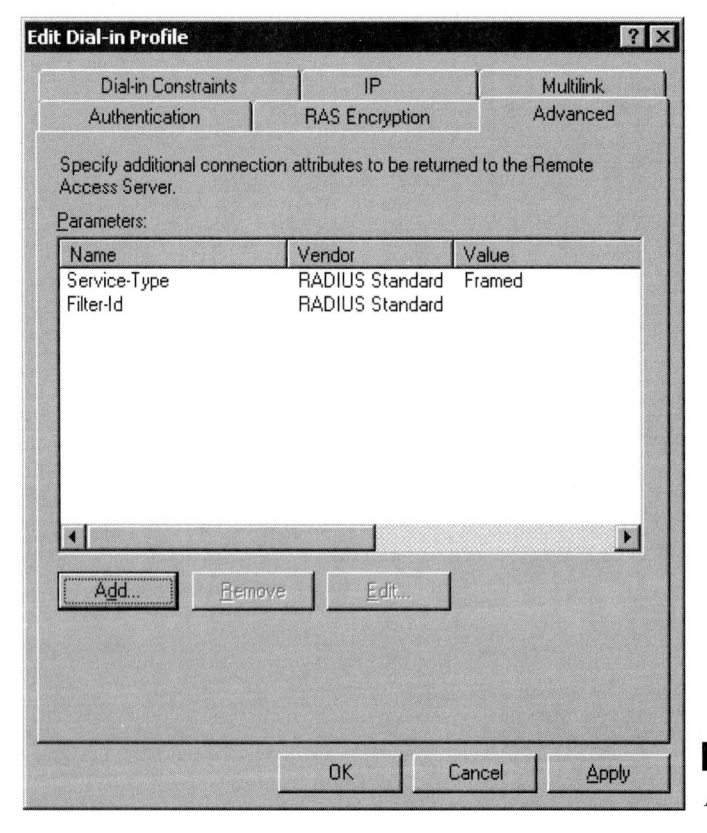

FIGURE 14.18

Add Attribute

click the Add button and select the attribute from the list that is provided, as shown in Figure 14.18.

As you can see, you have a number of options to choose from, and depending on which attribute you choose, you may have to enter additional information for the specific attribute.

Creating a New Remote Access Policy

You can create new remote access policies by right-clicking Remote Access Policies in the console tree and clicking New Remote Access Policy. Remember that a remote access policy allows you to specify a group of actions to be applied to a group of users. You can create as many new remote access policies as you desire; however, planning is of the utmost importance before implementing new policies.

When you click New Remote Access Policy, you are taken through several steps that allow you to establish the policy. Figure 14.19 shows the first window, where you simply enter a friendly name for the policy.

Once you enter the friendly name and click Next, the Add Remote Access Policy window appears. Click the Add button to enter conditions that must be met. In Figure 14.20, two restrictions have been added: The user must call a specific number, and the user can access the remote access server only from 7:00 a.m. to 10:00 p.m. Monday–Friday.

Next, the permissions window appears. You have two radio buttons where you choose to either grant remote access permission or deny remote access permission, based on the policy conditions you choose. In the exam-

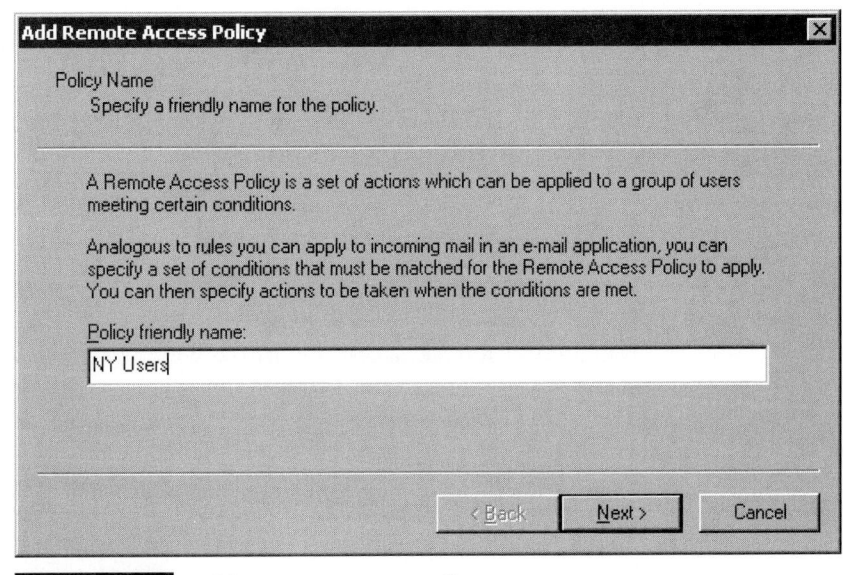

FIGURE 14.19 Add Remote Access Policy

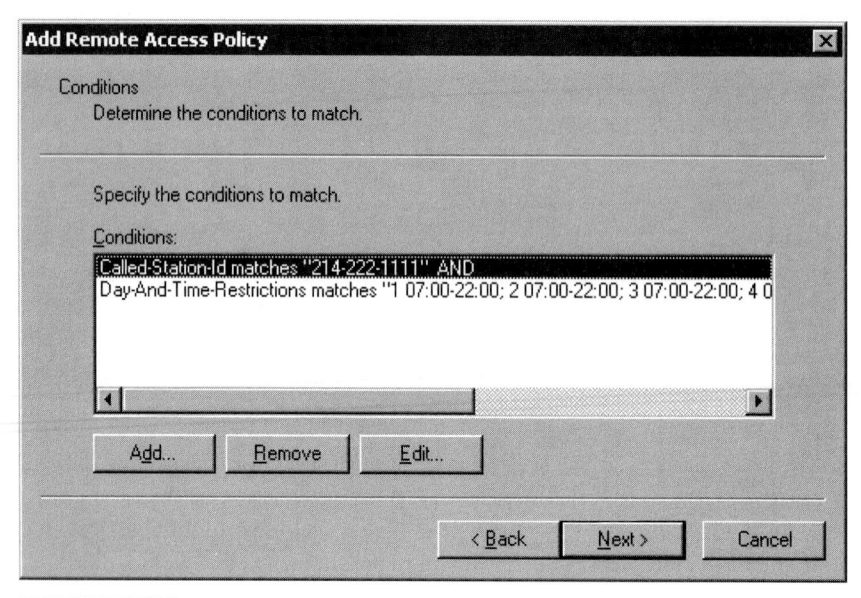

FIGURE 14.20 Policy Conditions

ple in Figure 14.20, I have made a restriction concerning the number and day and time. With this type of permission, I would want to grant remote access permission if the conditions are met. You can, however, use the condition(s) you select in a reverse method—if the conditions are met, you can choose to deny remote access permissions.

When you click the Next button, a window appears telling you that you can edit the profile you have created at this time by clicking the edit button. This action presents you with the same properties sheet we examined in the previous section. You can edit and further refine the policy now, or click Finish. Once you click Finish, the new policy appears in the details pane of the console. You can right-click the new policy and select Properties to edit the policy at any desired time.

Summary

The routing and remote access service in Windows 2000 is a superior service that enables remote clients to access the remote access server, and the entire network if desired. Remote access clients can use network resources as though they are directly connected to the network. The routing and remote access service is integrated in Windows 2000 and supports many protocols and new security features, such as IPSec and MPPE. This service also supports policies that allow you to further refine how your network users access the remote access server.

FIFTEEN

Connecting with Apple and Novell Systems

One of the most important and often complex tasks in networking and communication is integration with other operating systems. Very few networks have the luxury of upgrading all of their computers and servers to Windows 2000 at one time, so it is very important that Windows 2000 offers not only downlevel compatibility with older Windows operating systems, but also integration strategies with other operating systems such as Apple Macintosh and Novell NetWare. This interoperability feature allows networks to gradually move to Windows 2000, or remain as a mixed environment if they so choose. This chapter explores interoperability in Windows 2000 with Apple Macintosh and Novell NetWare computers.

Apple Macintosh Interoperability

The Macintosh operating system is the major operating system offered by Apple. The Macintosh OS has been around for several years, and you are likely to see Macintosh computers in most larger networking environments. With lower prices and the new iMac's popularity, Macintosh computers will continue to be used in networking environments. Windows NT 4.0 offered Services for Macintosh, which allowed Macintosh clients to log onto the Windows NT network and share files and folders. Windows 2000 extends this support by offering additional features to integrate the Macintosh client more fully into the Windows 2000 environment. The following sections show you the interoperability features that are now available and how to configure your Windows 2000 Server to support Macintosh clients.

Installing the Services for Macintosh

In order to integrate Macintosh clients with Windows 2000, you must install File Services for Macintosh on a Windows 2000 Server domain controller to which the Macintosh clients will log on. This service must be installed on an NTFS volume. To install Services for Macintosh, access Add/Remove Programs in Control Panel. Click Add/Remove Windows Components, and click Next when the wizard begins. In the Windows Components scroll box, double-click Other Network File and Print Services, then click the File Services for Macintosh check box and click OK (see Chapter 22 to learn more about Print Services for Macintosh). Click Next, then Windows installs the component. Click Finish to complete the installation.

Macintosh User Accounts

You create Macintosh user accounts just as you would any other type of account through the Active Directory (see Chapter 18). Macintosh clients can log on to a Windows 2000 Server as either a guest (if the guest account is enabled), as a user with a clear-text password (if clear text passwords are allowed), or as a user with an encrypted password. Clear-text passwords are built in to the AppleShare client, but you can use encryption that is offered by Windows 2000 Services for Macintosh.

Once Services for Macintosh are installed and a user account is created for the Macintosh client, the client can log on to the Windows 2000 Server. On the Macintosh computer, access Chooser, click AppleShare, then either access the Windows 2000 Server that appears or click Server IP Address and enter the IP address of the server (this option varies depending on which Mac OS version is in use.) When prompted, enter the username and password and click OK. Once the Macintosh client logs on to the Windows 2000 Server for the first time, it will attempt to reconnect each time the system is booted. Once the client is connected, the Macintosh user can access the Microsoft UAM (User Authentication Module) Volume that appears on the Macintosh desktop. The User Authentication Module prompts the user to log on to the Windows 2000 Server at boot-up by presenting a user name and password dialog box. The standard UAM is built in and uses clear text. If you want to use encryption, you can install the Microsoft UAM. However, users of Macintosh system 7.1 or earlier may experience some problems (such as hard locks), so make certain that encryption is needed before implementing the Microsoft UAM on system 7.1 or earlier. To install the MS UAM, open the Microsoft UAM Volume on the desktop and either run the installer program or drag the AppleShare folder to the System Folder on the hard drive. Once this is done, the user will be able to use Microsoft Authentication when logging onto the Windows 2000 Server.

Configuring AppleTalk

To configure AppleTalk on a Windows 2000 Server, right-click My Network Places and click Properties, then right-click Local Area Connection. Click on AppleTalk and click Properties. The General Property sheet provides you with an Accept inbound connections on this adapter check box and the default AppleTalk zone. You can change either of these as needed, although they are normally configured appropriately.

Windows 2000 can also provide AppleTalk routing support by providing routing and seed routing support to the AppleTalk router. AppleTalk routers function by broadcasting network addresses and related information and also "seed" the network, which means establishing and initializing network address information for the AppleTalk network. You can enable AppleTalk routing support once Services for Macintosh is installed by accessing the routing and remote access console. Expand the server, right-

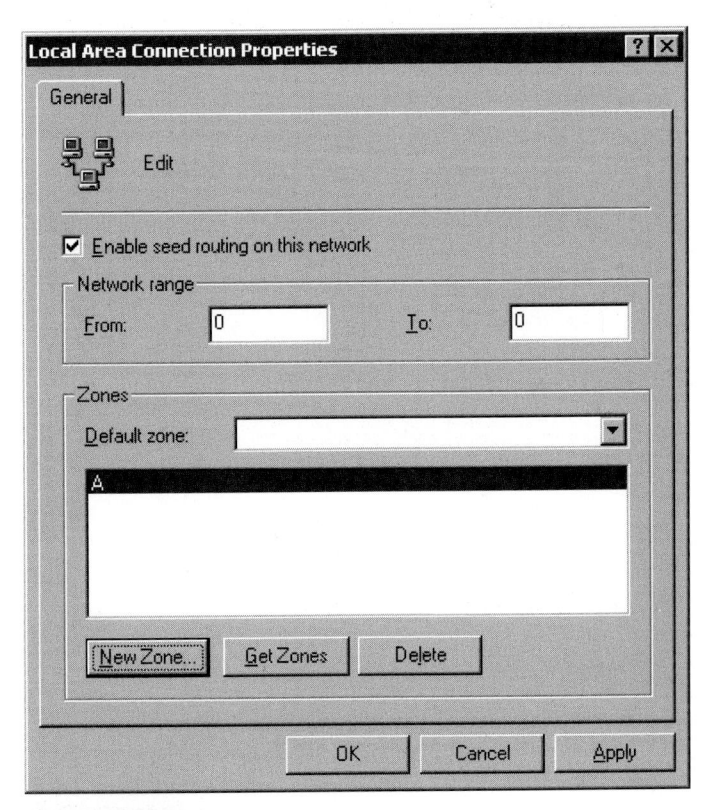

FIGURE 15.1 AppleTalk Routing

click AppleTalk routing, and click Enable AppleTalk Routing. Next, you can right-click on the adapter where AppleTalk routing is enabled (in the details pane) and click Properties. The Properties sheet, shown in Figure 15.1, allows you to enable seed routing on the network and enter a network range. You can also configure additional AppleTalk zones if necessary.

Windows 2000 also supports AppleTalk Remote Access Protocol (ARAP) so that Macintosh users can have dial-up access. ARAP is automatically installed with Services for Macintosh if routing and remote access (RRAS) is installed on the server. ARAP addresses are dynamically assigned to dial-in clients and callback functionality is provided as well. To configure ARAP, open the routing and remote access console, right-click on your server, and click Properties. You will see that an AppleTalk Properties sheet now exists, shown in Figure 15.2.

As with other RAS clients, you can allow AppleTalk clients to access the entire network or the server only. You can also click the "Password must be entered manually (ARAP only)" check box in order to force remote users to manually enter their passwords during the ARAP connection. This is simply an increased security feature.

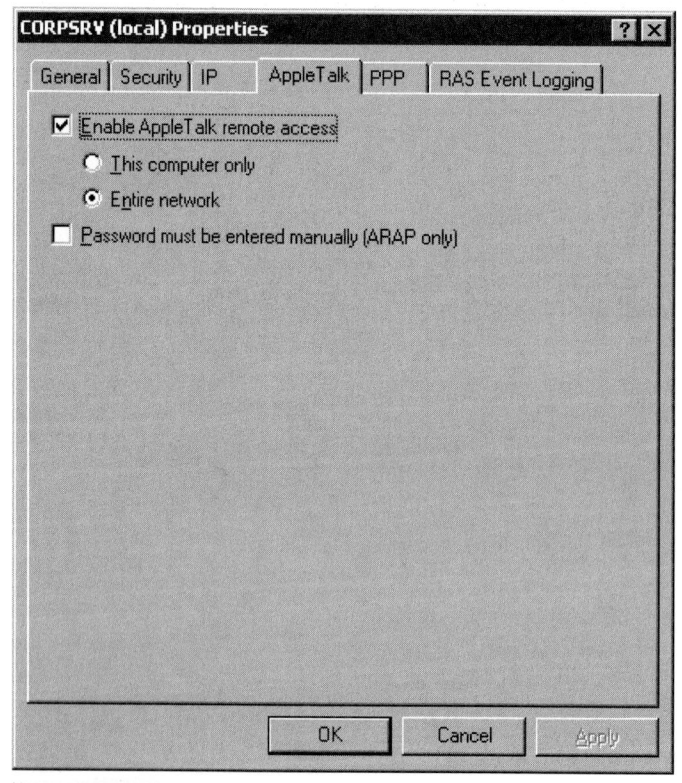

FIGURE 15.2 AppleTalk Properties

Creating and Managing Macintosh Accessible Volumes

You must create shared volumes that Macintosh clients can access. To do this, follow these steps:

1. Click Start → Programs → Administrative Tools → Computer Management.
2. Double-click System Tools, then double-click Shared Folders.
3. Right-click Shares and click New File Share. The Create Shared Folder Wizard begins.
4. In the Folder Location window, expand the drive(s) to select a folder to share, or type a new folder name in the dialog box to create a new folder, as shown in Figure 15.3. Make your selections and click Next.
5. The Set Permissions window appears, shown in Figure 15.4. Click the appropriate radio button to select the permissions you want to use and click Next.
6. The Name the Shared Folder and Control Computer Access window appears, shown in Figure 15.5. You can alter the share name and type a description if desired. At the bottom of the window you must select which operating systems can access the folder. Microsoft Windows is

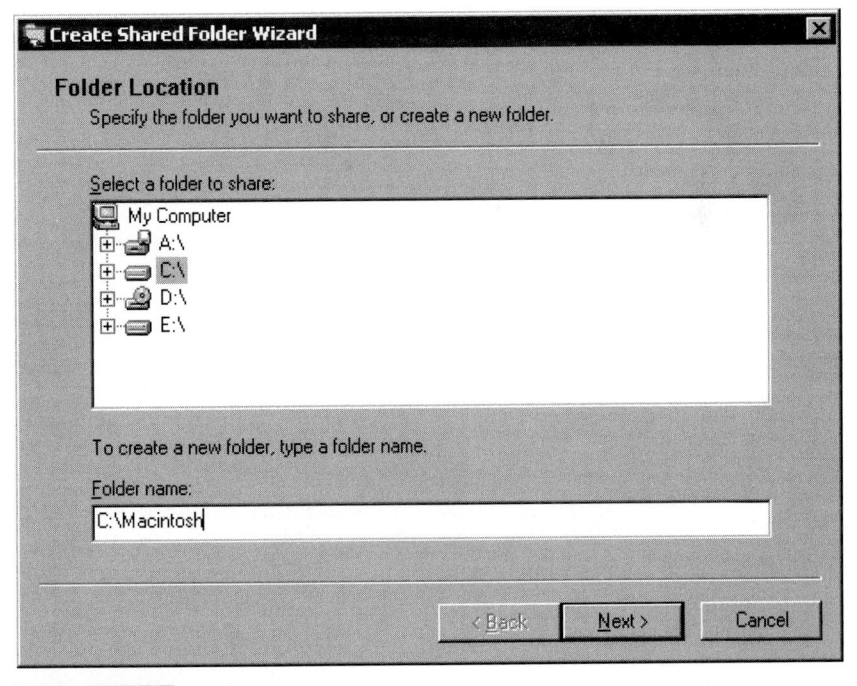

FIGURE 15.3 Folder Location

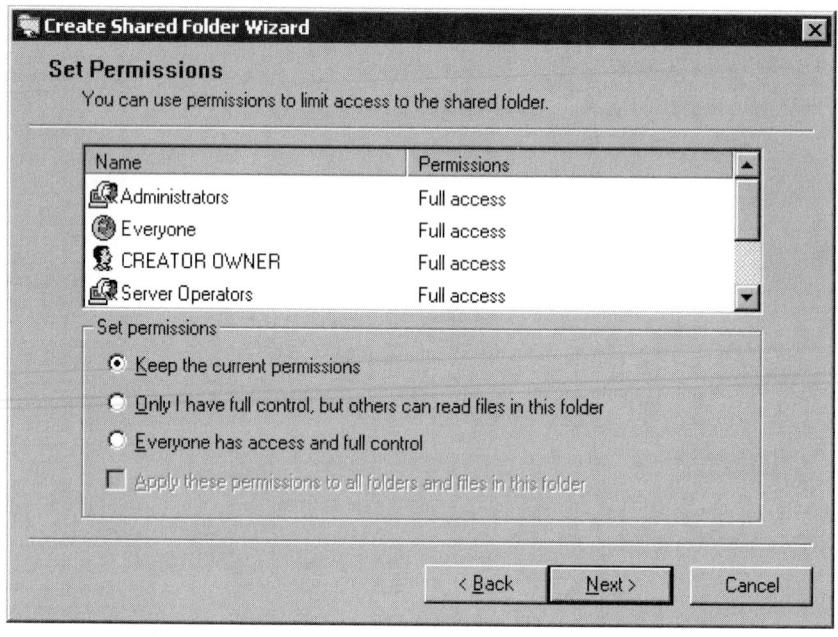

FIGURE 15.4 Set Permissions

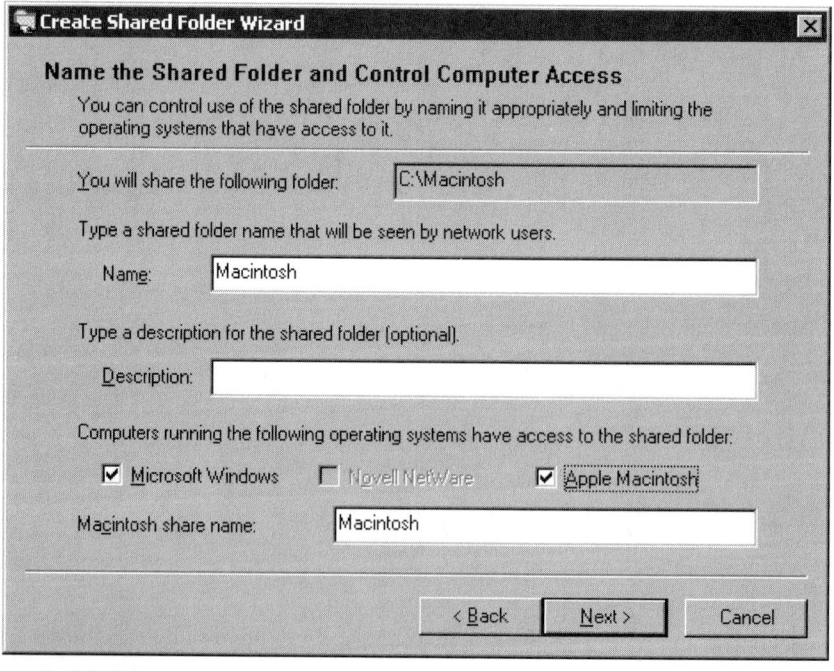

FIGURE 15.5 Shared Folder and Computer Access

selected by default. To allow Macintosh clients to access the share, click the Apple Macintosh check box. You must select this check box for any folder you want Macintosh clients to be able to access. Click Next.

7. A summary appears. Click Finish.

Once the folder is created, you can access the folder's properties sheet to further configure information about the shared folder. In the Computer Management console, double-click Shares, then right-click the Macintosh volume. You can choose to Stop Sharing the volume, or you can select Properties. The Properties sheet, shown in Figure 15.6, contains two tabs, General and Security. The General Properties sheet allows you to limit the number of users allowed, and you can also password protect the volume so that the clients must enter a password to access the share. To do this, type the password in the password box. You can also use the appropriate check boxes to configure the volume for read only and guest access if desired. The Security tab allows you to configure additional security restrictions and options for the share. See Chapter 20 to learn more about shared resource security.

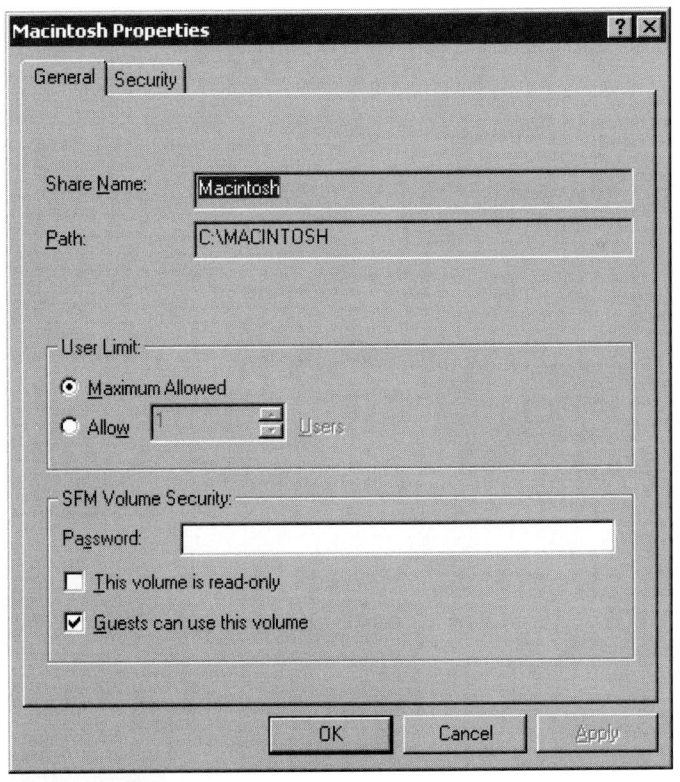

FIGURE 15.6 Share Properties

You can also configure your overall file server for Macintosh by right-clicking on Shared Folders in the console tree and clicking Configure File Server for Macintosh. This action opens a properties sheet where you can configure additional settings. The Configuration Property sheet, shown in Figure 15.7, allows you to enter a logon message that Macintosh clients will see when logging onto the system. You can also click the Allow workstations to save password checkbox, so the Macintosh computers can store their passwords—this action is less secure however. You can also set the type of authentication to be used, which can be either Microsoft only, Apple Clear Text, Apple Encrypted, Apple Clear Text or Microsoft, or Apple Encrypted or Microsoft. Keep in mind that clear text provides very little security while encryption protects your passwords and is very hard to break. Which authentication method you select will depend on the security needs of your network and your corporate policies. Finally, you can limit the number of Macintosh sessions if desired.

The File Association Property sheet provides a list of Macintosh document extensions that can be associated with file types if necessary. The

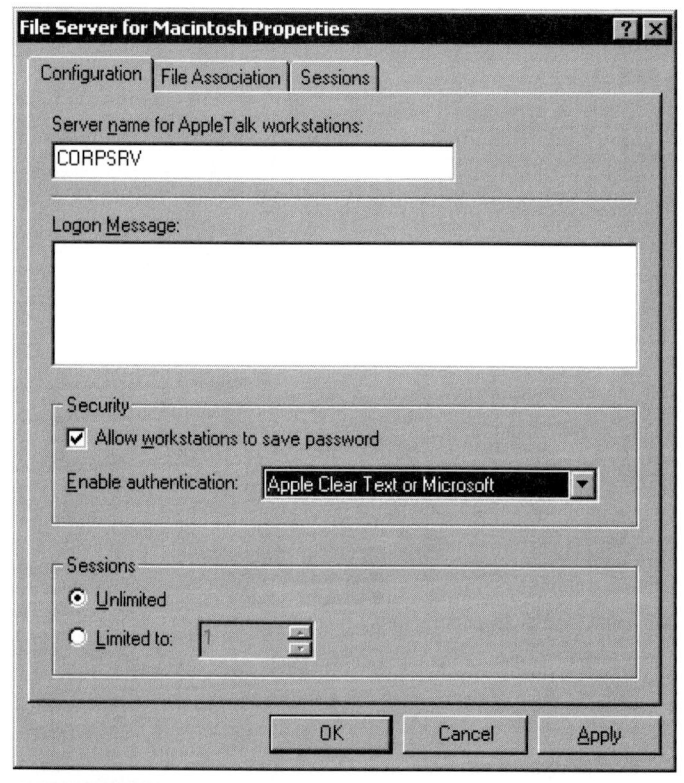

FIGURE 15.7 Configuration Properties

Sessions Property sheet allows you to monitor the Macintosh sessions and send a message to Macintosh users that are connected.

Interoperability with Novell NetWare

Novell NetWare is a leading provider of network server software and client operating systems. Due to the market share owned by NetWare, Microsoft has implemented several features that allow Windows 2000 computers to integrate into a NetWare environment or interoperate with the NetWare environment in mixed network settings.

As in earlier versions of Windows, the NWLink protocol, which is an IPX/SPX compatible transport protocol, is included for connectivity with Novell systems. NWLink can also be used to connect Windows operating systems as well. Client Services for NetWare (CSNW) and Gateway Services for NetWare (GSNW) are included in Windows 2000 as in Windows NT; however, the two services are now combined and simply called Gateway (and Client) Services for NetWare (GSNW). The client services feature is included in Windows 2000 Professional as CSNW, and this service allows Windows 2000 workstations to make direct connections to file and printer resources on NetWare 2.x, 3.x, 4.x, and 5.x software. GSNW allows a Windows 2000 Server to act as a gateway to NetWare 3.x, 4.x, and 5.x software. The gateway feature allows Windows clients to access the NetWare resources through the Windows 2000 Server gateway. File and Print Services (FPNW) is also available as a separate product. FPNW enables a computer running Windows 2000 Server to provide file and print services to NetWare client computers so that the client computers can access the server's shares and print resources. No additional configuration for the NetWare client is needed.

Installing NWLink

You can install the NWLink protocol by right-clicking on My Network Places and clicking Properties, then right-clicking on the local area connection where you want to install NWLink and clicking Properties. Click the Install button. The Select Network Component Type appears. Click on the Protocol icon, then click the Add button. Select NWLink IPX/SPX Compatible Transport Protocol from the list and click OK.

Configuring NWLink

After NWLink is installed, you can select it in the Local Area Connection Properties sheet and click the Properties button. This action gives you a single tab, shown in Figure 15.8.

There are three components involved in configuring NWLink: frame type, network number, and internal network number. When you install NWLink, the

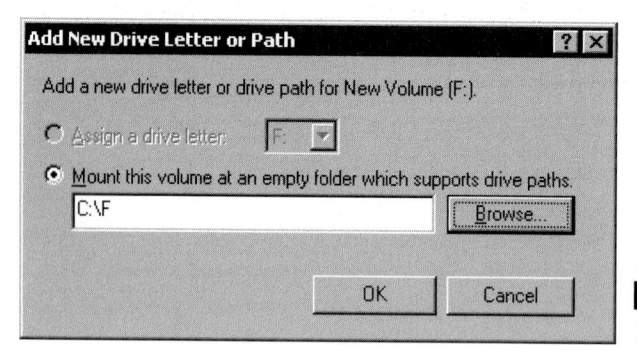

FIGURE 15.8
NWLink Properties

network number and frame type are automatically selected by Windows 2000, and a default network number is also supplied. If GSNW or IPX Routing is used, you will need to change the default internal number to the correct internal number for your network. The Frame Type tells the computer how the network adapter card should format data, which must match the frame type of the NetWare server so communication can take place. An incorrect frame type is a common communication problem in mixed Windows and NetWare environments. Windows will attempt to autodetect the network frame type, but you can also click the Manual frame type detection and enter the frame type as needed by using the Add button. In most cases, Windows 2000 Server will be able to autodetect the frame type. The Network number is required for each frame type and must be unique for each segment of the network. All computers on each segment must use the same network number for communication to take place. Windows 2000 automatically detects a network number during NWLink installation, and you can use the ipxroute config command at the command prompt to gain this information.

Installing GSNW

To install Gateway Services for NetWare Networks, access the Properties sheet for the network connection on which you want to install GSNW, then click Install. In the list that appears, select the Client icon then click the Add button. From that list, select Gateway (and Client) Services for NetWare and click OK.

Configuring GSNW

You can configure GSNW by accessing it in the control panel. If you double-click on the icon, you are provided a single Property sheet which can be configured, as shown in Figure 15.9.

You can select a preferred NetWare sever to log in to by using the drop-down box and selecting the server from the list. Or you can leave this configured as "none" so that you are logged on to the nearest available

FIGURE 15.9

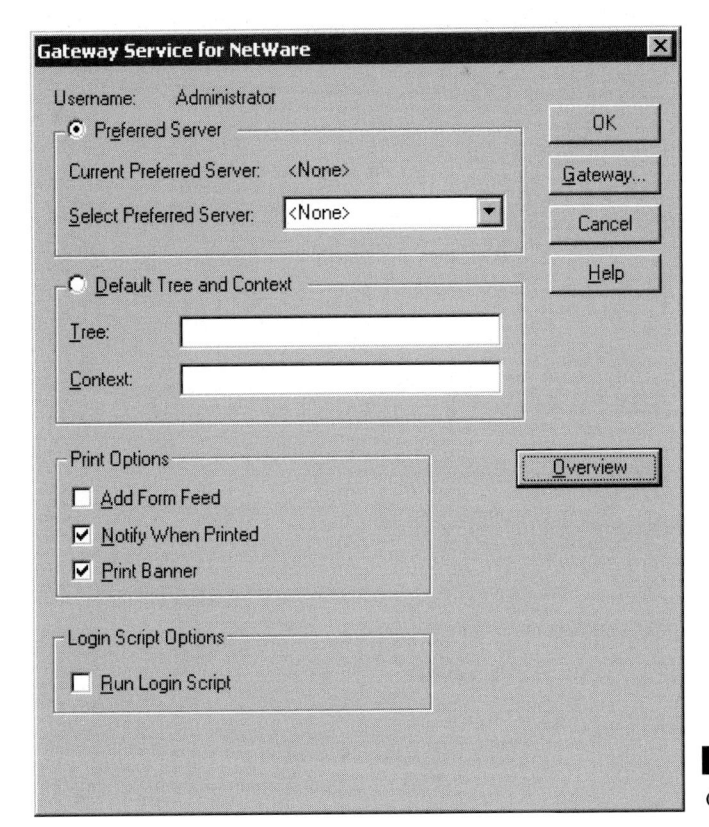

GSNW Properties

NetWare server when you log on to the network. You can also set a default tree and context. You do not need to do this unless you are in an NDS environment (such as a single Windows 2000 Server in a NetWare environment); otherwise, your server will use the Active Directory. You can also use this page to configure NetWare print options. Click the appropriate check box to Add Form Feed, Notify When Printed, or Print Banner. If you are using a logon script, you can select this check box at the bottom of the window so that the script will be run.

If you click the Gateway button, you can enable the NetWare gateway so that NetWare file and printing resources can be shared on the Microsoft network. The Configure Gateway window, shown in Figure 15.10, allows you to configure the gateway by clicking the enable gateway button and entering a gateway account and password.

You use the share dialog box at the bottom of the window to add NetWare shares to which Windows clients can gain access. Click the Add button to add a share to list. The Add button gives you a New Share window where you can enter the share's name, network path, and drive letter to use. You can also use the New Share window to limit the number of user sessions if desired.

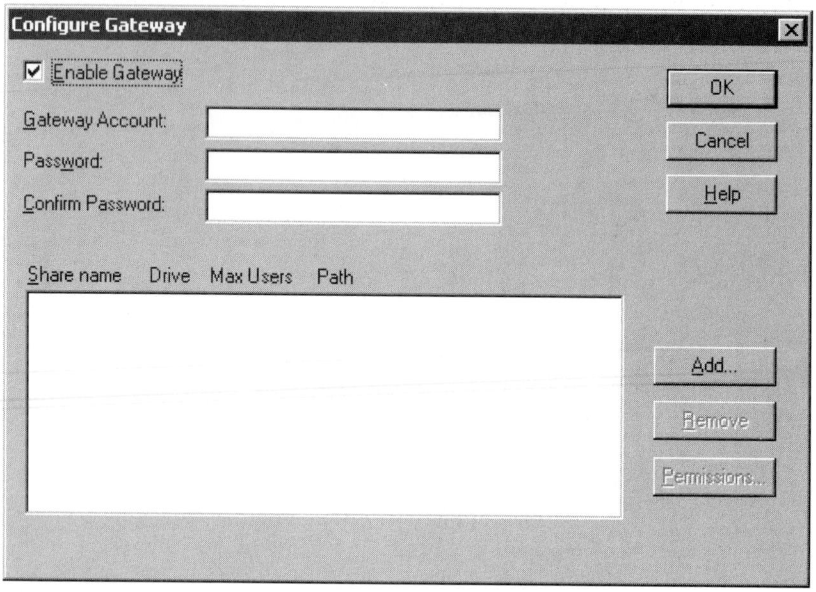

FIGURE 15.10 Configure Gateway

Directory Service Migration Tool

As mentioned earlier, Novell is Microsoft's greatest competitor in server software and directory services. For NetWare environments that want to migrate from Novell's NDS to the Active Directory, Windows 2000 Server includes a Directory Service Migration Tool. The Directory Service Migration tool allows you to copy objects from NDS or bindery-based servers and paste those objects into the Active Directory. The migration tool accomplishes this action by making an offline model of the NDS resources and an offline model of the Active Directory. The objects can then be moved to the Active Directory, modified and appropriately mapped as needed, then added to the online Actice Directory. The Directory Service Migration tool runs on all Windows 2000 client platforms.

You can install the Directory Service Migration Tool by accessing Add/Remove Programs in Control Panel, then accesing Add/Remove Windows components. In the option list that appears, double-click Networking Services, then select Directory Service Migration Tool from the list. Click OK then click Next. The tool is installed on your system, then click Finish. If Gateway Services for NetWare is not installed when you install the tool, it will be automatically installed.

Once the installation is complete, you can access the tool by clicking Start ➤ Programs ➤ Admistrative Tools ➤ Directory Service Migration Tool.

From the snap-in, you can connect to the NDS and begin migrating objects. Included in the snap-in is a sample project which you can view for assistance.

Summary

Interoperability with Apple and Novell systems is available in Windows 2000 Server to help integrate networking environments and operating systems. Windows 2000 Server supports Macintosh clients through the use of the AppleTalk protocol and Services for Macintosh. This feature allows Macintosh clients to integrate into the Windows 2000 environment. Windows 2000 continues to support Novell clients through the use of the NWLink protocol with GSNW, which allows Windows clients to access resources on a Novell network.

SIXTEEN

Overview of Windows 2000 Security Features

The importance of security in networking environments cannot be understated. Over the years, security has become more complex, and networking environments have to incorporate a variety of employees with differing access needs, intranet access, and even Internet access. Windows 2000 Server offers several new security features to accommodate the changes in the way networks operate and the security needs facing complex networks today. This chapter explores these new features. You will also find that additional chapters, such as Chapter 17 and Chapter 20 examine other security specific issues.

New Security Features in Windows 2000

Network security involves three major factors to be effective. First, the network must be able to keep unauthorized people out of the network. This task has become more complicated as companies have employed the use of intranets, web access, remote access, and even public web hosting. Before the LAN integration with the Internet, companies were isolated islands, but security has become much more complex in today's integrated networks, and keeping unauthorized users out of the network has become just as complex. A second security factor is the authentication of users on the network. Just as the network must keep unauthorized users out of the network, authorized users must be able to securely log on to the network. Finally, authenticated users must be able to gain access to network resources. This issue alone can become complicated since each user needs access to certain resources to complete his or her work while the user does not need access to others. For example, a typical user needs to access network files and printers, but does not need to access personnel information. Windows 2000 Server provides the following security features to accomplish effective security measures for each of these needs:

- NTFS permissions for files and folders (see Chapter 20).
- Authentication through Kerberos V5 (with password or Smart Card), Secure Socket Layer/Transport Layer Security (SSL/TLS), or NTLM (for previous versions of Windows).
- Active Directory Object-based Access Control (see Chapters 9 and 20).
- Group Policy (see Chapter 19).
- Encrypting File Systems (EFS) for protection of locally stored data.
- Security Templates.
- Certificates.

Authentication

Authentication is the process of verifying a user's identity and allowing the user access to the network. After authentication is complete, the user becomes a part of the network system and can both access resources and share local resources, as permitted by the system administrator. Windows 2000 provides single sign-on, which means a user has to log on to the network only one time. Once the user is authenticated, he or she may access the network resources he or she has permission to access. This feature allows only one logon for a single username and password (or smart card). The authentication process contains both an interactive logon, where the user provides a valid domain password or local computer password, and a network authentication, which confirms the user's identity to any network service the user accesses. The following sections explore the types of authentication that are supported in Windows 2000 Server.

Kerberos V5

The Kerberos Version 5 protocol is the primary security protocol in Windows 2000. Kerberos V5 verifies a user's identity for both the user and network services. This process of identification is known as "mutual authentication" and can be used with either password logon or smart card logon. A smart card is like other magnetic cards such as an ATM or credit card. A smart card reader is installed on the client machine and the card is inserted into the reader for logon access.

Kerberos V5 functions by issuing tickets for network service. The tickets include an encrypted password so that the user's identity can be confirmed. When a user logs on using a password or smart card, the information is passed to the Key Distribution Center (KDC) on a Windows 2000 domain controller. The KDC provides a ticket granting ticket (TGT) to the client. The client can then use this TGT to access the ticket granting service (TGS) to reach domain resources. This process is all part of the Kerberos V5 protocol built into Windows 2000, and except for the password or smart card logon, the process is invisible to the user. Every Windows 2000 domain controller is a KDC and can provide user authentication via the Kerberos V5 protocol.

Secure Socket Layer/Transport Layer Security (SSL/TLS)

SSL/TLS is most often used for communication across unsecure networks such as the Internet. Windows 2000 supports authentication vial SSL/TLS by accepting X.509 version 3 certificates issued by a certification authority (CA).

NT LAN Manager (NTLM)

Windows 2000 supports NTLM authentication for previous versions of Windows. NTLM was the primary authentication protocol for Windows NT 4.0. Upon the server installation, NTLM is automatically available because Windows 2000 installs by default in mixed-mode. If you have no need for NTLM, you can disable it by switching your domain to native mode.

Active Directory Object-based Access Control

Once users are authenticated, you can control what resources they access within the Active Directory through object-based access control. This feature allows you to assign security descriptors to objects in the Active Directory. The descriptor lists the groups of users or individual users that have been granted access to the object and the permissions each group or individual user has for the object. Through the object's properties, you can also permit or deny access to specific attributes of the object. Common objects that can be managed using object-based access control are folders, files, printers, and other resources within the Active Directory.

Encrypting File System

EFS can be used to encrypt local data stored on NTFS volumes. EFS uses public key encryption and allows users to both encrypt and decrypt files.

EFS provides an additional level of security in case a nonauthorized user gains access to the network. For example, if Sally works with highly sensitive documents located on a file server, she can encrypt those documents when she is not using them so that they cannot be compromised by other network users. Users can take advantage of EFS easily—it is transparent to the user since the system both encrypts and decrypts the files as needed, and it is built-into the new NTFS offered by Windows 2000. Because EFS is a feature of NTFS, FAT volumes do not support EFS. Files are encrypted by using a file encryption key, which is also used to decrypt the files upon demand. Again, the users do not have to understand the process to work with the actual encryption keys—the system handles this task automatically.

EFS also provides data recovery support. EFS can be used only if the local computer is configured with at least one recovery key. The file that is encrypted is available using the recovery key so that no private information is revealed to the person recovering the data. The following sections show you how to use EFS.

Encrypting or Decrypting a File or Folder

You can encrypt either files or folders, but encrypting a folder actually encrypts all of the contents within the folder and not the folder itself. Right-click on the file or folder and click Properties. On the General Property sheet, click the Advanced button. In the Compress or Encrypt Attributes section, click the Encrypt contents to secure data check box, then click OK, as shown in Figure 16.1.

Once the file or folder is encrypted, it does not appear differently to the user and can be opened and read by the user without any additional steps. However, other users cannot access the file. To stop encrypting the

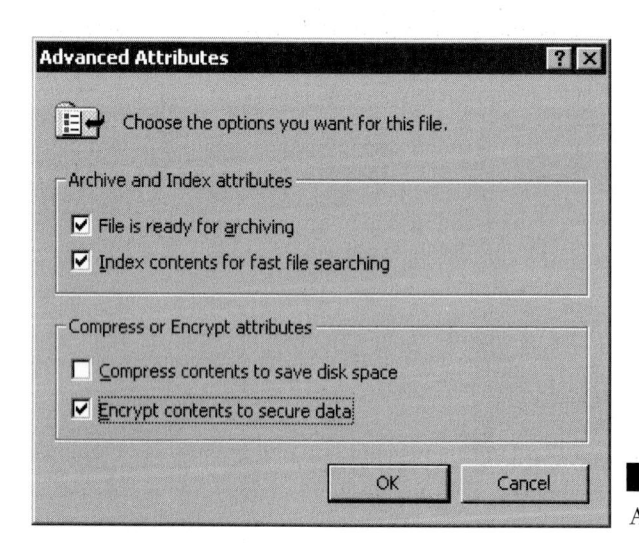

FIGURE 16.1

Advanced Attributes

file or folder, simply uncheck the check box in the Advanced Attributes. You can copy an encrypted file or folder to another volume, as long as the volume is formatted with NTFS; if the volume is FAT, the encryption will be lost. Also, if you move or copy an encrypted file or folder to another computer, that computer must have your certificate and private key available to decrypt the file or folder.

Configuring Recovery Agents

You can add recovery agents if you are logged on as administrator and if the Group Policy Snap-in and Public Key Policies extensions are installed on your computer. To add a recovery agent for a domain, follow these steps:

1. Click Start ➤ Programs ➤ Administrative Tools ➤ Computer Management.
2. Expand System Tools, expand Group Policy, expand Computer Configuration, expand Windows Settings, and expand Public Key Policies, as shown in Figure 16.2.

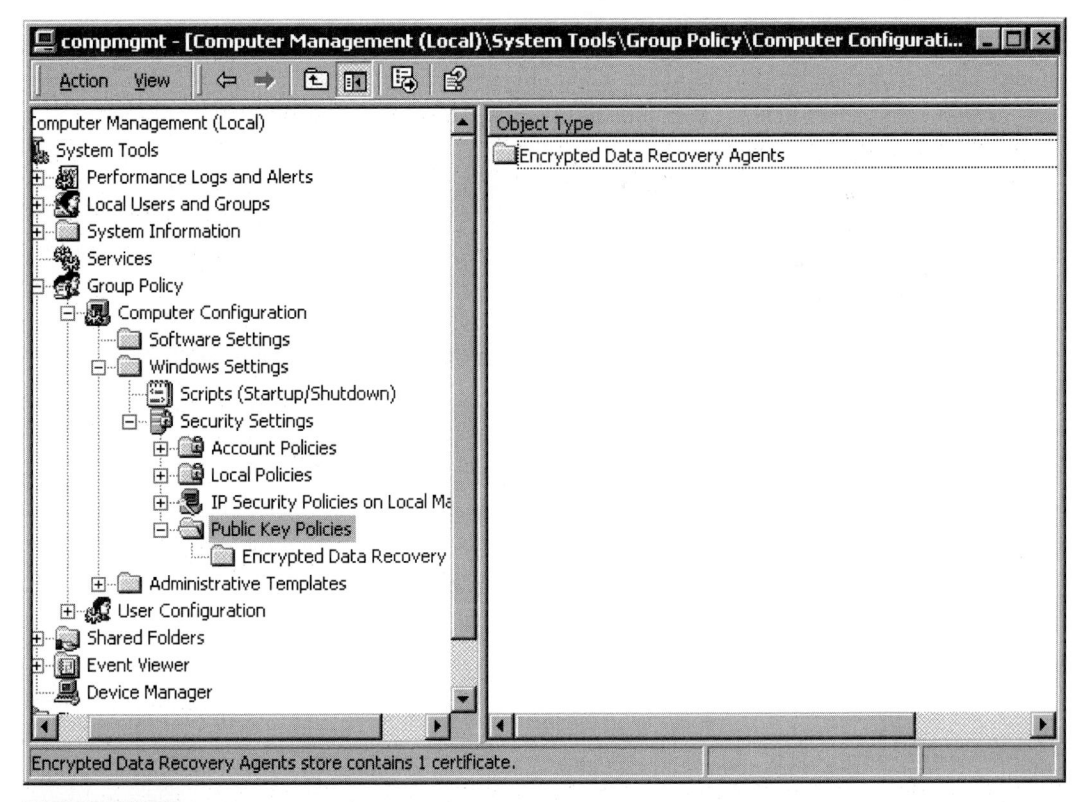

FIGURE 16.2 Public Key Policies

3. In the details pane, right-click Encrypted Data Recovery Agents and click Add.
4. The Add Recovery Agent appears. Follow the instructions that appear on the screen.

Security Policies

Windows 2000 Server provides a streamlined, central management location for the configuration of security settings through the Security template snap-in. From this location, you can define security settings for the users on your network. The template allows you to set the security configuration for your network. The following sections show you how to configure the security policy to meet your organization's needs.

The Security Template Snap-in

You can access the Security Template snap-in through the Group Policy snap-in, the Computer Management snap-in, or you can open the MMC and select the snap-in from the list. Once you open the snap-in, you will see the Security Templates container. If you expand this, you will see the different categories and a description of each, as shown in Figure 16.3.

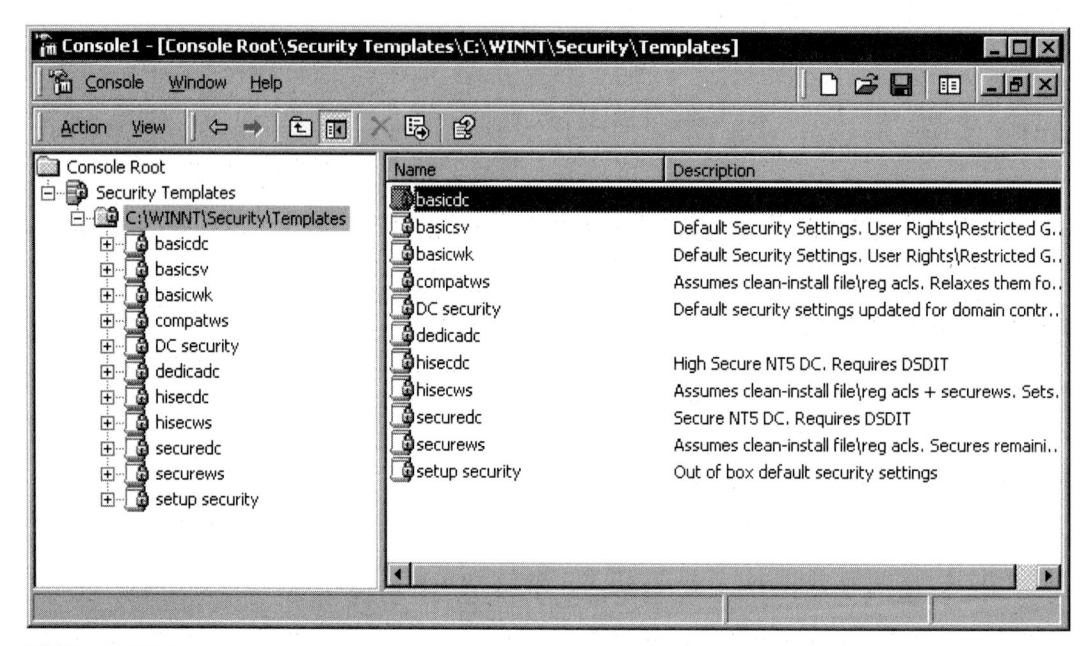

FIGURE 16.3 Security Template Snap-in

Configuring the Policies

For each policy category in the Security Templates snap-in, you can expand the policy to see the configurable options. For example, if you expand "basicsv," which is default security settings for user rights and restricted groups, you can see what policy options you can make. The options include Account Policies, Local Policies, Event Log, as well as others. If you expand one of these, for example, Account Policies, you can see the policies within that container that you can configure, as shown in Figure 16.4.

If you double-click one of the policies, for example, Password Policy, the objects appear that you can configure, such as minimum and maximum password ages, minimum password length, and so forth, as shown in Figure 16–5.

If you double-click on each attribute in the details pane, you can either select a configuration for the attribute or exclude the setting from the configuration. For example, the Maximum password age attribute, in Figure 16.6, has a setting of 42 days. This setting can be changed as desired.

To configure the Security Template, work through the categories and configure each attribute as desired for your network environment. You can also create additional security templates by right-clicking on the security

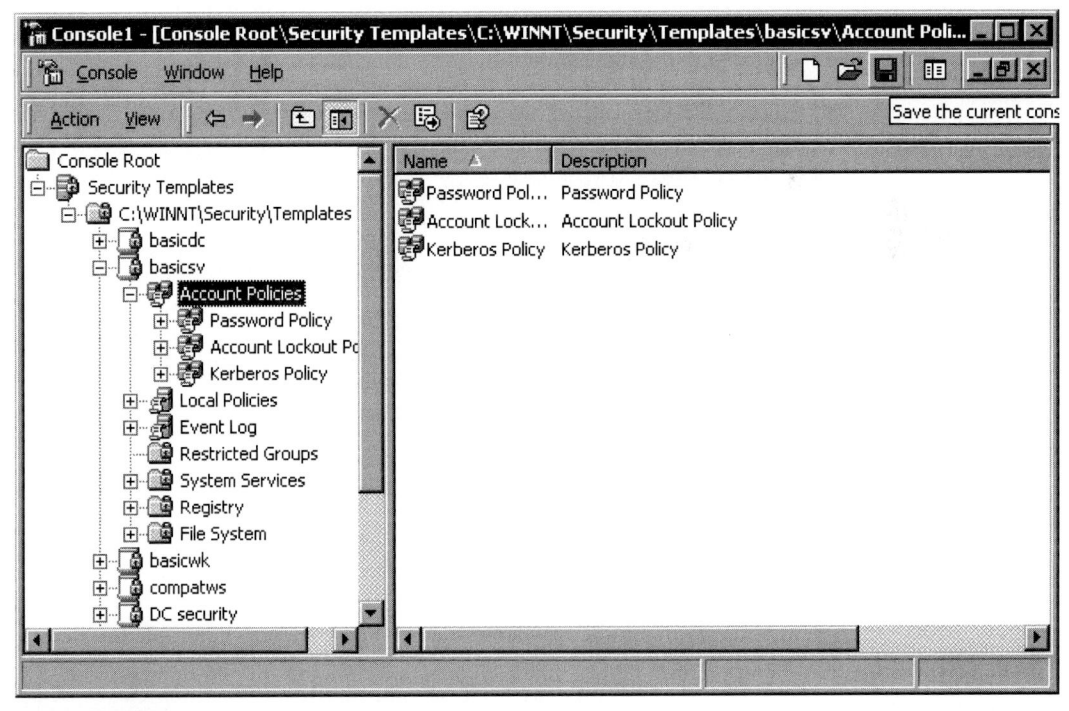

FIGURE 16.4 Account Policies

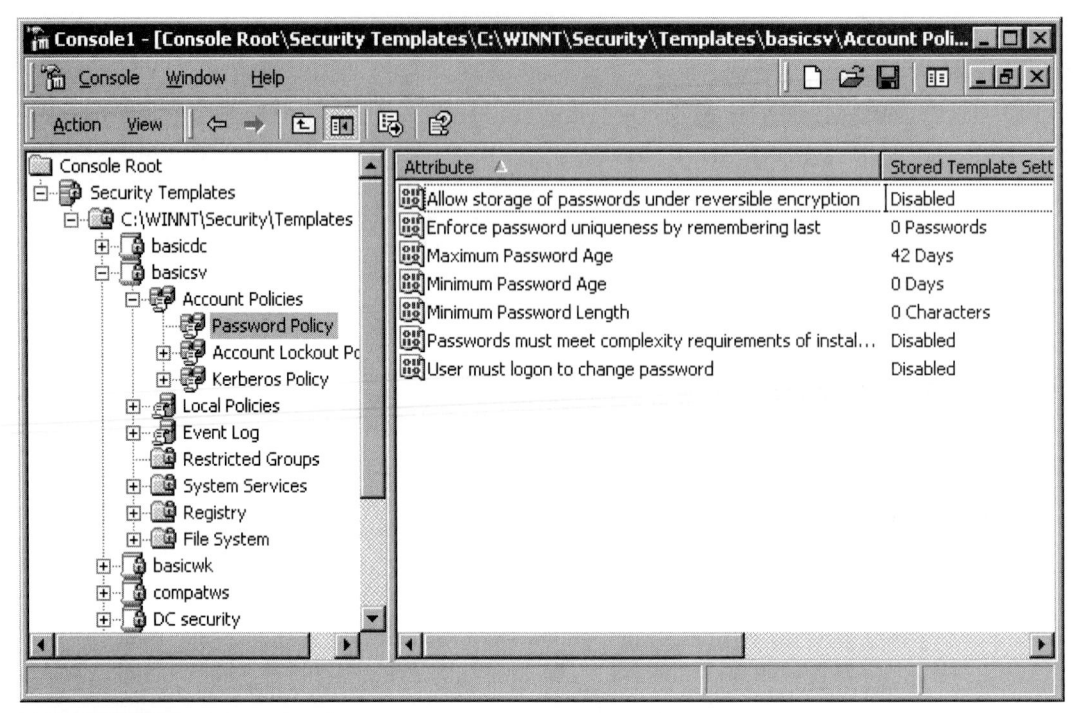

FIGURE 16.5 Password Policy

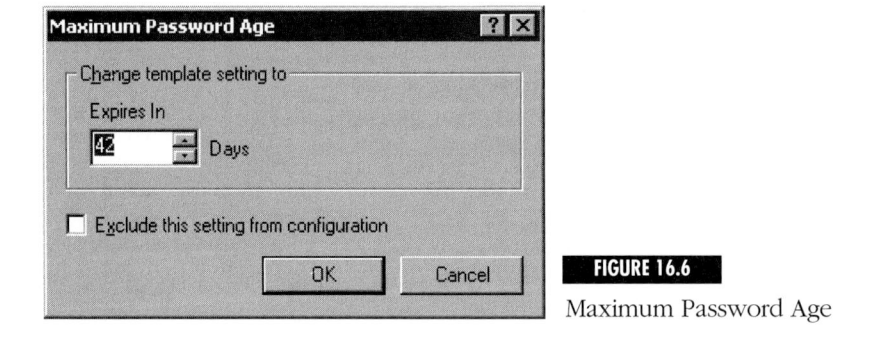

FIGURE 16.6 Maximum Password Age

templates default location in the console tree and clicking New Template. This action will prompt you to name the template; then the new template will be added to the template list.

The Security Configuration and Analysis Snap-in

The Security Configuration and Analysis snap-in allows you to review your security configuration and perform an analysis of the security templates so

three • Networking

that any discrepancies can be resolved. To start the snap-in, open the MMC and add the snap-in from the snap-in list. To open a database, right-click on Security Configuration and Analysis in the left pane and click Open database. Select the database from the list and click Open.

Once the database is open, you can right-click on Security Configuration and Analysis in the left pane and click Analyze System Now

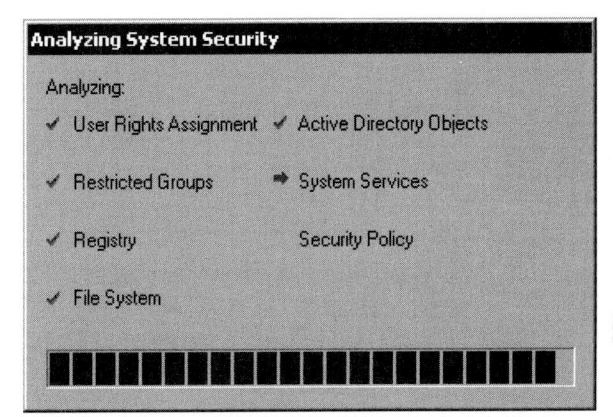

FIGURE 16.7

Analyzing System Security

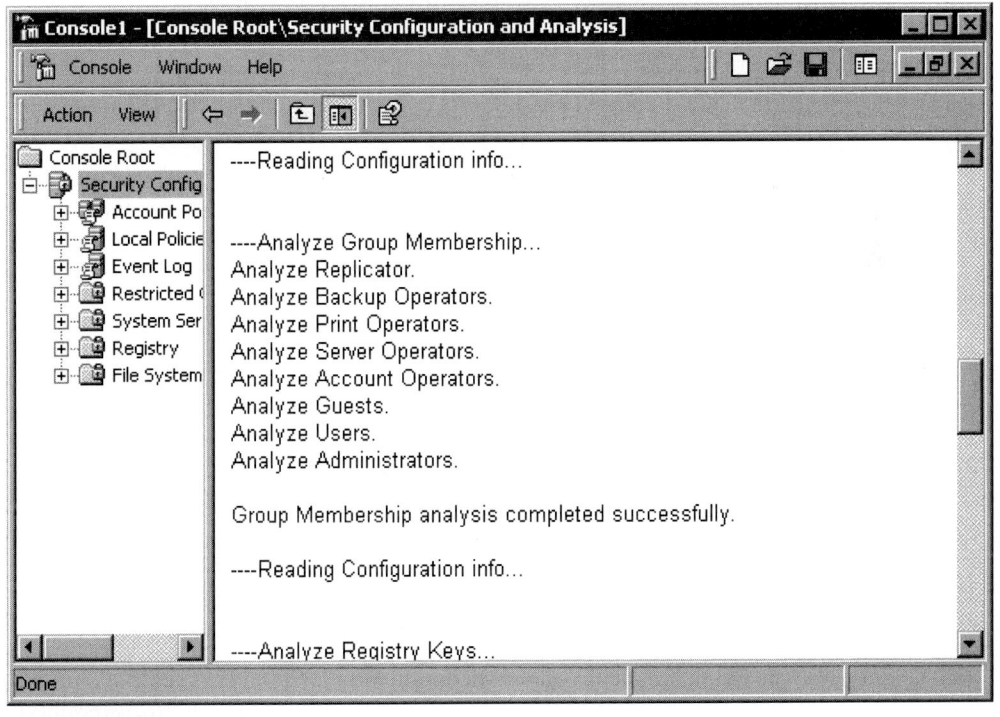

FIGURE 16.8 Log File View

or Configure System Now. If you click Analyze system now, the security configuration for the system is analyzed, as shown in Figure 16.7.

Once the configuration is complete, you can right-click Security Configuration and Analysis and click View Log File to review your system's security. The log file is displayed in the details pane, as shown in Figure 16–8.

Certificates

A certificate is a digitally signed comment that binds the value of a public cryptographic key to a person, device, or service that holds the corresponding private key. The most common certificates used today are based on the X.509 standard, and this is the certificate technology used in Windows 2000. The object that is assigned the certificate is called a "subject" while the issuer and signer of the certificate is called the certificate authority (CA). Certificates are typically used for web server authentication and secure e-mail, but they can also be used for logon purposes in Windows 2000 domains for increased security. This feature is particularly useful since it replaces the need for passwords which may be easily compromised. It is beyond the scope of this book to fully explore the deployment and configuration of certificate services. If you are planning a deployment, consult the Windows 2000 resource kit or a book that is soley devoted to certificate services in Windows 2000. The following sections give you an overview of certificate services configuration.

Installing the Certificate Authority

You can manage your certificates as well as the certificates of your users through the Certificates snap-in. To install the Certificate Authority, follow these steps:

1. Access Add/Remove Windows Components in Add/Remove Programs in Control Panel.
2. From the selection list, click Certificate Services, then click Next.
3. The Windows Component Wizard provides you with an Authority Type Selection, shown in Figure 16.9. You can choose from Enterprise root CA, Enterprise Subordinate CA, Standalone root CA, or Standalone Subordinate CA. The description of each appears in the right dialog box. Make your selection and click Next.
4. Enter the CA Identifying Information in the window that appears, as shown in Figure 16.10. Click Next when you are done.
5. The Data Storage Location window appears, shown in Figure 16.11. You can choose to accept the defaults, or change them as needed.

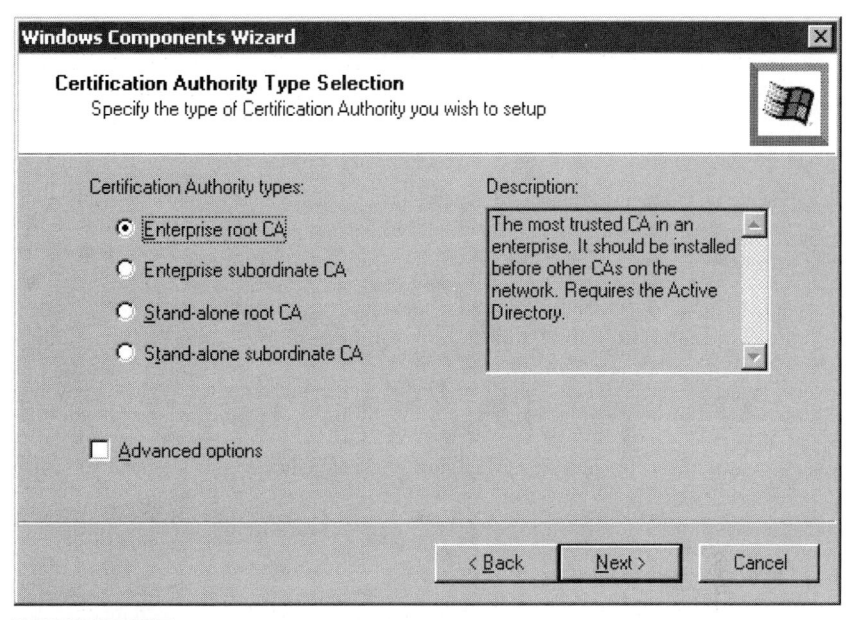

FIGURE 16.9 Authority Type Selection

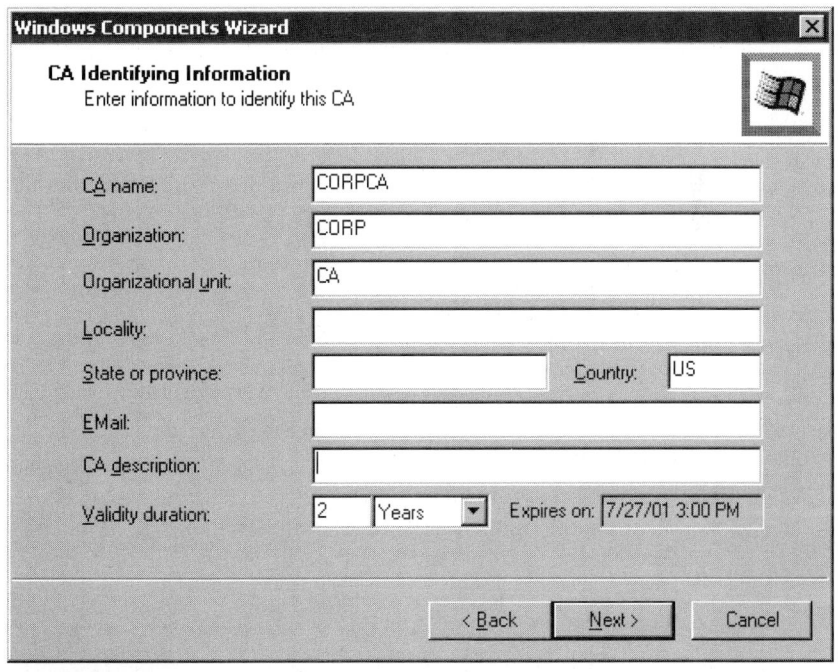

FIGURE 16.10 CA Identifying Information

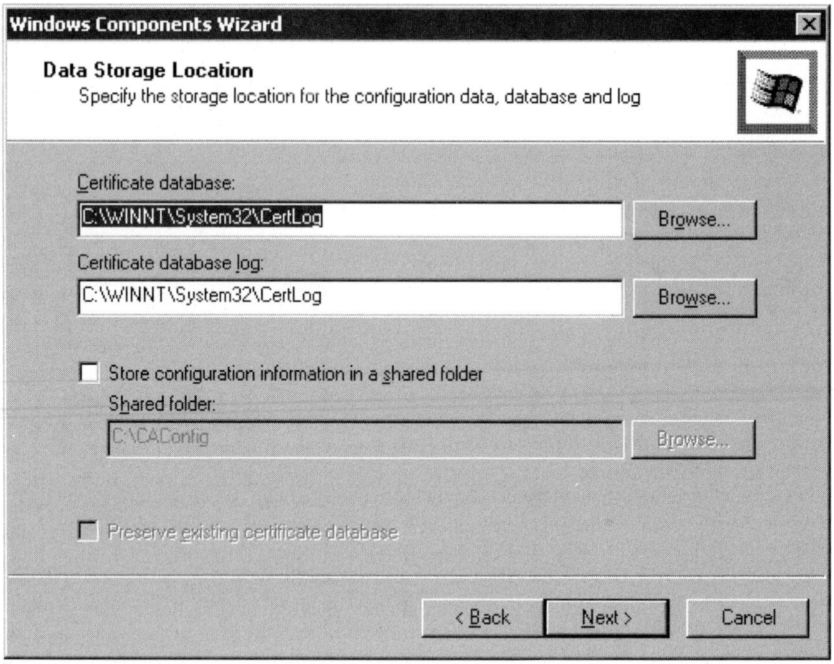

FIGURE 16.11 Data Storage Location

You can also store the configuration information in a shared folder. Click Next.

6. Setup will stop the WWW service while the installation takes place. The files are copied and configured. Click Finish.

Managing Certificates

The management of certificate and certificate services is performed through the Certification Authority MMC snap-in, which is available by clicking Start ➜ Programs ➜ Administrative Tools ➜ Certificate Authority. The snap-in provides you with folders for Revoked Certificates, Issued Certificates, Pending Requests, Failed Requests, and Policy Settings, as shown in Figure 16.12.

This snap-in is easy to use and you can see which certificates have been issued, which have been revoked, and so forth. If you right-click a certificate that has been issued or is pending, you can choose to revoke that certificate. You can also right-click on Policy Settings and issue a new certificate, based on the policy of your choice. If you right-click on the certificate account, you can start or stop the service or choose to backup or restore the CA.

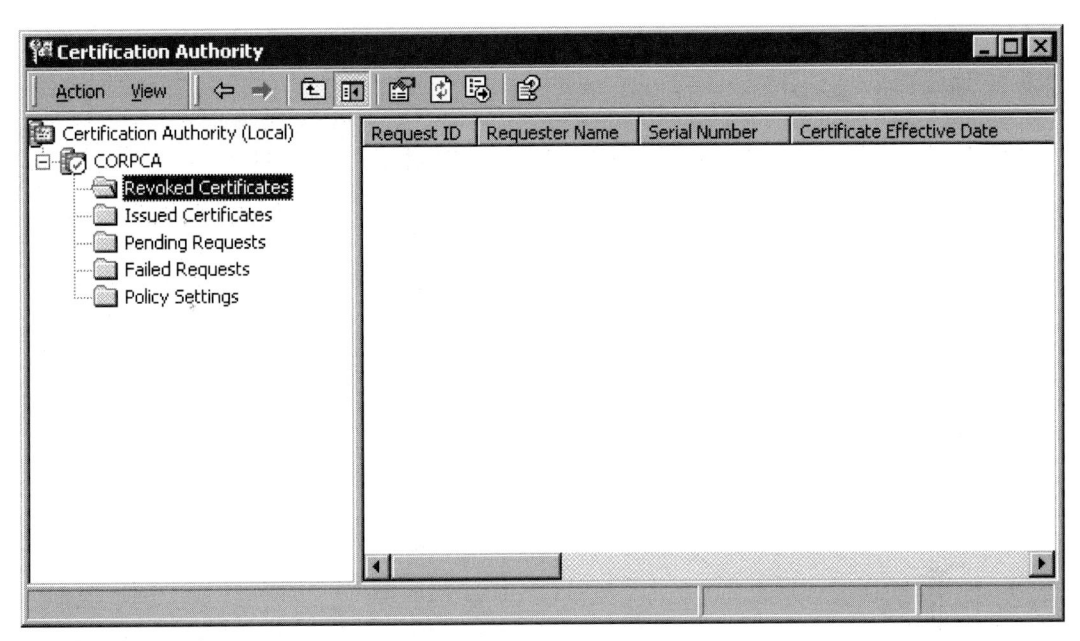

FIGURE 16.12 Certificate Authority

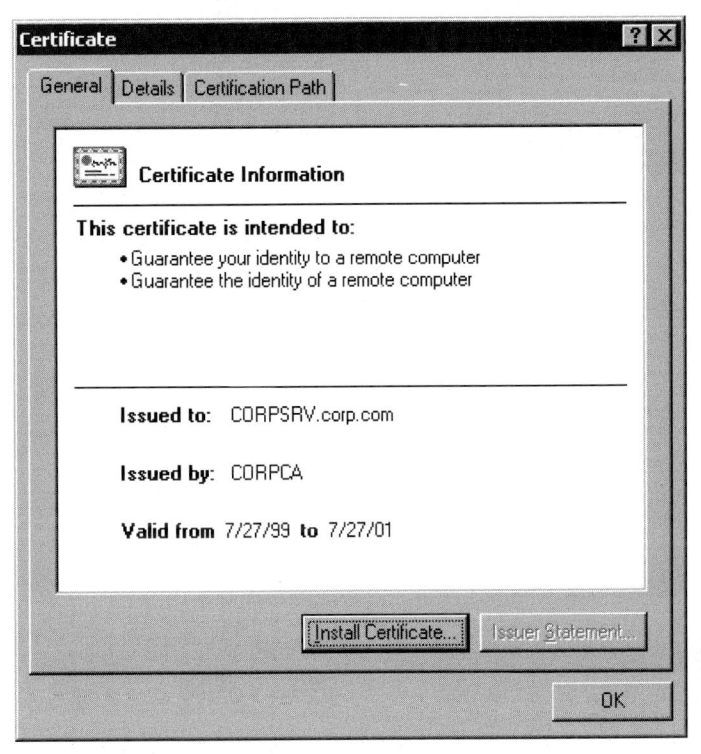

FIGURE 16.13 General Properties

FIGURE 16.14 Details Properties

    For a certificate, you can right-click on it to view its properties sheets by clicking Open. Each certificate has a General, Details, and Certification Path tab. The General Properties sheet, shown in Figure 16.13, gives you general information about the certificate and who it is issued to. You can also click on the Install Certificate button to install the certificate.

    The Details Properties sheet, shown in Figure 16.14, gives you details about the certificate, such as the serial number, its validity dates, and so forth. You can use the Show dropdown menu to only list certain aspects of the details if desired.

    Finally, the Certification Path Properties page gives you the certification path to the CA and a status of the certificate.

    The CA is managed from the Certificate Authority, but users can manage their certificates through the Certificates MMC snap-in. This snap-in can be manually added to the MMC, and when it is selected, the snap-in will prompt you to manage certificates for your user account, service account, or computer account, as shown in Figure 16.15.

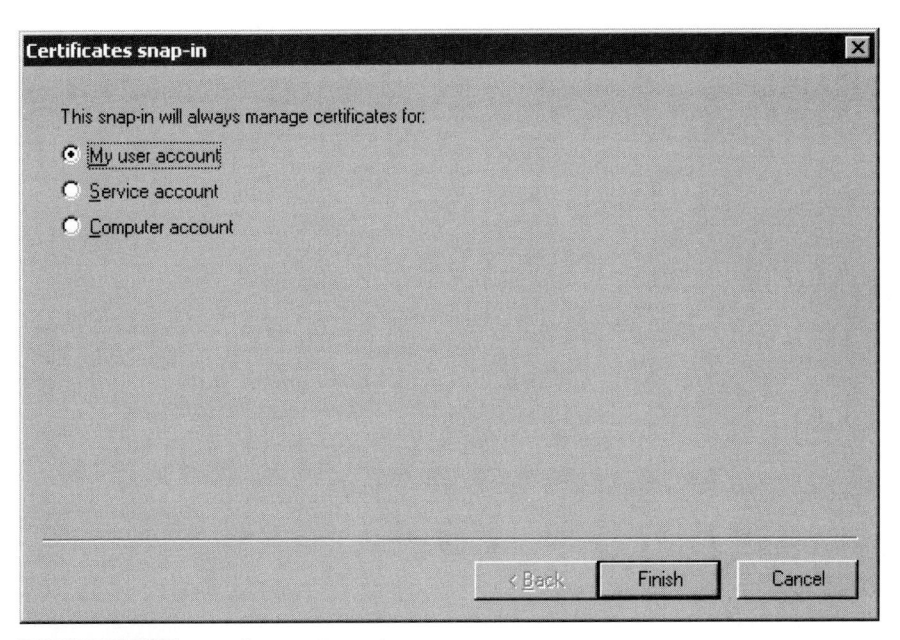

FIGURE 16.15 Certificates Snap-in

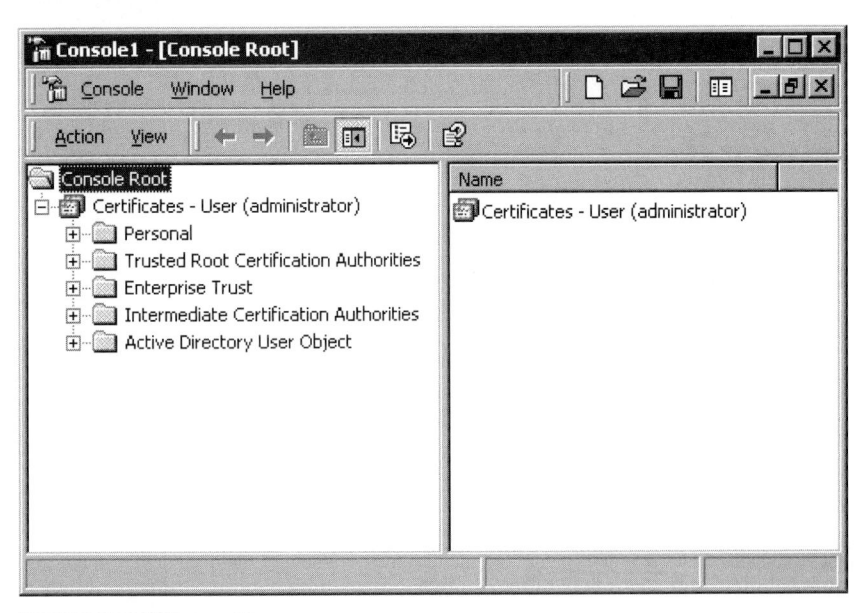

FIGURE 16.16 Certificates

Once you make your selection, the snap-in will display the chosen account and the certificate folders, such as personal, trusted root CA, Enterprise trust and so forth, as shown in Figure 16.16.

From this snap-in, you can right-click on any certificate that is available for the account and perform a number of actions, such as request a new key, renew a certificate, delete a certificate, or review the certificate's properties. You can learn more about certificate deployment planning and usage from the Windows 2000 Resource Kit on your Windows 2000 Server CD-ROM.

Summary

Windows 2000 provides advanced security features that enable networks to provide a high level of security against intruders and integrate with other networks or the Internet easily. Windows 2000 provides Kerberos V5 protocol for security, EFS, Security Templates, and a built-in Certificate Authority. These powerful features enable any networking environment, regardless of its needs, to be able to design an effective security plan to protect both network users and network resources.

SEVENTEEN

IP Security

Windows 2000 provides advanced security solutions through Kerberos, EFS, and digital certificates. However, these security solutions do not provide complete protection. While Windows 2000 security does provide a high amount of access control and data encryption, these solutions still do not protect the network from individuals who manage to gain access to the network. IP Security is an additional security feature offered in Windows 2000 that can both further protect the network against intruders and protect data as it travels along the network cabling. This feature, combined with other Windows 2000 security strategies, enables data to be protected as it is stored and as it is transferred over the network. This chapter gives an overview of IP Security and shows how to configure IP Security on your Windows 2000 Server.

IP Security Features

IP Security (IPSec) provides protection from attacks against the network by using cryptographic protection. This protection functions in a point to point manner in that only the sending and receiving computers have to know about the IP Security protection when it is needed. IP Security gives you the ability to protect communication flowing between different groups of computers, such as workgroups, domains, intranets, extranets, and so forth. This type of protection is accomplished using cryptography-based algorithms and keys. The algorithm uses a mathematical process to "scramble" the data, which is then interpreted or read by a key that can understand the algorithm. This combination makes data captured during transit extremely difficult to decipher. In addition to the algorithm and key defense, IPSec also provides the following features:

- Key Generation. For IPSec to function, both the sending and receiving computers must have the same shared key. This key cannot be sent across the network because this would be a security breach. So, key generation is performed by the algorithm. IPSec uses the algorithm to provide the key information for the encryption key. This way, the key can be generated on each computer without having to be sent across the network.
- Key Lengths. IPSec provides the ability to use longer key lengths for greater security protection. Longer keys are much more difficult to break, so you can generate longer keys for greater security.
- Dynamic Re-Keying. You can configure IPSec to generate new keys during a communication session. IPSec functions by encrypting data on the packet level, so during transit, a key can be used for part of the data, and then a new key can be generated for another portion of the data. In the case of a key being captured, only part of the data can be breached.

IPSec also uses an Authentication Header (AH) and the Encapsulating Security Payload (ESP) to provide security on a packet by packet level. The AH provides authentication, integrity, and anti-replay for both the IP header and data carried in the packet. AH does not encrypt the data, but it does protect the data from being modified. ESP provides the encryption for the data.

IPSec Policy Agent

IPSec functions by using a policy agent that contains the IPSec information. This information can be used to perform IPSec services, and the policy agent starts each time Windows 2000 is started. If the policy agent cannot find a policy in the Active Directory or if the agent cannot connect to the Active Directory, the agent waits to be assigned to a policy or to be activated. The policy agent retrieves the needed policy from the Active Directory if the computer is a member of the domain, or it can be retrieved from the registry if the computer is a standalone. Once the policy is retrieved, it is sent to the IPSec driver. The driver takes the IP Filter List(s) from the policy, and a security negotiation with a peer begins. Once the negotiation is completed, the driver secures the IP packets for transit, then routes the packets to the receiving computer. Once the receiving computer receives the packets, the driver on the receiving computer decrypts the packets, passes them to the TCP/IP driver, which then passes them to the needed application. This process is transparent to the users.

As you can imagine, the process can get tricky between different domains with different administrators involved in the IPSec policy process. If IPSec will be used across domains, a standard network policy for IPSec should be implemented.

Tunneling with IPSec

IPSec also provides tunneling with the Layer 2 Tunneling Protocol (L2TP). Tunneling is a feature that hides or encapsulates the original packet inside of a new packet. The new packet contains IP and routing information so that the hidden packet can reach the appropriate destination. Once the tunneled packet reaches its destination, the encapsulation is removed and the packet is sent onto its final destination. IPSec allows you to use L2TP or ESP for virtual private networking. This way, tunneled packets can take advantage of the IPSec security features so that tunneled packets are both encapsulated and encrypted for transit.

Configuring IPSec

Now that you have an understanding of IPSec and the security benefits you can gain, the rest of the chapter takes a look at how you configure and manage IPSec on your Windows 2000 Server. As with most other Windows 2000 components, you can manage IPSec from a centralized MMC snap-in, IP Security Policy Management. You can also implement IPSec features with other security systems provided in Windows 2000. Refer to Chapter 16 for more information.

To open the console, start MMC, click the Console menu, then click Add/Remove Snap-in. On the Add/Remove snap-in page, click the Add button, and click IP Security Policy Management, then click the Add button. The Select Computer window appears, shown in Figure 17.1.

You can select to manage either the local computer's IPSec policy or the policy for the entire domain or another domain or computer for which you have administrative rights.

Make your selection and click the Finish button. The console window appears, shown in Figure 17.2. In this figure, the selection to manage the domain was configured.

The following sections examine the configuration issues and actions you can perform.

Chapter seventeen • IP Security

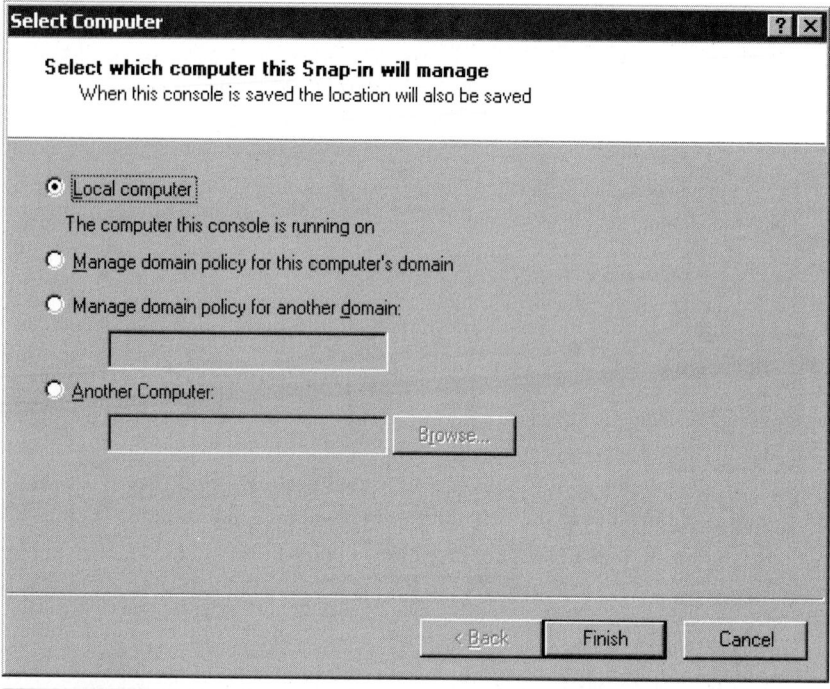

FIGURE 17.1 Select Computer

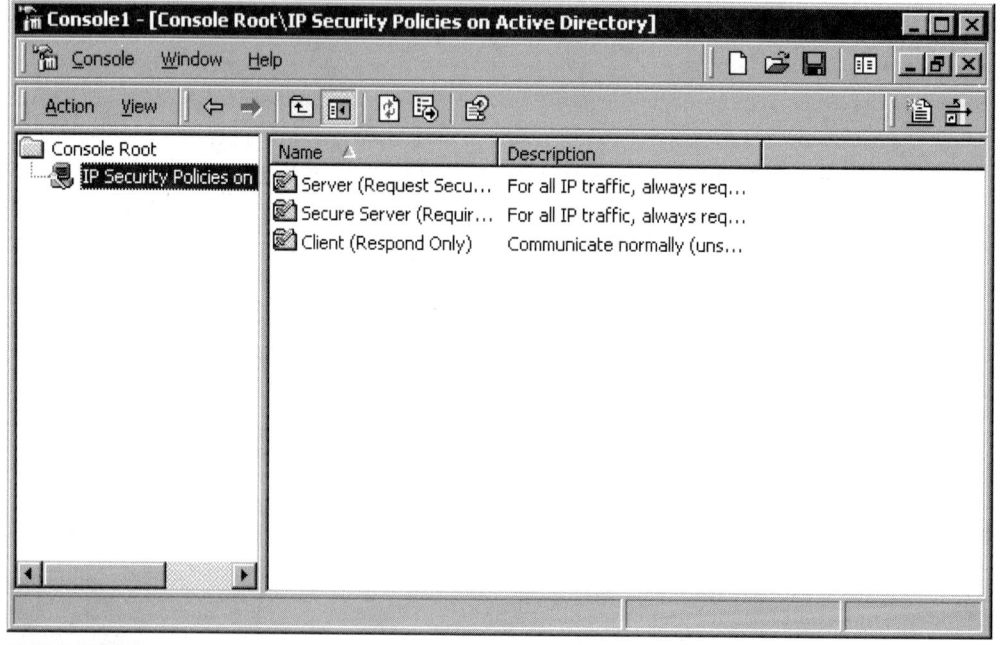

FIGURE 17.2 IP Security Policies on Active Directory

three • Networking **303**

Creating an IP Security Policy

To create an IP Security policy, follow these steps:

1. Right-click IP Security Policies in the left console pane and click Create IP Security Policy.
2. The IP Security Policy Wizard begins. Click Next.
3. The IP Security Policy Name window appears. Type a name for the policy and a description if desired and click Next.
4. The Requests for Secure Communication window appears. You have the option of either enabling or disabling the default response rule. This rule specifies how the server responds to remote computers when a security request is made when no other overriding rules apply. You should leave the default rule activated or secure communication will fail if no other rule is in effect. Click Next.
5. The Default Response Rule Authentication Method window appears, shown in Figure 17.3. You can choose to use Kerberos V5, which is the default for Windows 2000, or you can click the appropriate radio button to use a certificate or you can use a previously shared key. Make your selection and click Next.

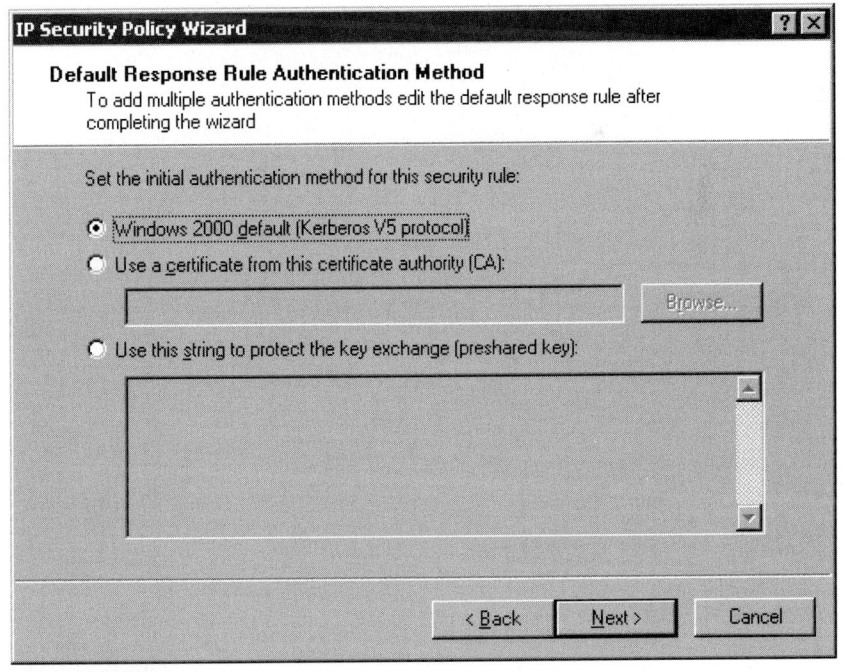

FIGURE 17.3 Default Response Rule Authentication Method

6. A summary window appears. Review your configuration. By default, an Edit properties check box is selected that allows you to edit the properties once the wizard completes. Click Finish.

The properties for the policy appear, shown in Figure 17.4. You have two tabs: Rules and General.

On the Rules tab, the default rule is listed if you chose to keep the default rule during the policy wizard. You can add new rules by clicking the Add button (see the following section). The General tab, shown in Figure 17.5, gives you the name of the policy, the description, and a check for policy changes box. This allows the system to check for policy updates in case you make changes. The default check time is 180 minutes, but you can change this by entering a new value in the box.

If you click the Advanced button, shown in Figure 17.6, you are presented with Key Exchange Settings. You can use this window to configure special settings for key exchanges. You can click the Master key Perfect Forward Secrecy check box to ensure that no master keys or master keying material is reused. You can also change the default authentication and key generation time of 480 minutes. A shorter time provides more key generation and higher security, but you may experience a performance loss due to serv-

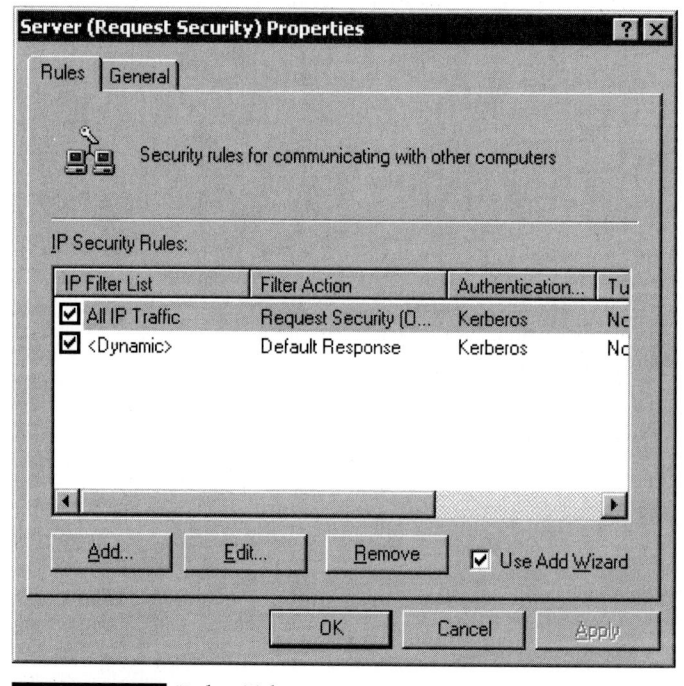

FIGURE 17.4 Rules Tab

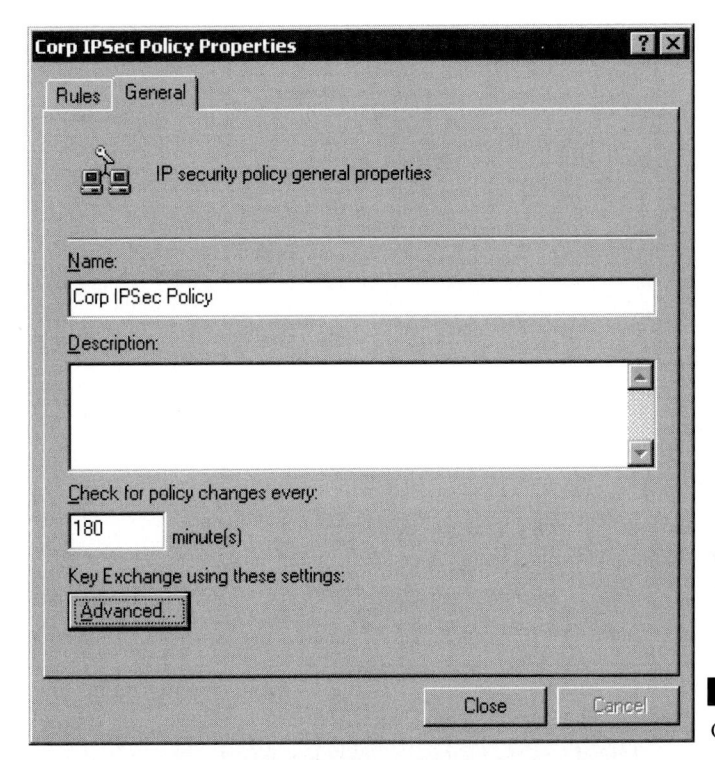

FIGURE 17.5
General Tab

FIGURE 17.6
Key Exchange Settings

er overhead. Or you can configure the Authenticate and generate a new key after every X sessions. The default is 0, but you can use this if you want a new key created after a predefined number of IPSec communication sessions.

If you click the Methods button, shown in Figure 17.7, you see the identity protection methods and encryption types that are in effect. You can click the Add button to configure additional algorithms if needed.

FIGURE 17.7

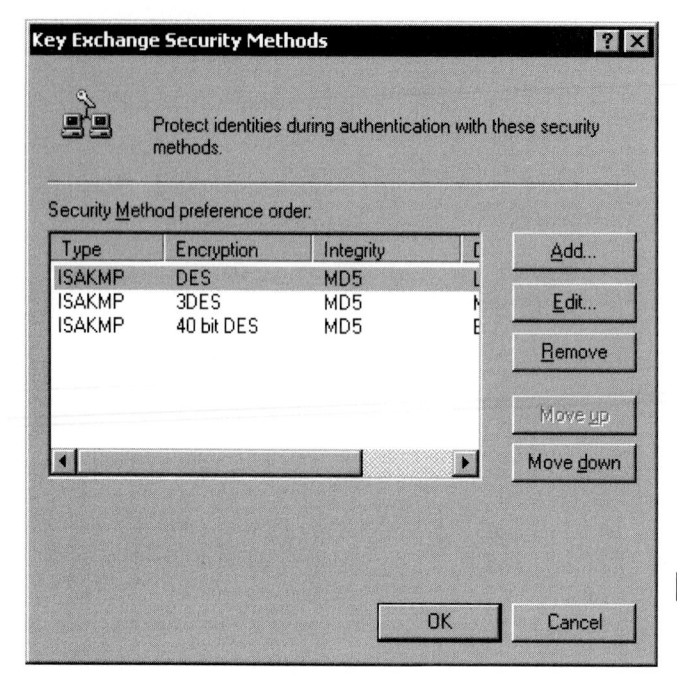

Key Exchange Security Methods

Creating New IPSec Policy Rules

You can create new rules for policies as needed. Policy rules define how the policy behaves in your environment and what is allowed under that particular policy. Right-click on the policy in the details pane of the console that you want to create a new rule and click Properties. On the rules tab, click Add, then follow these steps:

1. On the welcome screen, click Next.
2. The Tunnel Endpoint window appears, shown in Figure 17.8. If this rule applies to IPSec using L2TP tunneling, you can click the appropriate radio button and specify the DNS name of the computer where the tunnel ends, or you can specify the computer name by its IP address. Remember that the tunnel endpoint is the computer where the encapsulated packet is stripped and sent onto its final destination, so the tunnel ends at that computer. If the policy is not for tunneling, click the This rule does not specify a tunnel and click Next.
3. The Network Type window appears. The rule has to be applied to either all network connections, LAN connections only, or Remote Access connections. Make your selection and click Next.
4. The Authentication Method window appears. This is the same window you first saw when creating the policy. Choose either Windows 2000

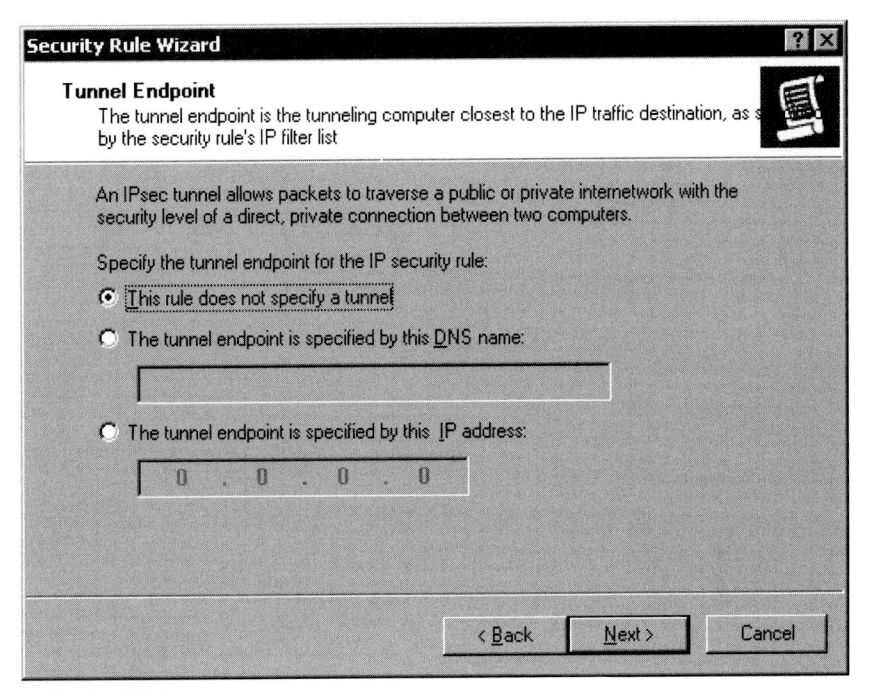

FIGURE 17.8 Tunnel Endpoint

default (Kerberos V5) or a certificate, or a preshared key and click Next.

5. The IP Filter List window appears, shown in Figure 17.9. You can specify the type of IP traffic the rule applies to. By default, All IP traffic is selected, but you can click the Remove button if you want the rule to apply to only certain kinds of IP traffic.

6. If you click the Add button, you can add filters as needed. When you click the Add button, a window appears, shown in Figure 17.10, which lets you add filters. If you click the Add button on this window, a new wizard begins (within the current wizard) that helps you configure IP filters. Click Next on the welcome screen.

7. On the IP Traffic Source window, use the drop down menu to specify the source address of the IP traffic. You can select from My IP Address, Any IP Address, A specific DNS Name, A specific IP Address, or A specific IP Subnet. Make your selection and click Next.

8. On the IP Traffic Destination window, use the drop down menu to specify the destination address of the IP traffic. You can select from My IP Address, Any IP Address, A specific DNS Name, A specific IP Address, or A specific IP Subnet. Make your selection and click Next.

9. The IP Protocol Type window appears. Use the drop down menu to

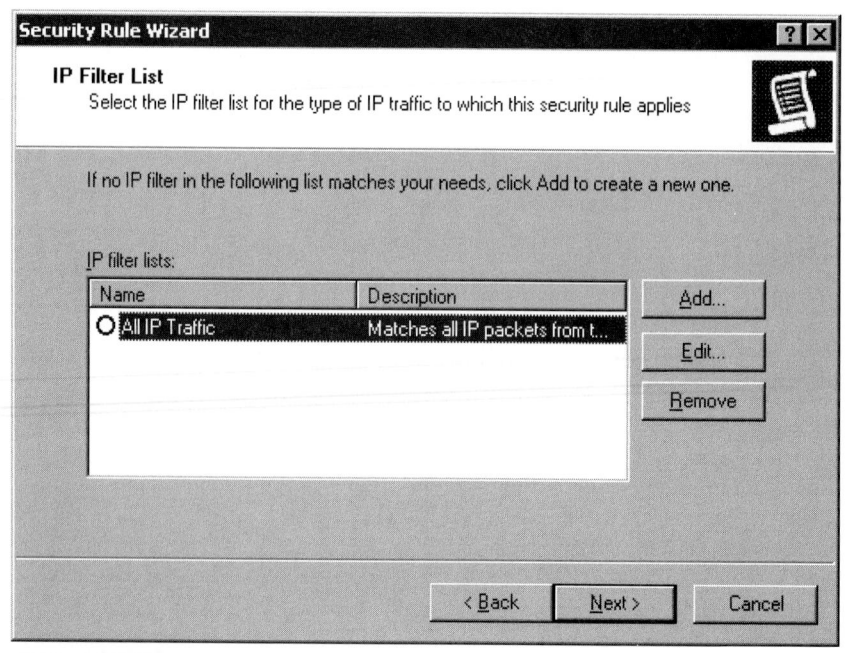

FIGURE 17.9 IP Filter List

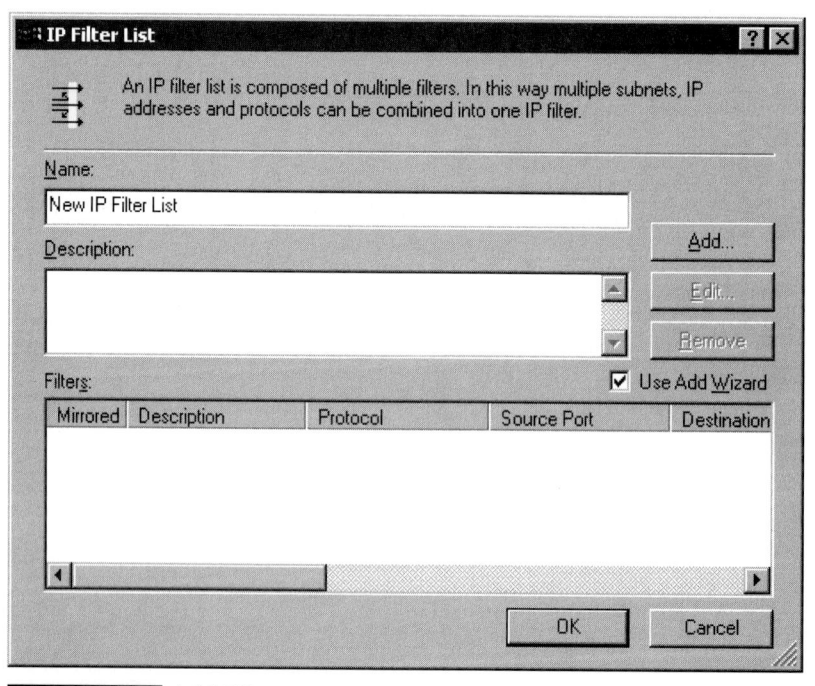

FIGURE 17.10 Add Filters

three • Networking

select the type of IP protocol you want to filter. The selections are any, EGP, HMP, ICMP, Other, RAW, RDP, RVD, TCP, UDP, or XNS-IDP. Make your selection and click Next.

10. The IP Protocol Port window appears. Use the radio buttons to configure the from and to IP ports. You can allow "any" or specify a particular port as needed. Make your selections and click Next.
11. Click the Finish button.
12. Once you click Finish, the IP filter you created appears in the list. You can click the Add button to add more filters or click Close.
13. Once you click Close, this returns you to the main wizard. Click Next.
14. The Filter Action window appears, shown in Figure 17.11. You can select either Require Security or Request Security as they appear in the list, or you can click the Add button to set a different action. If you click the Add button, you will be presented with another wizard similar to the filter wizard. Make your selections and click Next.
15. A summary window appears. Click Finish.

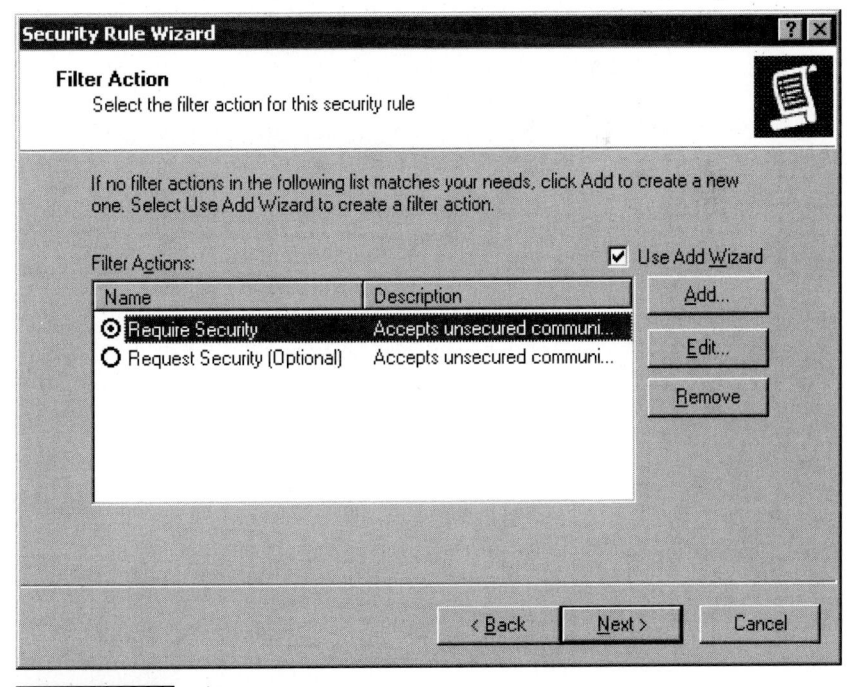

FIGURE 17.11 Filter Action

Managing Filter Lists

Once you configure various filters, you can manage them from one location within the IP Security Policies console. If you right-click on IP Security Policies in the console window and click Manage IP Filter Lists and Filter Actions, you are presented with Manage IP Filter Lists and Manage Filter Actions tabs. The Manage IP Filter Lists tab, shown in Figure 17.12, gives you a listing of the available IP Filter Lists that are shared by all IP security polices that are configured.

If you click the Add button, you can create new filters for use by all of your policies. This action launches the filter wizard as explained in the previous sections. If you click the Manage Filter Actions tab, shown in Figure 17.13, you manage the way your IP filters behave.

The list tells you which filter actions are in effect for all IP Security polices. You can add new ones by clicking the Add button. This action launches the IP Security Filter Action Wizard. To complete the wizard, follow these steps:

1. Click Next on the welcome screen.
2. Name the filter action and provide a description if desired. Click Next.

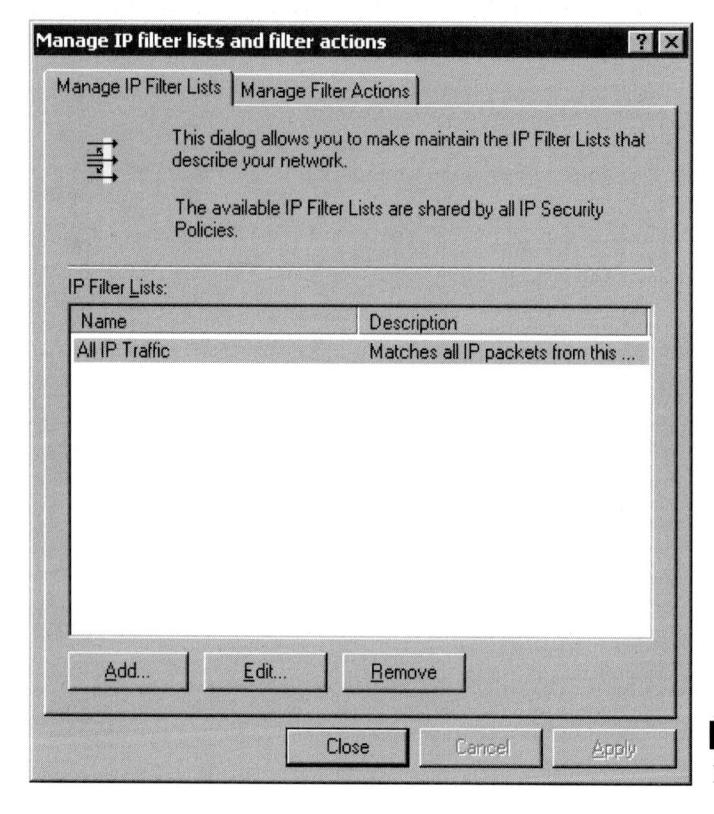

FIGURE 17.12
Filter Lists

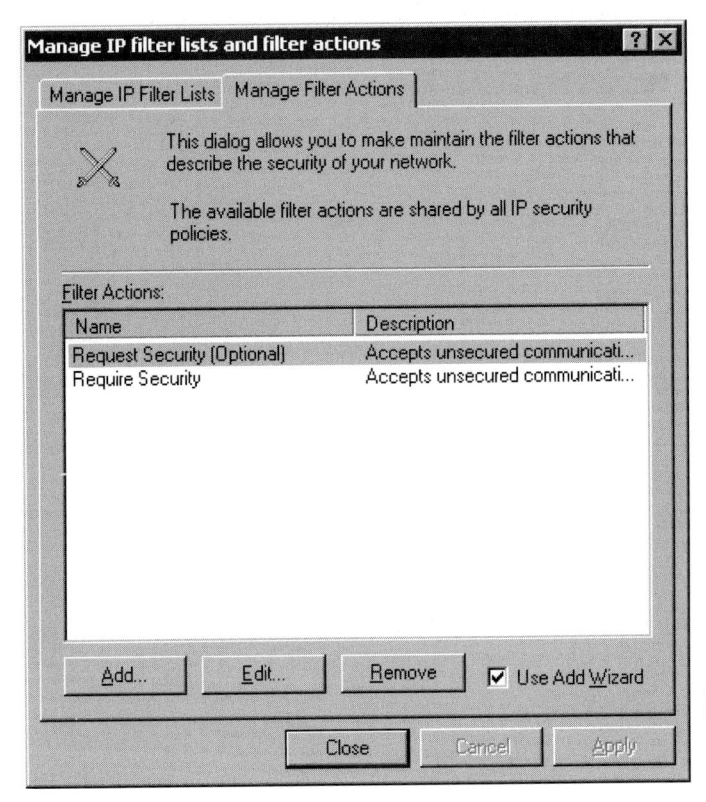

FIGURE 17.13

Manage Filter Actions

3. The Filter Action General Options window appears. You have three radio buttons to choose from. You can choose to either permit, block, or negotiate security. Make your selection and click Next.

4. If you selected permit or block, a summary window appears. Click Finish to finish the wizard. If you select negotiate security, the Communicating with computers that do not support IPSec window appears. This window presents you with two radio buttons for you to choose from. You can either select to not communicate with computers that do not support IPSec, or you can specify to fall back to unsecured communication. Click Next.

5. The IP Traffic Security window appears, shown in Figure 17.14. You have the options of selecting either high, medium, or custom security for the filter. If you choose custom, another window appears that allows you to choose the type of encryption you would like to use. Make your selections and click Next.

6. A summary window appears. Click Finish.

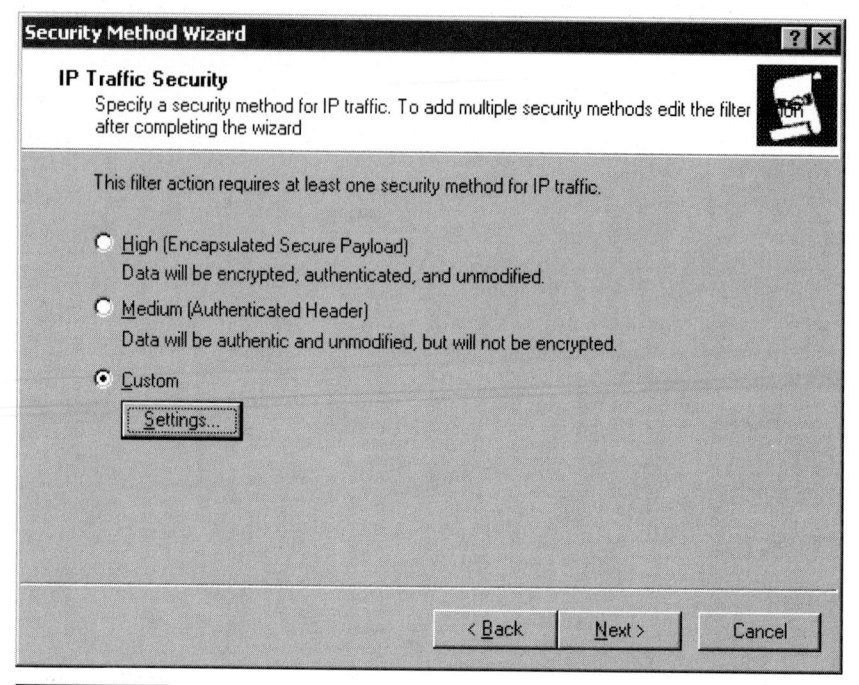

FIGURE 17.14 IP Traffic Security

Checking Policy Integrity

You check your policy integrity to see whether there are conflicts or contradictions between security policies that are in effect. To check for policy integrity, right-click IP Security Policies in the left console pane, point to All Tasks, and click Check Policy Integrity. The system checks the policy integrity and gives either a verification message or a report about integrity problems.

Restoring Default Policies

You can easily restore Windows 2000's default security policies if necessary. Right-click IP Security Policies in the left console pane, point to All Tasks, and click Restore Default Policies. A dialog box appears asking if you are sure. Click Yes to continue or No to quit.

Importing or Exporting Policies

You can import or export security polices as needed. Right-click IP Security Policies in the left console pane, point to All Tasks, and click either import or export policy. An Explorer based window appears so that you can select the location for either the import or export action.

Summary

IP Security provides an additional layer of security when used in conjunction with Windows 2000 security or remote access. IPSec provides data encryption at the packet level when it travels along the network wire and functions using an algorithm and mathematical key so that data cannot be read without the appropriate key. As the security needs of organizations have become more complex, IPSec is just one of the many security features offered in Windows 2000.

PART FOUR

Managing Clients and Performance

In This Part

▶ **CHAPTER 18**
Configuring User, Computer, and Group Accounts

▶ **CHAPTER 19**
Configuring Profiles and Policies

▶ **CHAPTER 20**
Managing Shared Resources

▶ **CHAPTER 21**
Additional Client Technologies

▶ **CHAPTER 22**
Printing

▶ **CHAPTER 23**
Auditing

▶ **CHAPTER 24**
Performance Monitor and Network Monitor

As an administrator, one of the time consuming aspects of your job can be managing network client(s) and shared resources. In this section, you learn about the new features Windows 2000 Server offers to manage clients and resources more efficiently. You will learn how to configure user, computer, and group accounts in the Active Directory, profiles and policies, printing, and a number of additional client technologies, such as Intellimirror. This section also reviews the use of Performance Monitor and Network Monitor in Windows 2000 Server.

EIGHTEEN

Configuring User, Computer, and Group Accounts

Managing User, Computer, and Group accounts is a task that consumes quite a bit of time for network administrators. For the most part, creating, configuring, and managing user, computer, and group accounts is not that different in Windows 2000 from what it was in Windows NT— there are more options you can configure, but the tasks remain much the same. As you have seen, User Manager for Domains is no longer present in Windows 2000; now you manage user, computer, and group accounts within the Active Directory Users and Computers snap-in. This chapter shows how to create, configure, and manage user, computer, and group accounts in Windows 2000 Server.

Understanding User and Computer Accounts in Windows 2000

Both user and computer accounts are enabled to provide access rights as well as restrictions to both network users and computers residing on the network. Windows 2000 provides two different kinds of user accounts: domain user accounts and local user accounts. A domain user account allows a user to log on to a Windows 2000 domain and access domain resources. When a user logs on to the domain, the user account and password is checked against the Security ID (SID) for the account. If the account is valid, the account is then authenticated by a domain controller and the user is provided an access token. The user account information is replicated to the other domain controllers so that the user can access domain resources. The local user account allows the user to log on to a particular computer and gain access to resources that exist on that machine. The local computer account is created only in the computer's security database, and this account information is not replicated to domain controllers. Users who log on to a local computer using a local computer account will not be able to access resources that exist on the domain.

Windows 2000 contains two Builtin accounts, the administrator account and the guest account. The guest account is disabled by default and can be enabled and assigned a password as needed. You can rename the guest account but you cannot delete it.

It is important to remember when creating user accounts that user logon names must be unique, the names cannot contain more than 20 characters, and these characters are not valid: " / \ [ ] : ; | = , + * ? < >. User logon names are not case sensitive.

User Accounts

In this section, I explore how to create, configure, and manage user accounts. The following sections show you how to complete various tasks related to User Accounts.

Creating Domain User Accounts

To create a User Account, follow these steps:

1. Click Start ➛ Programs ➛ Adminsitrative Tools ➛ Active Directory Users and Computers.
2. Expand the domain in the console.
3. Right-click the Users container, or the OU where you want to create a user account, point to New, and click User, or simply click on the New User icon on the taskbar. The Create New Object (User) appears, shown in Figure 18.1. Enter the user's name and logon name. The downlevel logon name, which will be used with earlier Windows servers, such as NT, is automatically displayed then click Next.
4. In the next window, type the password for the user and click the appropriate check boxes options as desired, as shown in Figure 18.2. You have the options of choosing User must change password at next logon, User cannot change password, Password never expires, or Account disabled. Make your selection(s) and click Next.

four • Managing Clients and Performance

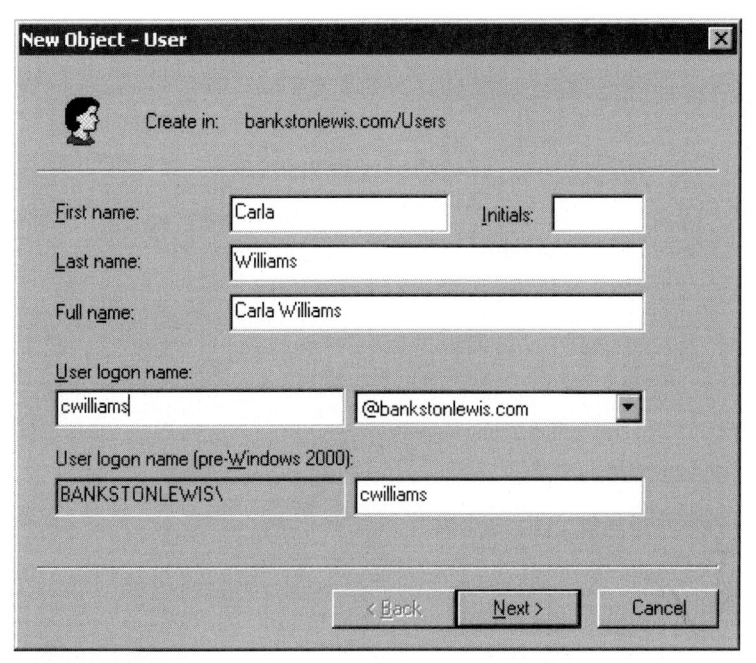

FIGURE 18.1 Create New Object (User)

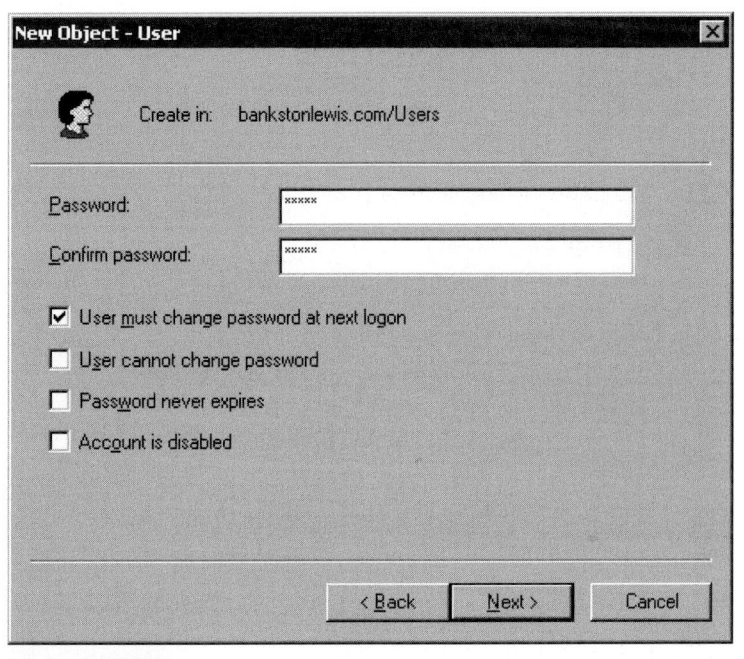

FIGURE 18.2 Password window

5. A summary page appears, shown in Figure 18.3. Review the account and click the Finish button to create the account or click the Back button to make changes.

Configuring Account Properties

Once a user account is created, you can configure additional information about the account that defines more information about the user and gives the user certain rights and access privileges. To configure a user account, find the user account you want to configure, right-click it, and select properties. The properties sheet for the user account opens and contains eight tabs. Other tabs may appear depending on your system configuration. The following sections show you what you can configure on each page.

GENERAL

On the General page, shown in Figure 18.4, you can enter additional information about the user such as a description for the user, office information, telephone, e-mail, and the user's home page if one exists. You can click on the Other buttons to enter additional information or additional web access pages if desired.

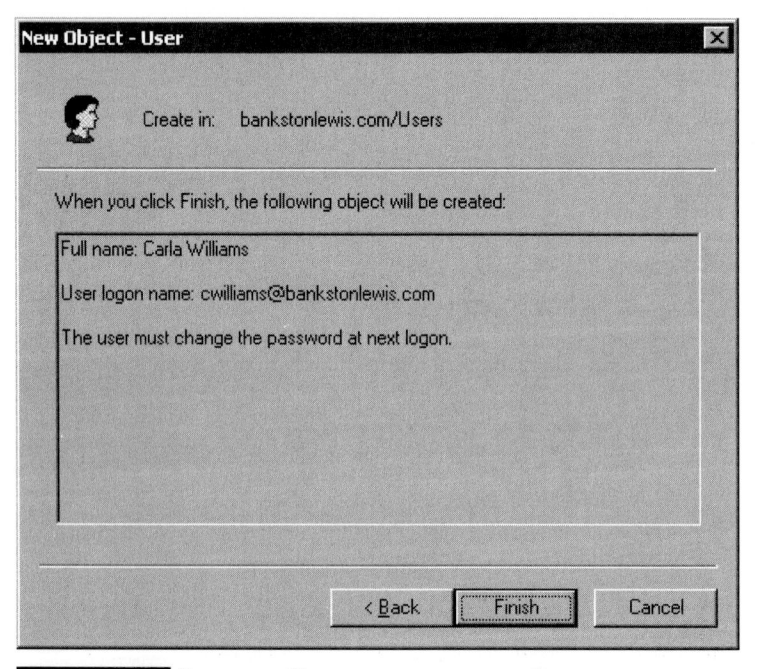

FIGURE 18.3 Summary Page

FIGURE 18.4 General Properties

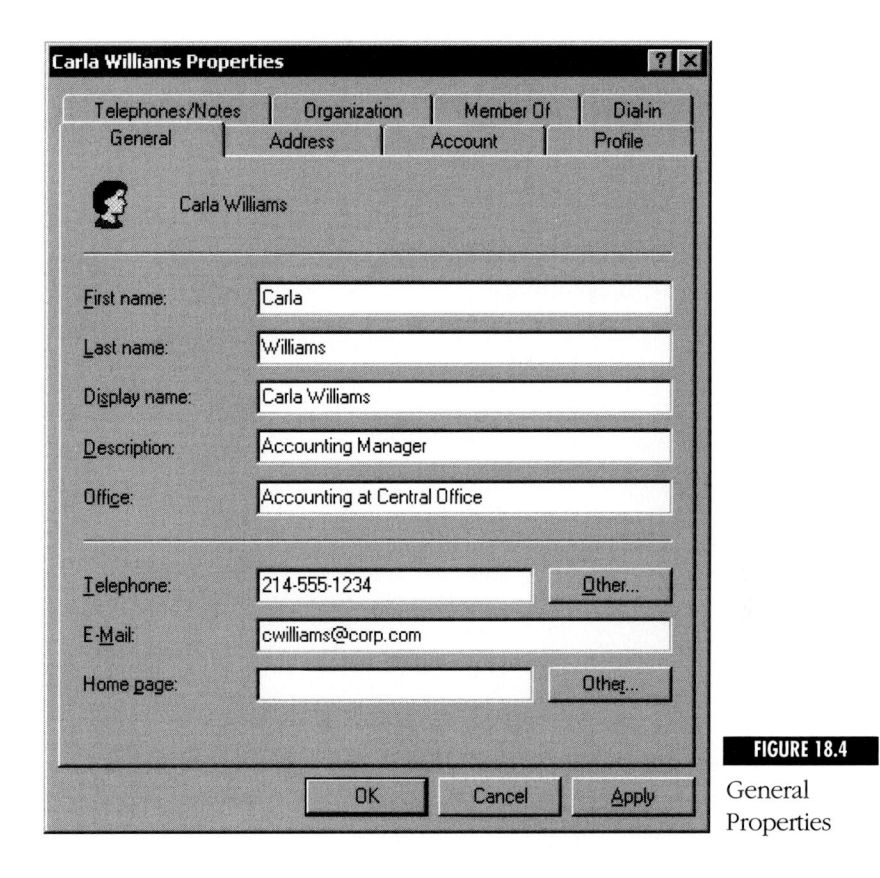

ADDRESS

On the Address Properties sheet, shown in Figure 18.5, you can enter the address of the user by entering the data in the boxes provided. Use the Country/Region drop-down menu to select the appropriate country or region.

ACCOUNT

The Account Properties sheet, shown in Figure 18.6 displays the user's logon name and downlevel logon name. On this page, you have the following account options you can enter for the user:

- User must change password at next logon.
- User cannot change password.
- Password never expires.
- Save password as encrypted clear text.
- Account disabled.
- User must log on using a smart card.

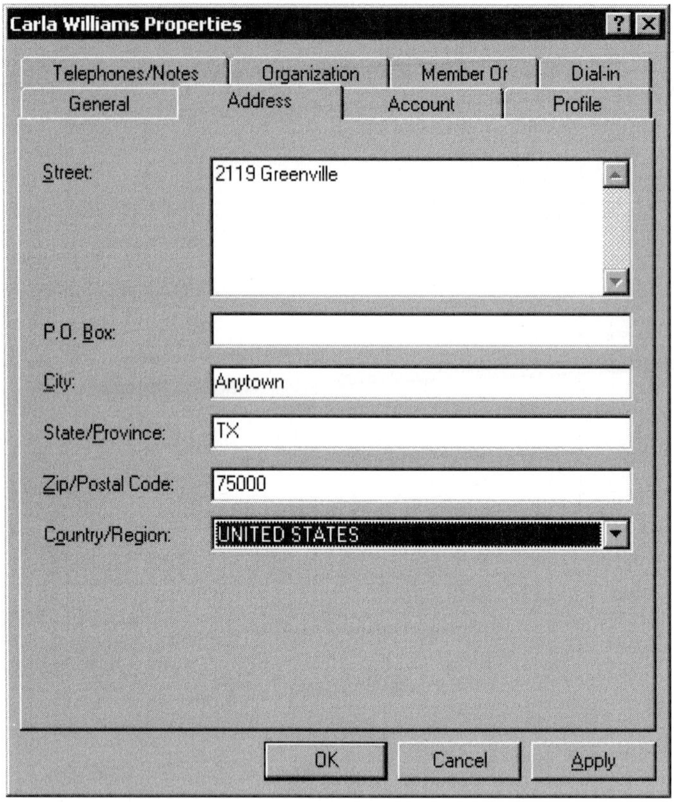

FIGURE 18.5 Address Properties

- Account is trusted for delegation.
- Account is sensitive and cannot be delegated.
- Use DES encryption types for this account (DES is Data Encryption Standard which are encryption algorithms used to provide confidentiality).
- Don't require Kerberos Preauthentication (which encrypts the password as it is being sent to the authentication server).

At the bottom of the screen, you can also set an expiration date for the account if the account is temporary and you want it to expire. To set the expiration date, click the End of radio button, then use the drop down menu to select the expiration date for the account.

If you click on the Logon hours button, you can restrict logon access to certain days and hours of the week if desired. The Logon hours page, shown in Figure 18.7, presents you with a grid representing each day and each hour of the week. Blue grids allow logon while white grids restrict logon. To make changes, click on the grid sections for the day(s) and

four • Managing Clients and Performance **323**

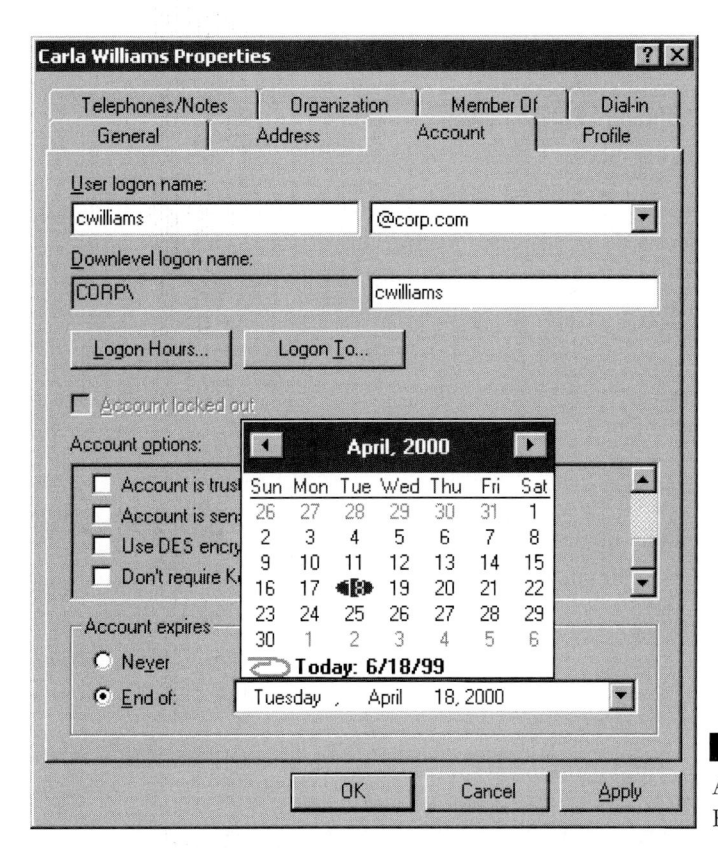

FIGURE 18.6 Account Properties

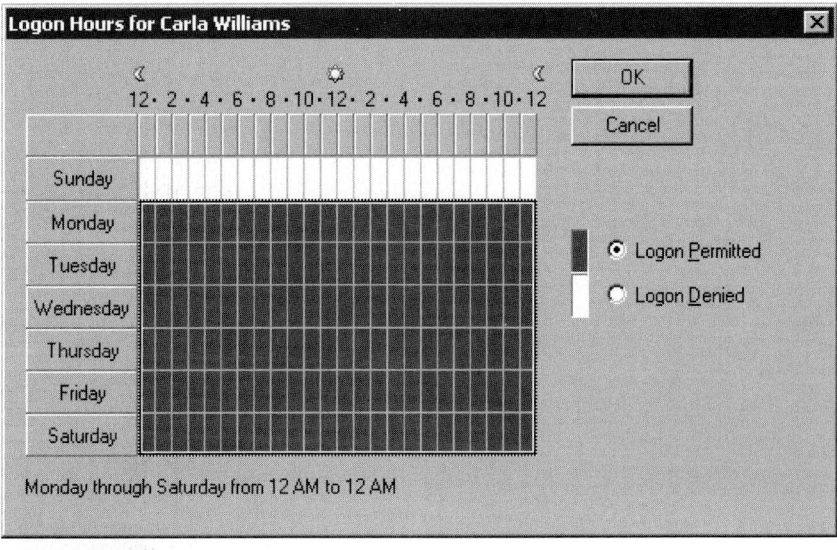

FIGURE 18.7 Logon Hours

hours(s) and select either the Logon Permitted or Logon Denied radio buttons. In the example in Figure 18.7, this user has 24-hour access Monday through Saturday, but no logon access on Sundays.

If you click the Logon To button, you can restrict the workstations the user can log on to. This window, shown in Figure 18.8, allows you to click the User may log on to these workstations button, then add the workstation NetBIOS names. Once this is done, the user is restricted to the workstations in the list. Even if additional workstations are added in the future, the user will still be restricted to the specified workstations in his or her account properties unless they are changed.

PROFILE

On the Profile sheet, you can enter the profile path, logon script, and home directory path if profiles are enabled for the user. You can also enter the network path to a shared documents folder if desired.

TELEPHONE/NOTES

The Telephone/Notes sheet allows you to enter additional phone numbers, such as home, mobile, fax, IP Phone, and pager numbers. A Comments section is provided where you can type comments related to the user's contact information.

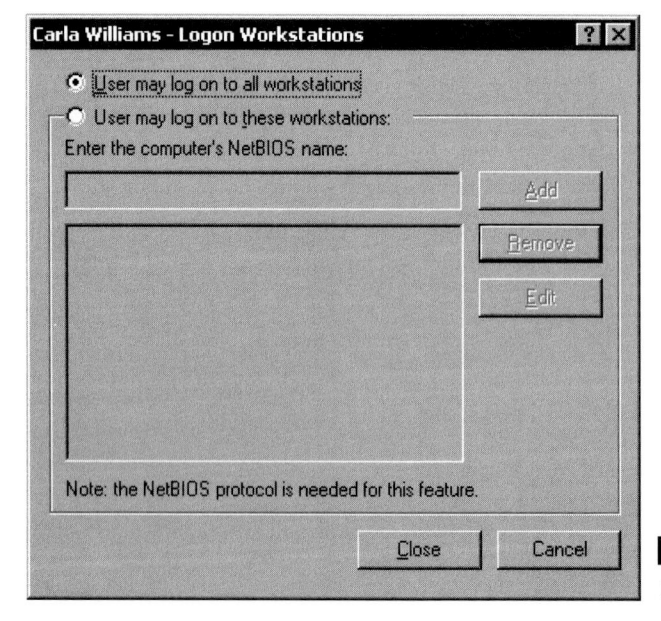

FIGURE 18.8

Logon Workstations

ORGANIZATION

The Organization page, shown in Figure 18.9, allows you to enter information about the user's place in the organization including the user's manager and the names of other employees who report to that user.

MEMBER OF

The Member Of page, shown in Figure 18.10, allows you to configure the groups the user belongs to. If you click the Add button, you are presented with a list of groups from the Active Directory. Select a group you want the user to belong to, click Add, then click OK. The new groups you select will appear in the Member of list.

DIAL-IN

The Dial-in sheet, shown in Figure 18.11, allows you to configure remote access for the user if desired. At the top of the window, you can click Allow

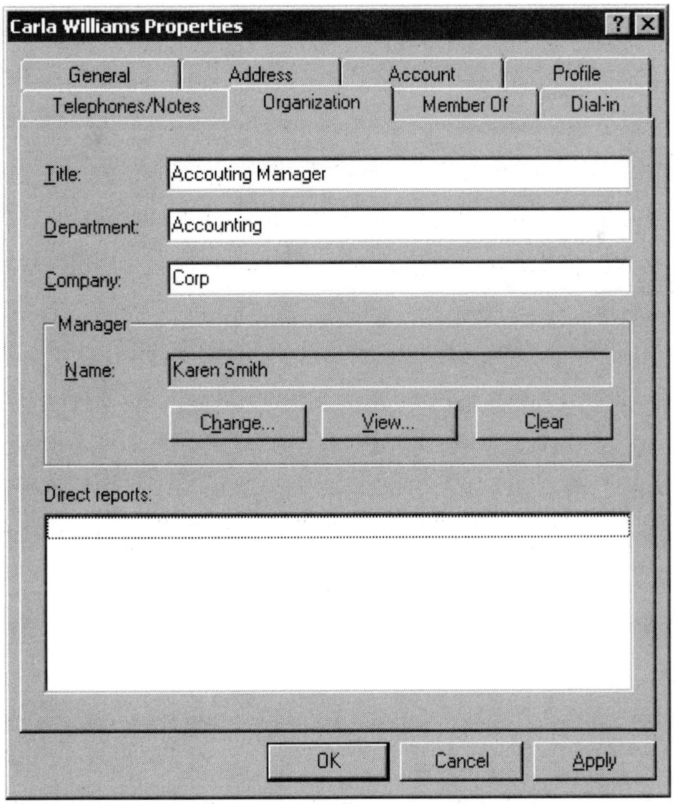

FIGURE 18.9
Organization Page

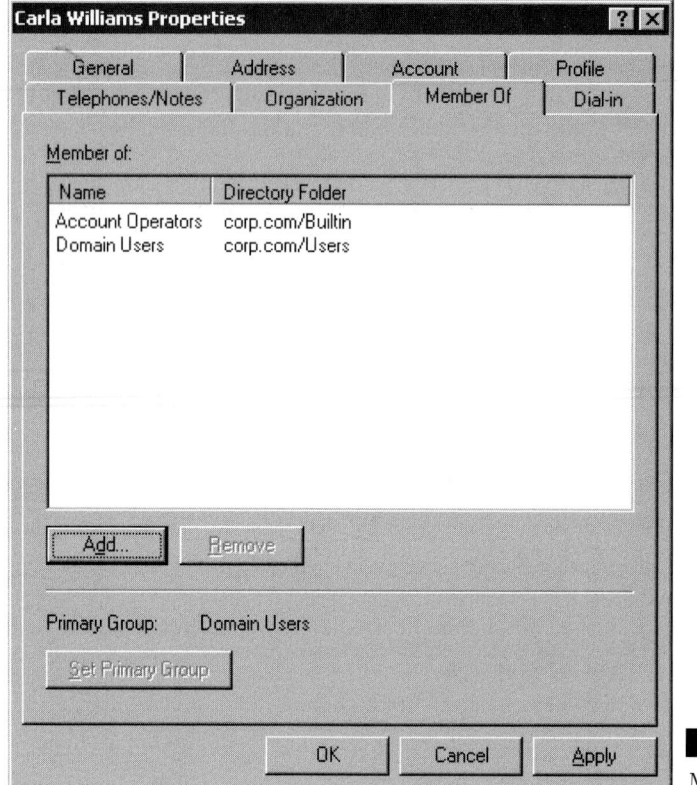

FIGURE 18.10
Member Of

access to allow the user to access the remote access server through a dial-up connection or VPN. You can also allow callback options by clicking the appropriate radio button in the middle of the screen. Depending on the configuration of remote access, you may also assign a static IP address to the user and assign a static route. By default, dial-in access is denied to the user until you enable it on this property sheet. See Chapter 14 for more information about routing and remote access.

Managing User Accounts

You can easily perform a number of other actions concerning user accounts by right-clicking the user account icon in the details pane, shown in Figure 18.12. This option allows you to quickly disable the account, reset the password, move the account to a different location in the directory, open the user's home page (if a home page is configured in the properties sheet), or send the user an e-mail (if the e-mail address is configured in the properties sheet). If you disable an account, a red X appears over the account object

FIGURE 18.11 Dial-In Properties

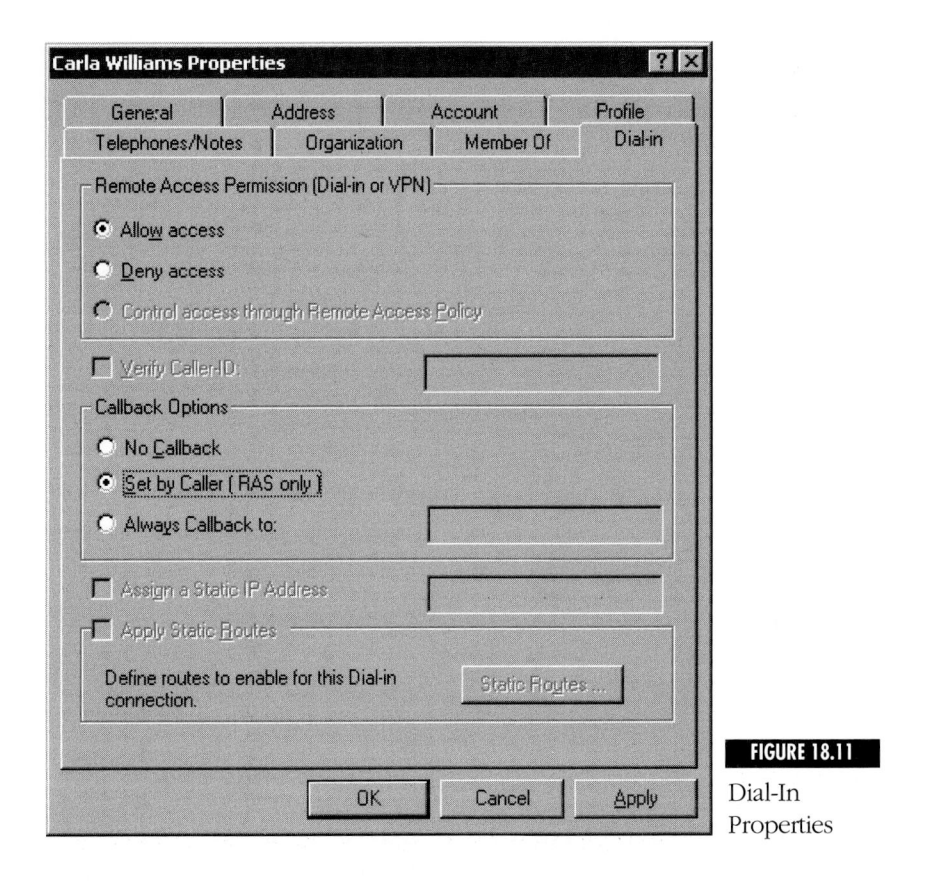

in the directory, as you can see in Figure 18.12. You can also delete or rename an account if needed. If you rename an account, you are renaming the Active Directory object name—the user still logs on with the same user name and password that were originally configured. If you need to change a user's logon name, access the properties sheet and change the logon name on the Account page.

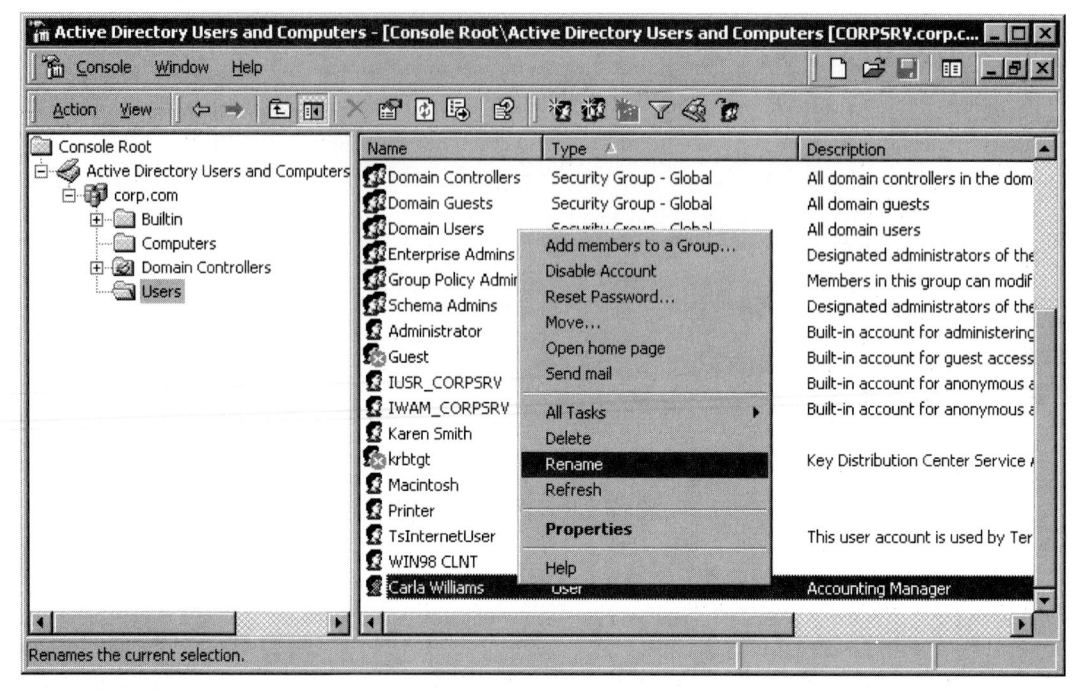

FIGURE 18.12 Account Management

Configuring and Managing Computer Accounts

Just as user accounts represent an actual user, computer accounts represent an actual computer on the network. Each Windows 2000 and Windows NT (server and workstation) computer in the domain has a computer account that can be used by administrators for auditing as well as permissions and restrictions. Since Windows 95/98 computers do not have the security features of Windows 2000 or Windows NT computers, they are not assigned computer accounts in Windows 2000, but they can log on to a Windows 2000 domain and use the domain resources. The following sections show you how to configure computer accounts.

Configuring Computer Account Properties

Each Windows 2000 or Windows NT computer in the domain appears in the Computers OU in the Active Directory Users and Computers snap-in. To access a computer account's properties, right-click on the account and click Properties. The properties sheet contains five tabs and are explained in the following sections.

GENERAL

The General Properties sheet, shown in Figure 18.13 provides the DNS and downlevel name of the computer as well as the role the computer plays on the network. You can enter a description for the computer if desired, and if you want the computer to be trusted for delegation, click the check box. Trusted for Delegation means that this computer account can be trusted to delegate other responsibilities to that computer. For example, you can delegate control of another folder to that particular computer account. Generally, however, it is best to delegate control of objects to user accounts instead of computer accounts.

OPERATING SYSTEM

The Operating System sheet tells you what operating system the computer is running and what service pack (if any) has been applied.

MEMBER OF

The Member Of page is the same as seen in user account properties. You can click the Add button to add the computer to other groups.

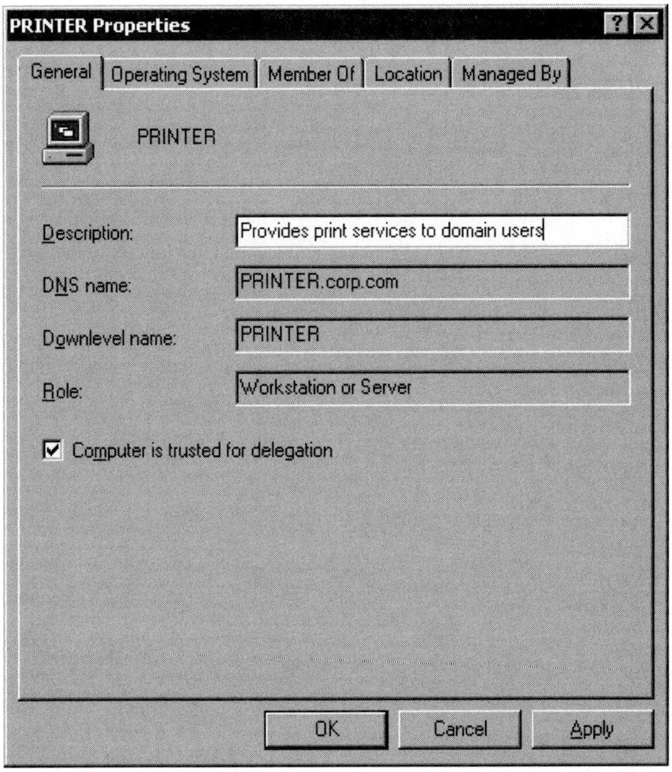

FIGURE 18.13 General Properties

LOCATION

The Location page allows you to enter the location of the computer account within the Active Directory.

MANAGED BY

The Managed By page, shown in Figure 18.14, allows you to enter information for the user who manages the computer. You can enter the user's name and contact information in the appropriate fields. When you provide a manager's name, the additional information is taken from that user's account in the Active Directory.

Managing Computer Accounts

There are several actions you can perform within the Active Directory Users and Computers snap-in that allow you to easily manage computer accounts. If you right-click on the Computers object in the console tree, you can choose to delegate control, find a computer, or add a new computer to the object. If you right-click a computer account in the details pane, you can

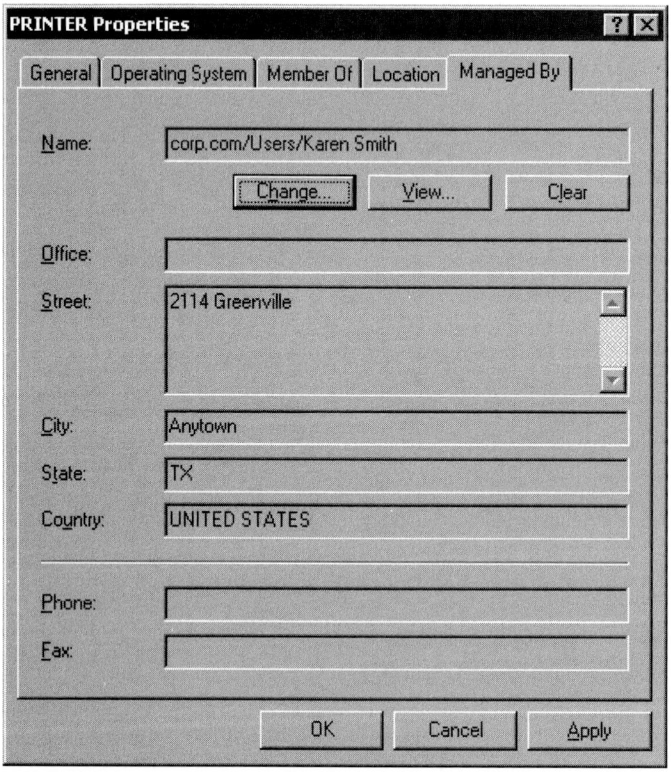

FIGURE 18.14

Managed By

disable the computer account, reset the account, move the account, or manage the account. If you disable an account, users will not be able to log on to the domain from that computer. Also, you can choose to place the computer account in a different OU by clicking Move. If you click Manage, you (as the administrator) are given management control and the Computer Management snap-in opens. At this point, you can manage the computer as though you are sitting at the computer by running system tools or configuring storage features.

Understanding Groups

Groups in Windows 2000 enable you to manage users more easily. You can give a group of users access to a particular resource in one action instead of having to give each user access to the resource. This organizational method saves administrative time and reduces the possibilities of errors. Additionally, members of a particular group can be members of other groups as well, and groups can be members of other groups (called nesting). However, adding groups to other groups should be done with care since permissions will become more complicated.

Types of Groups

Windows 2000 supports two group types—security groups and distribution groups. Both group types are stored in the Active Directory. The security groups are used to assign resource permissions to the groups while the distribution groups are used for non-security purposes. Applications use distribution groups for functions such as sending e-mail messages, and they cannot be used to assign permissions. Programs designed to work with the Active Directory make use of distribution groups. Also, a security group has all of the capabilities of a distribution group and more.

Group Scopes

Group scopes define how you can use the group to assign permissions. The scope determines how you can assign permissions to the group for resource access. There are three available group scopes in Windows 2000: global groups, local groups, and universal groups. Each of these is described in the following list:

- Global groups: members of global groups come from one domain but can access resources in any domain for which the group has permission.
- Local groups: members can come from any domain, but members can access only resources in the local domain. Local groups are used to

assign permissions to resources; then you can place global groups in local groups so that those resources can be accessed by the global group members.
- Universal Groups: members can come from any domain and can access resources in any domain. In Windows 2000, universal groups are available only in native mode, not in mixed mode.

For each group, there are group membership rules that apply. The rules define what members a group can contain and what groups the group can be a member of. The following list defines rules that govern group membership for each scope:

- Global groups: can contain user accounts and global groups from the same domain. The global group can be a member of a universal and domain local group in any domain.
- Domain Local: can contain user accounts, universal groups, and global groups from any domain. The domain local group can be a member of other domain local groups in the same domain.
- Universal: can contain user accounts, universal groups, and global groups from any domain. The universal group can be a member of any domain local or universal groups in any domain.

Understanding Builtin Groups

Windows 2000 includes several Builtin groups that are automatically created and configured upon installation. The Builtin groups are created in the Active Directory, and you can add or remove users from these groups as needed. By default, the groups do not have any rights to access resources. You can assign these rights by adding the Builtin groups to global groups or domain local groups. Windows 2000 includes the following Builtin global groups:

- Domain Users: The Domain Users group is automatically added to the Users domain local group. By default, the Administrator is a member and each new member added to the Active Directory becomes a member of this group.
- Domain Admins: The Domain Admins group is automatically added to the Administrators domain local group to allow group members to perform administrative tasks.
- Domain Guests: The Domain Guests group is automatically added to the domain local group.
- Enterprise Admins: The Enterprise Admins group is designed for users who need to have administrative control over the domain. The Enterprise Admins group can be added to the Administrators domain local group in each domain in the Enterprise.

Windows 2000 also provides Builtin domain local groups to provide users' rights and permissions for tasks on domain controllers and the Active Directory. There are a number of Builtin domain local groups. The following list explains some of the most common ones:

- Users: can perform tasks for which you have granted rights to resources.
- Account Operators: can create, delete, and modify user accounts and other groups, with the exception of the Administrators group.
- Backup Operators: can back up and restore all domain controllers by using Windows Backup.
- Administrators: can perform all domain administrative tasks on domain controllers.
- Print Operators: can set up and manage network printers that exist on domain controllers.

Configuring Groups

Like user accounts, group accounts are easy to create and configure. The following sections show you how to create and configure groups.

Creating a New Group

To create a new group, follow these steps:

1. Click Start → Programs → Administrative Tools → Active Directory Users and Computers.
2. Expand the server name and right-click on OU where you want to add a new group. Point to New, then click Group.
3. The Create New Object (Group) window appears, shown in Figure 18.15. Type the name of the new group, and then assign the group scope, either domain local, global, or universal. On group type, leave the default Security radio button selected. Click OK. The new group appears in the details pane in the console.

Configuring Group Properties

Once the new group is created, you can right-click on the object's icon and click Properties. This action opens the Properties sheet for the group which contains four tabs. The following sections explain what you can configure on each tab.

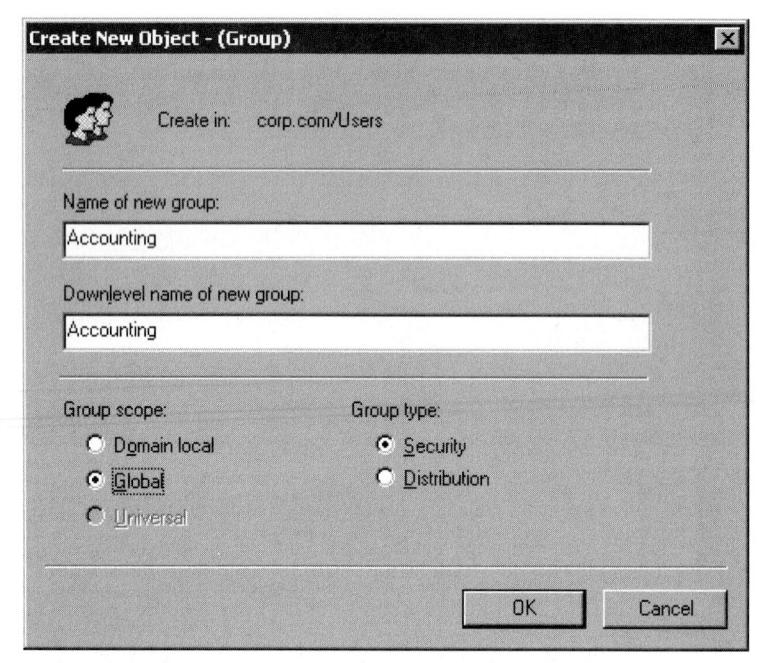

FIGURE 18.15 Create New Group

GENERAL

On the General sheet, shown in Figure 18.16, you can enter a description for the group and an e-mail address. For example, if the group has an e-mail address such as accounting@corp.com, then every member of the group will receive the e-mail sent to the group. The General tab also displays the scope and type of the group.

MEMBERS

The Members sheet, shown in Figure 18.17, gives you a listing of the current members of the group. If this is a new group, you will need to use this tab to add members to the group. If you click the Add button, you can select and add members to the group from the Active Directory.

MEMBER OF

The Member Of sheet (Figure 18.18) looks the same as the Members sheet, but on this tab, you add the groups that this group is a member of. For example, the accounting group can be a member of the Corporate group. This action, called nesting, gives group members additional rights by assigning them other group rights through the primary group. This feature should

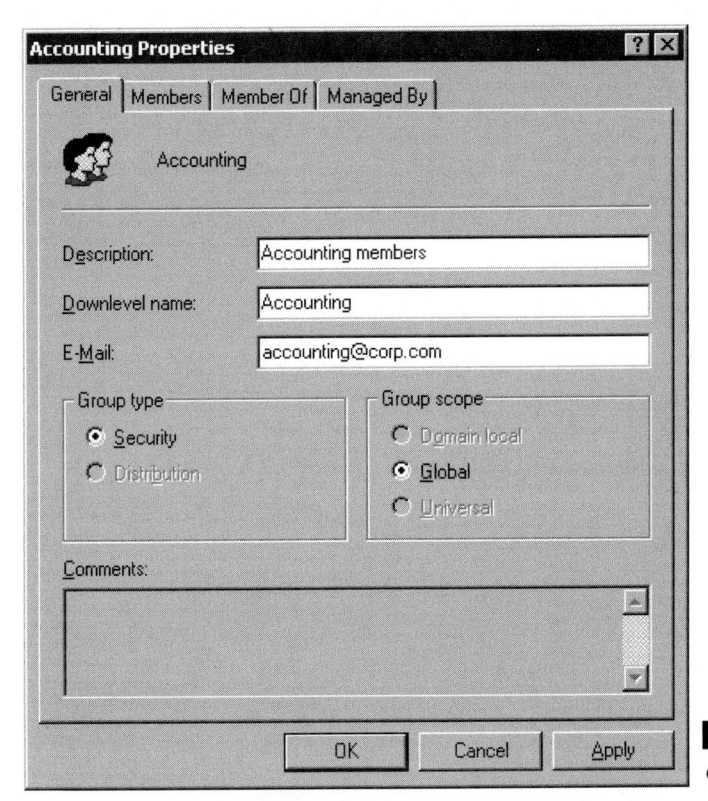

FIGURE 18.16
General Tab

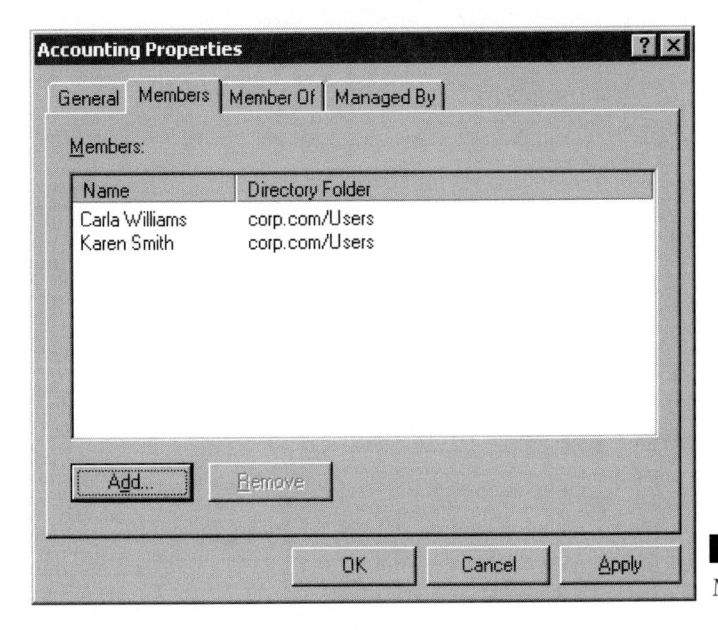

FIGURE 18.17
Members Tab

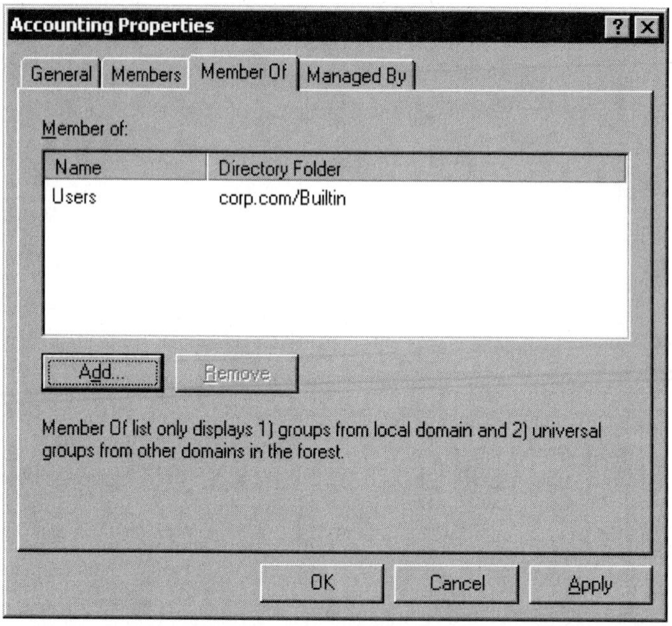

FIGURE 18.18
Member Of

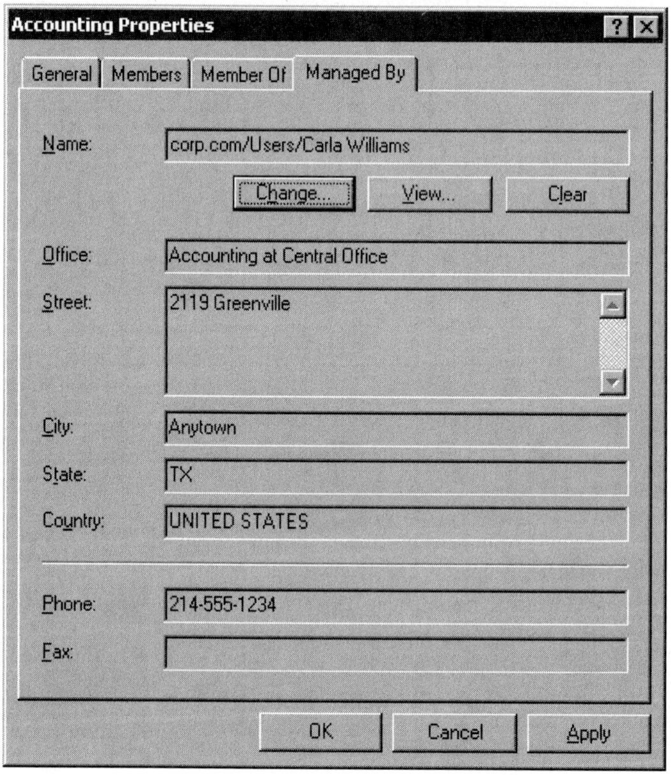

FIGURE 18.19
Managed By

be used with caution since multiple groups within multiple groups can become administratively difficult. Also, conflicting rights and troubleshooting problems can arise. To add the group to another group, simply click the Add button and select the desired groups from the Active Directory.

MANAGED BY

On the Managed By sheet, you can use the Change button to select a user from the Active Directory who will manage the group. Once you do this, the user's name, address, phone, and fax are entered automatically from the user's account in the Active Directory, as shown in Figure 18.19.

ALL TASKS

The All Tasks menu for each group allows you to either move the group to a different location or send e-mail. You can access All Tasks by right-clicking on the group object in the right console pane, point to All Tasks, then either choose Move or Send mail, as shown in Figure 18.20.

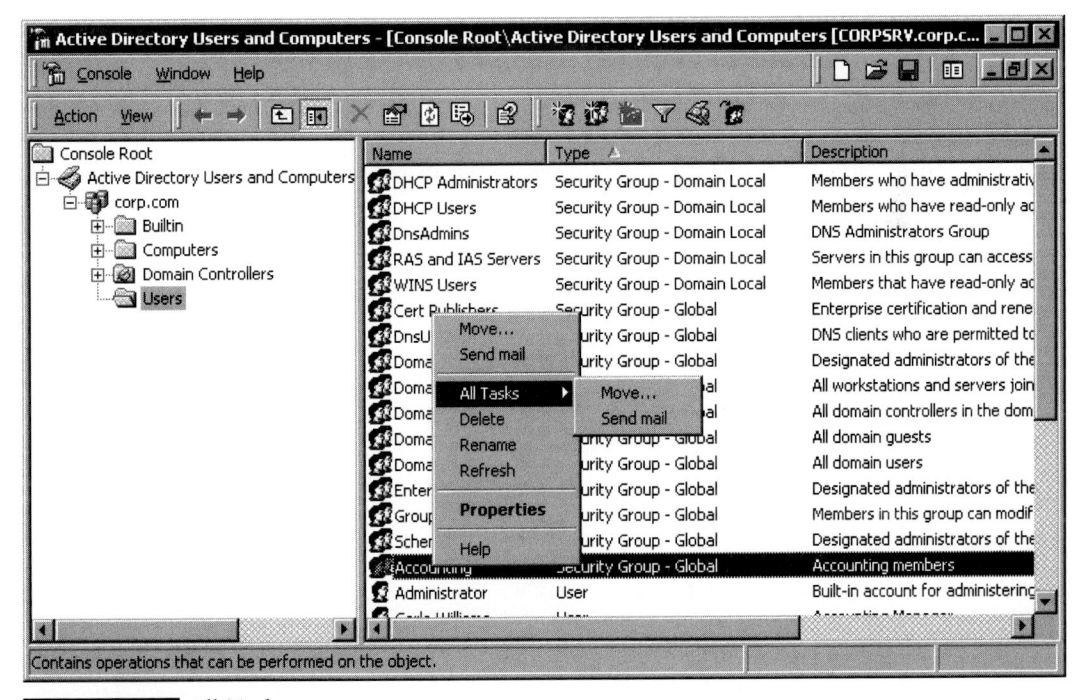

FIGURE 18.20 All Tasks

Summary

Configuring and Managing user, computer, and group accounts within the Active Directory Users and Computers snap-in is easy. From this single interface, you can perform a variety of actions and configure user and computer accounts for your domain. Additionally, you can manage remote computers and add users and computers to appropriate groups. By using group organization, you can define what resources users can access on the network while reducing administrative time and burden.

NINETEEN

Configuring Profiles and Policies

As network environments have grown over the past several years, the need to manage what users can do and what aspects of the operating system they can control has become very important. In many environments, multiple employees use the same computer, yet need to have their own settings preserved. Also, many networks find it useful to restrict the users from certain aspects of the operating system. In Windows 2000, you can accomplish these tasks, as well as several others, through the implementation of user profiles and group policies. In this chapter, you learn how to configure both of these in Windows 2000 Server.

Understanding User Profiles

A user profile gives the user a predefined set of operating system settings. When a user logs on to a Windows 2000 Server, the profile is applied to the computer to which the user logs on. Because the user's profile can be stored on the server, the user can log on to any workstation and receive the same settings. A user profile can control any number of system components, such as the user's desktop, printers, network connections, and a host of others.

There are three different kinds of profiles. First, each computer has a local user profile. The first time a user logs on to a computer, a local profile for that user is created and stored on the computer's hard disk. Any specific system changes the user makes are stored in the local profile and are specific to that computer.

Second, you can implement roaming user profiles. A roaming user profile "roams" with the user in that the user can log on to any workstation in the networking environment and still receive his or her profile. The roaming user profile is stored on the server and is applied to the computer when the user logs on. Changes made to the profile are stored on the server so that the most current version can always be applied. System administrators manage roaming user profiles.

Finally, you can also implement mandatory user profiles. A mandatory user profile is a roaming user profile that is "mandated" or required. Mandatory user profiles are used to specify a particular group of settings that must be applied for a particular user or a group of users. Users cannot make changes to mandatory profiles, and the settings are applied each time the user logs on to the network, regardless of the workstation.

Managing User Profiles

For the most part, user profiles are easy to manage and take care of themselves in Windows 2000. The following sections point out the major management functions you may need to perform concerning user profiles.

Setting Up a Roaming User Profile

A roaming user profile stores the user's profile on a server so that the profile information can be transferred to any computer when the user logs on. This feature allows the user to log on to different workstations and still receive the same desktop and system settings. To set up a roaming user profile, follow these steps:

1. On the desired server, create a share with an intuitive name (such as "Profiles." The share should have the path of *server_name**share_name*.
2. Open the Active Directory Users and Computers snap-in, then expand the desired OU. Right-click on the desired user object and click Properties.
3. Click on the Profile tab.
4. In the Profile path dialog box, type the path of the shared folder where the user profile will be stored, as shown in Figure 19.1.

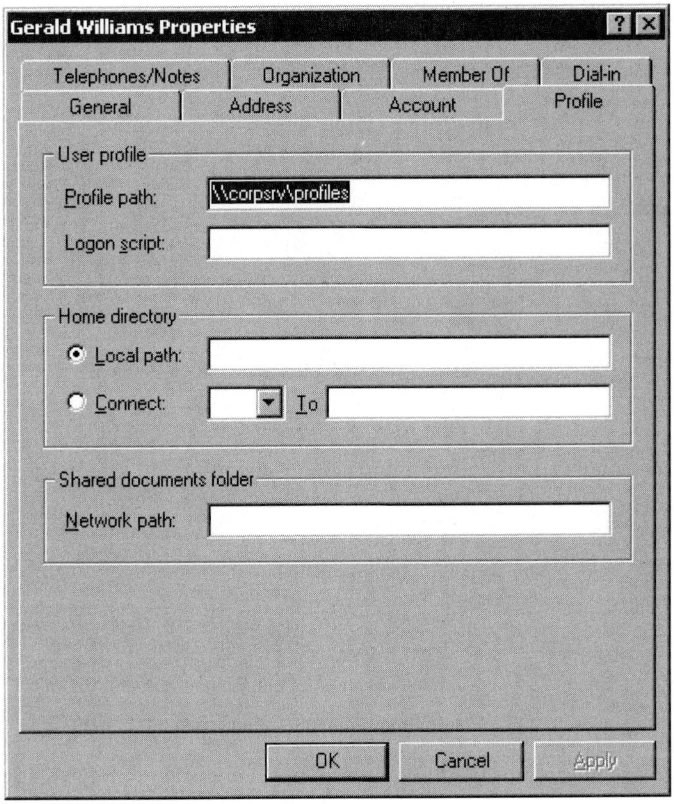

FIGURE 19.1
Profile Path

Configuring a Custom Roaming User Profile

You can choose to customize a roaming user profile, and then assign it to multiple users so that those users will have the same system settings when logged on to a computer on the network. You can perform this action by creating a template that contains the roaming settings that you want to apply to the users, and then copying that profile to the users' profile folder. Follow these steps:

1. Create a user account in the Active Directory Users and Computers that can serve as the template account.
2. Log on using the template account and set the desired desktop and system settings. Log off. Windows 2000 creates a user profile on the computer in C:\WINNT\Profiles\user_name. This profile can then be used as your template.

FIGURE 19.2
Select the Template Account

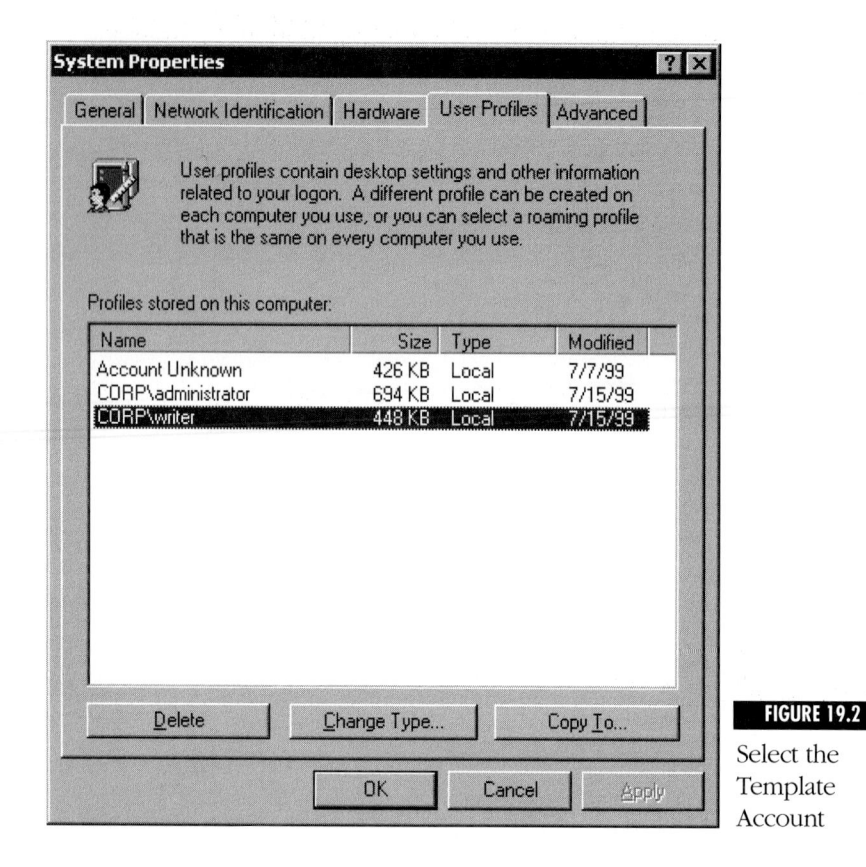

3. Right-click My Computer and click Properties. Click on the User Profiles tab.
4. In the list that appears, select the template account, shown in Figure 19.2.
5. Click the Copy To button.
6. In the Copy To dialog box, type the path to the server and the user logon name (such as *server_name**share_name**user_logon_name*) so that the profile is copied. You can also click the Change button under Permitted to Use to change the user account, as shown in Figure 19.3.

Making a Profile Mandatory

The registry portion of user profiles is named NTUSER.DAT. Users can make changes to their profiles, and the profile changes are stored in the registry. If you want the profile to be mandatory, rename NTUSER.DAT to

FIGURE 19.3
Copy To

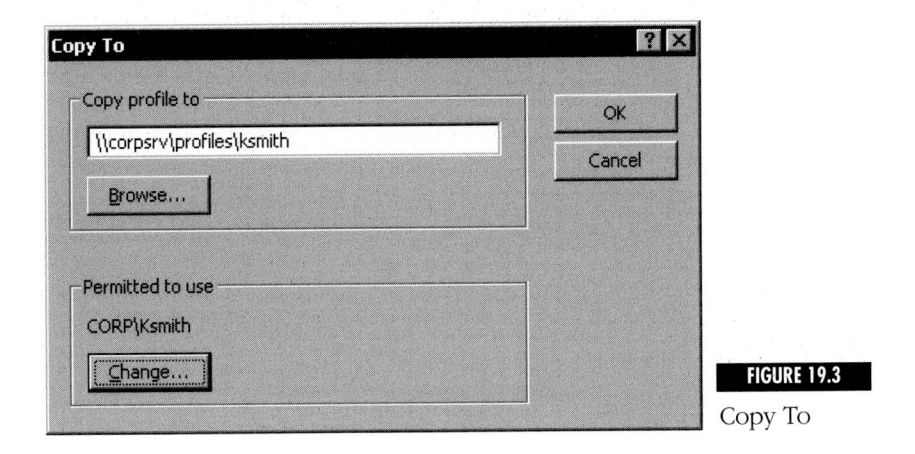

NTUSER.MAN. The .MAN extension makes the profile read-only. This way, the profile can be applied, but any changes the user makes are not saved and the next time the user logs on, he or she will receive the same mandatory profile.

Understanding Group Policies

Group policies are applied to Active Directory objects and are defined as a set of configuration settings that govern the actions users can perform with that Active Directory object. Group policies are used to control the user's work environment and to prevent the user from making configuration changes to his or her system. Microsoft designed group policies to give administrators more control over the Active Directory objects and to lower downtime due to misconfiguration caused by end users.

Generally, group policies are applied at the site and domain level of the Active Directory, but can also be applied at the OU level. The policies determine how the objects and child objects behave, and users within those objects can be given a preset configuration for their systems, such as customized Start menus and access to applications. The group policy can also automatically place certain files and folders within folders (such as My Documents) on the user's computer when he or she logs on. For example, the marketing group can have the company's marketing guidelines placed in a user's My Documents folder each time he or she logs onto the system. In short, group policies are an effective way to implement and maintain corporate policies for a particular organization. Group policies can affect any number of network components and Active Directory objects.

Aside from their ability to customize a network environment, group policies can also enforce security and enhance the user's work and productivity. In very secure environments, group policies can control what resources users access and how users access data through Windows 2000 security features. Additionally, group policies can make a user's work easier by automatically delivering applications to the user's Start menu, automating common tasks, automatically delivering files and folders to the user, and automatically updating applications and services.

Understanding Group Policy Components

In order to implement group policies, you will need to become familiar with the components of group policies—Group Policy Objects, Group Policy Containers, and Group Policy Templates. The following sections introduce these components.

Group Policy Objects

Group Policy Objects (GPO) contain the configuration settings for a particular Active Directory object. The GPO is then applied to a site, domain, or OU. The GPO can be applied to multiple sites, domains, or OUs, and multiple GPOs can also be used. GPOs store group policy configuration information in two locations: Group Policy Containers (GPC) and Group Policy Templates (GPT).

GROUP POLICY CONTAINERS

Group Policy Containers (GCPs) are Active Directory objects that contain property information and subcontainers for GPOs. GPCs contain version information to ensure that the information in the GPO synchronizes with the GPC and also status information so that you can determine whether the GPO is enabled or disabled. Data that is small and does not change frequently is stored in GPCs, and GPCs also contain class store information for GPO application deployment.

GROUP POLICY TEMPLATES

The Group Policy Templates (GPTs) reside in the system volume folder (Sysvol) of domain controllers and is actually a folder structure for the GPO. GPTs contain all of the software policies, scripts, file and application deployment, security information, and additional system setting information for the GPO.

Group Policy Structure

Before implementing group policies, you should have a firm understanding of their structure and how multiple policies affect each other. This structure, known as inheritance, determines how group policies are implemented for the user or computer. The inheritance structure is the site, then domain, then the OU, as shown in Figure 19.4.

Windows 2000 first examines any site group policy and applies the policy to the computer or user. Next, Windows 2000 examines any domain policy and applies it to the computer or user. Likewise, Windows 2000 examines any OU group policy and applies it to the computer or user. With this struc-

Site Group Policy

↓

Domain Group Policy

↓

OU Group Policy

↓

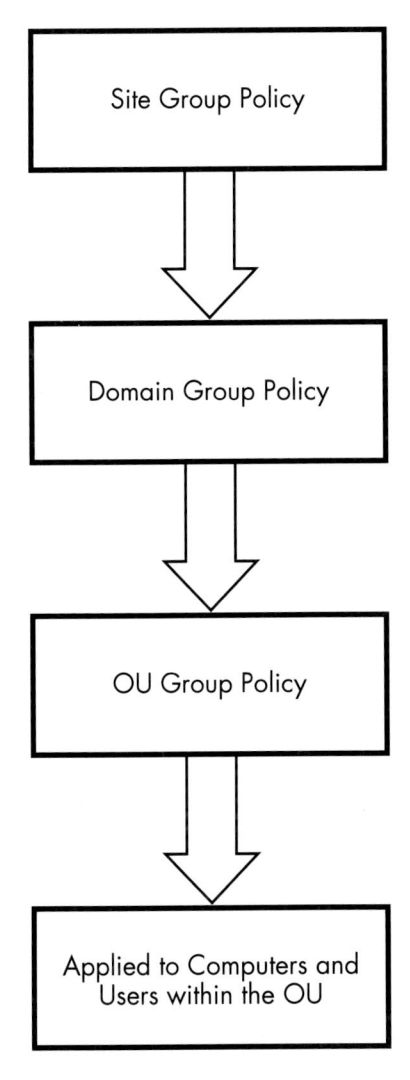

Applied to Computers and Users within the OU

FIGURE 19.4

Group Policy Inheritance

ture, the policy closest to the user or computer can override any policies above it. For example, if a domain has a group policy and an OU has a group policy, the OU policy will override the domain policy for the objects contained in that OU. If there is a conflict between a user policy and a computer policy in the OU, the user policy will override the computer policy.

You can change this default inheritance processing if desired so that no overriding occurs. This action allows higher level GPOs to go into effect without a child container that has a GPO to override it. You can also choose to block inheritance so that parent containers do not override child containers. If there is a conflict between a No Override and Block Inheritance, the No Override will take precedence over the Block Inheritance. You can block inheritance and apply no override settings by accessing the Group Policy Properties sheet of the OU within the Active Directory.

Configuring Group Policies

Group policies are configured and managed within the Group Policy MMC snap-in. You can also manage group policies for specific domains and OUs

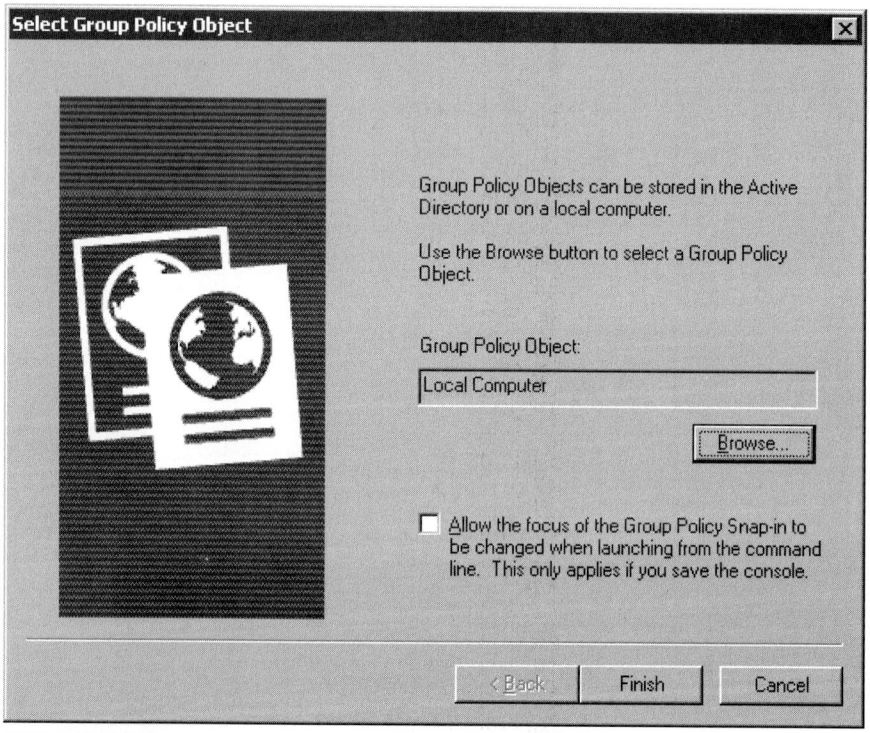

FIGURE 19.5 Select Group Policy Object

within the Active Directory snap-ins. To open the Group Policy MMC snap-in, click Start ➤ Run, then type MMC and click OK. On the Console menu, click Add/Remove snap-in, then click the Add button. From the snap-in list that appears, click Group Policy, then click Add. The Select Group Policy Object window appears, shown in Figure 19.5.

Use this window to select the group policy you want to administer. You can select either the local computer policy, or if you click the Browse button, you are taken to a Browse for a Group Policy Object window, shown in Figure 19.6. Use the tabs to select either Domain/OUs, Sites, Computers, or All. Select the policy from the list and click OK.

Once you select the GPO that you want to administer, click Finish. Click OK on the Add/Remove Snap-in window to open the snap-in. The snap-in now displays the policy you want to administer, as shown in Figure 19.7.

Working with Administrative Templates

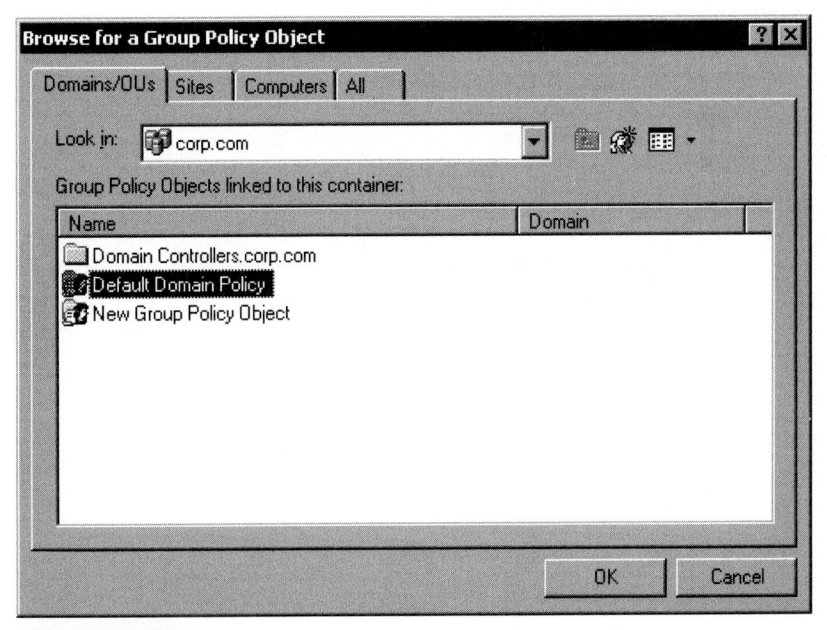

Once you open the Group Policy snap-in for the group policy you want to configure, you can add or remove administrative templates as needed for either the computer or user container. Administrative templates give you an easy way to enable the components you want to allow or disallow within the GPO. The following sections show you how to use and configure administrative templates.

FIGURE 19.6 Browse for a Group Policy Object

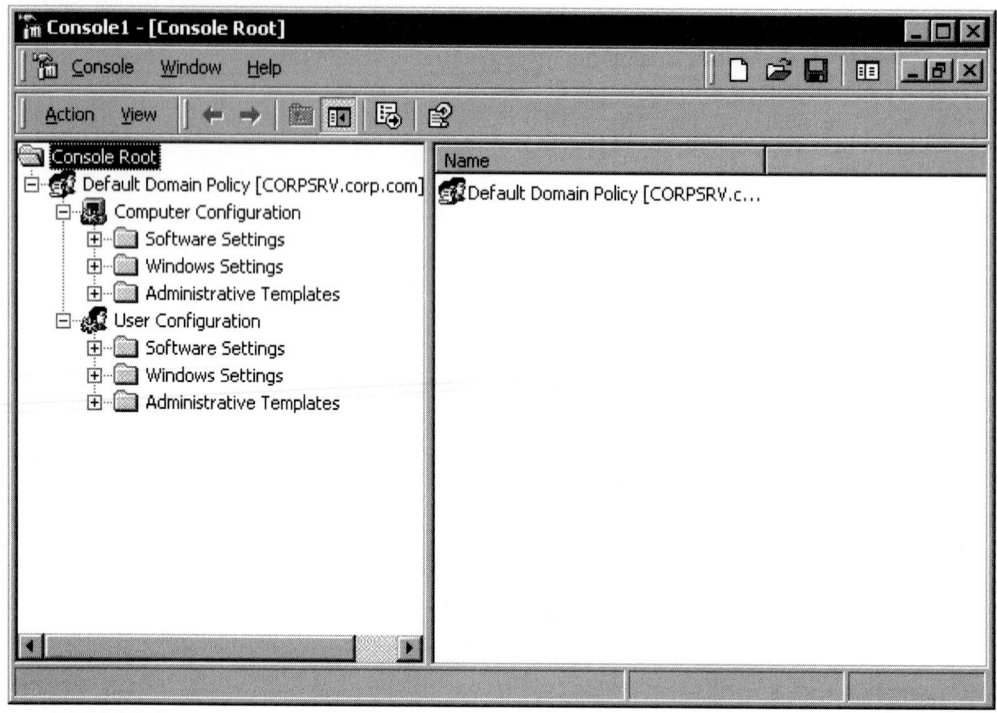

[Screenshot of Console1 - [Console Root] showing Group Policy snap-in with Default Domain Policy [CORPSRV.corp.com], Computer Configuration (Software Settings, Windows Settings, Administrative Templates) and User Configuration (Software Settings, Windows Settings, Administrative Templates).]

FIGURE 19.7 Group Policy Snap-in

ADDING OR REMOVING AN ADMINISTRATIVE TEMPLATE

To add or remove an administrative template, follow these steps:

1. In the Group Policy MMC snap-in, expand either the computer configuration or User configuration as needed.
2. Right-click the Administrative templates object and click Add/Remove templates. The Add/Remove templates window appears, shown in Figure 19.8. Select the kind of policy template you want to add or remove and click either the Add or Remove button.
3. If you clicked the Add button, a Policy Template window appears that will allow you to select the .adm file you would like to add, as shown in Figure 19.9. Select the .adm file you would like to add and click Open.

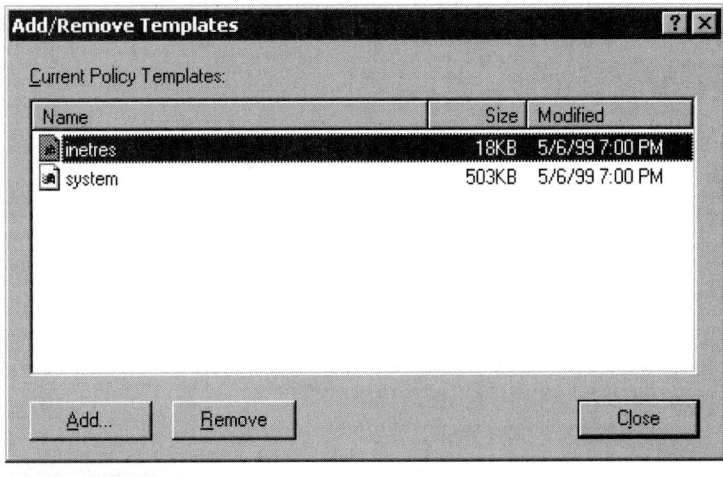

FIGURE 19.8 Policy Template Add/Remove

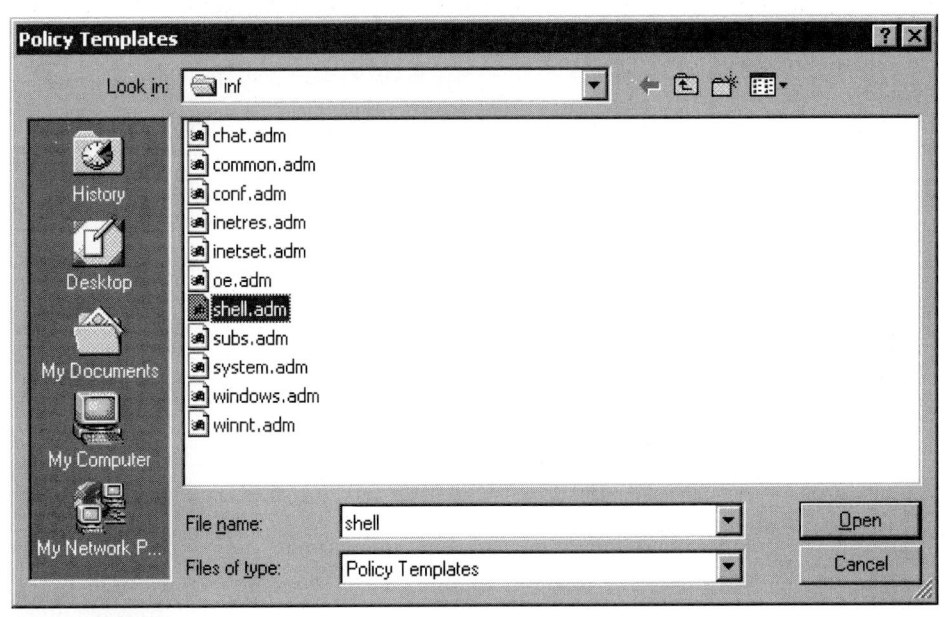

FIGURE 19.9 Policy Template File Selection

Setting Policies Using Administrative Templates

Once you have added or removed the administrative templates you want to use, you can edit each .adm file to enable or disable each component for the GPO. If you expand the Administrative templates container in either the

350   Chapter nineteen • Configuring Profiles and Policies

computer or user container, you can see that you have several templates to use to configure your policy. Depending on what .adm templates you have selected to use, you can create policies for system, network, printers, windows components, and other areas that affect the users desktop. If you double-click one of the folders, the MMC details pane will show you which .adm files exist. For example, if you double-click printers, you will see the various .adm files appear in the detail pane, shown in Figure 19.10.

If you double-click the template files, a window opens that allows you to either enable or disable the feature. For example, in Figure 19.11, by clicking the check box, printers are allowed to be published by this policy.

You will notice that the check boxes have three states: checked, unchecked, and checked but dimmed. If the box is checked, the feature is enabled. If the box is unchecked, the feature is disabled. If the box is checked but dimmed, then the policy is not configured and will not affect registry settings for the policy.

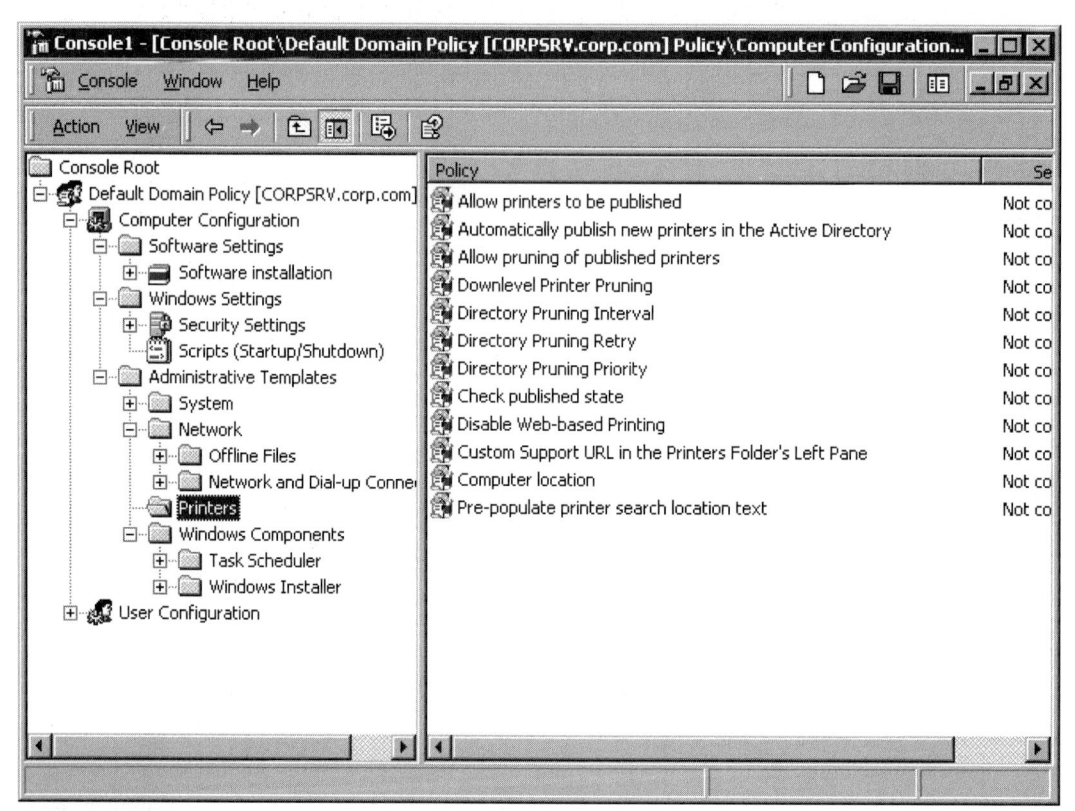

FIGURE 19.10   Templates appear in the details pane.

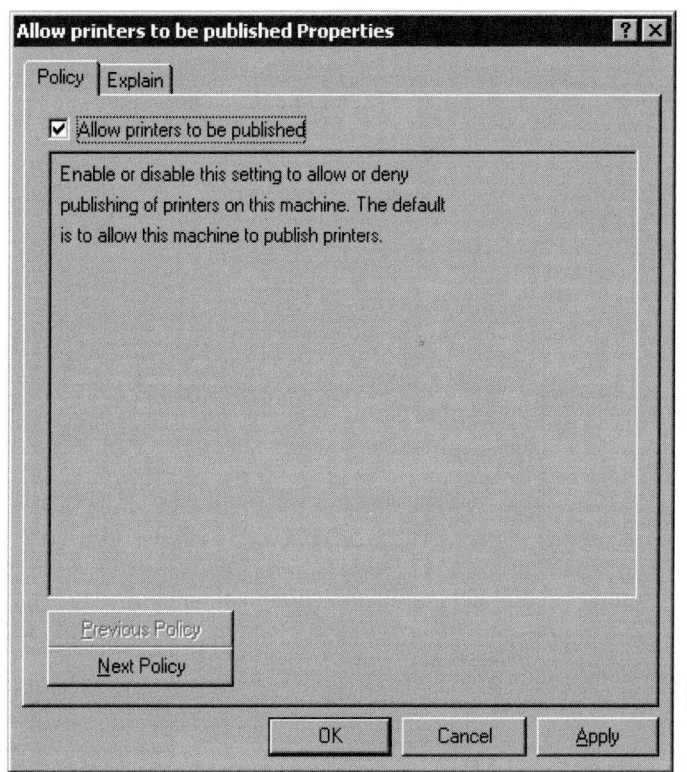

FIGURE 19.11
Template Properties

Configuring Software Settings

As with Administrative Templates, both the Computer Configuration and the User Configuration containers have a Software Settings object. If you expand Software settings, you can see the Software Installation object, which looks like a box with a CD-ROM inside. The software installation tool is one of the three Application Management tools included in Windows 2000; the other two are Windows Installer and Add/Remove Programs in Control Panel. The software installation tool in the Group Policy snap-in is used to deploy software and software updates to the users.

When you assign an application to users, the assignment is advertised to the user the next time he or she logs on to the workstation. The application is installed the first time the user activates the application (such as selecting it from the Start menu) or by activating a document associated with the application.

When you assign an application to computers, the application is advertised and installation takes place when it is safe to install the software, such as when there is no activity on the computer.

You can also publish an application to users instead of assigning the application. This feature allows the application to be advertised, but it does not appear on the users computer for installation. The user can choose to install the package by using Add/Remove programs in Control Panel, but installation is not required.

If you right-click on Software installation, point to New, then click New Package. You can browse your computer to add a software installation package to the snap-in. The packages are created using Windows Installer (*.msi files). You can also manage the general properties of the software installation tool by right-clicking Software Installation and clicking Properties. The properties sheets allow you to define the default behavior of software installation. On the General sheet, shown in Figure 19.12, you can specify a default package location.

For new packages, you have the option of displaying the Deploy Software dialog box, publishing the package, assigning the package, or configuring package properties. The installation user interface options allow you to select either a basic or maximum setting. The basic setting provides a basic display to the user concerning the software's installation progress as it is being installed. The maximum setting provides all screens and dialog

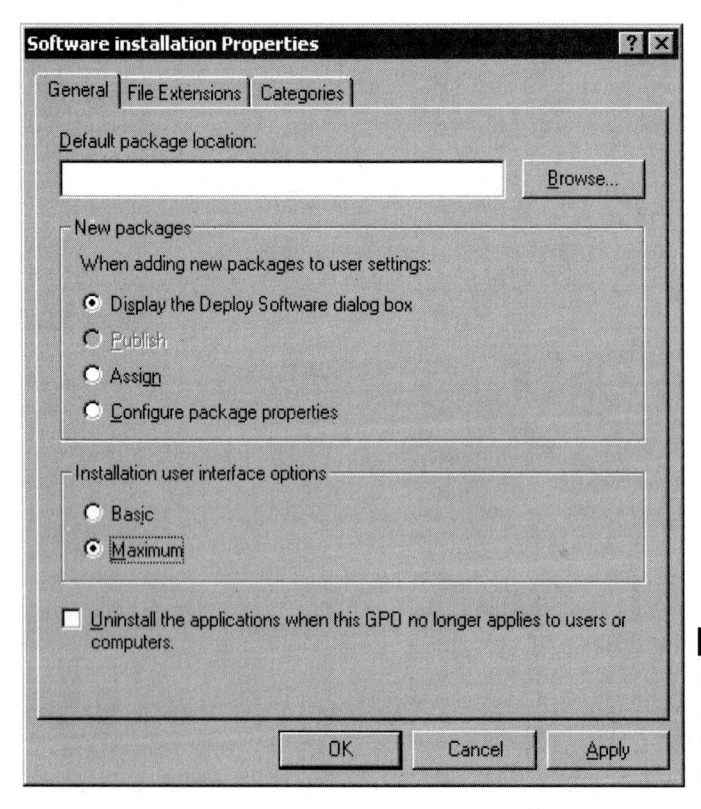

FIGURE 19.12

Software Installation General Properties

FIGURE 19.13
Software Installation File Extensions Properties

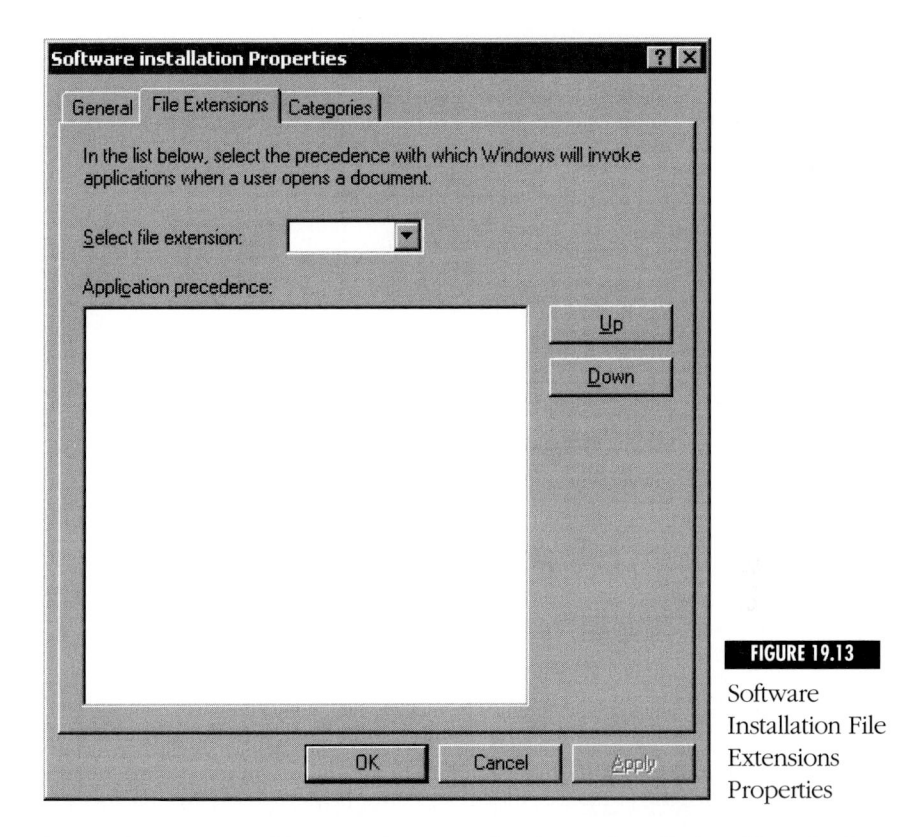

boxes that you would see under normal software installation. You also have the option of clicking the Uninstall the applications when this GPO no longer applies to users or computers. This setting is helpful if applications are specific to certain groups and not to others.

The File Extension Property sheet, shown in Figure 19.13, allows you to set precedence with the application and file extensions. For example, .doc documents are opened by Word, but you can also specify that other documents, such as .txt files be opened by Word before using any other application (such as Notepad).

The Categories sheet allows you to create categories in which software can be organized as needed. Use the Add, Modify, and Remove buttons to create and manage software categories.

Configuring Windows Settings

If you expand Windows Settings in either Computer Configuration or User Configuration, you can set additional Windows settings, specifically security settings and scripts. If you expand security settings, shown in Figure 19.14,

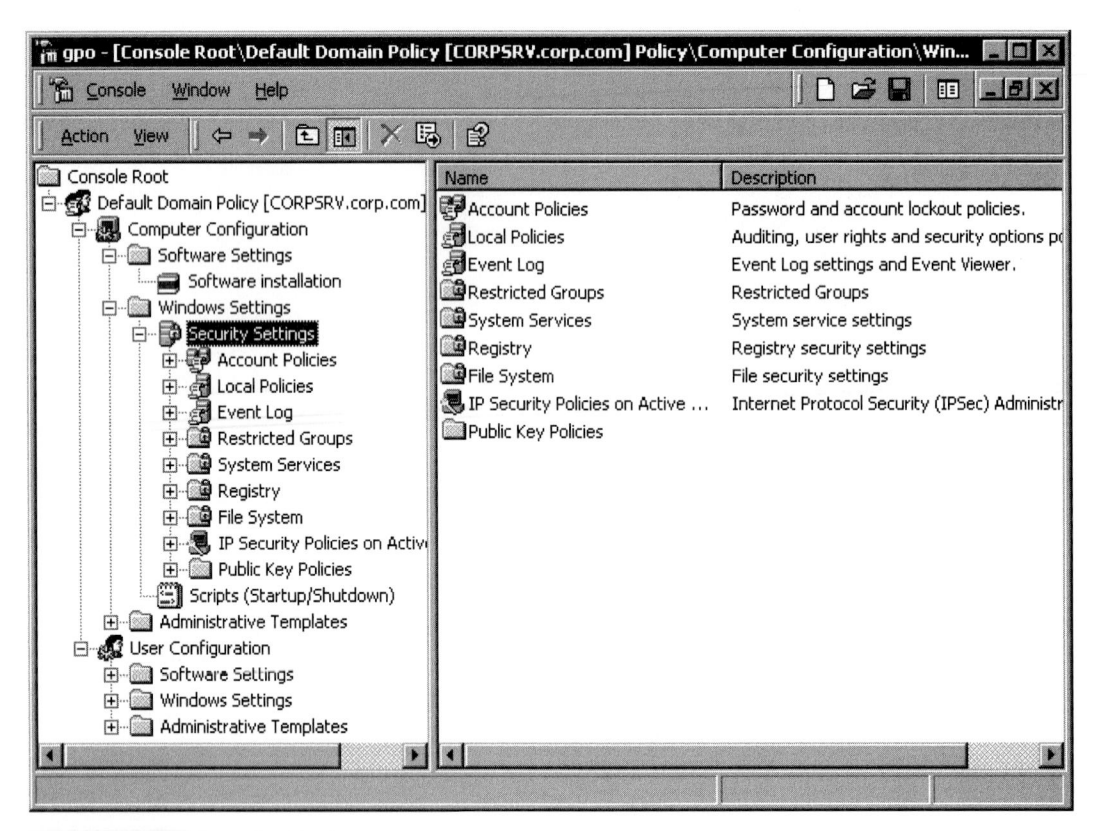

354   Chapter nineteen • Configuring Profiles and Policies

FIGURE 19.14   Security Setting

you can see that there are a number of configuration options you can set for the group policy. For example, if you expand Account Policies, and then expand Password Policy, you can see what configuration options you can change, as shown in Figure 19.15.

If you wanted to change, for example, the maximum password age, double-click on the object in the details pane. A dialog box appears that allows you to change the age at which passwords expire.

The other options that appear under Security Settings function in a similar manner. Each object has configurable properties that you can change to meet the requirements of your group policy.

Under Windows Settings, you also have the option to run Startup or Shutdown scripts. If you double-click on scripts in the left pane, you can add a batch file to the policy that can run at startup or shutdown as needed. You can use the Windows Scripting Host, which is included in Windows 2000, or you can run Visual Basic scripts or even JS Scripts.

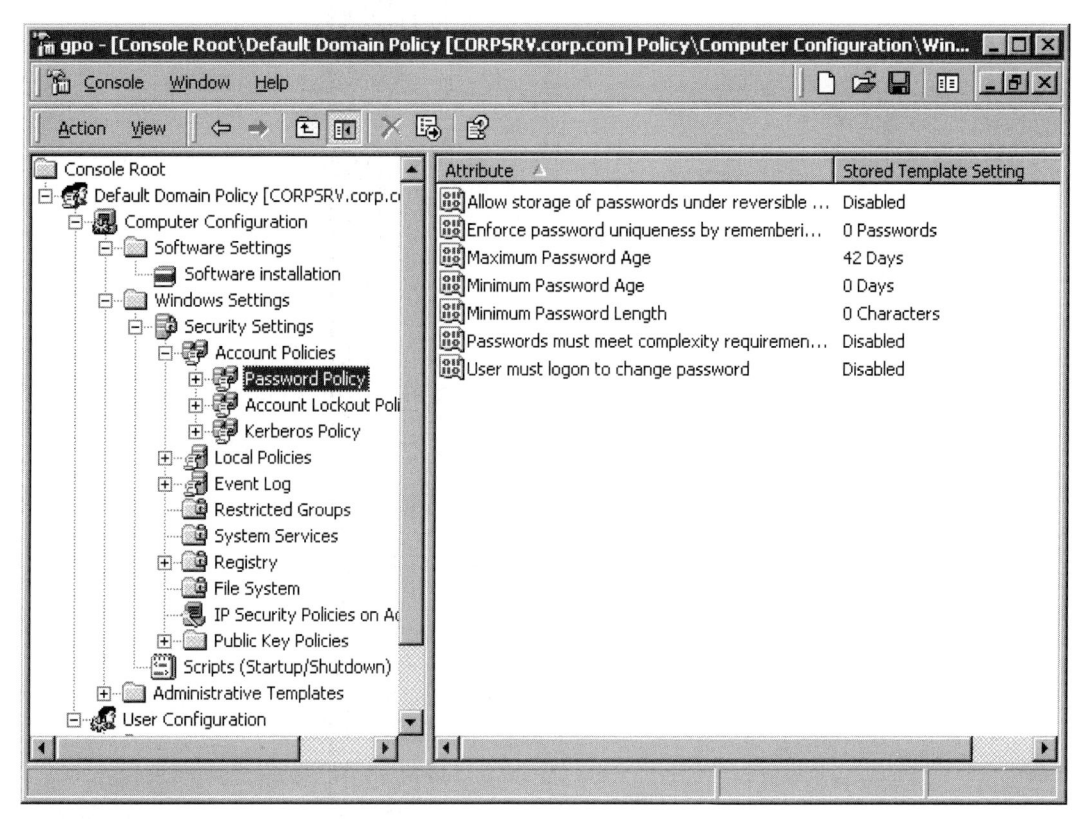

FIGURE 19.15 Available Password Policies

Configuring GPO General Properties

Aside from setting the configuration options for the group policy, you can also manage the general properties for the GPO. If you right-click the policy name in the left console window and select Properties, a three-tab property sheet opens.

On the General Properties page, shown in Figure 19.16, a summary of information about the GPO is provided.

You can use the two check boxes at the bottom of the screen to disable portions of the policy. For example, if the policy applies only to the users and not to the computers, you can select the Disable Computer Configuration settings check box. This action improves performance because the computer portion of the policy does not have to be parsed when a user logs on to the system and the policy is applied.

356 Chapter nineteen • Configuring Profiles and Policies

FIGURE 19.16
Policy General Properties

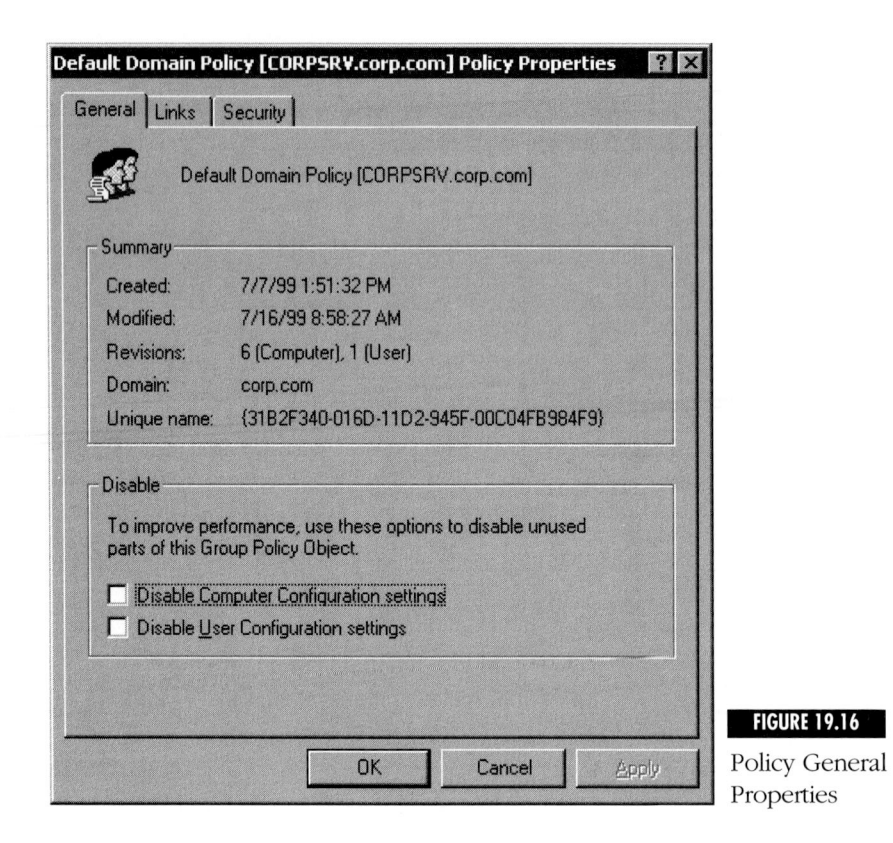

The Links Properties sheet, shown in Figure 19.17, allows you to configure links for sites, domains, and OUs that use this particular group policy.

Finally, the Security tab, shown in Figure 19.18, allows you to set security features for the members of the group policy. You can use this tab to filter the group policy as well. The policies that you configure in the GPO apply only to users that have Read permissions for the GPO. You can filter the GPO by removing Read permission from a specific group so that the policy will not apply to that group.

For example, in Figure 19.18, if you did not want the group policy to apply to the Domain Admins, you could simply remove Read permission, which takes away the policy settings for that group. You can also click the Advanced button to view additional permissions that may be present for the object. This action provides you with a typical advanced permissions window as you have seen in other configuration areas of Windows 2000 Server.

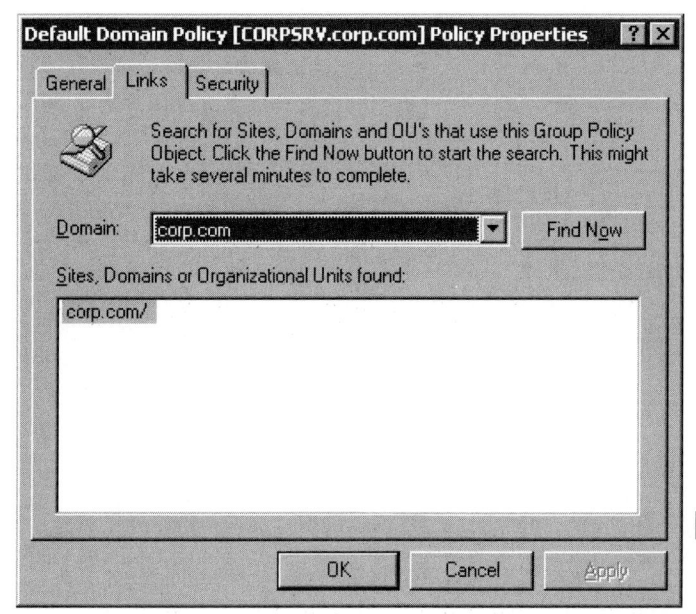

FIGURE 19.17
Policy Links Properties

FIGURE 19.18
Policy Security Properties

Summary

User and computer polices are effective ways to control what users can and cannot do with their computers. Aside from the control features, polices can also be used to implement a standardized desktop and operating system for all employees. Mandatory profiles can also be used so that users cannot change their system configuration. Windows 2000 also introduces group policy, a feature that works with the Active Directory to assign a standardized policy to a site, domain, or OU. This feature makes management not only of Active Directory containers but also of the user and computers that reside within those containers much easier and customizable.

TWENTY

Managing Shared Resources

The ability to share files and other information is a major reason for networking. Users can access each others' files and folders over the network, which gives you increased productivity while saving time. This simple idea, like most components of networking, has become rather complex over the years. The importance of securing certain resources and keeping unauthorized users from gaining access or changing the resource has been an ever-present security problem. Microsoft's answer to this problem has been NTFS permissions, which allow you to have more granular control over shared resources along with the Distributed File System, which helps users find the resources they need. This chapter explores the management of shared folders and files and the implementation of the Distributed File System.

NTFS Permissions

NTFS permissions allow you to control what resources the network users can access and what they can do with those resources once they access them. You can control a folder with NTFS permissions, and you can also control each file within a folder with NTFS permissions. In this manner, a user may be able to access a folder and some files within the folder, but not necessarily all of the files. NTFS permissions are available only on volumes that are formatted with NTFS—FAT and FAT32 volumes do not maintain any of the NTFS permissions, and this is one reason NTFS is the file system of choice.

▶ *For Review*

NTFS permissions

NTFS permissions in Windows 2000 work the same as in Windows NT. For individual files, you can assign the following permissions:

- Read—the user can read the file, view its attributes, permissions, and owner.
- Write—the user can perform any Read function, but can also edit the file and change its attributes.
- Read and Execute—the user can perform all actions of the Read function, but can also run applications.
- Modify—the user can perform all the actions of both Read and Read and Execute, and the user can modify or delete the file.
- Full Control—the user can perform any action permitted by all other permissions, and the user can change permissions and take ownership.

For folders, you can assign the following permissions:

- Read—the user can view the files and subfolders within the folder and view the folder ownership, attributes, and permissions.
- Write—the user can create new files and subfolders within the folder and make changes to the folder attributes. The user can also view the folder ownership and permissions.
- List Folder Contents—the user can see the names of files and subfolders in the folder.
- Read and Execute—the user can perform all actions of the Read and List Folder Contents permissions, and the user can move through the folders to other files and folders without permission for each folder.
- Modify—the user can perform all actions of the Write and Read and Execute permissions, and the user can delete the folder.
- Full Control—the user can perform all action provided by the other permissions, and the user can change the folder permissions, take ownership, and delete any subfolders and files.

In addition to all of these permissions, you can also deny a user access to a file or folder.

For each file and folder, NTFS maintains an access control list (ACL) that contains a list of user and group accounts that have been granted access rights to the file or folder. When a user wants to access a file or folder, the ACL is checked to see if the user has access rights, and if so, what access rights the user has.

You can assign permissions to each user and to each group the user belongs to. Once this is done, the user will have what is called "effective permissions" for each resource, based on the combined NTFS permissions. NTFS permissions are cumulative—if a user has Read permission assigned for a resource, but also has group membership in a group that has Modify permission for the resource, then the user's effective permissions are Read and Modify. The only exception to this rule is Deny. If a user has Read access to a file but is a member of a group that is denied access to the same file, then the user has no access—Deny overrides any other permissions. Also, file permissions override folder permissions. If a user has Read access to a folder, but full control over a file in that folder, then the user will retain the full control permission for the file and will not be reduced to Read because the file is contained in the folder.

Another issue with NTFS permissions you should keep in mind is "inheritance." By default, subfolder and files inherit the NTFS permissions of the parent folder. You can prevent inheritance on subfolders if desired. When you perform this action, the subfolder becomes the new parent folder for all other folders and files contained in that folder. For example, if a folder has Write permission, but there is a subfolder you want to have Read Only permission, then you block inheritance and assign Read permission to that subfolder. This subfolder then becomes a new parent folder, and everything within this folder will have Read permission.

Finally, you should have firm understanding about moving and copying files and folders and the effect these actions have on NTFS permissions. When you copy a file or folder to a different NTFS volume, the file or folder receives the permissions of the destination folder. For example, if you have a file called "Companyinfo" that has Read permission, then the file is copied to a folder that has Modify permission, the file will receive the Modify permission. Windows 2000 considers the copied file a "new" file, and therefore it inherits the permissions of the destination folder. In order to copy a file to another NTFS volume, you must have Write permission for the destination folder and you will become the Creator Owner of that file. Of course, if you copy a file or folder to a FAT or FAT32 volume, all NTFS permission are lost.

Next, if you move a file or folder within the same NTFS volume, the file or folder retains its NTFS permissions. You must have Write permission for the destination folder to move a file or folder into it, and you must have Modify permission for either the file or folder you are moving. If you move a file or folder to a different NTFS volume, the file or folder will inherit the permissions of the destination folder. You must have Write permission for the destination folder to move the file or folder to it, and you must have Modify permission for the file or folder you are moving. As with copying files, any file or folder that is moved to a FAT or FAT32 volume loses all of its NTFS permissions.

Assigning NTFS Permissions

By default, when a volume is formatted with NTFS, the Everyone group has full control permission. You should change this setting so that you can control what resources are accessed by what users or groups and what rights those users and groups have to that resource. As with most administrative tasks, organization is of key importance. Groups exist so that you can assign access rights to groups instead of individual users. Also, it is usually best to assign NTFS permissions to a folder, and then add appropriate documents to that folder. This action will make your job much easier. To set the NTFS permissions for a shared file or folder, right click on the shared folder and click Properties. Click on the Sharing tab, shown in Figure 20.1.

On this page, you can see the shared folder's name and the user limit (if one has been configured). To set permissions for the folder, click the Permissions button. This action opens a Share Permissions page, shown in Figure 20.2.

This window shows what permissions are given to the Everyone group. If you want to deny all permissions, click the Deny Full Control check box, which denies all NTFS permission for this group. Click the Add button to add other groups. A window from the Active Directory Users and

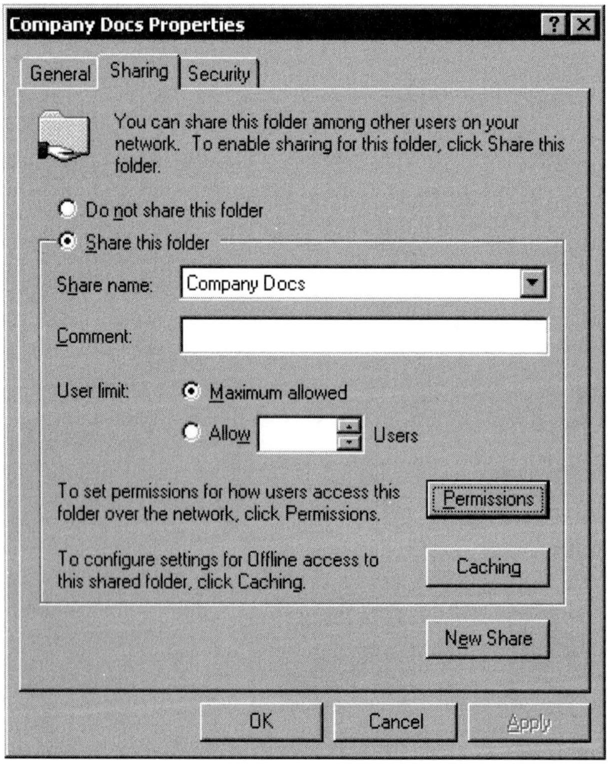

FIGURE 20.1
Sharing Tab

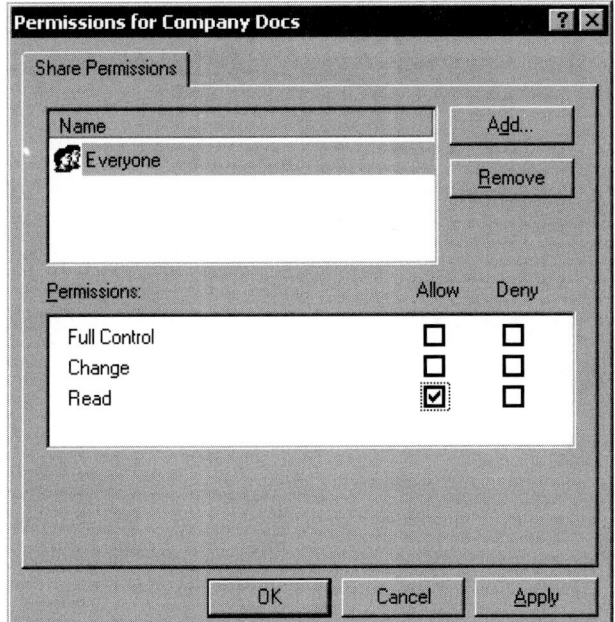

FIGURE 20.2
Share Permissions

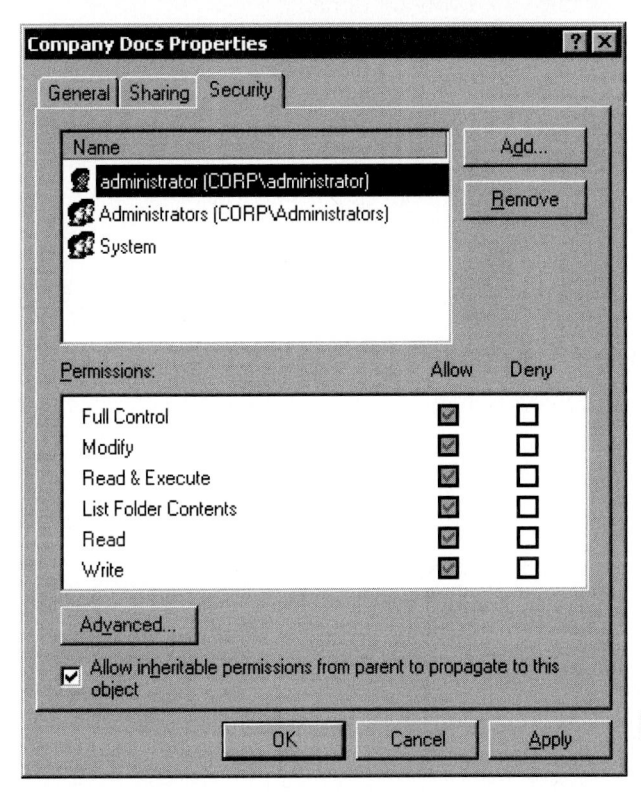

FIGURE 20.3
Security Tab

FIGURE 20.4 Security Pop-up Window

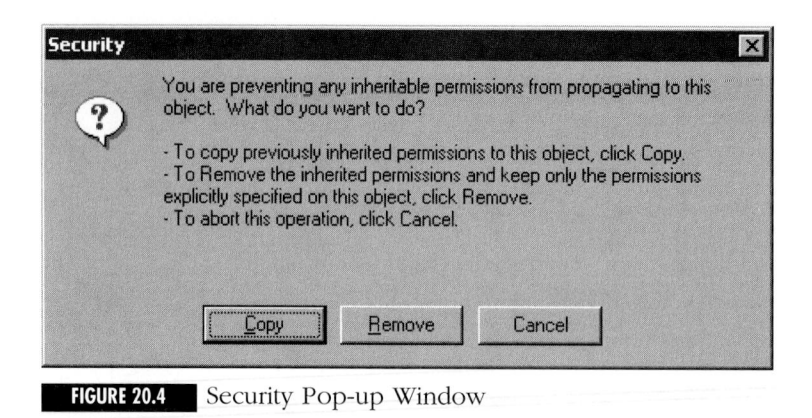

Computers appears, which allows you to select which groups you want to add permissions for. Select the group, click the Add button, and repeat the process until you have all groups that you want to include. Click OK when you are done. The new group(s) now appear on the Share Permissions page. Click the check boxes to assign what permissions you want to give, then click OK when you are done.

If you click the Security tab for the folder's properties, you can further define access rights for the folder, as shown in Figure 20.3.

Administrator and System groups are included by default with Full Control. You can add other groups and assign access rights as needed. This feature allows you to fine tune the rights you want to assign to individual groups. Also, at the bottom of the window, you can clear the Allow inheritable permissions from parent to propagate to this object check box to block inheritance. If you clear the check box, a security box appears asking what action you want to complete, as shown in Figure 20.4.

Advanced Access Permissions

Generally, the NTFS permissions you assign to users or groups for resource access are all you need to effectively manage a share. However, Windows 2000 provides additional access permissions if a specific type of access permissions is needed. These advanced access permissions are available by clicking the Advanced button on the Security tab of the shared resource's properties, shown in Figure 20.5.

You can click the Add button to add another user or group for which you want to define additional rights. For example, if I wanted to define advanced rights for a user, Karen Smith, I would click the Add button, select her user account, and click OK. Then, a permissions list will appear so I can select what rights I want to assign to Karen Smith, as shown in Figure 20.6.

Table 20.1 explains the fourteen entries that are available.

four • Managing Clients and Performance

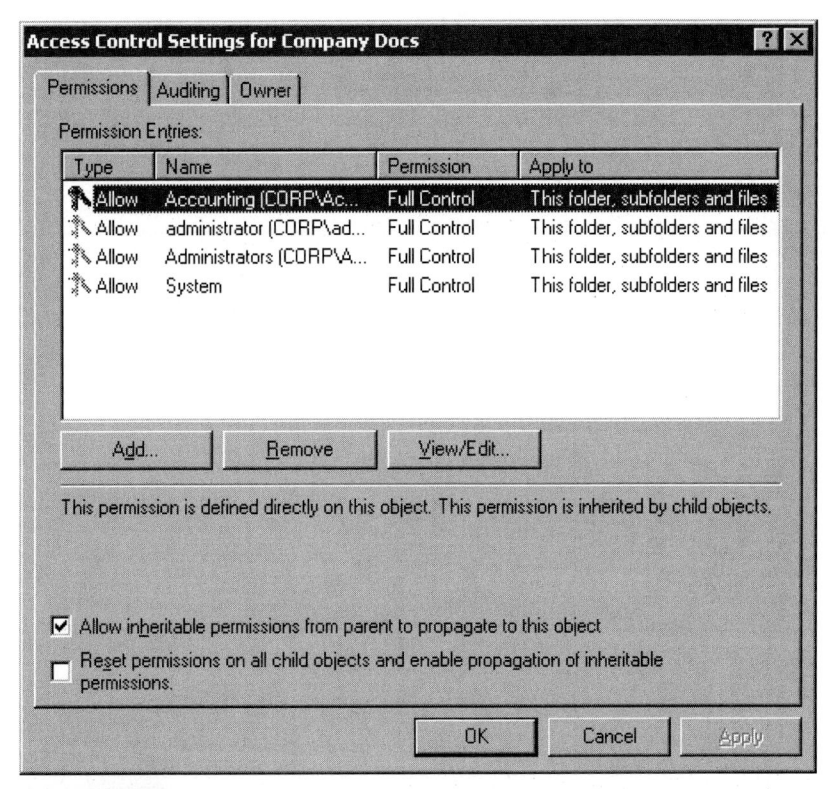

FIGURE 20.5 Access Control Settings

TABLE 20.1 Advanced Permission Entries

Permission Entry	Description
Traverse Folder/Execute File	Allows you to move through subfolders and execute files within those folders.
List Folder/Read Data	Allows you to list folder contents and read folder data.
Read Attributes	Allows you to read attributes.
Read Extended Attributes	Allows you to read all folder attributes.
Create Files/Write Data	Allows you to create files within the folder and write data to existing files.
Create Folders/Append Data	Allows you to create additional subfolders and append information to existing data.
Write Attributes	Allows you to write attributes for the folder.
Write Extended Attributes	Allows you to write extended attributes for the folder.
Delete Subfolders and Files	Allows you to delete any files and subfolders within the parent folder.

Permission Entry	Description
Delete	Allows you to delete any information within the folder and the folder itself.
Read Permissions	Allows you to read data within the folder and subfolders.
Change Permissions	Allows you to change ownership of the folder.
Take Ownership	Allows you to take ownership of the folder.

You can grant or deny any of these permissions to the selected user or group. Two particularly useful ones are Change Permissions and Take Ownership. You can give users or other administrators the ability to change the permissions of a shared folder without giving the person Full Control permission. This action allows the user to assign permissions for the folder without having the power to delete the folder or write to it. Another useful permission is Take Ownership. You can assign this permission to someone who can take ownership of the folder if the current owner either becomes unavailable or leaves the company. Yet you can still restrict the new owner

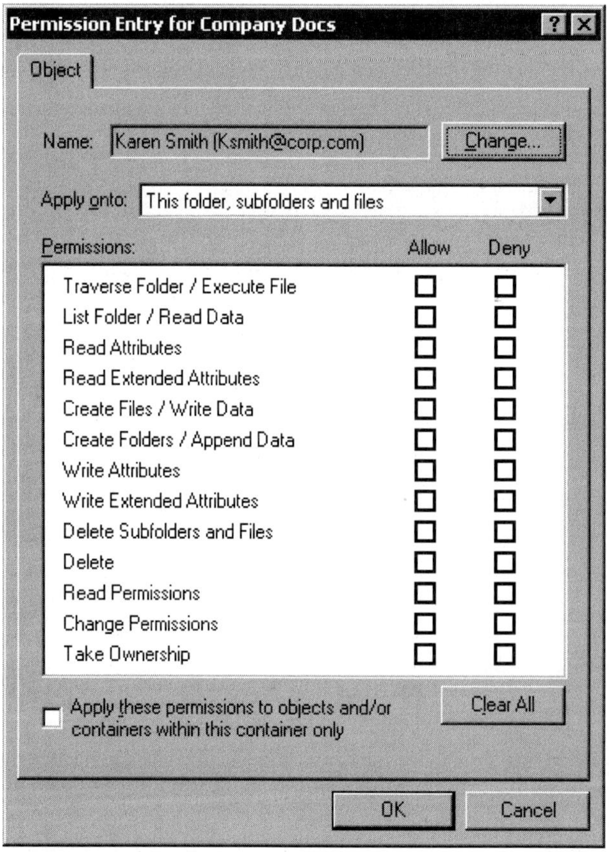

FIGURE 20.6

Permission Entry

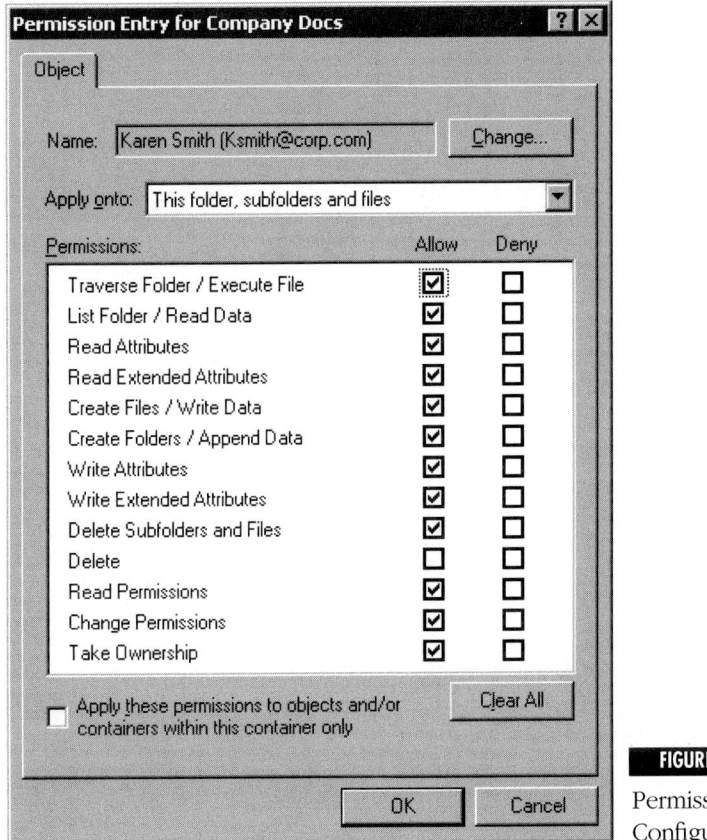

FIGURE 20.7
Permission Entry Configuration

from deleting the folder. As you can see in Figure 20.7, the user Karen Smith can perform almost any action on this share, with the exception of deleting the folder.

Additionally, you can select the check box at the bottom of the window to allow these permissions to become effective for all files and subfolders within that particular folder. Once the advanced permissions are configured, the Security sheet of the folder's properties sheets displays the user and provides a note telling you that additional permissions are present for the user but are only viewable by pressing the Advanced button, as shown in Figure 20.8.

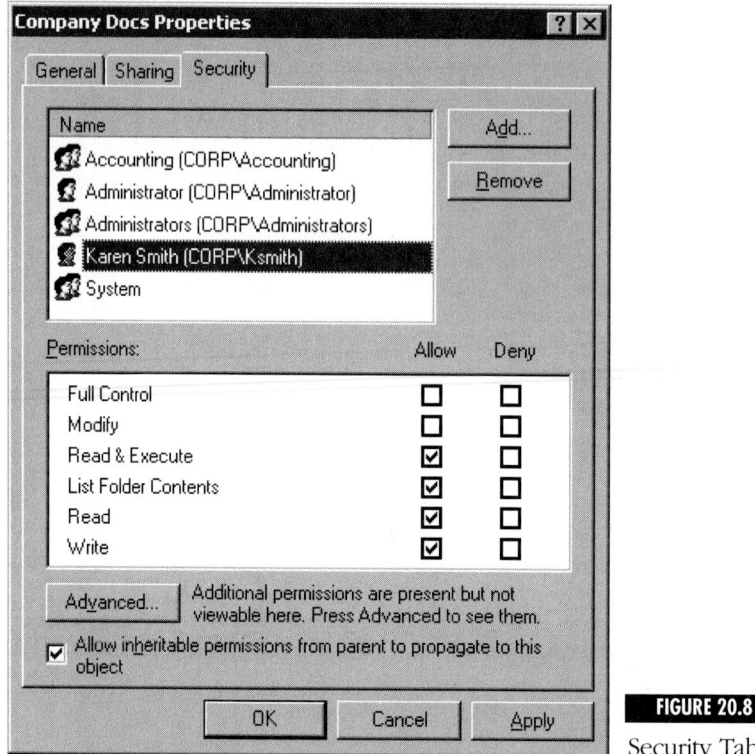

FIGURE 20.8
Security Tab

Managing Shared Folders

NTFS permissions work with shares to give you a full plate of security options. By combining shared folder permissions and NTFS permissions, you have a great deal of control over what users and groups can do with the information in shared folders. NTFS permissions, however, do not work on FAT or FAT32 volumes, but shared folders do. You can place a shared folder on a FAT or FAT32 volume and still control what users can access in the share. The default shared folder permission is Full Control assigned to the Everyone group, which is a setting you should change. A problem with Shared Folder permissions, however, is that the permissions apply only to the folder—not the files and subfolders within the folder. Obviously, shared folder permissions provide less security than NTFS permissions.

The shared folder permissions are Read, Change, and Full Control. You can allow or deny these permissions, just as you can in NTFS permissions. As with NTFS permissions, folder permissions are cumulative: If a user has Read permission but is a member of a group that has Full Control permission, the user has Full Control. The Deny permissions feature over-

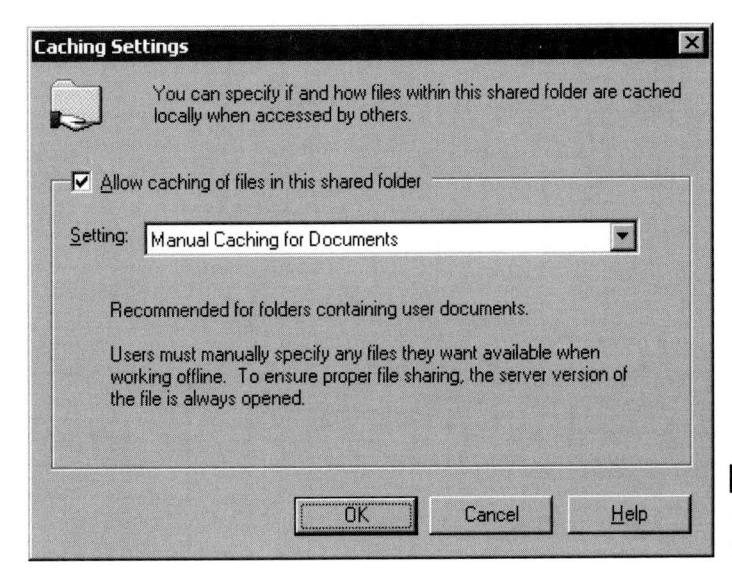

four • Managing Clients and Performance

FIGURE 20.9 Caching Settings

rides all other permissions. If you copy or move a shared folder between FAT or FAT32 volumes, the folder is no longer shared in the new location.

You can easily share any folder by right-clicking on the folder and clicking Sharing. The folder's properties sheet will open to the Sharing tab, and you can click the Share this folder radio button to share the folder. Shared folders appear on your drive with a hand icon under them. Click the permissions button to assign folder permissions. Generally, a good idea when using NTFS permissions is to leave the default folder permissions for the folder and define the access permission through NTFS using the Security tab. You can also click the Caching button to configure offline caching, shown in Figure 20.9.

To allow offline caching of shared folder information, click the Allow caching of files in this shared folder check box. In the Setting dropdown menu, you have three choices: Automatic Caching for Documents, Automatic Caching for Programs, and Manual Caching for Documents. Automatic caching for both documents and programs automatically downloads files and programs to the user so that the user can access the documents and programs should the shared folder become unavailable. The cached version is automatically updated with newer versions as they become available. The manual caching feature forces users to manually cache the specific files they want when working offline or if the shared folder becomes available. This feature requires more work on the part of the user, but less work on the part of the server.

Distributed File System

In large enterprise network environments, the number of shared folders and the servers that contain them can become overwhelming for users. Aside from the organization of the Active Directory, Windows 2000 includes the Distributed File System to help users easily locate shared folders and files,

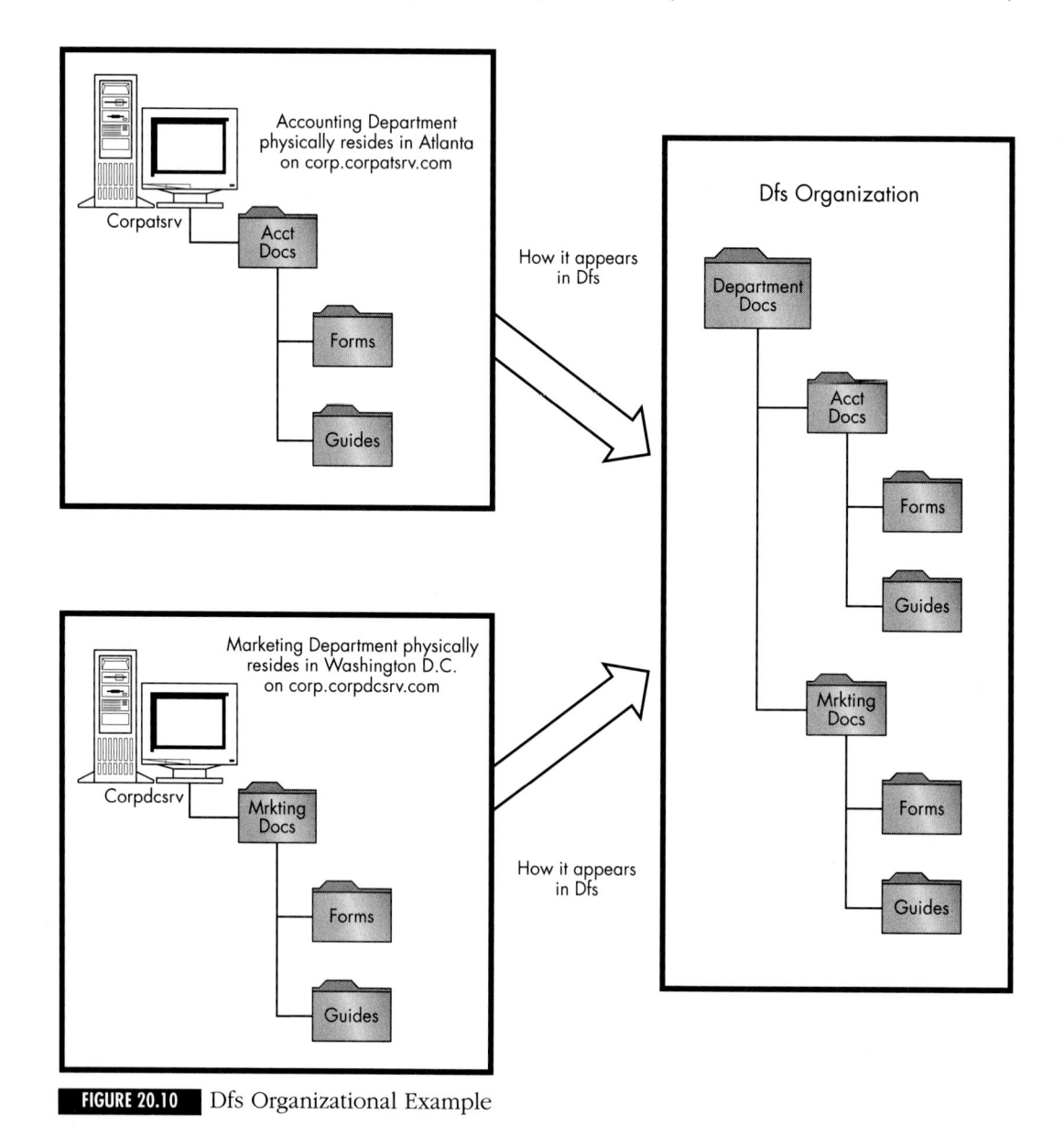

FIGURE 20.10 Dfs Organizational Example

regardless of their physical location on the network. The Distributed File System (Dfs) is a single hierarchy file system that provides a logical tree structure for all files and folders within an Enterprise. This tree structure allows users to have one point of reference to locate files and folders without having to know where the files and folders actually reside on the network.

Dfs begins with a root of the Dfs tree and extends itself by child nodes using branches or leaves. Branches contain leaves, and the leaves do not extend any further. Child nodes can be organized in any manner desired, such as by department or even office. Figure 20.10 shows you an example of the actual network place of certain folders and how those folders and files appear in Dfs. As you can see Dfs makes finding network resources much easier.

This structure is particularly useful in organizations that have multiple sites and multiple servers in each site that contain shared resources. With Dfs, the actual network architecture is transparent to users, which makes finding the desired folder and resource much easier.

There are two types of Dfs: standalone and fault tolerant. Standalone Dfs stores the Dfs topology on a single server that is accessed by users. After connecting to the Dfs root server, users simply browse the structure to locate the desired resource without having to know what server actually holds the Dfs resource. However, if the Dfs root or any server within the Dfs structure fails, users will not be able to gain access to resources. A fault-tolerant Dfs stores the topology structure in the Active Directory. The child nodes can then point to multiple identical shared folders for fault tolerance.

Only clients that support Dfs can use the features. Clients running Windows 2000, Windows NT, and Windows 98 have built-in Dfs supports. The Dfs client for Windows 95 is also available for download from microsoft.com.

Configuring Dfs

To setup and configure Dfs in Windows 2000, you use the Dfs MMC snap-in that is available in Start ➤ Programs ➤ Administrative Tools. The following sections show you how to set up and configure Dfs on your server.

CONNECTING TO AN EXITING Dfs ROOT

If you want to connect to an exisiting Dfs root, follow these steps:

1. Click Start ➤ Programs ➤ Administrative Tools ➤ Distributed File System. The MMC snap-in opens.
2. Click the Action menu and click Connect to an Existing Dfs Root.
3. A window appears asking you to select an existing Dfs root to manage, or you can type the name of the Dfs root in the window provided, as shown in Figure 20.11.
4. Click OK when you are done.

FIGURE 20.11
Connect to an Existing Dfs Root

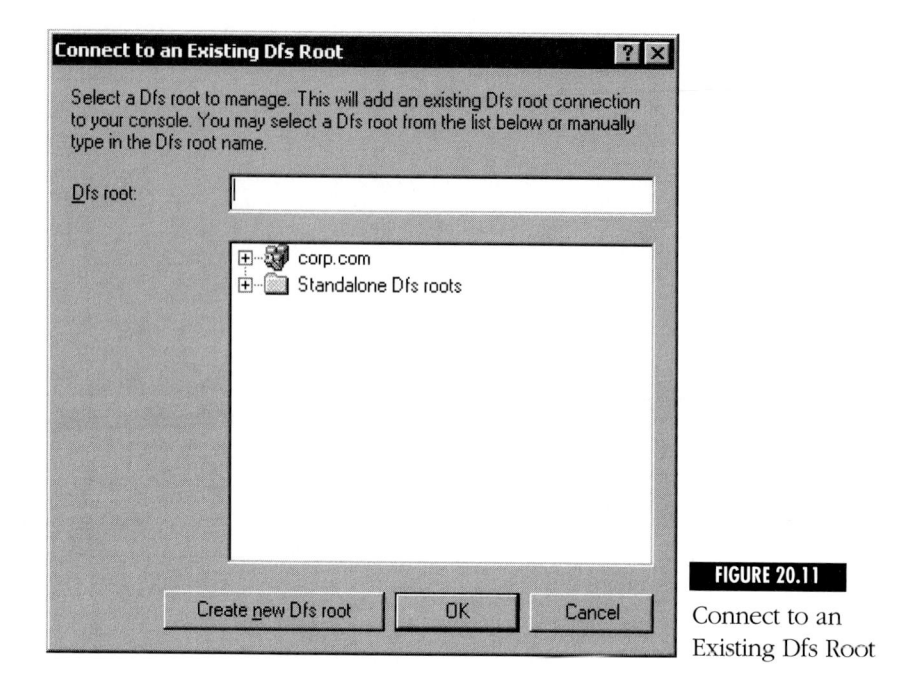

CREATING A NEW Dfs ROOT VOLUME

To create a new Dfs root volume on your server, follow these steps:

1. Click Start → Programs → Administrative Tools → Distributed File System.
2. Click the Action menu, then select New Dfs Root Volume. The Dfs Root Wizard begins.
3. Click Next on the Welcome screen.
4. The Select Dfs Root Type window appears, shown in Figure 20.12. Click either the Create a fault-tolerant Dfs root or Create a standalone Dfs root radio button for the type of Dfs root you want to create. Click Next.
5. The Select Domain to Host Dfs appears. Select the domain where you want the Dfs root to exist and click Next.
6. The Specify Server to Host Dfs window appears. Enter the name of the server that will host the Dfs root and click Next.
7. The Select Share for Dfs Root Volume appears. Use the dropdown menu to select an existing share that will house the Dfs root volume, or click the Create New Share radio button and enter the path and share new to create a new share for the Dfs root volume, shown in Figure 20.13. Click Next.

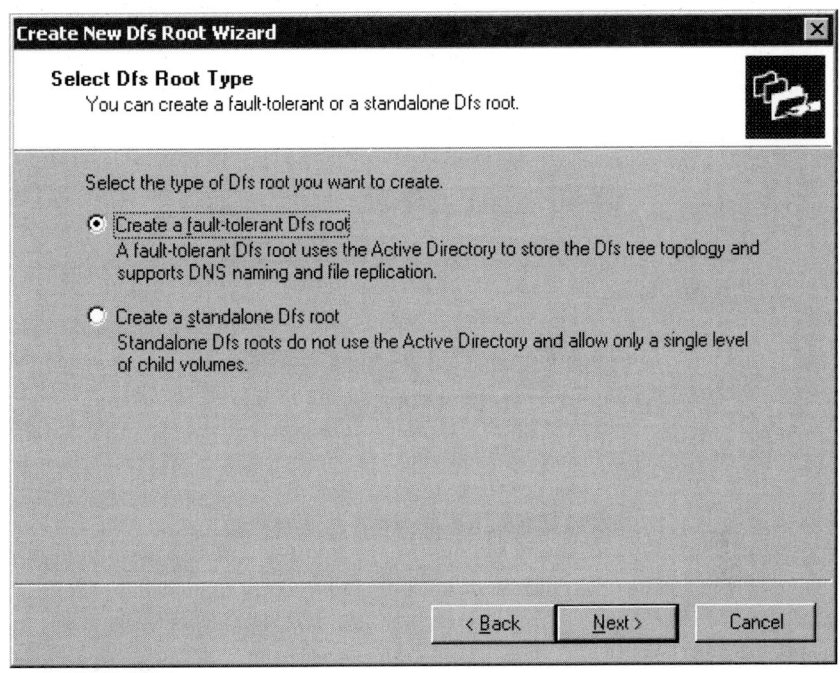

FIGURE 20.12 Select Dfs Root Type

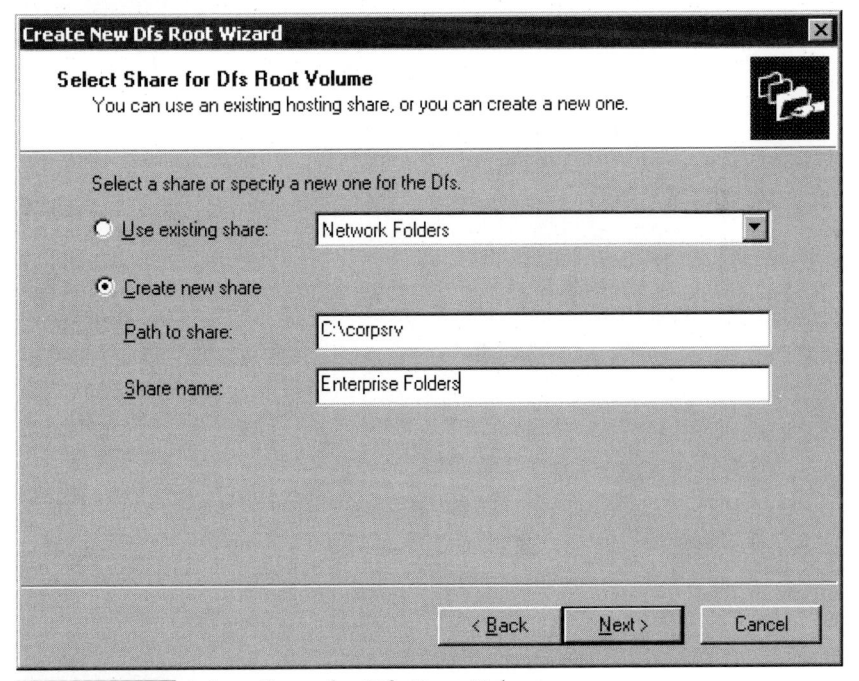

FIGURE 20.13 Select Share for Dfs Root Volume

8. The Provide Dfs Root Name window appears. Enter a different name for the share if desired. Use the Add the Dfs root to my current console check box if you want the root to appear in the Distributed File System MMC snap-in, as shown in Figure 20.14. Click Next.

9. A summary window appears. Review your configuration and click Finish, or click Back to make changes. The new Dfs root now appears in the MMC console.

CONFIGURING DFS PROPERTIES

You can access the general properties of the Dfs root by right-clicking on the Dfs root in the console and clicking Properties. The properties sheets provide you with a General tab and a Security tab. The General page provides you with a dialog box where you can enter a comment if desired and also a setting for client Dfs cache. This setting, which is 300 by default, specifies the number of seconds that client systems cache the referral by the Dfs root server to the replica set. On the Security page, you can configure security for Dfs access and modification as needed. This Security page is the same as you have seen for files and folders earlier in this chapter.

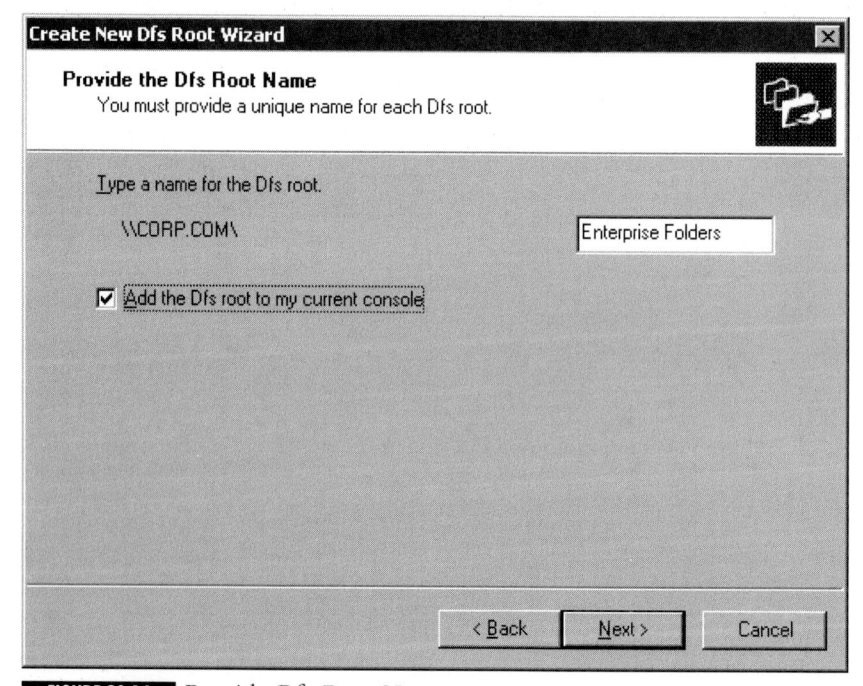

FIGURE 20.14 Provide Dfs Root Name

CREATING A NEW DFS CHILD NODE

If you right-click on the Dfs root, you will see several options to further define the Dfs structure. First, you can add a new Dfs child node. When you select this option, an Add to Dfs window appears, shown in Figure 20.15. Enter the name of the child node and the network path the user will send to in order to reach the child node. You can also add a comment if desired and enter a different value for the cached Dfs referal. The default is 1800 seconds.

Once you have configured child nodes, they appear in the Dfs console, shown in Figure 20.16.

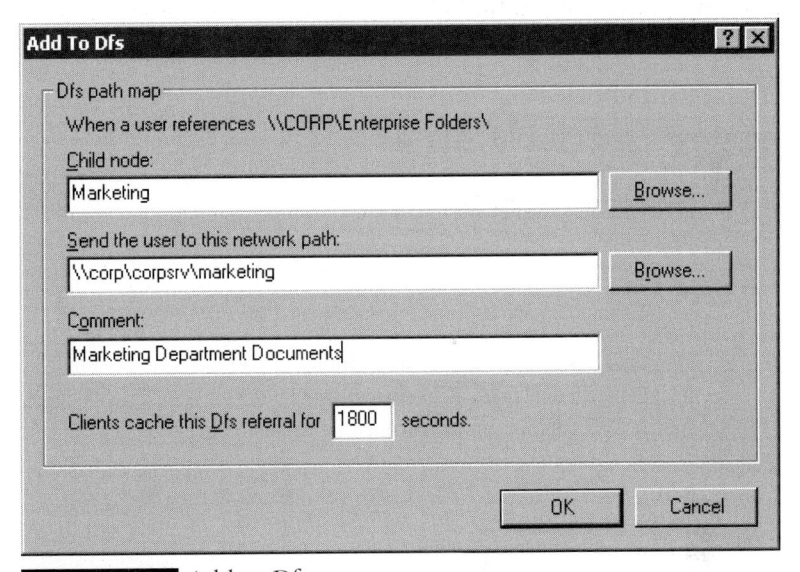

FIGURE 20.15 Add to Dfs

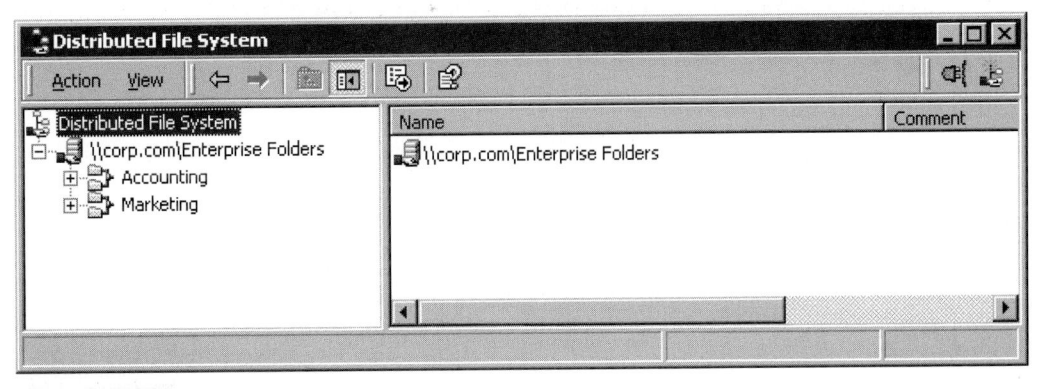

FIGURE 20.16 Dfs Console

CREATING A NEW ROOT REPLICA MEMBER

You can create a new root replica member by right-clicking on the root volume and clicking New Root Replica Member. This action begins the Create New Dfs Root Wizard that appeared earlier in the chapter. Follow the wizard's instructions to create the new Dfs root.

OTHER ACTIONS

You can also perform a variety of other actions by right-clicking on the Dfs root. Aside from creating a new child node or replica member, you can also delete the connection to the Dfs root, delete the Dfs root, check status, and open the Dfs root to view its contents. Likewise, you can right-click on a child node to see a list of configuration options. You can create a new Dfs replica member, remove the child node from the Dfs, check Status, or open the child node.

Summary

Windows 2000 provides you with flexible security for network shares through folder permissions and NTFS permissions. With NTFS permissions, you can control what files and folders users can access and what functions they can perform with those files and folders. The Distributed File System (Dfs) provided with Windows 2000 makes the organization of folders easy in an enterprise environment. Through the use of Dfs, users can easily locate shared folders on various servers without having to know the physical design of the network or the actual server location of folder and files. These features provide you with complex sharing capabilities with ease of administration.

TWENTY-ONE

Additional Client Technologies

As you have seen in previous chapters, Windows 2000 seeks to make end-users' work much easier by transparently implementing services and technologies that reduce client problems and network downtime. This chapter explores some additional technologies included in Windows 2000 Server that help users work more efficiently and help reduce the Total Cost of Ownership for Microsoft networks.

Intellimirror

Intellimirror is loosely defined as a collection of Windows 2000 technologies that are designed to make certain that a user's documents, programs, and desktop settings follow, or "mirror," the user, no matter what workstation the user is working at or whether or not the user is even connected to the network. Workstations running Windows 2000 Professional can take full advantage of the Intellimirror technologies. This initiative reduces the Total Cost of Ownership by reducing user downtime: No matter where the user is, he or she can access the tools needed for work. Intellimirror "mirrors" data between the server and the client machine. The mirror is a two-way process in that everything on the client computer is mirrored to the server, and the settings, documents, and programs can then be mirrored back to the client, regardless of the machine he or she is working at.

If a user is not connected to a server, then the client can still work on cached copies of the documents on his or her computer. When the user reconnects to the server, the documents are synchronized with the server so that the server always has the most current version.

The technologies that make up Intellimirror can function independently of each other so that administrators can implement all of the features, or only certain features as desired. This entire suite of technologies, however, all make up the Intellimirror initiative. The technologies included in Intellimirror are:

- Active Directory: this central location stores information about the user and Intellimirror technologies in use.
- Group Policy: you learned about Group Policy in Chapter 19. System, documents, and software settings can all be implemented for the user by using group policies.
- Offline Folders and Files: when a folder or file is shared, you can use the offline feature so that a cached copy of the folder and files is stored on the client computer. If the client is not connected to the network, he or she can still work on the files by using the cached copy. See Chapter 20.
- Disk Quotas: Disk Quotas can be implemented so that documents are automatically moved to another physical disk when the first disk becomes full.
- Roaming User Profiles: Roaming User Profiles follow the user from computer to computer so that the user always has the same system settings. See Chapter 19.
- Windows Installer: Windows Installer can be used to configure packages for automatic software installation and updates. These installations and updates can be delivered to a user's workstation without input from the user.
- Remote Installation Service: the Remote Installation Service can be used to automatically install Windows 2000 Professional or operating system updates to the user's computer. Remote Installation Service is explored later in this chapter.
- Synchronization Manager: the Synchronization Manager ensures that server side and client side documents are synchronized automatically. This feature makes certain that the mirror is always accurate. Synchronization Manager is explored later in this chapter.

All of these features work independently, yet they are all considered a part of the Intellimirror technology. Let's consider an example of how Intellimirror can benefit the organization and user. A new employee, Dawn Lewis, has just joined Corp, a large financial services organization. When Dawn logs on to her computer for the first time, the Active Directory account recognizes her account, the group policiy she belongs to, and a Roaming user profile established for her.

Company documents that she needs are automatically downloaded into her My Documents folder. When Dawn makes some changes to her system to customize her desktop to her preference and needs, those settings are saved in her profile on the server and she receives those settings each time she logs on, even if she uses a different workstation. The documents she uses are cached on her system so that when she takes her laptop home to finish some work in the evenings, she can work on the cached copy. The next day, when she connects to the network, the Synchronization Manager sees the changes on her laptop and updates the document copies on the server. When Dawn takes a business trip to another Corp office, she can even use one of their computers and receive her same settings, applications, and documents, just as if the information was stored on the local machine. Basically, whatever Dawn decides to do, her documents, software, and system preferences follow her.

Remote Installation Services

Remote Installation Services allows you to remotely set up client computers running Windows 2000 Professional without having to physically visit the workstations. This feature allows you to install operating systems on remote-boot client computers that are connected to the network. Remote Installation Services are considered a part of Intellimirror and are designed to reduce administrative overhead and client downtime. Remote Installation Services make use of Active Directory as well as DNS and DHCP. The client computer can be booted remotely using a boot floppy, or without a floppy if the computer is equipped with a Pre-Boot Execution (PXE) boot ROM. The workstation will contact the DHCP server that has Boot Information Negotiation Layer (BINL) extensions enabled. The server provides an IP address for the workstation, and BINL will refer the workstation to the server that performs the Remote Installation so that a bootable image of the operating system can be downloaded to the client for installation. To set up Remote Installation Services, you must have administrative privileges to run the wizard. Also, Windows 2000 Professional is the only operating system supported by remote installation and modifications to the installation image are not supported. The client computer must have enough disk space for the installation. Remote Installation will format only enough of the client computer's drive for the installation—any additional space will remain unformatted.

Setting Up Remote Installation Services

Remote Installation Services are not installed on the server by default, so you will need to install Remote Installation Services first. Double-click Add/Remove Programs in Control Panel, then click on the Add/Remove

Windows Components button. This action will start the Windows Components Wizard. Click Next on the Welcome Screen. On the Windows Components screen that appears, click the Remote Installation Service, shown in Figure 21.1, and then click Next. Windows 2000 Server installs the component. Click the Finish button when it appears, and click Yes to restart your computer.

Once the computer reboots, click Start → Programs → Configure Your Server. The opening screen will prompt you to Finish Setup. Click the Finish Setup button. The Remote Installation Services Setup Wizard begins. Follow these steps to complete the installation:

1. On the Welcome screen, note that an active DHCP and DNS server must be present on your network. You will need the Windows 2000 Professional CD-ROM or shared installation files for the remote install. Click Next.

2. The Remote Installation Folder Location window appears. The default path is C:\RemoteInstall. The Remote Installation folder cannot be installed on the same drive as the server operating system. Click Browse to change the location or click Next.

3. The Initial Settings window appears. By default, you need to configure Remote Installation Services to support client computers, but you can

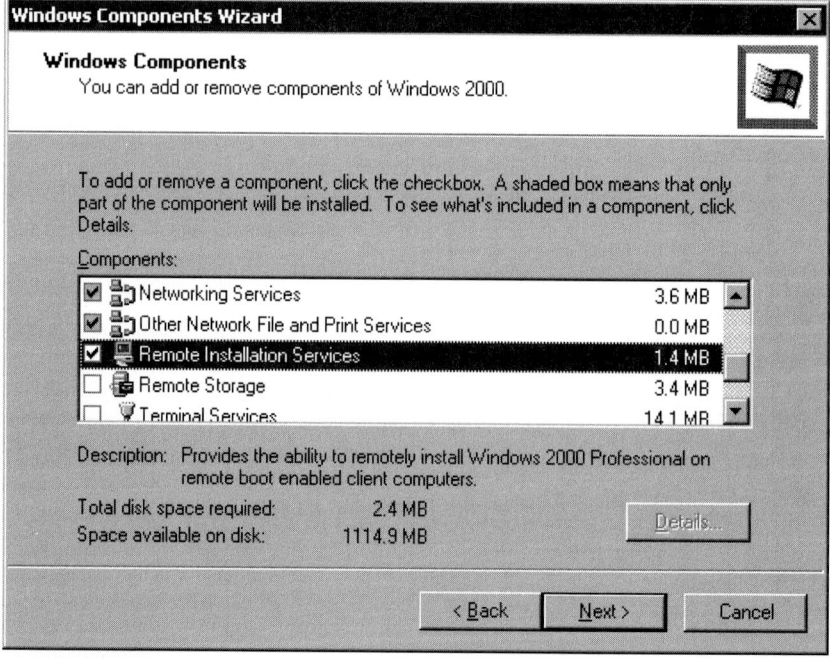

FIGURE 21.1 Remote Installation Services Component Installation

four • Managing Clients and Performance

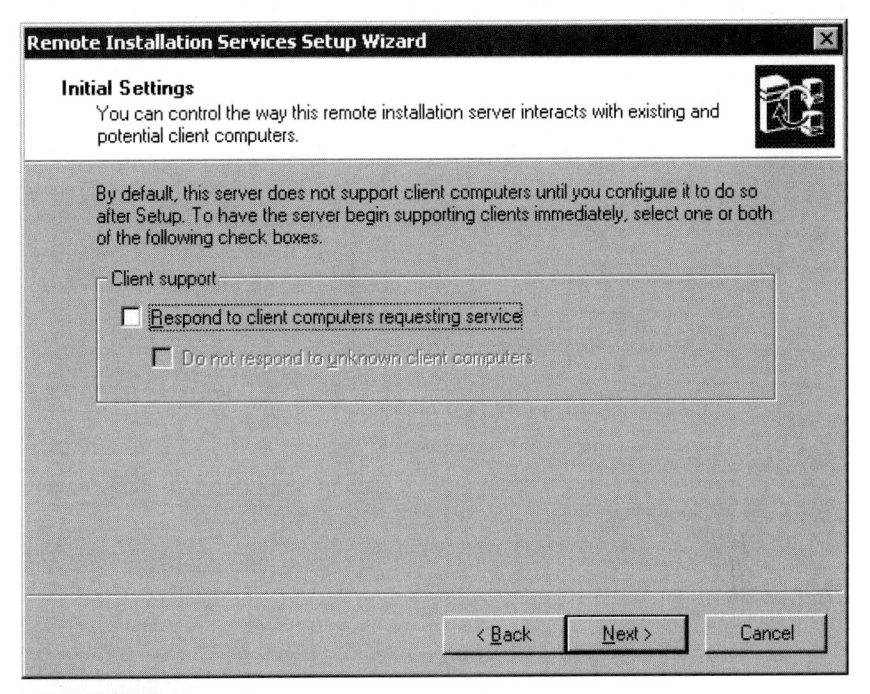

FIGURE 21.2 Initial Settings

click the Respond to client computers requesting service check box, as shown in Figure 21.2 so that you have client support immediately if desired. You can also click the Do not respond to unknown client computers check box if desired. Make your selections and click Next.

4. The Installation Source Files Location window appears. Enter the path to the installation source files, such as the Windows 2000 Professional CD-ROM or exiting share, and click Next.

5. The Windows Installation Image Folder Name appears. Enter the name for the image folder. The default is win2000pro. Click Next.

6. The Friendly Description and Help Text window appears. In the Friendly Description dialog box, type a friendly name (such as Windows 2000 Professional) and type any help text you wish to include in the Help text dialog box. Click Next.

7. A summary window appears. Review the settings you configured and click Finish. Remote Installation files are copied and installed.

Configuring General Remote Install Properties

Once you have installed Remote Installation Services, you manage it by accessing the Active Directory Users and Computers MMC snap-in. Expand the appropriate domain; then select the OU that contains the server that runs the Remote Installation Services (such as the Domain Controllers OU). Right-click the server object that runs the Remote Installation Services, then click Properties. On the Properties sheet, click the Remote Install tab, shown in Figure 21.3.

In the Client Support section, you see the same check boxes you saw during setup. If you did not select both or either boxes during setup, do so now. Click the Respond to client computers requesting service check box and the Do not respond to unknown client computers check box if desired. In the Check Server section, you can click the Verify Server to perform an integrity check if the server is experiencing problems. If you click the Verify Server button, a Check Server Wizard begins. Click Next to run the wizard, which will check for problems and log errors. You may need the installation

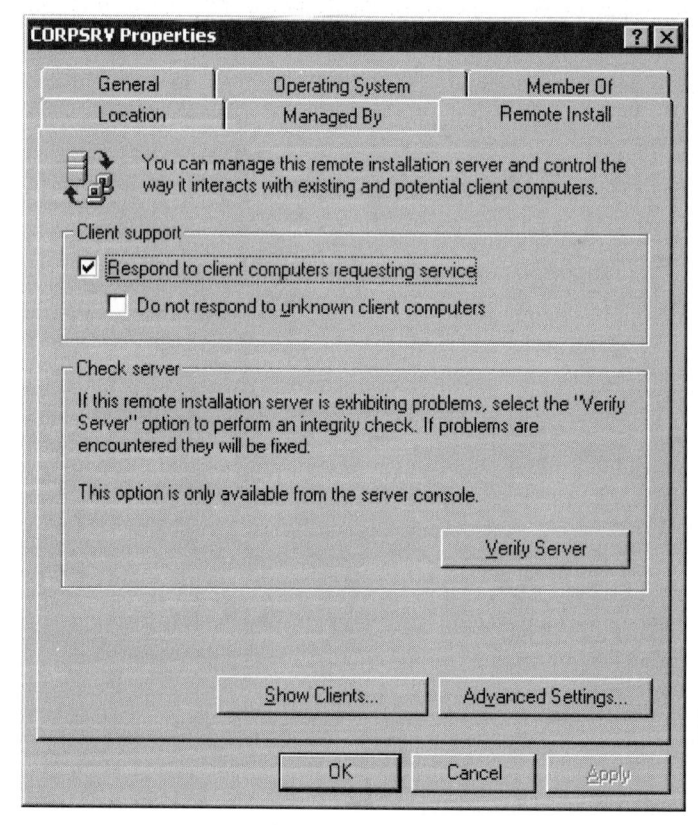

FIGURE 21.3

Remote Install Properties Page

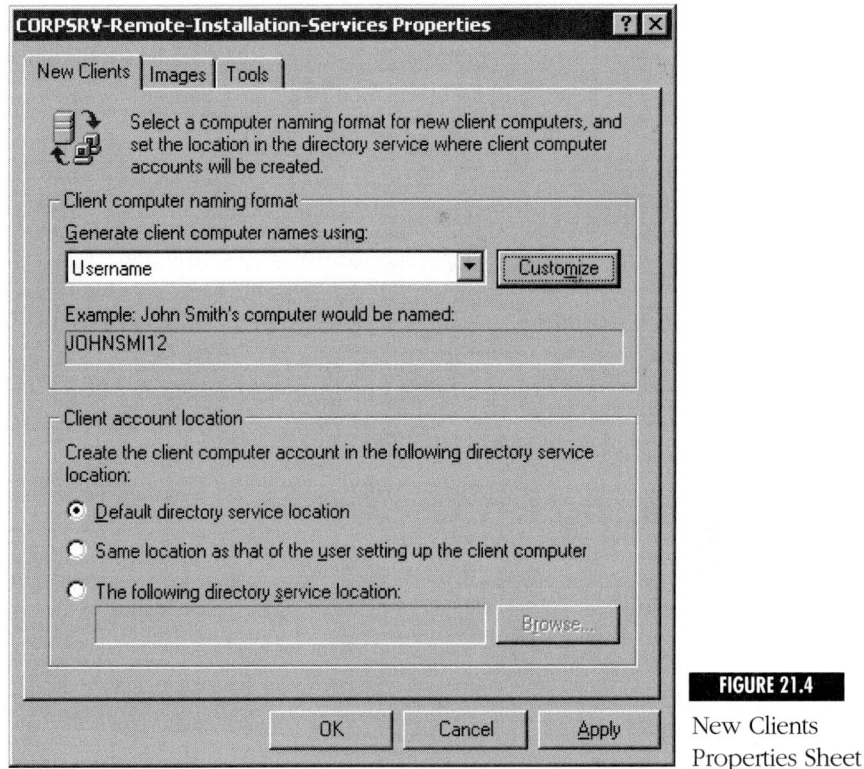

FIGURE 21.4 New Clients Properties Sheet

CD of Windows 2000 Professional to replace problem files. Click Next to begin. If problems are found, the server will attempt to correct them and may prompt you for more information. Once the wizard completes, click the Finish button to un-pause or restart the Remote Installation Services.

You can click the Show Clients button to see a list of Remote Install clients from the Active Directory, and you can further configure the Remote Install server's settings by clicking the Advanced Settings button. This action opens a Remote Installation Services Properties sheet with three property sheets.

On the New Clients Properties sheet, shown in Figure 21.4, you can perform several actions to configure the client computer.

First, you can determine a scheme for naming new client computers. If you click the Generate client computer names using the dropdown menu, you can select one of the following naming schemes:

- First initial, last name (such as CWILLIAMS24)
- Last name, first initial (such as WILLIAMSC24)
- First name, last initial (such as CARLAW24)
- Last initial, first name (such as WCARLA24)

- Username (such as CARLAWILL24)
- NP Plus MAC (such as NP649826115638 using the computer's MAC address)
- Custom

If you select Custom, or click the Custom button, the Computer Account Generation window appears, shown in Figure 21.5. You can use the % variables to determine what scheme you want to use to generate computer names. Enter the format in the provided dialog box and click OK.

On the New Clients Property page, you can also use the radio buttons at the bottom of the window to determine where the client computer account should be located. You can choose from Default Directory Service Location, Same location as that of the user setting up the client computer, or you can click "The following directory service location" to enter a specific location.

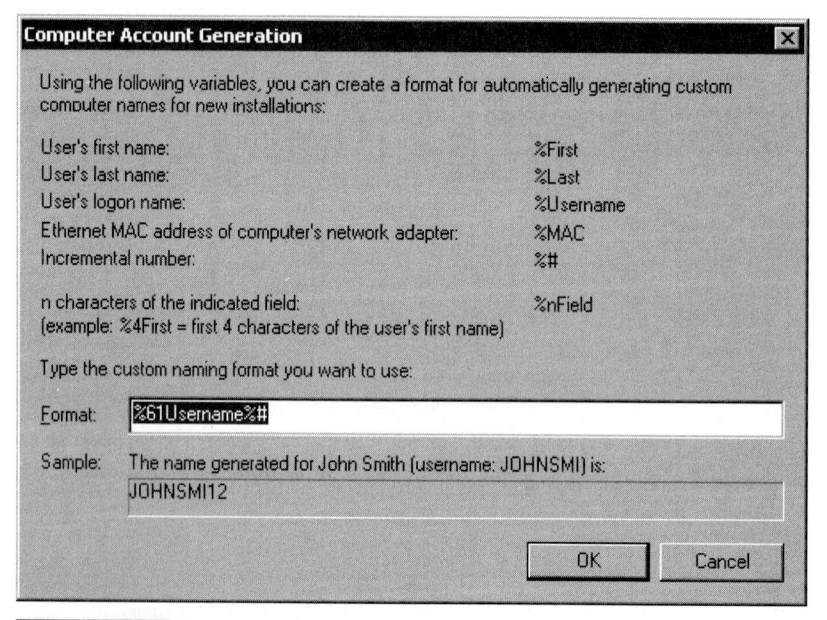

On the Images Property sheet, shown in Figure 21.6, you can see the images that are currently available for client installations.

If you click the Add button, you can add a new answer file or installation image. To add a new answer file or installation image, follow these steps:

1. On the New Answer File or Installation screen, shown in Figure 21.7, click either Associate a new answer file to an existing image, or Add a

FIGURE 21.5 Computer Account Generation

four • Managing Clients and Performance **385**

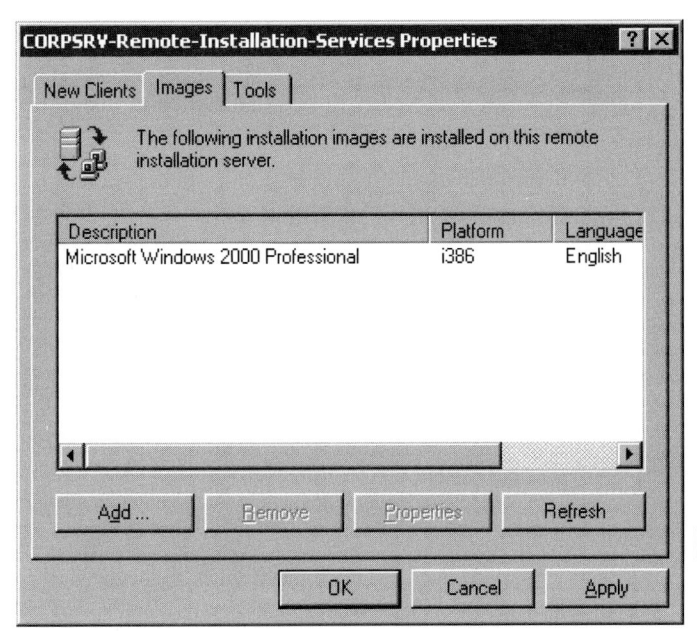

FIGURE 21.6 Images Properties Page

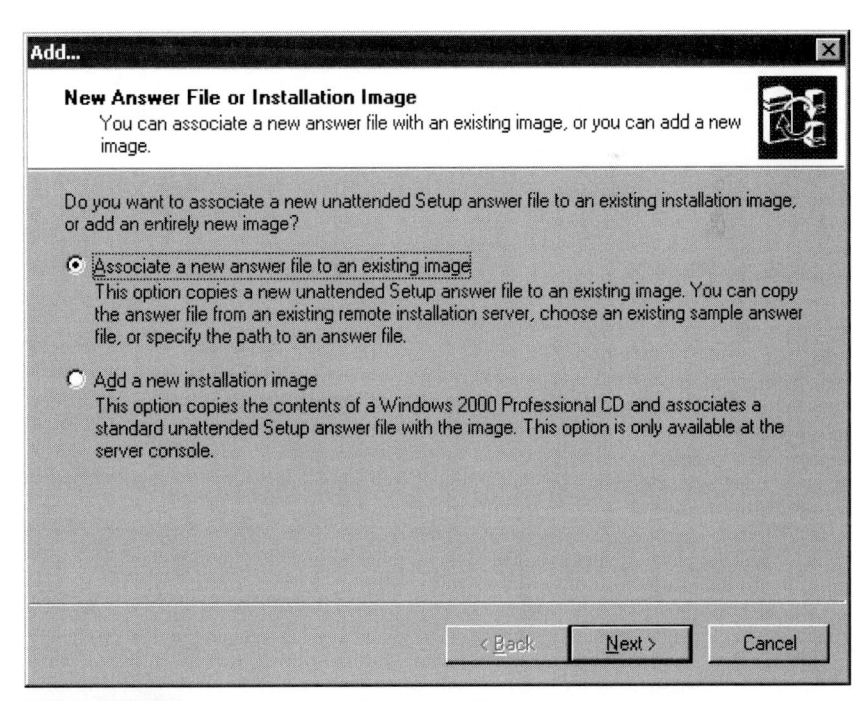

FIGURE 21.7 New Answer File or Installation Image

new installation image. If you click the Add a new installation image, another wizard begins that prompts for the location of the setup files, and then the file copy process begins again after you name the package, as in the initial Remote Installation setup. Make your selection and click Next.

2. If you clicked Associate a new answer file to an existing image in Step 1, the Unattended Setup Answer File Source window appears. Click the source of the answer file you want to use by clicking the appropriate radio button, as shown in Figure 21.8, and then click Next.

3. If you clicked another server or alternate location, the wizard will prompt you for the path to that location or server. If you clicked the Windows Image Sample Files radio button, the wizard presents you with a list of answer files that are available for association. Select the image you want to use from the list and click Next.

4. The Select a Sample Answer File window appears. Select the unattended answer file from the list you want to associate with the image, and then click Next.

5. The Friendly Description and Help Text window appears. Type in a friendly name and help text as desired and click Next.

6. A summary window appears. Review your settings and click Finish.

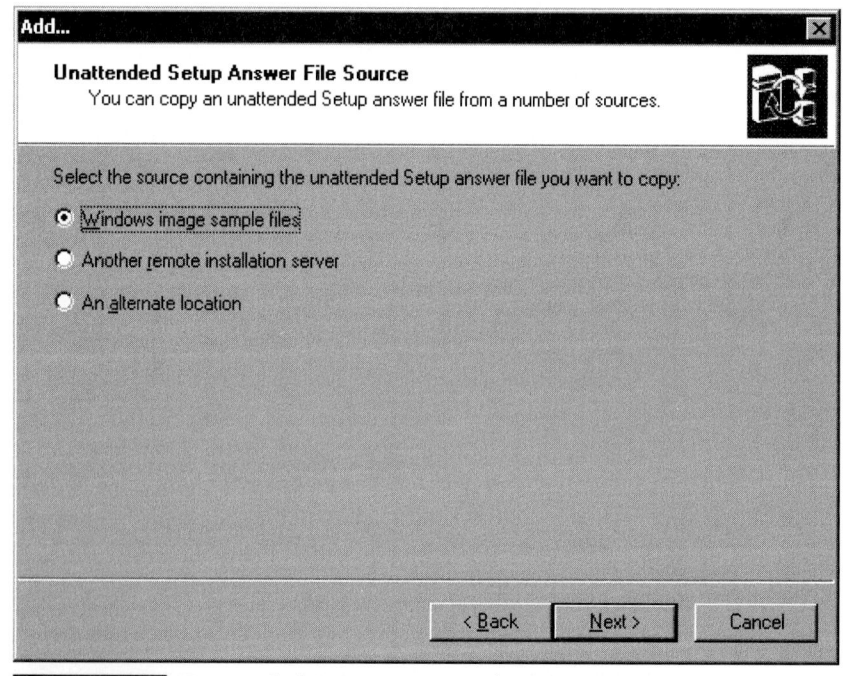

FIGURE 21.8 Unattended Setup Answer File Source

four • Managing Clients and Performance

The final Remote Installation Services Properties tab is Tools. This page lists any maintenance and troubleshooting tools that are installed on the server and that are available for use with Remote Installation.

Creating a Remote Client Boot Disk

To create a remote client boot disk to be used by client computers, follow these steps:

1. Click Start → Run.
2. Type the UNC path of the RBFG.exe utility that exists in the installation files that were created during Remote Installation setup. The typical path will be *server_name*\RemoteInstall\Admin\I386\RBFG.EXE. Or you can simply browse to the folder location and double-click RBFG.exe. This action opens the Windows 2000 Remote Boot Disk Generator window shown in Figure 21.9.
3. Insert a formatted disk into the server's disk drive; then click the Create Disk button.
4. You may want to click the Adapter List button to review the network PCI-based network adapters that are supported.
5. Click Close when you are done.

Invoking a Network Service Boot

To start the Remote Installation process, the client computer should be booted using a remote boot floppy disk, or the boot will happen automatically on remote-boot enabled computers. In the fields provided, enter a

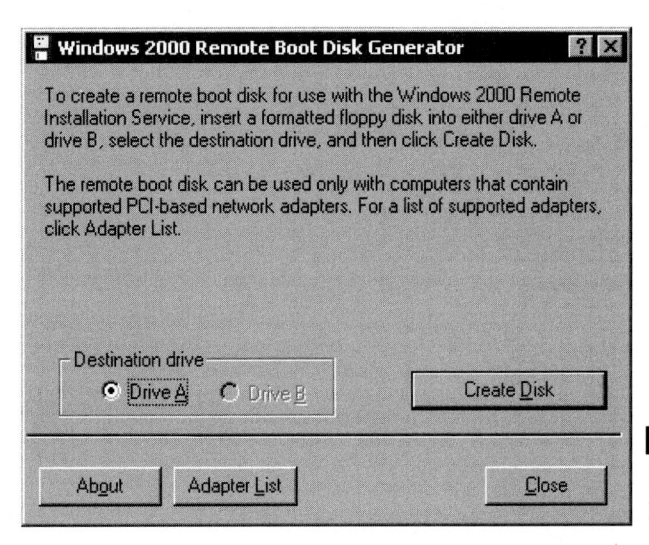

FIGURE 21.9
Remote Boot Disk Generator

valid username and password and domain name using the tab key to move between fields. The Client Installation Wizard will offer the following options:

- Automatic Setup: with this option, the client is not offered any installation options: all of the options are designated by the administrator.
- Custom Setup: the user can define a unique computer name and specify where the computer account should be created in the Active Directory.
- Restart from Previous Setup Attempt: use this option to continue installing after a previous installation attempt.
- Maintenance and Troubleshooting: use this option to access tools from the Client Installation Wizard to attempt to solve problems.

Creating a Remote Installation Preparation Image

You can create a Remote Installation Preparation Image (RIPrep) once a workstation is configured and applications are installed as desired. This process creates an image of all system settings and configuration as well as installed applications so the image can be installed on other workstations. Run the remote installation service on a chosen client computer, then configure the system and install any applications desired. This process requires that all applications and files be installed on the single boot partition of C:\ on the source client computer; Once this is done, you are ready to run the RIPrep utility. Follow these steps:

1. On the client computer, click Start → Run.
2. Type the UNC path of the RIPrep.exe utility, which is typically *server_name**share_name*\RemoteInstall\Admin\I386\RIPrep.exe. Or, you can browse to the appropriate folder and launch RIPrep.exe by double-clicking it.
3. Read the Welcome screen and click Next.
4. Type the folder name of the Remote Installation server where the RIPrep file will be copied and click Next.
5. Type a friendly name and help text in the appropriate dialog boxes if desired, and click Next.
6. Make sure all applications are closed and click Next.
7. Review the summary page and click Next.
8. The image is replicated to the server, and the workstation will shut down once the replication process is complete.

Synchronization Manager

The Synchronization Manger is also a part of the Intellimirror technologies. The Synchronization Manager is used to make certain that a user's off-line files are synchronized with the server copy once changes are made while working off-line. This ensures that the cached copy and the server copy are exactly the same. Synchronization Manager can be set to synchronize files at the following times:

- Every time a user logs on or logs off the computer—or both.
- At specific intervals during computer idle time.
- At scheduled times.
- Any combinations of the above three.

You can use Synchronization Manager to have certain files synchronized at one time and other files synchronized at another. For example, files that change on a daily basis can be synchronized every two hours while files that rarely change can be synchronized on a daily basis. Synchronization Manager can synchronize off-line files, folders, and even Web pages.

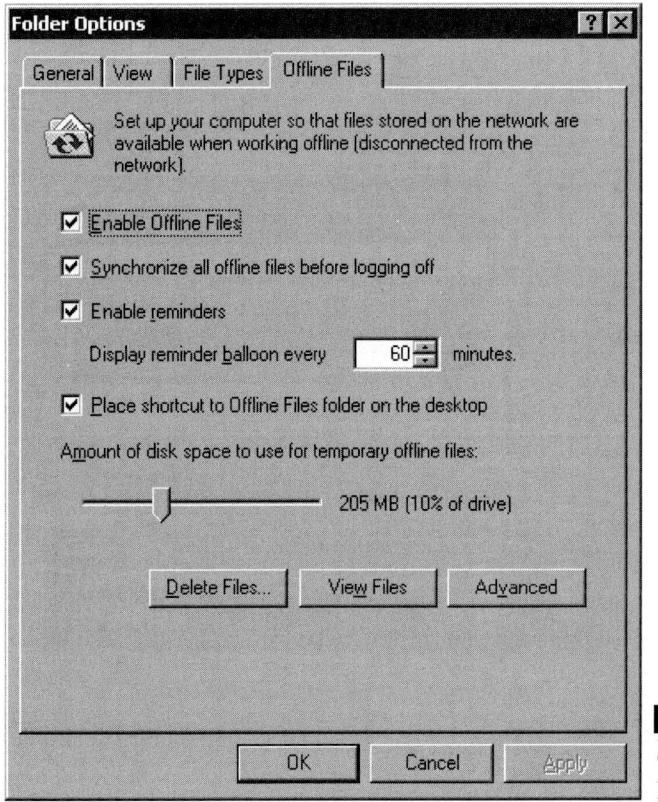

FIGURE 21.10
Offline Files Properties

Setting Up Client Computers to Use Offline Files

Before using Synchronization Manager, your computer must be configured to use off-line files. To configure your computer to use off-line files, follow these steps:

1. Open My Computer.
2. Click the Tools menu; then click Folder Options.
3. On the Offline Files tab, click the Enable Offline Files check box, as shown in Figure 21.10.

Making a File or Folder Available Offline

To make a file or folder available off-line, follow these steps:

1. In My Computer or My Network Places, click the file or folder you want to make available off-line.
2. On the File Menu, click Make Available Offline.

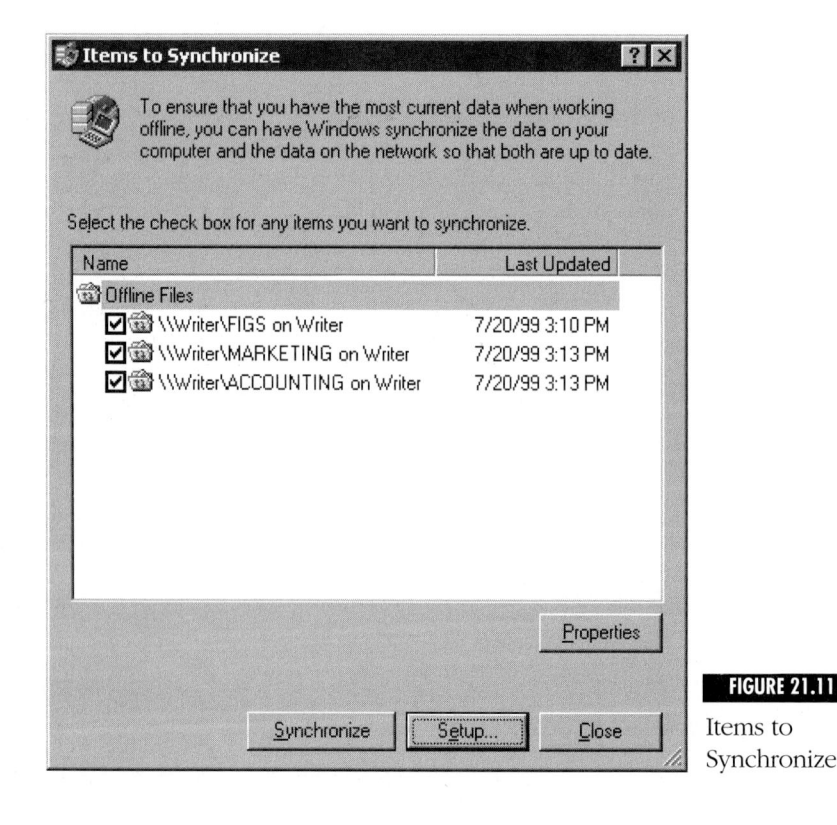

FIGURE 21.11
Items to Synchronize

Setting Up Synchronization Manager

To set up Synchronization Manager, click Start ➤ Programs ➤ Accessories ➤ Synchronize. The Items to Synchronize window opens, shown in Figure 21.11. Click the Setup button.

After clicking the Setup button, the Synchronization Settings Properties pages appear. On the Logon/Logoff page, shown in Figure 21.12, use the dropdown menu to select the manner in which the computer is connected. In the Synchronize the following checked items, select items that you want to synchronize by clicking the check box next to the item. At the bottom of the window, you can select whether to synchronize when you log on or log off your computer (or both), and you can click the Ask me before synchronizing the items check box if desired.

On the On Idle Property page, shown in Figure 21.13, you can configure which files or folders you want synchronized when your computer is idle. Select the items by clicking the check boxes next to them, and then click the Synchronize the selected items while my computer is idle check box.

If you click the Advanced button on this page, shown in Figure 21.14, you can configure how many minutes of idle time should pass before synchronization occurs. You can also configure the amount of time to pass

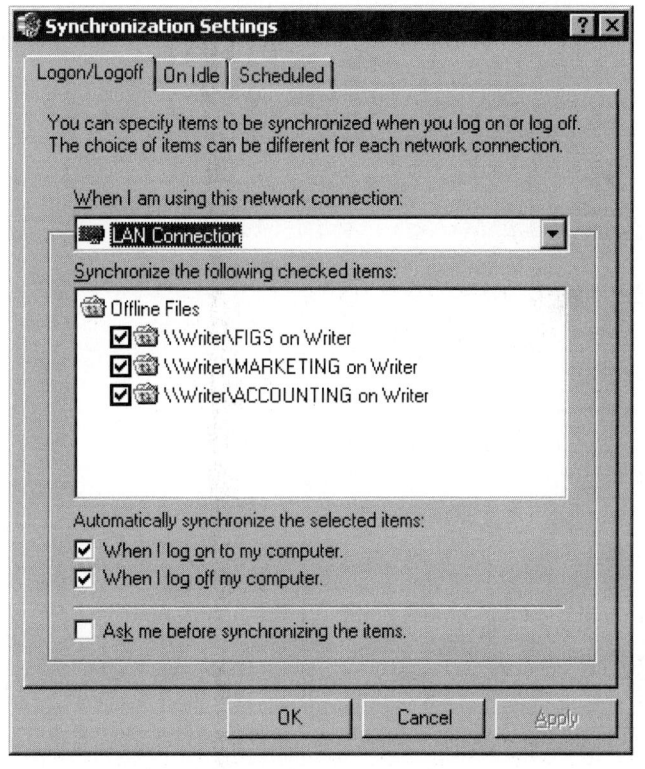

FIGURE 21.12
Logon/Logoff Properties

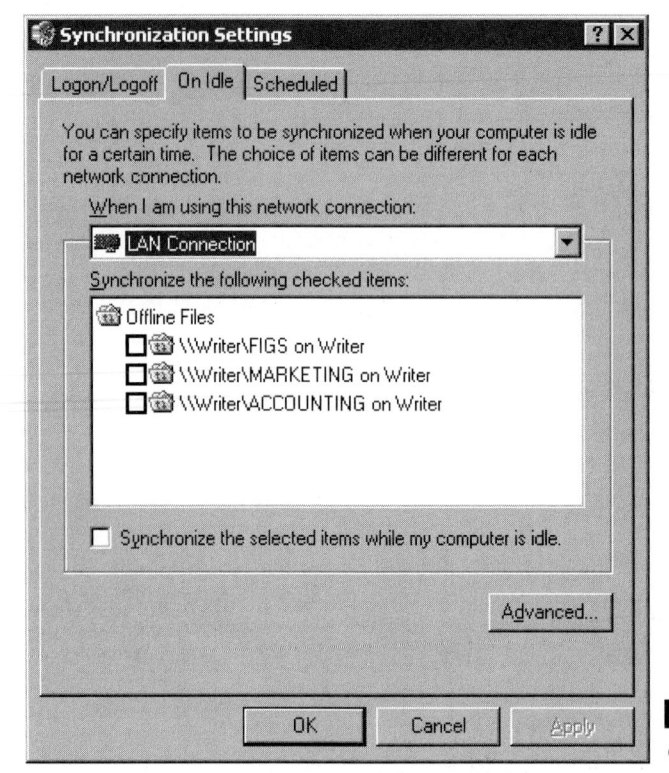

FIGURE 21.13
On Idle Properties

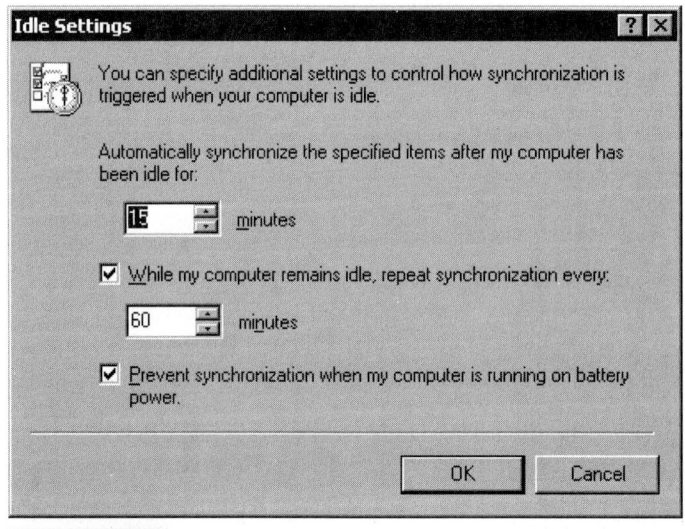

FIGURE 21.14 Idle Settings

four • Managing Clients and Performance

while your computer is idle for resynchronization to occur (such as every 60 minutes). You can also use the Prevent synchronization when my computer is running on battery power check box if necessary.

On the Scheduled Property page, shown in Figure 21.15, you can add or remove scheduled synchronization tasks from your schedule.

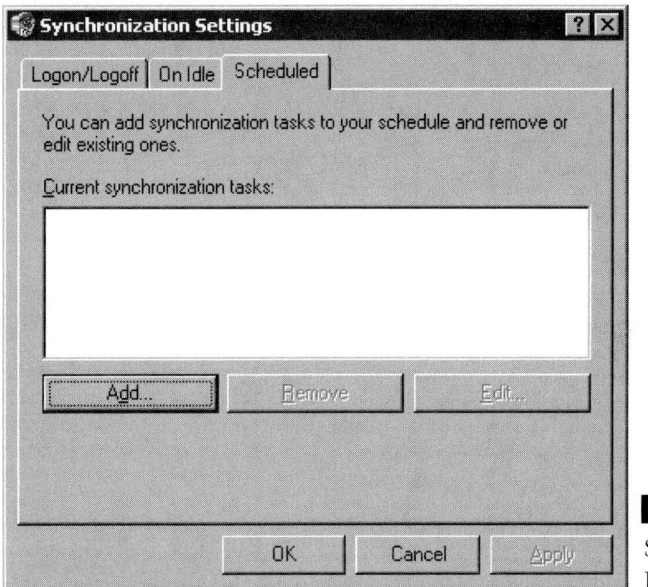

FIGURE 21.15 Scheduled Properties

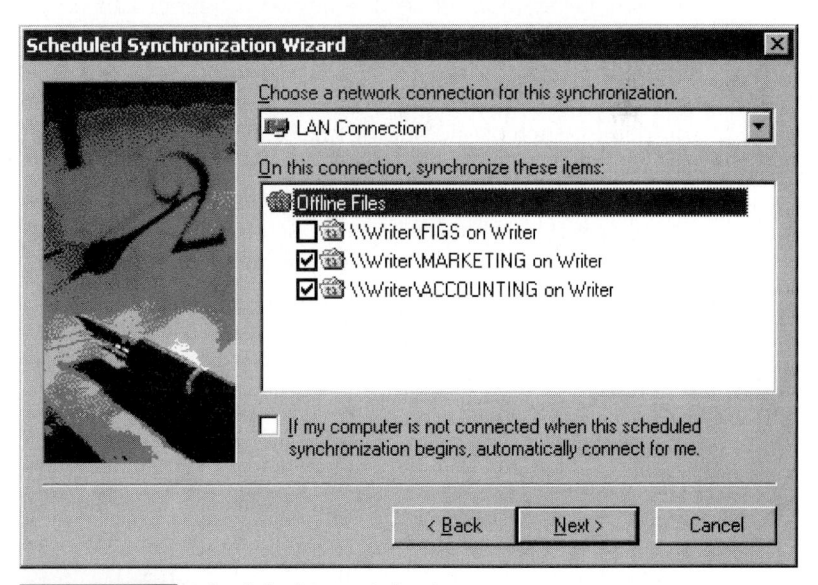

FIGURE 21.16 Scheduled Item Selection

If you click the Add button, the Scheduled Synchronization Wizard begins. To complete the wizard, follow these steps:

1. Click Next on the Welcome Screen.
2. In the next window, shown in Figure 21.16, select the items for which you want to schedule synchronization by clicking the boxes beside the items. You can also select the "If my computer is not connected when this scheduled synchronization begins, automatically connect for me" check box if desired. Make your selections and click Next.
3. On the synchronization schedule window, adjust the start time and start date, and select either the every day, weekdays, or click the Every button and adjust the number of days desired. Make your selection and click Next.
4. Type a name for the schedule and click Next.
5. Review your settings and click Finish.

Indexing Service

The Microsoft Indexing Service provided with Windows 2000 Server provides full text searching capabilities for text files, Microsoft Office 95 and later documents, HTML documents, and Internet mail and news documents (with IIS installed). The indexing service takes information from the documents and organizes it so that keyword queries can be performed through the Windows 2000 search function, Indexing Service query, or from a Web browser. The indexing service takes information from both a document's contents, or the actual words in a document, as well as the document's properties, such as the author's name. This feature allows you to search for a particular word or phrase and find all documents that contain that word or phrase, or you can search for all documents by a particular author. The indexing service requires an initial setup and configuration, but after that, its services are automatic, and it can even recover from a system crash or power failure.

The indexing service works by scanning documents. This process, which creates an inventory, determines what documents should be indexed. After you install the indexing service, a full scan will be run the first time, which means that the service takes a full inventory of the document in cataloged folders and adds them to the list of documents that will be indexed. The indexing service will also run a full scan if a new folder is added to the index catalog or if a serious error has occurred. The index service can also run an incremental scan. An incremental scan looks for changes in documents and updates the catalog as needed. Whenever a document is changed, it sends a notification to the indexing service so that it can be re-indexed. If the change notifications are lost, or if the service is shut down, the service performs the incremental scan to determine which documents have changed and need to be re-indexed.

Installing the Indexing Service

You install the Indexing Service just as you do any other service in Windows 2000, through the Add/Remove Programs option in Control Panel. Double-click the icon, and then click Add/Remove Windows components. Select Microsoft Index Service from the list and click OK. The service will be installed on your machine.

Configuring the Indexing Service

Once installation is complete, you can configure the indexing service. Click Start ➤ Programs ➤ Administrative Tools ➤ Computer Management. Expand Server Applications and Services to reach the Indexing service, shown in Figure 21.17.

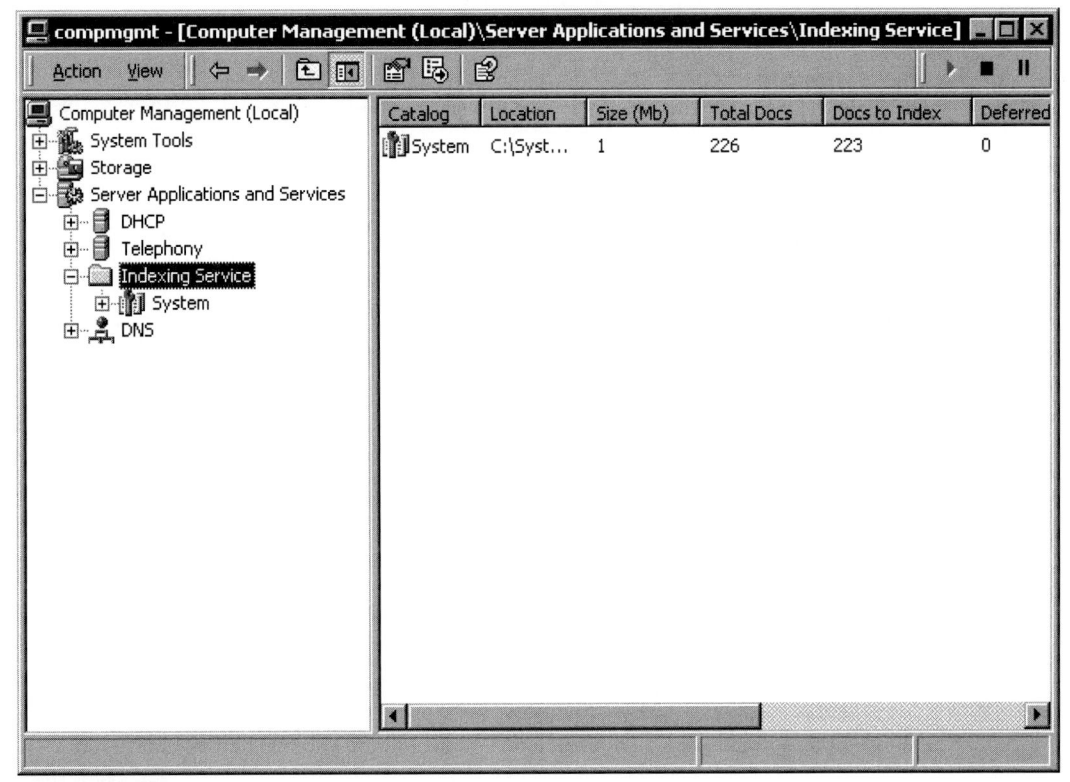

FIGURE 21.17 Indexing Service in Computer Management

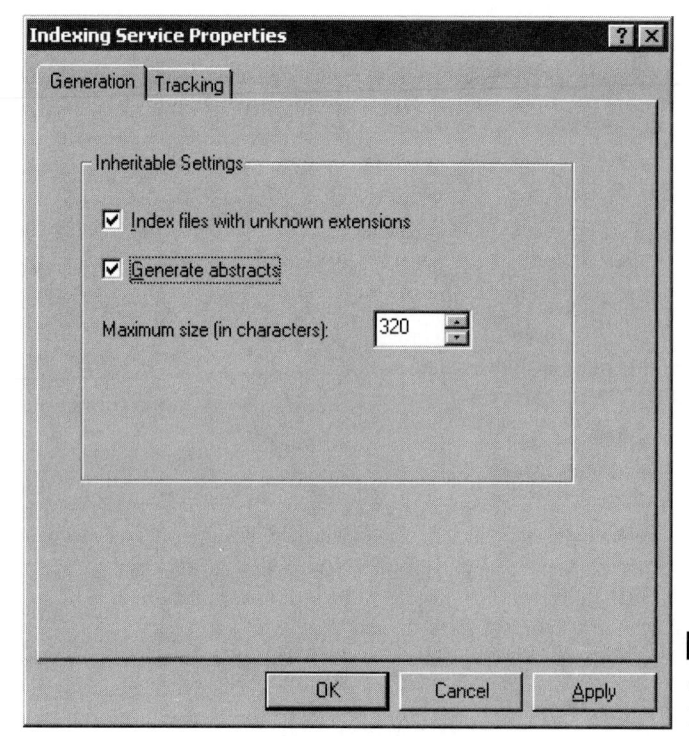

FIGURE 21.18 Generation Properties Page

To begin the service configuration, right-click on the Indexing Service object and click Properties. The Properties sheets contain two tabs: Generation and Tracking.

On the Generation Property sheet, as shown in Figure 21.18, you have two options. First, you can choose to index documents with unknown extensions. In this case, the indexing service does not have filters for these types of documents, but the service will attempt to extract whatever information it can and index. Click the check box if you want to use this option. Next, you have the option to generate abstracts. An abstract is a summary of the information found in the document. The Indexing service can generate an abstract that can be displayed with search requests so that readers can learn more about the document. If you choose this option, you can adjust the maximum abstract size permitted (in characters). The default setting is 320.

On the Tracking Properties page, shown in Figure 22-19, you can select the Add Network Share Alias Automatically check box. This feature tells the indexing service that you want to use the share name of any shared directory as the alias for that directory.

FIGURE 21.19
Tracking Properties Page

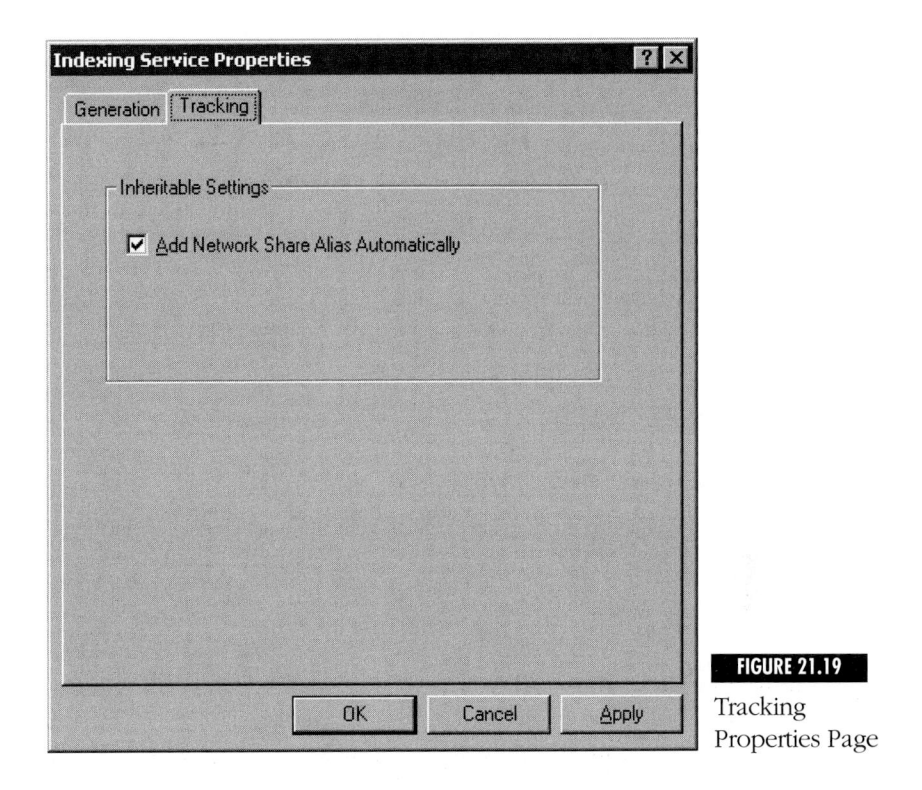

Creating a New Catalog

By default, a System catalog is created when you install the indexing service. The catalog stores all indexing information. The catalog(s) appears in the console tree under the indexing service object. You can create a new catalog by right-clicking the indexing service object in the console, pointing to New, and then clicking Catalog. A dialog box appears asking you to enter a name for the catalog and a storage location for the catalog. Enter this information and click OK to create the new catalog. Once the catalog is added, the indexing service will need to be stopped and restarted. You can both stop and restart the service by right-clicking on the indexing service object in the console and clicking either Stop or Start.

Performing Manual Catalog Scans

You can manually perform a full or incremental catalog scan as desired. This action is useful when there has been some problem with the server or service being down and allows you to make certain that the index is up-to-date. In the console tree, expand Indexing Service, and then expand the catalog you want to scan. Click the Directories folder. Select the directory in the details pane you want to scan. Click the Action Menu, point to All Tasks, and then click either Rescan (Full) or Rescan (Incremental).

Checking Indexing Service Performance

You can run an indexing service performance check and make some adjustments if desired. In the console, right-click Indexing Service and click Stop. Then, point to All Tasks and click Tune Performance. The Indexing Service Usage window appears, shown in Figure 21.20.

Click the radio button that best describes how the indexing service is used on this server and click OK. If you click the Customize radio button, click the Customize button to configure the desired setting. A Desired Performance window appears, shown in Figure 21.21. Use the sliders to adjust the level of indexing performance you want, from lazy to instant for both indexing and querying, and then click OK. Keep in mind that excessive indexing and querying may cause performance problems.

Click OK on the main window, then restart the indexing service.

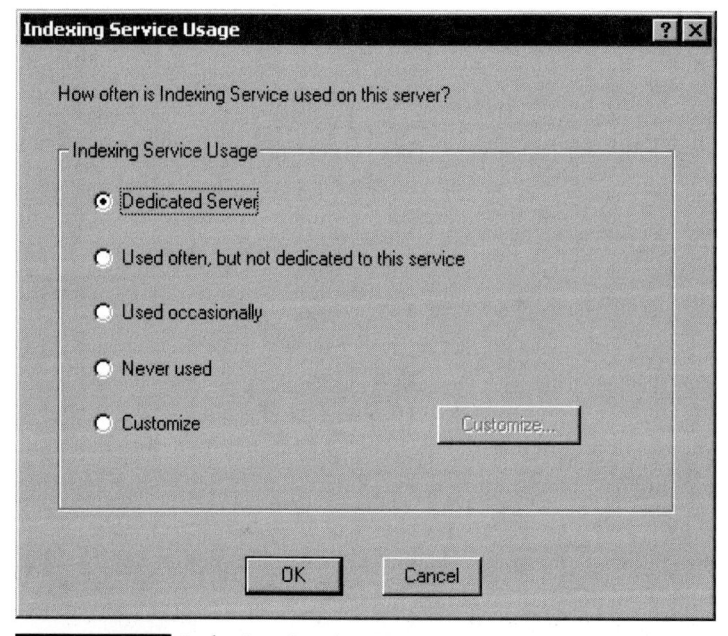

FIGURE 21.20 Indexing Service Usage

FIGURE 21.21
Desired Performance

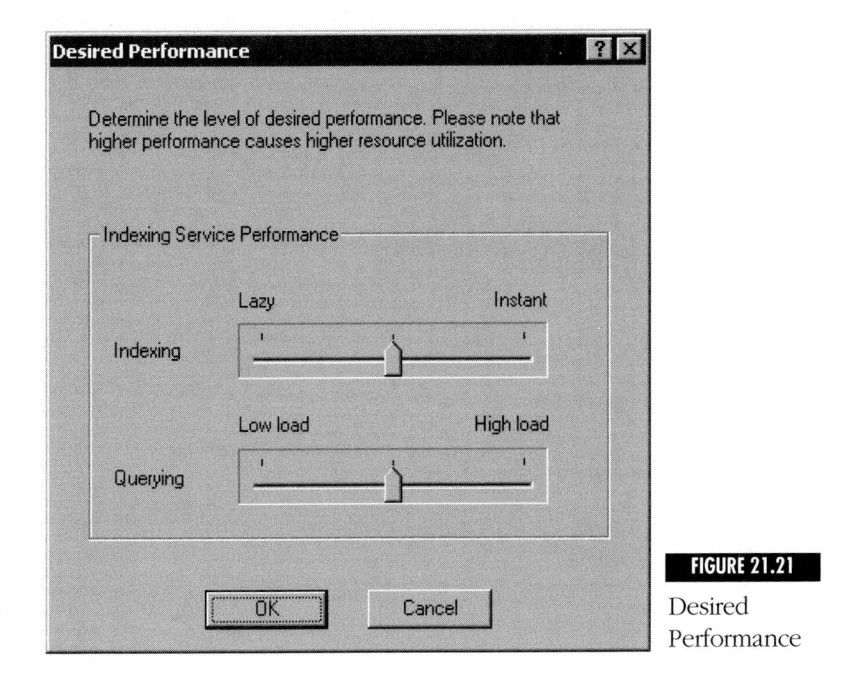

Retrieving a List of Unindexed Documents

As an administrator, it will be helpful to know which documents the indexing service could not index. You can easily retrieve a list of unindexed documents by expanding the Indexing Service object in the console and clicking Query the Catalog. In the query line, type @Unfiltered=True, and then click the Go button, as shown in Figure 21.22. The unindexed documents will appear in the list.

Preventing an NTFS Directory or Document from Being Indexed

To prevent an NTFS directory or document from being indexed, access Windows Explorer in Start ➤ Programs ➤ Accessories ➤ Windows Explorer. Select the folder or document you do not want indexed; then click File ➤ Properties. On the General tab, click the Advanced button, and then clear the Index Contents for fast file searching check box. Click OK, then OK again.

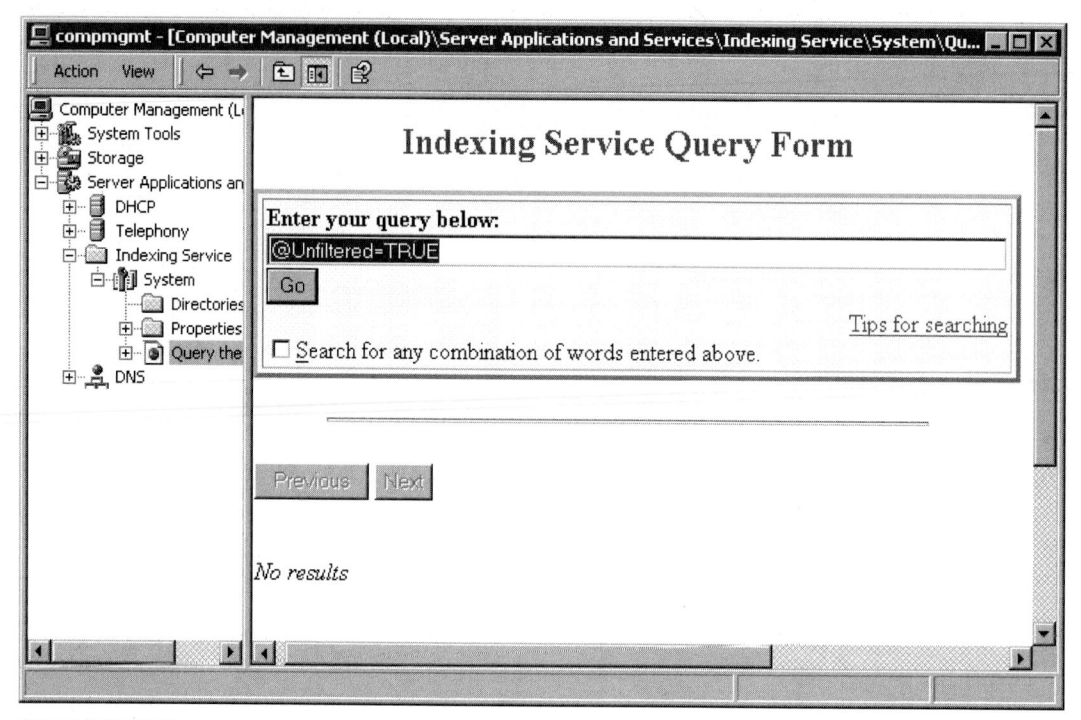

FIGURE 21.22   Indexing Service Query Form

Summary

Windows 2000 Server provides several additional technologies and services to increase client productivity and reduce downtime. Intellimirror is a collection of Windows 2000 technologies designed to enable a user's desktop settings, documents, and programs to follow him or her regardless of the workstation in use. The Remote Installation Services enable administrators to remote-boot workstations and install Windows 2000 Professional automatically. Windows 2000 supports off-line folders and documents so that users can work with file folders while not connected to the network. The off-line folders and documents can then be synchronized with the server copy. Finally, Windows 2000 provides an indexing service so that folders and files can be indexed, which allows users to perform full text searches for needed documents.

TWENTY-TWO

Printing

At first glance, setting up and managing print devices and printer pools on a network seems like an easy task. However, resolving print problems consumes much time, and many large environments have a dedicated administrator just to manage printing. It was once thought that computer networking would eliminate the need for printed pages—a paperless office. Yet the reality is that users depend on printing as much now as they ever have and print performance in any network is very important. In this chapter, we explore how Windows 2000 Server handles printing, and you learn about some new print features as well.

Printing Overview

Windows 2000 supports a variety of network printing options that allow you great flexibility and more ease of administration concerning printers. In Windows 2000, you can share printer resources across the network, use a Windows 2000 Server as a dedicated print server, and a wide variety of network client operating systems can print to Windows 2000. Windows 2000 even supports printing across the Internet. Except for the new features in Windows 2000, the printing process remains virtually the same as it did in Windows NT.

▶ *For Review*

Printer or Print Device?

If you have worked with Windows at all, it is important to keep in mind the Microsoft definition of a printer. This helps reduce any confusion when learning about Microsoft printing. A "print device" is the actual physical hardware—the printer sitting on a table somewhere on the network. A "printer" is defined as the software interface. So, when you "set up a printer," you are actually configuring the software on your server that runs the print device.

In order to review the process, let's consider an example of what happens when a Windows client prints a document. Diane, a typical user, needs to print a Word document that she has been writing. When she clicks print, Word calls the Graphics Device Interface (GDI), which calls the printer driver for the printer. Word, the GDI, and the driver, render the print job in the printer language, and the print job gets passed to the client spooler. The client spooler then makes a Remote Procedure Call (RPC) to the print server. After negotiation, the document is sent over the network to the print server's spooler. The server then queries the print processor concerning the print job. The print processor recognizes the job's data type and accepts the print job. The print server determines whether modifications to the job are needed to make it print correctly, and then the print job is passed to the print monitors. A two-way communication between the print monitor and the actual print device occurs, and the print job is passed to the port that connects to the actual print device. The printer receives the print job, converts it to a bitmap format, and then prints Diane's Word document.

New Windows 2000 Print Features

There are several new printing features available in Windows 2000. Most of these features are designed to make printing easier for clients (regardless of the operating system used), and to enable more printing options for network environments. The following list explains the new printing features:

- Remote Port: Windows 2000 makes printer administration easier by including remote port administration. Printers connected to any Windows 2000 computer can be configured and administered remotely without having to walk to the physical server.
- Standard Port Monitor: using the new standard port monitor, a Windows 2000 print server can print to network interface printers using TCP/IP. This feature replaces LPRMON for TCP/IP printers connected directly to the network with a network adapter. This new port monitor feature is 50 percent faster than LPRMON.
- Internet Printing: Windows 2000 integrates printing with the Internet. Client computers running Windows 2000 can print to Windows 2000

four • Managing Clients and Performance **403**

print servers using a URL, just as they would to contact a Web site. You can pause, resume, and delete print jobs over the Internet as well.
- Active Directory: printers can be stored in the Active Directory so that users can easily find which printer they want to use. You can also perform Active Directory searches to find specific printers, such as color printers or laser printers.
- Additional User Settings: users can change document defaults more easily and even change printers when they click on print.
- Monitoring: Performance Monitor now includes a Print Queue object that allows you to set up various counters to closely monitor printing performance.
- Macintosh and UNIX: new Windows 2000 features supports printing to Macintosh and UNIX printers.

Setting Up Printers

You can set up printers in Windows 2000 Server by clicking Start ➤ Settings ➤ Printers, or by double-clicking the Printers icon in control panel. The Add Printer Wizard appears in the printer folder to help you set up printers connected directly to your server or printers connected to servers on the network.

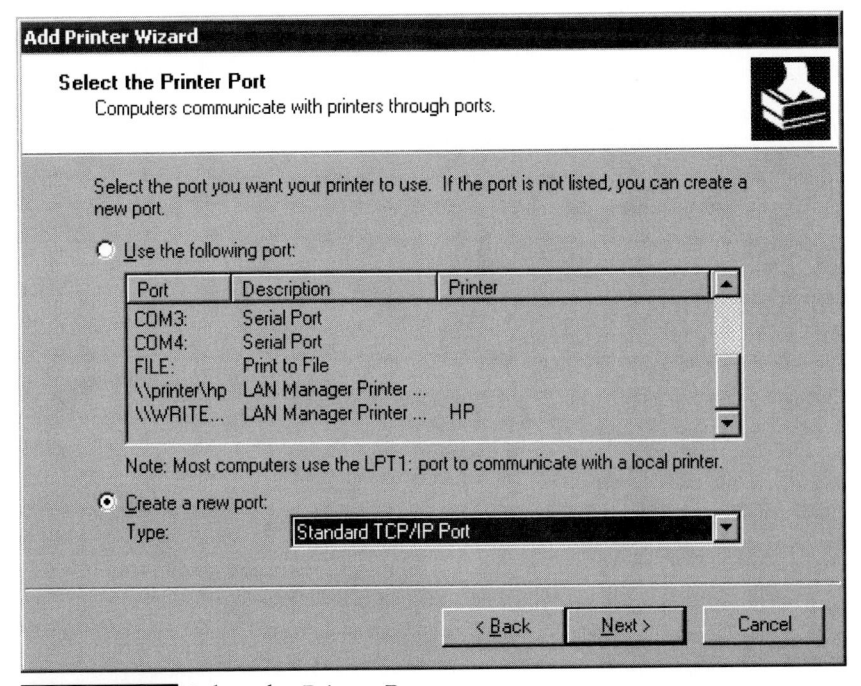

FIGURE 22.1 Select the Printer Port

The wizard attempts to detect your print device automatically, and you may need to provide drivers for the printer. All local printers, network printers, and network-interface print devices can be installed by using this wizard.

You can use the wizard to configure additional printer ports as well. The Select the Printer Port wizard window, shown in Figure 22.1, allows you to select the port you want to use from the list, or you can use the Create a new port radio button.

In the Create a new port dropdown menu, you can select AppleTalk Printing Device, Local Port, LPR Port, and Standard TCP/IP Port. If you click the Standard TCP/IP Port options, a wizard begins to help you configure the port. After the welcome screen, the Add Port window appears, shown in Figure 22.2, where you enter the printer name or IP address and the port name. The TCP/IP port can be used to easily configure network printers.

Printer Properties

Once you install printers on your server, an icon for each printer appears in the Printers folder. You can access the properties pages for the printers by right-clicking on the printer icon and clicking Properties. The following sections explain what you can configure on each page.

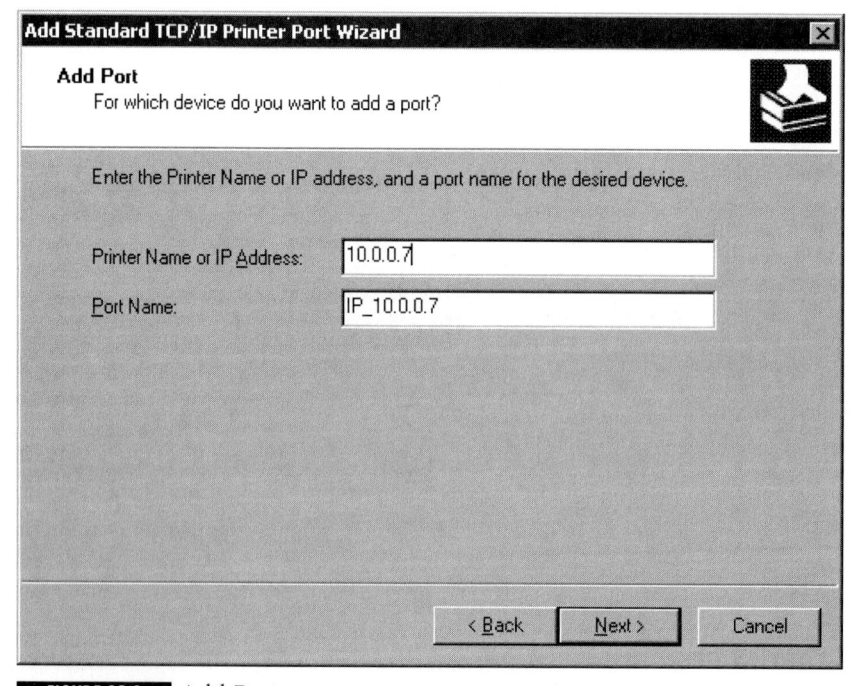

FIGURE 22.2 Add Port

GENERAL

On the General Properties page, shown in Figure 22.3, you can enter location information and comments if desired. The page lists the features of the printer. You can use the Print Test Page button to print a test page on the printer, and you can also click the Printing Preferences button to adjust the page layout (either portrait or landscape) and the color (either color or grayscale.)

If you click the Printing Preference button and then click the Advanced tab, you are provided with a tree structure of color advanced options, shown in Figure 22.4. You can click on a feature, and a drop-down menu will appear so that you can adjust it as desired.

SHARING

The Sharing tab, shown in Figure 22.5, allows you to either share the printer or not by clicking the appropriate radio button. If you share the printer, you

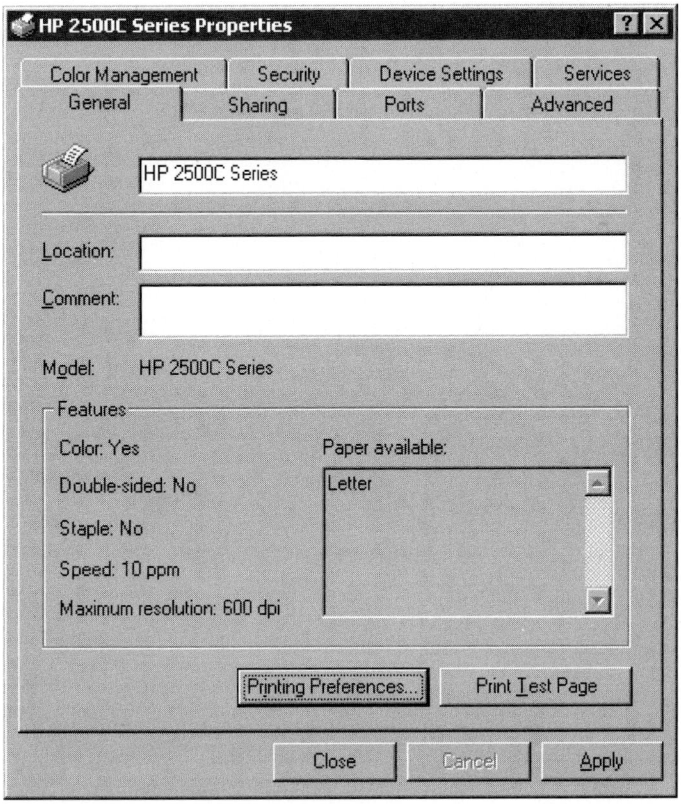

FIGURE 22.3 General Properties

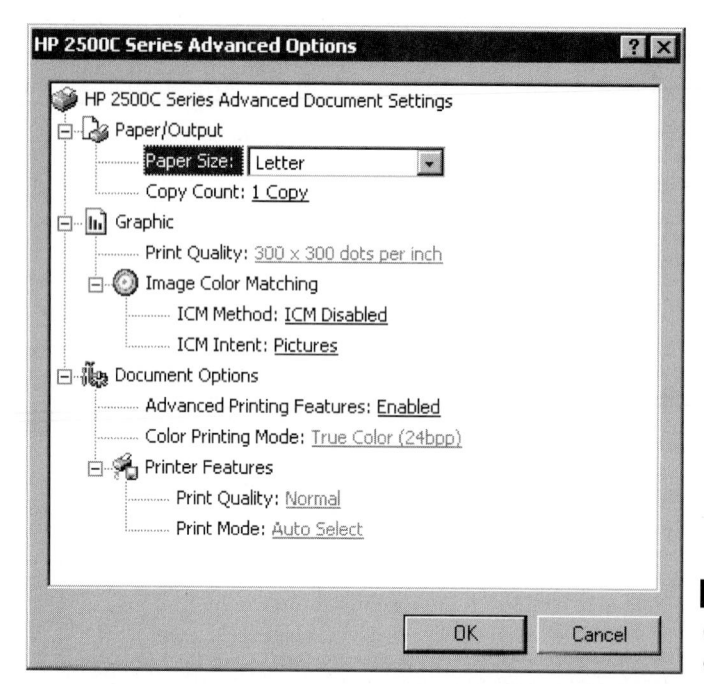

FIGURE 22.4
Color Advanced Options

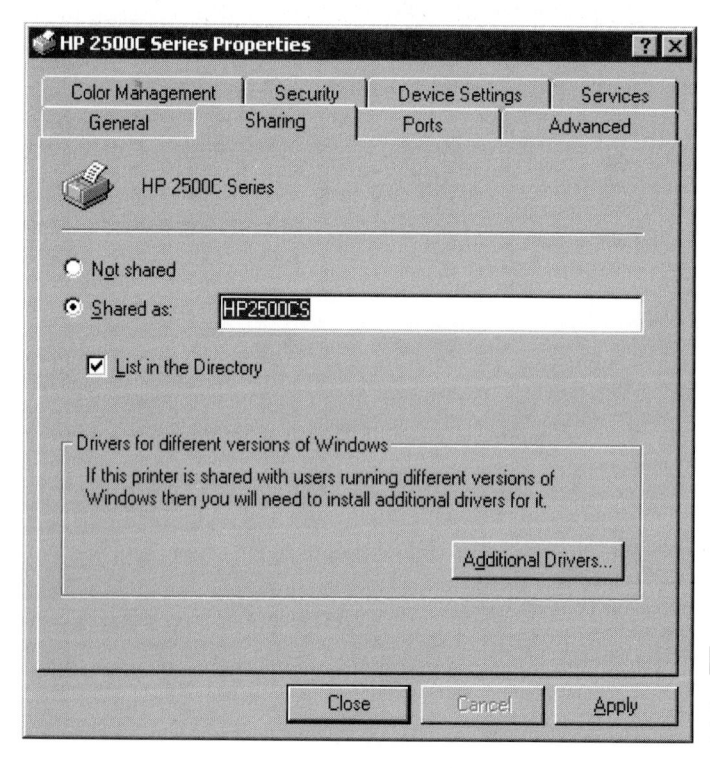

FIGURE 22.5
Sharing Properties

can click the List in Directory check box to add the printer to the Active Directory.

If you click the Additional Drivers button, you can install additional drivers from the printer so that users on other operating systems can download the drivers automatically and connect to the printer. Simply select the system you want to be able to download the drivers and click OK.

PORTS

On the Ports Property sheet, shown in Figure 22.6, you can select which ports the server should use to print to the device. Documents print to the first free port that is checked. You can select additional ports for use, add a new port, delete a port, or click the Configure Port button. At the bottom of the window, you can enable printer pooling. A printer pool contains two or more of the same print devices connected to the same server that appear as one print device. When a job is sent to the pool, the first available print device in the pool prints the job.

If you click the Configure Port button, shown in Figure 22.7, you can adjust the port name, the protocol for use (either RAW or LPR), and the RAW

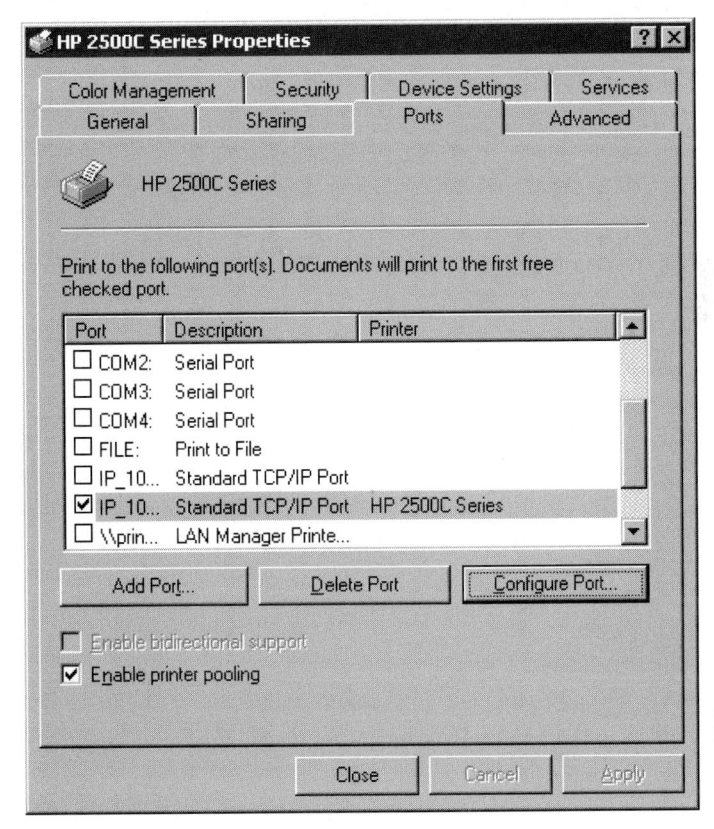

FIGURE 22.6

Ports Properties

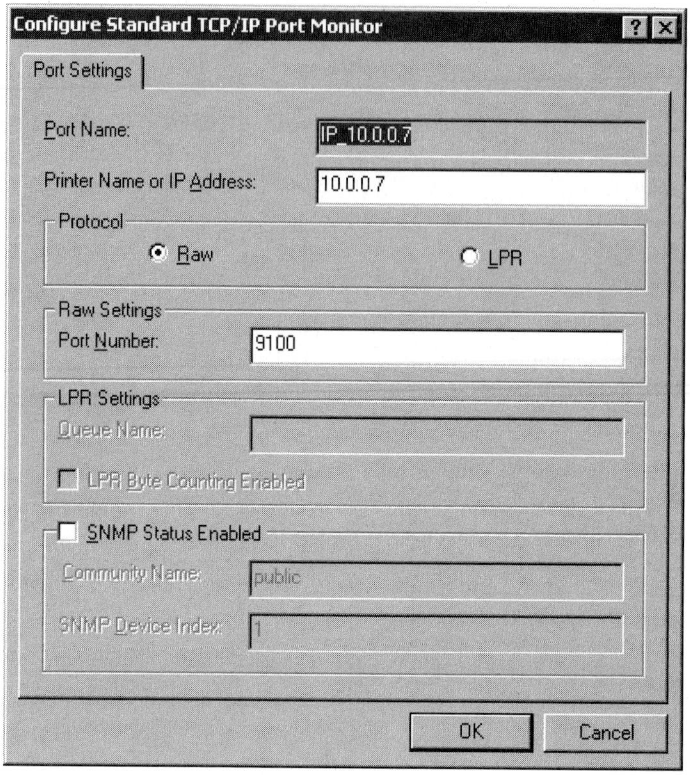

FIGURE 22.7

Configure Port Properties

and LPR settings, and you can enable the port for SNMP (Simple Network Management Protocol) if you are using SNMP in your environment.

ADVANCED

The Advanced Properties sheet, shown in Figure 22.8, allows you to configure several actions that determine how the printer behaves. First, you can allow the printer to be always available or available only during certain hours of the day, which you set by using the scroll boxes. You can also adjust the priority. The priority range is 1 to 99 with 1 being the lowest and 99 being the highest. Higher priority documents print before lower priority documents. With multiple printers connected to the same port, a printer that has a priority of 2 will always print before the printer with a priority of 1. This feature allows you to send critical documents to a certain printer with a higher priority and less critical documents to the lower priority printer.

You can use the New Driver button to configure a new driver for the printer. This action launches a wizard that helps you select the correct driver for your print device. In the middle of the window, you can adjust how documents are spooled. You can choose to spool the documents so that the pro-

four • Managing Clients and Performance

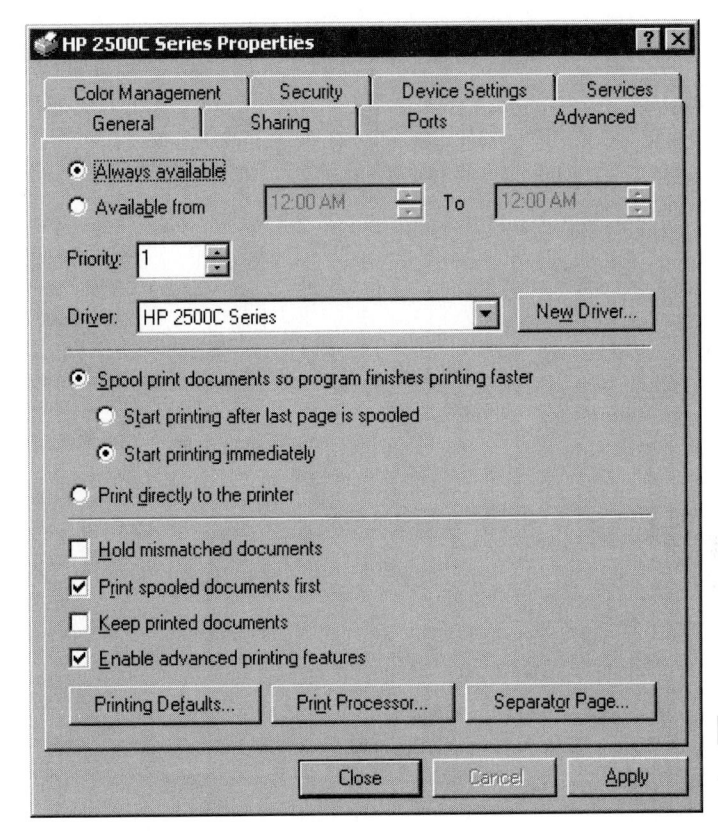

FIGURE 22.8 Advanced Properties

gram finishes printing faster, and then you can select to either start printing after the last page is spooled or start printing immediately. You can choose to print directly to the printer, but this action may slow performance.

The final check boxes at the bottom of the screen allow you to select other options, such as hold mismatched documents, print spooled documents first, keep printed documents, or enable advanced printing features.

The Printing Defaults button allows you to adjust the print layout, as you saw on the General Properties sheet. The Print Processor button allows you to select from a list a different print processor, if one is available. Finally, the Separator page button allows you to set a separator page to be printed between each document.

COLOR MANAGEMENT

The Color Management properties page allows you to associate color profiles with your printer. You have two options. First, you have an automatic setting, which is recommended. The automatic setting allows Windows to select the best color profile from a list of associated color profiles. You can also click the Manual radio button to select a color profile if desired. Click the Add button to

FIGURE 22.9
Color Management Properties

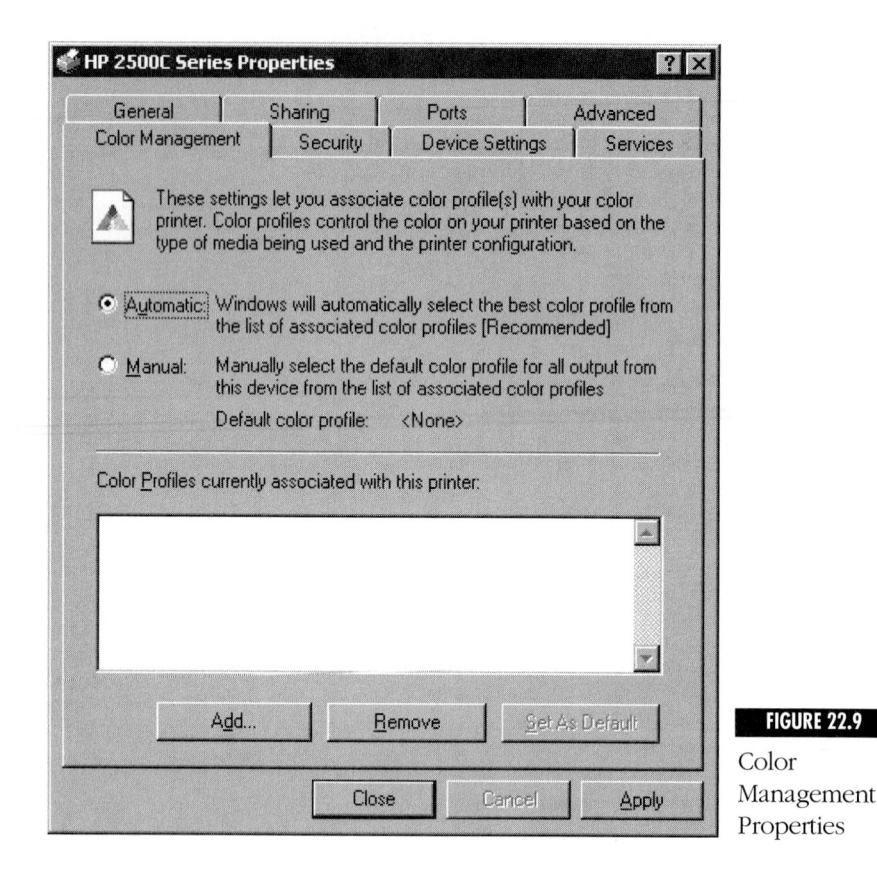

select the color profile from a list that appears. However, you should have a specific reason to manually change the color profile before doing so, because this may cause printing problems. Also, this properties sheet may not appear with all print device models.

SECURITY

The Security Properties page is the same page you have seen in other Windows 2000 components. The permissions are for print, manage printers, and manage documents. You can use the Add button to select users and groups from the Active Directory that you want to manage the printer. By default, the Everyone group has print permission. This can also be changed if you want only specific users or groups to access the printer.

DEVICE SETTINGS

The Device Settings Properties page allows you to set the form to tray assignments for the printer. By selecting each option, shown in Figure 22.10, you can use the drop-down menu to select the setting you desire.

four • Managing Clients and Performance 411

FIGURE 22.10
Device Settings

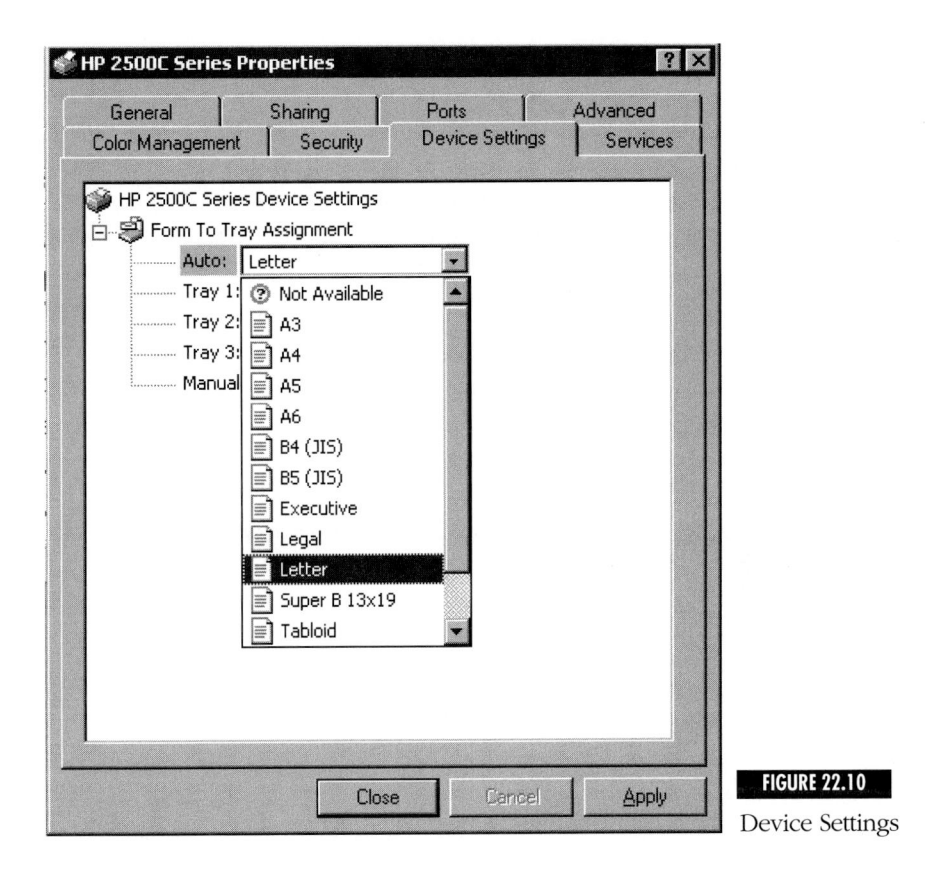

Setting Up Client Computers

In order to print to network printers, client computers must be set up to connect to the desired printer, and the correct printer drivers must be installed. For Windows 2000, Windows NT, Windows 95, and Windows 98, you only need to make a connection to the shared printer. Windows 2000 Server will automatically download the appropriate driver for the printer to the client, assuming that the appropriate print drivers are on the server. Client computers running older Microsoft operating systems must manually install the print drivers on the computer. For non-Windows clients, such as NetWare, UNIX, and Macintosh, various tasks must be performed in order for the clients to connect, as explained in the following list:

- NetWare: FPNW services must be installed on the server. FPNW is an optional component not included with Windows 2000 Server.
- UNIX: UNIX requires TCP/IP printing (also called Line Printer Daemon). This service is included in Windows 2000 but must be installed.

- Macintosh: Service for Macintosh must be installed for Macintosh clients to connect to network printers.

Clients can connect to network printers in a variety of ways. First, clients can use the Add Printer Wizard and select the network printer they want to install. Client Computers running Windows 2000 can use the Active Directory to find the desired printer, UNC naming convention, or they can simply browse the network. Windows 2000 clients can also use a Web browser by typing http://*server_name*/printers. Clients running Windows NT 4.0, Windows 95, or Windows 98 can connect to a printer using the UNC naming convention or the Add Printer Wizard. Clients running older Microsoft operating systems can use the Print Manager feature or the Net Use command line feature to connect.

Printing to Macintosh and UNIX Servers

In Windows 2000, you can now print to Macintosh and UNIX servers. In order to use this feature, you need to install the service(s) by using Add/Remove Programs in Control Panel, click Add/Remove Windows Components, double-clicking Other Network File and Print Services, and then selecting either Print Services for Macintosh or Print Services for UNIX, or both.

Once the Print Services for Macintosh is installed, you can use the Add New Printer Wizard in the Printers folder. Select to add a new local printer, click Next, and then click the create new port button and select AppleTalk Printing Devices. The wizard will search for AppleTalk printing devices on the network and allow you to install the printer. Then, Windows clients can print to the Macintosh server.

The same process applies to UNIX. Instead of selecting the AppleTalk Printing Device for the new port, configure a TCP/IP port for the connection to the UNIX server to which the printer is attached to.

Summary

Windows 2000 provides a full range of printing features that make network printing easier to manage and easier for clients to use. Client computers using Windows 2000 have the additional options of finding the printers they want to use in the Active Directory and using a Web browser. Windows 2000 Server also supports printing over the Internet. A wide variety of drivers and support for various printer vendors makes the installation, configuration, and management of network printers easier and more flexible than in previous versions of Windows.

TWENTY-THREE

Auditing

As an administrator, once you have Windows 2000 Server up and running the way you want, a lot of your time is spent monitoring the server as well as clients. This monitoring process, called auditing, allows you to track the activities of your users as well as the events that occur on the server. Auditing can help you make decisions about the needs of your network and help you solve certain problems your environment may be experiencing. This chapter shows you how to set up auditing on your Windows 2000 Server so that the auditing process is effective and returns the kind of information that will be helpful to you.

Auditing in Windows 2000

In order for auditing to be effective in Windows 2000, you create an audit policy that returns the information to you that you need. The audit policy defines what information is written to the Windows 2000 Security log, which allows you to view the events that you want to track. These events can be any number of things, such as failed logon attempts, changes in group memberships, changes in security settings, and even actions by certain users that you specify. By default, auditing is turned off in Windows 2000, and once you turn it on, you will have to decide which computers on the network you want to audit, and what kind of information about those computers you want returned to you. You can audit events separately on each computer.

Before creating an auditing policy, you will need to determine which events you want to audit for particular computers or users. The best bet is to audit events that pertain to sensitive information or security. Also, it is a good idea to audit resource access by the Everyone group so that you audit anyone who logs on to the network.

Configuring Auditing

Audit policies are based on the role of the computer on the network. For member or standalone servers or computers running Windows 2000 Professional, you create an audit policy for each individual computer. For domain controllers, an audit policy is set for all domain controllers in the domain. You then configure a group policy for the domain so that it applies to all domain controllers. In order to set up auditing, you must have Manage Auditing and Security log user rights for the computer where you want to configure an audit policy or examine the audit log. The Administrators group has these rights by default.

SETTING AN AUDIT POLICY

To set an audit policy on a computer that is not a domain controller, open the MMC and Add the Group Policy Snap-in. Expand the console tree to

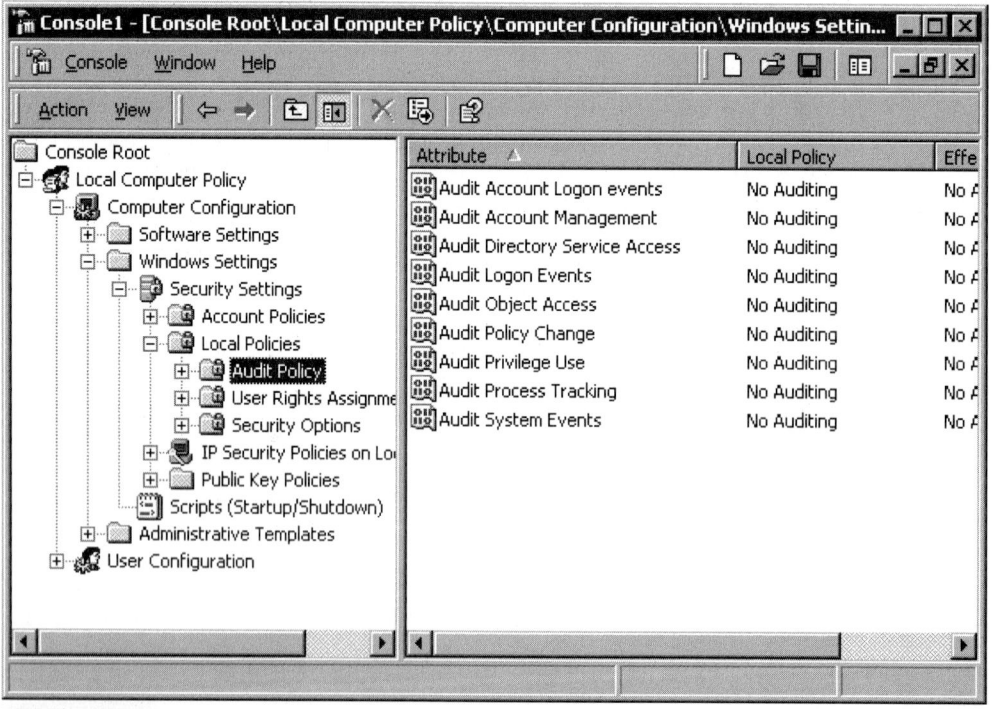

FIGURE 23.1 Audit Policy

four • Managing Clients and Performance   **415**

Local Computer Policy → Computer Configuration → Windows Settings → Security Settings → Local Policies → Audit Policy, as shown in Figure 23.1.

You can see in the details pane the available policy components that you can choose to audit. Table 23.1 gives you an overview of each policy component.

TABLE 23.1 Auditing Components

Event	Description
Account Logon	Records either successful or failed logon attempts (or both)
Account Management	Records changes, creations, or deletions of user or group accounts. Also, changes are recorded if an account is renamed, disabled, enabled, or a password is reset.
Directory Services Access	Records access to Active Directory objects. You configure in the Active Directory which objects are audited.
Logon Events	Records user logon or log off.
Object Access	Records if a user gains access to a file, folder, or printer. You configure which files, folders, and printers you want audited.
Policy Change	Records changes made to a user's security options, user rights, and audit policies.
Privilege Use	Records an action by the user to the local system, such as changing the system date.
Process Tracking	Records when a program performs an action. This feature is useful for programmers who want to audit the events of a program operation.
System Events	Records when an event occurs that affects Windows 2000 security or the security.

To set the audit policy, double-click on each attribute in the console tree details pane. As you can see in Figure 23.1, by default, each attribute is not configured. Once you double-click on an attribute, a dialog box appears, shown in Figure 23.2, that allows you to configure the attribute for auditing. By default, the Exclude this setting from configuration check box is selected. If you clear the check box, you can select to audit either successful attempts,

FIGURE 23.2
Audit Account Logon Events

audit failed attempts, or both. For example, in the Audit Account Logon Events attribute, you may want to audit only failed attempts so that the security log is not written to every time a user logs on to the network.

Once you configure each attribute, the MMC details pane will provide you with a template setting for each attribute according to the way you configured it. The setting will state either "Not Configured", "Failure", "Success", or "Success, Failure," as shown in Figure 23.3.

Once you have configured the attributes as desired, the audit policy will become active once you restart your server, or you may type secedit/RefreshPolicy/MACHINE_POLICY at the command prompt and press Enter. If you do not manually refresh your policy settings by using one of these two methods, it will start automatically when policy propagation occurs on your server, which happens every eight hours by default.

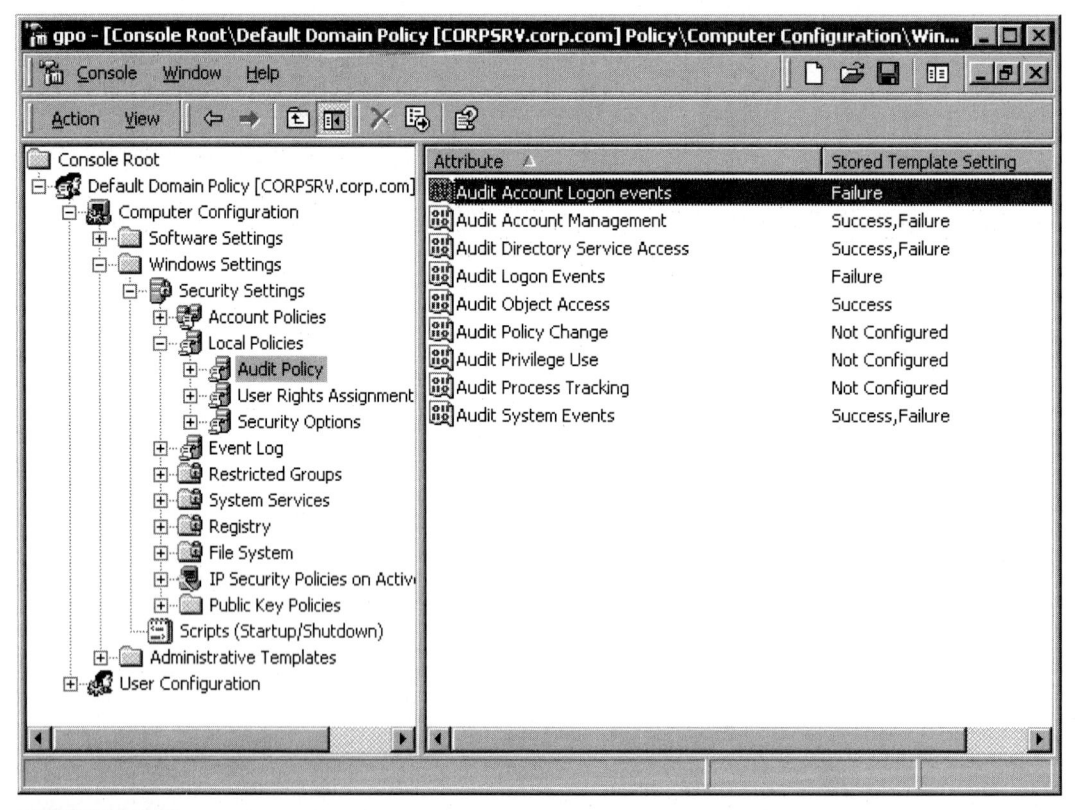

FIGURE 23.3 Stored Template Settings

Auditing File and Folder Access

You can set up auditing on NTFS partitions so that you can see who is accessing which files and folders. This is useful to determine what files and folders are mostly accessed by users, and it can help you determine whether security breaches are occurring. In order to audit file and folder access, you must configure the Audit Object Access in your audit policy.

To configure a specific file or folder for auditing, follow these steps:

1. For the file or folder you want to audit, right-click on the file or folder and click Properties.
2. Click the Security tab, and then click the Advanced button. The Access Control Settings window appears.
3. Click the Auditing tab.
4. Click the Add button, then select the user(s) whose files or folders you wish to audit and click OK.

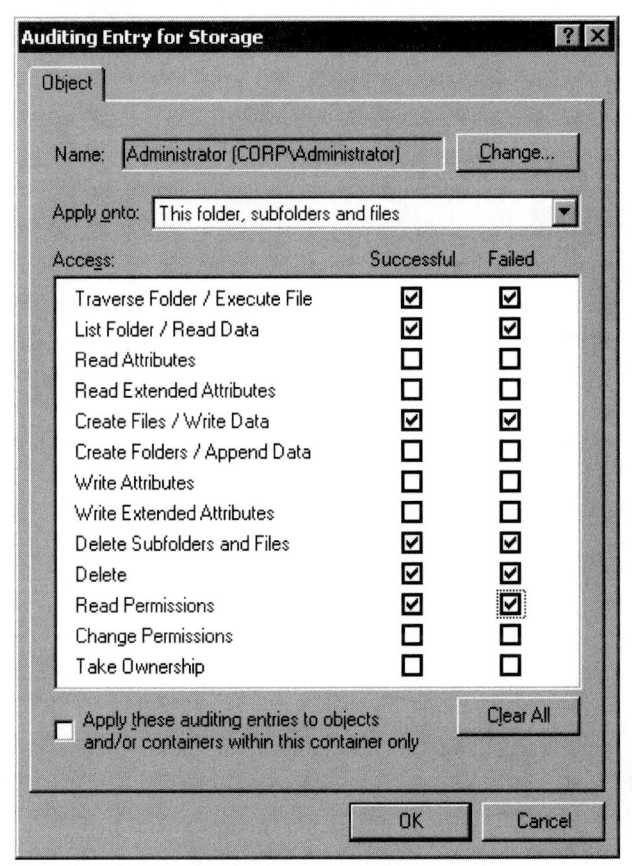

FIGURE 23.4
Auditing Entry Dialog Box

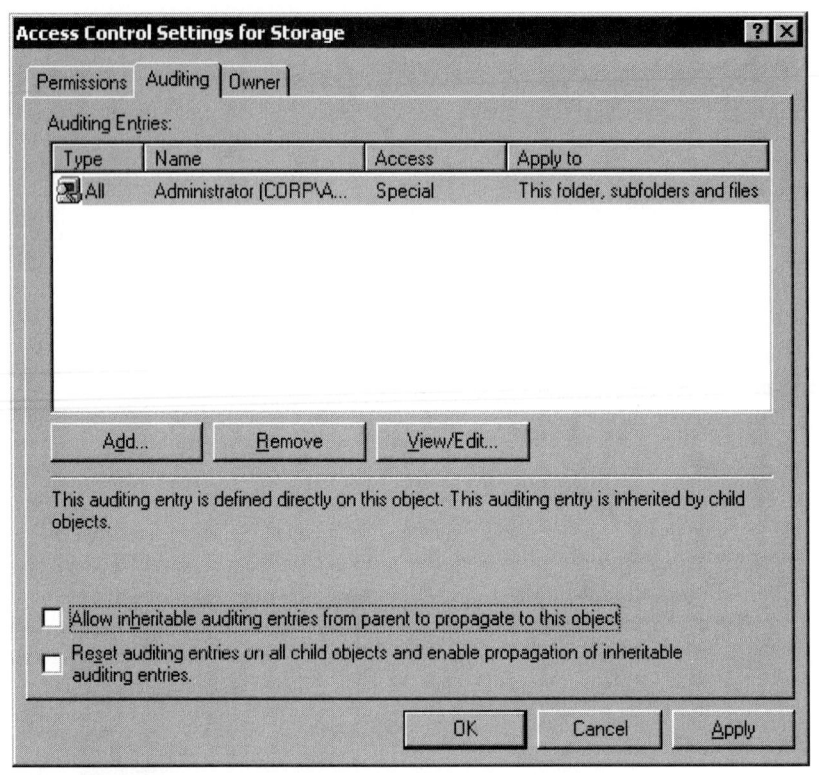

FIGURE 23.5 Auditing Properties

5. The Auditing Entry dialog box appears, shown in Figure 23.4. Select either the Successful check box or the Failed check boxes for the events that you want to audit for the file or folder. You can also click the Apply these auditing entries to objects and/or containers within this container only if you wish to limit the auditing to the specific folder. Click OK when you are done.
6. By default, the auditing changes made to a parent folder apply to all child folders and all files in the child folders. To change this, clear the Allow inheritable auditing entries from parent to propagate to this object check box, as shown in Figure 23.5.
7. Click OK.

Auditing Access to Active Directory Objects

Just as you can audit access to files and folders, you can audit objects in the Active Directory. This information tells you who is accessing which Active Directory object. As with file and folder access, you must set the audit policy for specific objects, such as OUs, user, computers, printers, and so forth. In order to use Active Directory object auditing, you must enable auditing of Directory Service in your auditing policy.

To enable auditing of Active Directory objects, follow these steps:

1. Click Start ➤ Programs ➤ Administrative Tools ➤ Active Directory Users and Computers.
2. Right-click on the Object you want to audit, click Properties, and then click on the Security tab.
3. Click the Advanced button; then click the Auditing tab. Click Add.
4. Select the user(s) that you want to audit for this object and click OK.
5. On the Auditing Entry window that appears, make your selections by using the Successful or Failed check boxes for the entries. Click OK.

Auditing Printer Access

As with files, folders, and Active Directory objects, you can audit printer access by accessing the printer's properties sheet, clicking the Security tab, clicking the Advanced button, clicking the Auditing tab, and add the user

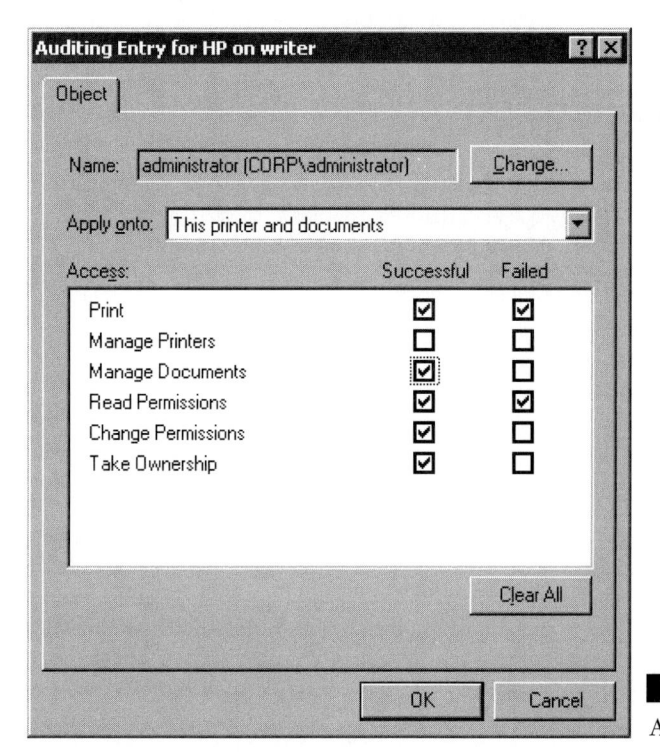

FIGURE 23.6

Auditing Entry

who will audit the printer. This Action provides you with an Auditing Entry dialog box, shown in Figure 23.6.

Click the Successful or Failed check boxes to configure the audit as desired. Click OK.

Configuring Logs

Audit events, as well as other events in Windows 2000, are stored in various logs that you can view through Event Viewer. There are three major logs: application, security, and system. The Application log contains warnings, errors, and general information that programs generate. The Security log contains information about auditing events, and the System log contains warnings, errors, and general information that the server generates about operations. Other logs, such as DNS and Directory Service may be present,

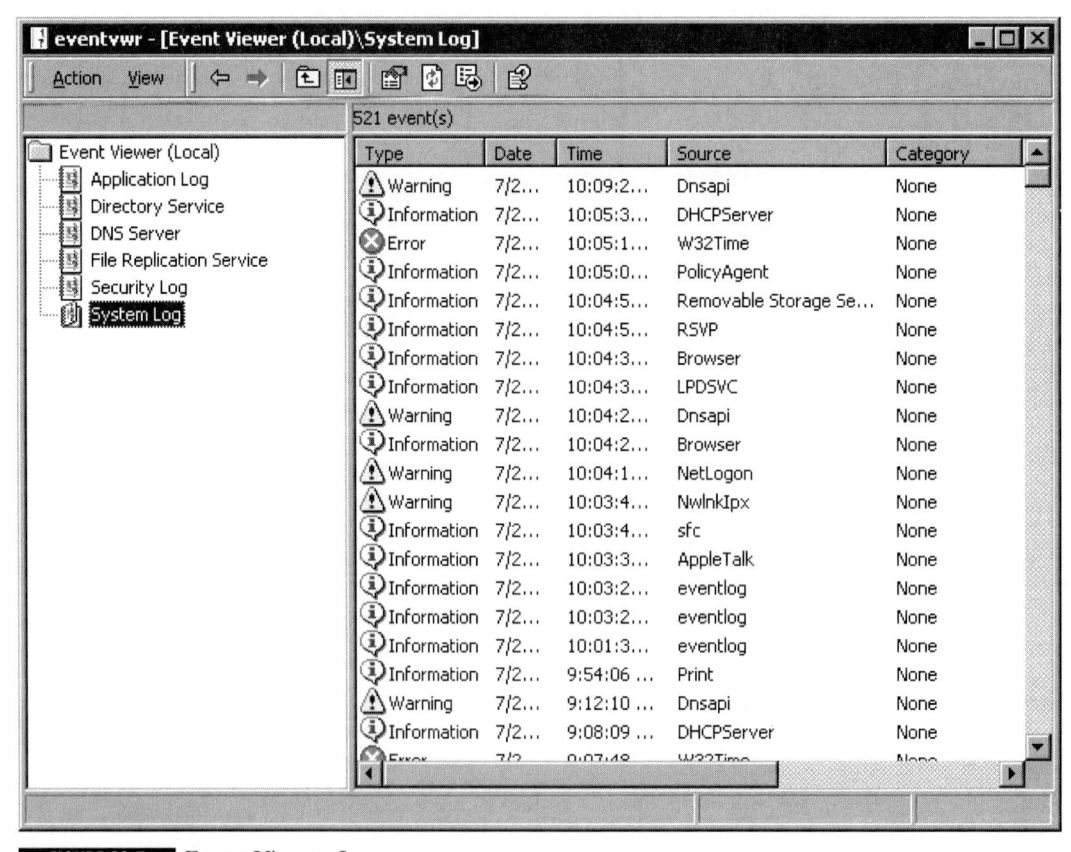

FIGURE 23.7 Event Viewer Logs

four • Managing Clients and Performance **421**

depending on your server's configuration. In Event Viewer, you can click on each log to view the log contents, as shown in Figure 23.7, and you can double-click an entry to read more about it.

Event Viewer automatically displays all events for the given log. To make the log easier to read to and find the information you want, you can filter the log. Select the log you want to filter, then click View ➤ Filter. This action opens the Filter Properties for the log, shown in Figure 23.8. You have a number of ways to filter events. First, you can filter events by the dates by using the drop-down dialog boxes and changing the To and From filter dates. This will give all of the events for the specified time period. Next, you can use the Types check boxes to filter the types of events you want to view. You can choose from information, warning, error, success audit, or failure audit.

You can also find specific events by clicking View ➤ Find. The Find window, as shown in Figure 23.9, allows you to specify the type of event that you want to find. You can also adjust the Up or Down radio buttons to tell Event Viewer which direction in the entry list to search.

Finally, you can access the Properties sheet for each log by right-clicking on it. On the General tab, shown in Figure 23.10, you can adjust the

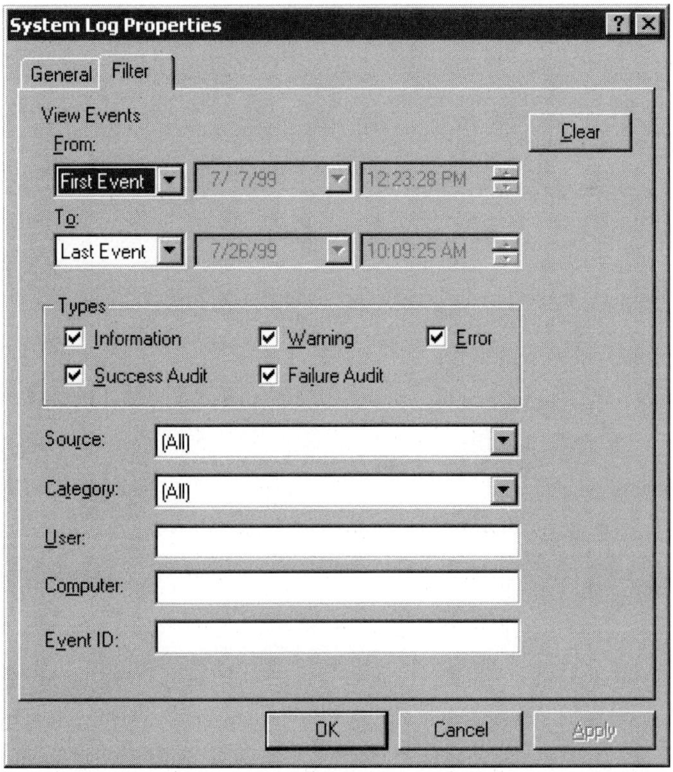

FIGURE 23.8

Filter Properties

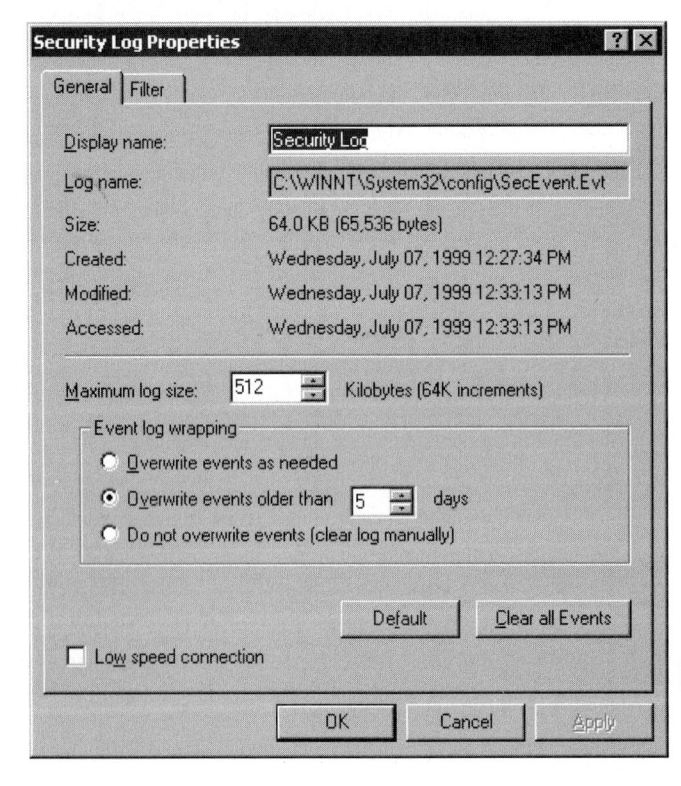

FIGURE 23.9
Find Event

FIGURE 23.10
General Properties

maximum log size, and you can choose what to do when the log becomes full. By default, the maximum log is 512 K; use the dialog box to change this default setting if desired. In the Event Log Wrapping section, you can choose to overwrite events as needed, overwrite events older than X days, or not to overwrite events. If you choose not to overwrite events, you must clear the log manually. Windows 2000 will stop writing events once the log becomes full.

Summary

Windows 2000 allows you to audit various events that occur on the server. You can use the audit policy, which is created in the Group Policy snap-in, to audit a variety of events, such as access to objects and even the Active Directory. The Windows 2000 Event Viewer allows you to examine and manipulate the various logs to meet your auditing needs so that you can view how users are accessing resources. Auditing is an important management feature to help you monitor and control your Windows 2000 network.

TWENTY-FOUR

Performance Monitor and Network Monitor

As you have seen throughout this book, Windows 2000 Server provides you with many administrative tools and wizards to make your work as a systems administrator easier and more manageable. Beside the tools and wizards to help you accomplish various configuration tasks, Windows 2000 includes Performance Monitor and Network Monitor to help you track the performance of your server as well as the network connection. This chapter shows you how to set up and use these tools in Windows 2000.

Performance Monitor

As in Windows NT 4.0, Performance Monitor continues to be an important part of Windows 2000. Performance Monitor is used to check your system's performance (or the performance of another system) by examining system components such as the processor, RAM, etc. You can access Performance Monitor by clicking Start ➤ Programs ➤ Administrative Tools ➤ Performance. The Performance Monitor MMC snap-in opens, as shown in Figure 24.1.

The interface for Performance Monitor is slightly different in Windows 2000 Server from what it was in Windows NT Server, but it works in the same manner. The following sections show you how to configure and use Performance Monitor.

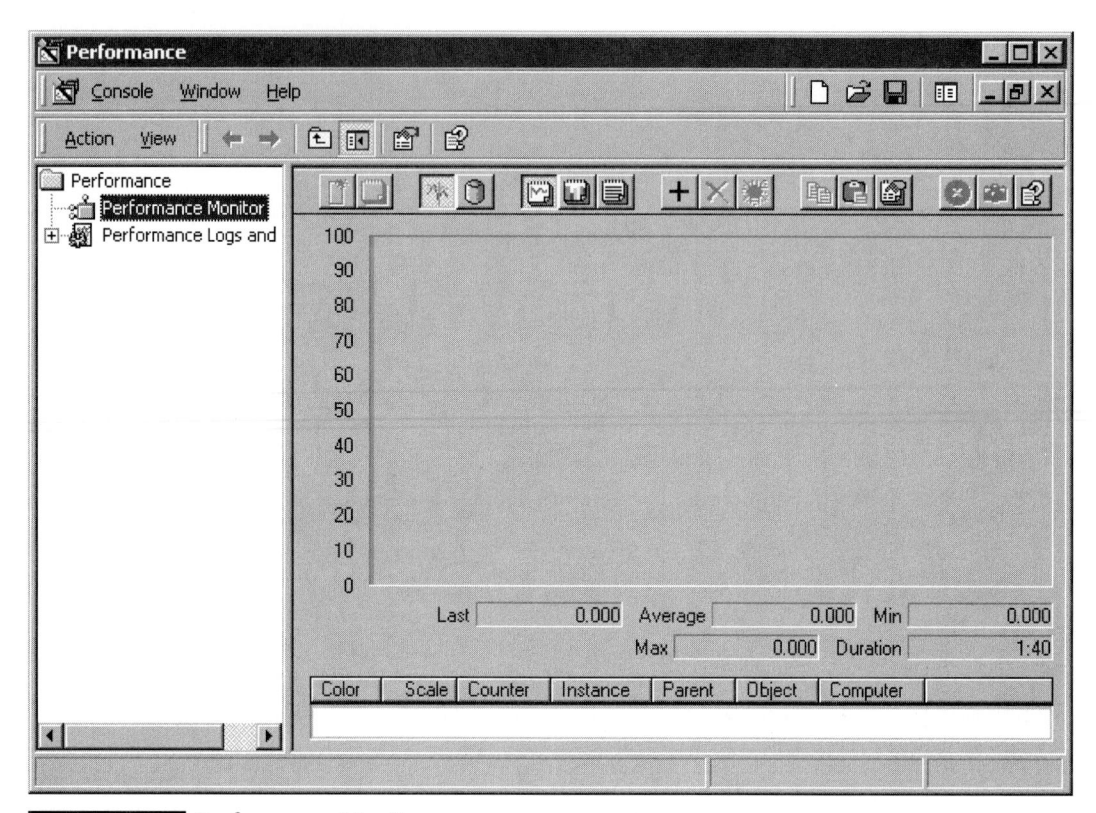

FIGURE 24.1 Performance Monitor

Using Counters

Counters are Performance Monitor components that track information about individual system components and report information back to you about that component's performance. You add the counters you want to track and view information about as needed. To add a counter, follow these steps:

In Performance Monitor, click the Add Counter button in the details pane, or simply right-click on the graph area and click Add Counters.

The Add Counters window appears, shown in Figure 24.2. You can select which counters for which computer you want to add by clicking either the Use local computer counters or Select counters from this computer and using the drop-down list. On the Performance object drop-down menu, click the type of object you want, such as Processor, System, TCP, PhysicalDisk, and so forth.

In the Performance Counters dialog box, select the counter you want and click Add. Continue this process to select all counters you want. When you are done, click Close. For each counter, you can also click the Explain button to learn more about the counter.

four • Managing Clients and Performance **427**

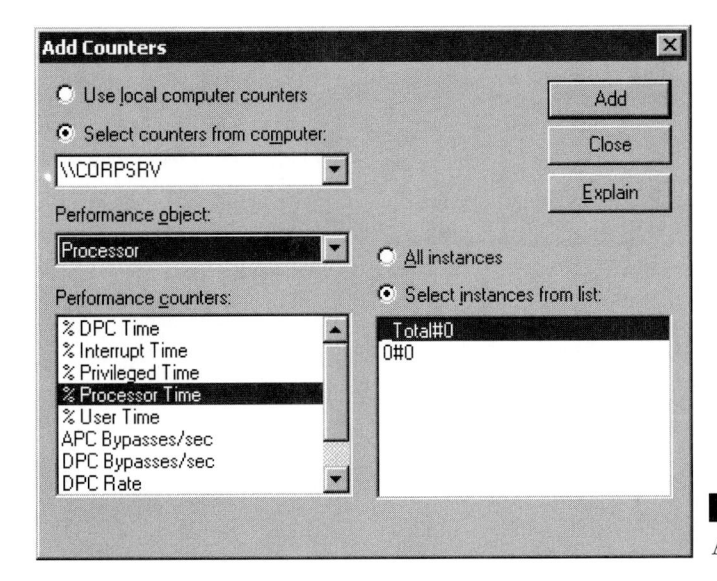

FIGURE 24.2
Add Counters

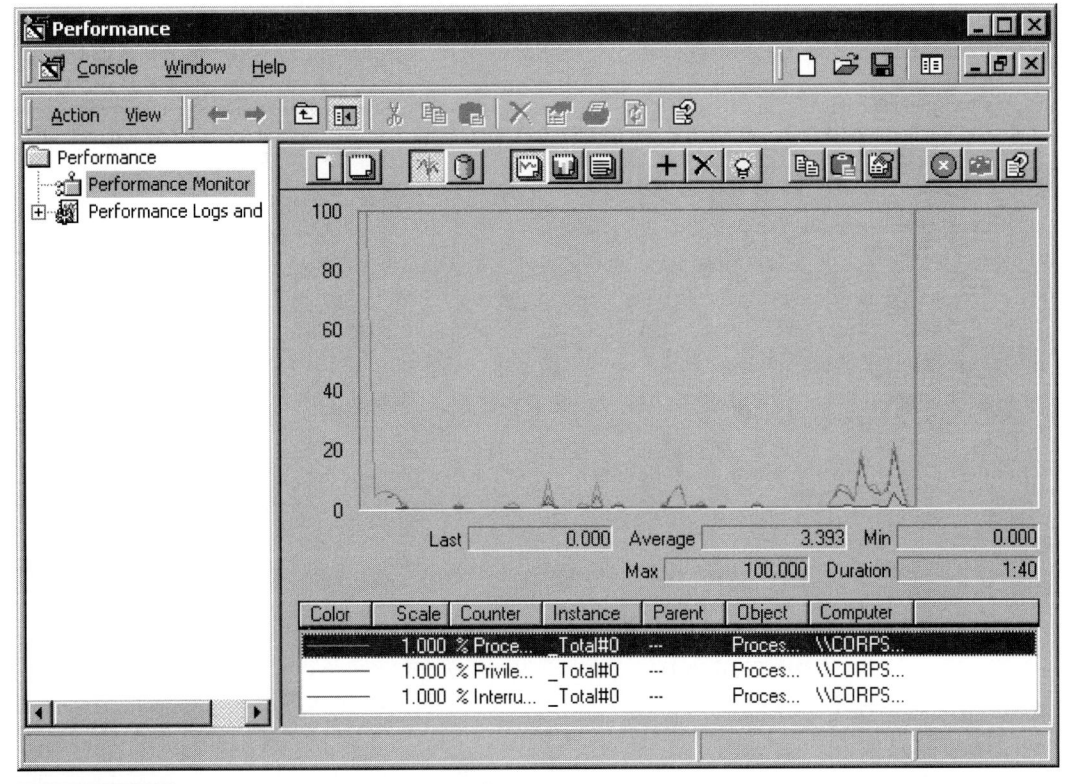

FIGURE 24.3 Performance Monitor Graph

Performance Monitor displays each counter in a different color and begins tracking the performance of the counter in the graph window, shown in Figure 24.3.

Once you have counters running Performance Monitor, you can easily delete any counter you choose by selecting the counter at the bottom of the details pane and clicking the Delete button (X) on the toolbar.

Because there are many counters for each object, it is often difficult to determine which counter should be used for a particular problem. Table 24.1 lists some of the major problems you might experience and tells you which counter you should use in Performance Monitor.

TABLE 24.1 Common Performance Problems and Counters that should be used.

Problem	Counters that should be used
Slow Processor Speed	Processor\ Interrupts/sec, Processor\ % Processor Time, Process\ % Processor Time, System\ Processor Queue Length
Memory Problems	Memory\ Available Bytes, Memory\ Pages/sec
Slow Network Performance	Network Interface\ Bytes Total/sec, Network Interface\ Bytes Sent/sec, Network Interface\ Bytes Received/sec, Server\ bytes total/sec, Server\ Bytes Received/sec, Server\ Bytes Sent/sec, Network Segment\ % Network Utilization
Printer Problems	Print Queue\ Bytes Printed/sec, Print Queue\ Job Errors

Performance Monitor Properties

You can configure the properties for a Performance Monitor graph. This feature allows you to view, save, and use the performance monitor in a way that is beneficial to you. You can access the graph's properties by right-clicking on the graph in the details pane and clicking Properties. The following sections tell you what you can do on each page.

GENERAL

On the General Properties page, shown in Figure 24.4, you can configure several options. First, you can select the Type of display to view, such as a graph, histogram, or a report. You can use the check boxes to add or remove the legend, value bar, or toolbar. On Appearance, you can use the dropdown menu to select either flat or 3D appearance, and you can also apply a Border style using the dropdown menu if desired. You can change the Report value type from default to current, average, minimum, or maximum by clicking the desired radio button, and finally, you can adjust the Update time as desired.

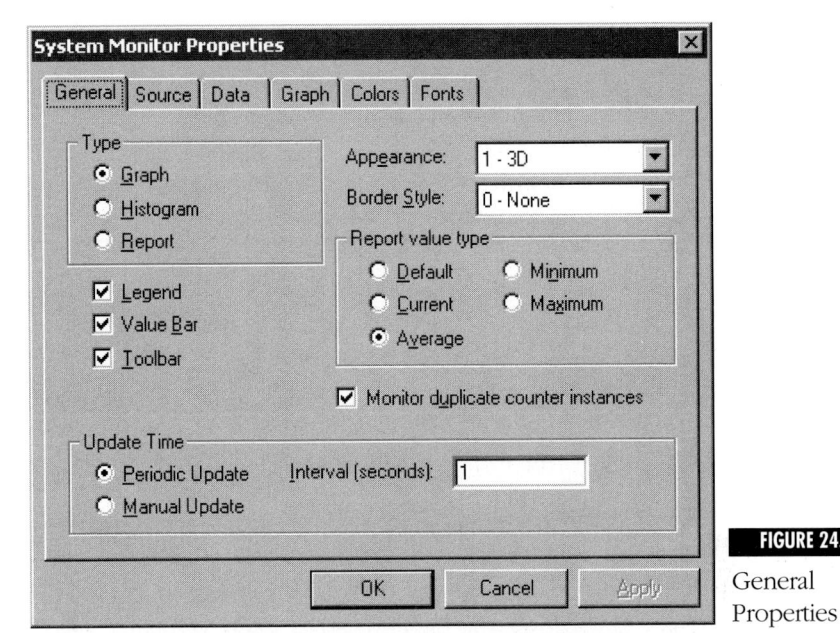

FIGURE 24.4
General Properties

FIGURE 24.5
Source Properties

SOURCE

You can choose the data source for the performance chart by using the Source Properties page, shown in Figure 24.5. You have the option of using the current activity or clicking log file to view a saved log file. If you choose to view a log file, you can use the Time Range section to select a range of time you wish to view from the log file.

DATA

The Data Properties sheet, shown in Figure 24.6, provides you with a list of current counters that are active. You can use the Add button to add more counters or the Delete button to remove counters. Also, you can adjust the color of the counter and graph bar width as desired by using the drop-down boxes.

GRAPH

The Graph Properties sheet allows you to adjust how you want to view the graph. You can provide a title for the graph, a Y-axis label, and you can choose to view either a vertical or horizontal grid. Also, you can adjust the graph scale as desired.

COLORS AND FONTS

The Colors Properties sheet and the Fonts Properties sheet both allow you to adjust the graph colors and fonts as desired.

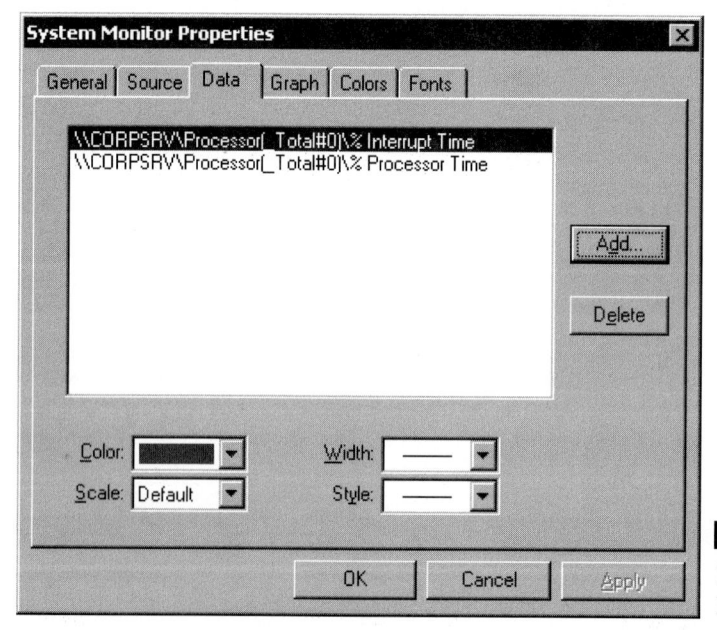

FIGURE 24.6 Data Properties

Performance Logs and Alerts

Windows 2000 Performance Monitor logs allow you to record data about the system (or a remote system's) activity. You can configure logging to occur on either an automatic or manual basis, or even on a schedule. Log counters can be saved as HTML files and later viewed with any Web browser. You can also set alerts on counters so that a particular action happens when that counter's performance falls too low. An alert can be configured to send a message, run a program, or even start a log. The following sections show you how to use logs and alerts.

CONFIGURING COUNTER LOGS

To configure a new counter log, follow these steps:

1. In Performance Monitor, click Performance Logs and Alerts in the left pane.
2. Click Counter Logs. Any existing logs appear in the details pane. A green icon tells you that the log is running while a red icon tells you that the log has stopped.

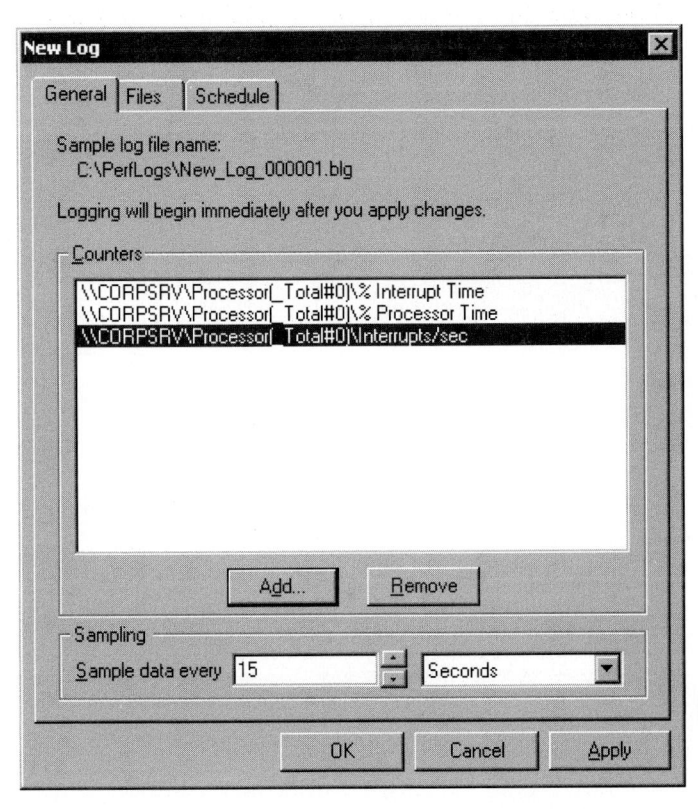

FIGURE 24.7 General Properties Page

3. In the details pane, right-click on the blank window, point to New, then click Create New Log Settings. If you wanted to create a counter log from saved data, you would choose Create log settings from...

4. A dialog box appears asking you for the name of the New Log settings. Type a name and click OK.

5. The properties sheets for the log appear. On the General Properties page, as shown in Figure 24.7, click the Add button to add new counters to the log. By default, data is sampled every 15 seconds, but you can change this default by adjusting the dropdown boxes.

6. Click on the Files Properties page, as shown in Figure 24.8. Use the dropdown menu to adjust the type of log file you want to create. You have the choices of either text file (CSV), text file (TSV), binary file, or binary circular file. Next, you can use the radio buttons to allow the log to grow to maximum size or you can specify the size limit of the log. Finally, you can adjust the log file naming convention and default storage location if needed.

7. Click the Schedule Properties page, shown in Figure 24.9. You can adjust the radio buttons to either manually start the log or allow the

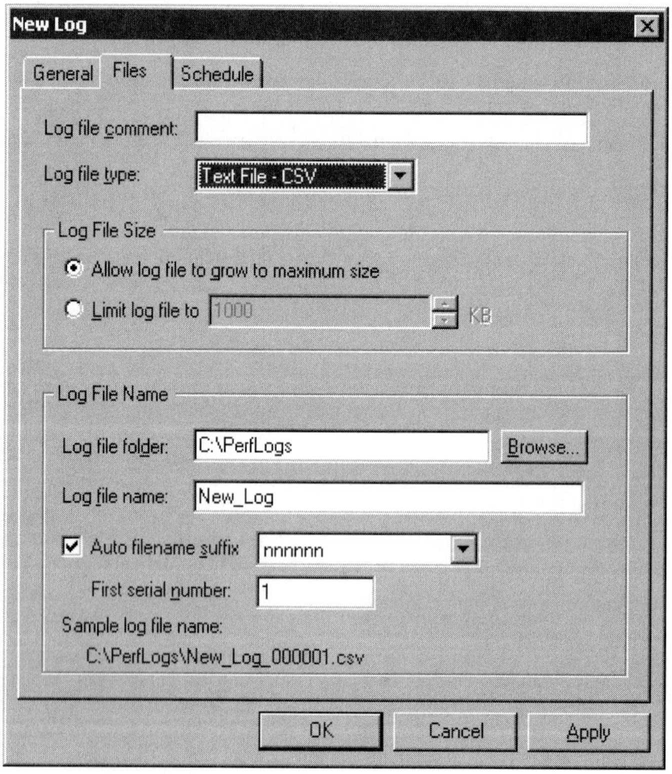

FIGURE 24.8

Files Properties Page

four • Managing Clients and Performance **433**

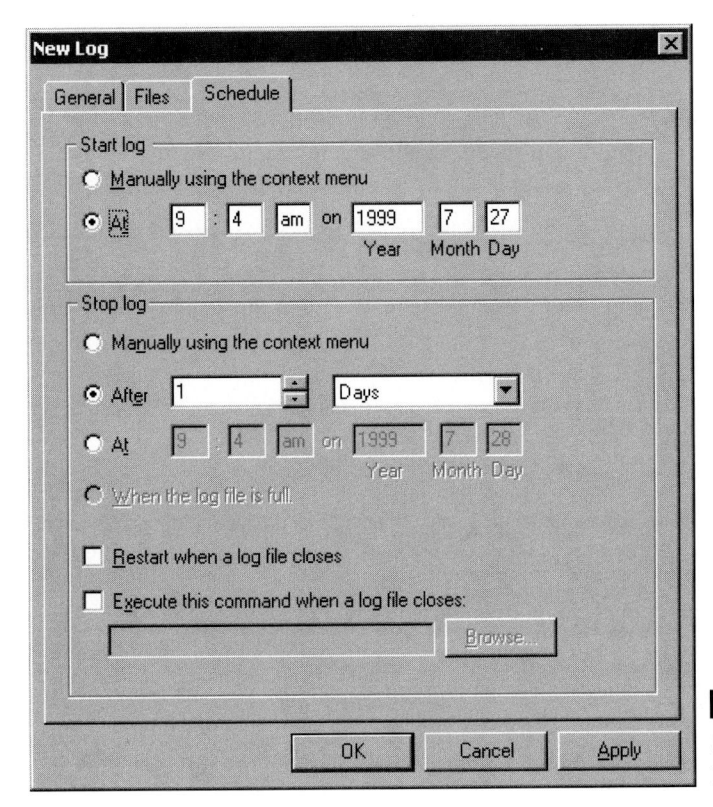

FIGURE 24.9 Schedule Properties Page

log to start at the specified time. Likewise, you can use the radio buttons to stop the log as desired.

8. Click OK when you are done.

CONFIGURING PERFORMANCE ALERTS

To create a performance alert, follow these steps:

1. In Performance Monitor, click Performance Logs and Alerts in the left pane.
2. Click Alerts. Any existing alerts appear in the details pane. A green icon tells you that the alert is running while a red icon tells you that the alert has stopped.
3. In the details pane, right-click on the blank window, point to New, and then click Create New Alert Settings. If you wanted to create an alert from saved data, you would choose Create alert settings from…

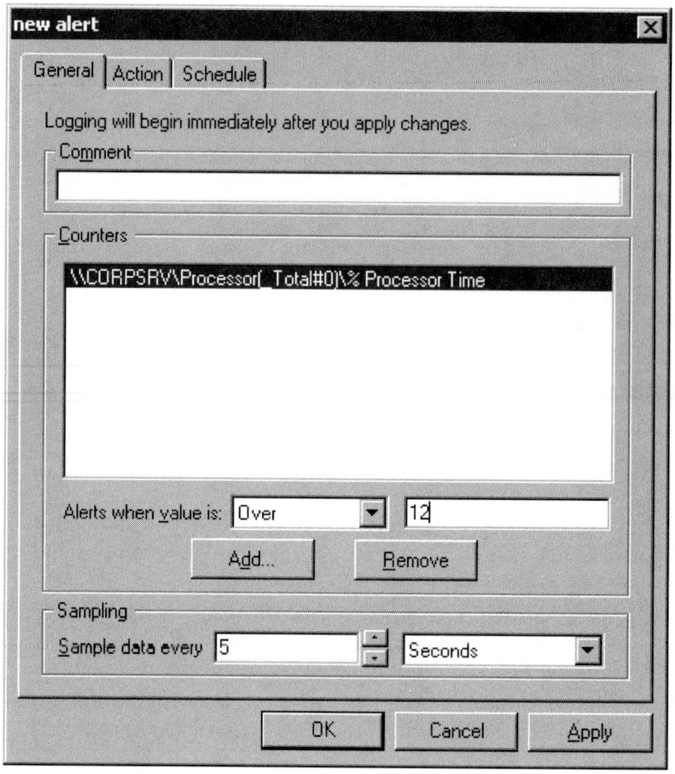

FIGURE 24.10 General Properties Page

4. A dialog box appears asking you for the name of the New Alert settings. Type a name and click OK.
5. The Alert Properties sheets appear. On the General Property sheet, shown in Figure 24.10, you can add counters for which you want to set up an alert. After you add the counter(s), use the dropdown button to change the alert value to either Over or Under, and then enter a number in the dialog box. Also, you can adjust the data sampling interval if desired.
6. On the Action Properties page, shown in Figure 24.11, you select how you want the system to handle the alert. Use the check boxes to select to either log an entry in the application event log, send a network message to, or execute the command file.
7. On the Schedule Properties sheet, you configure the schedule to start and stop the log as desired. This is the same window as in Figure 24.9.
8. Click OK when you are done.

FIGURE 24.11 Action Properties

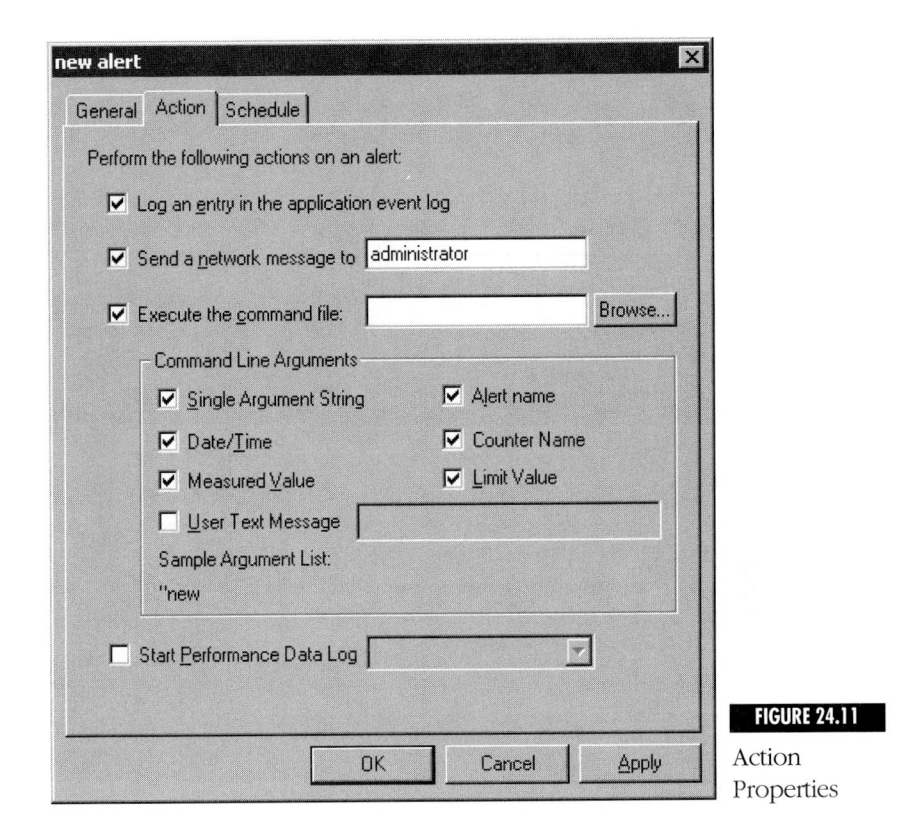

Network Monitor

Just as you use Performance Monitor to examine the performance of your server, you can use Network Monitor to examine the performance of your network. Network Monitor is used to help you track down network problems, such as network bottlenecks and transmission errors. Network Monitor captures data frames that are received from the network. You can save captured frames from the network and have them analyzed by network analysts. Also, you can use Microsoft's Systems Management Server (SMS) to capture frames sent to and from all computers on a network segment so that you can run a detailed analysis of your network. The Network Monitor included in Windows 2000 Server is a scaled-down version of the Network Monitor included with SMS.

Installing Network Monitor

You install Network Monitor by using the Add/Remove Windows Components in Add/Remove Programs in Control Panel. Once this is done, you will need to install the Network Monitor driver. To perform this action, follow these steps:

1. Right-click My Network Places and click Properties.
2. Right-click Local Area Connection and click Properties.
3. Click the Install button. In the Select Network Component Type window, select Protocol, and then click Add.
4. Select Network Monitor Driver in the window provided and click OK. You may be prompted for your Windows 2000 Server installation files.

Using Network Monitor

Once Network Monitor is installed, you can access it from Start → Programs → Administrative Tools → Network Monitor. Network Monitor works by capturing data frames from the network. To start a capture, click on the Capture menu and click Start. Network Monitor will begin capturing the data, as you can see in Figure 24.12.

The capture gives you information such as the type of transmissions that are taking place, the frames being sent, the number of broadcast mes-

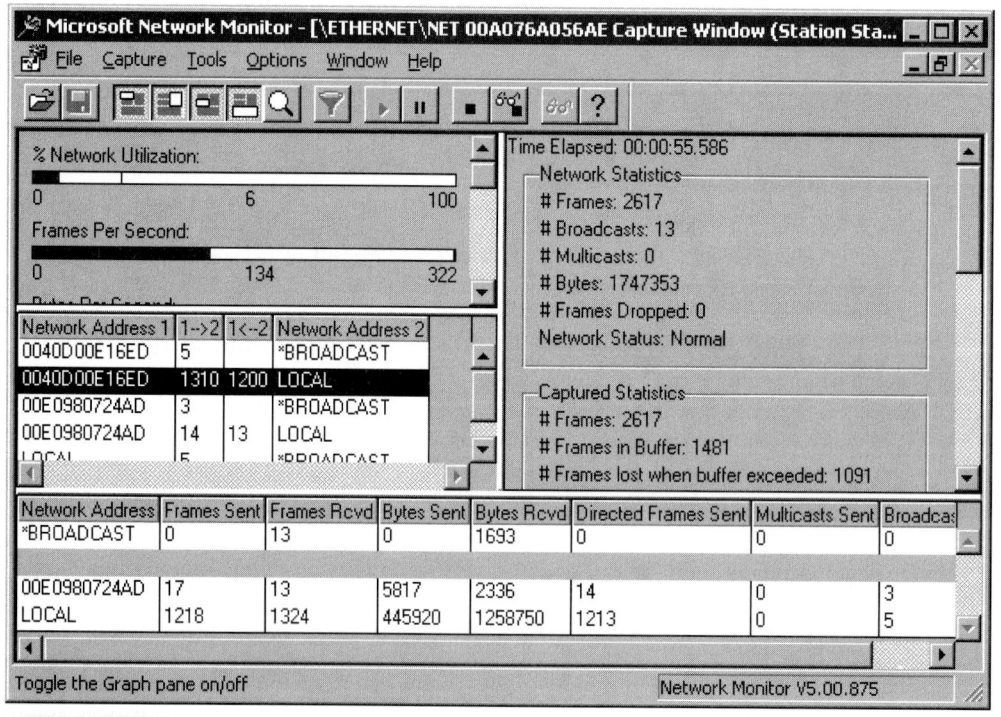

FIGURE 24.12 Network Monitor Data Capture

four • Managing Clients and Performance   **437**

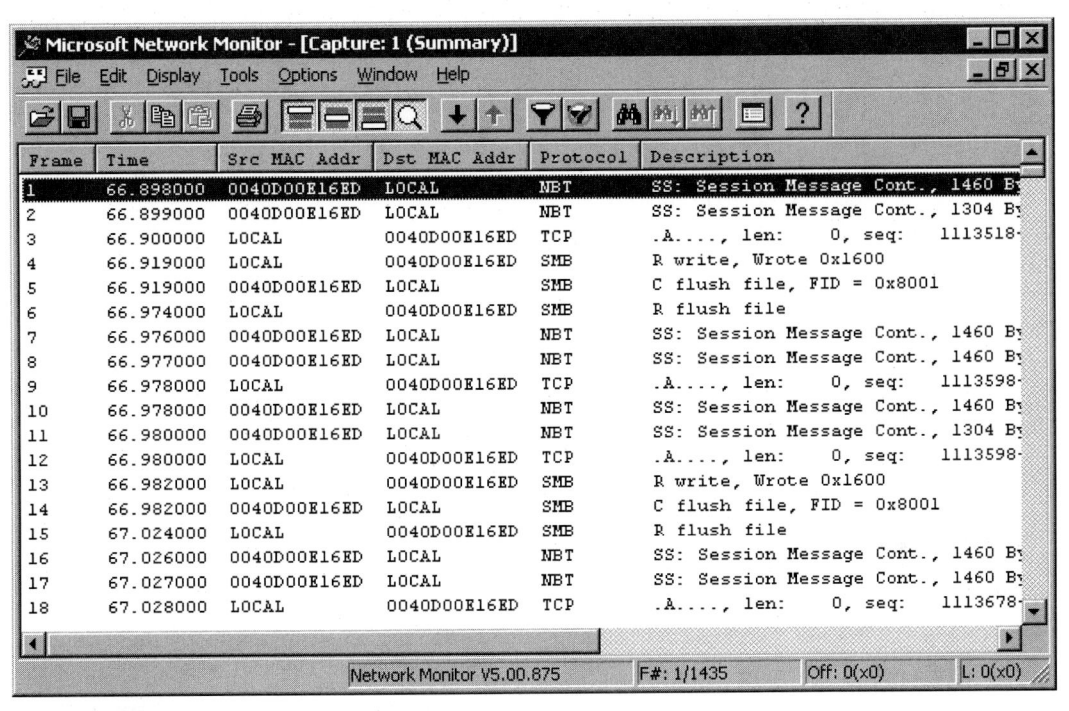

FIGURE 24.13 Capture Data Summary

sages, the frames dropped, etc. Once you capture the data for a period of time, you use the Capture menu to stop the capture. On the Capture menu, you can either use stop and view or you can simply stop the capture, and then click Display Captured Data. This feature provides you with a summary window of the network communication that includes the frame, time, the sender's MAC address, the destination MAC address, the protocol used, and a description, as shown in Figure 24.13.

You can also use the capture menu to configure filters and triggers for data capture. This feature allows you to control what kind of data frames are captured. The Tools menu also lists several tools, but most of them are available only with the full version of Network Monitor with SMS. For more information about Network Monitor, including filters and triggers, refer to the resource kit on your Windows 2000 Server CD-ROM.

Summary

Performance Monitor and Network Monitor are effective tools to help you solve performance problems with your server and your network.

Performance Monitor allows you to set up performance counters to view the performance of various system components. With Network Monitor, you can capture data frames and examine the network transmissions. The full version of Network Monitor is available with SMS and can capture all network traffic on a subnet.

INDEX

Accessories, 40
   accessibility features, 41
   address book, 43
   Communications Menu, 41
   Synchronize, 43
   System Tools, 41-42, 92
   Windows Explorer, 43
ACL (Access Control List) *see* Active Directory
Active Directory, 6-7
   Access Control List (ACL), 157, 360
   Administrative Tools, 51-52, 164
      Domains and Trusts, 52, 168-172
      Schema, 52, 178
      Sites and Services, 52, 172-178
      Users and Computers, 52, 164-168
   auditing, 418-419
   contacts, 168
   Design, 159-161
      extensible schema, 156, 159-160
      global catalog, 7, 52, 159
      namespace, 160
      naming conventions, 160-161
   Directory Service Migration Tool, 280-281
   DNS integration/standard naming, 10, 156, 216
   and Domain Controllers, 24
   hierarchy structure, 6
   HTTP, 156
   Installation, 161-164
      from the command line, 161
      using Administrative Tools, 161-164
   integration with Remote Access, 251
   and Intellimirror, 378
   LDAP, 156
   Macintosh user accounts, 270
   and Message Queuing Services, 8
   multimaster replication, 158-159
   Organization, 156-158
      domain, 157
      forest, 157, 176
      objects, 157, 418-419
      organizational units, 157
      sites, 158
      tree, 157
   and print services, 12, 403
   and review of users/groups, 23
   scalability, 156
   security, 156, 202
   see also Group policies; Naming conventions/Active Directory
Active Server Pages (ASP), 8
Address book, 43
Address Pool, DHCP terminology, 200
Administrative tools, 43-51
   Component Services, 43
   Computer Management, 43-45, 76, 273-275
   Configure Your Server option, 45-46, 161-164
   Data Sources, 46
   DHCP Manager, 46-47, 201
   Directory Service Migration Tool, 280-281
   Distributed File System, 48
   DNS Management, 48
   Event Viewer, 48, 420, 421
   File Manager, 48
   Internet Services Manager, 49
   Licensing, 49
   Performance Monitor, 49
   Routing and Remote Access, 50
   Terminal Services Licensing, 51
   WINS, 51
Appearance Property Sheet, 101
Apple Macintosh Interoperability, 269-270
   creating/managing Macintosh accessible volumes, 273-277
   File Services installation, 270
   Macintosh User Accounts, 270-271
   print features, 403, 412
AppleTalk, 189
   configuration, 271-272
Application Management Tools
   Add/Remove Programs, 351
   Application Installation Service, 7
   Software Installation, 351-353

Index

Windows Installer, 351, 353-355
 and Intellimirror, 378
ASR *see* Restore/Recovery
Asynchronous Transfer Mode (ATM), 10
Auditing
 and Active Directory Objects, 418-419
 Application log, 420
 configuration/set policy, 414-417
 Event Viewer, 48, 420, 421
 on NTFS partitions, 417-418
 policy, 413-414
 Security log, 420
 System log, 420

Background Property Sheet, 101
Backup
 default options/changing defaults, 129-130
 of DHCP database, 210
 Emergency Repair Disk (ERD), 129
 operations
  using a batch file, 131
  using the command line, 130-131
 options in Windows 2000 Server, 119
 in Systems Tools menu, 41, 121
 types, 120
  copy, 119
  daily, 120
  differential, 119
  incremental, 119
  normal, 119
 Utility, 12
 vs. remote storage, 133
 WINS database, 239
 Wizard, 121-125
 see also Restore/Recovery
Bridgehead server, 174-175

Caching, 369
 intelligent, 7
Certificates *see* Security
Certificates, Certificate Wizard, 9
CHARGEN, 186
Clustering, 13
CN (Common Name), 161
Communication Control *see* Qos
Component Services, 43
Control Panel in Windows 2000 Server, 37-40
 Accessibility Options, 38, 99-103
 Add/Remove Hardware, 38
 Add/Remove Programs, 38
 Administrative Tools, 39
 Date/Time, 39
 Display option, 39, 100, 101-103

Fast Find, 39
Fax, 39, 66-67
Folder options, 39, 103
Fonts, 40
Game Controllers, 40, 68
General tab global options, 100-101
Internet Options, 40, 104-106
Keyboard, 40, 68, 99-100
Licensing, 40
Mouse, 40, 68, 100
Network and Dial-Up Connections, 40
Phone and Modem, 40, 68-70
Power Options, 40
Printers, 40, 70-71
Regional Options, 40, 107-108
Scanners and Cameras, 40, 71
Scheduled Tasks, 40
Sound and Multimedia, 40, 100, 108-109
System, 40, 109-112
UPS, 40

Daytime, 186
DC (Domain ComponentName), 161
Desktop icons in Windows 2000 Server
 additional options, 36
 Internet Explorer, 36
 My Briefcase, 36
 My Computer, 37
 My Documents, 37
 My Network Places, 36-37
 Recycle Bin, 36
 Start Menu, 34-36
Device Manager, 60-61
 Device Properties Sheets
  Advanced Tab, 62-63
  Driver Property Sheet, 63
  General Tab, 61-62
  Modems Properties Sheet, 66
  Resources Property Sheet, 64-65
Dfs (Microsoft Distributed File System), 11, 48, 370-371
 child node creation, 375
 configuration, 371
 properties, 374
 root replica creation, 376
 root server, 371, 372-374
DHCP (Dynamic Host Configuration Protocol), 20-23, 184, 199
 address pool, 200
 authorizing a server, 202-203
 class options, 209
 configuring the server, 201-208
 database, 210

Index **441**

backup and restore, 210-211
default options, 209
exclusion range, 200, 206-207
installation, 201
lease, 200
leasing process
    DHCPACK step, 200
    DHCPDISCOVER step, 200
    DHCPOFFER step, 200
    DHCPREQUEST step, 200
Manager, reconciling the scope, 205-206
reservation, 200, 206
reserved client options, 209
scope, 200
    creation, 203-205
        multicast scope creation, 207-208
server
    options, 209
    properties, 201-202
server properties, conflict detection, 202
superscope, 200
    creation, 207
terminology, 200
Dial-up Connectivity *see* RAS
Directory, 6
Disk
    basic, 76, 77-78
    cleanup, 92-93
    defragmenter, 93
    Disk Management
        file systems, 75-76
        interface, 80-81
    dynamic, 76, 77
    error checking, 93
    Maintenance Wizard, 94
    on-line and off-line, 78
    quotas, 12, 82-83
    upgrade from basic to dynamic, 78-79
    volume properties, 81-83
    Web Sharing tab, 83
    Windows NT Disk Solutions, 77
    see also Volumes
Distributed file system *see* Dfs
Distributed Link Tracking, 12
DLC (Data Link Control), 189
DLL conflicts reduction, 7
DN (Distinguished Name) in Naming conventions/Active Directory, 160
DNS *see* Dynamic Domain Name System
Documents Menu, 35
Domains and Trusts/Active Directory snap-ins, 168-172

Domain Controllers
    changing, 168
    connecting to another domain controller, 171
    as a server role, 24
    see also Sites and Services
Domain mode, 169
    change, 169-170
domain trusts creation, 171
installation, 168-169
operations master change, 172
Trust relationships
    external nontransitive, 169
    external transitive, 169
    one-way, 169
UPN suffixes, 170-171
Driver Incompatibility Wizard, 14
Dual-boot configuration, 26-27
Dynamic Domain Name System (DNS), 10
    and the Active Directory, 156, 205, 216
    and DHCP, 20
    DNS management, 48
    dynamic feature, 216
    installation, 23, 216-218
    Management Console configuration adjustments
        clear the cache, 220
        connect to another computer, 219
        create a new zone, 219
        manually update a server, 219-220
        remove a DNS server, 219
        name servers (NS) records, 226
        properties configuration, 225-227
        start of authority (SOA), 226
    name checking methods, 222
    namespace, 160, 213-214
        host names, 214
        root domain, 214
        second-level domain, 214
        top-level domain, 214
    naming conventions, 160-161
    Properties configuration
        advanced, 222-223
        forwarders, 221
        interfaces, 220-221
        logging, 223-224
        monitoring, 224
        root hints, 223
        security, 225
    resource records, 228-229
    Unicode character support, 216
    WINS integration, 216
    zones, 214-216, 227-229
Dynamic HTML, 9

Echo, 186
Effects Property Sheet, 102
Enterprise Memory Architecture, 13
ERD *see* Backup
Event Viewer, 48, 420, 421
    log files, 43
Exclusion Range, DHCP terminology, 200

FAT (File Allocation Table) disks conversion, 20
Fibre Channel, 10-11
File copy schedule changes, for remote storage, 139
File System *see* Dfs
Filters, 309
    FilterKeys, 100
    managing filter lists, 310-312
Format/reformat drives, 75-76

Global catalog
    and Active Directory Schema, 52, 157, 159
    enabling/disabling, 173
Group Policies, 343-344
    Containers (GPC), 344
    Group Policy Snap-in, 346-347
        administrative templates, 347-350
        Editor, 7
        security policy, 288
    and Intellimirror, 378
    Objects (GPO), 344
        configuration/management, 355-357
    Structure, 345-346
    Templates (GPT), 344
Groups, 331
    builtin, 332
    configuration, 333-337
    membership rules, 332
    Scopes
        global, 331
        local, 331-332
        universal, 332
    Types
        distribution, 331
        security, 331
GSNW *see* Novell
GUI interface, 4
GUID (Globally Unique Identifier), 161

Hardware
    Configuration and Management
        Control Panel, 66-71
        Device Manager, 60-66, 109
        Hardware Profiles, 71-72, 109
        Plug and Play, 55-59

    System Information, 72-74
    installation steps, 56-57
    requirements for Windows 2000 Server installation, 17-18
    Resources folder, 73
    Wizard, 56, 109
        Add/Remove, 57-59
Help option, 35
HKEY_CLASSES_ROOT subkey, 116
HKEY_CURRENT_CONFIG, 116
HKEY_CURRENT_USER, 115
HKEY_LOCAL_MACHINE subtree, 115, 210
HKEY_USERS subkey, 115
HTTP
    and the Active Directory, 156
    HTTP 1.1, 9

Indexing Service, 9, 394-395
    installation/configuration, 395-397
    performance checking, 398
    System catalog, 397
    unindexed document list, 399
Intellimirror, 7, 377-379
Inter-Site Transports, configuration, 176-177
Interface/System Settings configuration, Start Menu and Task Bar, 97-99
Internet
    and DNS, 213
    "elective" standards, 186
    IP Telephony, 11
    Options
        Content Property Sheet, 105-106
        Control Panel or Explore Properties Sheet, 104
        General Property Sheet, 104
        Personal Information section, 106
    Printing Protocol (IPP), and Windows 2000 Server, 12
    Protocol (IP) address *see* Dynamic Name System
    Services Manager, 49
Internet Options, control panel or Explore Properties Sheet, Security Property Sheet, 105
IP Security, 299
    Filter lists, 309-312
    IPSec (IP Security), 299
        configuration, 301-301
        key generation/lengths/re-keying, 300
        policy agent, 300-310
        tunneling, 301
        see also Ras encryption
    policy creation, 303-305
        import/export policies, 312
        new rules, 306-310

Index

JAVA, and ASP, 8
Job Objects, 13

Kerberos Authentication, 13, 75
    and external transitive trusts, 169

LDAP, and the Active Directory, 156
Lease, DHCP terminology, 200
Library configuration/management
    changing media type, 140-141
    enabling a library/drive, 140
    insert/eject port, 144
    insert/eject/mount tape or disk, 144
    library cleaning, 142
        Cleaner Management Wizard, 142
    library door, 144
    library inventory creation, 141-142
    and removable storage, 140
LMHOSTS file import, 242

Macintosh services, 11
    see also Apple Macintosh Interoperability
Media
    copy sets, 139
    logical, 135
    managing, 139
    media pool, creation/deletion, 142-143
    physical, 135
        configuration/management, 143-144
    states
        physical (operational), 135
        side (usage), 135
    type changes for remote storage, 140-141
Message Queuing Services, 8
Metadata, 178
Microsoft Management Console (MMC), 4
MPPE (Microsoft Point-to-Point Encryption) see
    RAS encryption
Multibyte name checking method, 222
Multicasting, 207, 246, 251

Namespace see Dynamic Domain Name System
Naming conventions/Active Directory
    Distinguished Name (DN), 160-161
        CommonName (CN), 161
        DomainComponentName (DC), 161, 228
        OrganizationalUnitName (OU), 161
    Globally Unique Identifier (GUID), 161
    Relative Distinguished Names (RDN), 161
    User Principal Names (UPN), 161
NetBEUI, 189
NetBIOS see WINS
NetShow, 9

NetWare see Novell NetWare
Network Address Translator (NAT), 10
Network Monitor, 425, 435
    Driver, 190
    installation, 435-436
    use, 436-437
Network Neighborhood see Desktop icons/My
    Network Places
Novell NetWare Interoperability, 277
    Directory Service Migration Tool, 280-281
    GSNW (Gateway Services for NetWare
        Networks)
    install/configuration, 278-279
    Novell and Microsoft networks, 187
    NWLink install/configuration, 277-278
    printing, 411
NS (name servers) record, 226, 228
NTFS permissions, 359-360
    ACL (active control list), 360
    advanced access permissions, 364-367
    assignment, 362-363
    copy/move restrictions, 361
    effective permissions, 361
    enhancements, 11, 75
        encrypting/decrypting, 285-287
        and FAT disks conversion, 20, 361
        and SPF4 or 5, 19
    inheritance, 361
    managing shared folders, 368-369
    and NTFS directory/document index
        blocking, 399
    and NTFS partitions auditing, 417
NWLink, 187-188
    frame type, 187-188
    internal network number, 187
    network number, 187, 188
    see also Novell NetWare

Open Database Connectivity (ODBC), 46
Operations master, 172
Operator Requests for remote storage, 145-146
    deletion, 147
    display change, 147
    response, 146
OU (Organizational Unit), 6-7, 161-168
    see also Group Policies; Users and
        Computers/Active Directory snap-in

Packet Scheduler see QoS packet scheduler
Performance Monitor, 49, 425
    alerts, 433-434
    counters, 426-428
    graph configuration, 428-430

logs, 45, 431-433
Permissions
   Permission Wizard, 9
   see also NTFS permissions
Plug and Play, 55
   under Windows, 95
   under Windows NT, 55
   Windows 2000 features, 56
Printing, 401
   client computer set up, 411-412
   color management, 409-410
   new Windows 2000 features, 402-403
      active directory, 403
      additional user settings, 403
      internet printing, 402
      Macintosh and UNIX, 403
      monitoring, 403
      remote or standard port, 402, 407
   printer access auditing, 419-420
   printer properties, 404-407
   printer security, 71
   printer selection, 12
   printer set up, 403-404
   printer vs. print device, 402
Program files, 40-53
   Accessories, 40-43
   Active Directory Administrative Tools, 51-52
   Administrative Tools, 43-51
Programs Menu, 35
Protocol, 181
   Bandwidth Allocation Protocol (BAP)/
      Bandwidth Allocation Control Protocol
      (BACP), 251
   "bindings", 190
   Extensible Authentication Protocol (EAP), 251
   installation in Windows 2000 Server, 181-182
   Layer Two Tunneling (L2TP), 248, 251
      and IPSec, 301
   MS-CHAP Version 2, Microsoft Challenge
      Handshake
      Authentication Protocol version 2, 251
   Point to Point Tunneling (PPTP), 248-249
   suite, 183
   see also AppleTalk; DLC; NetBEUI; Network
      Monitor Driver; NWLink; Streams
      Environment; TCP/IP
Public Key Certificate Server, 14

QoS (Windows Quality of Service), 11
   Admission Control, 190-198
      installation, 192
      Packet Scheduler, 192

      subnet creation, 192
   policy configuration, 192-198
      Aggregate limits tab, 197, 198
      Flow limits properties sheet, 197, 198
      General properties sheet, 197
   properties sheet
      accounting, 195
      advanced, 195
      logging, 195
      servers, 195
      traffic, 193-195
Query policy selection, 173
Queued Work properties sheet, 145
Quote of the Day, 186

RAS/RRAS (Routing and Remote Access), 50, 247
   AppleTalk clients, 272
   configuration, 255-256
   console tree server name expansion
      dial-in clients, 258
      IP routing, 258-261
      ports, 258
      routing interfaces, 258
   Dial-up Connectivity, 248
      constraints, 262
   installation, 252-254
   Multilink, 265
   Ras encryption, 266
      IPSec (IP Security), 266
      MPPE (Microsoft Point-to-Point), 266
   remote access control/policies, 251, 261, 267-268
   routing, 251-252
   routing interfaces, 258
   server properties
      general, 255-256
      IP, 257
      PPP, 257
      RAS event logging, 258
      security, 256
   Virtual Private Networks (VPN), 248-250
      internet configuration, 250
      intranet configuration, 249
RDN (Relative Distinguished Names), 161
The Registry
   components
      data types, 115
      entry, 114
      hive, 114
      keys, 114
      subkeys, 114
      subtree, 114, 115-116

Index

editors
    Regedit, 118
    Regedt32, 16-117
  structure, 114-116
  Windows 2000 and NT, 113
REG_BINARY data type, 115
REG_DWORD data type, 115
REG_EXPAND_SZ data type, 115
REG_FULL_RESOURCE_DESCRIPTOR, 115
REG_MULTI_SZ, 115
REG_SZ data type, 115
Remote Installation Services, 379
  management, 382-387
  network service boot, 387-388
  remote client boot disk, 387
  RIPrep (Remote Installation Preparation Image), 388
  set up, 379-381
Remote/Removable storage, 133-134
  changing the file copy schedule, 139
  Command Line, 149-150
    allocate command, 149
    deallocate command, 149
    deletemedia command, 149-150
    dismount command, 150
    help command, 150
    mount command, 150
    view command, 150
  library configuration/management, 140-142
  managing media, 139
  and media classification, 135
  media pools configuration, 142-143
  operator request, 145-147
  Remote Storage Services (RSS), 12
  Removable Storage Manager (RSM), 12, 134
  Runaway recall limit setting, 138
  security configuration, 148
  set up, 135-136
  validation setting, 138
  Volume Management, 136
    adding a file rule, 136
    adding/removing volumes, 137
    basic file selection, 136
    changing file rule priority, 137
    changing/deleting a file rule, 137
  work queue, 144-146
  see also Storage concepts
Reservation, DHCP terminology, 200
Restore/Recovery
  Advanced System Recovery (ASR), 14
  ASR Preparation Wizard, 128-129
  "Authoritative Restore", 128
  of DHCP database, 210-211

Restore Wizard, 125-128
security, 287-288
Windows Backup tab, 128
WINS database, 239
RFC name checking method, 222
Run command, 34
Runaway recall limit, 138

Scalability, 12-13
  SMP scalability and I20 support, 13
Scope, DHCP terminology, 200
Screen Saver Property Sheet, 101
Search Menu, 35
Security, 283, 288
  Active Directory, 156
    Access Control List (ACL), 157, 285
    and DHCP server, 202-203
  Certificates, 292
    Authority installation, 292-294
    management, 294-298
  Configuration
    Editor template feature, 14
    Manager SP4, 19
    Removable Storage, 148
  for DNS service, 225
  EFS (Encrypting File System), 285-287
  IP Security Protocol, 14
  Kerberos Authentication, 13, 75, 284-285
  log and auditing policy, 413, 420-423
  new features, 283-284
  NTLM (NT LAN Manager), 285
  SSL/TLS (Secure Socket Layer/Transport Layer), 285
  Template snap-in, 289
    analysis of templates, 290-292
    policy configurations, 289-290
  see also IP Security
Server
  management, 4
  roles in Windows 2000 Server, 24
Service Pack 4(SP4)/ 5(SP5), 19
Settings
  Menu, 35
  Property Sheet, 102-103
Shared resources *see* NTFS permissions
Shut Down option, 34
Sites and Services/Active Directory snap-ins, 172-178
  changing forests, 176
  create a new domain controller in a site, 173
  enabling/disabling global catalog server, 173
  inter-site transports configuration, 176-177
  licensing computer change, 177

moving a domain controller between sites, 174
preferred bridgehead server designation, 174-175
removing a nonoperational server, 176
repairing a domain controller, 175
select a query policy, 173
site, 172-173
site access, 173
site creation/renaming, 176
subnet creation, 176
see also Group Policies
Smart card, 14
Snap-in, 4
SOA (start of authority) record, 226, 228
SQL, Transaction Services protecting updates, 9
Start Menu, 97-99
   Create Shortcut Wizard, 98
   Options tab, 98
   Taskbar options, 97-98
Startup and recovery, 112
StickyKeys, 99-100
Storage concepts, 133-135
   libraries, 134, 140-142
   media pools, 134-135, 142-143
   media states, 135
   remote storage, 133-134
Streaming Media, 9
Streams Environment, 190
Structured Query Language (SQL) data access, 46
Subnet Bandwidth Management (SBM) standard, 191
   see also QoS
Superscope, DHCP terminology, 200
Synchronization Manager, 389
   and Intellimirror, 378
   set up, 391-394
Synchronize, 43
System catalog, 397
System Information, 72-74
System Properties Sheets
   access, 109
   Advanced Property sheet
      environmental variables, 111
      performance, 110-111
      startup and recovery, 112
   General Properties sheet, 109
   Hardware Property Sheet, 109
   Network Identification, 109
   User Profiles, 109
Systems Tools
   backup, 41
   character map, 42
   disk cleanup, 42, 92-93
   disk defragmenter, 42, 93
   scheduled tasks, 42

TCP/IP (Transmission Control Protocol/Internet Protocol), 20, 182
   configuration, 184-185
   conflict detection, 202
   Default Gateway, 183
   IP Address, 183
      automatic private IP address feature, 184
      DHCP (Dynamic Host Configuration Protocol) assignment, 184
      manual assignment, 184
   as a protocol suite, 183
   Simple Services installation/configuration, 186-187
      CHARGEN, 186
      Daytime, 186
      Echo, 186
      Quote of the Day, 186
   Subnet Mask, 183
      manual assignment, 184
   and UNIX printing, 411
   utilities, 184
Togglekeys, 100
Transaction Services, 9
Trust relationships *see* Domains and Trusts

UNIX, printer support, 403, 411, 412
UPN (User Principal Names), 161, 170
User profiles, 339
   Local, 339-340
   Mandatory, 340, 342-343
   Roaming, 340
      and Intellimirror, 378
      set up/configuration, 340-342
   see also Group policies; NTFS permissions
Users and Computers/Accounts
   administrator account, 318
   computer accounts, 328
      management, 330-331
      properties configuration, 328-330
   domain user account, 317
      creation/configuration, 318-326
      management, 326-327
   guest account, 318
   local user account, 318
Users and Computers/Active Directory snap-in, 164-168
   adding an organizational unit, 165
   adding users/groups/shares, 168
   computer identification, 328-330

Index

delegating control of an organizational unit, 165-166
deleting control of an organizational unit, 167
finding an organizational unit, 167
moving an organizational unit, 167-168
Remote Installation Services management, 382
renaming an organizational unit, 168
see also Group policies; Groups

VBScript, and ASP, 8
Volumes
   Macintosh accessible, 273-277
   mirrored, 76
      breaking/repairing, 91
      creation, 90
      deletion, 90
      removal, 90
   RAID-5, 76
      creation, 91
      deletion, 91
      reactivation, 92
      repairing, 92
   simple
      change the drive letter/path, 86-87
      creation, 84-85
      deletion, 85-86
      extension, 86
   spanned, 76
      creation, 88
      deletion, 89
      extension, 89
   striped, 76
      configuration/management, 89
      creation, 89
      deletion, 89-90
   see also Remote/Removable Storage Volume Management
VPN *see* RAS

WAN networks, and sites, 172
Web Application Services, 8
Web Based Enterprise Management (WBEM), 7-8
   and SPF4, 19
WEB option configuration, 101-102
Web Publishing Services, 9
Windows 2000 Server installation
   as an Upgrade
      from Windows earlier than NT 4.0, 18
      from Windows NT 4.0, 18-23, 78
      implement DCCP, 20-23
      performing the Windows 2000 upgrade, 24-26

      review users/groups, 23
      Service Pack 4 or 5, 19
      TCP/IP, 20
   as a clean install, 26-30
      creating boot disks, 27
      dual-boot configuration, 26-27
      installation steps, 29-30
      installing from a network share, 27
      set up options/switches, 27-29
   hardware requirements, 17-18, 23
   importance of planning, 17, 30
Windows 2000 Server interface, 32-33
   desktop, 34-37
Windows 2000 Server new features
   as an MMC snap-in, 4
   application and publishing services, 8-9
   differences from Windows NT, 3
   dynamic DNS, 216
   file features, 11-12, 75-76, 103
   improved scalability, 12-13, 156
   and Internet Information Server, 9, 5.0
   management features, 4-8
   Microsoft's goals, 3
   networking components, 10-11, 153
   Plug and Play compliance, 14, 55
   print services, 12, 402-403, 412
   security tools/enhancements, 13-14, 283-284
   set up tools, 14
   see also Macintosh services
Windows Explorer, 43
Windows Scripting Host (WSH), 8
Windows Update, 36
WINS
   check database consistency, 238-239
   Configuration options
      adding servers to the Console, 233
      adjustable logging options, 236
      Name Record property sheet, 236
      properties sheet, 233-234, 235
      server statistics, 235
      server status, 234
   database backup/recovery, 239
   LMHOSTS file import, 242
   managing registrations, 240
   registered names check, 243
   Replication Tasks
      add a partner, 244
      force replication, 245
      replication partner properties, 245-246
   scavenge database, 238
   static mappings, 241
   tombstoning, 244

in Windows 2000 Server
implementation requirements, 232
installation, 233
WINS (Windows Internet Naming Service), 51, 231–231
integration with DNS, 216, 226

Work queue in remote storage, 144
states of operation, 144–145

XML, 9

Y2K fixes, 19

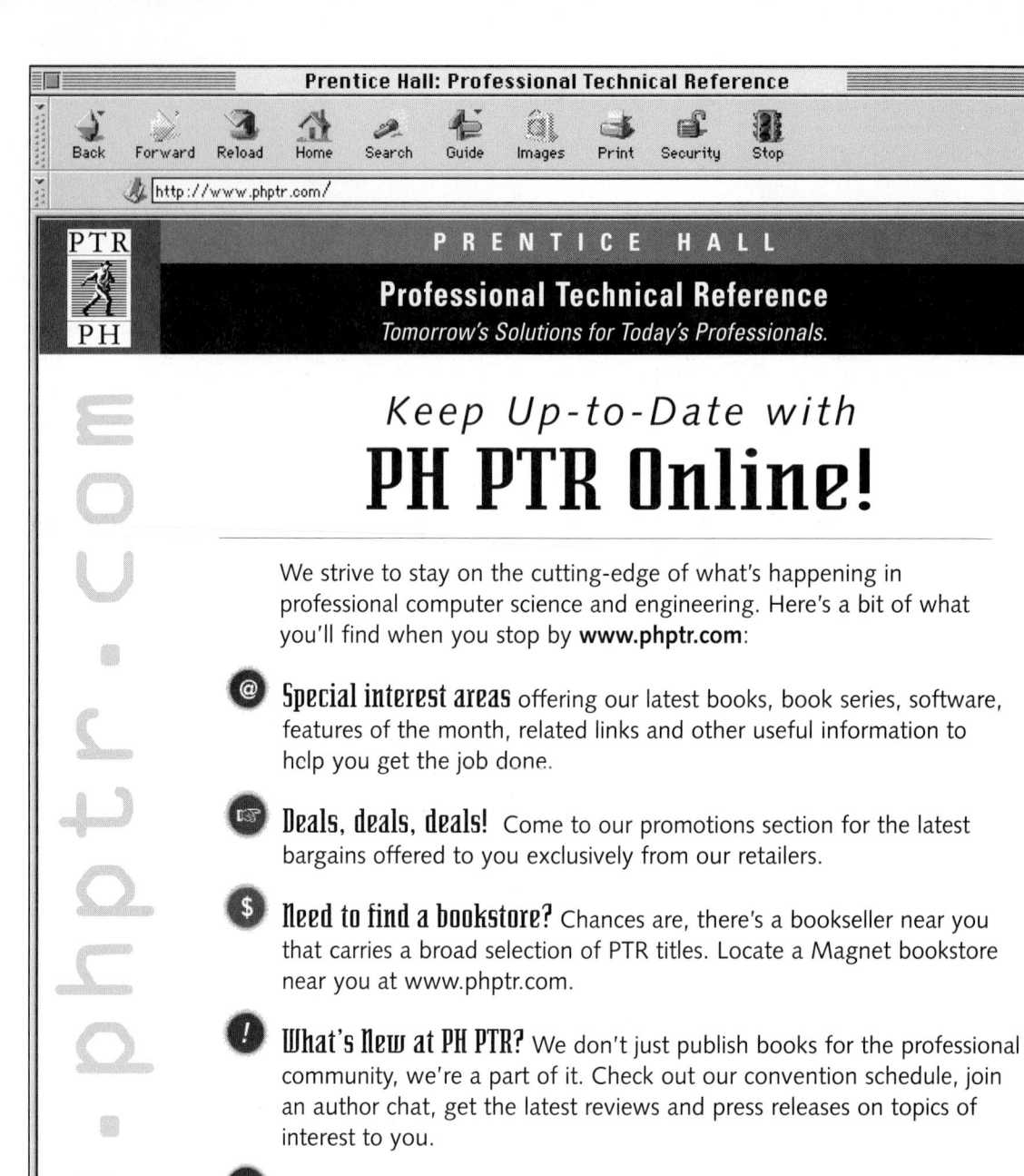

PRENTICE HALL
Professional Technical Reference
Tomorrow's Solutions for Today's Professionals.

Keep Up-to-Date with
PH PTR Online!

We strive to stay on the cutting-edge of what's happening in professional computer science and engineering. Here's a bit of what you'll find when you stop by **www.phptr.com**:

- **Special interest areas** offering our latest books, book series, software, features of the month, related links and other useful information to help you get the job done.

- **Deals, deals, deals!** Come to our promotions section for the latest bargains offered to you exclusively from our retailers.

- **Need to find a bookstore?** Chances are, there's a bookseller near you that carries a broad selection of PTR titles. Locate a Magnet bookstore near you at www.phptr.com.

- **What's New at PH PTR?** We don't just publish books for the professional community, we're a part of it. Check out our convention schedule, join an author chat, get the latest reviews and press releases on topics of interest to you.

- **Subscribe Today!** Join PH PTR's monthly email newsletter!

Want to be kept up-to-date on your area of interest? Choose a targeted category on our website, and we'll keep you informed of the latest PH PTR products, author events, reviews and conferences in your interest area.

Visit our mailroom to subscribe today! **http://www.phptr.com/mail_lists**